Contents

Dedication..4
Acknowledgments 4
Condition and Value..5
Illustrations 6
Julio T. Buel 7
T. H. Bate & Co. 20
Riley Haskell 26
W.D. Chapman 34
John H. Mann 84
Gardiner M. Skinner 88
Lysander S. Hill and Charles B. Hibbard..............97
William T.J. Lowe..105
Harry Comstock 121
Enterprise Manufacturing Co. 127
John B. McHarg 181
Henry Loftie 198
John Pepper & Sons 202
Welch & Graves 206
James T. Hastings 214
Charles R. Harris 220
Miscellaneous Manufacturers 225
Whence the Plug? by Sam Stinson......................277
Lure Manufacturers Before 1901........................282
A Brief History of the Patent Office 283
Patent Drawings of Unfound Lures 284
Patent Index 298
Company Index 300
Bibliography 303
About the Author...303

DEDICATION

In memory of my father, Ellwood Carter, who taught
me an appreciation of the outdoors

ACKNOWLEDGMENTS

I have been working on and off with this book for longer than I care to acknowledge and in the process, I'm sure I've left someone out of the following list of contributors. If you happen to be one of them, I apologize; please let me know so I can correct the oversight if and when another edition is printed.

I'd like to give a special thanks to **Tom Penniston,** Albany, WI, for allowing me to use some of his great old photos in the book (including the background for the cover). Also **Steve Lumpkin,** Chicago, IL, for information and original artwork; **Bob Bulkley,** Evansville, IN, for lots of photos and information; **Charles Atwood,** Evans, CO, for lots of information and photos; **Bob Pattridge,** Cleveland, NY, for Chapman photos and information; **Gerry Barrows,** Lockport, NY, for information and photos on New York manufacturers; **Drew Reese,** Reeds Springs, MO, information on Pflueger; **Robert Korman,** Mt. Pleasant, MI, information on Harry Comstock and others; **Dick Wilson,** Kent, OH, information on Pardee and photos; **Paul Lindner,** Fremont, MI, information on Michigan Manufacturers; **Rich Metcalf,** Syracuse, NY, information on J. H. Mann and H. Loftie; **Dudley Murphy,** Springfield, MO, for technical assistance and support; **Larry Honeywell,** Theresa, NY, for information on W. D. Chapman; **Aziel Lafave,** Theresa, NY, for showing my wife and me around Theresa and information on W. D. Chapman; **Bob Wentz,** Germansville, PA, for photos; **Bob Lang** of Lang's Sporting Collectibles Inc., Raymond, ME, for photos; **Karen Eppinger,** Dearborn, MI, for information on the Buel Co.; **Randall Anderson,** Bartlesville, OK, for photos; and the late **Richard Nissley,** Birmingham, MI, for lots of help and information.

Others who contributed information or photos, or allowed me to photograph lures from their collections are **Dr. Harold Herr,** Ephrata, PA; **John Savu,** Warren, OH; **Karl White,** Luther, OK; **Marc Wisotsky,** Brooklyn, NY; **Art Kimball,** Boulder Junction, WI; **Steve Hays,** Palmyra, N.Y.; **Jim Bourdon,** Croton on Hudson, NY; **Joseph Stagnitti,** Manlius, N.Y.; **Max Berry,** Washington, D. C.; **Raymond Heffington,** Deland, FL; **Jim Muma,** Belleville, IL; **Randy Gariglietti,** Arma, KS; **David Gaustad,** Spring Valley, CA; **Joel Anderson,** Gem Lake, MN; **Thomas Eichten,** Stillwater, MN; **Henry Norris,** Gladstone, MO; **Stephen Twitty,** Lewisburg, TN; **Edward Salensky,** Syracuse, NY; **Dave Bunner,** Columbus, OH; **Gibby Gibson,** Hermitage, TN; **Barry Taylor,** Emporia, VA; **Scott Ghinazzi,** Wisconsin Rapids, WI; **David Spengler,** Madison, WI; **Jack Leslie,** Mooresville, IN; **Richard Iseman,** Russell, PA; **Tom O'Hara,** Cedar Rapids, IA; **Dan Basore,** Warrenville, IL; **Donald J. Ash,** Rice Lake, WI; **Debbie Steimle,** Louisburg, KS; **Dick Streater,** Mercer Island, WA; and **Rick Edmisten,** Studio City, CA, for moral support.

I would also like to thank:
M. E. Maclean, Reference Librarian, Coburg Public Library, Coburg, Ontario, Canada;
Walter Font, Fort Wayne Indiana Historical Society;
Mercer County Historical Museum, Celina, OH;
Loree Bergerhouse, Tazewell County Genealogical Society, Pekin, IL;
Thomas J. Kernan, Rome Historical Society, Rome, NY;
Flower Memorial Library, Watertown, NY.
Isabel R. Muir, Four Rivers Historical Society, Natural Bridge, NY.

Last, but not least, I would like to thank my wife **Loretta** and our daughter **Robin** for the hard work they did on the book. I love them both very much.

19th Century Fishing Lures

A Collector's Guide to U.S. Lures Manufactured Prior to 1901

Arlan Carter

COLLECTOR BOOKS
A Division of Schroeder Publishing Co., Inc.

PREFACE

When I decided to do this book, I went to the local library and checked out a few books on publishing, talked to a few people who had published books, and then went out and bought some layout sheets, a waxer, and some blue pencils. I drew outlines with the blue pencils and then pasted in the pictures and text with the waxer. The book slowly began to take shape.

Somewhere along the line, Dudley Murphy (co-founder of the National Fishing Lure Collector's Club) casually suggested to me that perhaps I should buy a computer and enter the twentieth century — before it was over. I did, and things began to speed up. However, due to business interests and a bit of procrastination there were several years when nothing of any consequence was accomplished as far as the book was concerned.

I mention this in my own defense. I have been working on the book for quite awhile and some of my friends and acquaintances, and lately even strangers, have begun to goodnaturedly suggest that maybe they had missed the first edition but were definitely interested in the second edition. Well, for better or worse, here's the first edition. I hope you enjoy it as much as I enjoyed putting it together.

ABOUT THIS BOOK

The material in the book is a combination of photographs, catalog illustrations, and where available, a patent drawing of the lure. The major companies are arranged in a loose chronological order determined by the date of their first patent.

It is a foregone conclusion that this book will contain information that is incomplete and possibly even incorrect. After all, these lures are at least a hundred years old. I do hope, however, that the information contained herein will help you to understand better the beginnings of the lure industry and give you a better appreciation of the craftsmanship and beauty found in these old lures.

Individuals wishing to learn more about lure collecting would do well to contact the National Fishing Lure Collectors Club (NFLCC) HCR #3, Box 4012, Reed Spring, MO 65737 or www.nflcc.com on the Internet. I have belonged to the NFLCC for 20 years. The money you pay in dues will be the best investment you'll ever make in the hobby.

For a signed copy, send check or money order to Arlan Carter, P.O. Box 107, Fall Creek, WI 54742, or call 1-800-695-6017. Please include $29.95 plus $2.00 for postage and handling. Visa & MasterCard accepted.

The current values in this book should be used only as a guide. They are not intended to set prices, which vary from one section of the country to another. Auction prices as well as dealer prices vary greatly and are affected by condition and demand. Neither the author nor the publisher assumes responsibility for any losses which might be incurred as a result of consulting this guide.

Collector Books

P.O. Box 3009

Paducah, KY 42002-3009

www.collectorbooks.com

Copyright © 2000 by Arlan Carter

All rights reserved. No part of this book may be reproduced, stored in any retrieval system, or transmitted in any form, or by any means including but not limited to electronic, mechanical, photocopy, recording, or otherwise, without the written consent of the author and publisher.

Condition and Values

Condition: Probably 80 percent of the lures in this book are made of metal. Metal lures do not lend themselves well to the grading system used by the National Fishing Lure Collectors Club (NFLCC) or any other system I've seen published. Metal lures are generally deemed by collectors to be in acceptable or not acceptable condition. A lure is generally acceptable if it is free of bad dents and deep corrosion. Missing hooks and swivels, even shafts, on metal lures are not considered much of a detriment. They are easily replaced by ones that are indistinguishable from the originals. The paint, or lack thereof, on the back of a spinner is usually not of prime importance. An exception would be the Enterprise Manufacturing Company's spinners that have illustrations of frogs, crayfish, moths, etc. on their reverse sides. Paint on metal lures such as the Pflueger May Bug and Dixie Minnow is also very important, and this type of lure could probably be graded by the NFLCC system. Wood and rubber lures can be graded by the NFLCC system.

NFLCC Standard Lure Grading System

10	(NIB)	Unused w/original box or carton
9	(M) Mint	Unused w/o box
8	(EXC) Excellent	Very little or no age cracks; very minor defects
7	(VG) Very Good	Little age cracks; some minor defects
5-6	(G) Good	Some age cracks; starting to chip, small defects
3-4	(AVG) average	Some paint loss and/or chipping, showing age
2	(F) Fair	Major paint loss and/or defects much chipping
1	(P) Poor	Parts missing, poor color and/or major chipping
0	(R) Repaint	Original paint covered over in part or all

Conditions may be clarified by adding (+) or (-) ratings to the letter scale, or by adding ½ to the numerical scale.

Values: In most cases the values of lures in this book are based on the actual lure pictured. The reason for this is that many of the lures, especially the Enterprise Co., are found in several different grades. A plain nickel plated or tin spinner blade isn't worth nearly as much as a fancy embossed blade in the Clover Leaf pattern. Nor is a tin or nickel plated blade worth as much as a gold plated one. I have tried to show a variety of plain and fancy types.

Some lures do not have a value listed. In most cases this relates to the fact that the lure has changed hands so infrequently that a value has not been established. In other cases a catalog picture (cut) has been found illustrating the lure, but the lure itself has not been found. On a few occasions I have priced a catalog illustration. In these cases I was able to find an illustration of the lure but did not have access to the piece even though it may have been traded several times.

In the final analysis, lure values are highly subjective and very volatile. The prices in this book aren't meant to be exact. They do, or at least should, provide a relative value by which you can compare one lure to another.

ILLUSTRATIONS

From the 1888 edition of the Thos. H. Chubb Co. catalog

Illustration showing the office at the Thos. H. Chubb Company in Post Mills, Vt. Mr. Chubb is the gentleman in the center of the room reading the paper. The Chubb Company was primarily a rod manufacturer, but these illustrations would be typical of a lure manufacturing company during the same era. The company also made the famous Henshall-Van Antwerp Black Bass Reel.

The machine room. Note the large mechanical drop press at the left. This is the same type of press that would have been used to punch out metal spinners and spoons. The entire operation was powered by a single shaft located near the ceiling and extending the entire length of the factory. This shaft was powered by a single large steam engine or water turbine. All operations were driven by belts and pulleys connected to this shaft. Speeds were controlled by the size of the pulleys.

Tackle room. This is where all the finished products were kept.

Julio T. Buel

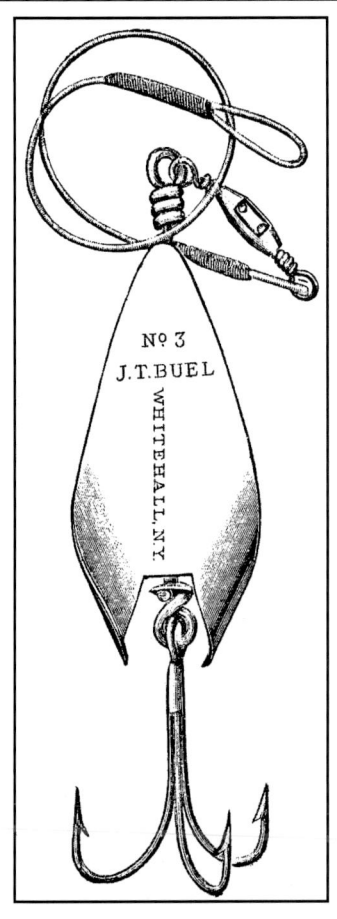

Were the nineteenth century lure manufacturing fraternity to have a designated founding father, Julio T. Buel would be the most likely candidate. He was granted five patents between 1852 and 1876. His 1852 patent is the first on record for an actual fishing lure. His second, in 1854, is for a weedless hook, another first; and an 1876 patent is for a spreading devise for use with two trolling spoons, also a first.

These patents were not only firsts, but also very practical and useful inventions. The fishing populace enthusiastically accepted the Buel patent lures, and during Julio's lifetime, he had to do little, if any, advertising. As a later trade catalog expounded, "J.T. Buel stamped upon fishing tackle is proof of honest material and perfect construction." That statement must have been true from the very beginning.

Julio was born in East Poultney, Vermont, in 1806. He had two brothers, Alexander and Harvey. In 1814, the family moved to Castleton, Vermont, where his father, Ezekiel, was a furrier. Julio learned the furrier trade at an early age while working in his father's shop.

He also developed a taste for fishing, and it was during his time in Castleton that Julio first became involved in the manufacture of fishing lures. The story has it that he accidently dropped a tablespoon overboard while fishing on Lake Bomoseen, a lake several miles north of town. As the spoon fluttered toward the bottom, a large lake trout came out of the depths and grabbed it, thus the inspiration for the trolling spoon. Julio manufactured these spoons on a small scale and sold them to the locals.

In 1827, at the age of 21, he left home and

moved to Whitehall, New York, where he opened his own furrier business. He specialized in making beaver hats, a type of hat resembling those worn by Abraham Lincoln. He also continued to make the trolling spoons, and they became so popular that in 1848, he quit the furrier trade and went into the full-time manufacture of fishing lures.

The sale of his lures was helped considerably by Henry William Herbert, a popular outdoor writer, who wrote under the pseudonym Frank Forester. Herbert sang the praises of the Buel Spoon and the orders came rolling in.

The employees of the new company tried in vain to keep pace with the orders, but it was a never-ending battle.

Julio operated the business out of a small brick building on Canal Street, and although he never caught up with the backlog of orders, he refused to expand or hire more employees. He insisted on a top-quality product, and during his lifetime, he produced one of the finest lures ever made. Genio C. Scott, in his 1875 book, *Fishing in American Waters,* states, "Foreigners have frequently swindled the anglers of this country by attaching hooks of inferior quality to spinning baits; but the domestic competition in the fishing-tackle business has become so strong that first-rate tackle of all kinds can be had at home; and the Buel feathered trolling-spoon, and those of M'Harg, are the best in the world for taking the principal fishes of our lakes and rivers."

Testimonials such as the above, and others from periodicals like *Forest and Stream* and *The American Angler* made it unnecessary for Julio to buy printed advertising.

His fame and esteem as a lure maker spread, and in 1876, at the centennial Exposition, he was awarded a medal for his contribution to the fledgling lure manufacturing business, a tribute well deserved.

Among Buel's employees were his brother Harvey and Charles B. Pike. Pike was a jeweller by trade and ideally suited to the lure manufacturing business. Buel sold the company to Pike in 1885. Julio T. Buel died in May, 1886.

South Canal Street in Whitehall, N.Y. (right side of photo). Buel had his shop here from 1848 until his death in 1886.

Although not generally within the time frame of this book, I believe a continued history of the J. T. Buel Co. might be helpful to collectors trying to determine the date of manufacture or origin of certain Buel look-alikes. The following information, as does much of this chapter's text, comes from *The Spooners*, a book published by the Eppinger Manufacturing Company (makers of the world-famous Daredevil), and written by Harvey W. Thompson. I thank them for allowing me to use this material. Charles Pike continued to operate out of the small brick building until 1902 when he replaced it with new, larger quarters. Two of Pike's employees were a jeweler named Guerdon Hardy and Nathan G. Fagan.

Hardy eventually left Pike to buy a business known as the Harder Company. The Harder Company was a Buel imitator operating in Whitehall at the time. An existing 1935 Harder catalog lists the firm's address in Whitehall. In 1957, Bill Roden of the *Adirondack Sportsman* wrote that Gordon Williams and Cy Woodbury had teamed up and bought the Harder Company and were continuing production from Diamond Point, which is on the east shore of Lake George, not far from Whitehall.

As for Fagen, he learned the trade and in 1912, he also left Pike. He joined William E. Koch who owned the Clover Leaf Hook Company. This merger formed the Northern Specialty Company. In 1958, Ruth Jackson, a former employee, and her husband bought the business from Fagan. At that time, the company was producing 600 different lures. In 1974, the Jacksons sold Northern Specialty to the Eppinger Manufacturing Company of Dearborn, Michigan.

The J. T. Buel Company left Whitehall in 1927 after a man named E. Hammond had purchased the company from Pike and moved it to Saratoga Springs, New York. The company continued to operate after the death of Hammond in 1932, until World War II. After the war, the company was purchased by Frank T. Dunn, grandson of a former employee. He moved the company to Canton, New York, but evidently had his problems because when he sold to J. M. Habib of Watertown, New York in 1959, the business had been inactive for almost 10 years. Habib continued to operate it until 1967, when he sold to the Eppinger Manufacturing Company.

Karen Eppinger of the Eppinger Manufacturing Co. demonstrates an old drop press once used by the J. T. Buel Company. The press does not have a tripping device; you just raise the punch and let it drop on the die.

Very early spoon marked "PATENT APPLIED FOR" No. 1. The back of the spoon is marked J.T. Buel, Whitehall, N.Y. This spoon is similar to the 1854 patent found on page 13 but does not have provisions for the weedless spring rod. $500.00 – 750.00.

J.T. Buel

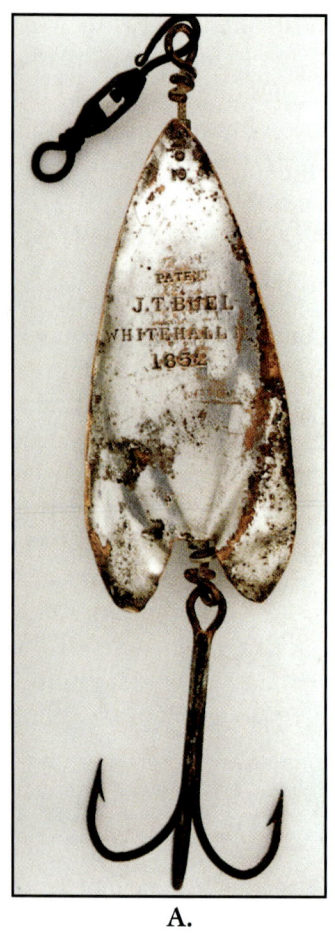

A.

B.

C.

A. An early version of the Buel "Arrowhead" spinner. Note the old snap-on swivel. It is marked "Patent - J. T. Buel - Whitehall - 1852." $75.00 – 100.00.

B. Another early version marked "J. T. Buel - patent April 6th - Whitehall, N. Y. - 1852." The stamping forms a '"T" on the face of the lure. $75.00 – 100.00.

C. The spinner on the left is marked "J. T. Buel - Whitehall N. Y." This is also stamped in a "T" design, but has no patent date. This model was catalogd in the late 1880 and the 1890s. $20.00 – 40.00.
The lure on the right shows up in the 1890s as the new "Buel" spinner. It has a deep notch at the bottom to accommodate a snap. The hook and swivel on this bait could be changed without the use of a pliers. It was sold for awhile in conjunction with the older model. Later "Arrowheads" all had removable hooks and swivels and were marked "J. T. Buel - Whitehall N.Y." in small letters. The one pictured shows the air chamber on the back side.

D. This is a very early spinner marked "J T. Buel - patent-1852 - J. Warrin Sole Maker." J. Warrin was a New York City tackle maker and reel manufacturer in the 1850s and probably before. The words "Sole Maker" are puzzling, because it is thought that J.T. Buel had always manufactured his own lures. It is possible that J. Warrin was licensed to make them. Note the unique removable hook. $200.00 – 250.00.

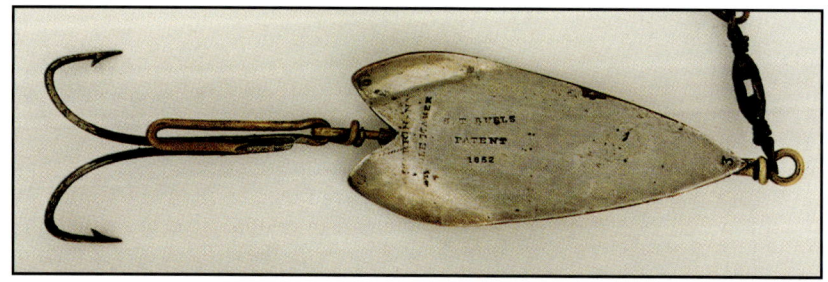

D.

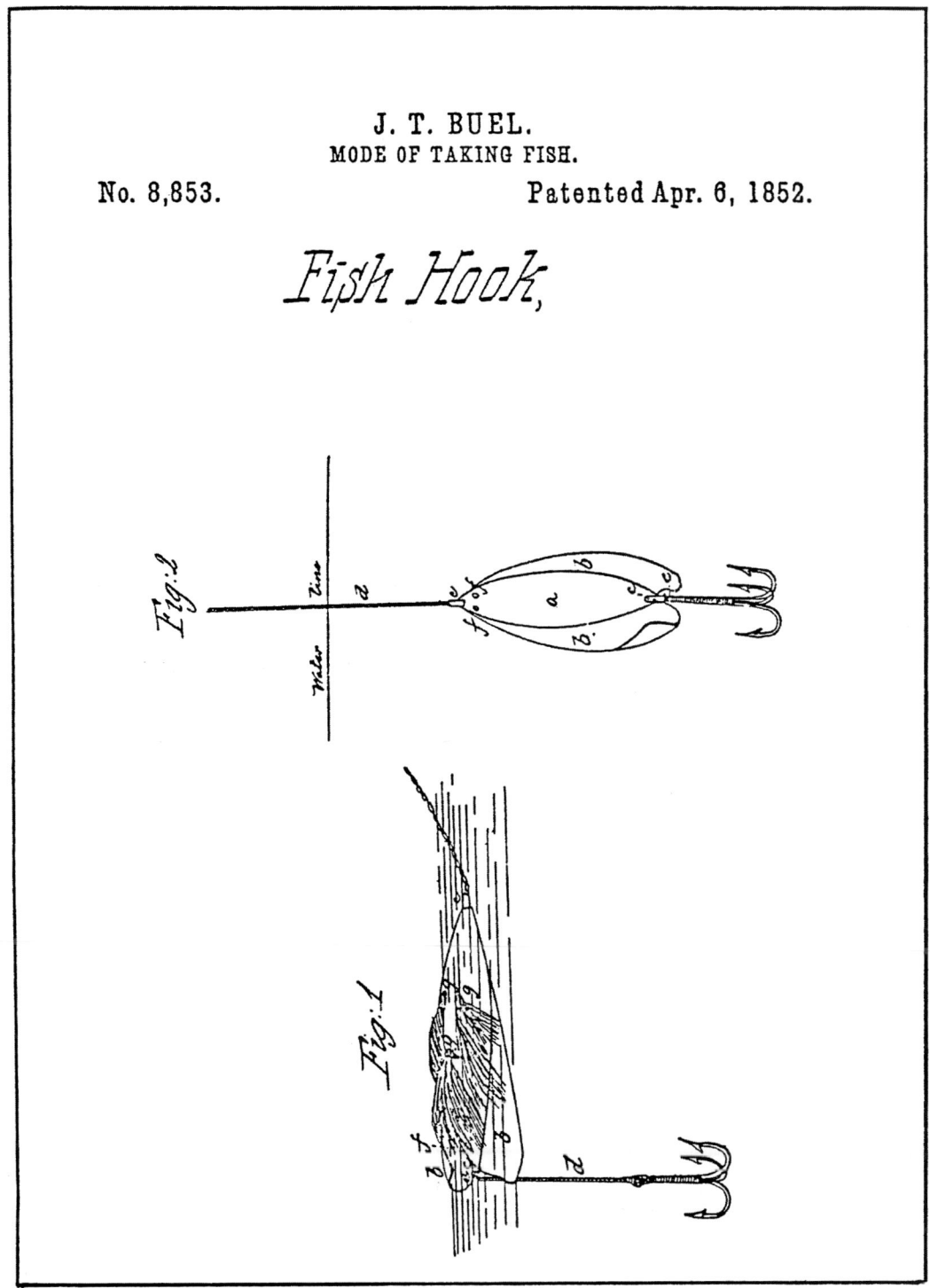

Buel's first patent. The main feature of the patent was an air chamber (a) that allowed water or air to enter through a small aperture (f), thus allowing the fisherman to have either a sinking or a floating lure. Another prominent part of the patent was a tube (c) running lengthwise in the lure through which the line (d) was passed and attached to the hook. This eliminated the use of a swivel. There were also provisions (g) in the body of the bait to attach feathers of different colors. Interestingly, lures found to date have a sealed air chamber and tube but no provisions for attaching feathers or allowing water to enter the chamber.

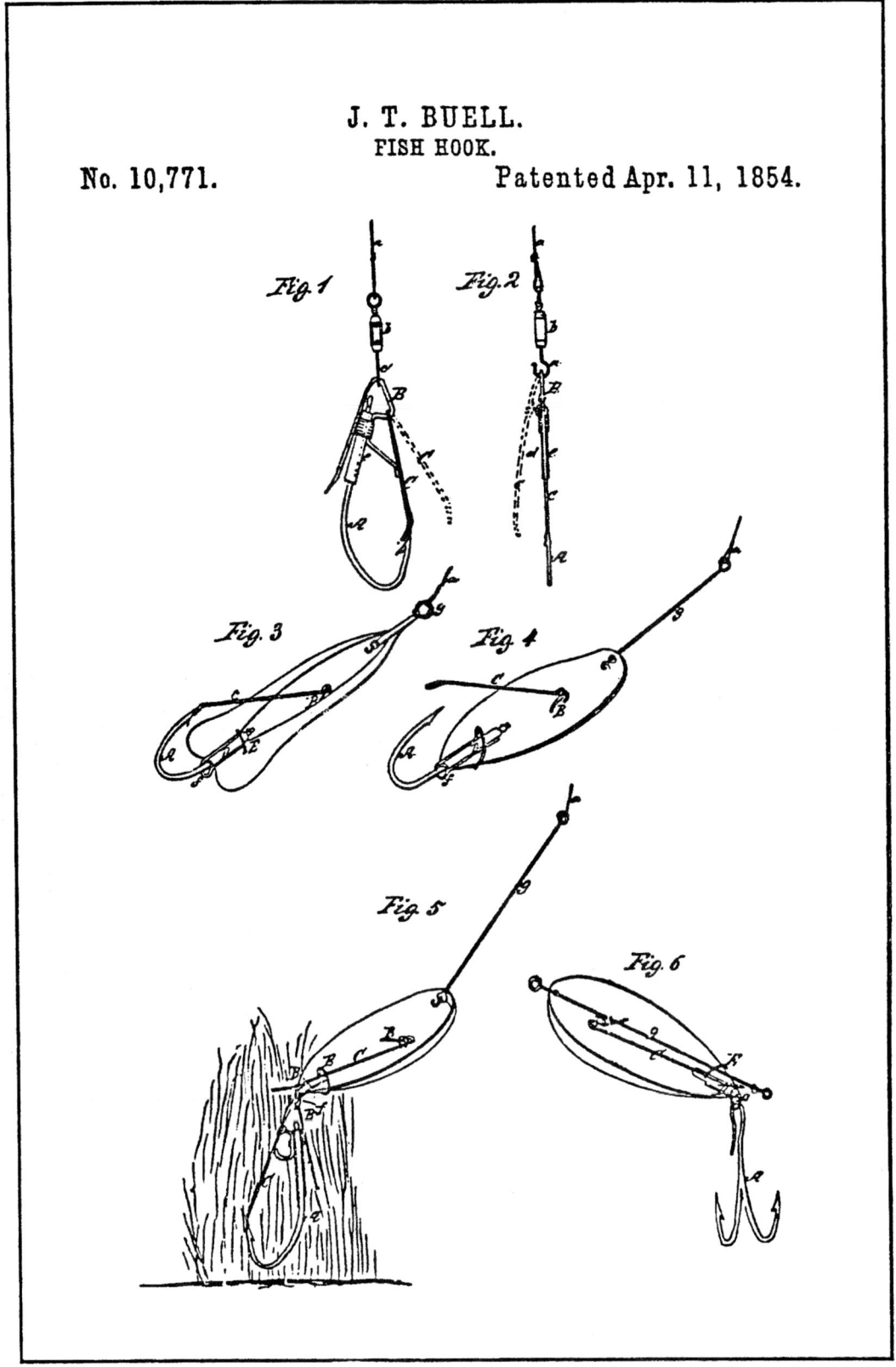

Buel's second patent. This patent demonstrates the use of a spring-rod to render a hook or lure weedless.

A.

B.

C.

A. A spoon-shaped lure marked "Patent - J. T. Buel - Whitehall - 1854." This lure is copper, and silver plated on the concave side. $750.00 – 1,000.00.

B. A view of the spoon with the spring-rod out of position. This configuration is illustrated in Fig. 4 of the patent on page 12. The wire post near the bottom of the lure can be bent over to hold the spring-rod when it is not in use.

C. A view of the spoon with the spring-rod in position.

D. Spring-rods used on a single hook. Their use is shown in Fig. 1 of the patent on page 12. The rod is indicated by the letter "**C.**" These rods are marked "Buel's Patent 1854." $20.00 – 30.00.

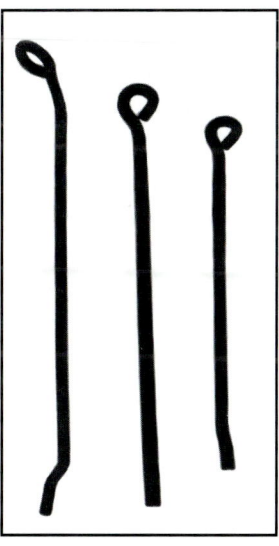

D.

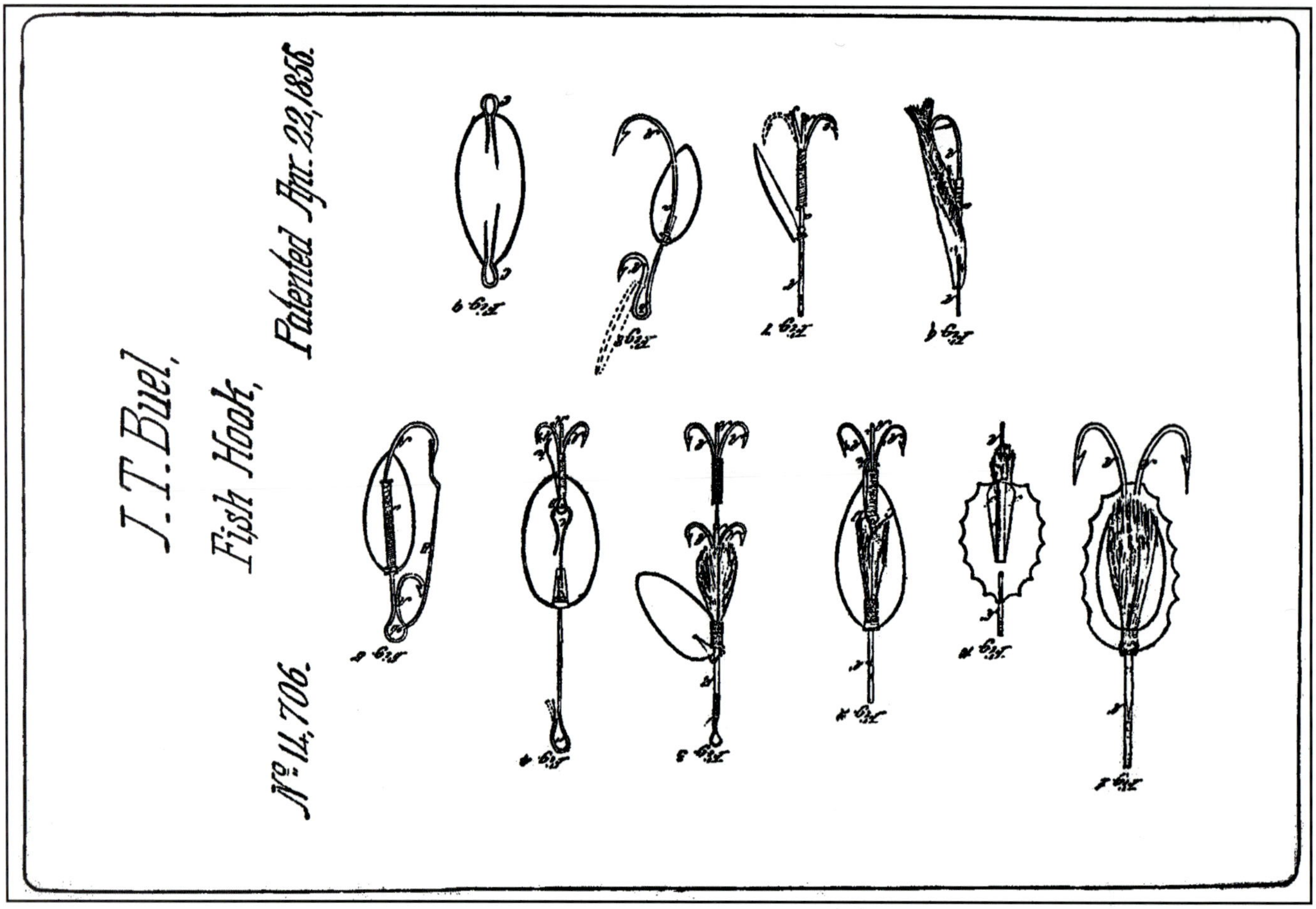

A.

A. Buel's April 22, 1856 patent. This is a fairly complicated patent that includes several features pertaining to the method of hook attachment. It also illustrates a way of interchanging spoons of different sizes and colors without removing the lure from the line.

B. This lure is marked J.T. Buel Patent April 6, 1852 and April 22, 1856. It is illustrated in Figures 5 and 8 of the patent above. The spoon on this lure can be removed or changed by sliding it off the smaller hook at the front of the shaft. The smaller hook also serves as an attachment for a minnow or other live bait. $500.00 – 750.00.

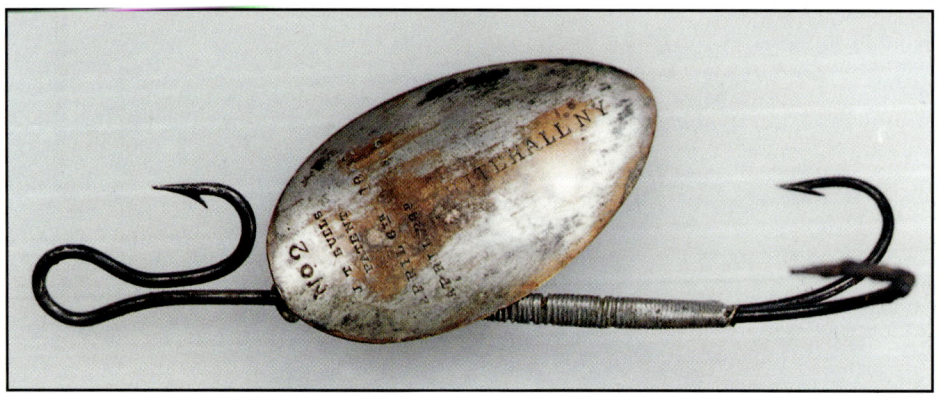

B.

J.T. Buel

A.

B.

C.

A. A spoon-shaped lure marked "Patent - J. T. Buel - Whitehall - 1854." This lure is copper, and silver plated on the concave side. $750.00 – 1,000.00.

B. A view of the spoon with the spring-rod out of position. This configuration is illustrated in Fig. 4 of the patent on page 12. The wire post near the bottom of the lure can be bent over to hold the spring-rod when it is not in use.

C. A view of the spoon with the spring-rod in position.

D. Spring rods used on a single hook. Their use is shown in Fig. 1 of the patent on page 12. The rod is indicated by the letter "**C.**" These rods are marked "Buel's Patent 1854." $20.00 – 30.00.

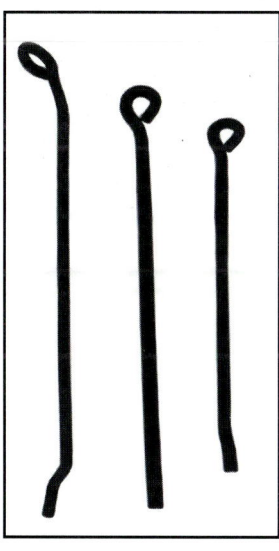

D.

13

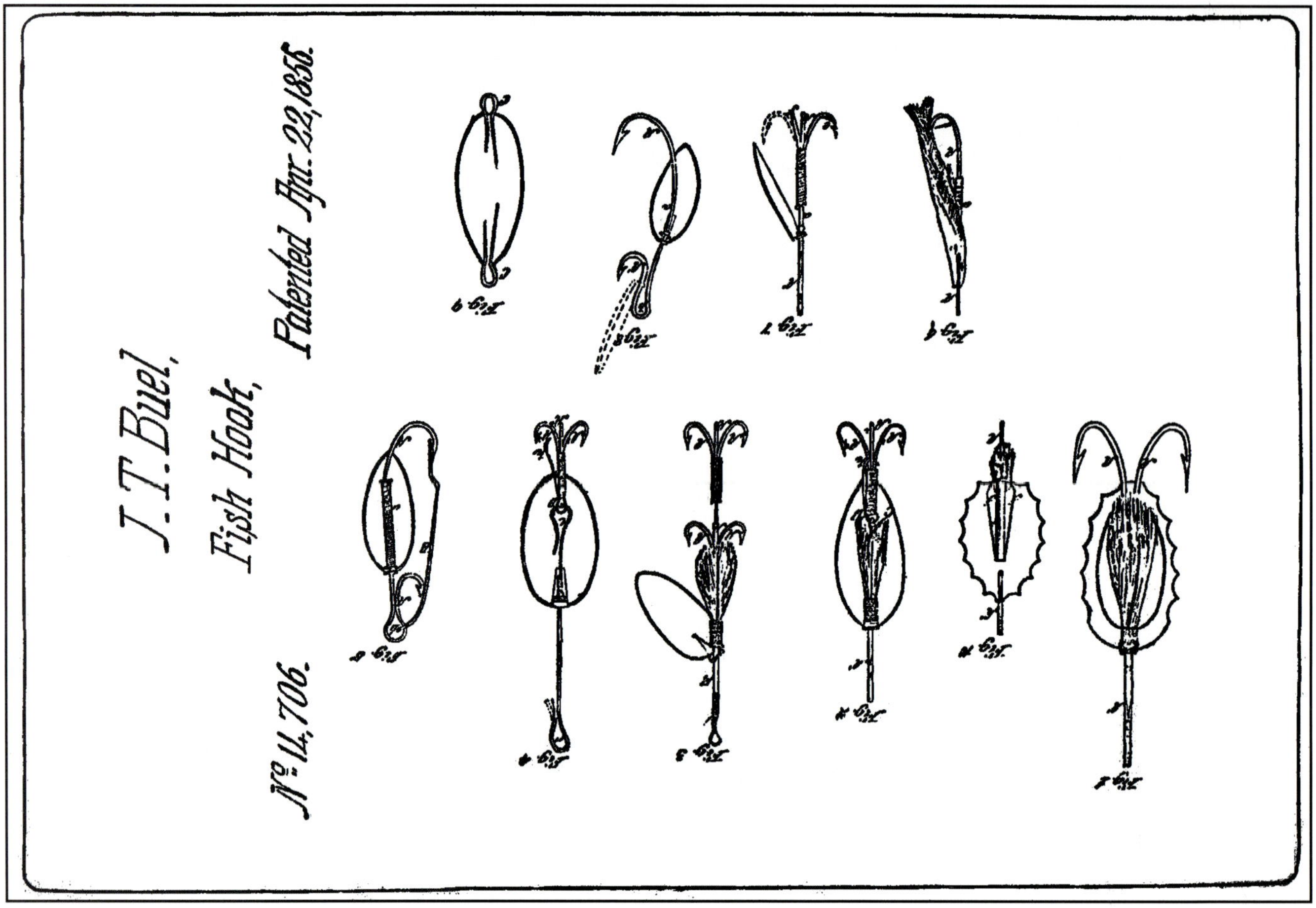

A. Buel's April 22, 1856 patent. This is a fairly complicated patent that includes several features pertaining to the method of hook attachment. It also illustrates a way of interchanging spoons of different sizes and colors without removing the lure from the line.

B. This lure is marked J.T. Buel Patent April 6, 1852 and April 22, 1856. It is illustrated in Figures 5 and 8 of the patent above. The spoon on this lure can be removed or changed by sliding it off the smaller hook at the front of the shaft. The smaller hook also serves as an attachment for a minnow or other live bait. $500.00 – 750.00.

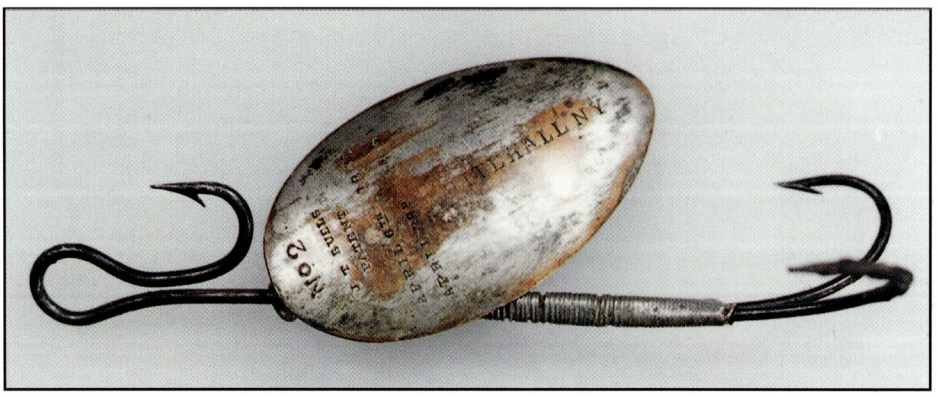

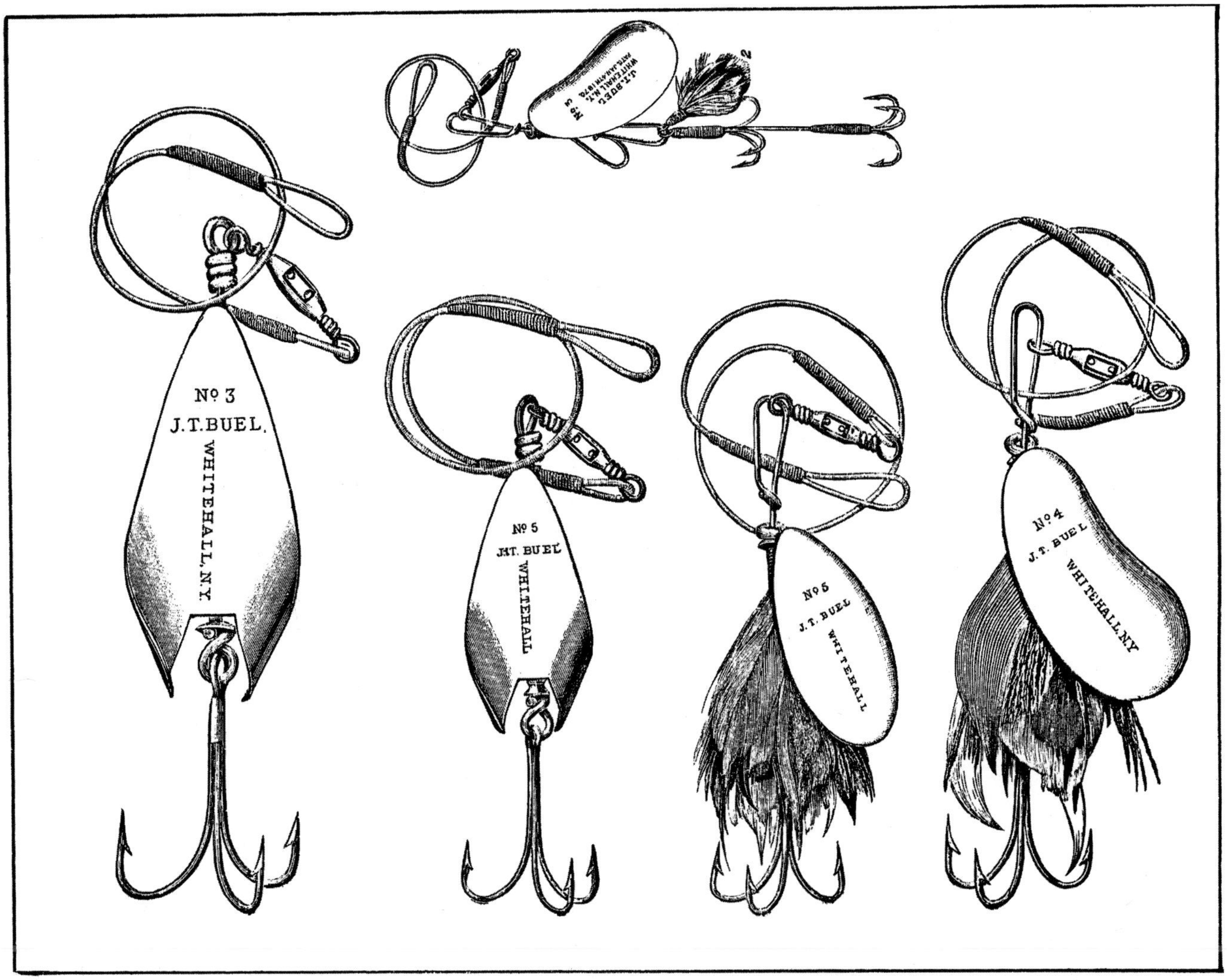

Page from an 1888 Thomas Chubb catalog. The top lure is one of the Jan. 4, 1876, patents shown on the next page. It is a fly spoon-bait hook combination. The two lures on the lower left are the 1852 "Arrowhead" spinners, The two on the right are fly spoons.

Ad from the Feb. 20, 1886, *American Angler*. Charles Pike was the owner of the J.T. Buel Co. at the time.

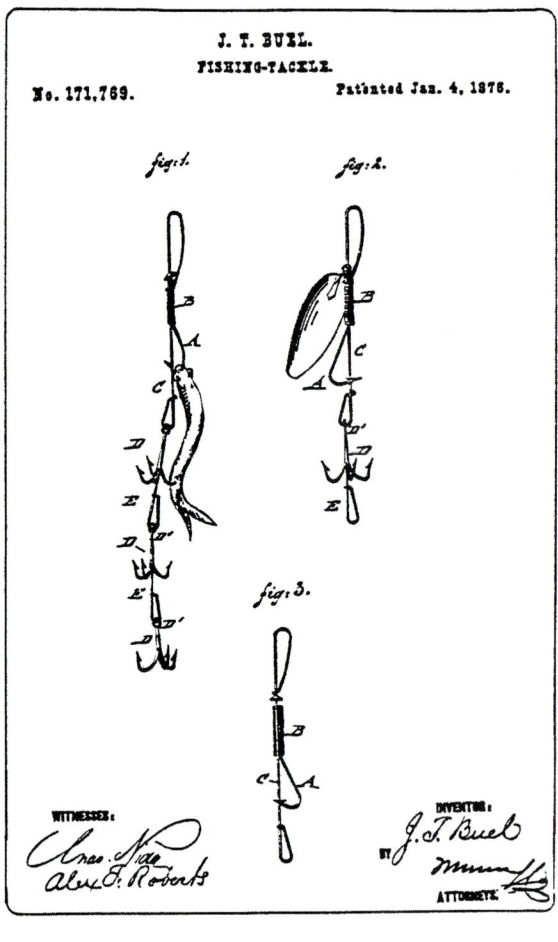

A.

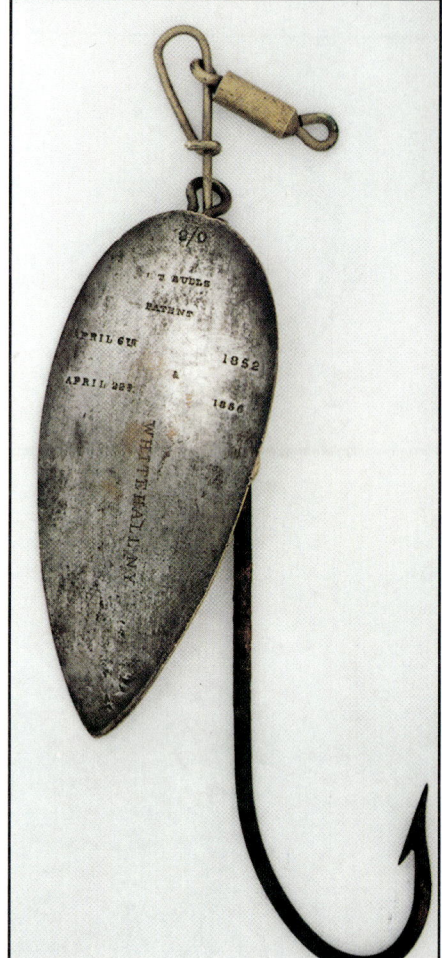

B.

A. Buel patent of Jan. 4, 1876. This patent is similar to the 1856 patent, but differs in that the upper hook is attached to a sliding wire ferrule that can be adjusted to accommodate different sized baits. The lower treble hooks can be attached or removed by means of a snap.

B. This bait is much like the regular fly spoon, except it is attached to the shaft in a reverse position. It is marked "J. T. Bucls - Patent - April 6th-1852 - Whitchall, N.Y." This lure has none of the features found in the 1852 and 1856 patents. $75.00 – 100.00.

C. A smaller version of the spoon above but with the patent dates stamped longitudinally on the spinner blade. Buel seemed to use every conceivable configuration for applying his name and patent dates to the lures. $75.00 – 100.00.

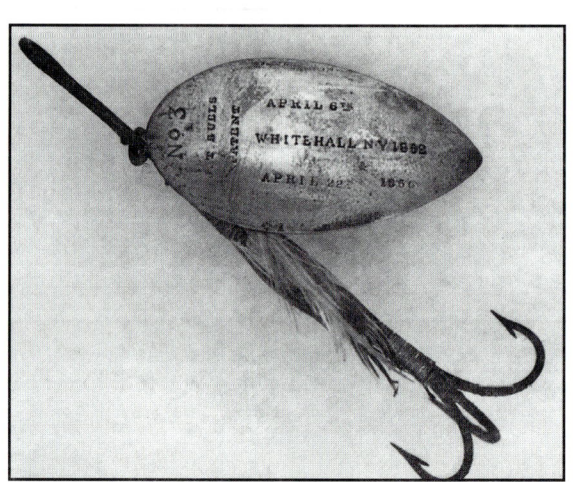

C.

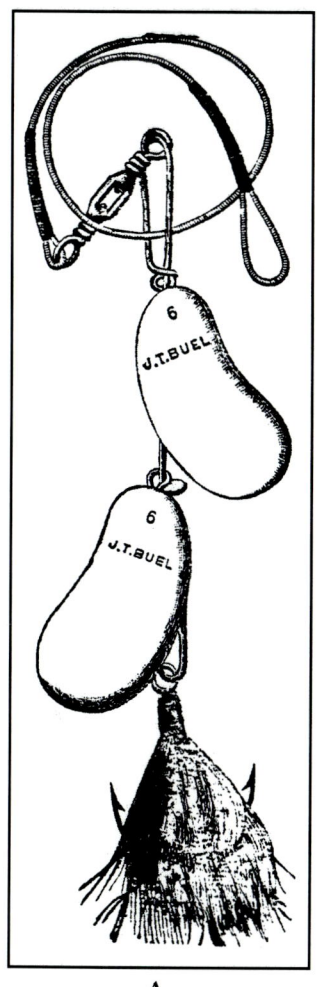

A. A cut from an 1895 H. H. Kiffe catalog showing Buel's two-bladed fly spoon. It was made in at least five sizes. $30.00 – 40.00.

B. Buel's Kidney Fly Spoon with old box. This lure was made in at least 11 sizes. $30.00 – 40.00; box $500.00+.

C. Buel's Fly Spoon. It was made in at least 12 sizes, including a 3/0 "Maskinonge Bait" with attached leader. $30.00 – 40.00.

A.

B.

C.

A.

A. This Buel spinner look-alike is marked "Pikes Spinner - Pat. Apl'd for." It is 3" long and made from two interlocking pieces of nickel plated brass. Charles Pike was an employee of Buel who bought the company in 1885. There is a good chance this lure was designed by Mr. Pike. $150.00 – 200.00.

B. Buel's other Jan. 4, 1876 patent.

C. These blades are all marked "H. W. Buel - Whitehall, N. Y." In all probability, they were made by Harvey Buel, Julio's half-brother, when and why are not known. $30.00 – 40.00 each.

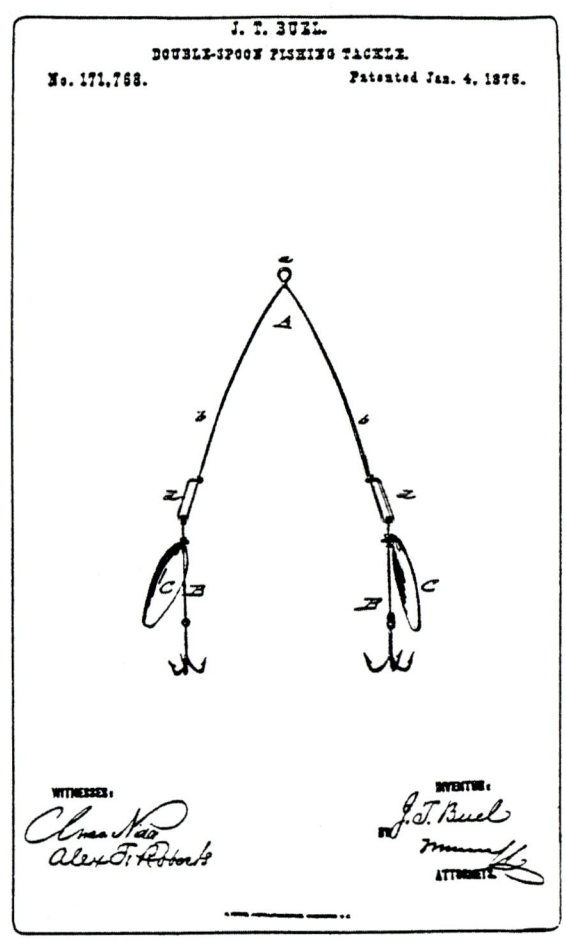

B.

C.

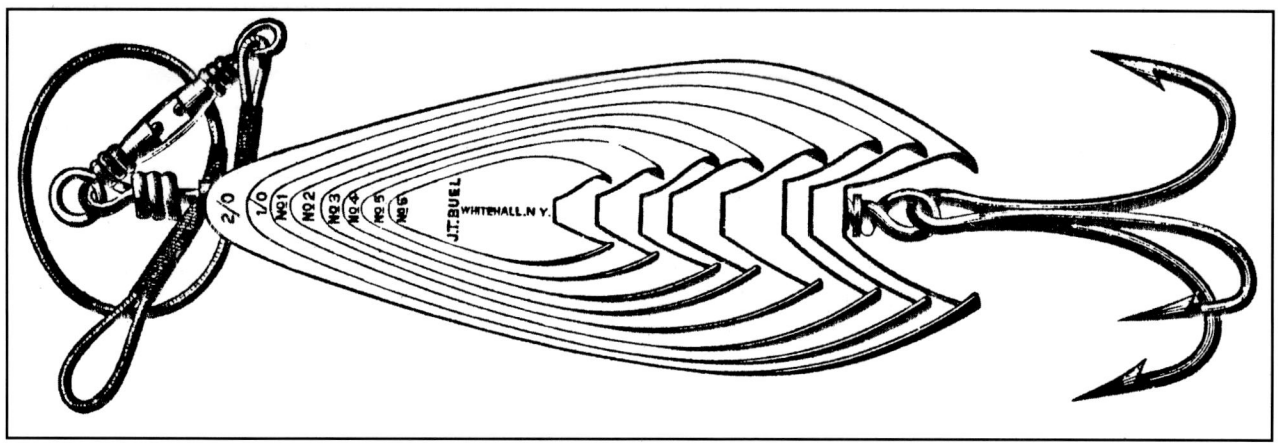

Cut showing the exact sizes of "Arrowhead" spinners in 1895. In later years they were available up to 6/0 and larger if special ordered.

Collector's Postscript

It is difficult to determine the age of Buel lures. His lack of advertising and the unavailability of nineteenth century catalogs makes it mostly a matter of guesswork. The baits bearing the patent dates appear to be the oldest, with the "T" pattern logo being the next in line. The common small print two-line logo first appears in the 1890s.

Most of the trade houses in the 1890s carried a small standard line of Buel lures, such as those illustrated in this chapter. I don't believe the line was expanded much until 1902 when Pike moved into larger quarters. However, this is just speculation, as I have not seen a catalog printed prior to 1900. By 1920, the Buel catalog contained well over a hundred items.

The most elusive baits seem to be those having patent dates. The 1854, 1856, and 1876 patent models appear to be almost nonexistent. A later twentieth century version of Buel's second 1876 patent (page 16) does show up occasionally. This does not have the sliding ferrule as shown in the patent drawing. Hopefully, in time, more information will surface to complete the J.T. Buel story.

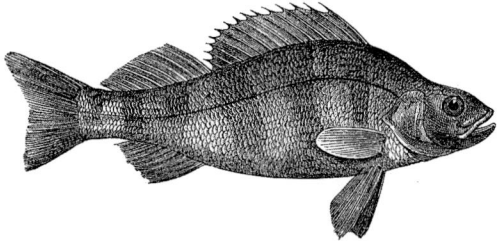

T. H. Bate & Co.

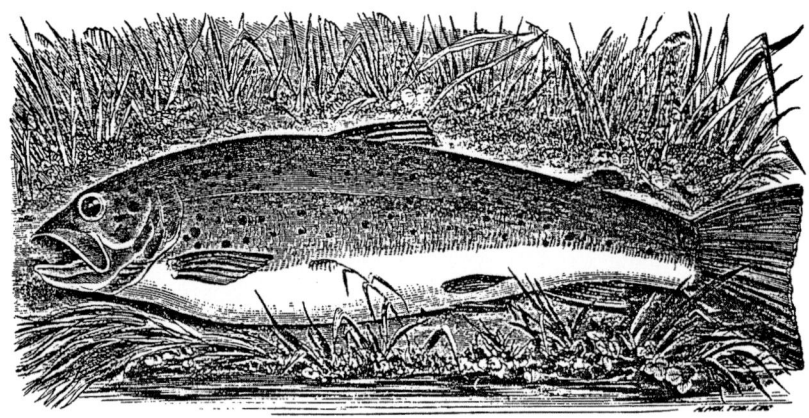

THOMAS H. BATE & CO.

No. 7 WARREN STREET,

NEW YORK,

MANUFACTURERS AND IMPORTERS OF

NEEDLES, FISH HOOKS,

FISHING RODS AND TACKLE

OF EVERY DESCRIPTION.

The Thomas H. Bate Company of New York City had its origin in England. In 1822, James and Thomas Bate of Redditch, England, owners of a needle and hook factory, sent a representative to New York for the purpose of establishing a tackle company in that city.

The new business was a success and continued to operate under the Bate name until 1873 when it became the William Mills and Son Company.

During the period between 1822 and 1873, the company underwent a number of name changes, all variations of the Bate name. The following information is from an old William Mills & Son catalog.

1822, T & J Bate; 1836, Thomas Bate; 1843, T & T. H. Bate; 1850, T. H. Bate & Co.; 1853, Thomas H. Bate; 1859, Thomas H. Bate & Co.

Reel collectors are probably more familiar with the Bate Company than lure collectors. The only lure bearing the Bate name that appears with any regularity is the Serpentine Spinner. This lure was originally patented by Charles DeSaxe of New York, N.Y. in 1855 and assigned to Thomas H. Bate.

T.H. Bate & Co.

A.

A. Large size Serpentine Minnow marked Patent applied for. This is a size No. 1. This size Serpentine Minnow is much harder to find than the smaller sizes. $300.00 – 400.00.

B. Patent for the Serpentine Minnow. Charles De Saxe assigned this patent to Thomas H. Bate.

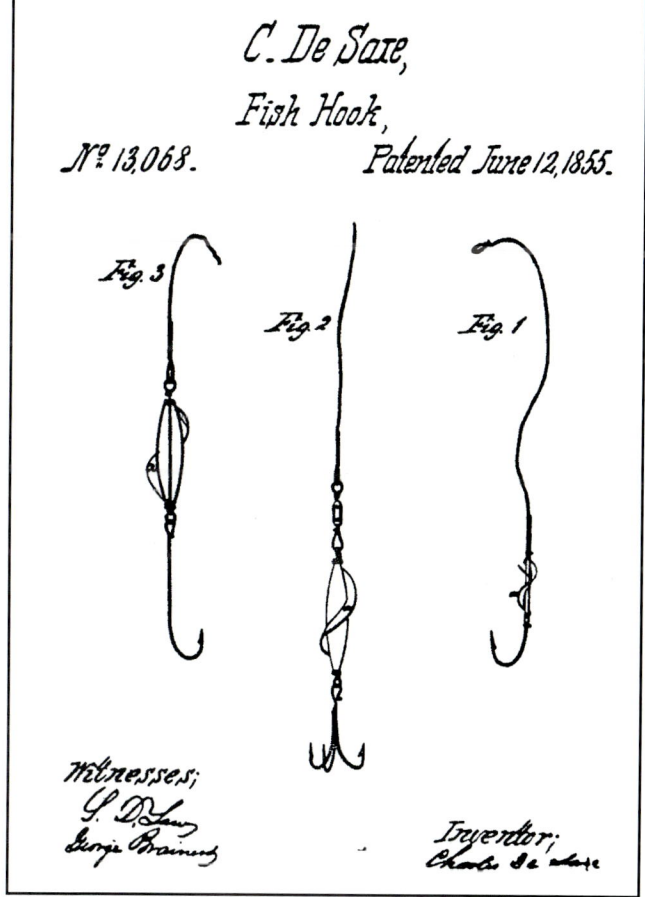

B.

T.H. Bate & Co.

A.

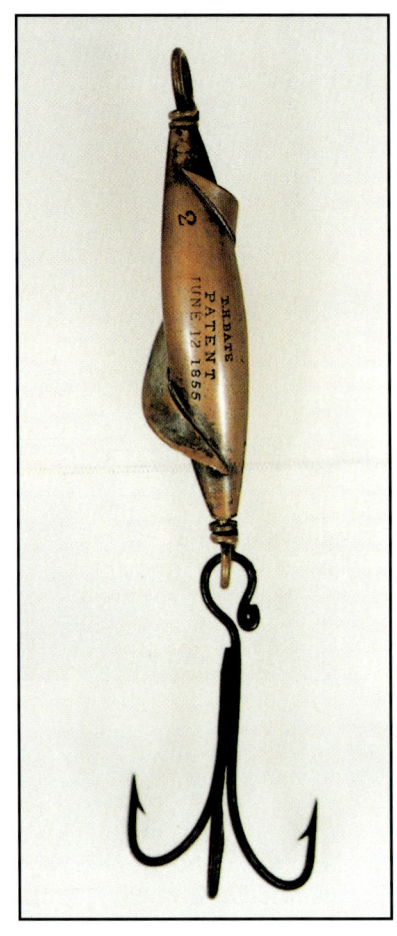

B.

A. Bate's Serpentine Spinner in size 3. This bait is marked T.H. BATE'S patent June 12, 1855. $150.00 – 200.00.

B. Bate Serpentine Spinner in size 2. This Bate is marked T.H. BATE (no "S") patent June 12, 1855. This appears to be the earlier of the two pictured.

C. Tin Squid pictured in the 1867 catalog. It was made in three sizes and had a brass tag attached marked T.H. BATE N.Y. $100.00 – 200.00.

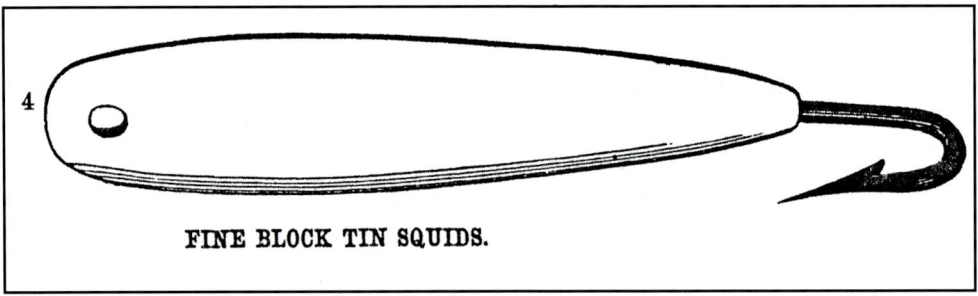

C.

T.H. Bate & Co.

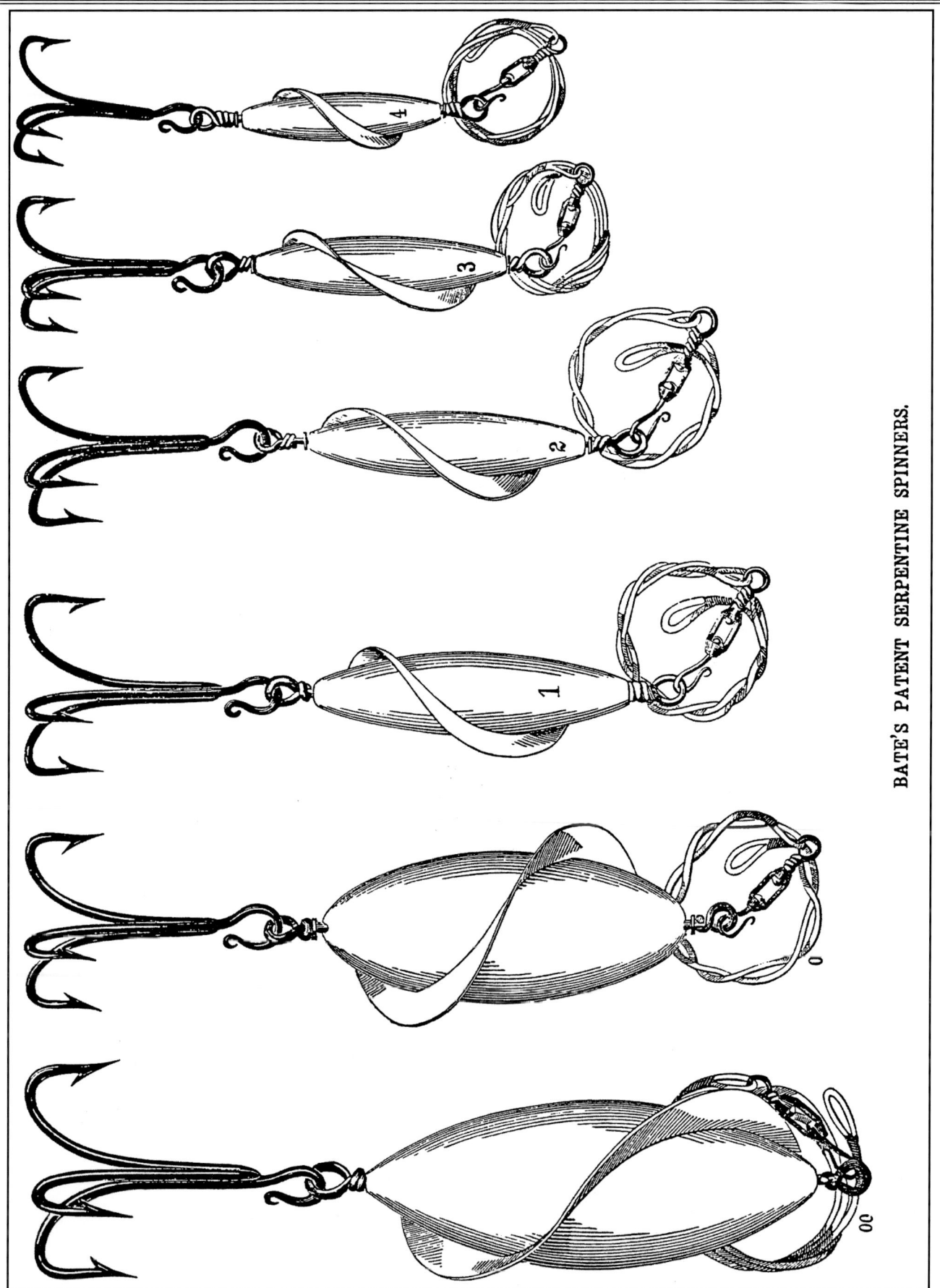

BATE'S PATENT SERPENTINE SPINNERS.

1867 catalog illustrations of the Bate's Serpentine Spinners. Shown actual size.

T.H. Bate & Co.

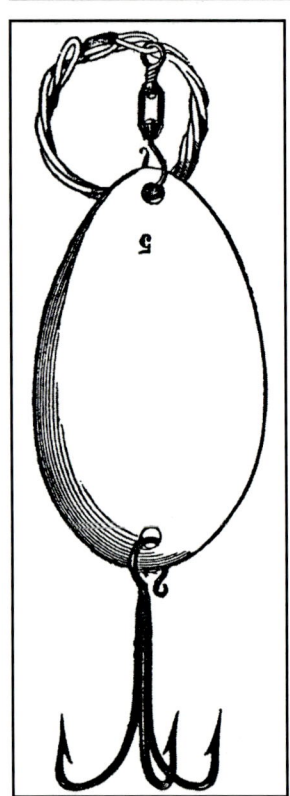

A. Cut from an 1867 catalog showing the "Treble Hook Spoon." They were made in five sizes.

B. Cut from the same catalog showing the "Single Hook Spoon." This spoon was also made in five sizes.

C. Cut of the "Lake Spoon." It was made in three sizes and had a brass body in the center of the spoon, probably for added weight.

D. No. 3 Lake Spoon. It is marked T.H. BATE N. Y. $200.00 – 250.00.

Collector's Postscript

Most of the illustrations for this chapter came from a copy of an 1867 Bates & Co. catalog. This catalog also contained lures patented by J.T. Buel and a variety of English lures and reels.

A.

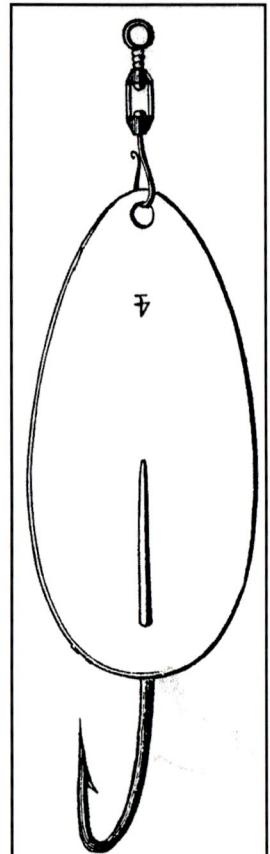

B.

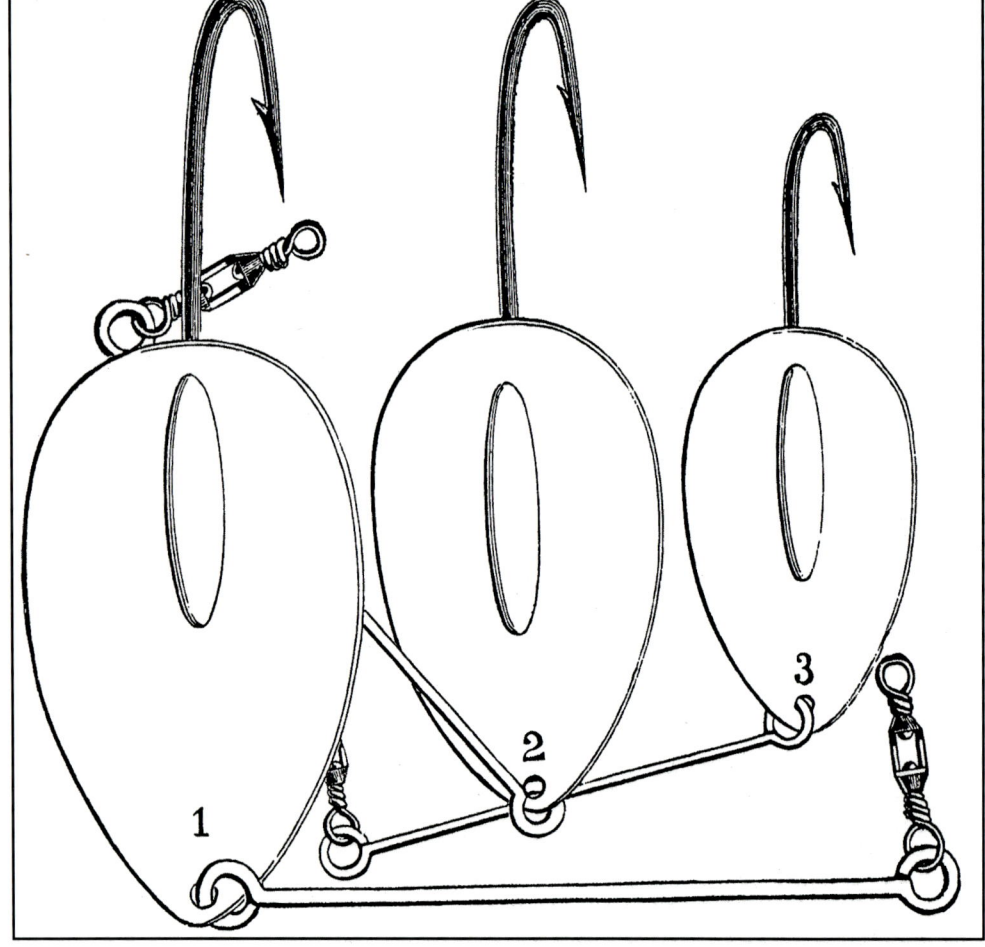

C.

D.

1855 T.H. Bate's poster. This poster is one of the earliest pieces of American angling advertising in existence. The background of the poster is brown "velvet" (flock). The image size is 16¼ by 20½. Printed on the medallion in the upper right corner is "First Prize at the World's Fair, New York 1853." In the bottom center circle is printed "Serpentine Spinner, Patent Applied For." It is copyrighted in 1855. Note the neat folding net on the left side.

Riley Haskell

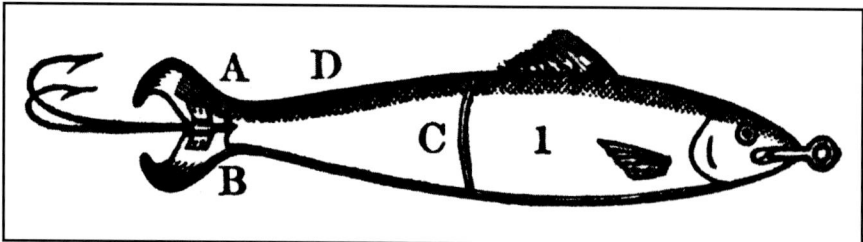

It is unfortunate that so little is known about Riley Haskell because he created one of the all-time great fishing lures. Hopefully, as time passes, more information will become available.

Riley's father was Foster Haskell. Foster came from one of the Eastern states at an early age and settled in Mentor, Ohio, on a farm where he lived until his death on May 21, 1873. His wife's name was Polly. She was the eldest of eight children of Scribner Huntoon, an early settler in Concord, New Hampshire. They had six children, Emily, Albert, William, George, Mrs. Alvin Daniels, and Riley. Polly died March 18, 1875.

The first mention found of Riley is in the June 24, 1858, copy of the *Painsville Telegraph*. It announced that Riley Haskell was opening a new gun shop in the basement of House's block and was ready to attend to all orders in the line of manufacturing or repairing rifles. On January 6, 1859, the *Telegraph* announced that he was moving to the premises one door east of the bank. The 1860 census lists Riley as living at Cowles House, N. W. corner of Main & St. Clair, Painsville, Ohio, age 33 years.

On September 29, 1859, the *Telegraph* once again announced, "PATENT FISHING HOOK — Riley Haskell has secured a patent on his angling improvement. The hooks are fixed to an artificial fish, the lower portion on the body spins, the fish is silver-plated and the whole thing is called, by way of a name, the "Trolling Bait." It is so neatly made as to resemble very nearly the natural fish."

Riley made these baits in three sizes. The smallest size, excluding the hooks, was 3½" long, and the other two, 4½" and 6" respectively. He used a combination of copper and brass to manufacture the lures. They have been found made entirely of copper and entirely of brass, but most are a combination of the two. A common configuration would be a copper body with brass fins and tail.

I took one of the lures to the Industrial Arts Department at the University of Wisconsin-Stout at Menomonie, Wisconsin, and showed it to Dr. Henry Thomas and Dick Klatt. They concluded that it had been stamped in four separate pieces and soldered together, with the fins and tail being inserted and soldered separately. Before stamping, the sheet metal was probably run through a roller press to apply the scale pattern. Riley's signature was then applied with a separate stamp to this sheet of metal. This could account for the odd placement of his signature on some lures.

Riley made his beautiful minnow for at least 16 years. I base this on the fact that Genio C. Scott in his 1875 book, *Fishing In American Waters,* states that the Haskell Trolling Bait can be had at most fishing tackle stores. He also mentions that he has heard good report of the bait's success.

Riley died at the age of 55 on June 24, 1882. The following is an obituary from the June 29, 1882 *Telegraph*. "Mr. Riley Haskell died of apoplexy Friday night at 2 p.m., June 24, 1882. The funeral services were conducted by Rev. W. B. Hendryx at the family residence in South Mentor last Sabbath afternoon. Mr. Haskell had the reputation of being the finest gunsmith in Northern Ohio. He was always a gentleman and will be greatly missed by those who knew him best!"

Among the items listed in his estate were eight unfinished reels. It's possible that, somewhere, probably on a dusty shelf or in a rusty tackle box, there sits a long neglected reel bearing the magic name "Riley Haskell."

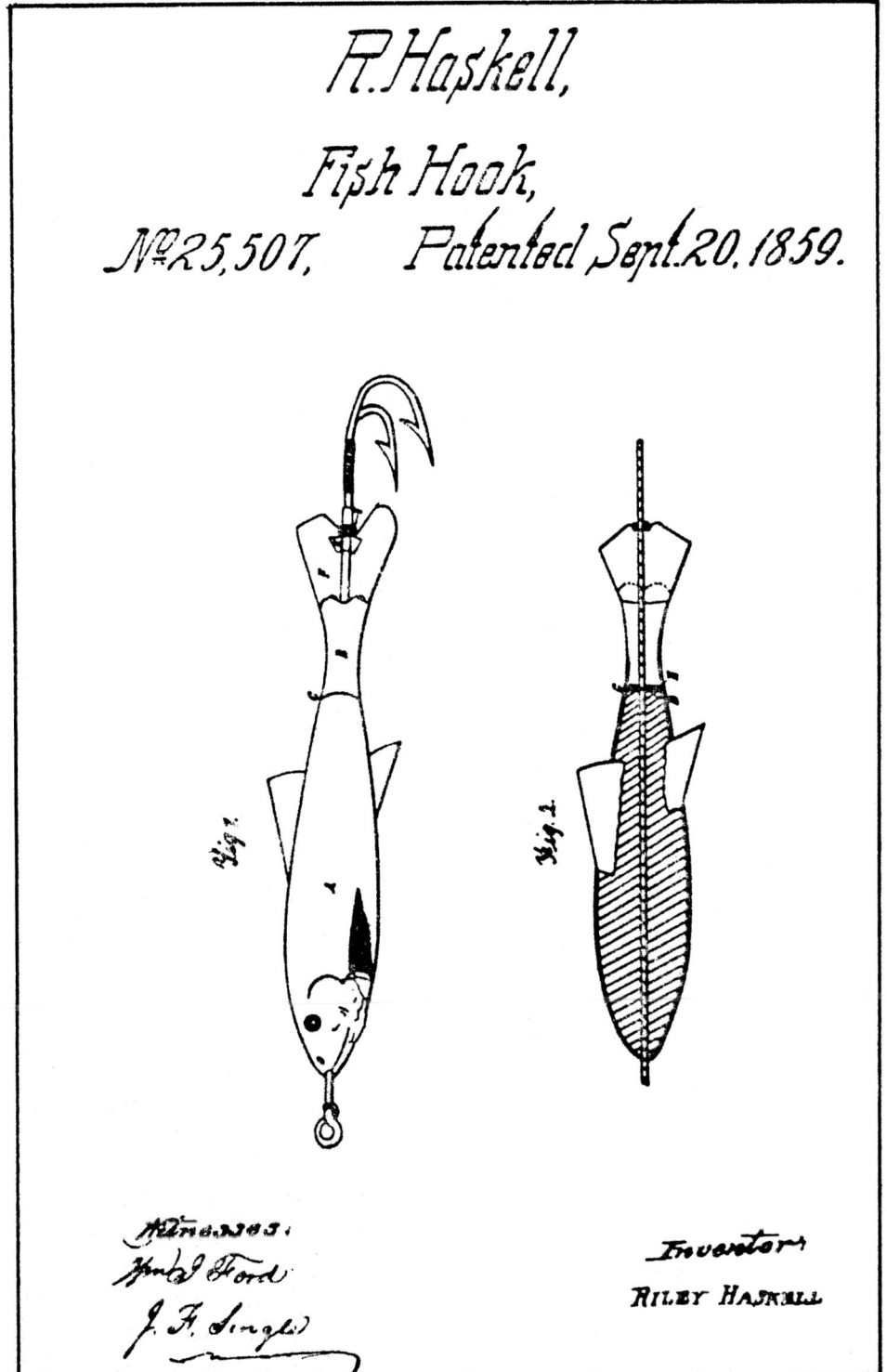

Riley Haskell's 1859 patent drawing. He states that the lure can also be made of India rubber, gutta percha, wood, etc.

A.

A. All three sizes of the Haskell Minnow. The smallest size (excluding the hook) is 3½". The medium size is 4½" and the large size is 6". $2,500.00+.

B. "The Dream Box." With the exception of the medium-sized minnow on the left, this is exactly the way this box was found.

B.

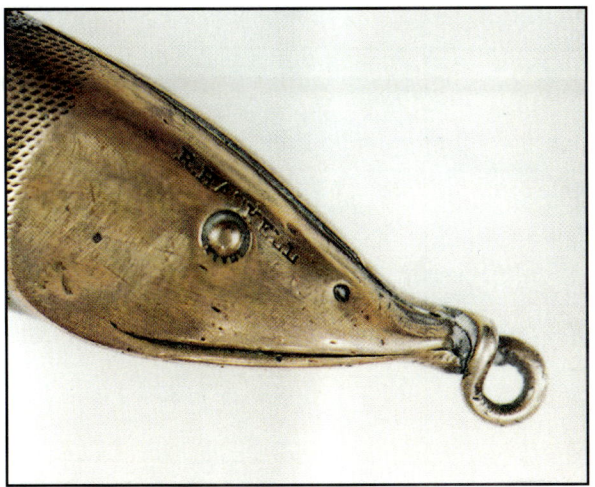

A.

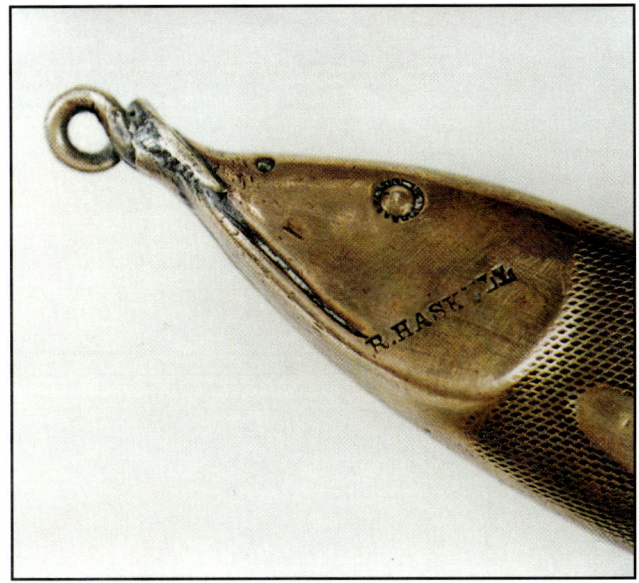

B.

A. & B. Close-up views of the large size (6") Minnow. It is unusual for the Haskell name to be stamped on the head of the lure.

C. & D. 3½" size with copper body and brass fins, showing back and front.

C.

D.

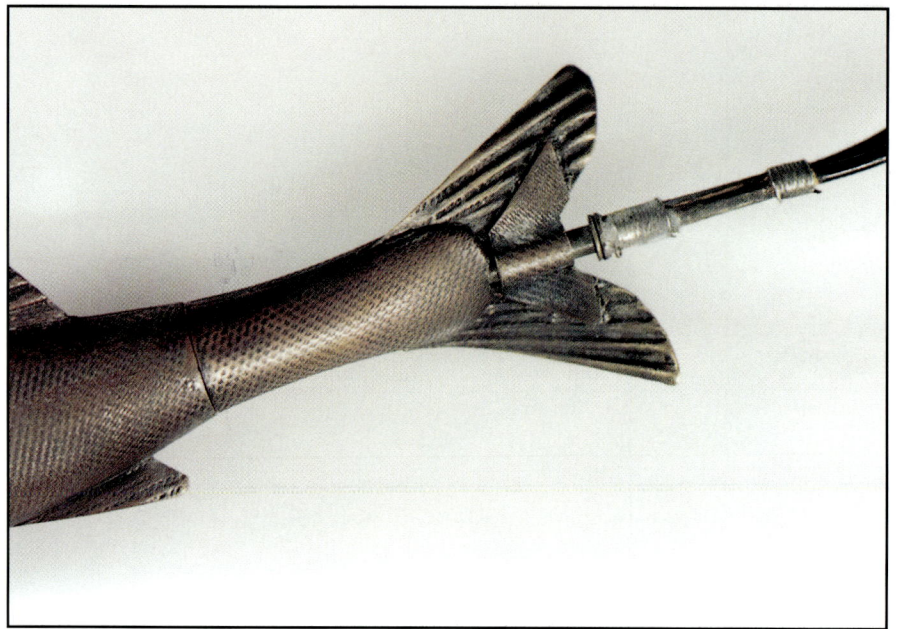

A.

A. Close up of the tail section on the 4½" size. Note how the hooks are both soldered and wound with brass wire.

B. 4½" model. Has unusual scale markings on the gill plate. The treble hook is not original.

C. Close-up of the front section of the 4½" size.

B.

C.

A.

B.

A. & B. Two 3½" minnows. Although all of the Haskell Minnows are very similar in appearance, they each have slight differences that make them unique. The two above have bottom fins that are a little longer and more pointed than normal.

C. & D. An all-brass 3½" minnow that doesn't have a scale pattern. A very unique and beautiful lure. Possibly an older model.

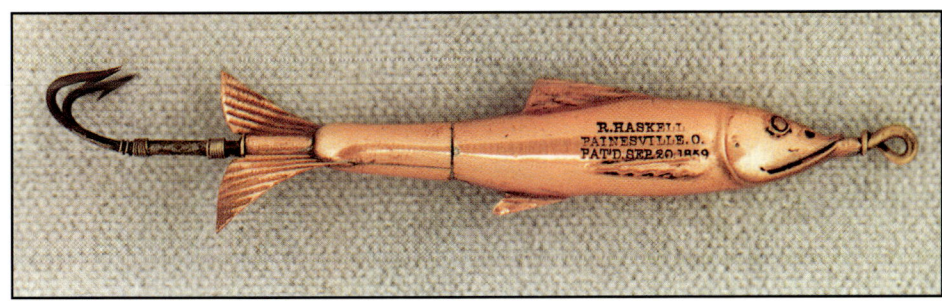

C.

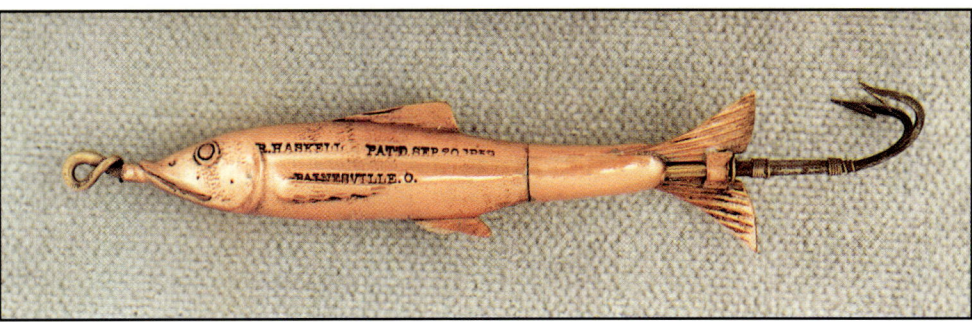

D.

Two views of a 4½" size. This lure is unusual because the scale finish extends to cover the whole head. Note the tiny hole in the gill plate; these are found on all Haskells.

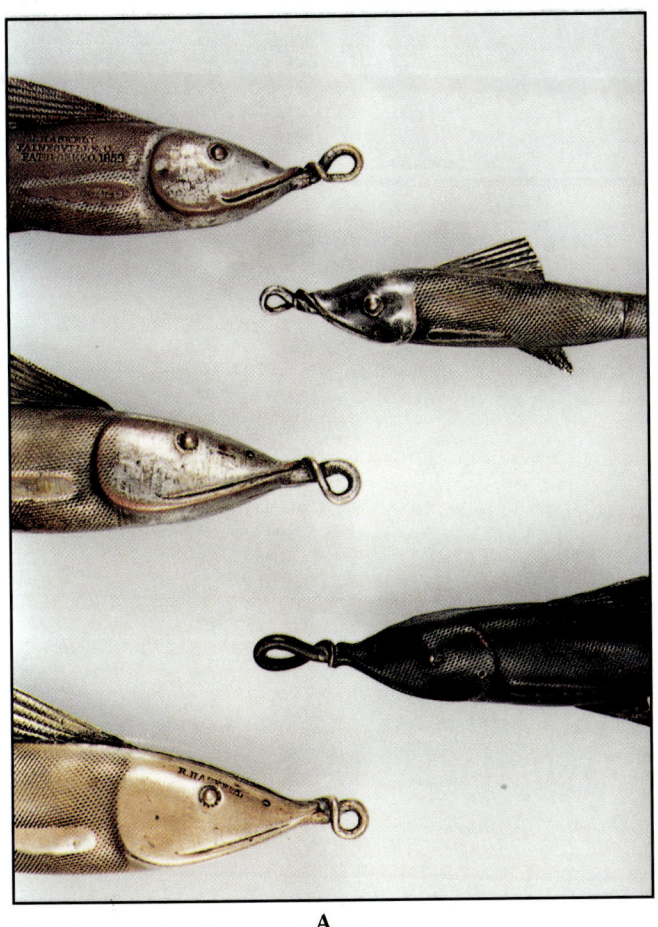

A. Five at once. Two 6" models, two 4½" models, and one 3½" model.

B. 4½" model with much of its silver plate remaining. Note the old clip-on swivel.

Collector's Postscript

All Haskells are rare and desirable, but the 6" size seems to be the most difficult to find. The 3½" and the 4½" sizes have been found in roughly equal quantities. Consider yourself lucky if you find one of these jewels.

W.D. Chapman

In 1818 Sylvester Bodman returned to Northampton, Massachusetts, to procure a team of horses. He had staked out a new home in what is now Theresa, New York, and needed a team to transport his family and belongings. His own horses were still in Theresa where Morse Stark was watching after his crops and livestock. He had very little success until he became acquainted with Dudley Chapman. Dudley who was from the nearby town of Deerfield had the much needed horses and decided to return with Sylvester to Theresa.

So it was that Dudley arrived in Theresa and settled on Road 42 near the Bodman's farm.

He married Sophronia Peck, and they were soon blessed with a baby boy. William Dudley was born in 1820, the first of five children born to the Chapmans. He had three sisters, Mary, Martha, one who died in infancy, and one brother named Simion.

Little is known of William's early life except that he was self-supporting by the age of 17 and was an avid fisherman and outdoorsman. Perhaps a better insight of William's youth can be gained by recalling an incident told to reporter Ernest G. Cook of the *Watertown Daily News* on the occasion of William's 89th birthday. This was in 1909.

"I was a young shaver when our folks moved from the farm into the settlement or village of Theresa on the Hoboken side of the river. One balmy June morning I was out in the back yard when a voice called to me from across the way. It was Jonathan Thompson, who started the first tannery here, and as I approached he said, 'This will be one of the best nights for fishing we will have this year and I am going down to Red Lake to try my luck; don't you want to go?' Well, wouldn't you want to go if you were a boy? I did and then happened to think it was Sunday and so it was out of the question for me and told Thompson so. 'Pshaw, your father won't care if we get the fish,' replied Thompson. 'I guess you don't know pa as well as I do,' I told him. 'He will tan my jacket if he finds out I have gone down to the lake with you on Sunday.'

"Father's commands, you know, were as strict as the laws of Medes and the Persians, but the temptation was too great and I decided to run the risk of the tanning for the chance to fish. We went down to the river in an old canoe, arriving at the lake in good season to collect plenty of fat pines for jacklights before dark. Others must have thought it would be good fishing, for soon two other boats came into the lake. 'Bill' Townsend was in one and he landed where we were. Soon it began to thunder and lightning and a fierce storm was about to break over us. Townsend said there would be no fishing and he would head for home.

"You just let them go," whispered Thompson to me, "and after they are gone we will go up to 'Uncle' Noah Ashle's shanty and stay there while it's storming and then we will try our luck.

"Well, we did have luck. I speared 18 muscallonge, and five of them would weigh 20 pounds each. We reached home the next morning and Thompson said, "Now you let me run this thing.

"So he put the finest fish on a string and led the way up to our place. When Father saw us he exclaimed, "Well, well boys, that is great luck!" And the licking never came. However, it was the last time in all my many days of fishing that I ever allowed myself to fish on Sunday."

On August 28, 1844, William married Mary Ryan of Theresa, by whom he had six children, of whom the eldest, Mary J., died at the age of 15, and

Picture of Theresa Falls on the Indian River, taken from an 1855 map. Note the maximum use of water power, main source of energy in the 19th century.

George B. at the age of three. Four survived, Ada A. (Mrs. Jason C. Morow), Ellen (Mrs. E.R. Stockwell), Byron W., and Lotta A. (Mrs. E.D. Perrins). Byron married Belle Simons of Medina, N.Y., and they had a son and a daughter, Jesse and Mary A. Later Byron became a partner in his father's business.

William learned the carpenter's trade early on but was soon involved in other endeavors. By 1860, he had established a large watch and jewelry business and was the owner of a steamboat on the Indian River.

The Indian River runs through Theresa in a northeasterly direction before emptying into Red Lake. It provided power and a means of transporting supplies and products for the early industries. William owned the second boat on the river. He purchased it on the Erie Canal around 1860, and had it transported overland to Theresa. It was operated for a short time and then sold. He also built and operated two other boats, The Lady of the Lake and Sir John Keach. The exact time frame during which William owned these boats is unknown.

It is known that on May 15, 1866, he was granted a patent for an improvement in fishing tackle. It is reasonable to assume that it was around this time that he started the fishing tackle manufacturing business. Business was great, and the W.D. Chapman Company soon grew to occupy a large three-story building in downtown Theresa. During the company's peak years, it did an annual business in excess of $60,000 and employed five salesmen to travel and call on the trade houses. There were also about a dozen girls to trim the fish hooks and several men to make the fish lures and other items. An article in the *Theresa Sentinel* for November 11, 1886, states that four agents would start out in January with a sample case worth $653. W.D. Chapman lures were very popular and sold well in every state and Canada.

Sometime between April 1875, and January 1876, son Byron joined the company as a partner. Thereafter, the business was known as W.D. Chapman and Son.

By 1886, the annual catalog boasted that W.D. Chapman and Son was the largest manufacturer of trolling baits in the United States. Indeed, this catalog lists (if you count the sizes) over 90 different lures, and this doesn't include the imported insects and minnows. William also invented and manufactured other items, including a revolving show case, desk letter file, and spring birdcage holder. He claimed the birdcage holder was the most profitable invention he had patented. During the heyday of the company, they used several tons of brass wire every year to manufacture the birdcage springs.

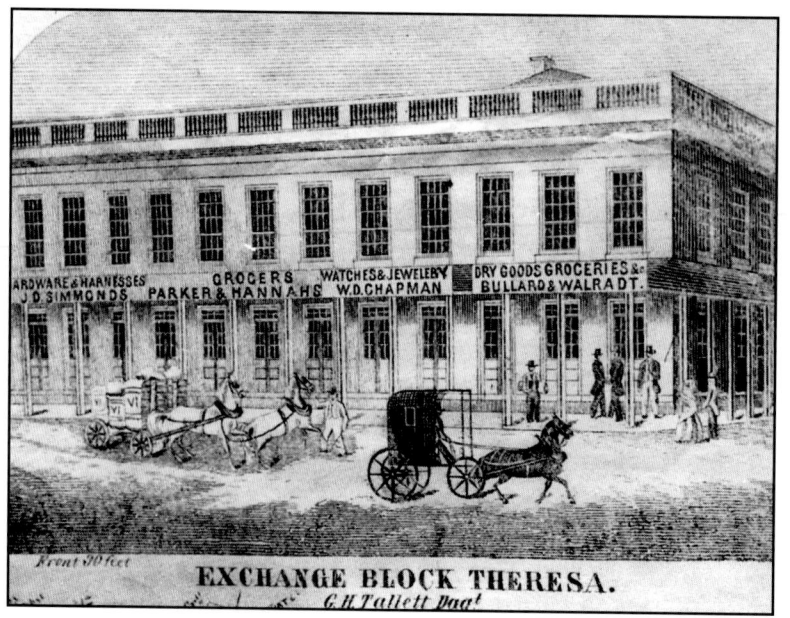

Exchange Block in Theresa. W.D. Chapman's shop is second from the right. Taken from an 1855 map.

By 1888 the fishing tackle division of the company had moved to Rochester, N.Y., and set up shop at 121 State Street. It was to be the beginning of the end.

On April 5, 1890, a devastating fire consumed the downtown district of Theresa, destroying 42 buildings, including W.D. Chapman and Son's jewelry and watchmaking company. All that remained were one tavern and the American Hotel. The Chapmans' loss was estimated at $3,000 for the building, part of which housed a harness shop, along with an undetermined loss of inventory. Chapman's octagon-shaped house which was nearby was almost destroyed. Dropping strips of carpeting from the roof and keeping a stream of water on them saved the structure.

All of the patterns and dyes used to make the patented items were destroyed, and as the fishing tackle business had already moved to Rochester, they never rebuilt. As for the tackle business, things did not fare as well in Rochester as they had in Theresa. The company soon suffered financial losses. Some said it was because of over-expansion and loss of control by the original founder. Whatever the reason, by 1897, the company had been sold to Gibson and Woodworth of 113 State Street in the same city. Perhaps the death of Byron in 1895 may have contributed to the decision. It isn't known at this time how long Gibson and Woodworth continued in the business, but is is interesting to note that in 1900, the Enterprise Manufacturing Co. (Pflueger) catalog carried the "Bass Bait" and the "Reversible Propeller," both long-time staples in the Chapman line.

An ad for the "Safe Deposit Minnow" confirms that William continued in the tackle business after Byron's death. The ad lists the mailing address as W.D. Chapman, Theresa, N.Y. A circular was available that listed other baits and sinkers. In 1907 he patented a bait which he named the "Omega" because, he said, it would be his last invention in that line. One of the witnesses listed on the patent was Bert Jarvis. Jarvis had worked for the aging Chapman as a handyman and boy Friday.

In 1943, Ernest G. Cook interviewed Jarvis concerning his employment by Chapman. This interview was prompted by a magazine article that had triggered a renewed interest in the famous Chapman baits. The interviewer was the

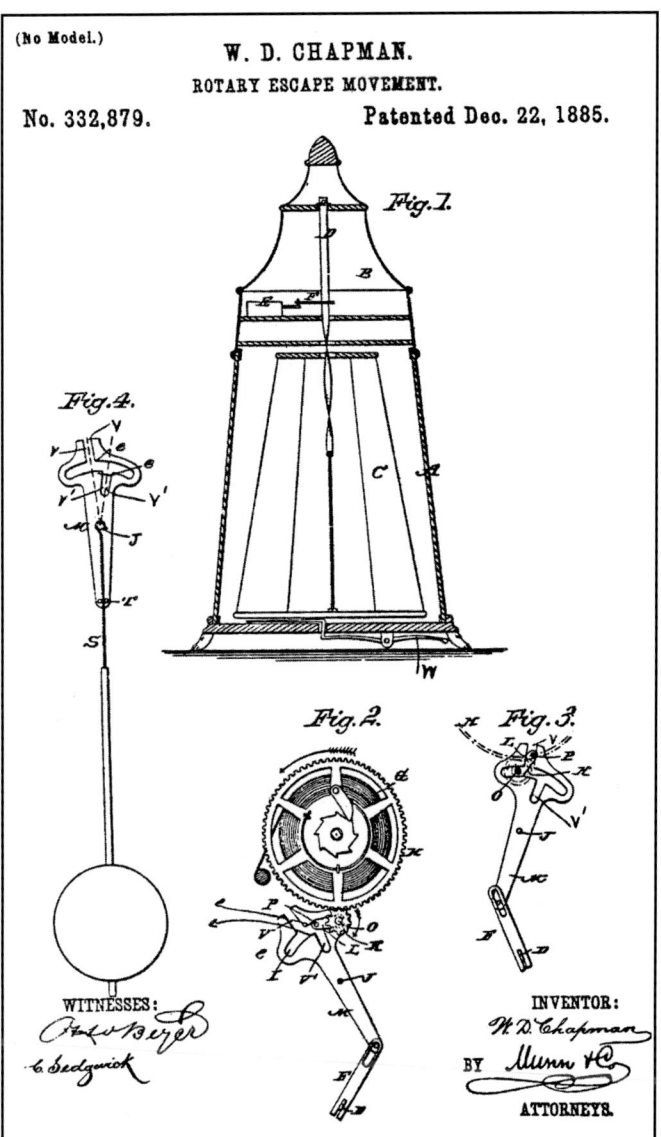

Patent for a wind-up mechanism to operate a revolving show case.

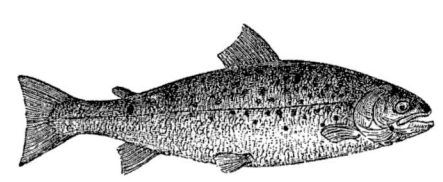

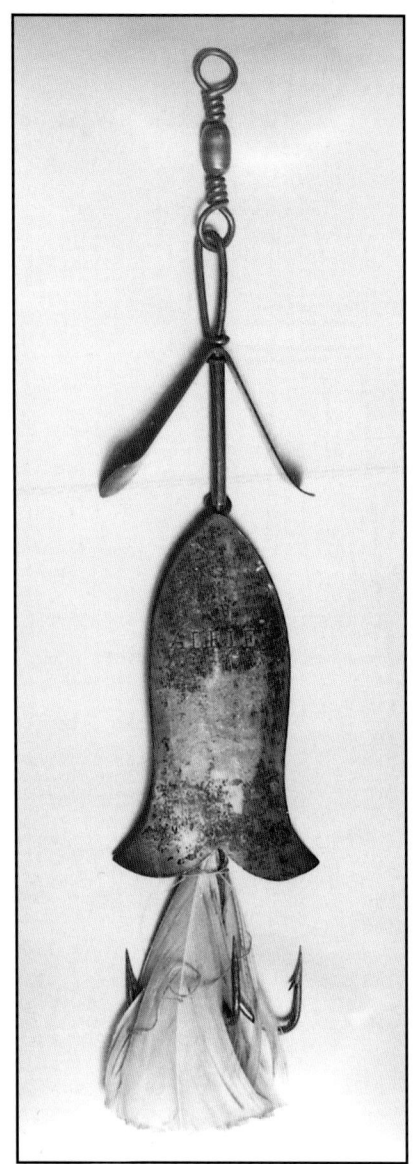

Top blade is marked "W.D. Chapman, Theresa, N.Y." Bottom blade is marked "ALFIE." Top blades are approximately 1" long, bottom blade 3" long. No size markings.

same Mr. Cook of the *Watertown Daily News* who had written the article about Chapman some 30 years earlier. The following is an excerpt from that interview.

"Well, I started in with Mr. Chapman, an old man at that time, with a long and very busy life behind him. He was still very active with his inventions. The work was never hard but I had to keep my wits about me and see that Mr. Chapman was supplied with such articles as he needed. Of course I learned to operate some the presses to turn out the spoons that were in use on the bait.

I remember that Mr. Chapman was seeking to bring out some new kinds of bait, some that would catch fish when other kinds would not attract. He would work to perfect some little part of the bait and the next day he would take me to the Indian Landing and I would get out his boat and away we would go down the Indian River, which would be a real holiday for me. Much of the time Mr. Chapman would tell me stories of his fishing trips when he was a boy and when an older youth and man. He was an expert fisherman.

"One day, after what seemed like weeks of preparation, he had a new model that he thought would be a winner. It was an imitation of a small fish, like pickerel, which had clusters of fish hooks attached on different sides of the bait. It would catch a fish if the fish ever as much as started to take a nibble from it. He thought it was perfection and we got out the boat one summer morning and started fishing with it. The water was rather low in the Indian River at that time and the weeds in the water were thick and high.

"I started to row the boat slowly as Mr. Chapman indicated and we were on the way downstream. It was a most discouraging day. That bait, loaded with hooks, would catch on the weeds and gather them in as a hay rake gathers hay in the meadow. Again and again we stopped the boat to clear the bait of weeds. And all the time we never caught a fish. We tried over and over again with different speeds of the boat, but all to no avail. Before we knew it we were far down the river and below the bluffs, that high ledge of rocks that come sheer out of the water.

"Mr. Chapman was discouraged, for the bait looked like a failure. We were so near the outlet of Red Lake that I proposed we row over and try the bait in the lake. He consented and soon we were on the waters of the lake. No weeds there and the bait worked to perfection. The old man was busy taking in the fish. The day of gloom and discouragement was changed instantly to one of joy and happiness. In certain waters the bait would be a success."

This story serves to illustrate the concern William had for the products he sold to the public. He, along with son Byron, manufactured fishing lures for at least 40 years.

They signed virtually every item they made.

In the early years, William used the mark I.X.L. as an indication of the pride he took in his lures. I.X.L. is a play on words (letters?) meaning I excel. And excel they did!

Chapman lures show a level of craftsmanship and creativity seldom seen in the tackle industry. The influence of their jewelry business is evident in many of the pieces. An abundant use of spirals, tapers, scallops, and sweeping curves, often incorporated into three-dimensional form, set them apart from the ordinary. Casual observers with little, if any, interest in fishing tackle are invariably impressed by the artistic qualities of these lures. The Chapmans were truly masters of their trade.

William's wife Mary died in 1904, and he spent his remaining years with his daughter Ellen (Mrs. E. Stockwell).

W.D. Chapman died in his sleep on July 9, 1909.

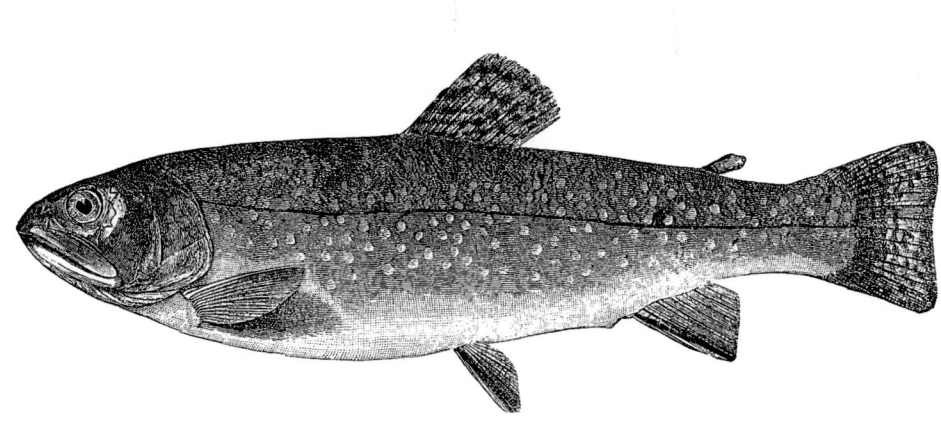

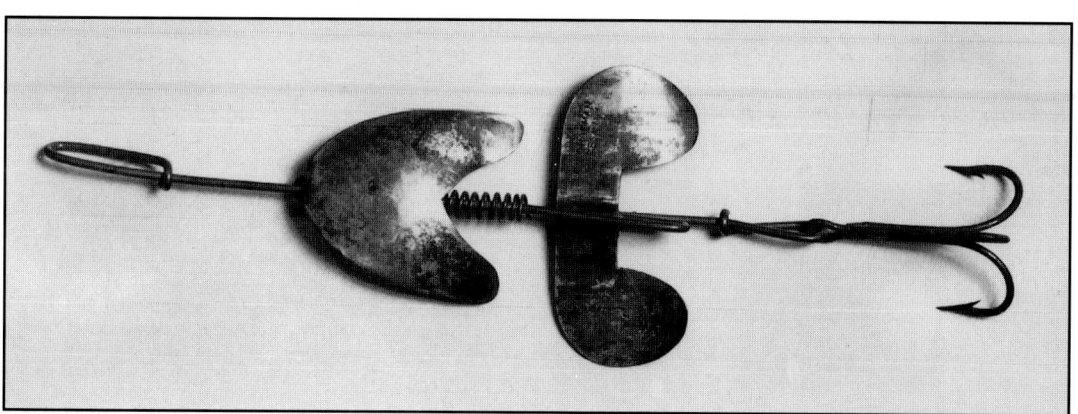

This lure has a bait holder with a spring retainer. The front blade is approximately 1½" long. The rear blade is approximately 2" wide x 1" long. The bottom blade is marked "W.D. Chapman, Theresa, N.Y." There is no size marking.

Cut from 1886 catalog showing rotating display case. Needed to be wound only twice a week.

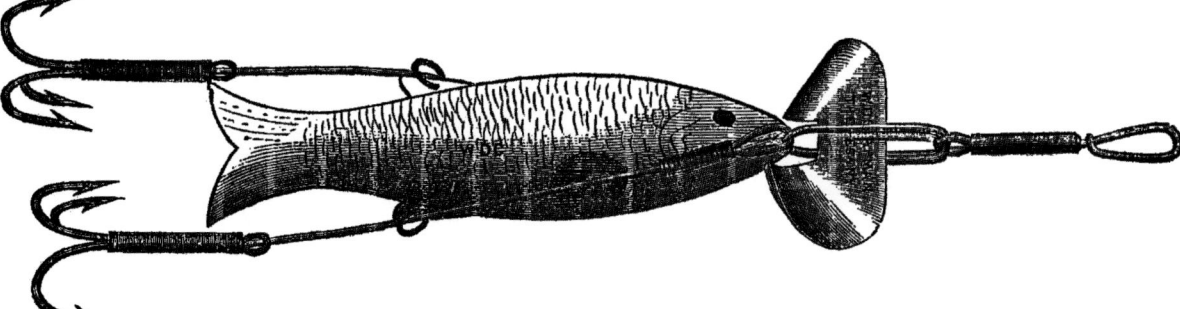

This is a *Forest and Stream* ad from April 1, 1875. The address shown is W.D. Chapman, Manufactory, Theresa, N.Y.

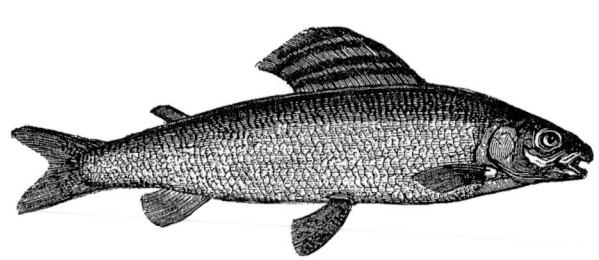

This ad from January 27, 1876, lists W.D. Chapman and Son, Theresa, N.Y. Sometime between the publication of the two ads, William's son Byron joined the company. From this time until Byron's death in 1895, the company was known as W.D. Chapman and Son Company.

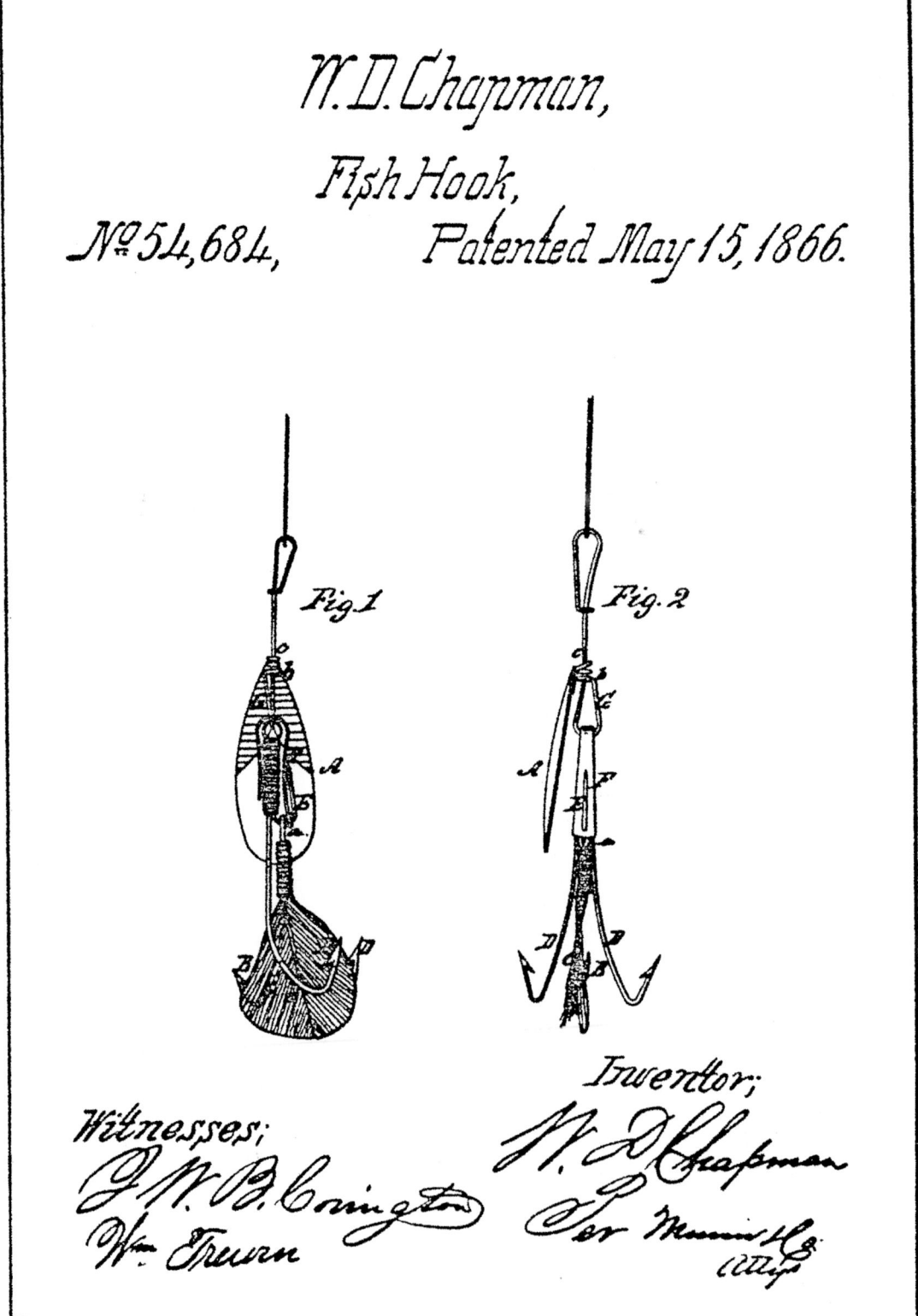

Official drawing of Chapman's first lure patent. This patent was for a method of changing hooks on the lure with supposed relative ease.

A. The component parts of the 1886 patent. The center hook-shaped piece has a hole in its lower end and is marked "W.D.C."

B. The assembled parts as used to attach a fly hook. The device is well made, but probably was too complicated to have been very popular.

C. Blade with patent device attached. Blade is 3" long by 1⅛" wide and marked "W.D. Chapman, Theresa, N.Y." Also has I.X.L stamped in center but has no size marking.

A.

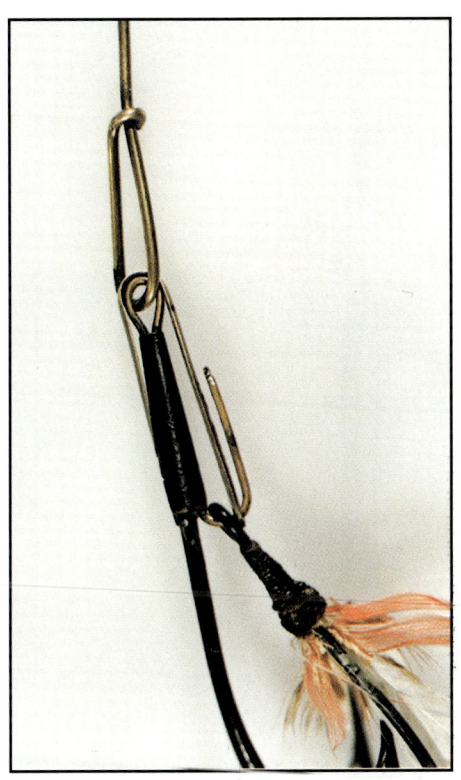

B.

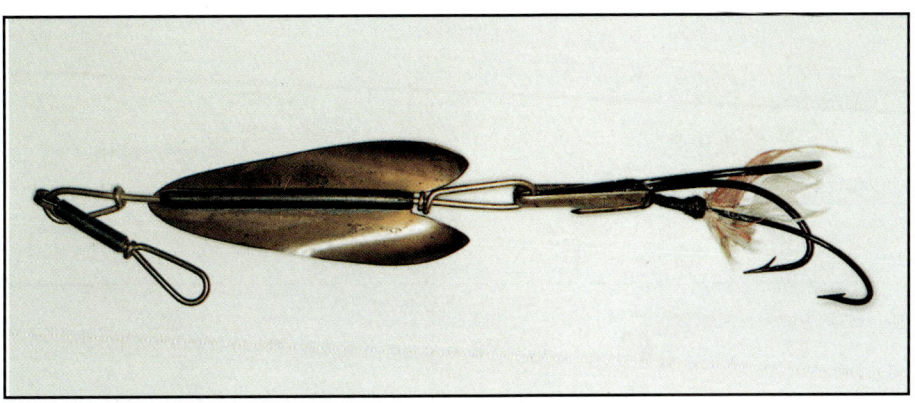

C.

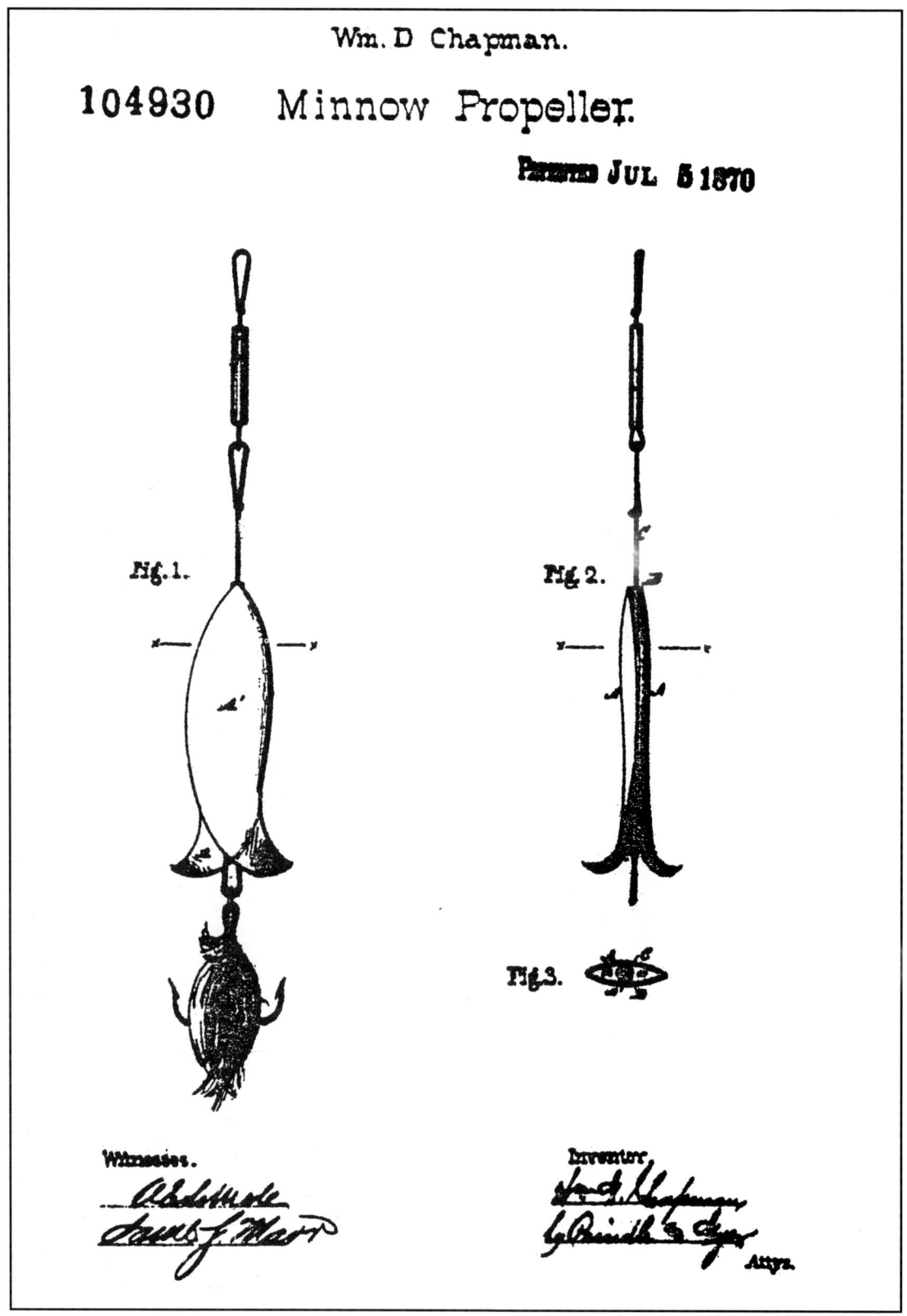

Chapman's second lure patent, the "Minnow Propeller." This lure is formed using fish-shaped halves soldered to a hollow tube. The bait must have been successful, because it was still being sold 25 years later.

W.D. Chapman

A. This 1871 patent is very similar to the "Minnow Propeller." The main difference is in the construction. In this patent the fins are inserted and soldered between spoon-shaped halves. There is no center shaft. Also, hooks are hung on the sides of this model.

B. 1870 patent model. 2¾" silverplated copper. Marked "W.D. Chapman, Theresa, N.Y. Patent May 4, 1870. Size 2"." This lure was made in at least seven sizes. $100.00 – 125.00.

C. Marked "W.D. Chapman, Theresa, N.Y. Patent May 4, 1870." This lure is constructed exactly like the 1871 patent, but is marked 1870. It is 3⅜" long and has a silver front and brass back. Also marked I.X.L. Size No. 1. $125.00 – 150.00.

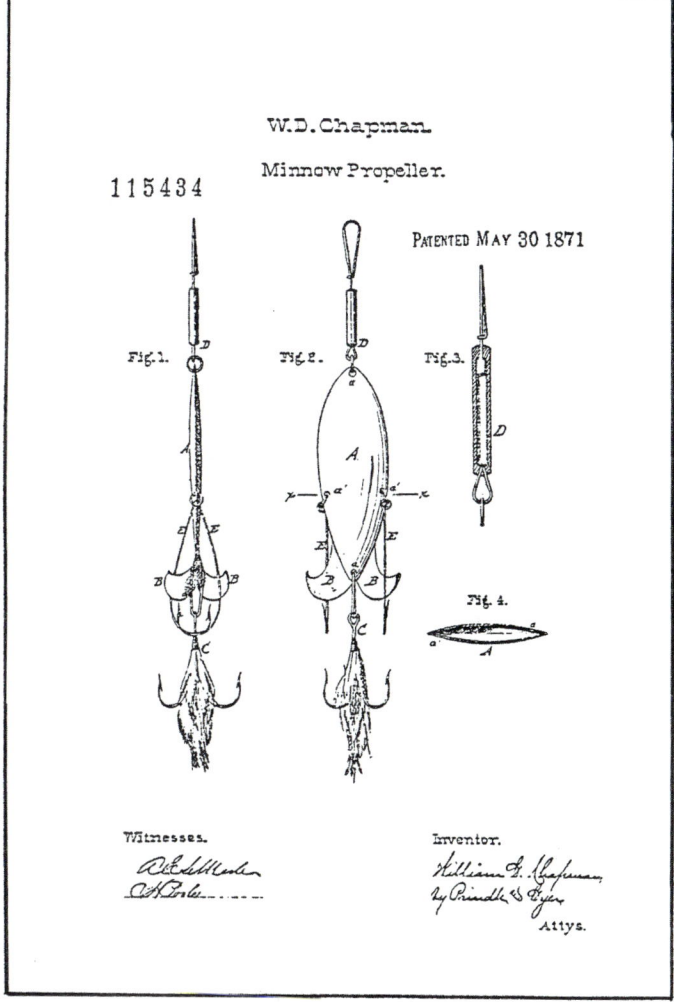

A.

B.

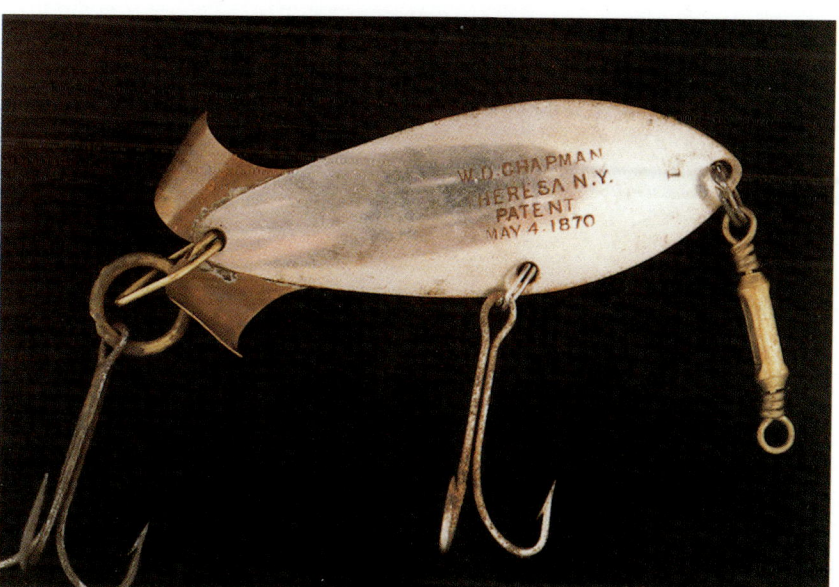

C.

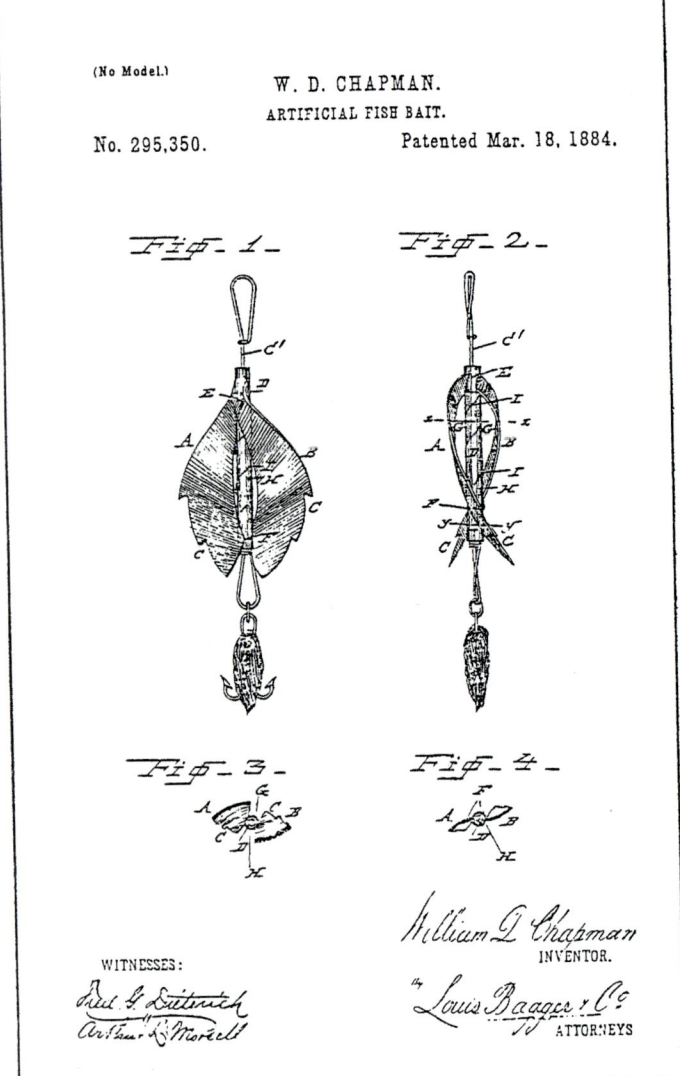

Patent for the "Allure." It was one of W.D. Chapman's most popular lures. It is also one of the lures most frequently found by collectors.

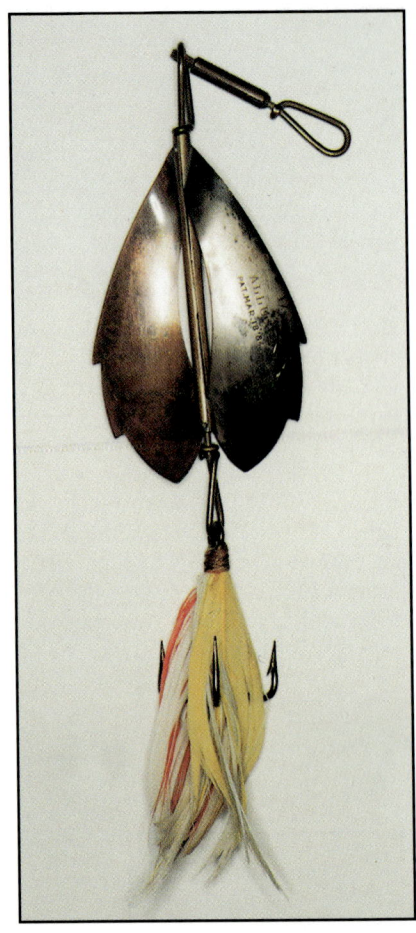

The "Allure" was made in at least five sizes: 3, 2, 1, 1/0 and 2/0. The 1886 catalog states, "These baits are a great favorite with sportsmen, and a very good bait where there are weeds, as they seldom clog." This lure was also made as a "fancy Allure," the only difference being the addition of a fancy fly instead of the traditional feathered treble hook. "Allures" were made of copper, silver plated on one side, with both sides polished. They are often found without the Chapman markings; probably a model sold to hardware stores and the general trade houses. $75.00   100.00.

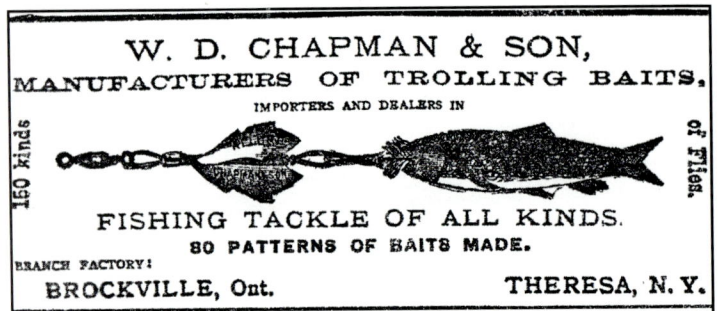

July 20, 1882, *Forest and Stream* ad depicting the Allure, two years before it was patented.

This "Allure" is constructed differently from most. The blades are stamped from a single piece of metal and then folded over at the top instead of being soldered to the shaft. Although marked "W.D. Chapman," I believe this is a later model. Most examples I have seen were nickel plated, a finish not used until later by Chapman. This type of "Allure" was also manufactured by J.T. Buel in the early twentieth century. $100.00 – 125.00.

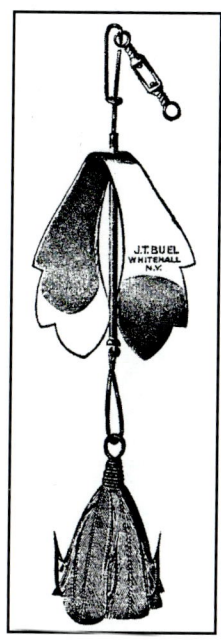

Buel's Allure

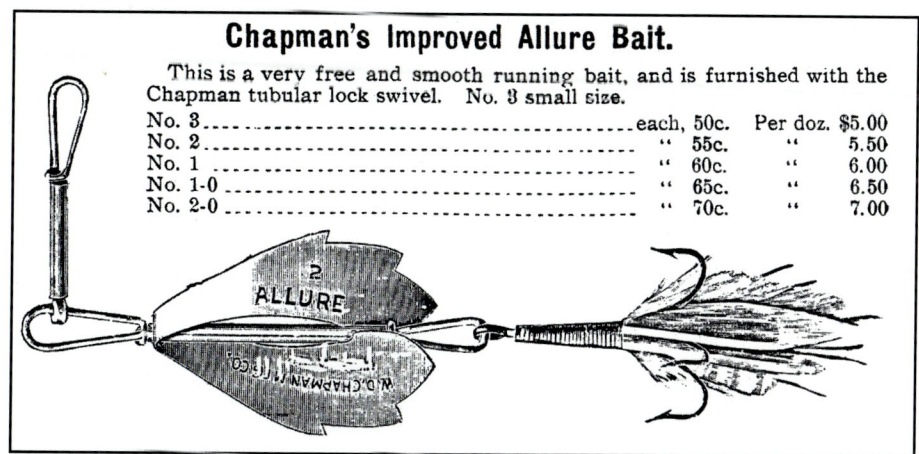

Illustration from a late 1890s trade catalog showing the "Improved Allure."

W.D. Chapman

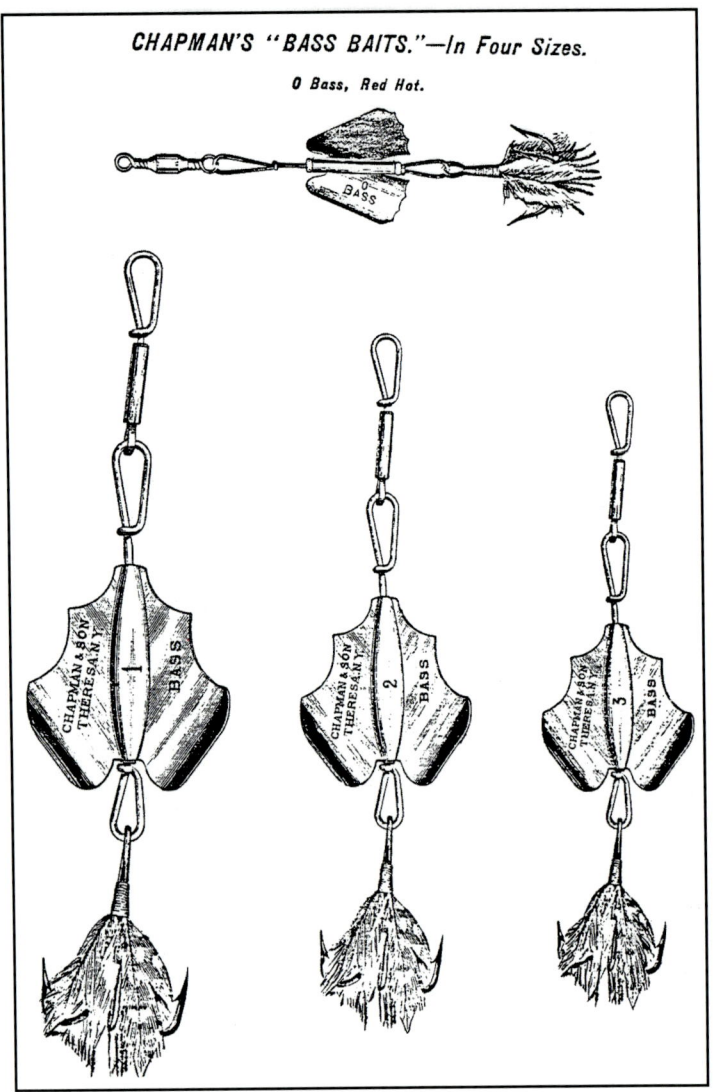

A.

B.

A. Catalog page (reduced in size) showing the popular "Bass Baits." This lure was a Chapman standard for many years. Interestingly, it is shown in the 1900 edition of the Enterprise Mfg. Co. Catalog (Pflueger) as the "Buckeye" spinner.

B. Although not listed in any available catalog, this lure appears to be a member of the "Bass Bait" family. It is marked W.D. Chapman, Theresa, N.Y. No. 4. It is $15/16$" long. $75.00 – 100.00.

C. The "Reversible Propeller," another long-time offering of the Chapmans. It was manufactured in two sizes, Nos. 2 and 3. It also was shown in the 1900 Pflueger catalog. Cut shown is reduced in size.

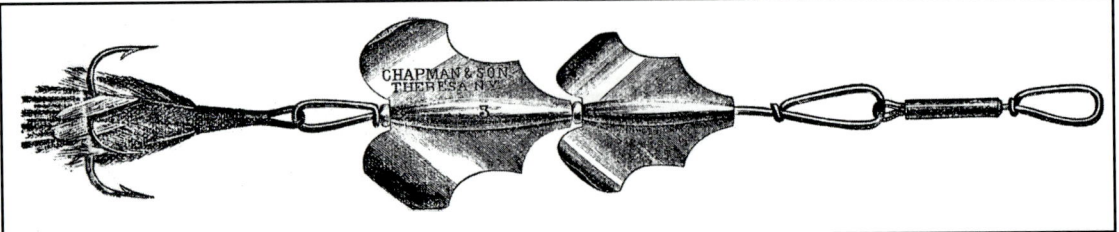

C.

A.

A. January 27, 1876, *Forest and Stream* ad. Note the tag line "New Articles for the Centennial Year."

B. Three sizes of the Bass bait. The smallest was 7/8" while the largest was 1 15/16" long. The catalog states, "Great favorites, as they never fail to play in the water. The 'O Bass' is especially good on the end of a leader with three or more flies, as it attracts the attention of the fish." $75.00 – 100.00.

B.

A.

B.

A. This early lure is marked Patent May, 1866. The hook on the shank of the double hook is part of the rather complicated 1866 patent. It is also marked W.D. Chapman, Theresa, N.Y. - I.X.L. $150.00 – 200.00.

B. This minnow harness is marked W.D. Chapman, Theresa, N.Y. NO. 3. The blade is 2¾" long with the overall length being 7½". The hook near the top was put through the head of the minnow and then secured with the spring on the shaft. One or both of the treble hooks (depending on the length of the minnow) were then placed in the tail. $200.00 – 250.00.

C. This fish-shaped bait has a unique curved lip that makes it spin in the water. It is marked W.D. Chapman, Theresa, N.Y. No. 1. It is made of brass and is 3½" long. Smaller versions of this lure were also made. $250.00 – 300.00.

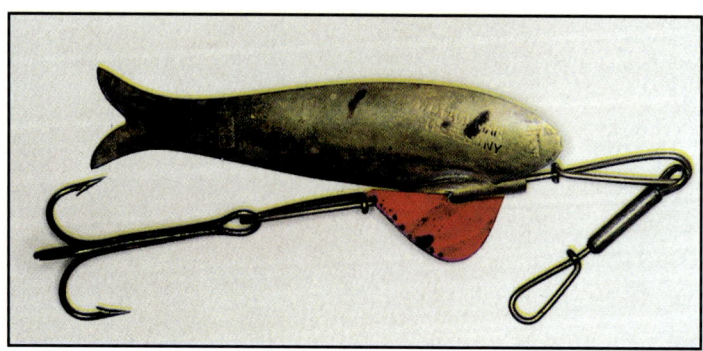

C.

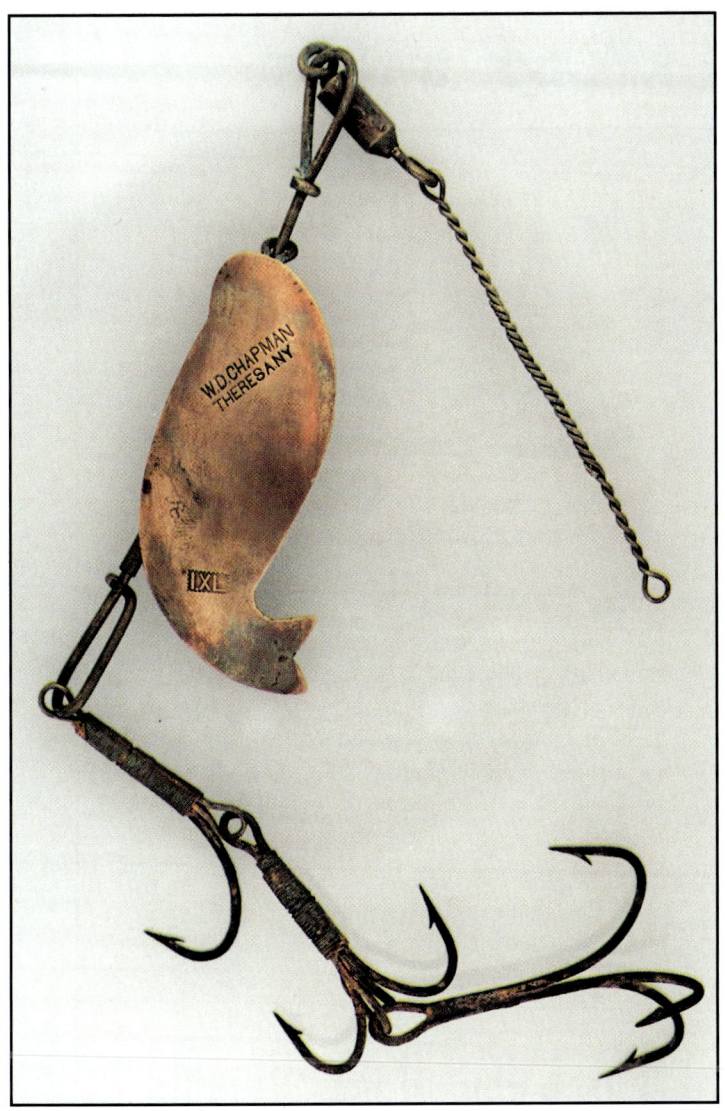

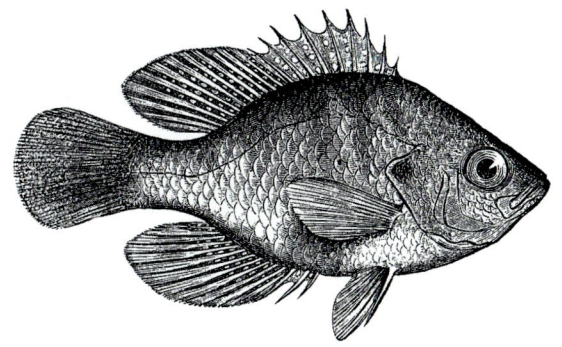

A.

A. This early lure's blade is 2½" long (9½" overall). It appears to be a bait holder. The marking I.X.L. appears on the tail. $300.00 – 400.00.

B. This lure is 2⁵⁄₁₆" long, copper on one side and brass on the other. It is also marked I.X.L. and has No. 3 stamped on the top. This lure was also made in a large Musky size and probably in other sizes as well. $150.00 – 250.00.

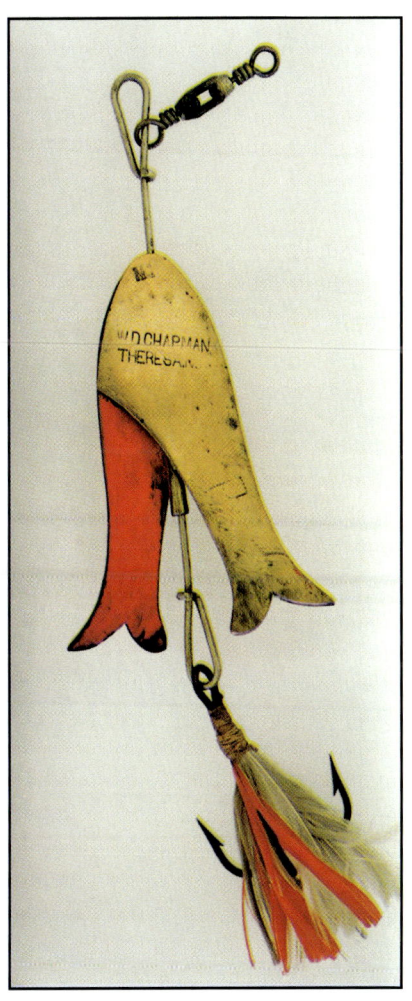

B.

CHAPMAN'S KILBY BAITS.

The Kilby Bass, Single.

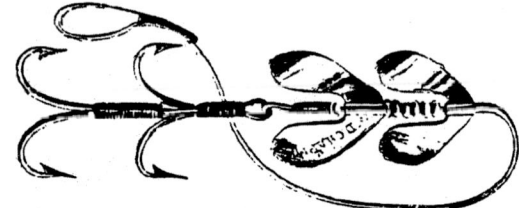

Made only in One Size. No. 2.

These baits have been in use two years and have given good satisfaction. The two Kilby Bass Baits have been changed so they will play on a wire snood instead of gimp, they will also be mounted with triple hooks and fly.

TRY THEM.

The Kilby Bass, Double

Made only in One Size. No. 3.

Kilby Minnow in One Size, No. 2, for General Fishing.

SEND FOR SAMPLES OF OUR GOODS.

Page from an 1880 W.D. Chapman catalog.

A.

A. Chapman's No. 2 "Kilby Minnow." Made in one size only. The hollow body is 2⅞" long. It is silverplated on one side and brass on the other. The blade is marked Chapman & Son, Theresa, N.Y. $1,500.00+.

B. Two "Kilby Bass Singles." These are strung on a length of gimp as shown in the catalog cut on the facing page. $100.00 – 150.00.

C. The "Kilby Bass Single." The blade is 1¼" long and was originally silverplated. It is marked W.D. Chapman, Theresa, N.Y. Chapman also produced a "Kilby Bass Double," which had two identical "Kilby" blades on a single shaft. $100.00 – 150.00.

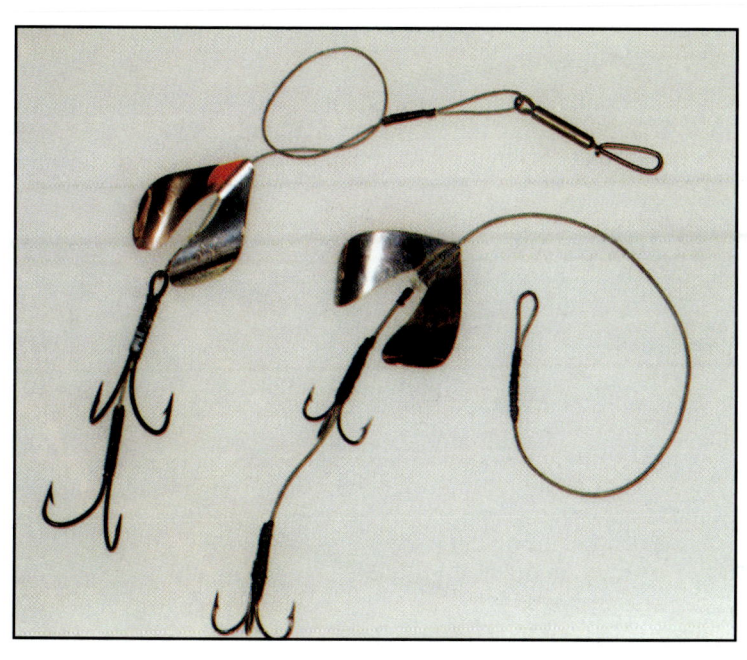

B.

C.

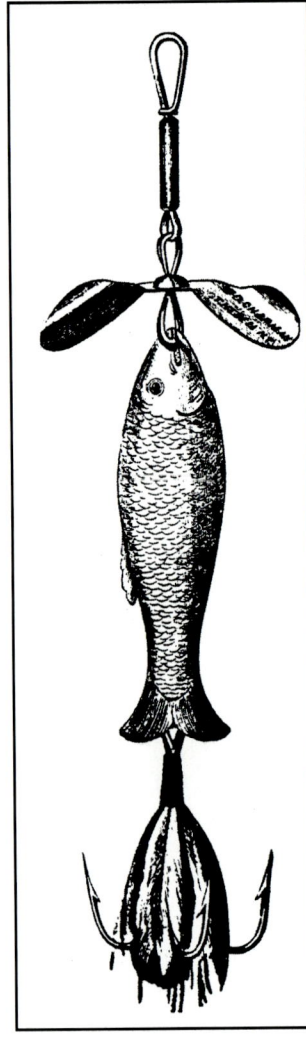

A. Early version of the "International Minnow." The illustration is from the 1880 catalog. Note the angle of the propeller as compared to the lure below. $1,000.00+.

B. Canvas pouch used by the Chapmans as a promotional item in the early 1890s. Note the pictured "Kilby Bass Single." The "150 Kinds of Trolling Baits" is rather misleading. This figure includes the various sizes as well as the individual lure. Some lures were made in as many as ten sizes. The lure in the pouch is the "Daisy Bait." $100.00 – 200.00.

C. The "International Minnow." Made in two sizes. The larger 2⅞" size is shown. The smaller size is 1⅞". This lure is similar to the "Kilby Minnow" but is not a hollow lure. It has a strap on the back of the minnow body that connects the hook with the line tie. It is marked Chapman & Son, Theresa, N.Y. $1,000.00+

A.

C.

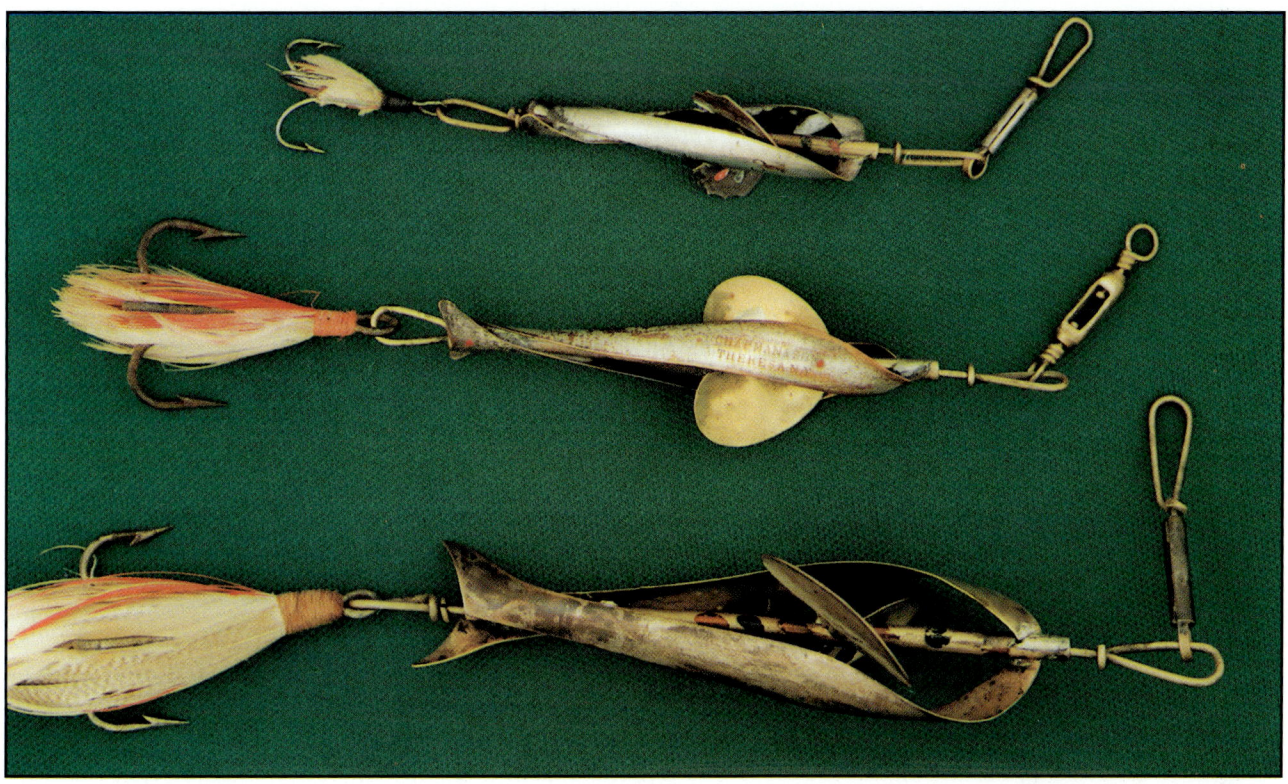

A.

A. Chapman's "New Combination" in three sizes. The 1886 catalog proclaims "Sportsmen say it is the most killing bait ever offered to the public." The sizes are (top to bottom) No. 3, 2½"; No. 2, 3½"; and No. 1, 4½". This lure was patented July 28, 1885. $750.00 – 1,000.00.

B. Advertisement from the May 9, 1885 issue of *The American Angler*. This lure is seldom found with the gimp leader and hook still intact.

B.

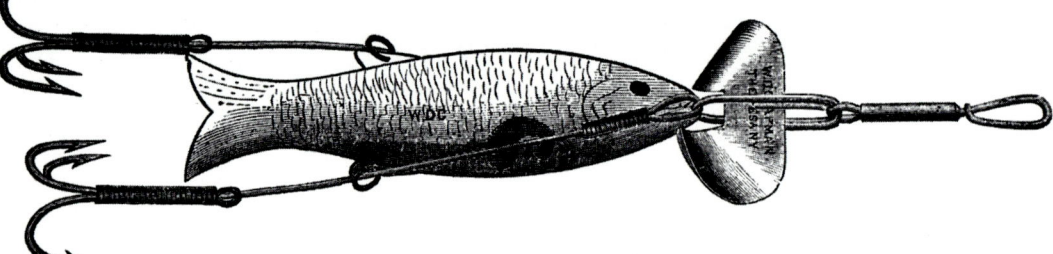

A.

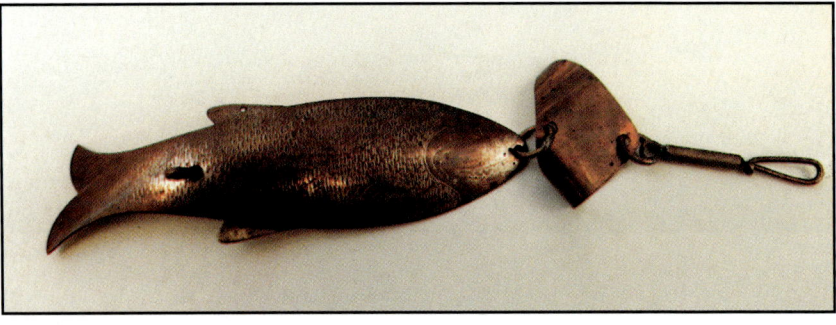

B.

D.

A. *Forest and Stream* ad from April 1, 1875, showing the "Boss" bait.

B. The "Boss" bait. The body of this lure is 4⅜" long and was silverplate over brass. Only traces of the silver remain. The spinner on the front is 1" long and is marked W.D. Chapman, Theresa, N.Y. No. 1. This spinner is attached in a different manner from the bait in the illustration. $2,500.00+.

C. Slide cover box for the "Boss" bait. This box is 7½" long and 2¼" wide. The cover has the same cut as is found on the *Forest and Stream* ad pictured above. Note the bright colors, very unusual for a box of this vintage.

D. Close-up view of the leaf pattern embossed on the side of the box. The purple inside section is embossed with a star pattern.

C.

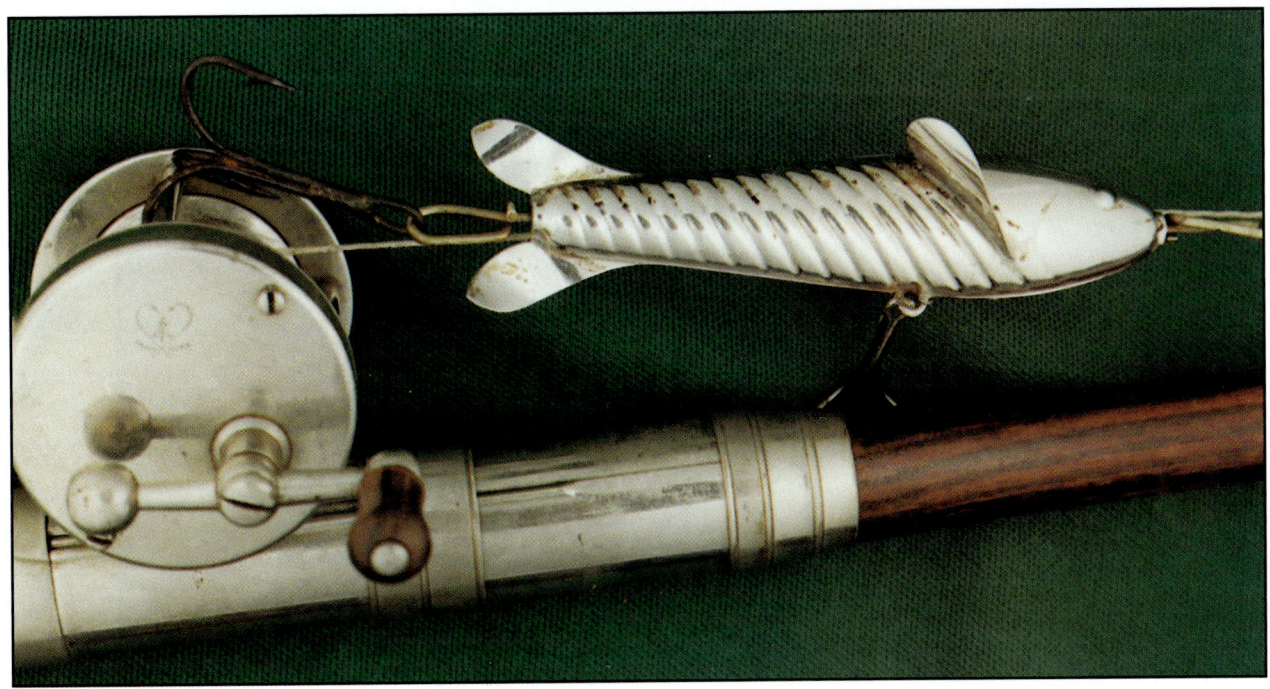

A.

A. The "Safe Deposit Minnow." This beautiful lure was manufactured in 1897 after the death of William's son, Byron. It is 4½" long, nickel plated, and is marked W.D. Chapman, Theresa, N.Y. No. 1/0. Two smaller versions of the "Safe Deposit Minnow" were made. They are shown on the next two pages. William evidently continued making baits under his own name after selling out to Gibson & Woodworth of Rochester, N.Y. $2,500.00+.

B. 1897 magazine ad with cut of the "Safe Deposit" minnow. The ad says "Make a deposit for these baits." Chapman must have been between ad agencies at the time.

B.

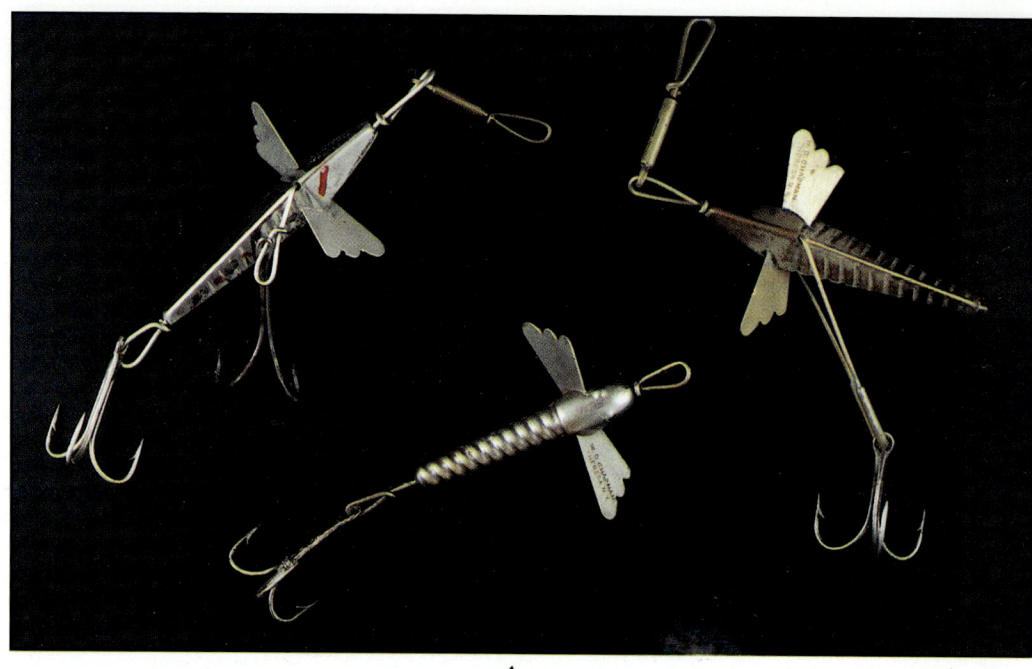

A.

A. Left: This four-sided Phantom type bait is marked W.D. Chapman, Theresa, N.Y. It is 2⅝" long and the hook is attached to a wire bail that can swivel a full 360 degrees. It is silverplated copper on one side and brass on the other. Center: This lure is the small size of the "Safe Deposit:" minnow (see ad below). It is 2⅛" long and appears to be nickel plated. It is marked W.D. Chapman, Theresa, N.Y. Right: This lure is the same as the other four-sided bait, but has a single wire hook attachment instead of a bait. This lure is also nickel plated which raises the possibility that these all may have been manufactured during the late 1890s after the death of son Byron. $1,000.00+ each.

B. Another four-sided lure like those above, but apparently using halves of the "Allure" as wings. Innovation was a strong Chapman asset. When I first started collecting, I often wondered if he ever made two lures alike. $1,000.00+.

C. Page from 1897 J. F. Marsters catalog.

B.

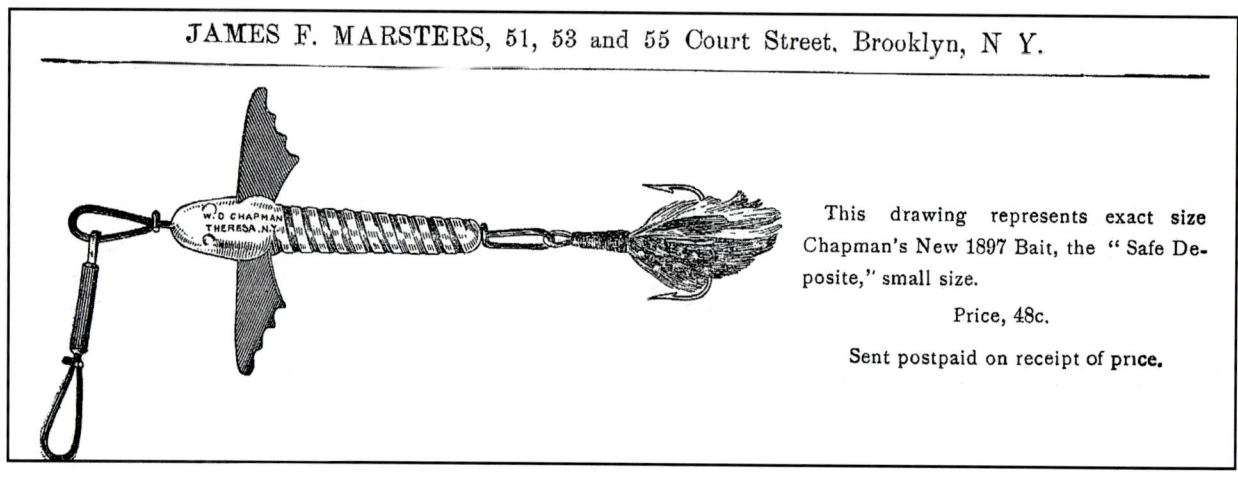

C.

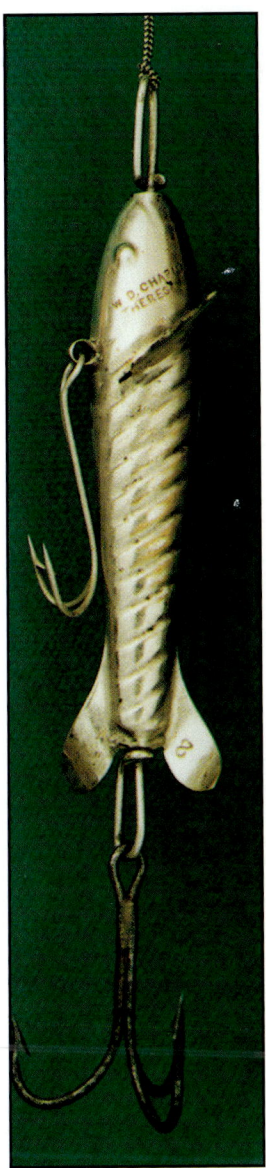

A.

B.

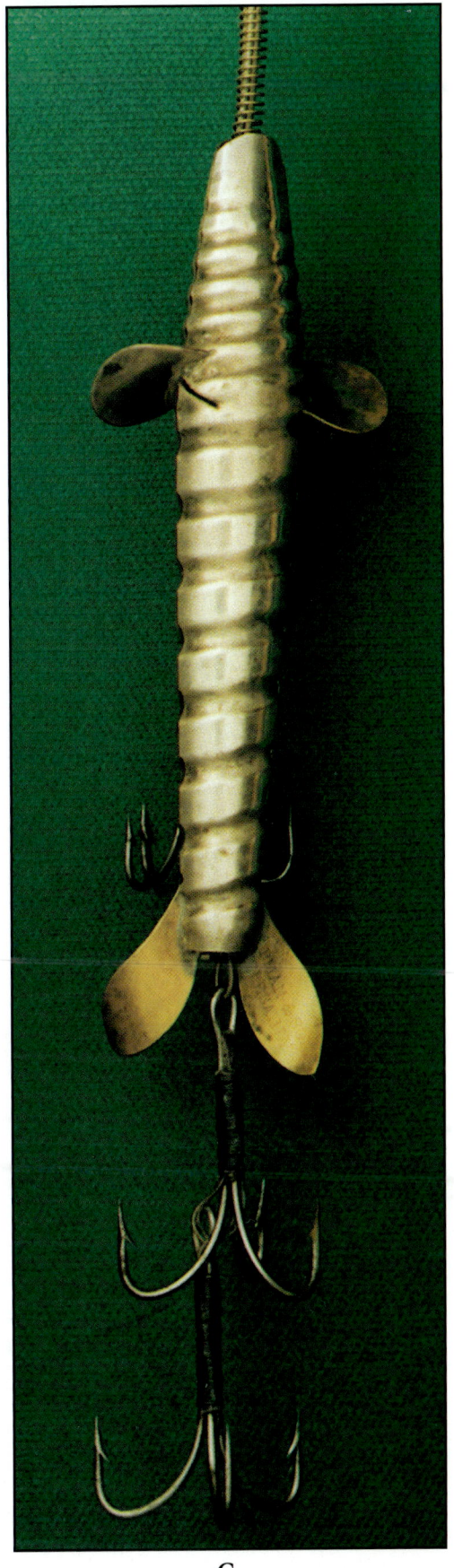

C.

A. The medium size of the "Safe Deposit" minnow. It is 3¼" long and has the No. 2 stamped on its tail. $2,500.00+.

B. This bait is 3⁵⁄₁₆" long and has two fins on each side that make it spin. It is silverplated copper and marked W.D. Chapman, Pat Apd for. There is a No. 3 stamped on the front. $1,000.00 – 1,500.00.

C. The "Threaded Minnow." This minnow came in three sizes. The one shown is 4⅞" long and is the largest of the three. These lures are shown in the 1886 catalog and also in a later Gibson & Woodworth catalog. This lure in another size and variation is shown on the next page. $500.00 – 750.00.

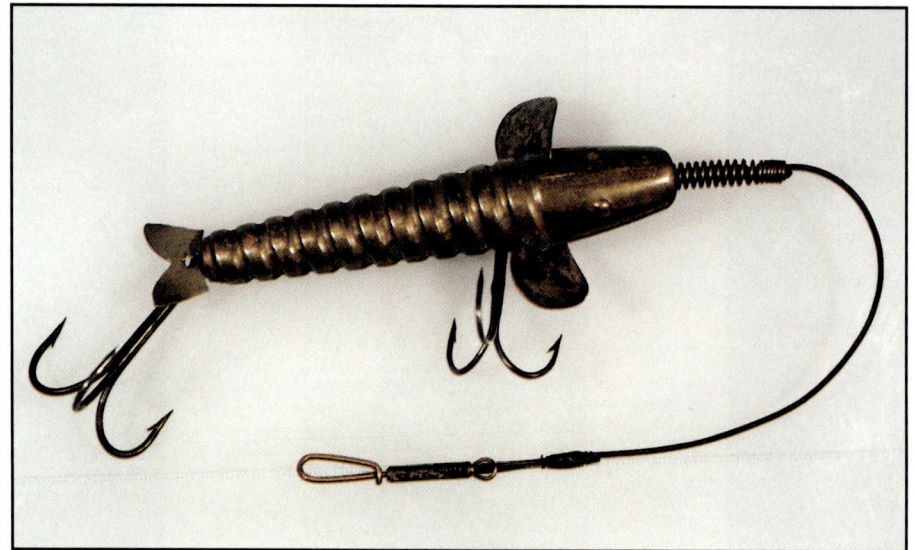

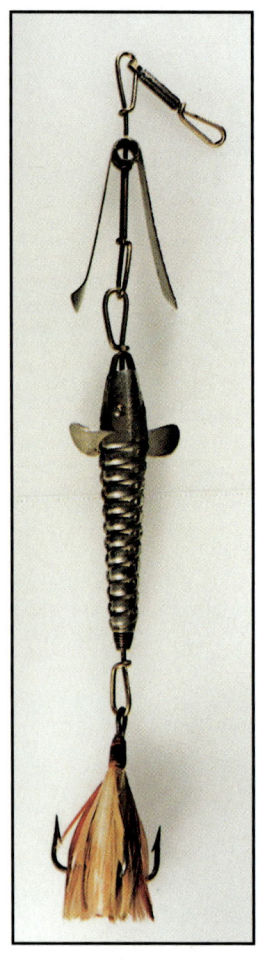

A.

B.

A. "Threaded Minnow" marked Chapman & Son, Theresa, N.Y. No. 2. This lure is 3½" long including the tail. Note the tail is not attached to the body as is the one featured on page 59 and in the cut at the bottom of the page. The tail is held in place by the gimp leader threaded through the body. The spring protruding from the mouth of the minnow is to protect the gimp leader from wear. $500.00 – 750.00.

B. This minnow has a solid shaft through it and a spring type bearing on the rear. It is also approximately 3½" long. The spinner on the front is 2¼" long and marked Chapman, Son & Co. Rochester, N.Y. Pat Ap'd For. $1,000.00 – 1,500.00.

C. Cut from Gibson & Woodworth catalog, circa 1896.

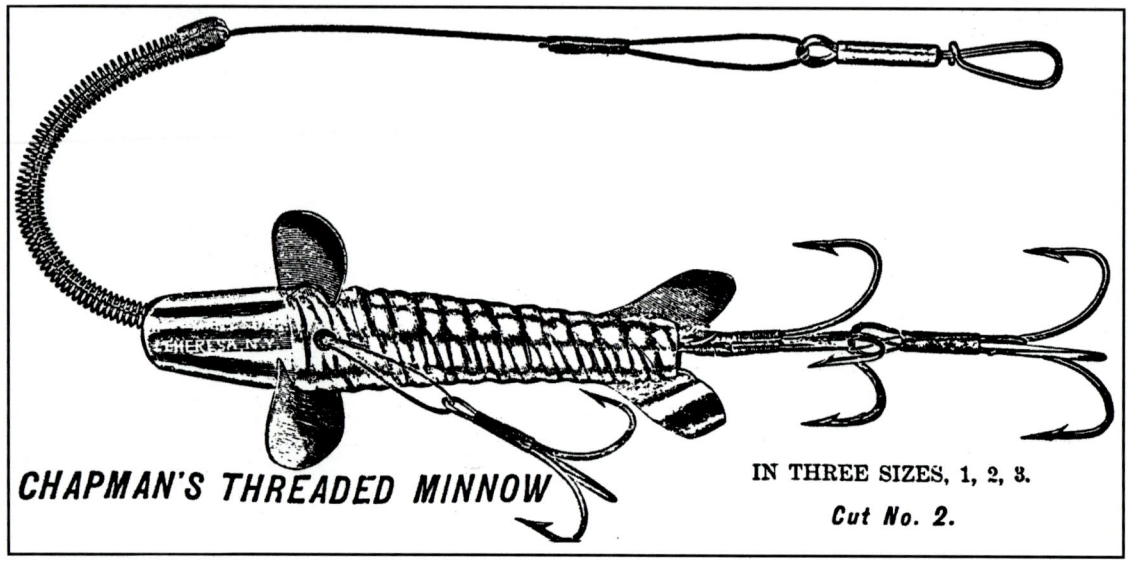

C.

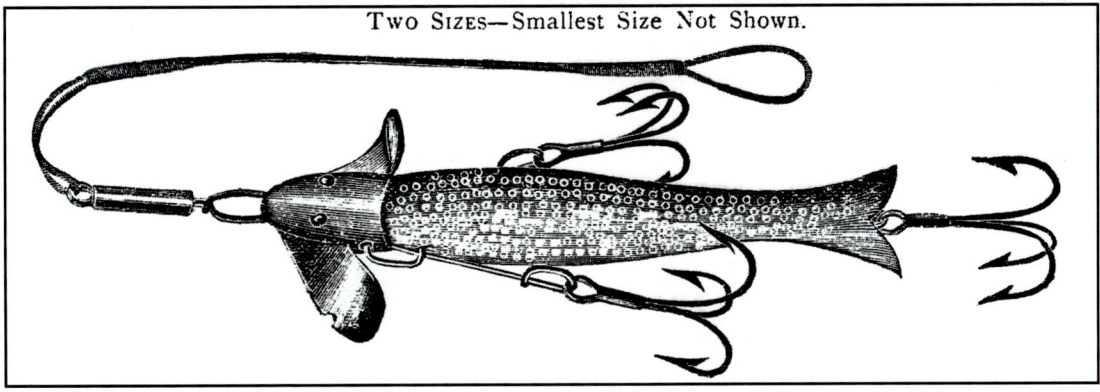

A.

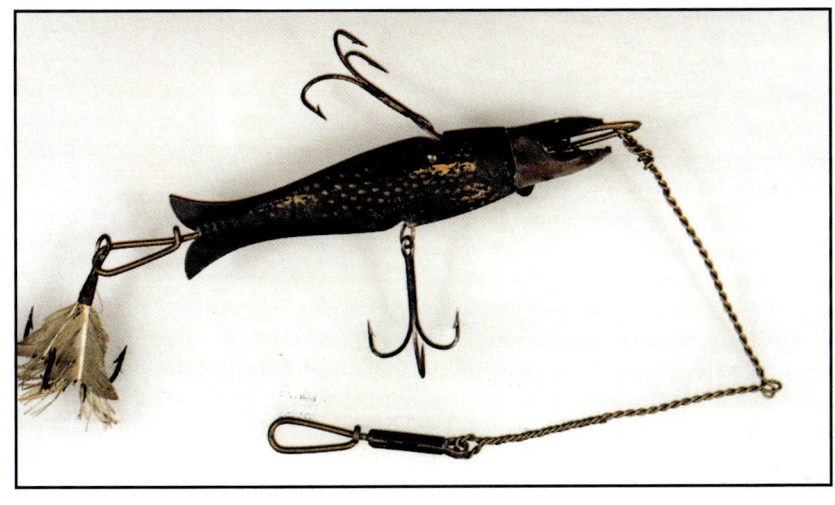

B.

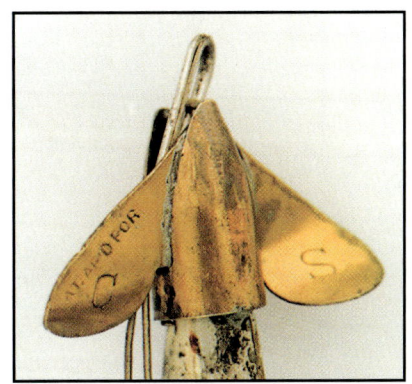

C.

A. Cut of the "Water Nymph" from the Gibson & Woodworth catalog, circa 1896.

B. "Water Nymph" with solid shaft through center and three sets of treble hooks. $500.00 – 750.00.

C. Close-up of unusual marking on "Water Nymph." The "C" and "S" indicate Chapman and Son.

D. Two-hook "Nymph" with wire through gimp leader. $500.00 – 750.00.

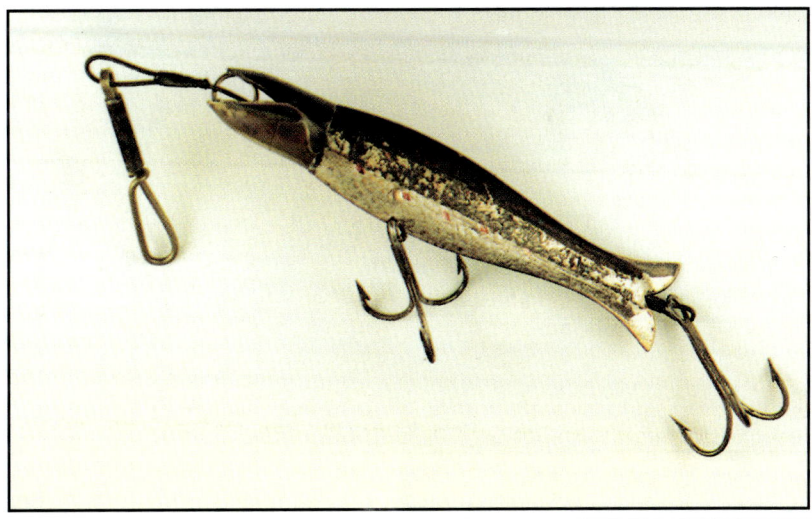

D.

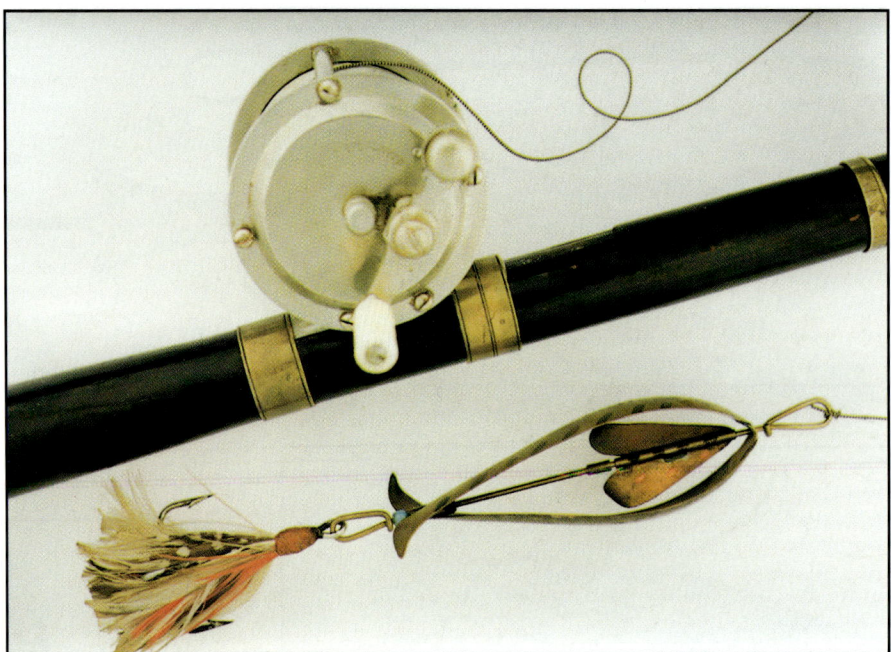

A.

A. This unique lure is 3⅞" in length and has a 1½" arrowhead-shaped spinner in its center. It was made in at least three sizes. The one pictured is a No. 1. Both the outer and inner blades are marked W.D. Chapman, Theresa, N.Y. It is designed so the outer blades spin opposite of the inner blades. W. D. Chapman patented this lure in 1907 and assigned the patent to Fred J. Sharp and Charles J. Smith of Watertown, N.Y. He named it the "Omega" because he said it would be his last patent of that type. It is not known if they manufactured it under the name of W.D. Chapman or if Chapman manufactured it for them; albeit his name is on the bait. The reel pictured is a Thomas Chubb. "Henshall-Van Antwerp," owned by Joel Anderson. $750.00 – 1,000.00.

B. Small version of the "Omega" bait. This lure is 2⁷⁄₁₆" long and marked W.D. Chapman, Theresa, N.Y., ALLURE. It has colored beads in the center instead of the arrowhead spinner. $750.00 – 1,000.00.

B.

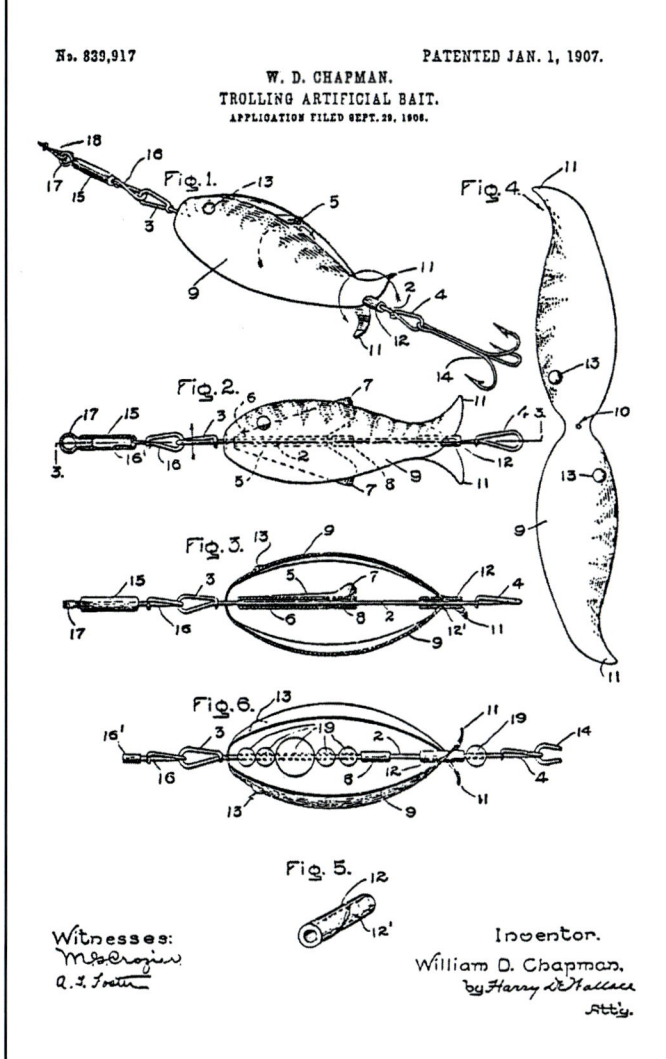

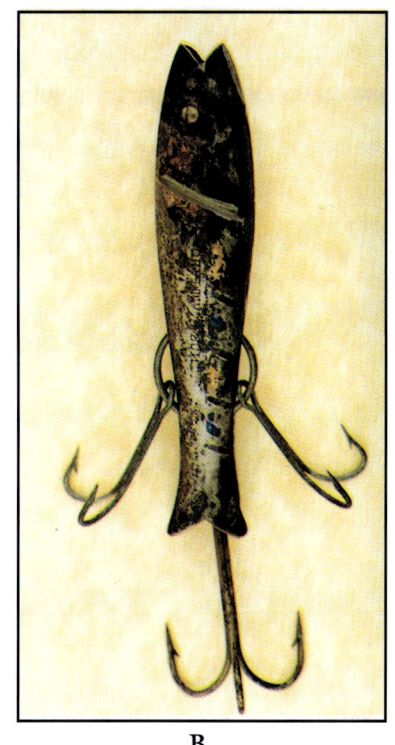

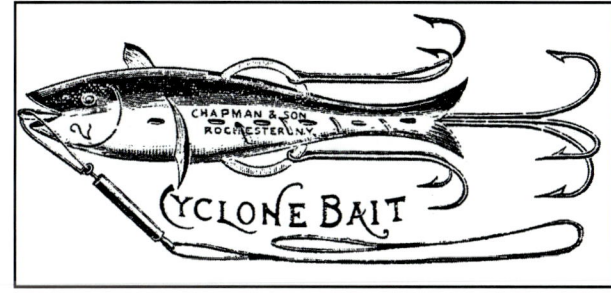

A.

B.

C.

A. Copy of the 1907 patent granted to Chapman for the "Omega" bait.

B. The "Cyclone Bait." This bait is 3⅜" long and is silverplated on one side. It has a slot extending from the tail to the center of the body. A ring in the center holds the hooks and line tie. The one pictured is missing the line tie. The lure is marked Chapman & Son, Rochester, N.Y. It has No. 2 stamped near the front. $1,000.00+.

C. Cut from the Gibson & Woodworth catalog showing the "Cyclone Bait."

D. This odd-shaped lure is marked W.D. Chapman, Theresa, N.Y. It is 3½" long.

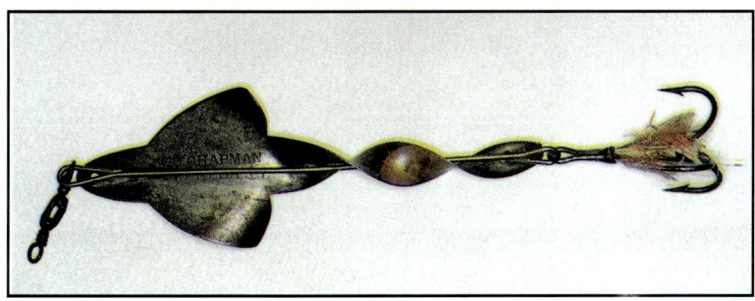

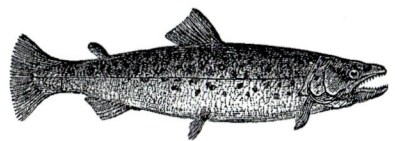

D.

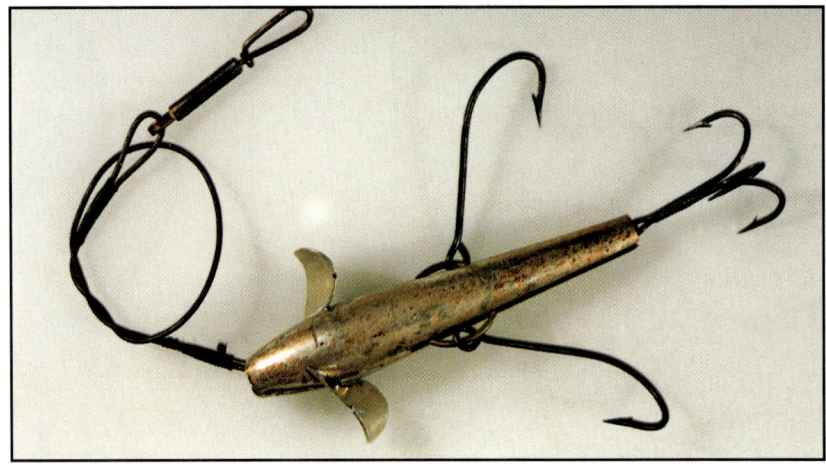

This Devon type lure is marked W.D. Chapman and Son, Theresa, N.Y. It is 3" long, silverplated copper on one side and brass on the other. It has a large No. 1 stamped between the blades. $500.00 – 750.00.

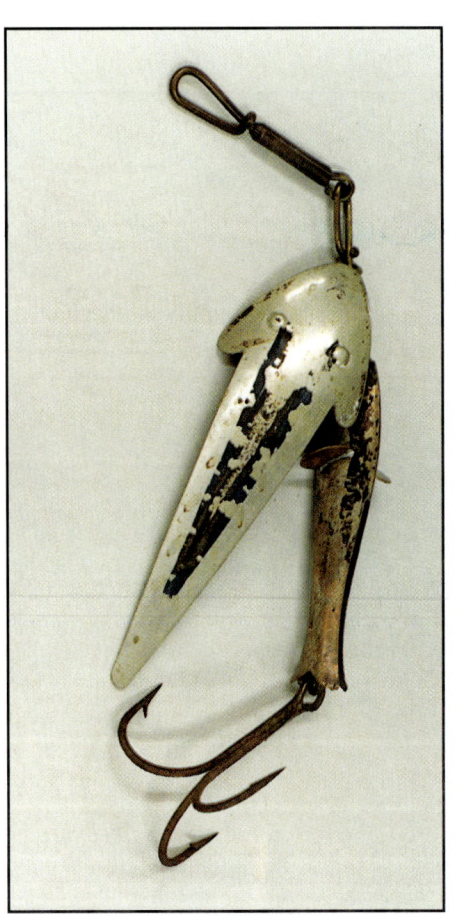 

These baits have blades approximately 3" long that appear to be made of German silver. They are marked W.D. Chapman, Theresa, N.Y. The one on the left is stamped 3/0 and has a Devon type minnow on the shaft. The other is wrapped with yarn. Left: $500.00 – 750.00. Right: $100.00 – 200.00.

A.

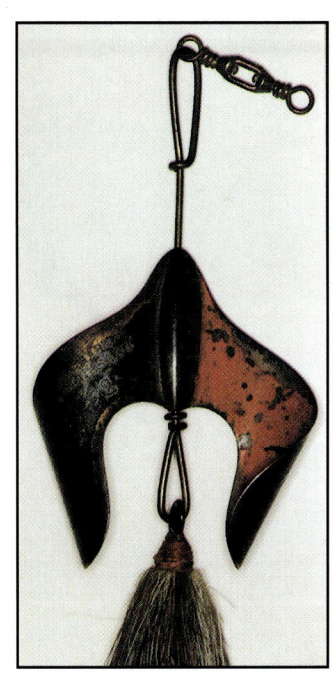

B.

A. This phantom-type lure is marked W.D. Chapman, Theresa, N.Y. The swivel is a typical Chapman type as shown in his patent of May 30, 1871. These swivels were not always used on his lures; indeed the 1886 catalog shows as many cuts with the standard square swivels as it does his own. $400.00 – 600.00.

B. This large lure is marked W.D. Chapman, Theresa, N.Y. It is similar to the Lowe bait but has a small hollow body whereas the Lowe does not. $250.00 – 350.00.

C. A large Propeller type lure marked W.D. Chapman, Theresa, N.Y. 1/0. This bait is also stamped "M" Allure. (Musky?) $250.00 – 350.00.

D. This very old teardrop-shaped lure is marked W.D. Chapman, Theresa, N.Y. It is 1½" long and is stamped I.X.L. at the top. $75.00 – 100.00.

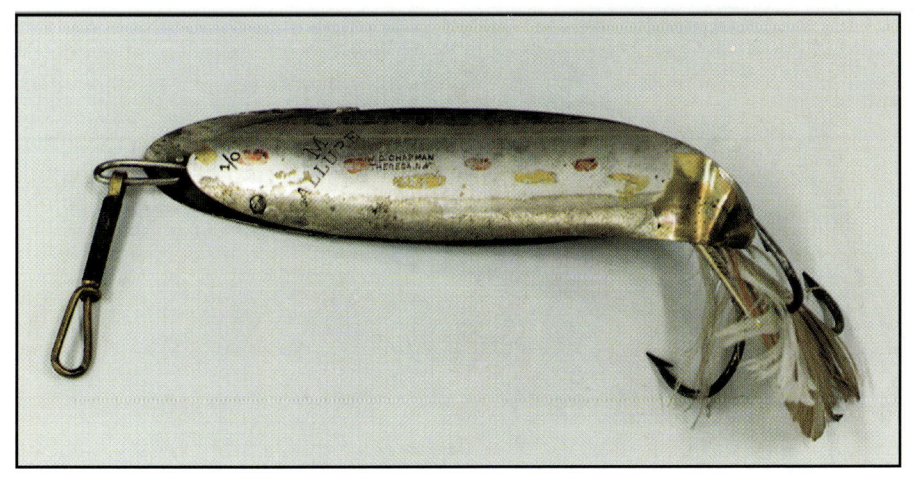

C.

D.

One version of the "German Propeller." It is 2⅞" long and is marked W.D. Chapman, Theresa, N.Y. 1/0. $150.00 – 250.00.

A 4" version of the "German Propeller," also marked W.D. Chapman, Theresa, N.Y. The attachment rings on this lure are soldered stationary, as is the tie ring on the other. It also has a raised, cigar-shaped piece attached to one side. $250.00 – 350.00.

Another "German Propeller" bait. This one is 3⅞" long and marked W.D. Chapman, Theresa, N.Y. It is made of brass and has an embossed, raised, copper piece attached to one side. $350.00 – 450.00.

A.

A. This unusual spinner appears to have been stamped from the same pattern as the "Kilby Minnow" or "International Minnow." It is 1½" long and is silver plated on one side. The reverse side is painted red. There are no markings. $200.00 – 250.00.

B. The "Hero Bait." The bait shown is marked Chapman & Son, Theresa, N.Y. No. 3. It is 2" long. The "Hero Bait" came in at least 4 sizes. The 1886 catalog states, "These baits are particularly successful in fishing for Large Mouth Bass." $50.00 – 75.00.

C. A variation of the "Hero Bait." This one is marked Chapman & Son, Theresa, N.Y. No. 1. $50.00 – 75.00.

B.

C.

W.D. Chapman

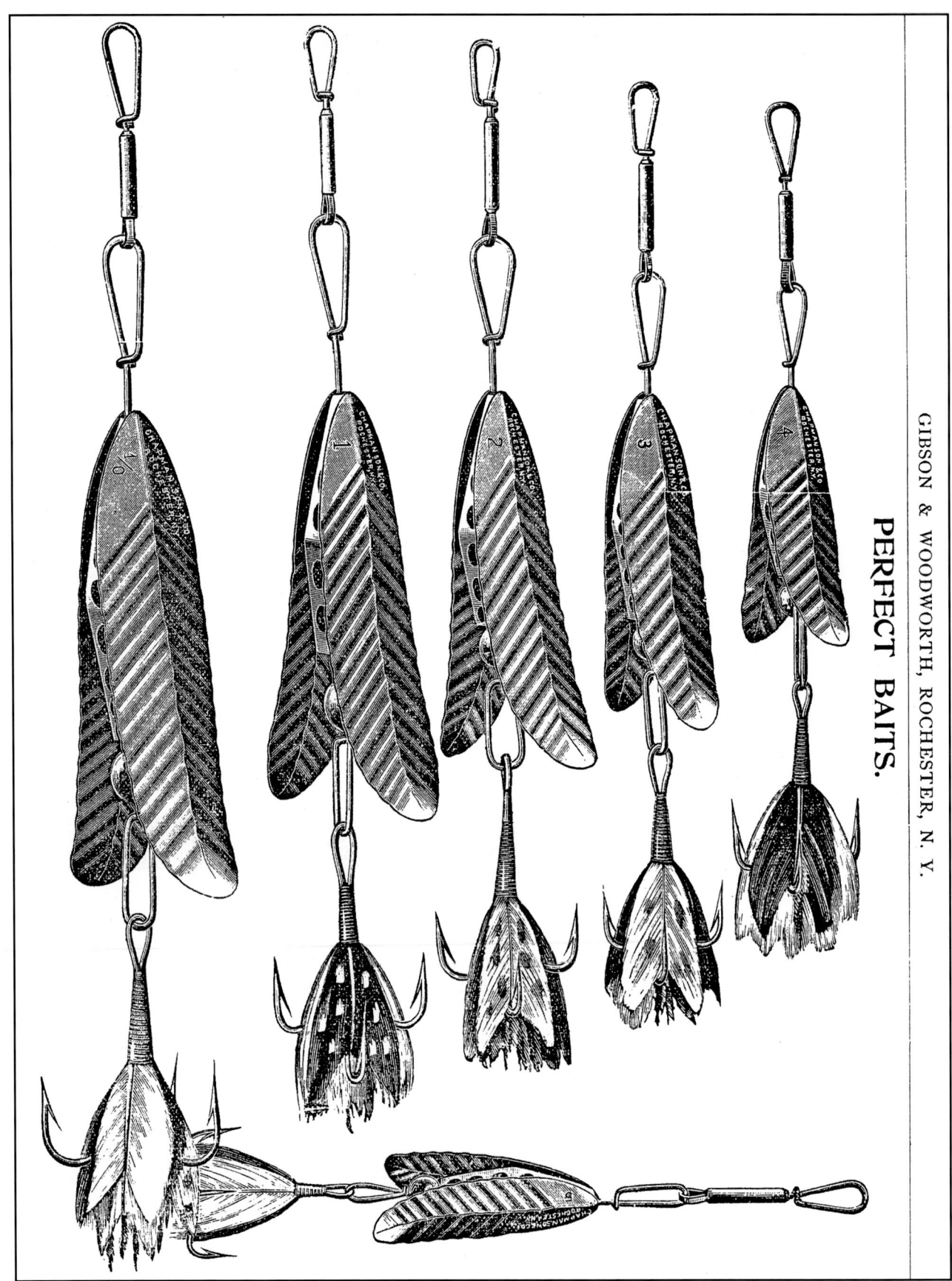

Page from 1890s Gibson & Woodworth catalog.

A.

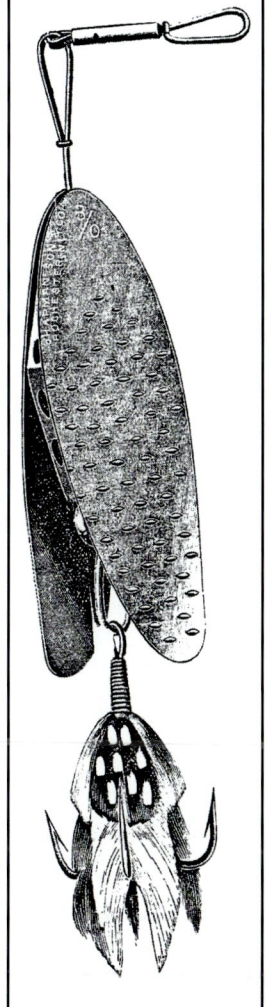

B.

A. The "Perfect Bait." This lure is similar to the "Minnow Propeller" described earlier. The main difference is the chamber between the blades and the willow leaf pattern. The bait shown is 2⅝" in length and is marked Chapman & Son, Theresa, N.Y. No. 2. It is made of brass and plated silver on one side. This lure was made in at least six sizes. $125.00 – 225.00.

B. Catalog cut of the "Electric Bait."

C. The "Electric Bait." This bait is also similar to the "Minnow Propeller." It has a chamber between the blades and a raised pattern of small bumps. The larger one pictured is marked Chapman Son & Co., Rochester, N.Y. on one blade. The other blade is stamped Pat Ap'd for No. 3/0. It is 3¾" long. The smaller one pictured has the same markings, except it is size No. 1. It is 2⅝" long. These lures are usually brass on one side and silver plated copper on the other. They were made in at least seven sizes. $100.00 – 200.00.

C.

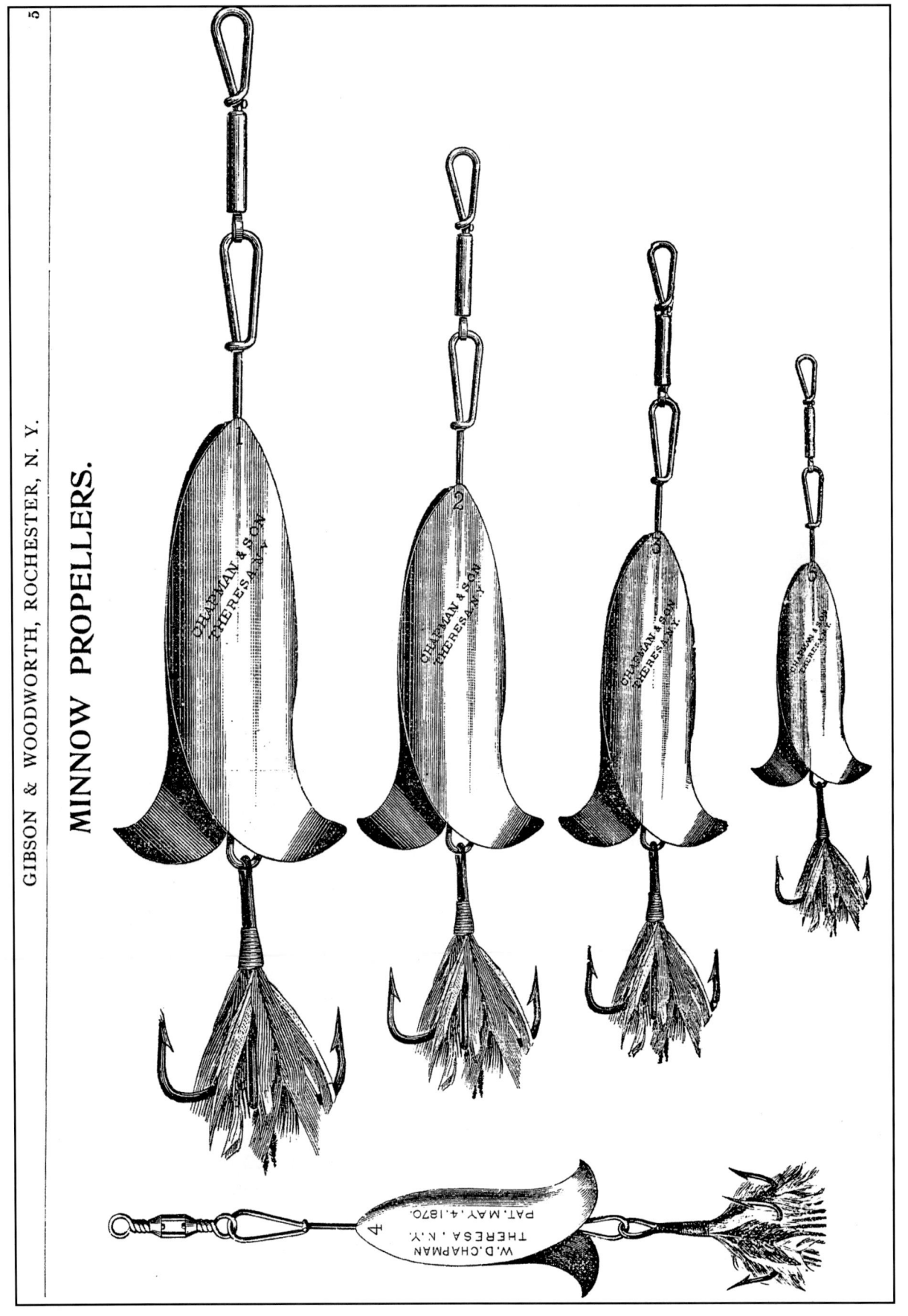

Page from 1890s Gibson & Woodworth catalog.

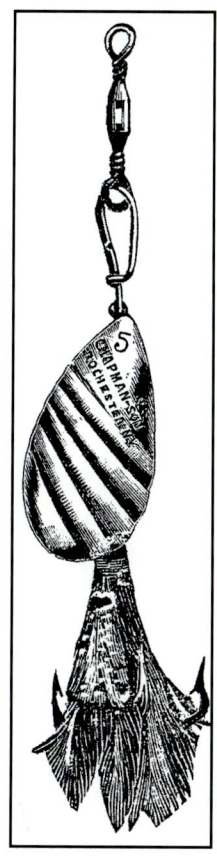

A.

B.

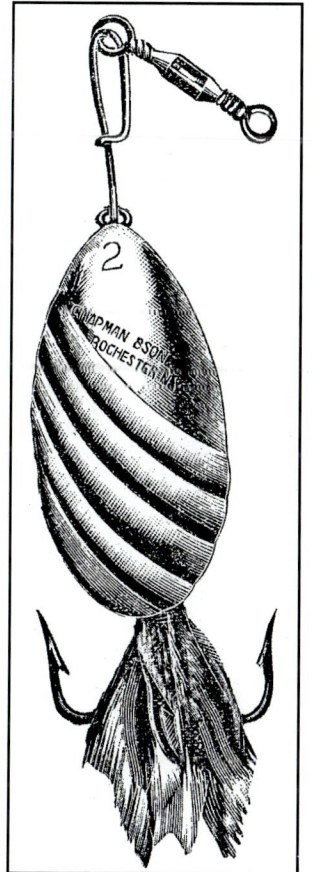

C.

D.

A. Catalog cut of the "Mascot Bait."

B. Another "Minnow Propeller" type lure. This bait is 3" long and is marked W.D. Chapman, Theresa, N.Y. No. 3. It is also stamped ALLURE with an inverted T. A small raised eye is near the front of each blade. $100.00 – 150.00.

C. Catalog cut of the "Mascot Bait."

D. The "Mascot Bait." This spinner is marked Chapman & Son, Theresa, N.Y. NO. 1/0. It is 2½" long and is made of copper. The back side is painted red. It came in at least seven sizes. $75.00 – 100.00.

A.

B.

C.

A. The "Excelsior" bait. This lure was new in 1886. It was made in at least five sizes. The one shown is marked Chapman & Son, Theresa, N.Y. No. 4. It is approximately 2" long. $125.00 – 175.00.

B. This bait is 1⅜" long and marked W.D. Chapman, Theresa, N.Y. $50.00 – 75.00.

C. This arrowhead-shaped lure is 1⅝" long and marked W.D. Chapman, Theresa, N.Y. No. 4. It is nickel plated and probably of a later vintage. $75.00 – 125.00.

D. Ad for an early "Water Nymph." The "Nymphs" shown earlier were made after 1892.

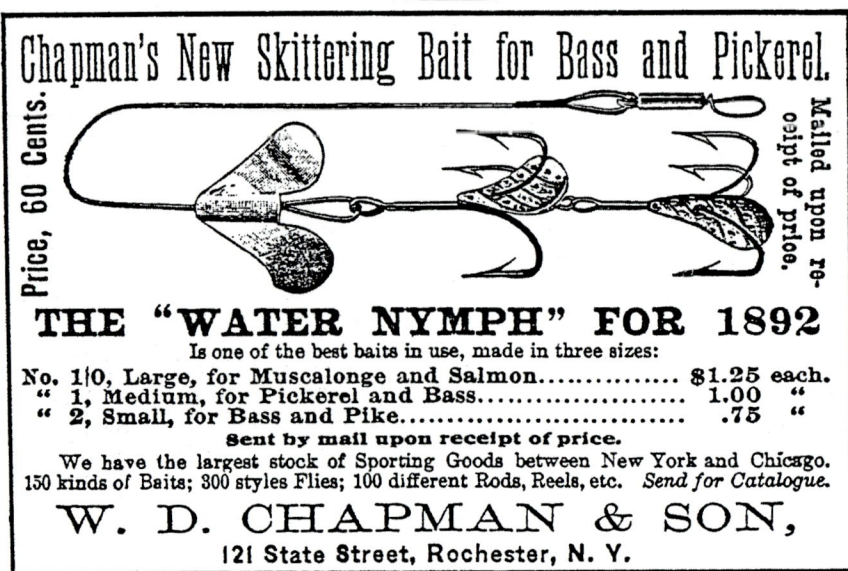

D.

A.

A. Cover of the Gibson and Woodworth catalog. This catalog is not dated, but appears to be circa 1895 – 1897.

B. These round spinners were made in at least four sizes. The large one pictured is 1¼" in diameter and marked W.D. Chapman. Theresa N.Y. No. 1/0. The smaller one is 1¹/₃₂" in diameter and is marked W.D. Chapman, Theresa N.Y. No. 2. $75.00 – 100.00.

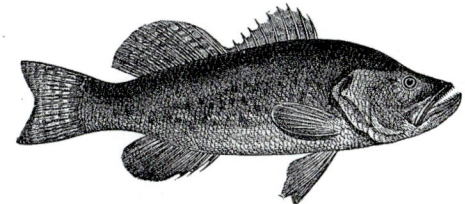

B.

A.

B.

C.

A. Chapman's "Daisy Bait." Manufactured in at least five sizes. The one pictured is marked Chapman & Son, Theresa N.Y. No. 3. It is 2" long. $50.00 – 75.00.

B. A variation of the "Daisy Bait." This spinner has a raised portion at the bottom of the bait. It is 2⅝" long and is marked Chapman & Son, Theresa N.Y. No. 1. $100.00 – 125.00.

C. A "Daisy Bait" in reverse. This large size bait is 3⅝" long and marked W.D. Chapman, Theresa, N.Y. $50.00 –75.00.

D. The "Montreal" bait. This bait was made in at least seven sizes. The one shown is 3¼" long and marked W.D. Chapman, Theresa, N.Y. $100.00 – 125.00.

D.

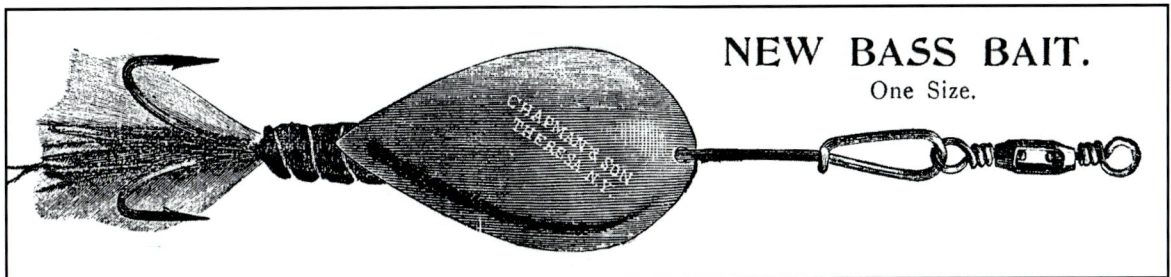

A.

A. Cut from the Woodworth and Gibson catalog showing a bait similar to the "Montreal" bait. This lure is attached to the shaft through a hole in the upper part of the blade rather than a wire loop.

B. Chapman's "Pike Oval" or "Thousand Island Oval" bait. This lure was made in at least six sizes. The one pictured is 1⅞" long and marked W.D. Chapman, Theresa, N.Y. No. 3. It is an early example of this lure and is also stamped I.X.L. with the 1866 patent date. The larger sizes may also be marked "1,000 Island Bait." $40.00 – 60.00.

C. A tandem spinner with small "Pike Oval" blades. The top blade is marked Chapman & Son, Rochester, N.Y. No. 3, and is 1½" long. The bottom blade is unmarked. $50.00 – 100.00.

D. The "Pickerel" bait. This bait was made in at least 10 sizes. The one shown is 1¹⁵⁄₁₆" long and marked Chapman & Son, Theresa, N.Y., No. 6. $40.00 – 60.00.

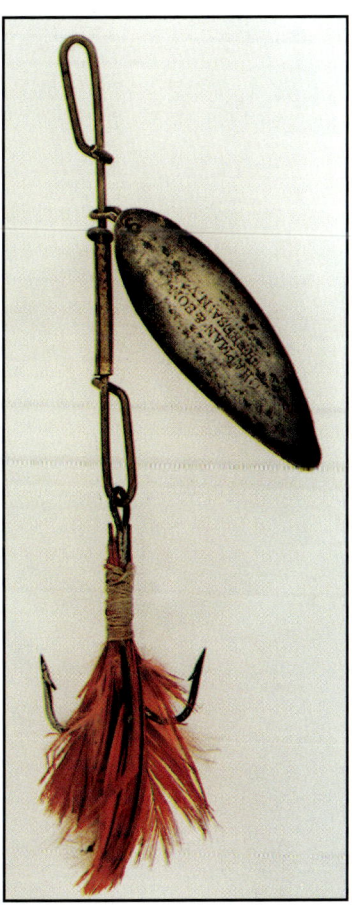

B.   **C.**   **D.**

 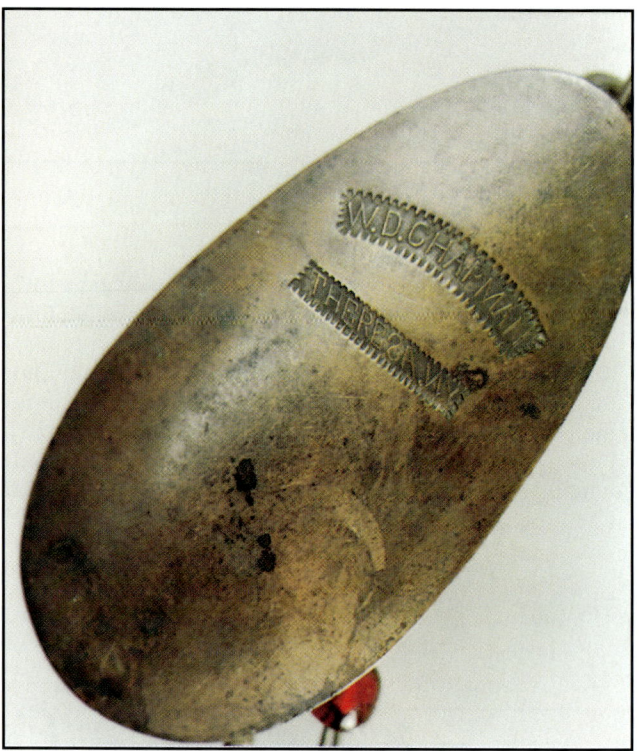

A.   Close-up of Pike at left.

A. Early "Pike" bait. The printing on the bait is markedly different from that on most Chapman baits. Note that the "s" in Theresa and the "N" in N.Y. are inverted. This lure is 2½" long and made of copper, silver plated on the back side. $150.00 – 250.00.

B. A spinner similar to the "Montreal" bait. This lure is 3½" long and marked W.D. Chapman, Theresa, N.Y. It came in at least two sizes. $100.00 – 125.00.

B.

A.

B.

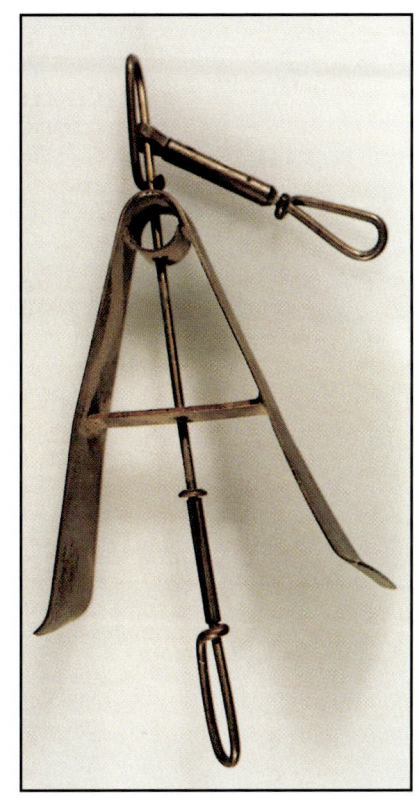

C.

A. The "Pike Kidney" or "1,000 Island Bait." The 1886 catalog states, "A great favorite with sportsmen at the Thousand Islands." It was made in at least seven sizes. The lure shown is 2¼" long and marked Chapman & Son, Rochester, N.Y. No. 1/0. "1,000 Island Bait" is stamped along the edge. $40.00 – 60.00.

B. This early lure has tandem 2" blades. The top blade is marked W.D. Chapman, Theresa, N.Y. No. 2. The bottom blade is marked "Montreal." $150.00 – 250.00.

C. This odd-shaped blade is 3" long and marked W.D. Chapman, Theresa, N.Y. It is made of brass with a copper cross bar. It may have been used in conjunction with another lure. $150.00 – 200.00.

D. Another lure resembling the one above, but smaller and without the cross bar. It is 2¼" long and marked Chapman, Son & Co., Rochester, N.Y. Pat Ap'd For. $150.00 – 200.00.

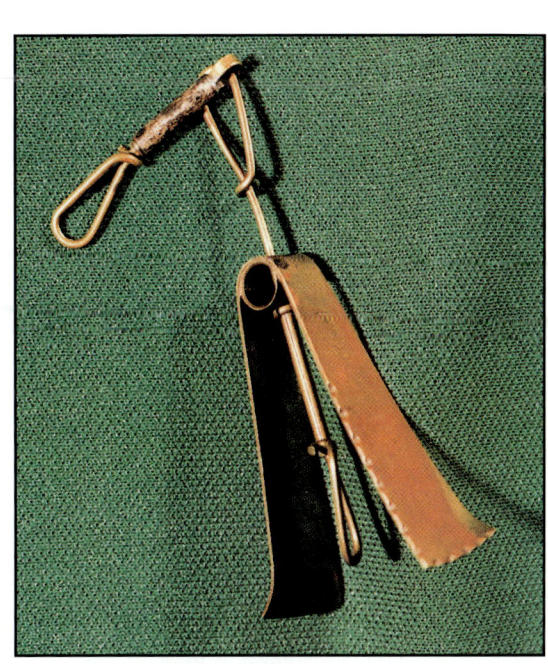

D.

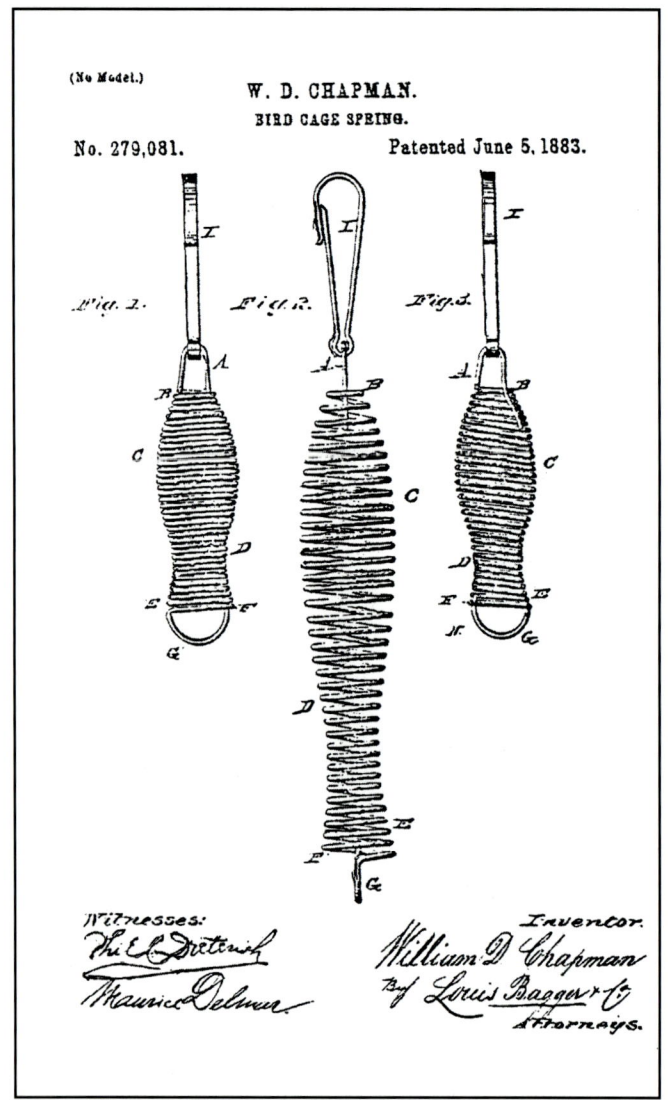

A.

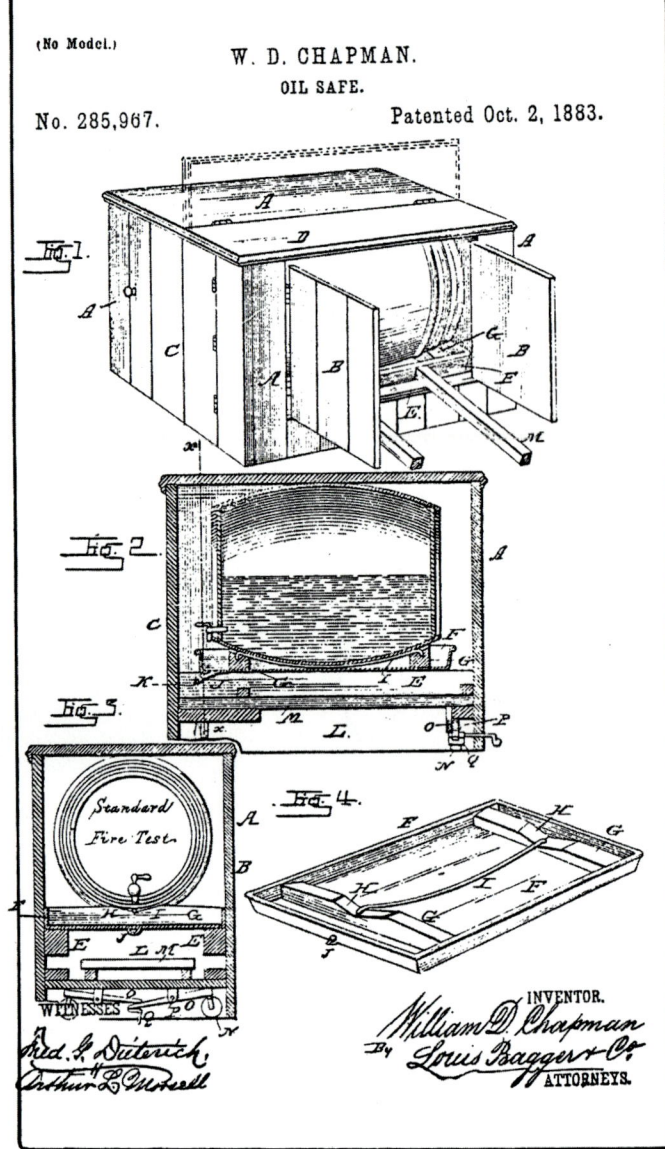

B.

C.

A. An 1883 patent for a bird cage spring. Chapman stated that this was the most financially successful of his patents. The patent date is stamped on the clip above the spring.

B. An 1883 patent for an oil safe, basically a box containing an oil barrel with a tray in the bottom to catch any leaking or spilled oil.

C. The "Mermaid" bait. This lure was made in at least five sizes. The larger sizes occasionally have "1,000 Island Bait" stamped on them. $50.00 – 75.00.

W.D. Chapman

A.

B.

C.

A. These lures were called, strangely enough, "Hooks to Spoon." They were manufactured in at least four sizes. The one shown is 3⅝" long and stamped Chapman & Son, Theresa, N.Y. No. 3/0. $100.00 – 150.00.

B. This odd spoon has an offset line tie. It is 2 9/15" long and marked W.D. Chapman, Theresa, N.Y. No. 1/0. It appears to be made of German silver. $100.00 – 150.00.

C. Rod tip manufactured by W.D. Chapman & Son, Theresa, N.Y. It is ⅝" long.

D. An 1884 patent for a stamping press. It was designed to stamp ornaments or letters in metal items.

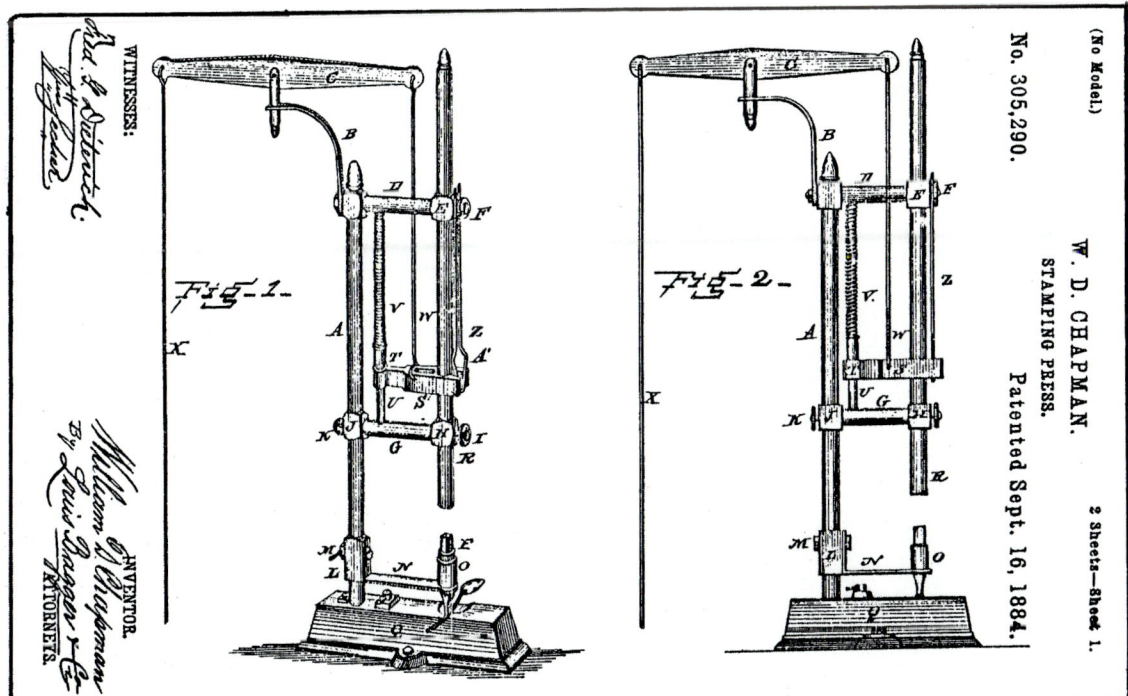

D.

W.D. Chapman

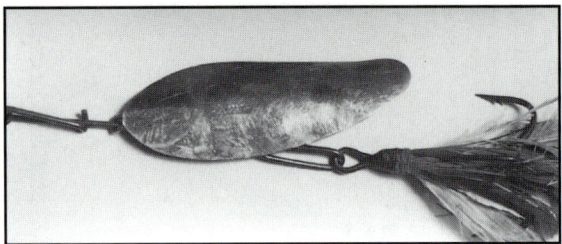

A.

A. This lure is 3⅞" long and marked W.D. Chapman, Theresa, N.Y. No. 1/0. $75.00 – 100.00.

B. These lures are similar to the more common Allure; the main difference is the way the blades are attached to the tubular shaft. On the Allure, the blades are soldered at the top and bottom of the tube, leaving a space in the center. The lures pictured have the blades soldered the full length of the tube. They are marked W.D. Chapman, Theresa, N.Y., with a large "M" stamped on one side. Double: $100.00 – 150.00; single: $75.00 – 100.00.

C. This early lure is 2⅜" long and marked W.D. Chapman, Theresa, N.Y., with "I.X.L." stamped at the top. $125.00 – 175.00.

D. Chapman fly rod spinners. These lures all have blades that are less than an inch long. They were also made in a couple of other patterns. $50.00 – 75.00 each.

B.

C.

D.

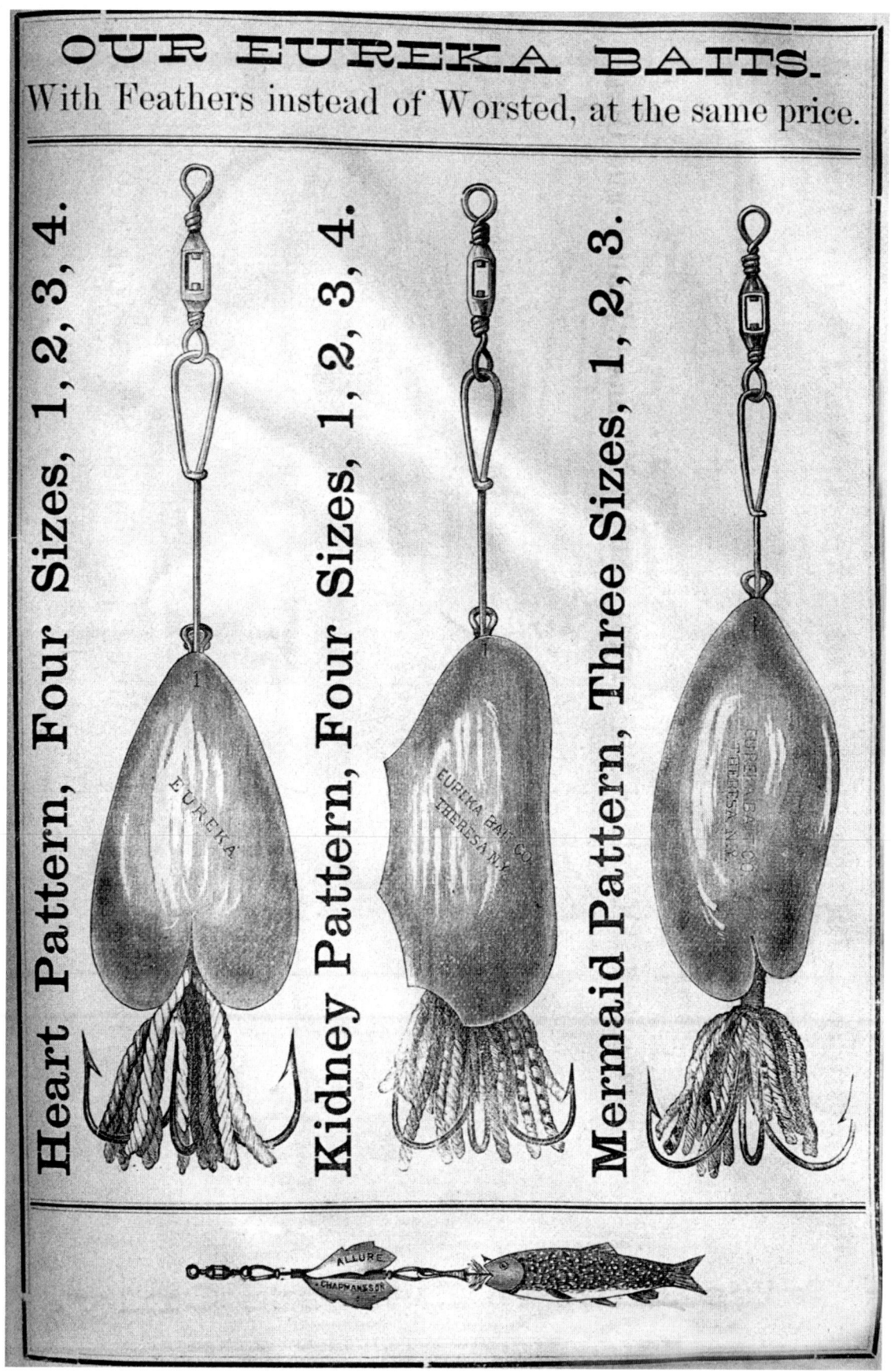

Page from the 1884 W.D. Chapman & Son catalog showing the inexpensive line of "Eureka" baits.

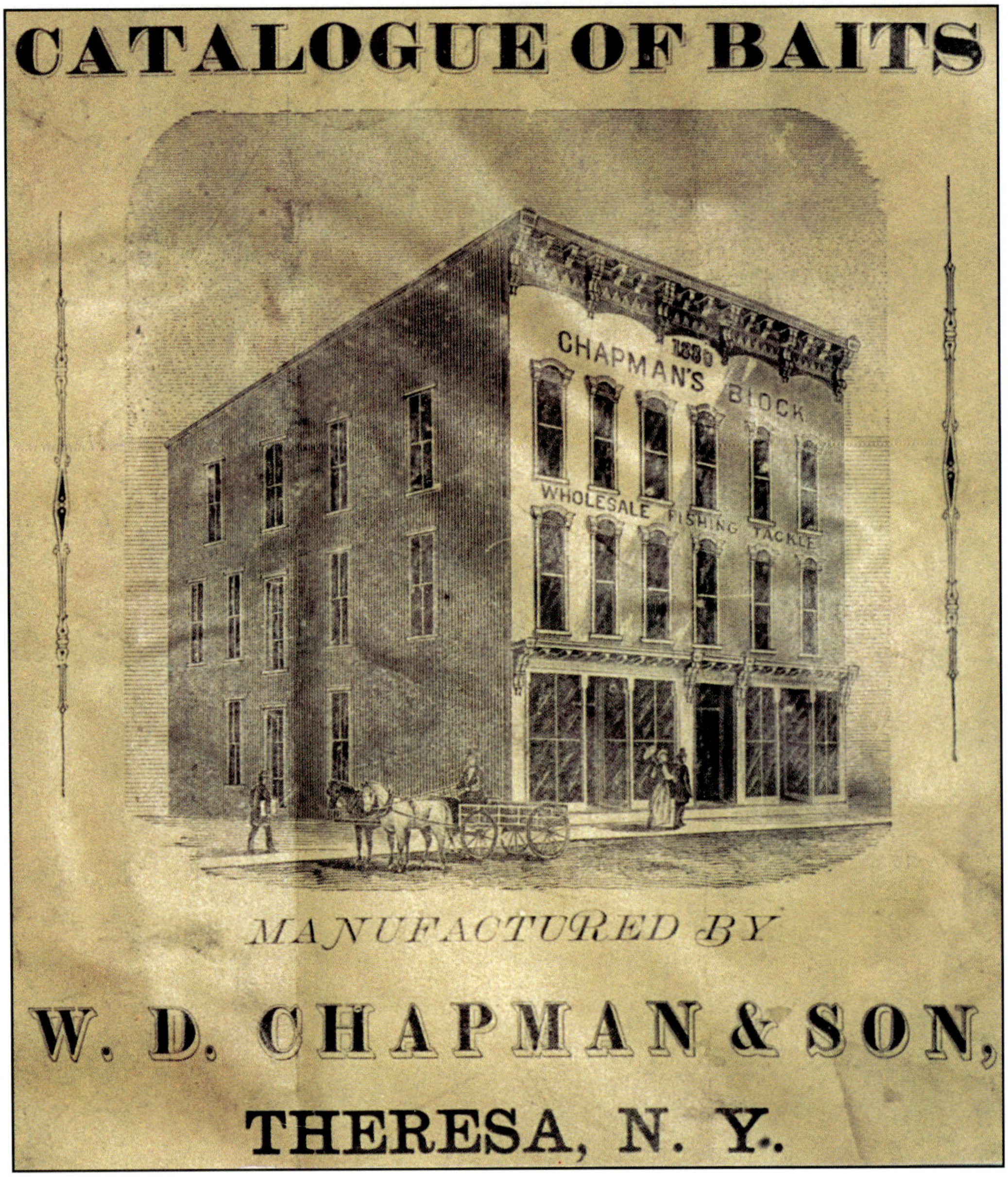

CATALOGUE OF BAITS
CHAPMAN'S BLOCK
WHOLESALE FISHING TACKLE
MANUFACTURED BY
W. D. CHAPMAN & SON,
THERESA, N. Y.

Catalog cut of Chapman's factory in 1884.

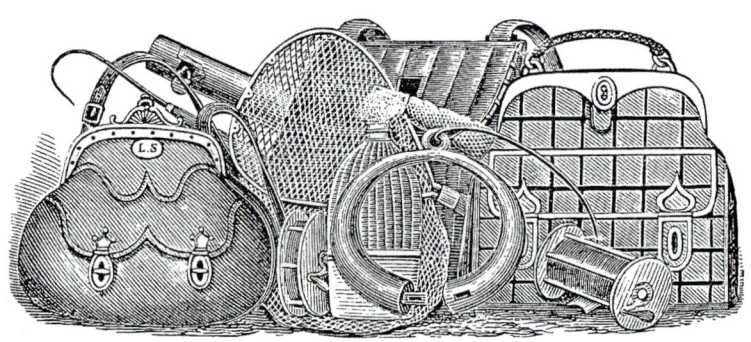

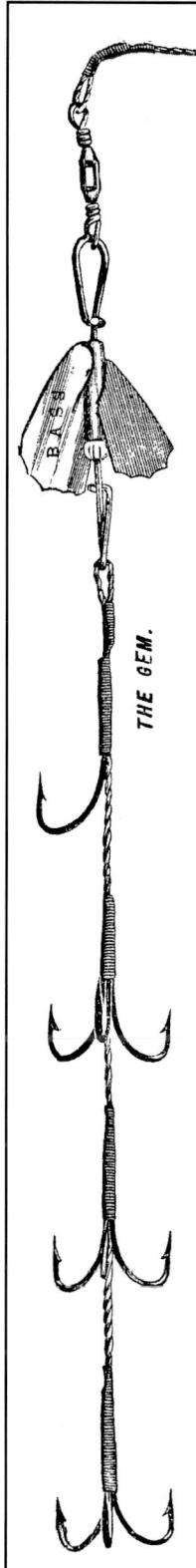

Collector's Postscript

Chapman lures can generally be dated by observing their markings. If a bait is marked W.D. Chapman, Theresa, N.Y., chances are it was manufactured before 1876. The letters I.X.L. stamped in conjunction with this marking indicate a very early lure. If it is marked Chapman & Son, Theresa, N.Y., it was manufactured between 1876 and 1887. If it is marked Chapman, Son, & Co., Rochester, N.Y., it was made after 1887. One exception would be the lures manufactured by W.D. Chapman after the death of son Byron in 1895. These lures would be marked the same as those before 1876. The "Safe Deposit" minnow and the folded, improved "Allure" would be in this time period. The four-sided "Helgramite" type lures are probably in this time period as well. These baits have been commonly found with a nickel finish, a finish not found on the earlier lures. The 1886 catalog states that they always ship silver except when otherwise ordered. Copper, oreide (imitation gold), or brass were available, but nickel is not mentioned.

There are no Chapman lures that could be termed "common," however some are found more frequently than others. Among those found with some frequency are the ALLURE, MERMAID, PIKE, PICKEREL, and BASS; also the ELECTRIC, PERFECT, and MINNOW PROPELLER in medium sizes.

The Pike, Kidney, Mermaid, and Heart patterns are often found marked "Eureka." These baits have a tinned finish of lesser quality than the regular line. To quote the catalog, "These baits are made so as to enable the dealers to furnish those that buy for quantity and not quality, although they are a splendid bait for the money."

The Chapmans also made a line of fly rod spinners. Unfortunately, most of them are unmarked, and therefore difficult to identify. They also imported a variety of English lures and carried a line of trade reels and other items to accommodate their customers.

John H. Mann

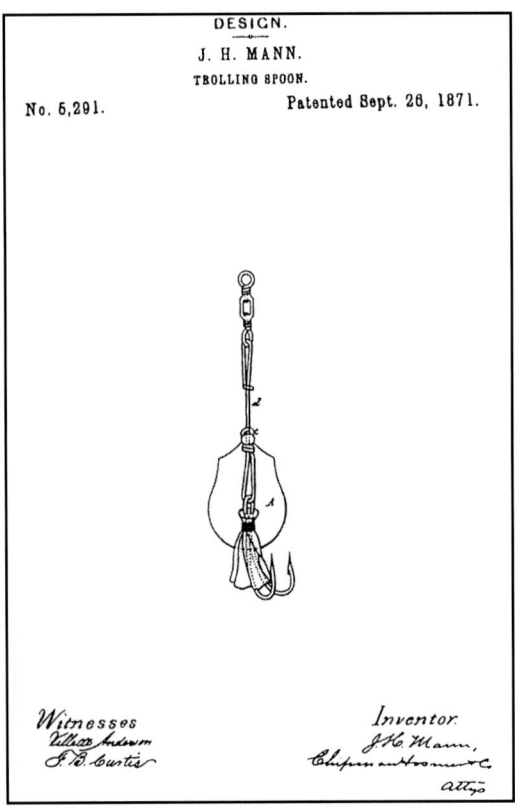

John Mann's first patent. It is a design patent for a shield or badge-shaped spinner.

John H. Mann was born in Peterboro, England on June 17, 1825, and came to this country in 1849, settling in Syracuse, N. Y.

In 1854 he married Annie Weber. They had eight children: Ann, Edward, Emily, William, Alice, George, Florence, and Isobel.

John Mann was in the grocery business from 1852 until his death. Sometime in the late 1850s he began operating a sporting goods business located a short distance from the grocery.

It is not known when he began to manufacture fishing lures, but he was issued a design patent on Sept. 26, 1871 for a shield, or badge, shaped spinner. A short time later on Nov. 21, 1871 he was issued a patent for an "Improvement in trolling spoons." This was for the application of glass washers or beads to support the eye or loop of a spinner blade on its shaft. He also manufactured a kidney-shaped lure that had a wire loop attached to control the distance that the blade was allowed to extend from the main shaft. This also may have been patented.

He produced another lure called "Mann's Perfect Revolving." This lure was advertised extensively in *Forest and Stream, Harper's Weekly*, and undoubtedly in other papers and magazines.

John H. Mann died of cancer August 3, 1892.

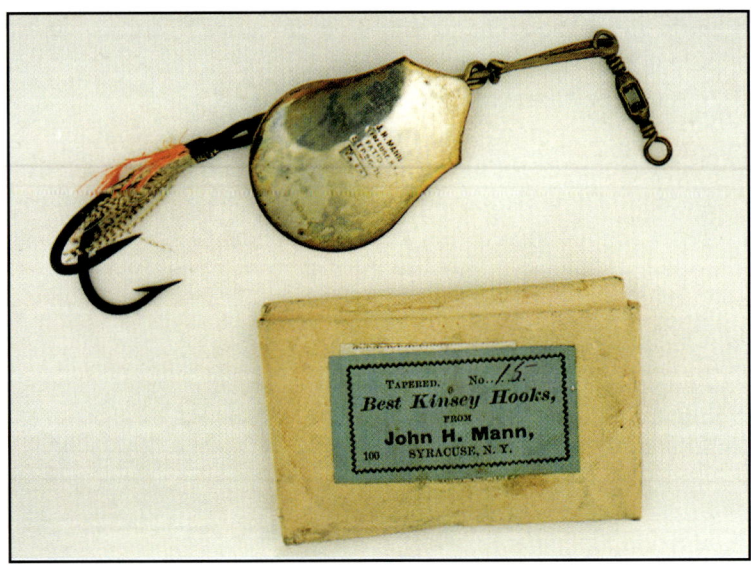

Example of the shield-shaped spinner blade. It was made in at least five sizes, and in silver, brass or copper. Also shown is an envelope of hooks manufactured or distributed by Mann. Lure, $75.00 – 100.00.

A.

A. Mann's Oval Trolling Spoon. This lure was made in two versions. One had a single fixed hook and the other had a double hook. It was made in at least three sizes and finished in silver or brass. $50.00 – 75.00.

B. John Mann's second patent. It is for the beads used as bearings on the main shaft.

C. An example of Mann's second patent using the clear glass beads as bearings. This lure is found in at least three different sizes and was also made in a single blade version. It was made in silver and brass. $50.00 – 75.00.

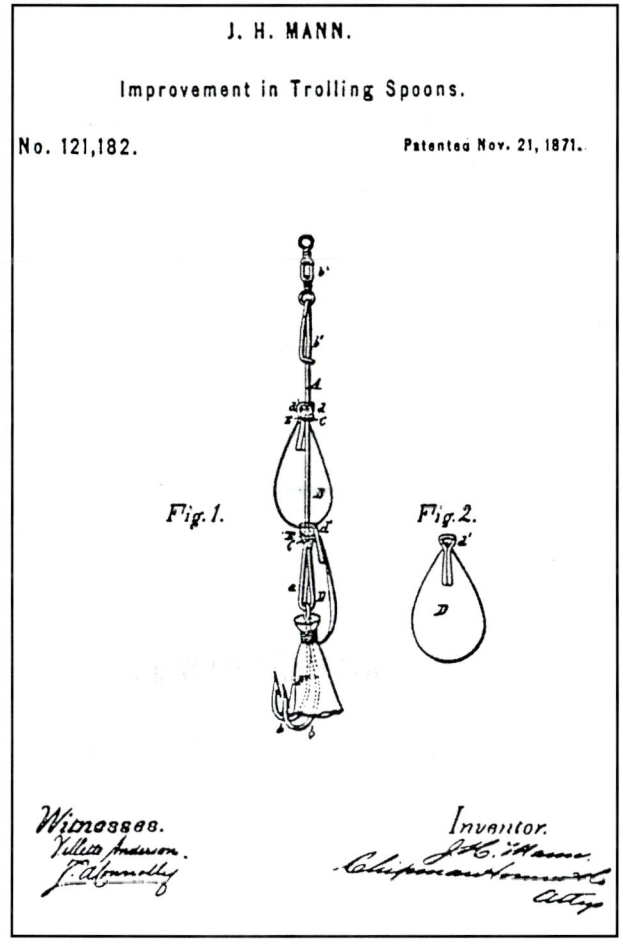

B.

C.

A.

B.

A. Advertisement for "Mann's Perfect Revolving." This bait was advertised in *Forest and Stream*, *Harper's Weekly*, and other publications. It was available in both a single and double configuration.

B. Detail of the reverse side of Perfect Revolving spoon. Note the patented clear glass bead.

C. The No. 22 Perfect Revolving spoon. The blade of this lure is 2½" long. The Perfect Revolving was available in silver, brass, and copper finish and also came in a tandem configuration. $50.00 – 75.00.

C.

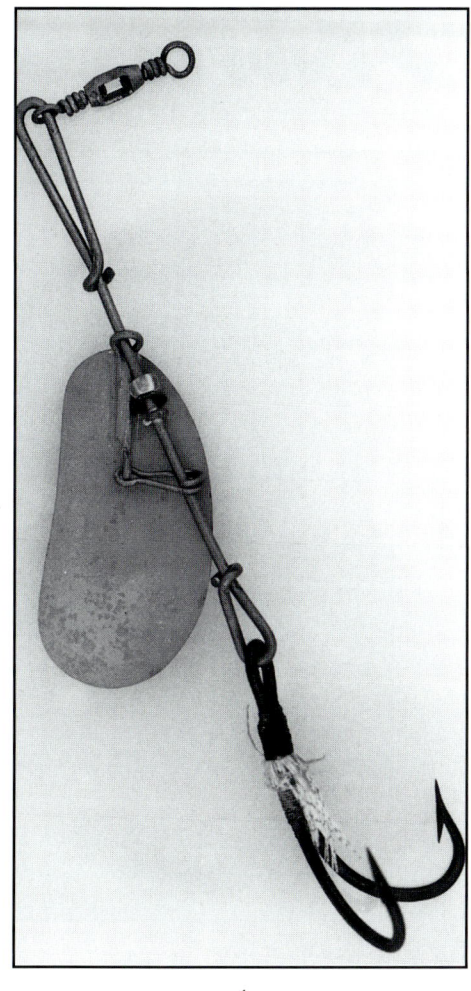

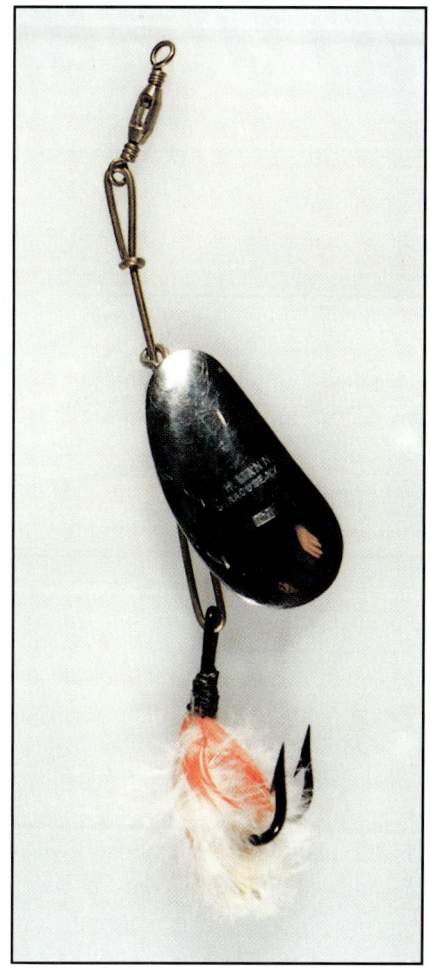

A.

B.

A. Kidney-shaped spinner with clip attached to control the amount of swing the blade has away from the shaft. It came in at least two sizes. $75.00 – 100.00.

B. Mann's kidney-shaped spinner. It came in at least five sizes and was available in silver, brass, and nickel. $30.00 – 50.00.

C. Early heart-shaped spinner marked J. H. Mann Syracuse N. Y. No. 14 It has the patented clear glass bead and familiar japanned double hook. $100.00 – 150.00.

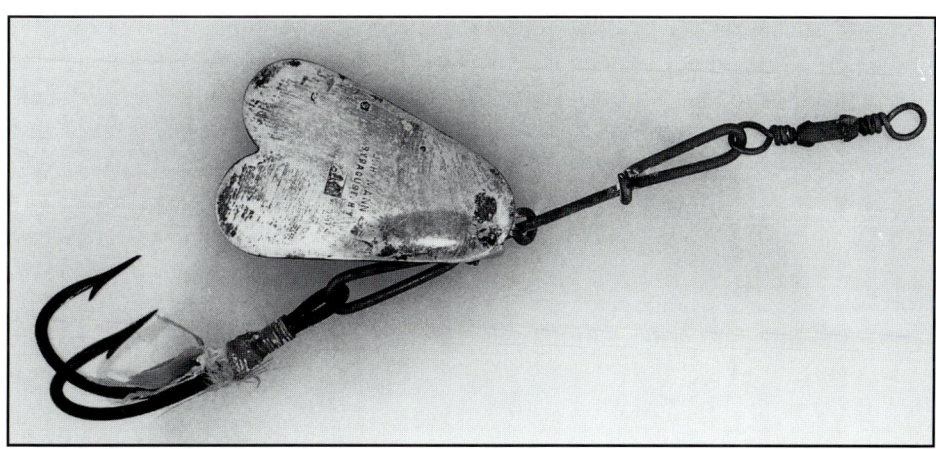

C.

Gardiner M. Skinner

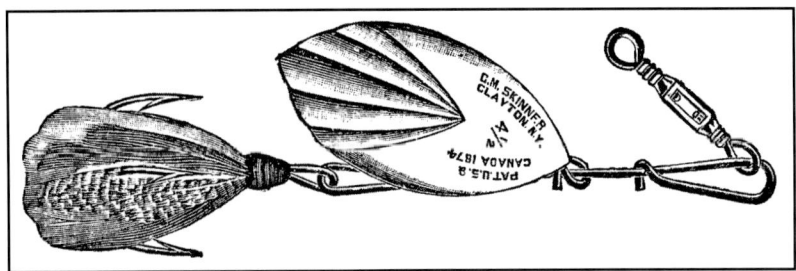

When Gardiner M. Skinner patented his fluted trolling spoon on August 4, 1874, he could not have foreseen that over 100 years later it would still be a popular fishing lure. It is still used on a number of musky bucktails, and until a few years ago, it could be purchased bearing his name and patent date. It ranks with South Bend's Bass Oreno and Creek Chub's Pikie Minnow as the lure most likely to be found in an old tackle box. This in itself is a testimonial to the popularity and fish catching ability of this great old spinner.

Gardiner's father was Sylvester Skinner. Sylvester was a native of New Britain, Connecticut. He later moved to Chenango County, New York, and finally to Gananoque, Ontario, where he died in 1875 at the age of 74. He was a manufacturer of hames, scythe snaths, and grain cradles. He was arrested at the time of the Patriot War, suspected of being in possession of correspondence of the Patriots and was wounded in his attempt to escape arrest. He married Amanda Stickney of Lowville, New York. Gardiner was their only child.

Gardiner Mills Skinner was born in Brockville, Ontario, on January 24, 1845. He married Mariana Girard, daughter of Peter and Elizabeth (Wilson) Girard, of Clayton, New York, on December 11, 1871. Gardiner and Mariana had four daughters: Glennie M., Ettie L., Eva L., and Mabel F.

He was living in Gananoque, Ontario, at the time he was granted the 1874 patent for a fluted spoon. He manufactured his lures in that city until 1879, when he moved the operation to James Street in Clayton, New York.

Over the years he obtained several patents to improve his fluted trolling spoon. The first was a patent granted on May 18, 1886 for what was basically a hammered design on the spoon. Two other patents issued in 1891 were for improvements in the way the blade was attached to the lure shaft. The last patent he received was in 1892 for an improved snap lock on the end of the lure shaft.

Skinner spoons were famous for their fine quality and in 1893 at the International Columbian Exposition, Gardiner was awarded the first prize diploma and medal for superior quality and progressive features.

In 1887 the original factory building burned down, and the business then moved to a building at 343 James Street. From this location the company continued to do business until 1962.

Gardner M. Skinner died on January 3, 1903.

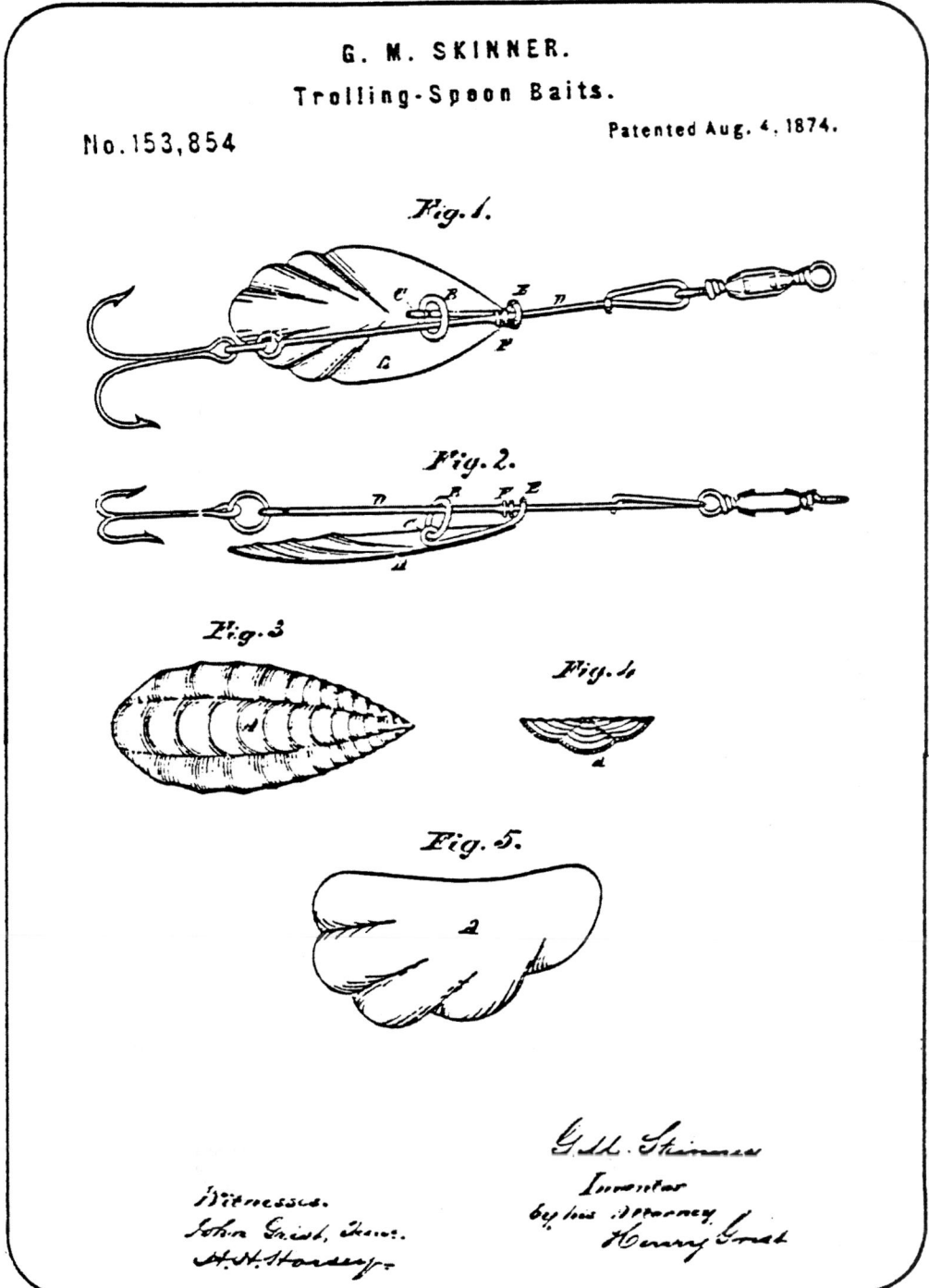

Skinner's 1874 patent. He made two claims in the patent description. The first was for a fluted or corrugated surface to cause refractory rays of light and therefore make the lure more attractive to fish. The second was a ring or loop to prevent the spoon from spinning in too large a circle about the shaft. I have not seen a Skinner spoon with this loop.

G.M. Skinner

A.

A. The common Fluted Spoon Bait. This lure was available in at least 10 sizes. The one shown is a Number 3 and the blade is approximately 1¼" in length. This lure was available in nickel, brass, enamel (white), copper, silver, and gold.

Skinner suggested that the Nos. 1 through 4 be used for Bass, Pickerel, Salmon, and all game fish; Nos. 5 and 6 for Pickerel, Muscallonge, Salmon, Blue Fish, and all game fish weighing from 3 pounds up; Nos. 7 and 8 for anything less than 40 pound Muscallonge. Although the nickel plated versions are very common (except the tiny no. 0), other finishes are difficult to find and command a higher price. $3.00 – 5.00.

B. Early ad from the May 11, 1876, issue of *Forest and Stream*.

C. The so-called "Turkey Wing." This lure is Skinner's version of the popular kidney spoon. It was made in at least five sizes, 14 through 18, and probably more. The 1879 Simmons Hardware Catalog lists two sizes, 15 and 17. The illustration in this catalog shows the lure with the inscription, "G.M. Skinner — Gananoque, Ont." This was the same year Skinner moved to Clayton, N.Y. $75.00 – 100.00.

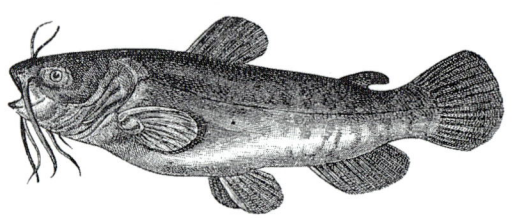

B.

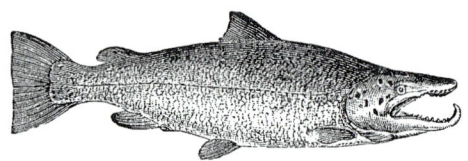

C.

G.M. Skinner

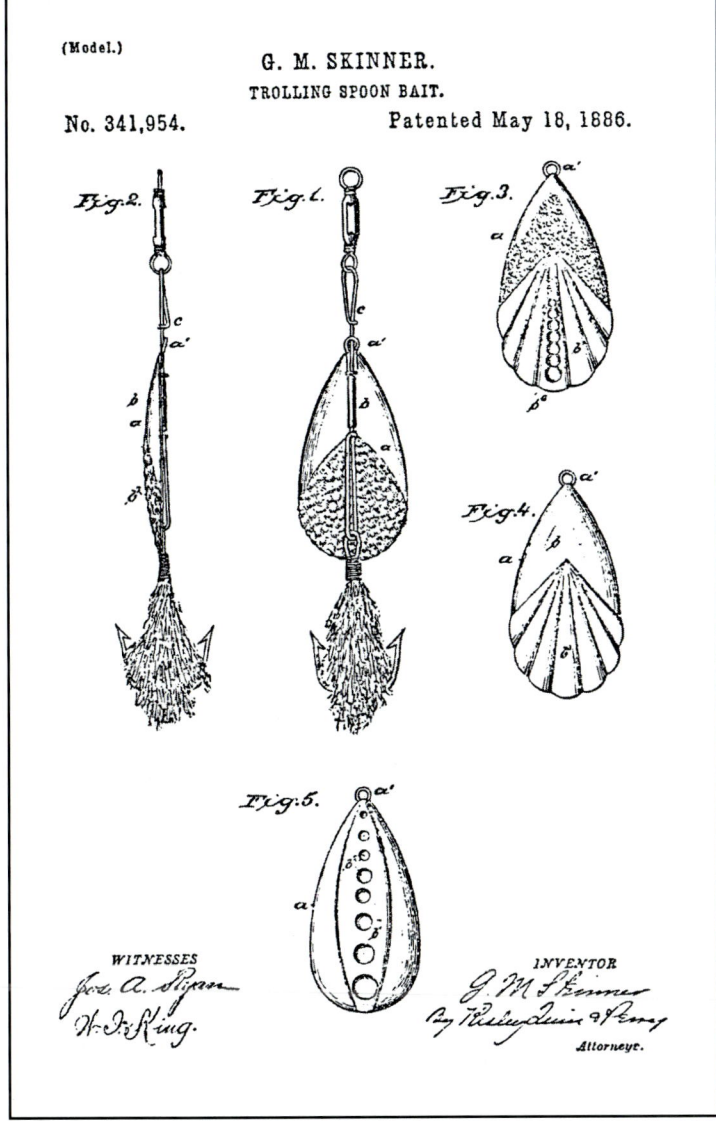

A.

B.

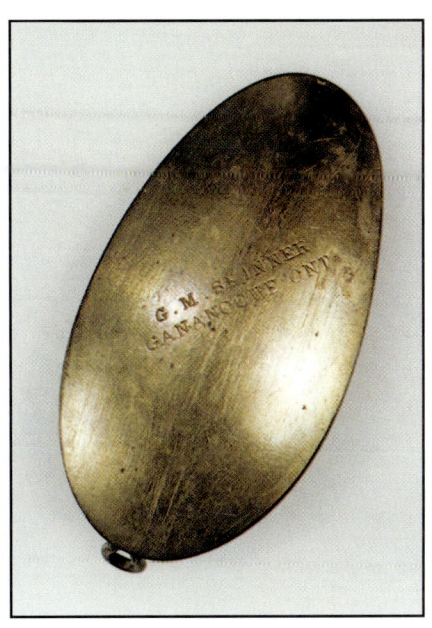

C.

A. This patent is basically for a spoon with a hammered design. Although it appears to be the first regular patent for a hammered spoon, W.T.J. Lowe of Buffalo, N.Y. was granted a design patent for a similar spoon on August 11, 1886.

B. An example of the 1886 patent. This spoon is 2 5/16" in length and marked G.M. Skinner, Clayton, N.Y. Patented May 18, 1886, and is silver plated. This spoon is commonly called the Turkey Foot. $75.00 – 125.00.

C. This spoon-shaped blade is 2 5/8" in length and marked G.M. Skinner - Gananoque, Ontario. $100.00 – 150.00.

G.M. Skinner

A.

A. The smaller bait is the number 9 St. Lawrence Muscallonge and Pickerel Bait. It is 3" long and nickel plated. It was available in nickel, brass, enamel, copper, silver, and gold, as were most of Skinner's baits. The larger example is the No. 12 extra large Muscallonge spoon. The blade on this spoon is 3¾" long and finished in copper. Note the double swivel; this was standard on this bait. The Muscallonge spoon was also available with a smaller No. 6 blade. $10.00 – 20.00.

B. An early spoon with the Canadian patent date of Jan. 6, 1874. It is also stamped G.M. Skinner – Gananoque, Ontario – Fluted Bait Patent. Interestingly, it is not a fluted spoon. $100.00 – 150.00.

C. G.M. Skinner's weedless casting spoon. Available in one size only, finished in brass, copper, nickel, and enamel. $20.00 – 30.00.

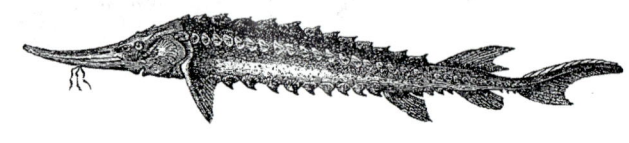

B.

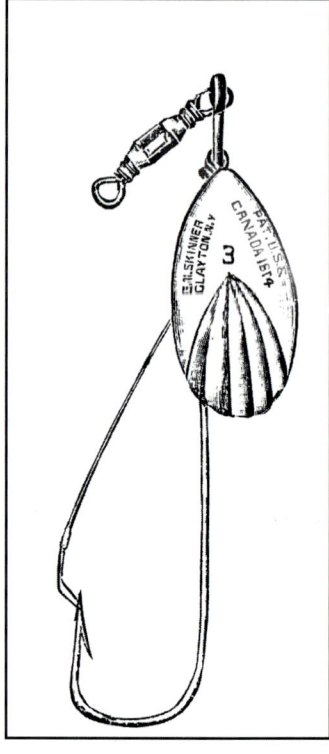

C.

92

A.

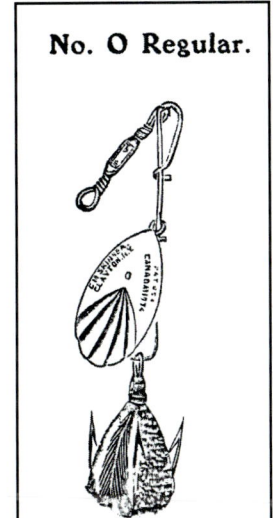

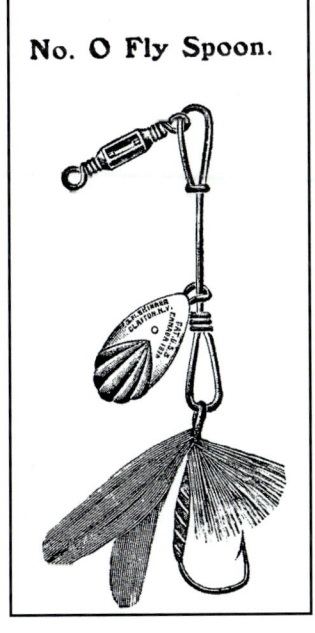

B.

A. The "Fly" spoon was offered in four sizes, and came in all finishes except silver. The catalog recommended size 2 for all-around fishing. $20.00 – 30.00.

B. These baits were made in one size only and are shown actual size. They were available in all finishes, and the "Fly" spoon used seven different fly patterns. $30.00 – 50.00.

C. "Skinner's New Casting Spoon." It was available in all finishes, and came in four sizes. $20.00 – 30.00.

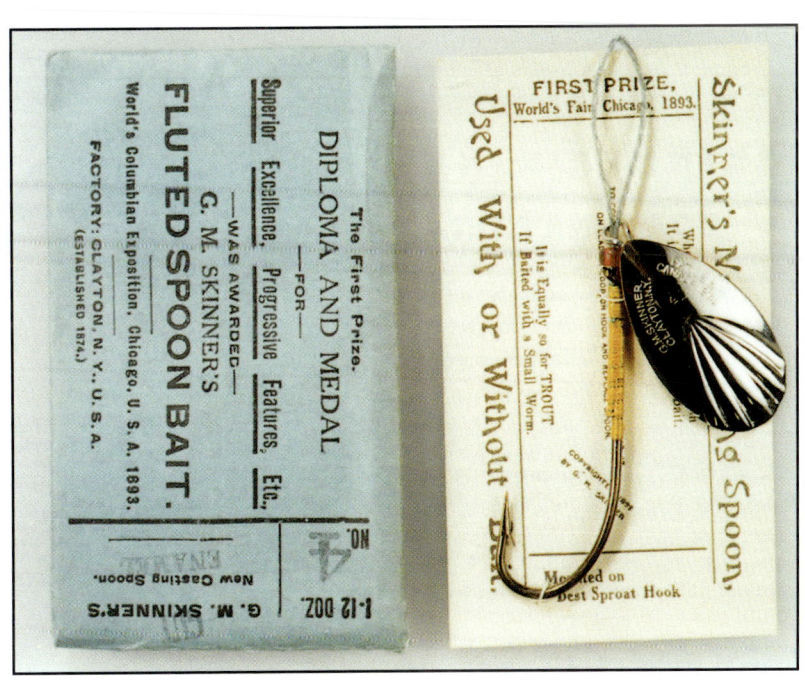

C.

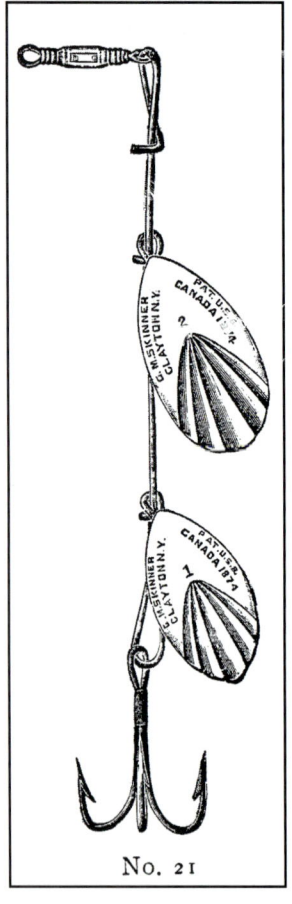

A.

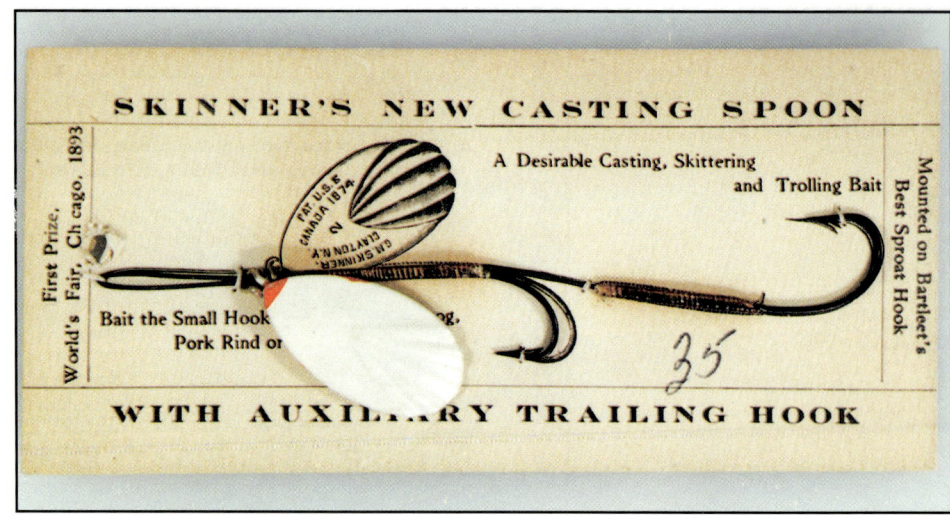

B.

A. G.M. Skinner's Double Trolling Spoon. Made in one size only, but available in all finishes. $40.00 – 60.00.

B. This spoon is virtually the same as the new casting spoon, but has a trailing hook for securing frogs, minnows, and other bait. It was made in three sizes and available in all finishes. $20.00 – 30.00.

C. Skinner's Combination Baits. These sets were packaged one assortment per box.

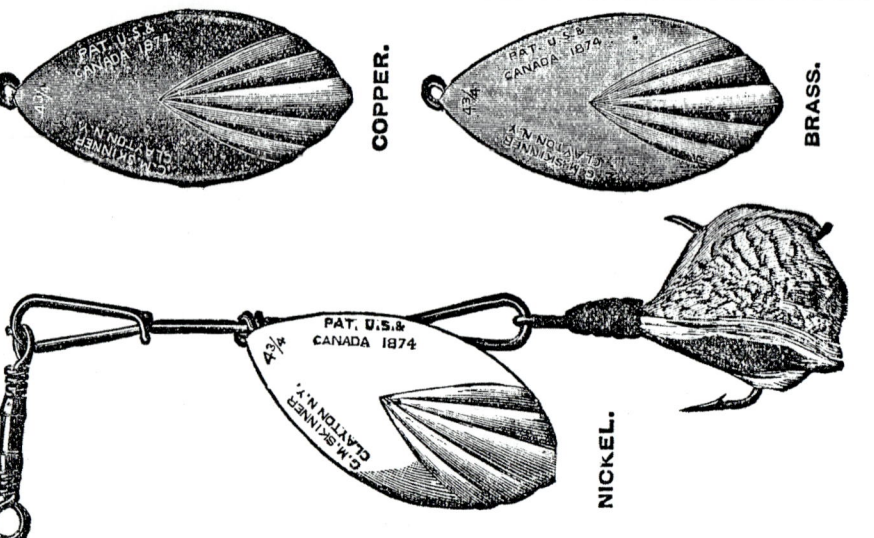

C.

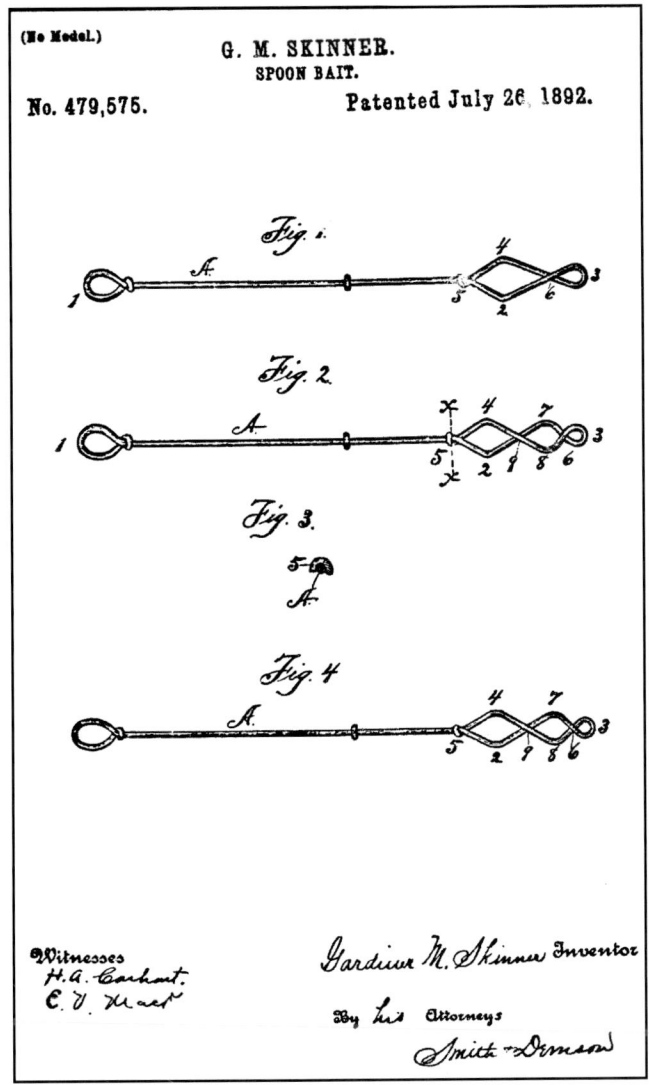

A.

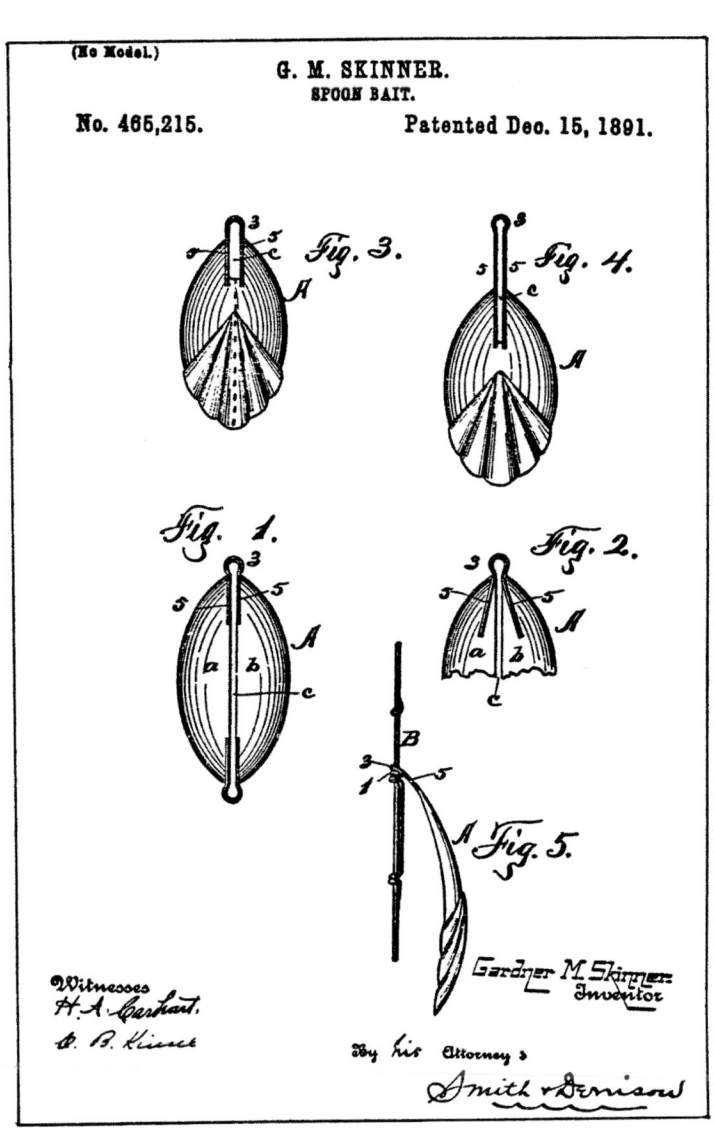

B.

A. Skinner claimed that the common snap hook on a spinner shaft was subject to opening when leverage was applied by a fish. He claimed the above patented snap would cure this problem. It is similar to a standard snap except for the twists in the wire which were supposed to prevent the hook from sliding up the shaft, where it could force open the snap. Sounds good, but I don't think many were manufactured.

B. This is another patent designed to prevent the fish from gathering leverage. The slot allows the blade to fold back out of the way when a fish is on. Figures 1 and 2 demonstrate how a blade can be made in two halves; each of a different material, while maintaining the slot in the center.

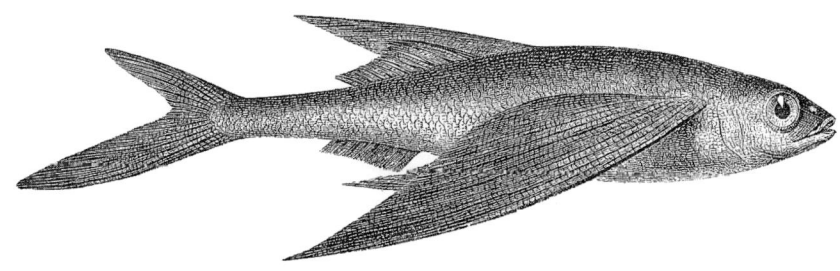

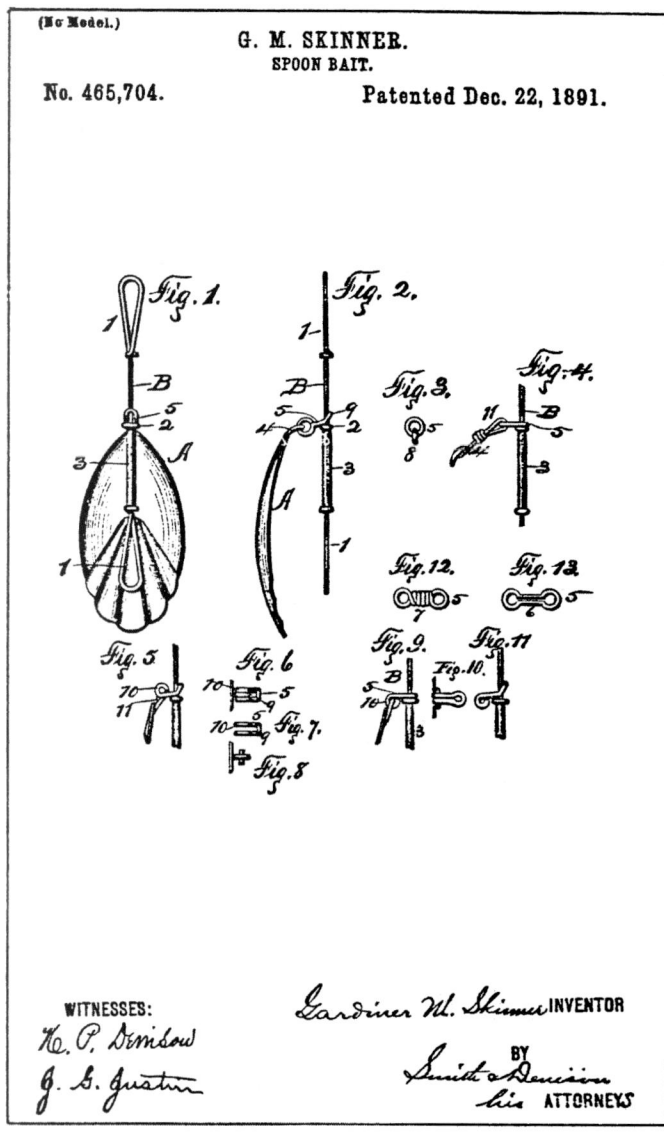

Collector's Postscript

Skinner fluted spoons in nickel plate are so abundant that they are almost a nuisance to collectors. Not so the rest of the Skinner baits. With the exception of the No. 9 and No. 12 Muscallonge spoons, most Skinners are, at best, difficult to find. The rarest are probably those marked Gananoque, Ontario. These were made before Gardiner moved to Clayton in 1880. Other scarce lures are the "Turkey Wing," Double Trolling Spoon, Weedless Casting Spoon, and the Combination Baits. Collecting a complete set of Skinner lures would be a challenge.

A.

A. This patent allows the blade to swivel in two directions, thus not interfering with a hooked fish.

B. Ad from an 1896 Wilkinson Co. Catalog. This ad recognizes the Skinner Spoon, but credits the hinge joint to J.M. Clark. Clark has been credited by many as the inventor of the Chicago rod, a short bait casting rod.

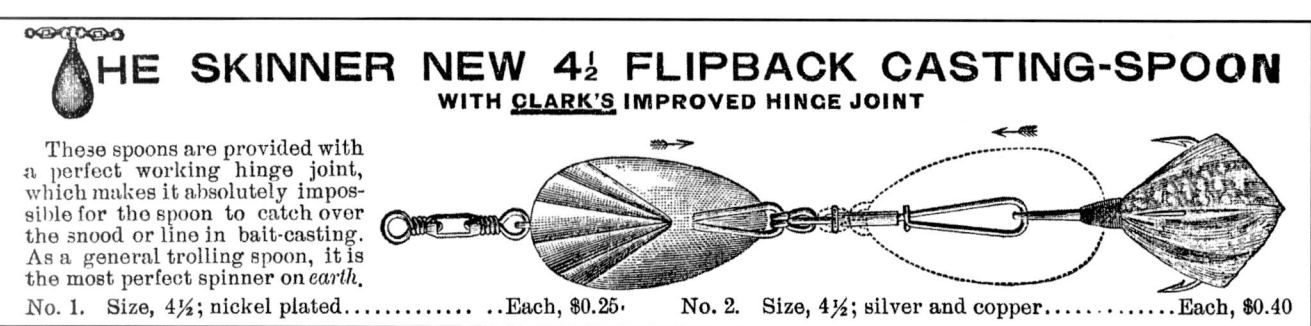

B.

Lysander S. Hill and Charles B. Hibbard

Little is known about Lysander S. Hill of Grand Rapids, Michigan. City directors list him as a jeweler and watchmaker in the 1860s and 1870s. He was granted his first patent for a fishing lure on May 23, 1876. This patent and subsequent patents all relate to methods of keeping a rotating spinner blade away from its main shaft while at the same time allowing it to close inward when a fish strikes. In 1879 he joined with Clark D. Spaulding to form the L.S. Hill and Co. at 21 Pearl Street in Grand Rapids.

Charles B. Hibbard joined the L.S. Hill and Co. in 1879. It is not known how long he was with them, but by 1882 the Grand Rapids city directory lists the C.B. Hibbard Fishing Tackle Co. It is apparent that Mr. Hibbard had formed his own company. In 1884 he was granted a patent for a spoon bait. This patent, like those of Hill, was also for a method of keeping the rotating spoon away from its main shaft.

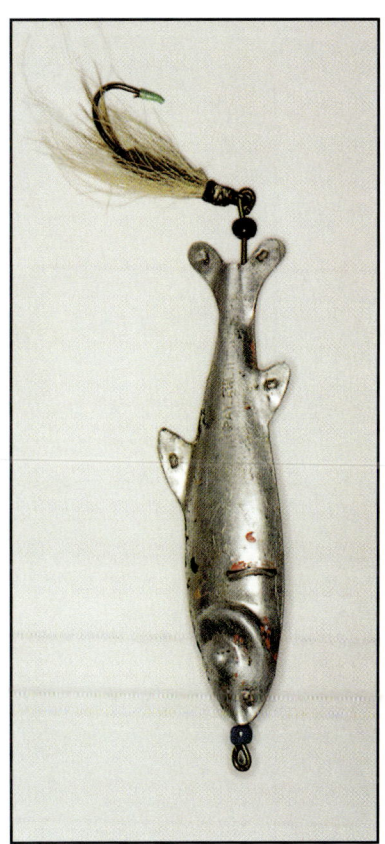

Hibbard Hollow metal minnow.

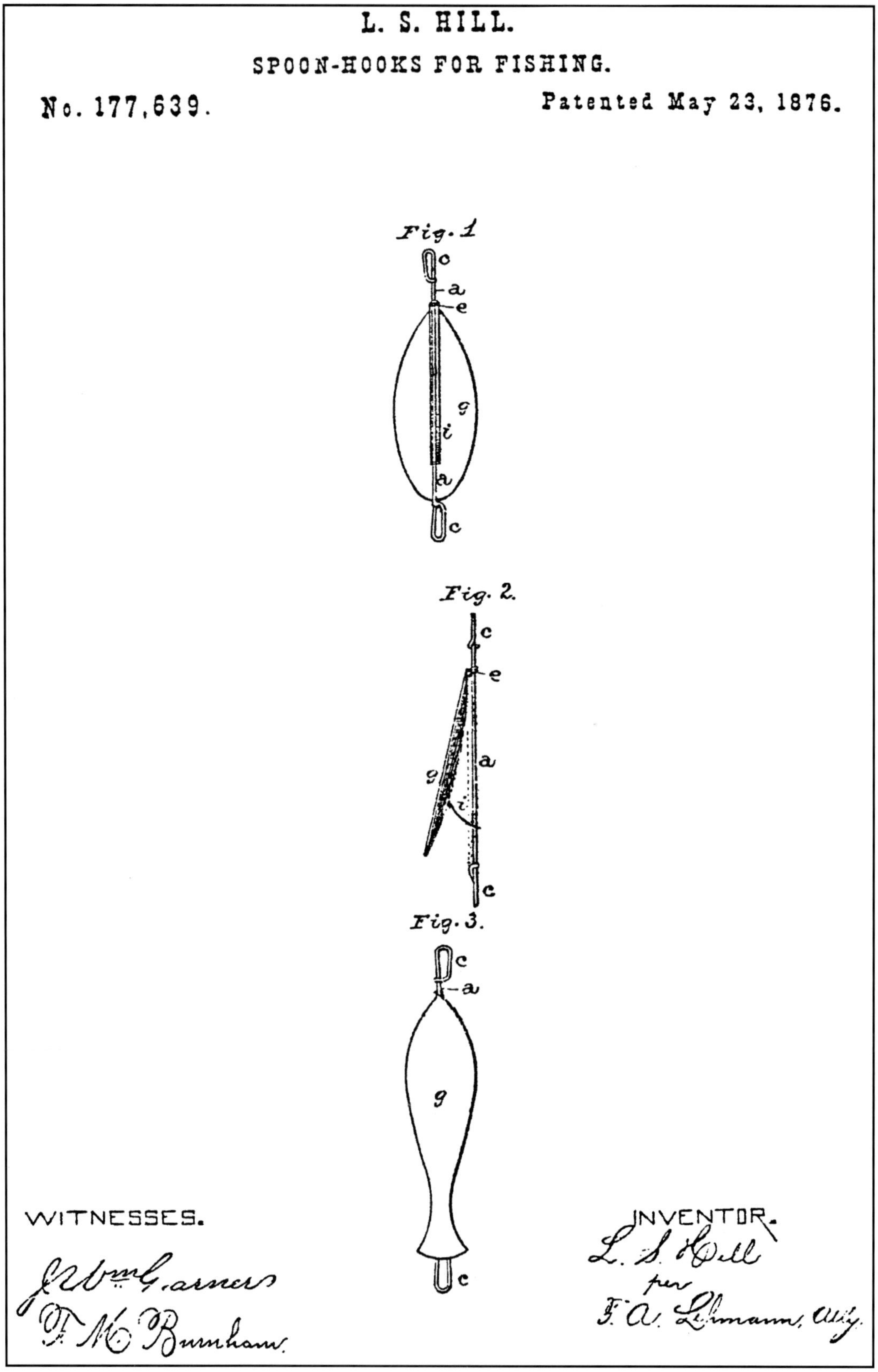

L. S. HILL.
SPOON-HOOKS FOR FISHING.

No. 177,639.   Patented May 23, 1876.

Fig. 1

Fig. 2

Fig. 3

WITNESSES.
Wm G. Arners
T. M. Burnham

INVENTOR.
L. S. Hill
per
F. A. Lehmann, Atty.

Hill's first patent, granted in 1876. It has a flat steel strip that keeps the spoon separated from the shaft.

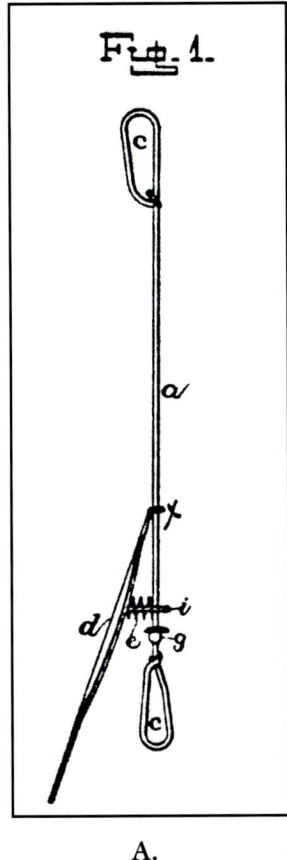

A.

B.

A. Portion of Hill's second patent drawing. This patent was granted on Feb. 4, 1879. It utilizes a spring to hold the spinner away from the shaft.

B. A single and a double Hill Spoon using the patented spring. Double: $75.00 – 100.00; Single, $50.00 – 75.00.

C. A large Number 5 spoon using the patented spring. $75.00 – 100.00.

C.

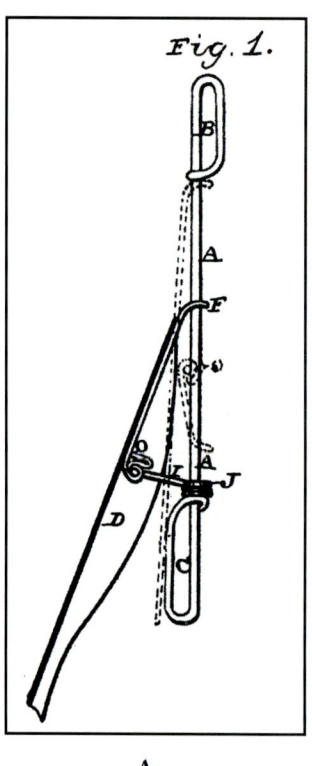

A.

A. Lysander S. Hill's third patent. This patent was granted on Nov. 7, 1882 and was witnessed by C.D. Spaulding. Spaulding was a partner in L.S. Hill and Co. This patent consisted of a rod that was hinged to the spoon and looped around the main shaft. The weight of the spoon against the bottom loop of the main shaft kept it (the spoon) away from the shaft but allowed it to close when any pressure (a fish?) was applied to it. Got that?

B. Spoon marked "Peerless Automatic." This spoon also has the Nov. 7, 82 patent date. It is 2⅝" long and appears to be silver plated. Its mechanism differs slightly from the 1882 patent drawing at left. $75.00 – 150.00.

C. Close-up view of the "Peerless Automatic" as described above.

B.

C.

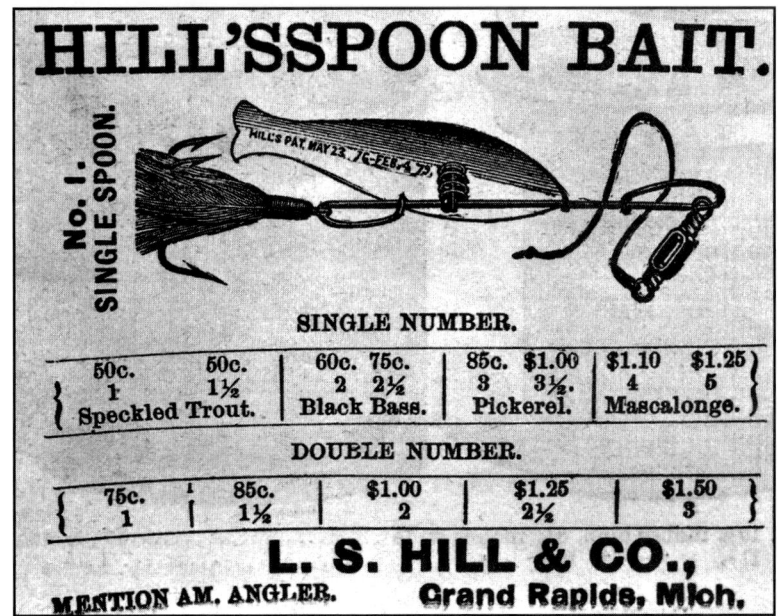

A.

A. Ad from an 1885 issue of the *American Angler*. The single spoons were available in eight sizes and made in silver or brass finish. They came with either treble or double hooks and could be found with or without feathered hooks. The double spoons were made in five sizes and were available with the same options as the single spoons. On both the single and the double spoons the model number on the blade also indicates its length, the Number 1 is 1" long, and the Number 5 is 5" long.

B. This tiny lure is only 1" long. It is marked with both the 1876 patent and the 1879 patent. It has No. 1 stamped on the tail; this is the model number and also indicates the length of the lure. $75.00 – 100.00.

C. This ad is from the Mar. 23, 1885 issue of the *American Angler*. The ad shows C.B. Hibbard's Mar. 25, 1884 patent spoon. It was made in seven sizes and came in copper, silver, and gold. Hibbard also manufactured a double spoon that was available in four sizes.

B.

C.

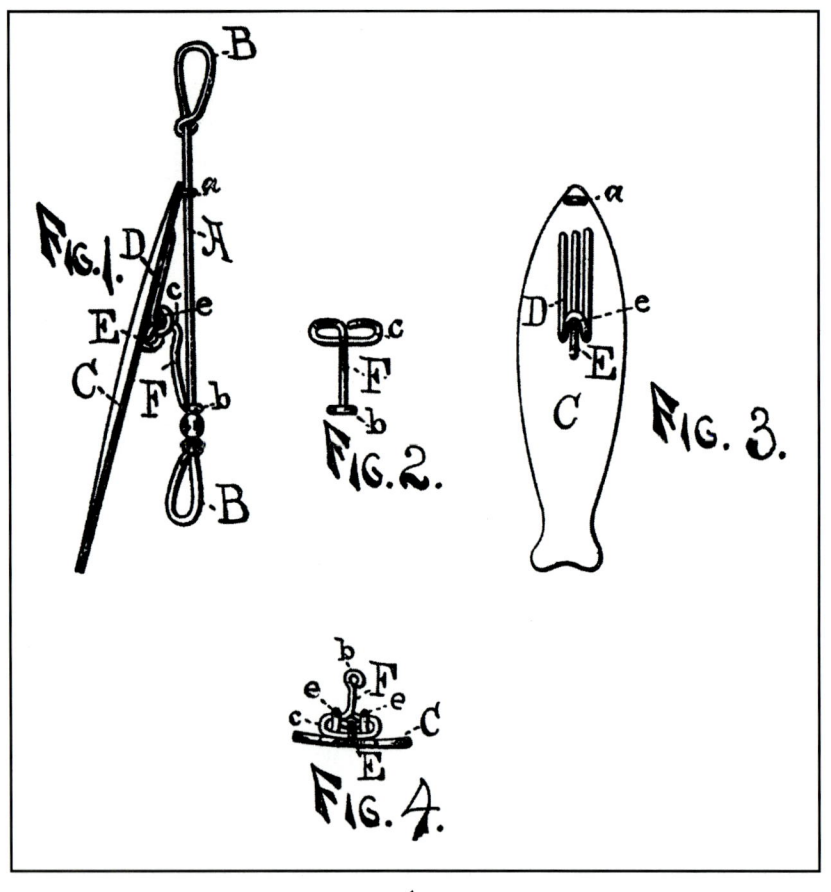

A.

B.

A. Charles B. Hibbard patent number 295,758. It was granted on March 25, 1884.

B. Hibbard spoon marked "C.B. HIBBARD - PAT. MARCH 25, 84. GD. RAPIDS, MICH. 3/2." The number designation "3/2" indicates the length of the blade (3½") just as it does on the L.S. Hill patent baits. $50.00 – 75.00.

C. Metal minnow manufactured by C.B. Hibbard. This minnow is of hollow construction and held together with soldered tabs. It is marked C.B. HIBBARD - GD RAPIDS - PAT. APL'D FOR. Size designation is No. 3. It was made in at least three sizes. Size 3 is 3⅜" long. $400.00 – 500.00.

D. Same lure with propeller on the front.

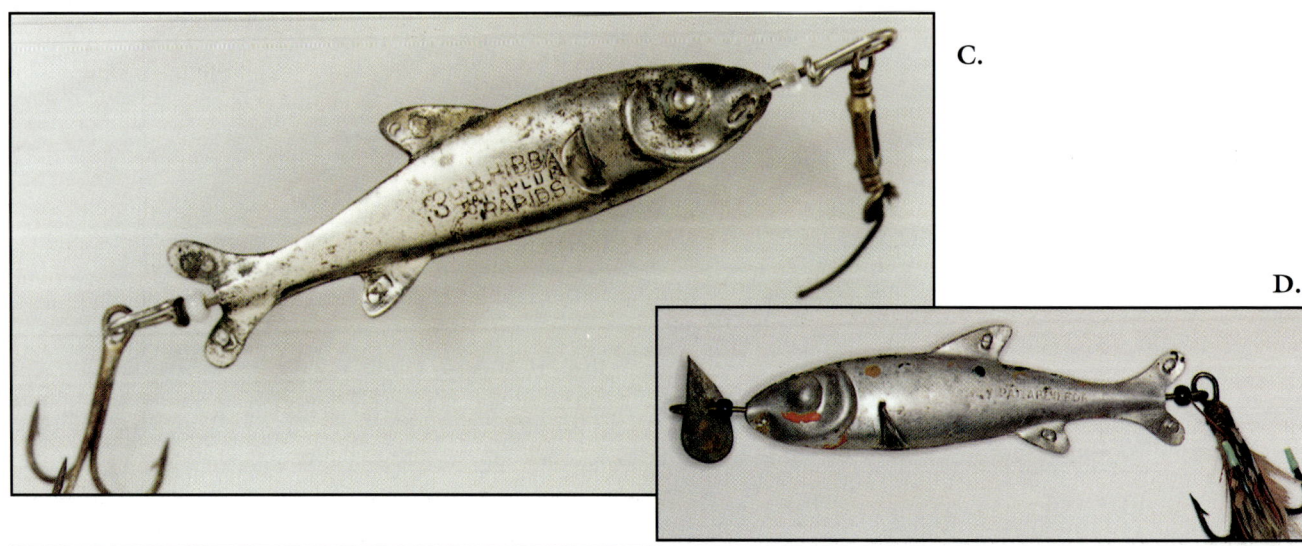

C.

D.

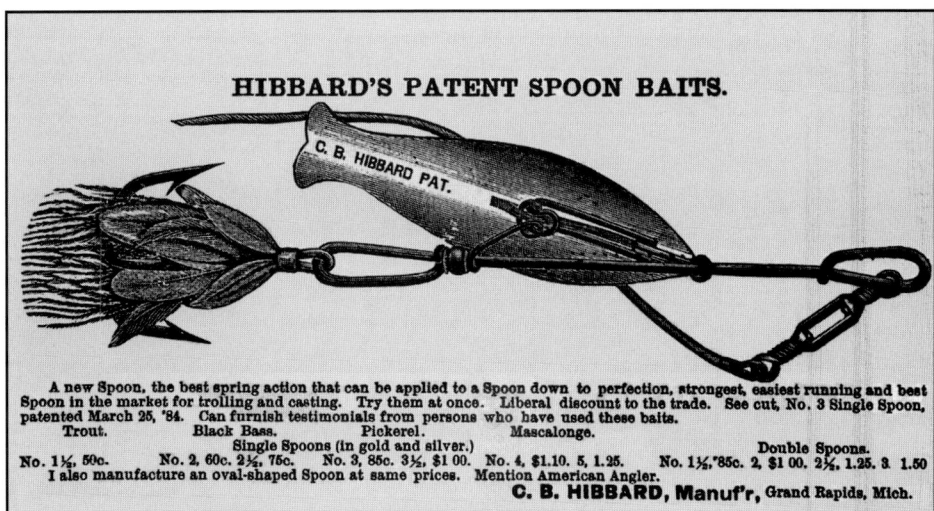

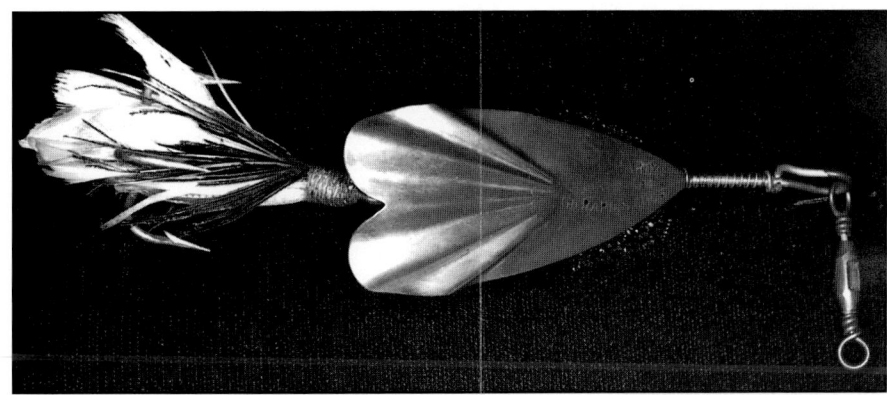

A. Advertisement from the May 16, 1885 *American Angler* magazine. Note that in this ad he states that he also manufactures an oval spoon at the same prices. The spoons ranged in price from 50 cents to $1.50, not a small sum at that time.

B. Heart-shaped lure marked C. B. HIBBARD - PAT MARCH 25, 84. GD RAPIDS MICH. No. 3. $100.00 – 150.00.

C. Three different types of tail designs used on the Hibbard spoons.

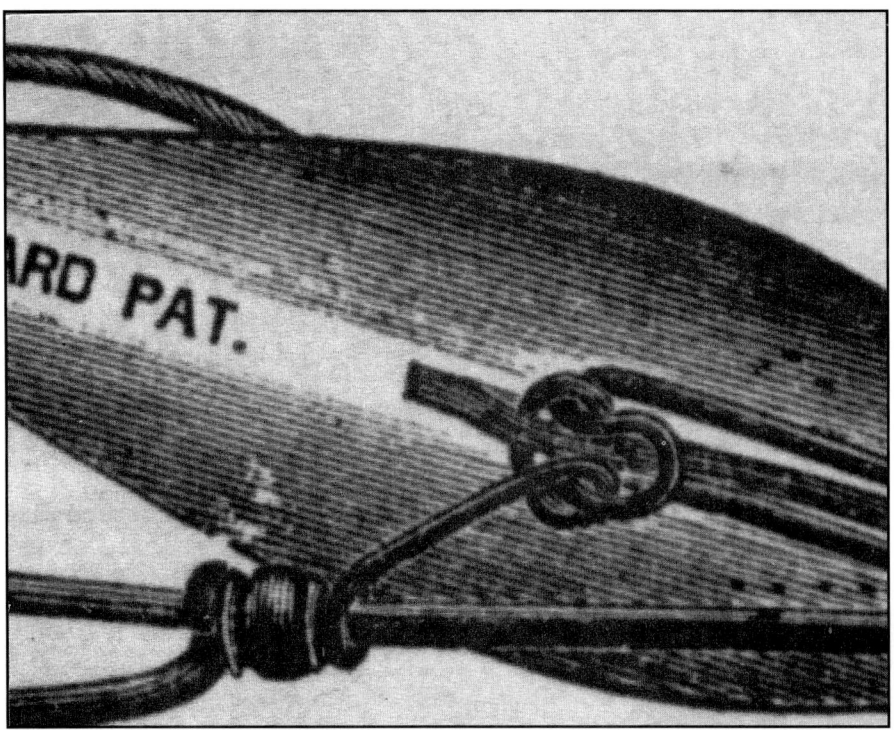

A.

A. Close-up view of C.B. Hibbard's March 25, 1884 patent.

B. Left: Drawing of L.S. Hill's May 23, 1876 patent.
Center: Drawing of L.S. Hill's February 4, 1879 patent.
Right: Drawing of L.S. Hill's November 7, 1882 patent.

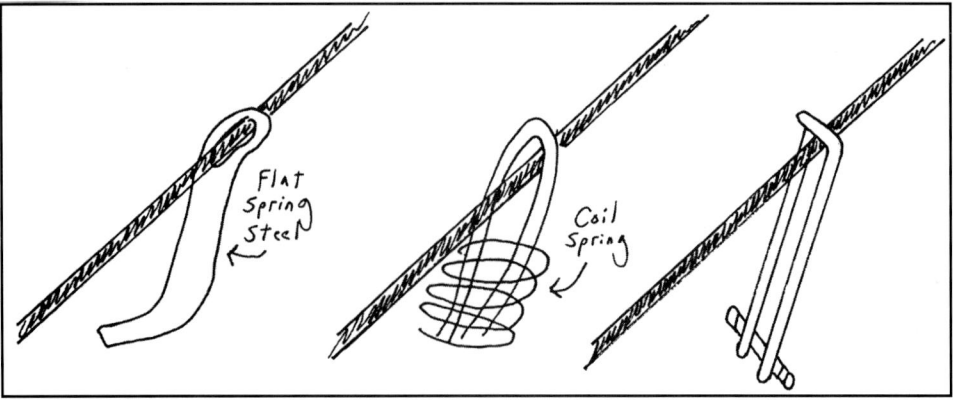

B.

William T. J. Lowe

William T. J. Lowe was born in Buffalo, New York, on July 2, 1840. During the Civil War he served in the New York Fifth Cavalry until a bullet wound in the stomach ended his tour of duty.

After the war he evidently returned to Buffalo where in 1876 he is found listed in the city directory as a silversmith at 284 Elm Street. In 1877 he is still listed as a silversmith but now located at 51 Sycamore Street. In 1878 he had two listings in the directory, one as a silversmith at 51 Sycamore, and the other as a trolling bait manufacturer at 277 Oak Street. The next year found Mr. Lowe manufacturing fishing tackle at 191 William Street; his home is listed at the same address, but there is no listing for the silversmith business.

In 1885 he is listed as "William T.J. Lowe manfr. fishing tackle=41 Bonck Ave." This is the first time he is listed at this address. By 1890 his business and residence were both listed at 1119 West Avenue. He continued to operate his business and live at this address until his death in 1915.

It is interesting to note that a short obituary published by the *Buffalo Evening News* on September 28, 1915 states, "Mr. Lowe was engaged in the plumbing business which he conducted up to his death." There is no mention of the tackle manufacturing. One could conclude that the plumbing business was his main source of income. It is odd, however, that the city directories list him for 39 years, first as a silversmith and then as a fishing tackle manufacturer, but never as a plumber. Strange.

During the many years he was in the tackle manufacturing business, he was granted at least three patents relating to lures.

The first was issued on April 25, 1882. It was for a coiled spring that held a spinner blade away from its shaft. This was a common theme for inventive lure manufacturers, and this was not the first nor was it the last that would try to solve the problem of revolving spinner blades straying too far or staying too close to the lure's main shaft.

His second patent was granted April 17, 1883. It was for an improvement on his first patent.

His third patent was a design patent issued

Aug. 11, 1885. It was for a spinner blade that was partially stamped in a dimpled or hammered pattern. This design was used before the turn of the century for lures sold to Abbey & Imbrie and other trade houses. It was also used later on his famous "Buffalo" baits. All of the Lowe spinners, including the early ones, were of superb quality. It appears that he sold most of his products to established trade houses at a wholesale level. I have never seen a W.T.J. Lowe catalog nor do I recall ever seeing a Lowe retail advertisement other than one found in an old Buffalo city directory.

After Lowe's death in 1915, the Enterprise Mfg. Co. continued to manufacture and market his lures. The 1916 Enterprise Mfg. Co. catalog has a picture of Mr. Lowe with this notation beneath it, "On Jan. 25, 1916 all trademark rights and good will of the business (W.T. J. Lowe) except Canada, were transferred to the Pfluegers, operating the Enterprise Mfg. Co. of Akron, Ohio."

W.T.J. Lowe died on September 27, 1915. He was survived by his wife Minnie, two sons, Harry and Charles, and a daughter, Mrs. W.J. Campbell.

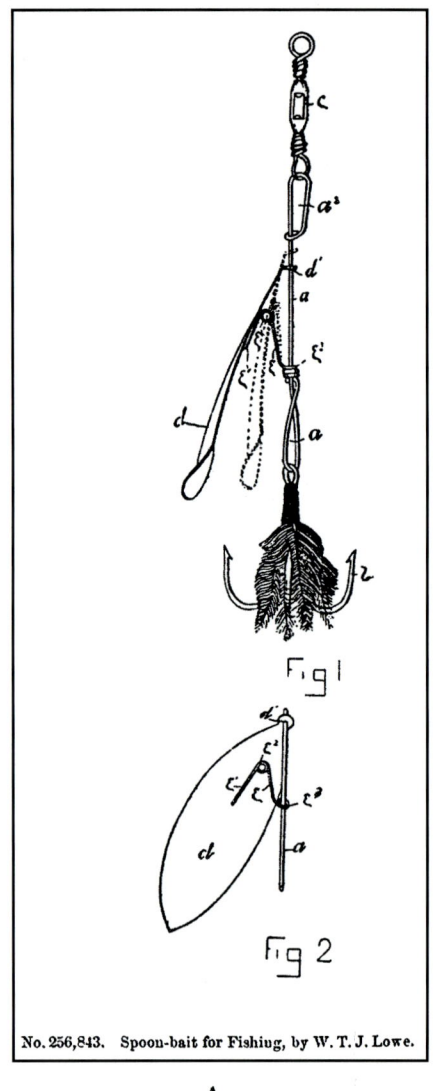

A.

B.

A. An abbreviated copy of Patent No. 256843, issued April 25, 1882, to W.T.J. Lowe. Patented in Canada January 28, 1882. The patent consists of a stiff wire with a coil in the center that, when attached to the spinner blade on one end and attached loosely to the shaft with a loop at the other, holds the blade at a predetermined distance from the shaft. This had been tried before, but Lowe thought this method would be stronger and allow more flexibility.

B. Spinner utilizing the 1882 patent. The blade on this lure is 2½" long. $75.00 – 100.00.

C. Another lure using the April 25, 1882 patent. This lure is marked "Eclipse" Lowe's Pat. Apr. 1882. $75.00 – 100.00.

C.

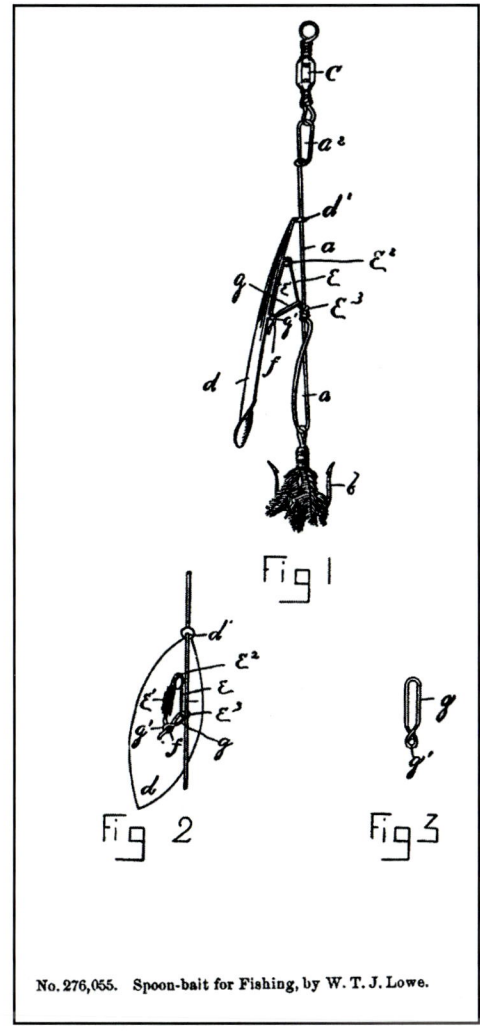

A.

B.

A. The drawing for Patent No. 276055, issued April 17, 1883. This is Lowe's second patent. This patent is an improvement on his first patent issued on April 25, 1882. It consists of a wire loop placed between the blade and the shaft. This prevents the blade from spreading too far from the shaft when the lure is rapidly trolled or pulled against a strong current.

B. Top view of the lure shown below. It clearly shows his early trademark. $75.00 – 100.00.

C. Underside of lure showing details of Lowe's second patent.

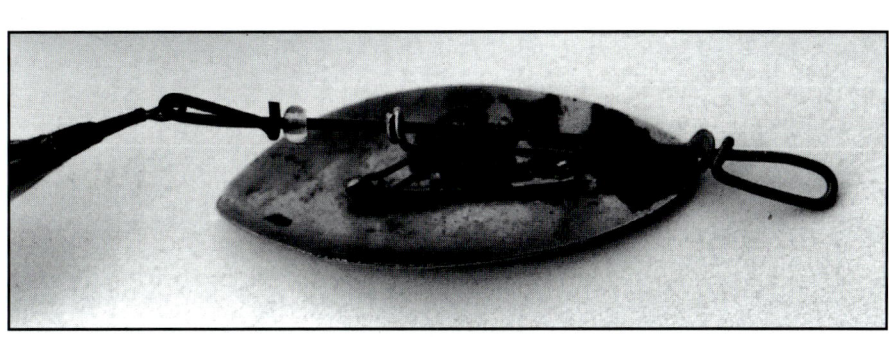

C.

A.

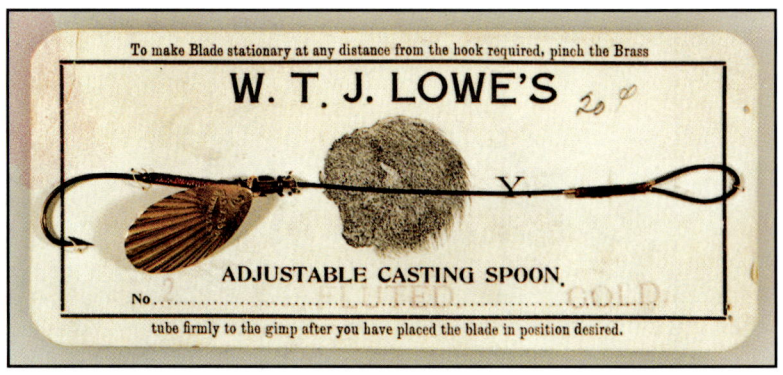

B.

A. A large peculiar shaped lure marked W.T.J. Lowe on the small body in the center. $75.00 – 100.00.

B. Lowe's Adjustable Casting Spoon. Note the Buffalo head with the N. and Y. on either side. Lowe later used an illustration of a full bodied standing buffalo as one of his trademarks. $75.00 – 100.00 w/card.

C. Heart-shaped spinner marked PAT APL'D FOR. $50.00 – 75.00.

D. Advertisement found in the Buffalo city directory.

C.

D.

W.T.J. Lowe

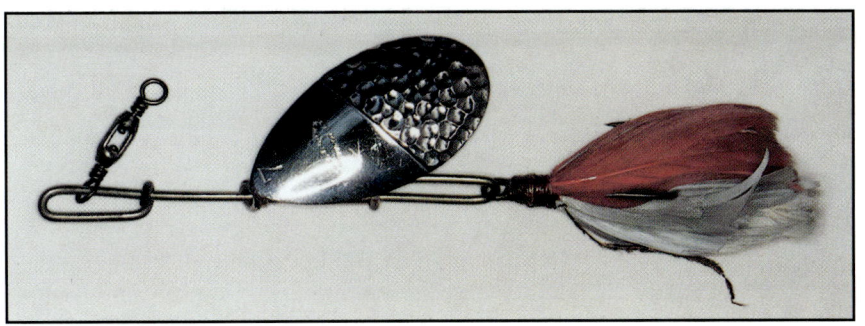

$10.00 – 20.00.

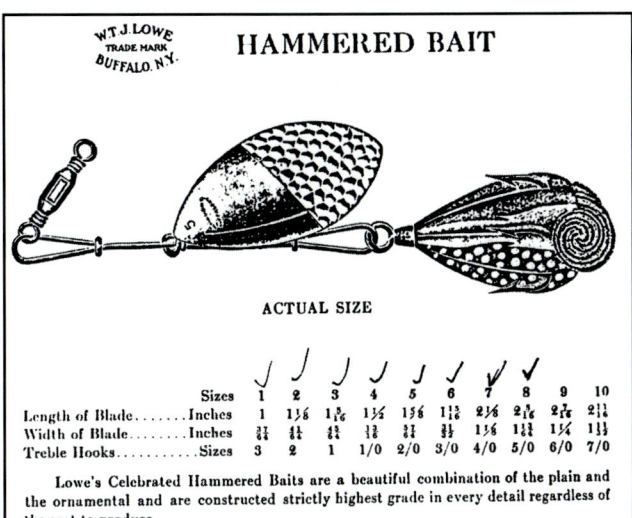

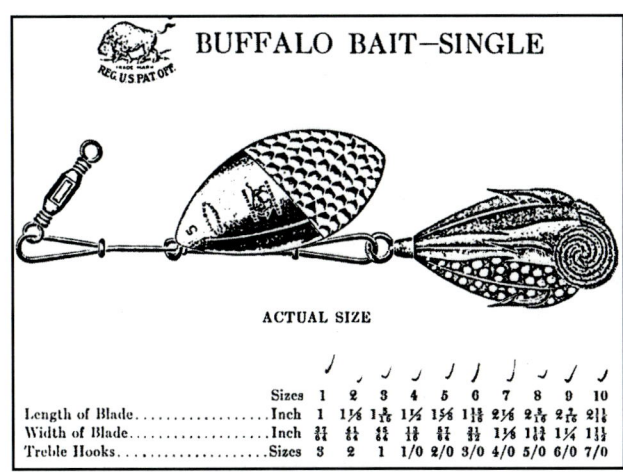

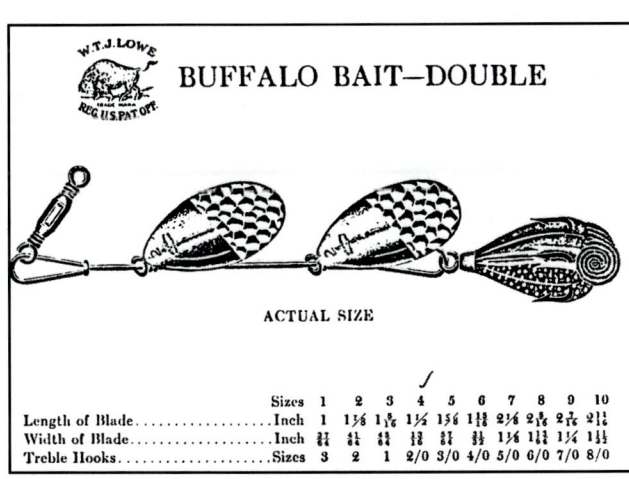

$10.00 – 20.00.

$20.00 – 30.00.

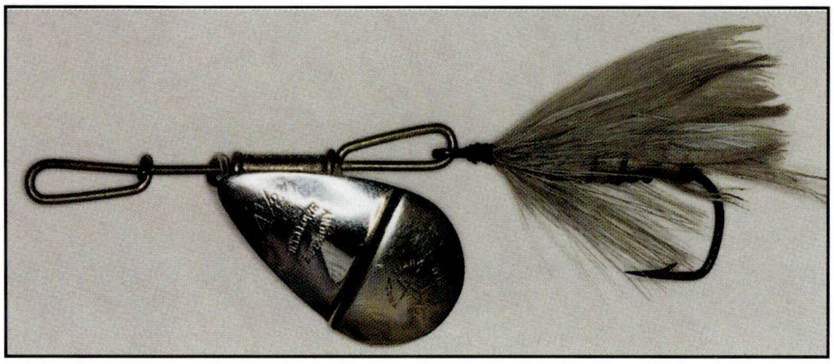

$20.00 – 30.00.

NEW FLY STAR SPOON

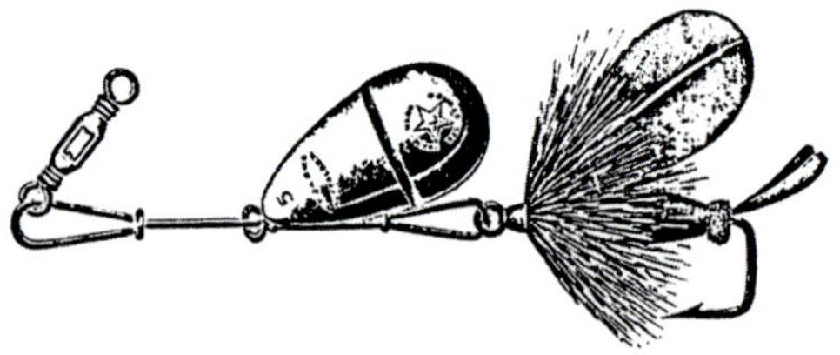

ACTUAL SIZE

	Sizes	6	5	4½	4
Length of Blade	Inches	1 1/32	1 5/64	1 7/32	1 11/32
Width of Blade	Inches	½	19/32	¾	13/16
Sneck Hooks Ringed	Sizes	1/0	1/0	2/0	2/0

Lowe's Celebrated New Fly Star Spoons make a decided hit with the angler who is partial to the fly. Can be used either as a cast or troll and has special attraction for Bass and Lake Trout.

Mounted on highly burnished spring brass wire shafts with a snap loop which will permit of the instant interchanging of flies.

Furnished with any of the following patterns of our highest grade flies tied on Hollow Point Sneck Hooks ringed, sizes as per chart above.

Royal Coachman	Cow Dung	Rube Wood
Seth Green	White Bucktail	White Miller
Red Ibis	Silver Doctor	Montreal
Professor	Grizzly King	Mixed White and Brown Bucktail
Coachman	Queen of Water	

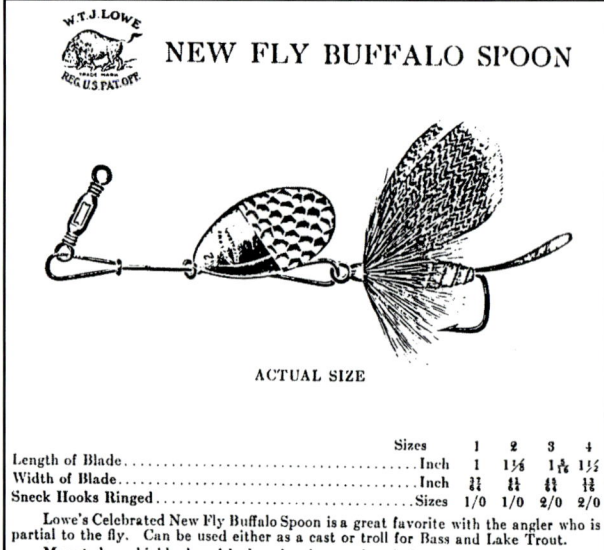

NEW FLY BUFFALO SPOON

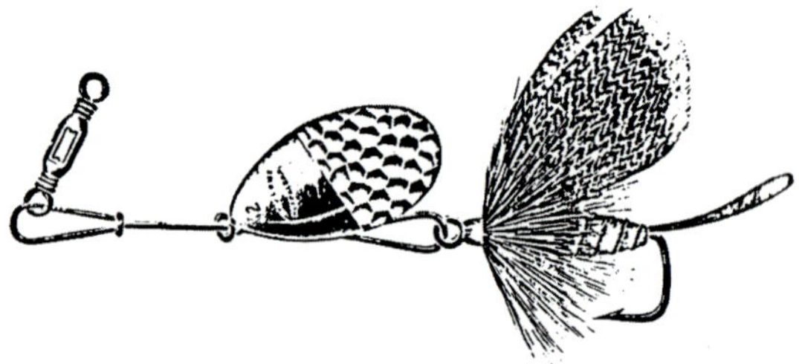

ACTUAL SIZE

	Sizes	1	2	3	4
Length of Blade	Inch	1	1⅛	1 5/16	1½
Width of Blade	Inch	37/64	41/64	43/64	13/16
Sneck Hooks Ringed	Sizes	1/0	1/0	2/0	2/0

Lowe's Celebrated New Fly Buffalo Spoon is a great favorite with the angler who is partial to the fly. Can be used either as a cast or troll for Bass and Lake Trout.

Mounted on highly burnished spring brass wire shafts with a snap loop which will permit of the instant interchanging of flies.

Furnished with any of the following patterns of our highest grade flies tied on Hollow Point Sneck Hooks ringed, sizes as per chart above.

Royal Coachman	Cow Dung	Rube Wood
Seth Green	White Bucktail	White Miller
Red Ibis	Silver Doctor	Montreal
Professor	Grizzly King	Mixed White and Brown Bucktail
Coachman	Queen of Water	

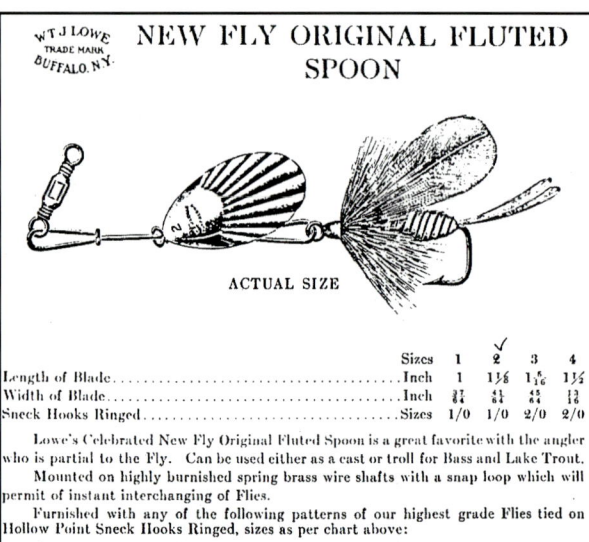

NEW FLY ORIGINAL FLUTED SPOON

W.T.J. LOWE TRADE MARK BUFFALO, N.Y.

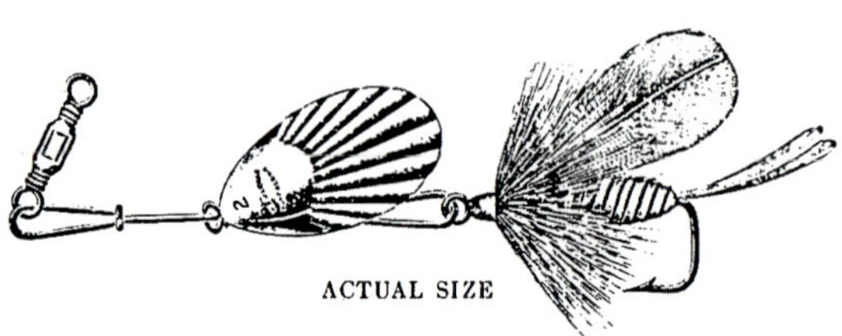

ACTUAL SIZE

	Sizes	1	2 ✓	3	4
Length of Blade	Inch	1	1⅛	1 5/16	1½
Width of Blade	Inch	37/64	41/64	45/64	13/16
Sneck Hooks Ringed	Sizes	1/0	1/0	2/0	2/0

Lowe's Celebrated New Fly Original Fluted Spoon is a great favorite with the angler who is partial to the Fly. Can be used either as a cast or troll for Bass and Lake Trout.

Mounted on highly burnished spring brass wire shafts with a snap loop which will permit of instant interchanging of Flies.

Furnished with any of the following patterns of our highest grade Flies tied on Hollow Point Sneck Hooks Ringed, sizes as per chart above:

Royal Coachman	Cow Dung	Rube Wood
Seth Green	White Bucktail	White Miller
Red Ibis	Silver Doctor	Montreal
Professor	Grizzly King	Mixed White and Brown Bucktail
Coachman	Queen of Water	

This lure was also made in a standard fluted pattern. (Like G.M. Skinner's design)

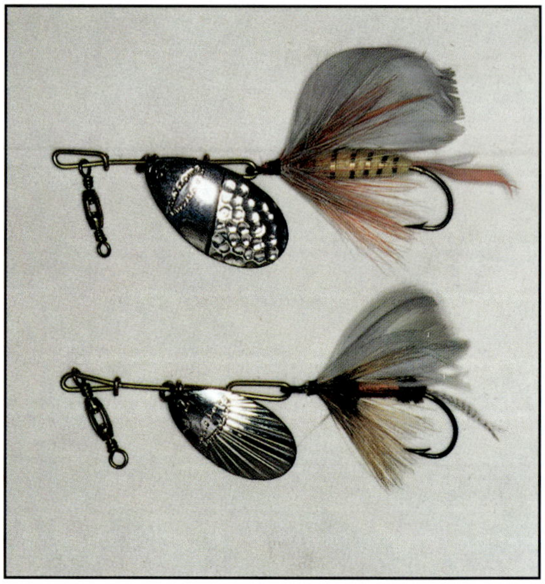

$20.00 – 30.00.

W.T.J. Lowe

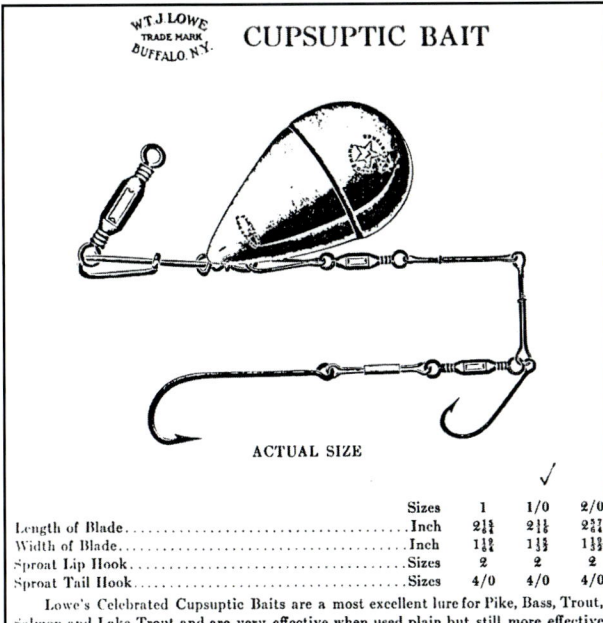

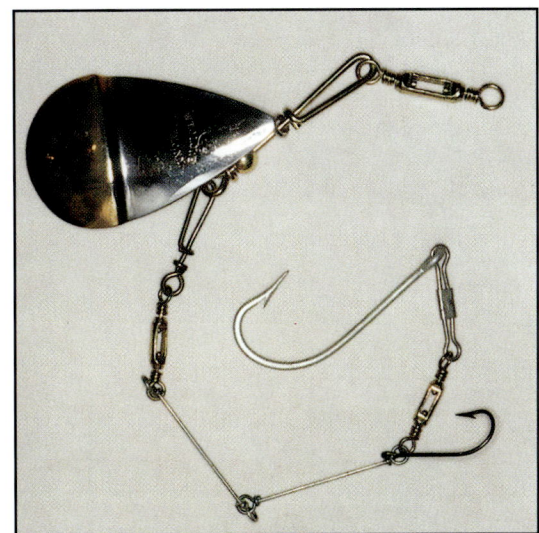

$40.00 – 60.00.

The Star blade on a beaded shaft. $40.00 – 60.00.

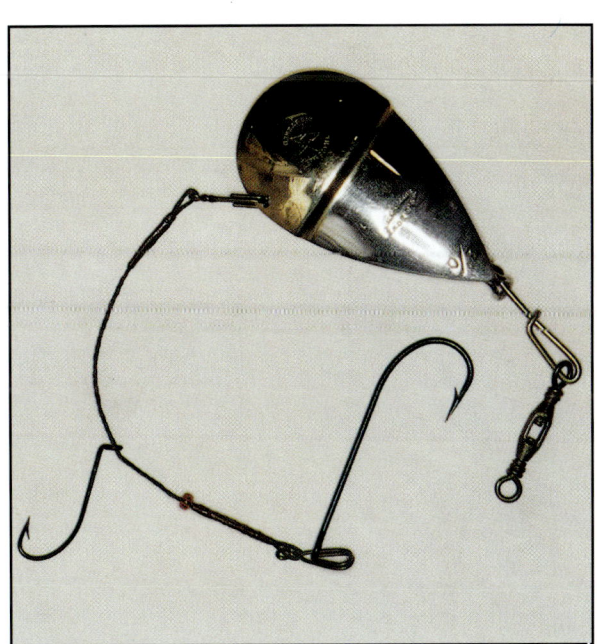

A variation of the Cupsuptic Bait. The harness is attached to the edge of the blade. $40.00 – 60.00.

W.T.J. Lowe

$20.00 – 30.00.

No. 10 Willow leaf spinner. Probably made in other sizes. $15.00 – 25.00.

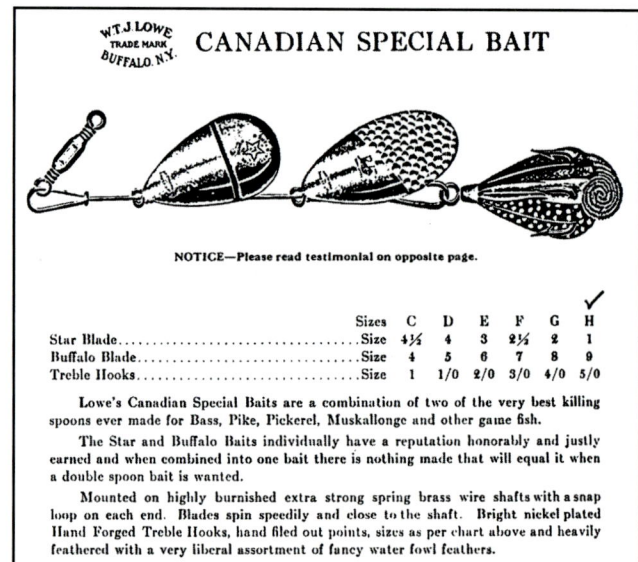

Tiny unmarked Star spinner. $10.00 – 20.00.

Star Bait with heavy duty shaft and large treble hook. No. 3/0. $30.00 – 50.00.

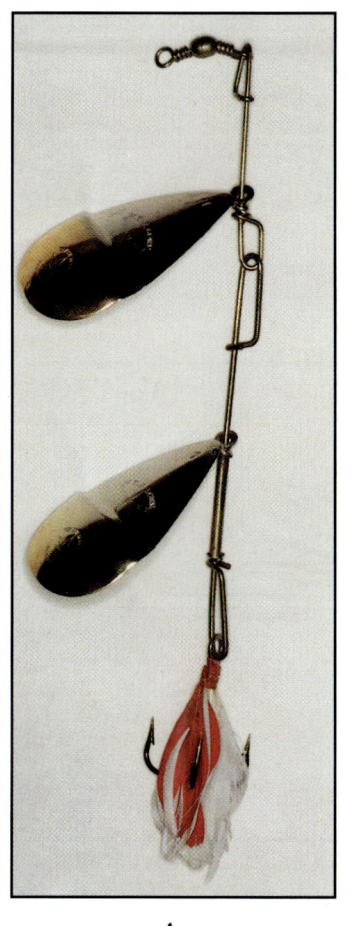

A.

B.

C.

A. A double Star Bait on a linked shaft. $25.00 – 35.00.

B. Kidney-shaped Hammered Bait. Gold on top half and nickel plate on bottom half. These came in at least eight sizes. $15.00 – 25.00.

C. Kidney-shaped Hammered Bait. Nickel plated. These came in at least eight sizes. Note the double hook. Lowe used both double and treble hooks on these lures. $10.00 – 20.00.

D. Kidney-shaped Hammered Bait. Gold and nickel plate. $20.00 – 30.00.

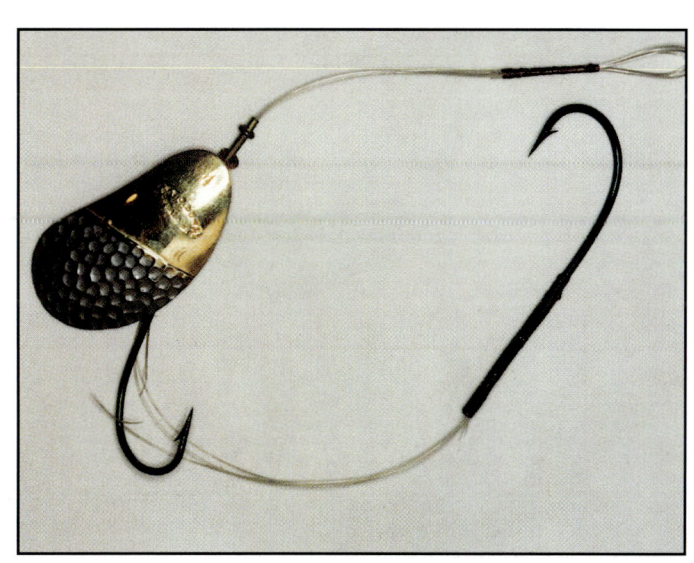

D.

W.T.J. Lowe

PLAIN LEAF—MUSKALLONGE BAIT

	Sizes	9	12
Length of Blade	Inch	3 1/4	3 1/2
Width of Blade	Inch	1 3/4	1 7/8
Treble Hooks	Sizes	6/0	7/0

Lowe's Celebrated Plain Leaf—Muskallonge Baits are constructed extra strong throughout and of the highest standard of quality of materials and workmanship possible to secure.

Very killing bait for Pickerel, Muskallonge and many other of the fresh and salt water game fishes.

Mounted on highly burnished extra strong spring brass wire shafts with a snap loop on each end. Blades spin speedily and close to the shaft. Extra stout bright nickel plated Hand Forged Treble Hooks, hand filed out points, sizes as per chart above and heavily feathered with a very liberal assortment of fancy water fowl feathers.

PRICE EACH

No.		Sizes	9	12
4100	Polished Gold Both Sides		1.00	1.20
4101	Polished Silver Convex—Red and Satin Sil. Concave			
4102	Polished Copper Convex—Red Concave		.50	.85
4103	Polished Brass Convex—Red Concave			
4104	White Enamel Both Sides with Red Tip			

Packed—Each blade is first wrapped in silver tissue paper and the Bait complete is also finally wrapped in silver tissue paper. One-half dozen in a fancy white card box. Six boxes (3 dozen Baits) in a carton.

$25.00 – 35.00.

$30.00 – 50.00.

FLUTED LEAF—MUSKALLONGE BAIT

	Sizes	9	12
Length of Blade	Inches	3 1/4	3 1/2
Width of Blade	Inches	1 3/4	1 7/8
Treble Hooks	Sizes	6/0	7/0

Lowe's Celebrated Fluted Leaf—Muskallonge Baits are constructed extra strong throughout and of the highest standard of quality of materials and workmanship possible to secure.

Recommended highly for Pickerel and Muskallonge, also many of the fresh and salt water game fishes.

Fluted blades mounted on highly burnished extra strong spring brass wire shafts with a snap loop on each end. Blades spin speedily and close to the shaft. Extra stout bright nickel plated Hand Forged Treble Hooks, hand filed out points, sizes as per chart above and heavily feathered with a very liberal assortment of fancy water fowl feathers.

PRICE EACH

No.		Sizes	9	12
3210	Polished Gold Both Sides		1.00	1.20
3211	Polished Silver Convex—Red and Satin Silver Concave			
3212	Polished Copper Convex—Red Concave		.50	.85
3213	Polished Brass Convex—Red Concave			
3214	White Enamel Both Sides with Red Tip			

LAKE SALMON AND MUSKALLONGE BAIT

		Size	1 ✓
Length of Blade	Inch		3 3/4
Width of Blade	Inch		2 3/8
Treble Hook	Size		10/0

Lowe's Lake Salmon or Muskallonge Baits are made exceptionally strong and the finish and workmanship of the standard Lowe quality.

Very generally used for Lake Salmon and Muskallonge trolling.

Mounted on highly burnished extra strong spring brass wire shafts. Blades spin speedily and close to the shaft. Extra stout bright nickel plated Hand Forged Treble Hooks, hand filed out points, size as per chart above and heavily feathered with a very liberal assortment of fancy water fowl feathers.

$30.00 – 50.00.

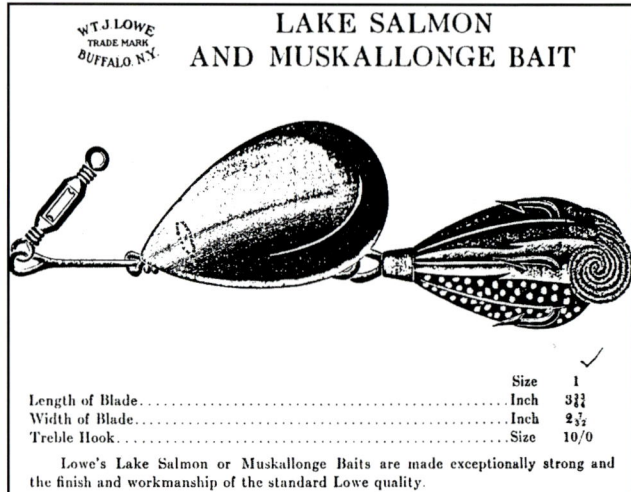

W.T.J. LOWE TRADE MARK BUFFALO N.Y.

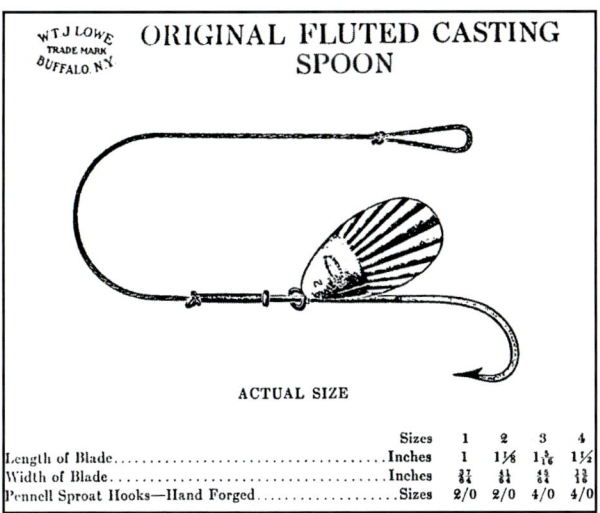

ORIGINAL FLUTED CASTING SPOON

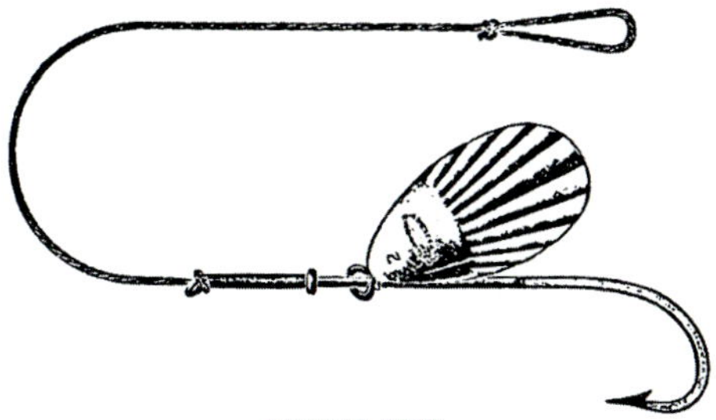

ACTUAL SIZE

	Sizes	1	2	3	4
Length of Blade	Inches	1	$1\frac{1}{8}$	$1\frac{5}{16}$	$1\frac{1}{2}$
Width of Blade	Inches	$\frac{37}{64}$	$\frac{41}{64}$	$\frac{45}{64}$	$\frac{13}{16}$
Pennell Sproat Hooks—Hand Forged	Sizes	2/0	2/0	4/0	4/0

Same finish as Fluted Casting Spoon below right.

W.T.J. LOWE TRADE MARK REG. U.S. PAT. OFF.

BUFFALO CASTING SPOON

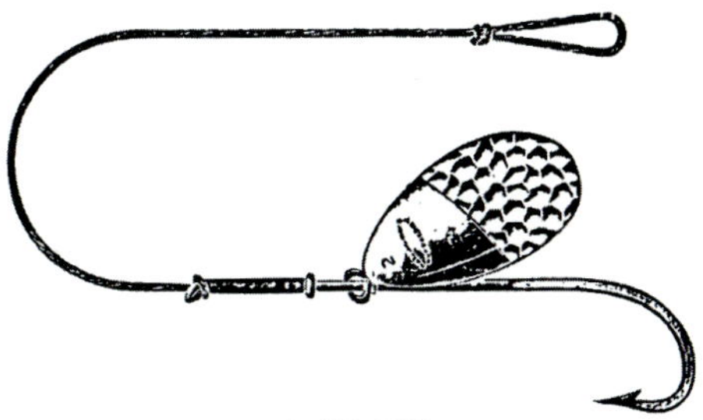

ACTUAL SIZE

	Sizes	1	2	3	4
Length of Blade	Inches	1	$1\frac{1}{8}$	$1\frac{5}{16}$	$1\frac{1}{2}$
Width of Blade	Inches	$\frac{37}{64}$	$\frac{41}{64}$	$\frac{45}{64}$	$\frac{13}{16}$
Pennell Sproat Hooks—Hand Forged	Sizes	2/0	2/0	4/0	4/0

Polished Silver and Gold both sides.

$20.00 – 30.00.

W.T.J. LOWE TRADE MARK REG. U.S. PAT. OFF.

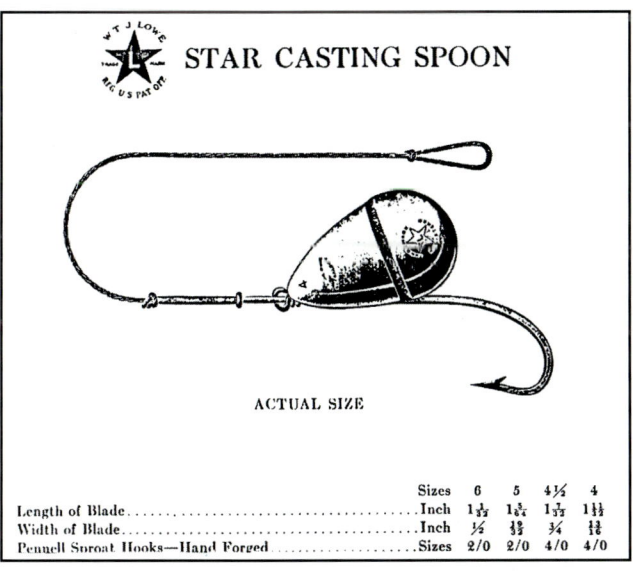

STAR CASTING SPOON

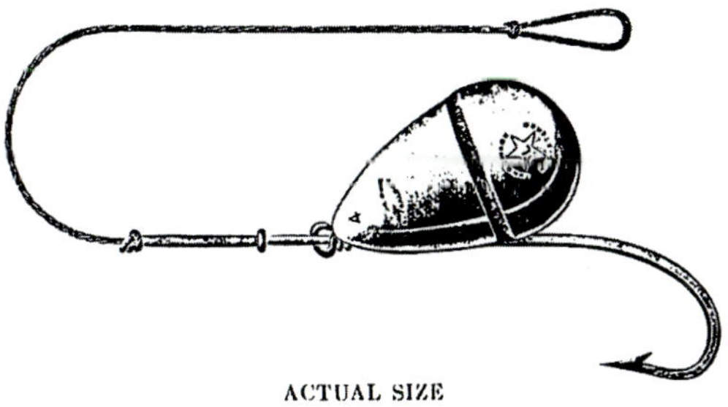

ACTUAL SIZE

	Sizes	6	5	$4\frac{1}{2}$	4
Length of Blade	Inch	$1\frac{1}{32}$	$1\frac{5}{64}$	$1\frac{7}{32}$	$1\frac{11}{32}$
Width of Blade	Inch	$\frac{1}{2}$	$\frac{19}{32}$	$\frac{3}{4}$	$\frac{13}{16}$
Pennell Sproat Hooks—Hand Forged	Sizes	2/0	2/0	4/0	4/0

Polished Silver and Gold convex, red concave. $20.00 – 30.00.

W.T.J. LOWE TRADE MARK BUFFALO N.Y.

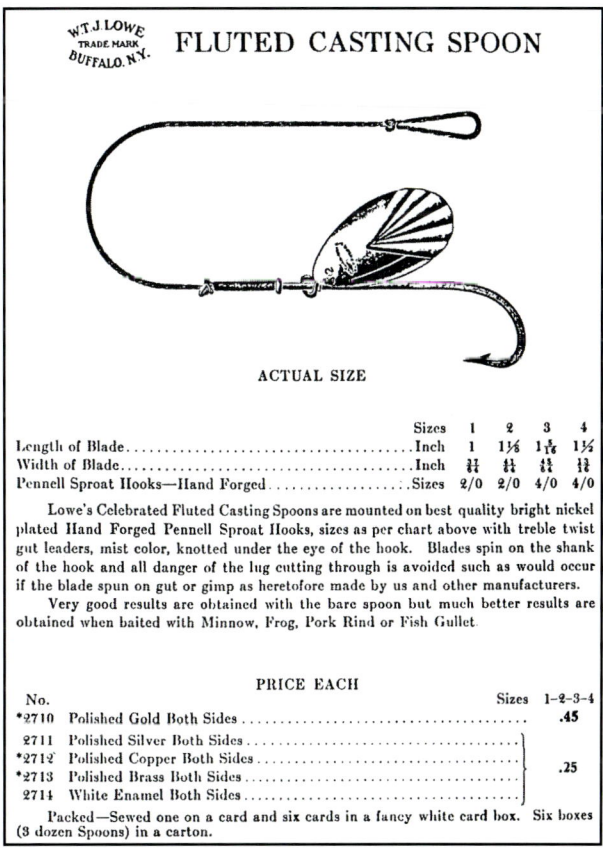

FLUTED CASTING SPOON

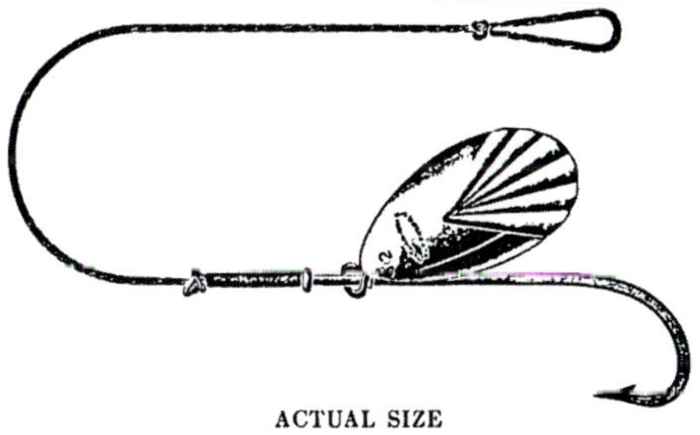

ACTUAL SIZE

	Sizes	1	2	3	4
Length of Blade	Inch	1	$1\frac{1}{8}$	$1\frac{5}{16}$	$1\frac{1}{2}$
Width of Blade	Inch	$\frac{37}{64}$	$\frac{41}{64}$	$\frac{45}{64}$	$\frac{13}{16}$
Pennell Sproat Hooks—Hand Forged	Sizes	2/0	2/0	4/0	4/0

Lowe's Celebrated Fluted Casting Spoons are mounted on best quality bright nickel plated Hand Forged Pennell Sproat Hooks, sizes as per chart above with treble twist gut leaders, mist color, knotted under the eye of the hook. Blades spin on the shank of the hook and all danger of the lug cutting through is avoided such as would occur if the blade spun on gut or gimp as heretofore made by us and other manufacturers.

Very good results are obtained with the bare spoon but much better results are obtained when baited with Minnow, Frog, Pork Rind or Fish Gullet.

PRICE EACH

No.		Sizes 1-2-3-4
*2710	Polished Gold Both Sides	.45
2711	Polished Silver Both Sides	.25
*2712	Polished Copper Both Sides	.25
*2713	Polished Brass Both Sides	.25
2714	White Enamel Both Sides	.25

Packed—Sewed one on a card and six cards in a fancy white card box. Six boxes (3 dozen Spoons) in a carton.

$20.00 – 30.00.

W.T.J. Lowe

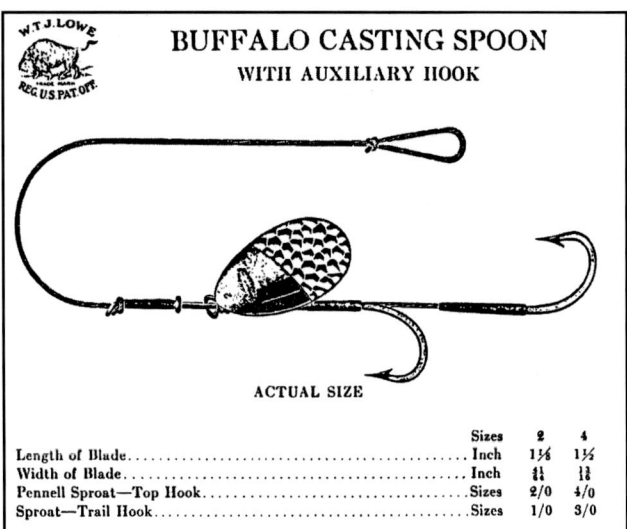

Polished Silver and Gold both sides. $20.00 – 30.00.

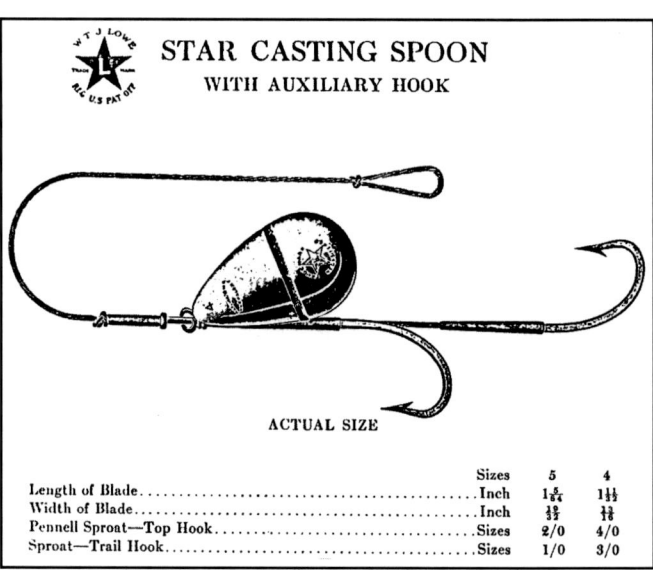

Polished Silver and Gold convex – red concave. $20.00 – 30.00.

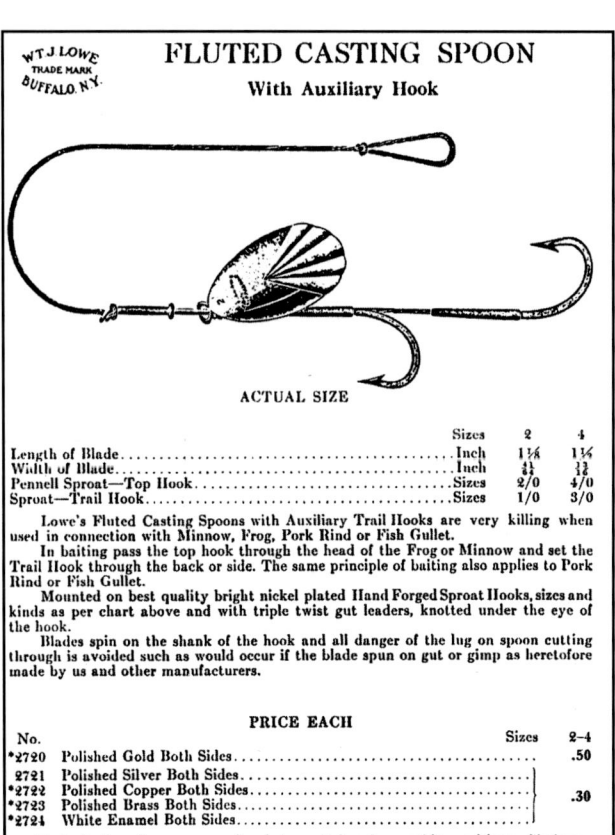

$20.00 – 30.00.

Harry Comstock

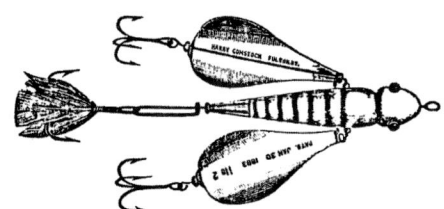

Harry Comstock in China for the Remington Arms Company.

Harry Comstock was born on July 16, 1838, in the the town of Junius, Seneca County, N.Y., to Joseph and Mary (Duers) Comstock. His given name was Harrison, a name he later dropped in favor of the more popular nickname, Harry. He had three sisters, Clarissa, Emily, and Theresa. His father, Joseph, was a shoemaker by trade, and no doubt Harry, being the only son, helped around the shop. The only record of his youth appears in the 1850 census, where he is listed as living in Junius with his parents and sisters.

Harry spent a good part of his adult life involved in the firearms business, first as an employee and salesman for the Remington Arms Company, and later as a gun designer and entrepreneur. It is, therefore, ironic that he should be remembered for the invention of a solitary fishing lure.

This single lure was, however, the legendary "Flying Helgramite," the harbinger for millions of wooden bass lures manufactured during the twentieth century.

On October 6, 1860, he married Ruth Palmer of Seneca Falls, N.Y. What he and his new bride did for the next 20 years is still a mystery. He and Ruth reappear in the 1880 census, this time in Fulton, N.Y., with a three-year-old son, also named Harry. Historical news articles written many years later indicated that he was involved in the firearms industry during this time. A short news item in the Jan. 30, 1886 issue of the *American Field* seems to corroborate this.

"Mr. Harry Comstock is well known to sportsmen as he visited every section of America which made any pretension to civilization; and having used up his own country he went to China some three years ago, from which he returned last fall. His experiences in China would fill a book; we hope he will give our readers a short series of articles descriptive of his travels through China, when introducing the Remington rifle to the Chinese Government."

An unconfirmed story relates that Harry sold so many rifles to the Chinese that Remington recalled him because they were unable to fill the orders.

Prior to his trip to China, Harry was granted a patent for the object of our interest: the "Flying

Helgramite." The patent was filed on Nov. 25, 1882, and granted Jan. 30, 1883.

The first known advertisement for the Helgramite appeared in the May 12, 1883 issue of the *American Angler*. The ad ran continuously through July 14, 1883. The *American Angler* was a popular weekly magazine devoted entirely to fishing. Harry's ad was rather elaborate for its time and must have been quite expensive. He sold the lure in three sizes and advertised that it would not "sink or snag." Truth in advertising had not yet arrived.

Harry's business acumen becomes apparent when reading the May 19, 1883 issue of the *American Angler*. In a letter to the editor (actually a lengthy article), he explains the life cycle of the helgramite and expounds on the fish-catching virtues of this insect. He points out that many anglers are unaware of the proper name for the helgramite and suggests that it should be the "Flying Helgramite," all this while running an ad in the same magazine for a lure called, appropriately, the "Flying Helgramite." Harry's explanation of the helgramite's metamorphosis is nearly a description of his new bait. "In from ten days to two weeks his transformation is complete, and he assumes a new dress throughout, and has not the least vague appearance of the once dingy, dirty insect crawling under your feet on the river bank. Now he has a pair of silken, almost transparent wings, fully three inches in length. The head has grown round and comely. The eyes deep red, large and glassy, protruding from the head. The shelly part, with the head, has assumed a pale green, and the body remains either the same dirty white or a dark brown."

Harry's new lure gets more publicity in the June 30, 1883 issue of the *American Angler* when they published a field test of the "Flying Helgramite." This type of article was rare in the 1800s, and Harry surely must have benefited from it. The story was authorized by "Black Bass," obviously a pen name. Prominent sportsmen of the period sometimes wrote articles using pseudonyms. The following is titled simply, "The Flying Helgramite."

"When requested by you to give this formidable looking bait a fair test, I gazed at it with some incredulous thoughts rambling in my head, but on hefting the lure I found him a much lighter weight champion than expected, and agreed to let the black bass tackle him.

Having a hard braided line I fastened the 'deceiver' on and chucked him overboard to sink or swim. I was trolling with live bait very slow, and found the helgramite kept well up in the water; the wings are excellent spinners, whirling rapidly; requiring but little forward motion of the boat to make them "buzz." Now how does it grapple a fish?

I tied the line around my leg, with one rod lying in the boat trolling live bait and casting with my fly rod when a tug-tug at my leg line convinced me of a strike, and hauling him in I don't know which was most astonished, the bass, myself, or the helgramite. The bass had stuck (sic) the tail hook and the wings had flopped around, one catching him under the gills and the other toward the dorsal fin. Of course he came without knowing just what had struck him. I caught another bass (two pounds) with same results, but had no chance for a further test as only live pickerel bait was the sure lure.

The flying helgramite is, I believe, as big and successful a 'hog' as the big-mouth bass himself, and when they meet it is just 'dog eat dog' anyhow. As a lure, I personally, would not like to use it, except like the boy after the woodchuck — woodchuck or no dinner. The fish don't seem to have a shadow of a chance, and I think it even more certain than the murderous gang. Its merits are lightness, unlikely to foul or snag, its spinning qualities and attractiveness, its grim death grip on the fish, and all being equal, I believe will kill its full share against any spoon bait.

I used the smallest size (No. 1), but believe if made at least two sizes smaller it would be more killing in bright waters and just as attractive and serviceable."

On July 21, 1883, a new ad for the Flying Helgramite appeared in the *American Angler*. It was basically the same ad Harry had been running since May 12, although it had been redrawn, and listed a new smaller size. The big difference, however, was that the manufacturer was no longer Harry Comstock, but the Enterprise Manufacturing Company (Pflueger) of Akron, Ohio. Harry is listed as Superintendent and General Agent, E.F. Plueger as Manager, and Ferdinand Schumacker as President. Although Harry was obviously an employee, his alliance with the Enterprise Manufacturing Co. was short lived. The final Enterprise ad was in the Nov. 10, 1883 issue; about the same time Harry is known to have journeyed to China for the Remington Arms Company.

In Harry's absence, the Enterprise Co. continued to manufacture the Flying Helgramite. Their 1885 catalog lists it in four sizes and available in luminous only. As a matter of fact, all of the items in the 1885 catalog were available in luminous finish.

It is interesting to note that the Enterprise ads in the *American Angler* were not for a luminous finish, although E.F. Pflueger had been granted a patent for luminous baits on Feb. 13, 1883. This would indicate that lures without the luminous finish were the earliest, but could have been manufactured by either Comstock or Enterprise. The 1886 – 1887 Enterprise catalog does not list the Flying Helgramite, although it does have a testimonial dated Aug. 19, 1884.

"For the first time I gave your Bait a trial, and I gave it a thorough one. I went with the Judge of the county, and we had royal sport. My first capture was a 7 pound black Bass; afterwards we took in many, varying from two to five pounds. My catch was pronounced here as unequaled. No one had ever seen a Bass of that size here. It was caught with your "Flying Helgramite," against a ____ and a ____ Spoon, and came out on top. I presented it to Judge Gillett on our return. Respectfully, G. P. Humphrey."

Harry's return from China in the fall of 1885 and the absence of the Flying Helgramite from the 1886 – 1887 Enterprise catalog is probably not coincidental. There is evidence of a lawsuit involving Harry and the Enterprise Co. Possibly, the Enterprise Co. had been manufacturing the lures without Harry's permission.

The Feb. 13, 1886 edition of the *American Field* ran this notation about one of his advertisements. Unfortunately, the ad itself was missing from the magazine.

"THE FLYING HELGRAMITE — The attention of our readers is drawn to the advertisement of Mr. Harry Comstock, offering for sale his patent for the manufacture of "The Flying Helgramite," which we know is regarded by those having tried it, and who are thoroughly competent to judge, as the very best bait they have used. A capitol opportunity is offered for a good investment."

The late 1800s found Harry involved once again in the firearms business. He had invented a shotgun known as the "Comstock Gun" and a Fulton businessman named John Hunter was interested in manufacturing it. However, before the deal was finalized, Mr. Hunter decided to manufacture the L.C. Smith shotgun, a gun well known and manufactured since 1880. Harry's relationship with Mr. Hunter must have lasted until 1889, because two gun patents granted to Harry on Nov. 12, 1889 were assigned to "The Hunter & Comstock Arms Co." Another patent dated March 4, 1890, was issued to Harry Comstock, no mention of the arms company. Harry spent his final years as a salesman or "commercial traveler" as they were called in those days.

The April 5, 1895 edition of the *Oswego Daily Palladium* issued this news special — "Harry Comstock, the inventor and great American traveler, committed suicide this afternoon by taking carbolic acid." An unfitting end for a very talented man.

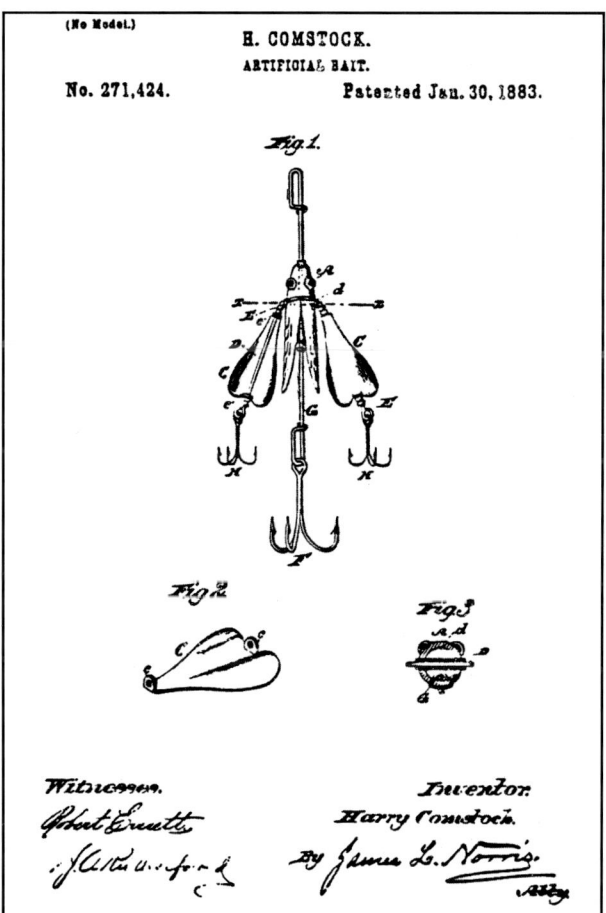

Patent for the "Flying Helgramite." This patent was granted to Harry Comstock on January 30, 1883.

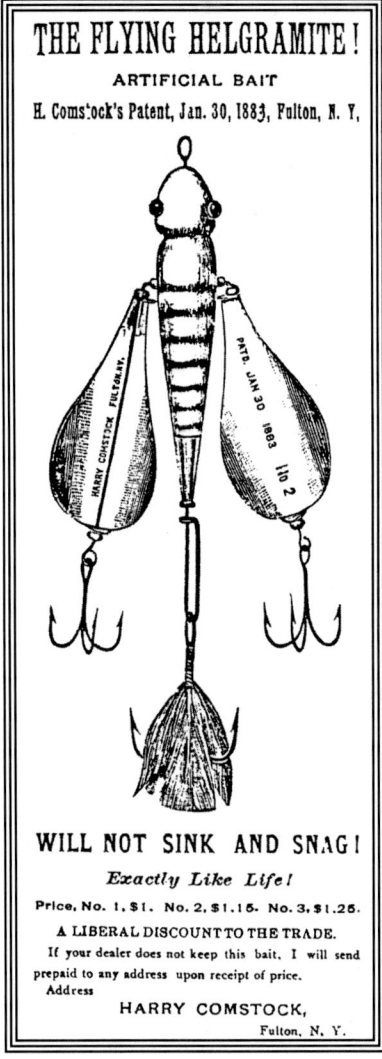

A.

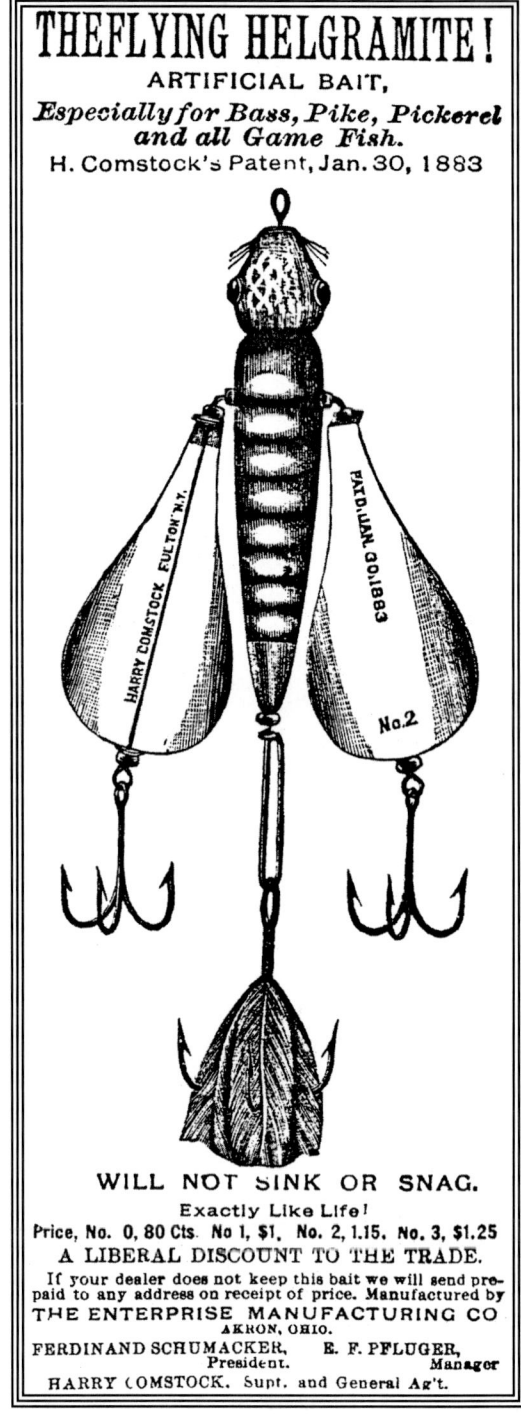

B.

A. Harry Comstock advertisement printed in the *American Angler* magazine from May 12, 1883 through July 21, 1883.

B. Enterprise Manufacturing Co. advertisement printed in the *American Angler* magazine from July 28, 1883 through Nov. 10, 1883. Note that Harry is now the superintendent and general agent for the company. Also note that the lure is now available in four sizes.

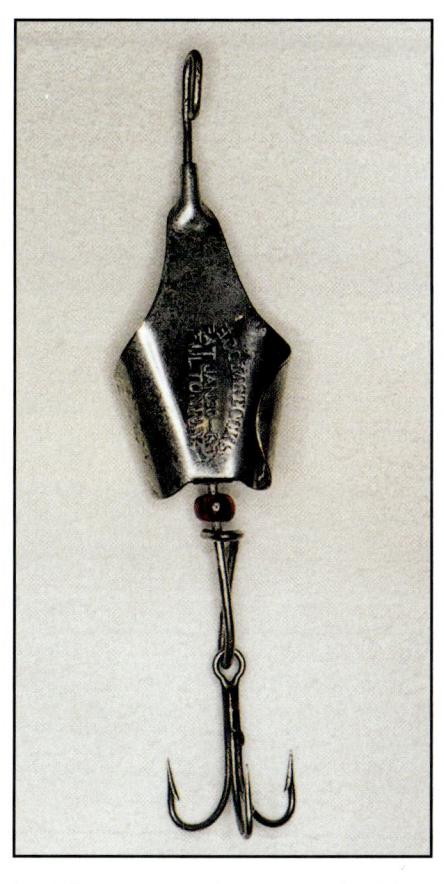

A.

B.

A. Helgramite wing lure. It was thought at one time that this lure was probably made from a broken Helgramite wing, but on further observation it appears that it is made the same way as the early Enterprise Mfg. Co. "Akron Spinner." The narrow end of the wing is formed into a tube and there is no hole present as would be the case if it were an actual Helgramite wing. It is probably an Enterprise product although it does not appear in any of the catalogs made available to me. $500.00 – 750.00.

B. Non-luminous Helgramite. Marked "H. Comstocks – Pat Jan 30-83 - Fulton, N.Y." $2,500.00+.

C. Helgramite marked "H. Comstock - Pat Jan 30-83." There is no "s" on Comstock nor any "Fulton, N.Y." $2,500.00+.

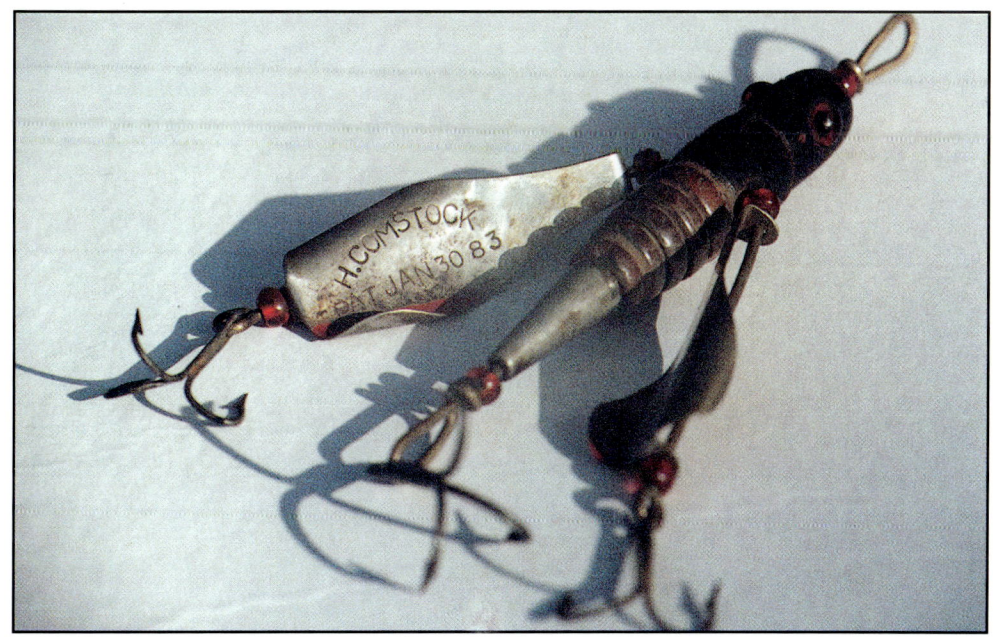

C.

A.

A. This version of the Flying Helgramite is somewhat of a mystery. The one shown here was an exhibit in a trial involving the Enterprise Manufacturing Company. The hook points have been clipped off so the lure could be safely handled. It appears to have wings utilizing the Enterprise Company's "Bass Bait." The "Bass Bait" was not listed as an Enterprise product until after 1887. By this time the company had stopped advertising the Comstock Flying Helgramite. The examples I have seen were non-luminous and painted a red-maroon color. The quality of these lures is not consistent with the quality of lures produced by Enterprise during the later part of the 1800s, nor is the color consistent with the Comstock Helgramite or the natural flying helgramite for that matter. Perhaps time and the assimilation of more information will determine this lure's proper place in the scheme of things.

B. Harry Comstock's "Flying Helgramite." This is the luminous Enterprise Co. version shown with a period rod and reel.

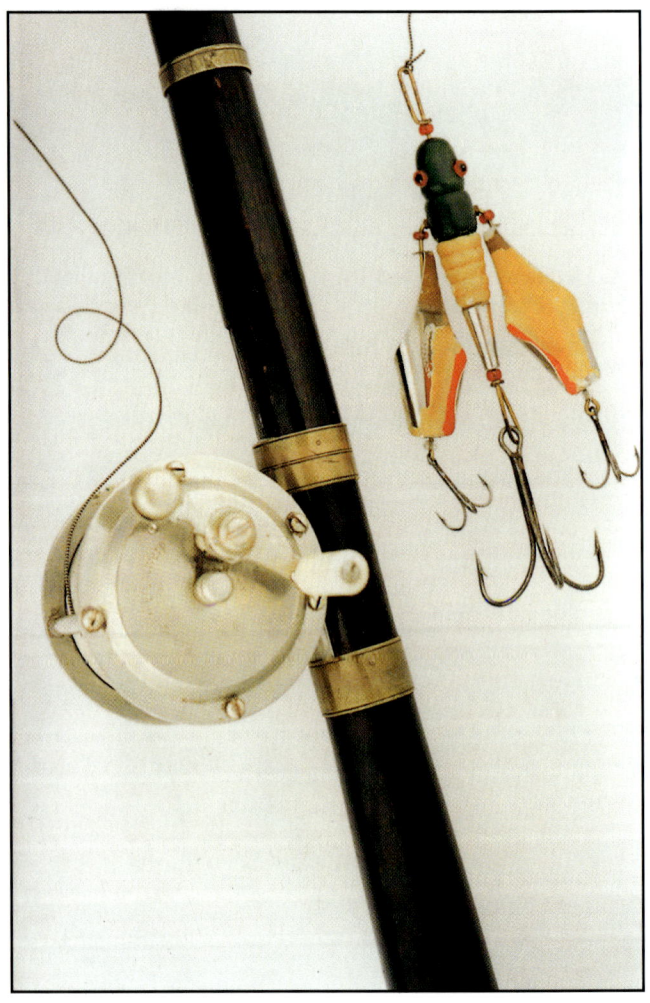

B.

COLLECTOR'S POSTSCRIPT

Harry Comstock's "Flying Helgramite" is truly one of the classic lures of all time. I believe it to be the first wooden "plug" type lure. It has all of the characteristics needed to qualify: glass eyes, wooden body, fish catching ability, and a reasonable production run. It is a joy to behold.

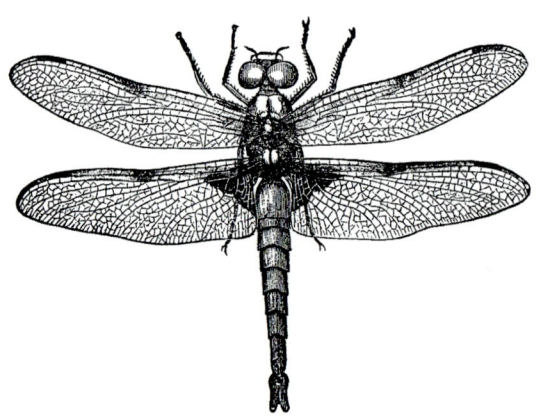

Long before Heddon, Creek Chub, or South Bend had their first products on the drawing board, there was an American company producing quality fishing lures by the tens of thousands. This company was the Enterprise Manufacturing Company of Akron, Ohio.

The Enterprise Manufacturing Company was co-founded in 1881 by Ernest F. Pflueger and Ferdinand Schumacher. An 1883 ad for the "Flying Helgramite" lists Schumacher as the president of the company, and Pflueger as the manager. Harry Comstock, inventor of the Flying Helgramite, was listed as superintendent and general agent (salesman). In 1883, Pflueger was granted a patent for the use of luminous paint on fishing lures. These luminous lures were the mainstay of the company for many years.

In 1886 the Enterprise Manufacturing Company was incorporated. Investors included A. L. Conger, George W. Crouse and Dr. B. F. Goodrich. In the same year the company bought out the American Fish Hook Company, a company that had been established in 1864. The Enterprise Co. used this date in future advertising as their founding year.

Under Pflueger's able leadership, the company grew dramatically. In 1885, the Enterprise Manufacturing Co. published a four-page catalog listing nine lures (all luminous) and a luminous bobber. By 1892 the catalog had expanded to 65 pages, and listed all manner of fishing tackle, including over one hundred lures. The luminous lures continued to be a mainstay of the company. Annual catalogs always had a list of testimonials from sporting goods dealers and important sportsmen of the day. A letter from President Grover Cleveland was used for a number of years. All of these testimonials extolled the virtues of the "luminous bait."

Ernest continued as the head of the company until his death on Sunday, Nov. 18, 1900. The *Akron Beacon Journal* of November 19, printed the following obituary.

"Mr. Pflueger was born in Baden Baden, Germany, in 1843, and came to America with his parents when but five years of age. The family lived in Buffalo, N.Y., where Mr. Pflueger attended school, and at an early age was apprenticed to a baker. After learning the trade, and not being suited with it, Mr. Pflueger served an apprenticeship as a

molder. He completed his apprenticeship at the age of 20 years.

He came to Akron 30 years ago, and engaged in the grocery business which he followed until 1881 with great success. In 1881 he organized The Enterprise Manufacturing Company for the manufacture of novelties. During his life Mr. Pflueger amassed a comfortable fortune.

Mr. Pflueger was married to Miss Julia Dunnebeck, of Erie, Pa., in 1863. To this union nine children were born, six of whom are living; Joseph, Ernest, George, Mrs. Ida M. West, Charles, and Julia.

Funeral services will be held at the family residence, 225 Carroll Street, Wednesday afternoon at 2:30 o'clock. Interment at Glendale."

Another early account states, "Orphaned in his childhood, he was brought to America by a brother and sister and spent his youth and early manhood in Buffalo. There he became a molder. He followed his craft in Buffalo and Erie, Pa., until 1868 when he came to Akron and started working for a stove company. A few years later he opened a grocery store on Howard Street.

Pflueger was constantly inventing something, all sorts of things. He took out over 50 patents, mostly covering harness trimmings, fishing tackle, illuminated bait, and other fishing paraphernalia. To manufacture some of these devises, he started a small concern called the Enterprise Works in 1881."

Collectors attempting to acquire a full set of early Pflueger lures will find the task confusing and at times exasperating.

Many of Pflueger's lures were available in four different grades. A quote from the 1892 – 1893 catalog states:

"You will note we make most patterns of Spoon Bait in four different grades thereby enabling the dealer to suit all classes of people in price, from the laborer to the capitalist. While we use different grades of metal, plating, and finish, according to the price of goods, we do not build any bait but what will give satisfaction.

Our First quality is unsurpassed for finish and grade of material used.

Our Second quality will compare favorably with some goods sold for "first."

Our Third quality we claim to be fully as good as other manufactures' so-called "second."

Our Fourth quality are goods that have a big run among the Hardware, Notion and Fancy Goods jobbers for country trade."

In preparing this chapter, I had available to me the following catalogs: 1885, 1886 – 1887, 1892 – 1893, 1894, 1895 – 1896, 1897, 1898, and 1900. You will note that there is a considerable gap between the 1886 – 1887 catalog and the 1892 catalog. It is possible that during this four-year period some lures may have been introduced and then dropped. As previously stated, it was during this time that the catalog grew from four pages to 65. This, of course, presents the possibility that there are some lures in collector's hands that may be Pfluegers, but are not identifiable as such. Time, and the availability of the missing catalogs, will probably correct this. To add to the confusion, many of the lower grade lures (those sold to the trade houses) were unmarked. They are Pflueger nonetheless.

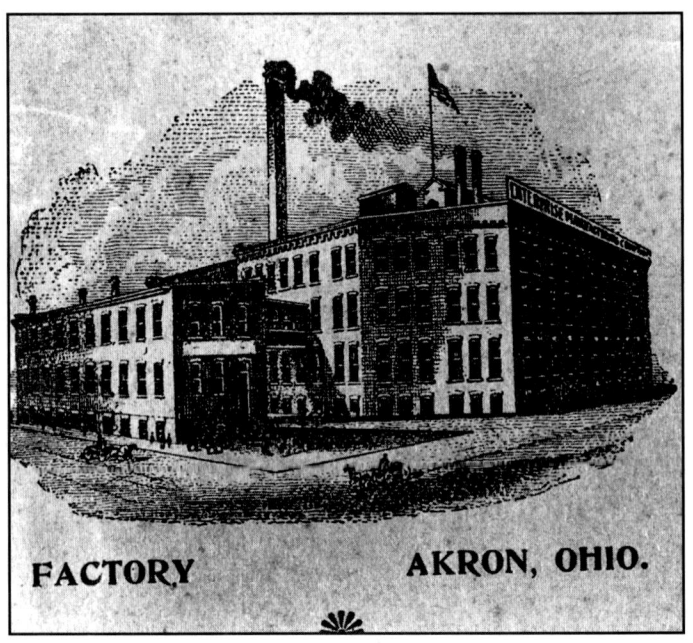

Cut from the 1897 catalog depicting the factory at Akron, Ohio. The 1892 – 1893 catalog pictured an additional factory at St. Paul, Minnesota. Subsequent catalogs show only the one in Akron.

A. Pflueger's first patent for the use of luminous paint. He proposed that small metal ornamental plates be finished with luminous paint attached to horses' harnesses, so the horses could be seen in the dark. He claimed that frequent serious and often fatal accidents were caused by the failure of people to identify horses in the dark. The compound he proposed to use was a paint or varnish composed of sulfide of calcium as a base, and a vehicle consisting of any siccative oil or paint varnish. This is the same compound he used on the fishing lures.

B. Pflueger's first patent relating to fishing lures. The patent had nothing to do with the lures shown in the patent drawing. His patent claim was a luminous finish to be applied to the baits and therefore increase their effectiveness at night. The patent was obviously a success; luminous baits are still being marketed today.

C. Advertisement from the 1883 Spring Trout addition of the *American Angler* magazine. Note that the address is E. F. Pflueger, not Enterprise Mfg.

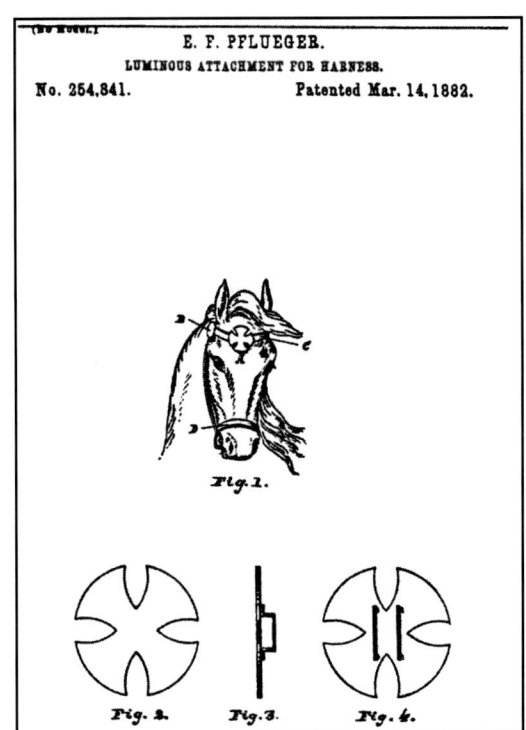

A.

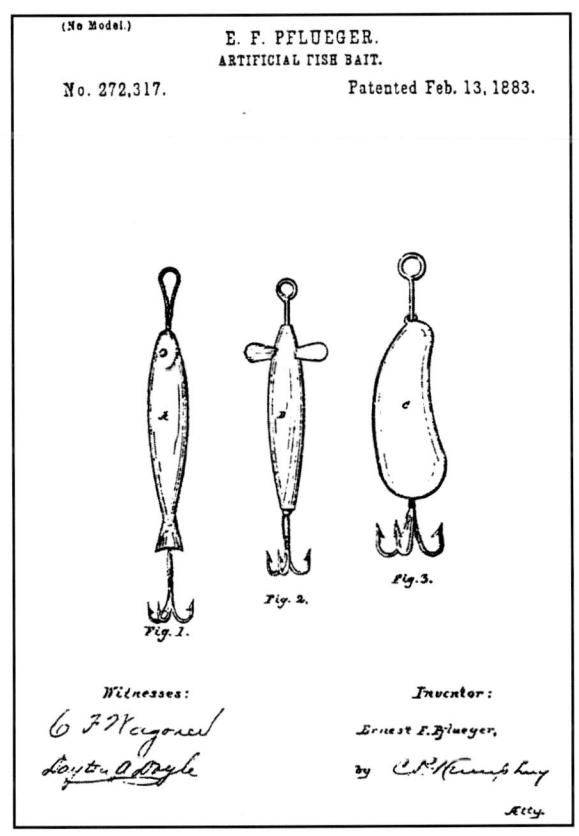

B.

C.

PFLUEGER'S PATENTS.

LUMINOUS SOFT RUBBER GRASSHOPPER.

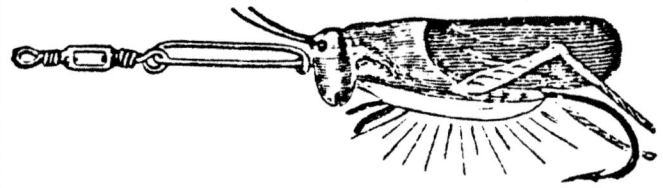

EXACT SIZE.

Assorted Colors. Price, 60 Cents Each. Samples sent postpaid to any address on receipt of price.

LUMINOUS SOFT RUBBER CRAWFISH.

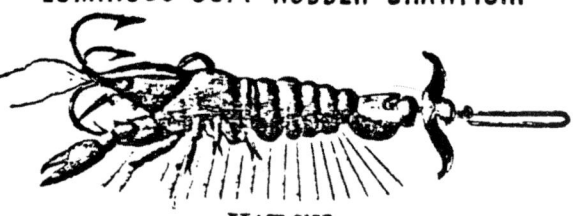

EXACT SIZE.

Price, 60 Cents Each. Samples sent postpaid on receipt of price. Either Treble or Single Hook.

Ho! Ye Bass Fishermen! Look at This!
LUMINOUS SOFT RUBBER FROGS.

The only Frog made having a Treble Feathered Hook, and working on a Swivel.

Single Hooks furnished if desired.

Making it easy to replace a broken Hook, and the Bait is a lasting one. Combined with Luminous qualities, it is a decided improvement over live Frogs.

EXACT SIZE.

Green and Brown. Price, 60 Cents Each. Samples sent postpaid on receipt of price.

LUMINOUS AKRON TROLLING SPOON.

—A— POSITIVE PROPELLER.

NEAT, CHEAP, DURABLE.

Cut Shows size of No. 2.

Price Each: No. 1, 50 Cents. No. 2, 55 Cents. No. 3, 60 Cents. No. 4, 65 Cents.

LUMINOUS KIDNEY SPOONS.

Regular Sizes: No. 1, 50 Cents. No. 2, 55 Cents. No. 3, 60 Cents. Samples sent postpaid on receipt of price.

LUMINOUS HARD AND SOFT RUBBER MINNOWS.

Above Cut Shows size No. 8.

The only Minnows made with Plated Rod and having Feathered Treble Hook. They are decorated to represent the ve Minnow to perfection, and are practicably indestructible.

Price Each: No. 7, 70 Cents. No. 8, 80 Cents. No. 9, 90 Cents. Samples sent postpaid on receipt of price.

Page from the 1885 Enterprise Manufacturing Co. catalog.

WOOD AND CORK FLOATS.

These are our regular size Floats, with luminous qualities, which act not only as a lure to the fish, but also enables the fisherman to see his float in the dark; also on cloudy days, where heretofore they were of no use in the dark. Every fisherman should try them and be convinced.

LUMINOUS FLOATS.

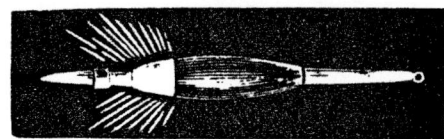

Assorted Sizes.

Price, 30 Cents. Samples sent postpaid, on receipt of price.

LUMINOUS SOFT RUBBER DOBSON.

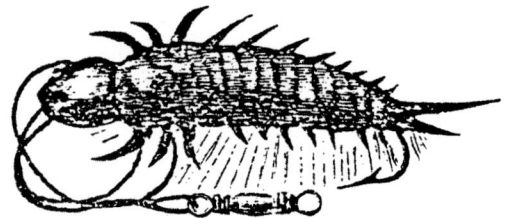

Cut Shows Size No. 1.—Made in Two Sizes.

Price, 60 Cents Each. Samples sent postpaid on receipt of price.

LUMINOUS FLYING HELGRAMITE.

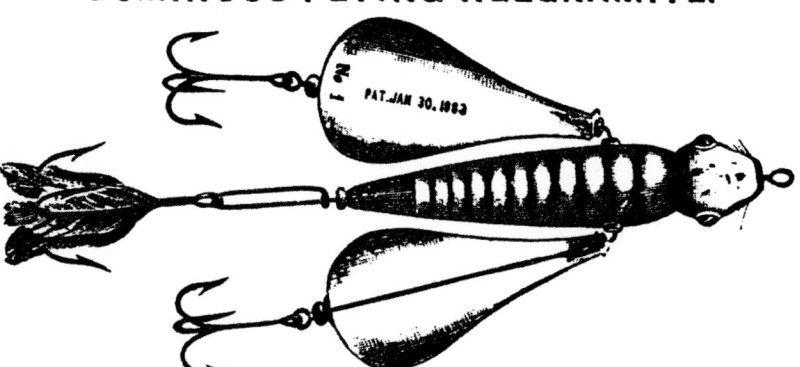

Cut of No. 1.

Price Each.
No. 0, - 80 Cents.
No. 1, - 85 Cents.

Price Each.
No. 2, - 90 Cents.
No. 3, - $1.00.

Samples sent postpaid to any address, on receipt of price.

LUMINOUS CRYSTAL MINNOW.

Size of No. 1.

Each Minnow has nickel-plated spoon and rod attached, making them revolve perfectly, even if against a very gentle current.

Finely decorated, and has feathered treble hook. Price, No. 1, 60 Cents; No. 2, 75 Cents.

THE PATENT LUMINOUS DEXTER SPOON and MINNOW COMBINED.

A most complete and practicable Spring.

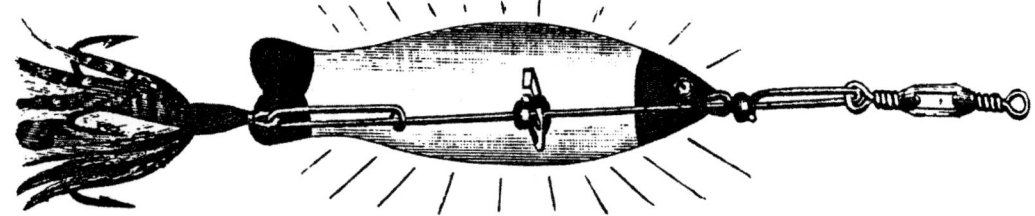

Having experimented for several years to find a simple yet durable and practical spring for spoon baits, we have struck the nail on the head at last, and think the sale it commands is abundant proof of its excellent catching qualities. **Price, 60 Cents.** Samples sent postpaid on receipt of price. Trolling Spoons, gold-plate, **15 Cents** each extra; silver-plate, **10 Cents** each extra.

Page from the 1885 Enterprise Manufacturing Co. catalog.

A.

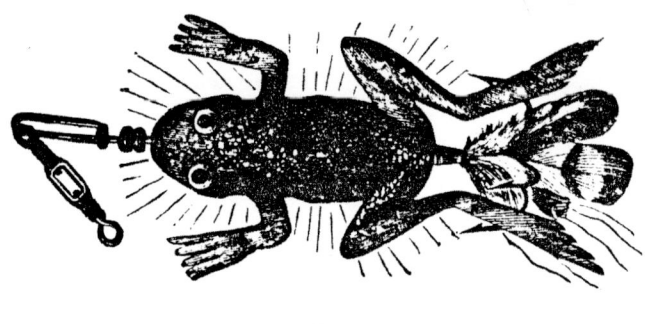

B.

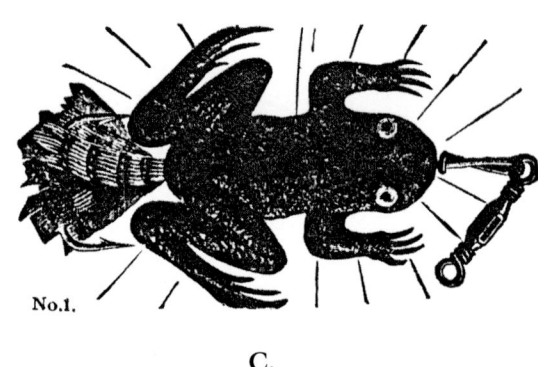

C.

A. An advertisement from the May 9, 1885 issue of *The American Angler*. This picture was also used on the cover of the 1885 and 1886 – 1887 catalogs. NOTE: The 1885 catalog contained a total of nine different lures; the Flying Helgramite, the Crystal Minnow, the Soft Rubber Grasshopper, the Soft Rubber Crawfish, the Soft Rubber Frog, the Akron Trolling Spoon, the Hard and Soft Rubber Minnows, the Soft Rubber Dobson, and the Dexter Spoon. All of these lures were luminous.
Additions to the 1886 – 1887 catalog were the Embossed Kidney Trolling Spoon, The Kidney Trolling Spoon, a second Frog, and the Royal Malleable Crystal Fly. A line of luminous flies had also been added, and the Soft Rubber Minnow was sporting a new windmill type propeller. Both catalogs had luminous bobbers. The Flying Helgramite was dropped for the 1886 – 1887 season after having a short production run. It had been introduced in 1883.

B. The Luminous Soft Rubber Frog. This frog was advertised in the 1885 catalog as "The only frog made having a treble feathered hook and working on a swivel. Making it easy to replace a broken hook." In the 1886 – 1887 catalog, this frog is listed as size 2. By 1892 it was designated the No. 714, and was available in luminous and non-luminous. It was absent from the 1894 catalog, but reappeared in the 1895 – 1896 issue. It remained in the line through 1900. In 1900 it is shown without the feathers on the treble and with a short gimp leader instead of a through shaft. The No. 714 frog is approximately 2½" long. $1,000.00+.

C. The No. 1 Luminous Soft Rubber Frog. This frog was introduced in the 1886 – 1887 catalog. It is different in shape than the 714, and is approximately 1⅝" long. By 1892, it was available in both luminous and non-luminous and was listed as 712. It was shown in the 1892 catalog without the feathered treble and with a short gimp leader. $1,000.00+.

ENTERPRISE MFG. CO.

A.

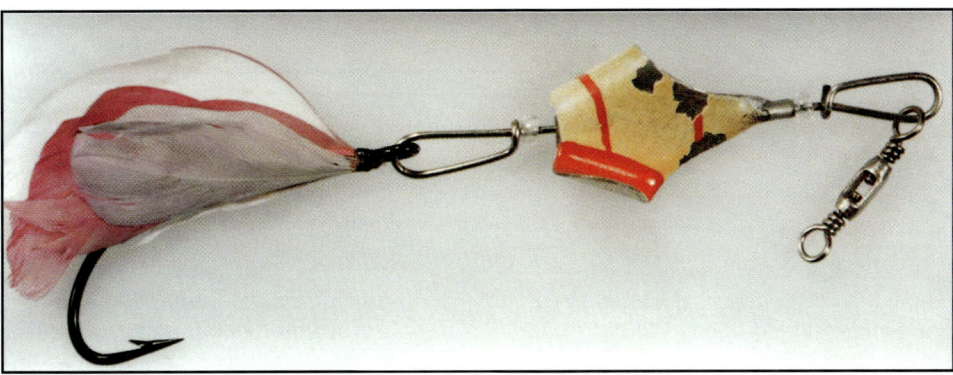

B.

A. The 1900 version of the No. 712 frog. Note the gimp leader and lack of feathers on the treble. $50.00 – 75.00.

B. The Luminous "Akron" trolling spoon. This lure was made until 1896. A non-luminous version was named the "Leader." A second quality model was the "Victor," and a third quality made of polished tin, was named the "Lone Star." $100.00 – 150.00.

C. Catalog cut of the Luminous Soft Rubber Dobson. The 1885 catalog lists it in two sizes; the cut shows the actual size of No. 1. In 1892 it was made in both luminous and non-luminous and both were designated No. 709. The 1894 catalog shows the luminous as No. 709 and the non-luminous as No. 759. These numbers were used through 1900. $50.00 – 75.00.

D. The top lure in the photo is the non-luminous No. 759. The bottom bait is the more common Dobson, the one manufactured into the 1940s. Notice the long leader on the No. 759. $50.00 – 75.00 (top); $10.00 – 20.00 (bottom)

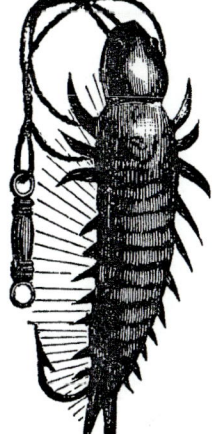

C.

D.

133

Enterprise Mfg. Co.

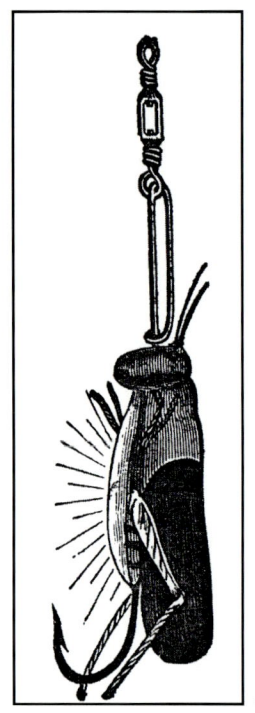

A.

B.

Above: The Luminous Soft Rubber Grasshopper. This lure was listed in the 1885 and 1886 – 1887 catalogs as being available in assorted colors. The early models had a through shaft with a clip on the front. In 1892 it is illustrated with a gimp leader. This is the one shown in the photo and the one found most frequently by collectors. Also, in 1892, the Grasshopper was listed as No. 710 and was available in both luminous and non-luminous. In 1894 the non-luminous version was listed as No. 760. These designations continued through 1900. **A.**, $200.00 – 250.00; **B.**, $50.00 – 75.00.

Below: The Luminous Soft Rubber Crawfish. In 1885 and 1886 – 1887, the Crawfish was available with either treble or single hook. By 1892 it was available in luminous and non-luminous and with a treble hook only. In 1894 the luminous model was listed as the No. 711 and the non-luminous 761. From 1885 until 1898, the Crawfish is illustrated as having a through shaft with a clip and a small propeller on the front. It is shown in 1900 with a short gimp leader; this is the one in the photo and the one most often encountered by collectors. **C.**, $50.00 – 75.00; **D.**, $200.00 – 250.00.

C.

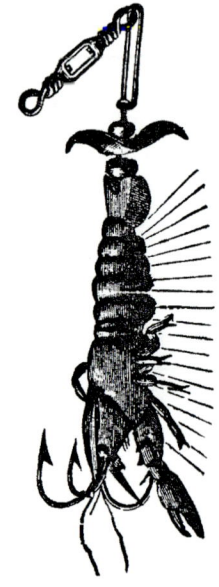

D.

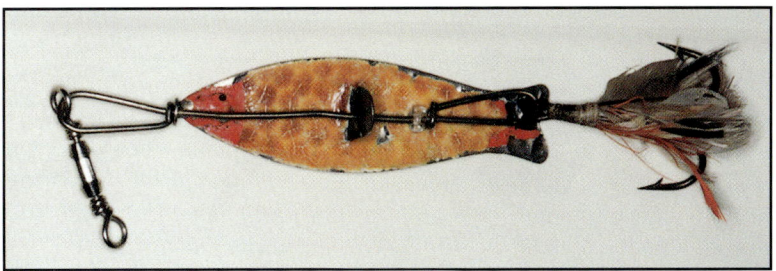

A.

A. Reverse view showing the luminous paint on the patent "Dexter Spoon and Minnow Combined." The 1885 catalog lists it as luminous only. In 1886, it was offered in both plain and embossed. By 1892, it was offered in both luminous and non-luminous. The luminous Dexter was listed as No. 610. The non-luminous was called the "Persuader" and designated the No. 611. Also listed were the No. 603 "Atlas," a less expensive version, and the No. 613 "Hawkeye." The Hawkeye was made of polished tin, a real cheapie. In 1895 – 1896, it listed only the No. 610, and by 1897, it was no longer in the line. It had a patented spring that held the spoon to the shaft. $200.00 – $300.00.

B. Reverse side of the No. 611 non-luminous "Persuader." This photo clearly shows the metal tab or spring that holds the blade against the main shaft. Note the notches on each side of the tab. These lures have been found with a string tied through these notches and around the tab. This would in effect keep the blade closer to the shaft. $150.00 – 200.00.

C. Top side of the No. 611 non-luminous "Persuader." This is the hammered finish. $150.00 – 200.00.

B.

C.

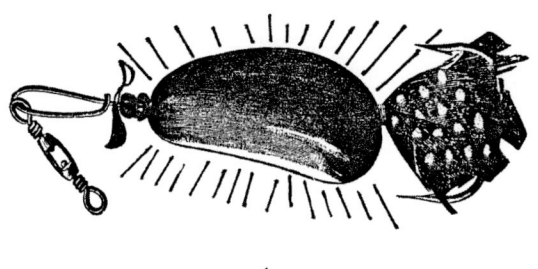
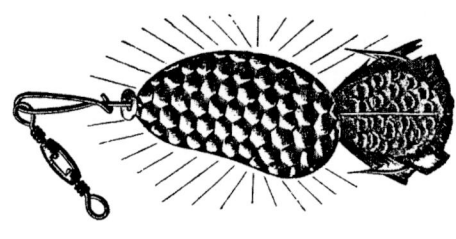

A. B.

A. The Luminous Kidney Trolling Spoon. This lure was in the 1885 catalog. It was available in three sizes and was finished in brass or nickel. Gold was available at extra cost. A distinguishing feature of the lure and other early Kidneys is that the eye is formed as part of the blade and not as a soldered loop. By 1892 it was called the "Nickel Plated Bait" and the small propeller on the front was gone. It was listed as No. 619 and was then available in seven sizes. The 1894 catalog did not list the 619, but it returned in the 1895 – 1896 issue featuring the patent reversible hinge lug (clevis). In 1897 it was referred to as a second quality non-luminous bait. It remained as such through 1900. $100.00 – 150.00.

B. The Luminous Embossed Kidney Trolling Spoon. This lure was introduced in the 1886 – 1887 catalog. It was available in six sizes and was finished in brass, nickel, or gold. By 1892 it was renamed the "Empire" and was listed as both luminous and non-luminous. The number designation of the luminous was 620 and the non-luminous, 621. In 1894 the "Empire" was sold as either plain or embossed. The 1895 – 1896 catalog calls the luminous 620 the "Empire," and the non-luminous 621 the "Enterprise Bait." Both were first-quality baits and remained so through 1900. $20.00 – 30.00.

C. The 1892 catalog lists the "Keystone" in seven sizes. It is a "second quality" bait and has an inexpensive swivel. The 1894 catalog does not list this lure, but it reappears in the 1895 – 1896 issue. That is the last time it is listed. $10.00 – 20.00.

D. The "Excelsior Spoon" was a "third quality" lure made of polished tin. The 1892 catalog lists it as being made in seven sizes and available with twisted leader or swivel. The 1894 catalog does not list it, but it was available again in 1895 – 1896 and remained in the line through 1900. $10.00 – $20.00.

E. This lure is the same as the "Keystone Spoon" but came with the addition of a gimp leader. Its time frame is the same as the "Keystone." $10.00 – 20.00.

NOTE: The Empire, Enterprise, Excelsior, and Keystone were all available as "Pike" baits. They are the same as their namesakes, except they have feathers attached to the main shaft instead of the treble hook. These were listed for the last time in the 1892 – 1893 catalog. After 1892 – 1893, all of the above lures remaining in the line used the patented clevis.

C.

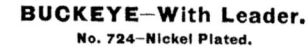
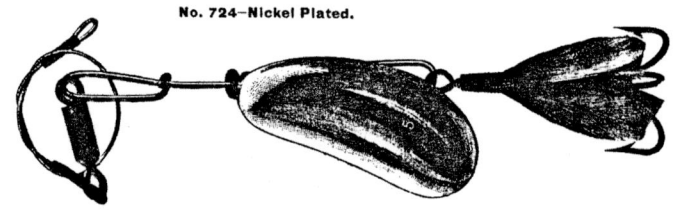

E. D.

ENTERPRISE MFG. CO.

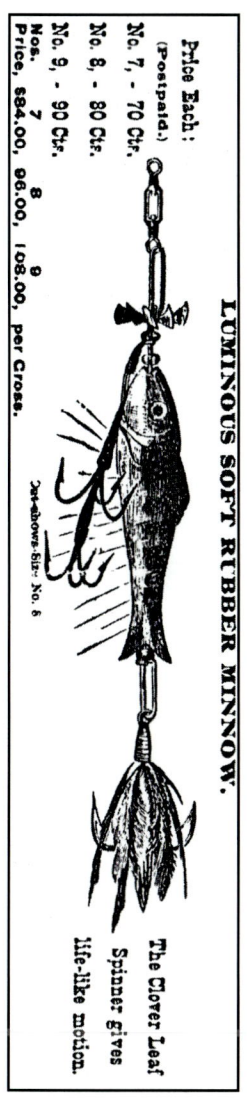

A.

B.

Note: The 1885 catalog lists the Luminous Hard and Soft Rubber Minnows in three sizes: Nos. 7, 8, and 9. These lures were 2", 2½", and 3" respectively. Early lures had a nickel plated shaft, and the Soft Rubber Minnows made between 1886 and 1892 were equipped with a clover leaf spinner. By 1892 the lures were available in both luminous and non-luminous. The 1894 catalog shows both the soft and hard rubber minnows without props. These baits continued in the line through 1900. It is difficult to tell the Hard Rubber Minnows from the Soft Rubber Minnows.

A. The 1886 – 1887 catalog lists the luminous soft rubber minnow as having a Clover Leaf propeller and the non-luminous hard rubber minnow without a prop (see catalog cut at left). These are non-luminous minnows with props. $350.00 – $500.00.

B. This hard or soft rubber minnow has metal fins and glass eyes. The 1900 catalog shows the hard and soft rubber minnows with fins. $300.00 – 400.00.

C. Later non-luminous version of the soft or hard rubber minnow. $75.00 – 100.00.

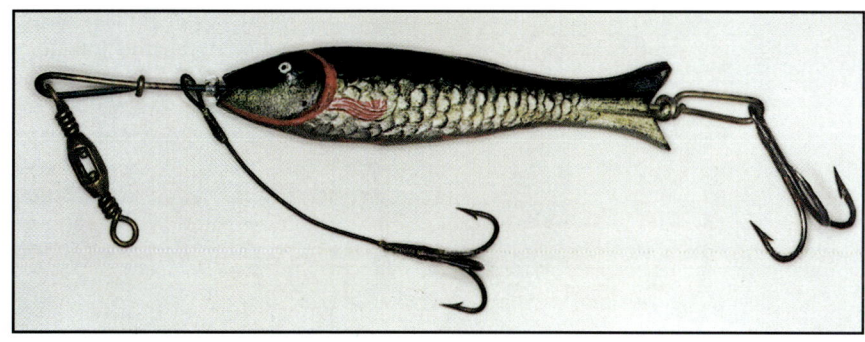

C.

A.

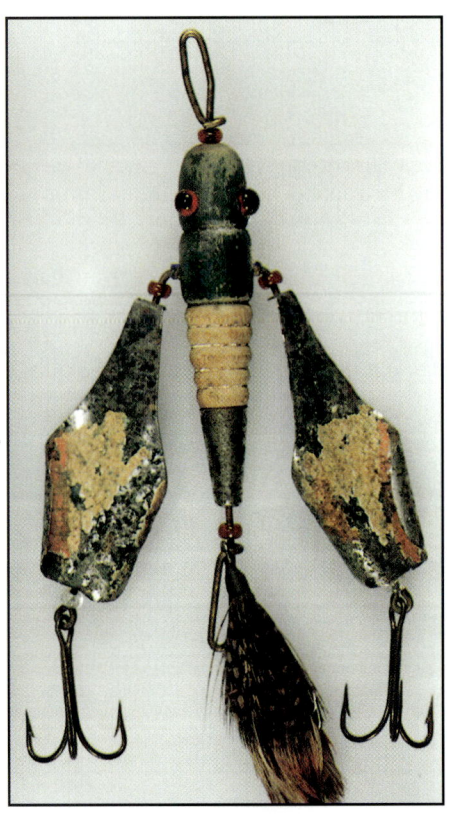

A. The luminous Flying Helgramite. This classic lure was made in at least four sizes: 0, 1, 2, and 3. The body lengths of the two shown in the above photograph are 1⅝" and 2⅜" respectively. I have seen one that was 2¹⁵⁄₁₆" in length; with the musky sized one on the opposite page (3⁵⁄₁₆") that accounts for the four sizes. However, things in those days were seldom exact, and I'm sure there are variations on these sizes. $2,500.00+.

The earliest appearance that I could find of the Helgramite as an Enterprise Mfg. Co. product was in the July 28, 1883, issue of *The American Angler*. This ad ran until Nov. 10, 1883, and made no reference to it being luminous. Its final appearance is in the Enterprise 1885 catalog. In this catalog it is available only in a luminous finish. For more information on the Flying Helgramite, see the previous chapter on Harry Comstock.

B. A veteran Helgramite still wearing some of its luminous paint. $2,500.00+.

B.

A.

B.

C.

Close-up views of the famous Flying Helgramite:
A. The longitudinal slot cut in the belly of the Helgramite was probably made to facilitate assembly of the lure. It eliminated the need for drilling blind holes which may have intersected and caused problems. Also, the small red eyes of the Helgramite had fine attached wires which were twisted together and then cut off even with the top of the slot. This held the eyes securely in place without glue. A wondrous lure, the Helgramite!
B. Close-up view showing the bright colors and segments of the body.
C. A large size Helgramite. The body on this lure is 3⁵⁄₁₆" long. It does not have a slot down the belly of the lure. $2,500.00+.

ENTERPRISE MFG. CO.

A.

B.

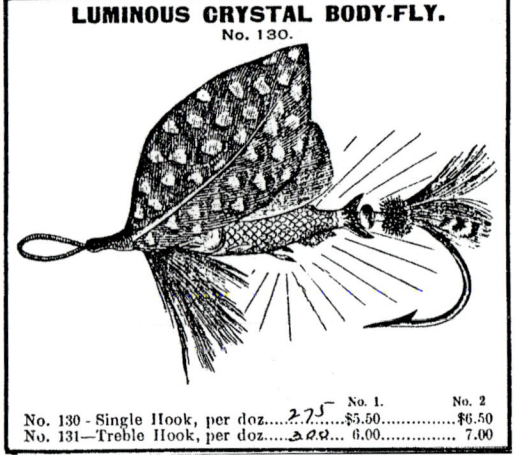

A. The Luminous Crystal Minnow. This may have been the first lure manufactured by the Enterprise Manufacturing Company. An article titled, "Whence the Plug?," written by Sam S. Stinson, and published in the May, 1918 issue of *The American Angler*, quotes Ernest A. Pflueger as saying that the Enterprise Company's first plug was manufactured in 1881. He goes on to state that the plug was a hollow glass minnow and was filled with a luminous substance. Ernest A. Pflueger was the grandson of Ernest F. Pflueger, and was president of the company at the time of the article. The Crystal Minnow appears to have been manufactured from a patent originally granted to Jorgen Irgens of Bergen, Norway, on Sept. 7, 1880. Enterprise may have bought the patent or was using it under license. Ernest F. Pflueger re-patented it on Aug. 28, 1883. The patent drawings are nearly identical. The Irgens' bait, along with the Pflueger patent, is shown later in this volume (p. 254). $1,000.00 – 1,250.00.

B. The Luminous Crystal Minnow was manufactured in two sizes. The smaller size is approx. 1¼" long. Early models had a nickel plated shaft and propeller. In the 1886 – 1887 catalog, it is referred to as the Luminous Malleable Crystal Minnow. By 1897 it was no longer listed in the catalog. $1,000.00 – 1,250.00.

C. First listed in the 1886 – 1887 catalog and called "The Royal Malleable Crystal Body Fly." It was made in two sizes, and with either single or treble hooks. The small size was approx. 1¼" long. It, too, was gone by 1897. It is a very rare lure. $1,500.00 – 2,000.00 each.

C.

Above: The May Bug Spoon. This beautiful lure was introduced into the line sometime between 1887 and 1892. It was made in only one size, but was available in either luminous or non-luminous. The 1895 – 1896 catalog states, "The body being separated from the wings gives life like action in the water." It was cataloged through 1900. In fact, it was still available in 1916. The later ones sometimes have a bulldog trademark on the wing. $800.00 – 1,250.00.

Below: The Pearl Phantom. This bait is found in the 1892 catalog and was listed through 1900. It was made in three sizes and can be readily identified by the metal eye on its tail. It was made of mother-of-pearl and painted in a perch stripe pattern. It is most often found with the paint missing. This lure was probably imported from Great Britain. $500.00 – 750.00.

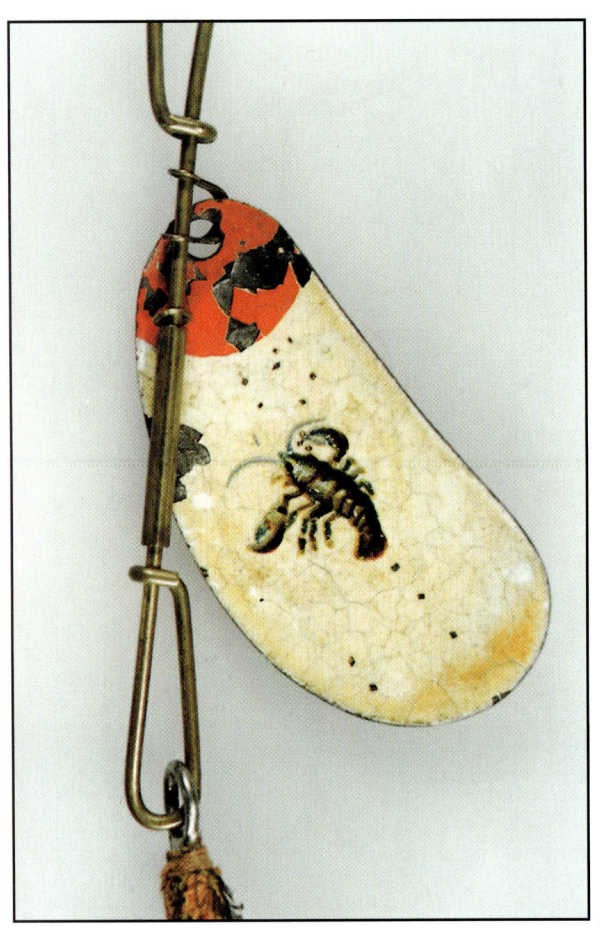

A.

B.

Enterprise started applying these figures to the reverse sides of spinners and spoons as early as 1894. Figures include a frog, crayfish, butterfly, moth, fly, beetle, and a sunburst. **A**. $30.00 – 50.00; **B. & C.** $50.00 – 75.00.

C.

ENTERPRISE MFG. CO.

A.

B.

A. & B. Frog and sunburst designs. The frog is one of the more common figures the collector is likely to find. **A.** $20.00 – $30.00; **B.** $25.00 – $35.00.

C. The Climax Bass Bait. Made in three sizes. Available in luminous, non-luminous, brass, copper, and nickel. First listed in 1894 and continued through 1900. $100.00 – 150.00.

C.

143

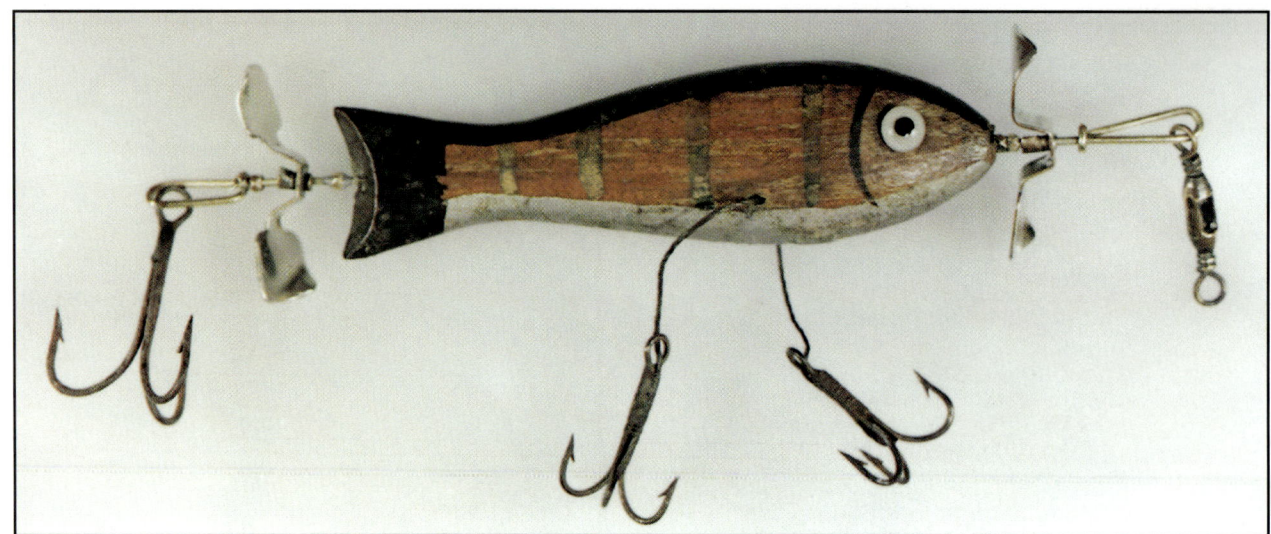

The Trory Minnow. This lure was first produced in 1899 and is illustrated in the 1900 – 1901 catalog. Its existence is the direct result of a fishing trip taken by Joseph E. Pflueger, then superintendent and vice president of the Enterprise Mfg. Co. $3,000.00+.

In 1908, a court action was instigated by the William Shakespeare Co. against the Enterprise Mfg. Co. concerning their use of a certain hook attachment device. During this trial, Joseph Pflueger was called upon to testify. The following is an excerpt from this testimony.

Question: How do you identify the Trory Minnow with the year 1899, was that the only bait you used in fishing during that year?
Answer: In the fall of 1898 I did a great deal of fishing on the lakes near Akron, and especially on the body of water known as Twin Lakes. There was a certain fisherman who worked in the File Works at Kent, whose name and address I am not familiar with, using a bait with which he was having great success. I was anxious to secure a sample of that bait, and did so through a friend by the name of Mr. Trory.

Q: Is the Trory bait you refer to as having been used during this season, the one illustrated in your 1900 – 1901 catalog?
A: It was similar, very similar, but not identical. The spinner blades were not of as neat a design as on the minnow which we made, the decorating of the minnow was not artistically done, and in many other ways it was a very crude bait, in fact a homemade bait.

Q: Kindly give the name of the man employed in the file works you referred to, and his address, also the name and address of Mr. Trory.
A: As stated in my answer to the first question, I am not in possession of the file maker's name and address, neither do I know how to secure it. Mr. Trory's address is Kent, Ohio.

The file maker, in all probability, was Samuel H. Friend, maker of the Pardee Minnow and Kent Frog (see page 267). The Trory was available in both luminous and non-luminous. After 1900 – 1901, it was made in a five hook version.

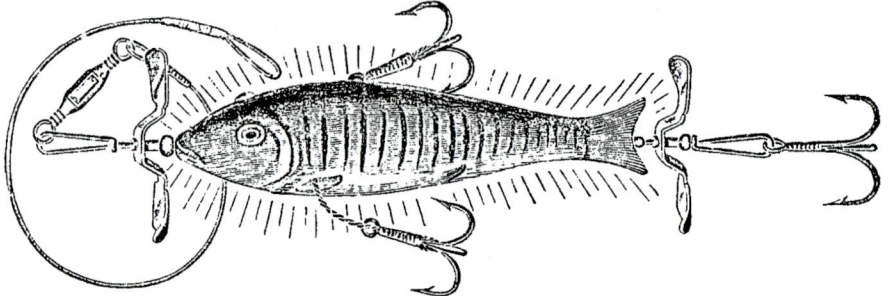

Cut of the Trory Minnow from the 1900 catalog (reduced size).

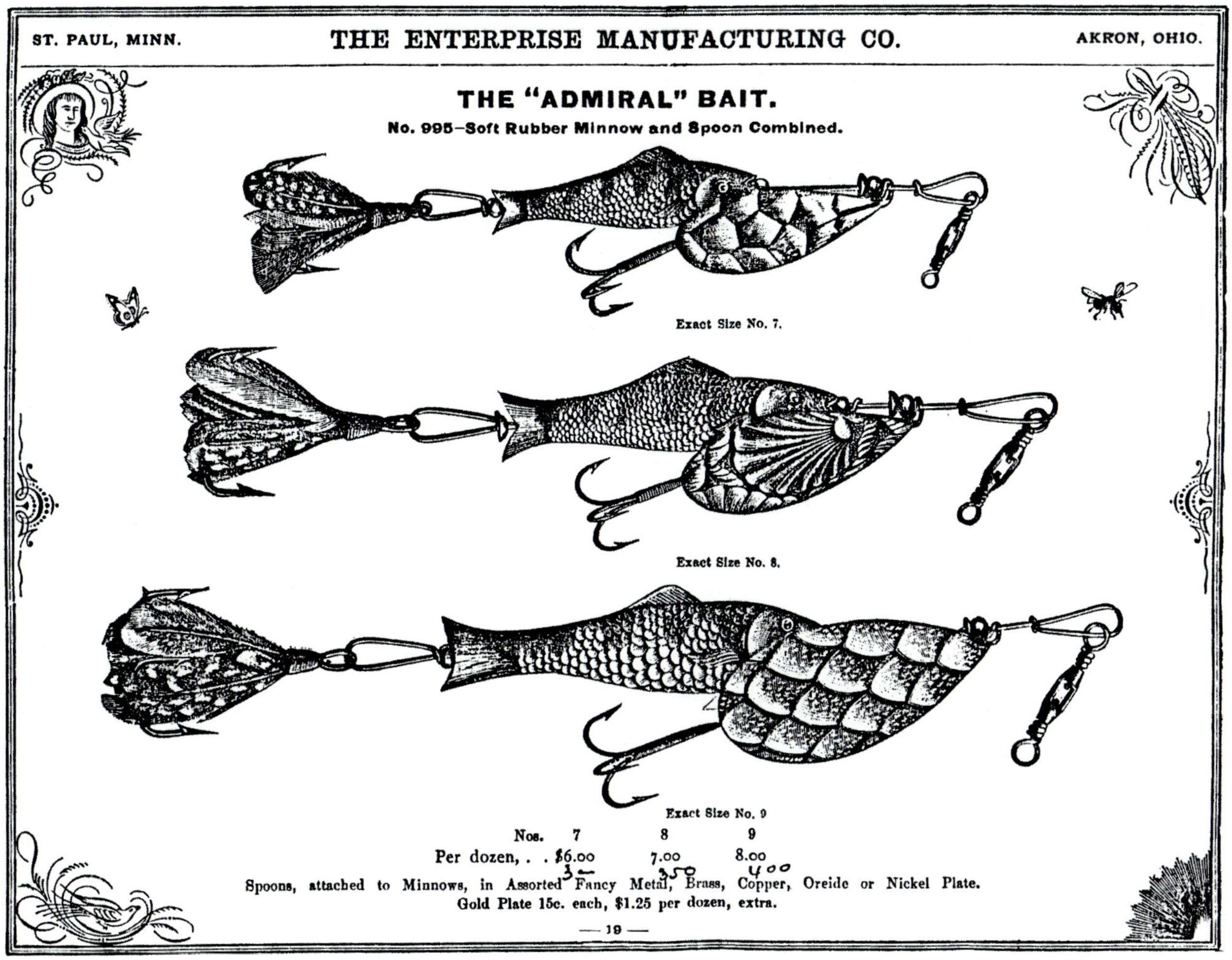

ENTERPRISE MFG. CO.

ST. PAUL, MINN. — THE ENTERPRISE MANUFACTURING CO. — **AKRON, OHIO.**

THE "ADMIRAL" BAIT.
No. 995—Soft Rubber Minnow and Spoon Combined.

Exact Size No. 7.

Exact Size No. 8.

Exact Size No. 9

Nos.	7	8	9
Per dozen,	$6.00	7.00	8.00

Spoons, attached to Minnows, in Assorted Fancy Metal, Brass, Copper, Oreide or Nickel Plate. Gold Plate 15c. each, $1.25 per dozen, extra.

— 19 —

A.

A. Page (reduced) from the 1892 catalog showing the "Admiral" bait. The Admiral bait was non-luminous and manufactured in three sizes: 2" (No. 7), 2½" (No. 8), and 3" (No. 9). The 1894 catalog features the bait with the new patented clevis. Its counterpart, the "Governor" bait, had a luminous belly and the attached spoon had a luminous paint applied to the reverse side. It was available in the same three sizes and was listed as No. 794.

B. Close-up of the small size "Admiral." This is an early lure with white glass eyes and soldered loop on the blade. Note the Clover Leaf pattern. $500.00 – 750.00.

B.

ENTERPRISE MFG. CO.

A.

A. 3" Admiral with the so called "Root" pattern blade. The 3" models of the Admiral and Governor were supplied with two trebles. $500.00 – 750.00.

B. Enlarged view of the beautiful Clover Leaf blade pattern. $500.00 – 750.00.

C. Early "Governor" with glass eyes and Sea Shell pattern blade. $500.00 – 750.00.

D. "Governor" still tied in its original box. The tag found in the box reads, "You must expose these goods to light and air before testing their luminosity in the dark." $500.00 – 750.00 without box.

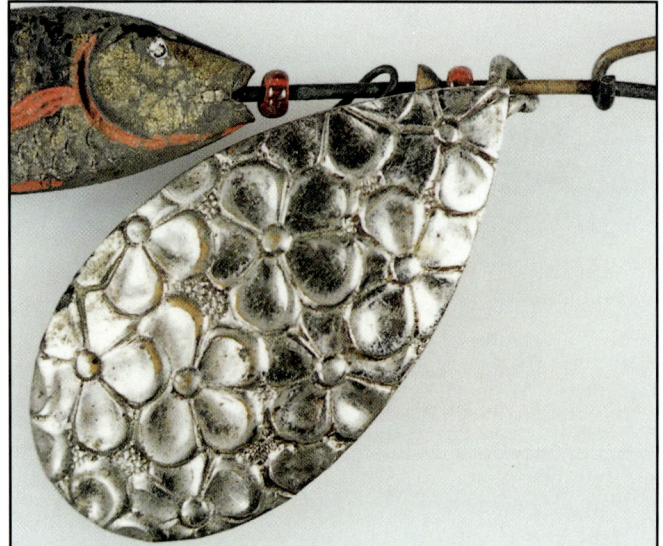

B.

C.

D.

146

ENTERPRISE MFG. CO.

A.

B.

THE MASKINONGÉ.

C.

A. The "Muskallonge Trolling Minnow." This large, soft rubber, minnow first appears sometime between 1887 and 1892. The 1892 – 1893 catalog calls it the Muskallonge Trolling Minnow, but in 1894, it is referred to as the "Muskallonge Killer". In the 1895 – 1896 catalog, it is called "The Muskallonge and Tarpon Killer," but by 1900 it is called the "Muskallonge Minnow." It remained in the line for many years. The last reference I could find was in the 1916 catalog. It is then listed as the "Didwel Minnow." It is a large bait, 7" in length. This photo shows it beside a medium (2½") length Admiral Minnow. It was available in both luminous and non-luminous through 1900. The 1916 "Didwel" was finished in Pflueger's "FLEXO" silver enamel with a green back. $500.00 – 750.00.

B. The "McMurray" spinner. This large spinner first appears in the 1894 catalog. It was 7" long and was originally available in luminous, non-luminous, nickel both sides, and brass both sides. The 1897 and 1898 catalogs list it in only luminous and nickel both sides. By 1900, it was being made in luminous and nickel both sides, plus red paint one side and copper both sides. This lure was later made in a variety of sizes. Early models are distinguished by the clip on the front which allows the swivel to be changed; later versions had a twisted wire eye. $20.00 – 40.00.

C. The "Bolt" Spoon. Available in luminous and non-luminous. This lure was made in one size and was in the line through 1900. $20.00 – 40.00.

A.

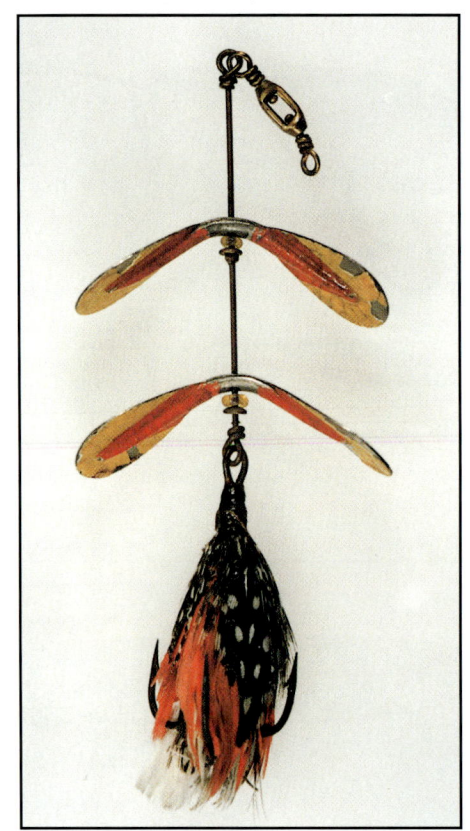

B.

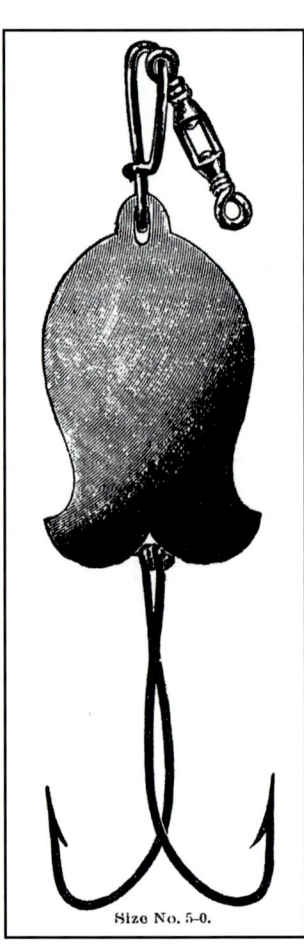

C.

A. "New Akron Spoon." This lure was introduced in the 1895 – 1896 catalog. It was made in two sizes and was available in luminous and non-luminous. It was still listed in the 1900 catalog. In 1900 its name was changed to the "New Akron Spinner." $100.00 – 125.00.

B. "Tandem Spinner." The 1900 catalog states, "This is the second season for the Tandem." It was made in two sizes and was finished in luminous and non-luminous. It had blades of copper, brass, and nickel. In later years, it was made in a variety of sizes. Early models had glass beads and square swivels. It must have been a fish catcher — they made it for the next 50 years. $30.00 – 50.00.

C. "Delevan." This bait first appeared in the 1894 catalog. It was made in three sizes, Nos. 3/0, 4/0, and 5/0, and was available in luminous and non-luminous. It continued in the line through 1900. $10.00 – 20.00.

A.

B.

A. "The Crescent Bait." This lure first appeared in the 1895 – 1896 catalog. It was made in six sizes and was available in luminous and non-luminous. It was also available in second and third quality. The price differential between first and third quality was quite severe. A No. 3 first quality luminous sold for $6.10 per dozen whereas No. 3 polished tin sold for $10.00 per gross. This lure could still be found in the 1900 catalog. $100.00 – 150.00.

B. "Pflueger's Combination changeable and Reversible Lug Trolling Spoon." The name of the lure is actually a self-description. It was made in seven sizes, each with three interchangeable blades. It first appeared in the 1895 – 1896 catalog and could still be found in the 1900 edition. $150.00 – 200.00.

C. "The Corrugated Spoon." First listed in the 1895 – 1896 catalog. It was made in nine sizes and finished in luminous and non-luminous. It was also available in second and third quality (nickel plate and polished tin). It was still available in 1900 but was named the "Coburg Bait." William Delany of Coburg, Ontario, was probably the inventor of this spoon. $15.00 – 30.00.

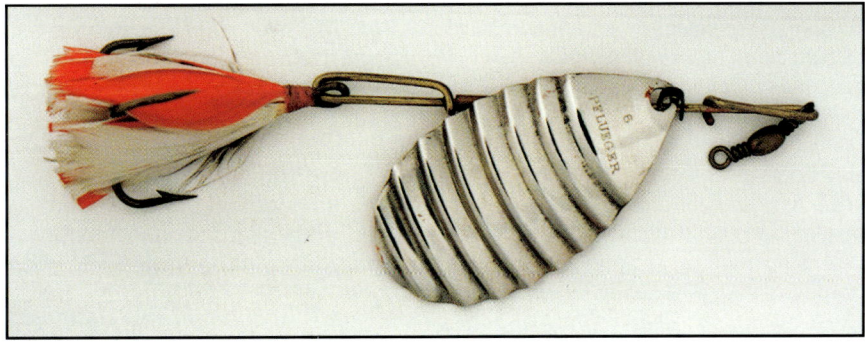

C.

Enterprise Mfg. Co.

A.

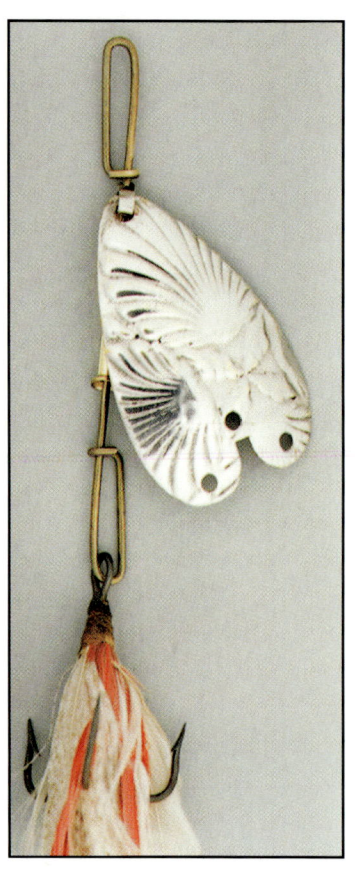

B.

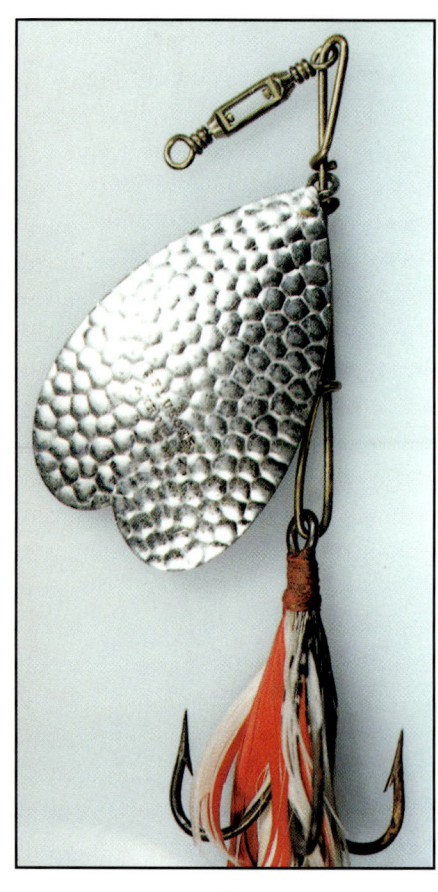

C.

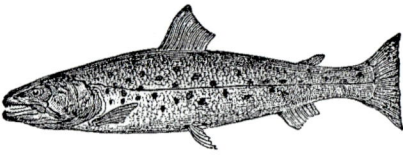

A. The "Acme" spoon. This spoon was introduced between 1887 and 1892. It was made in six sizes and had a luminous finish. A non-luminous version was named the "Rival." They were not available after 1892. Note the hole in the blade for the shaft. The patent date on the spoon (Feb. 13, 1883) is for the luminous paint. $30.00 – 50.00.

B. The "Windsor" spoon. This spoon was introduced between 1887 and 1892. It had a luminous finish and was available in six sizes. A non-luminous version was called the "Peerless" spoon. Early versions of these lures had a soldered eye instead of the patented hinge as shown. The holes in the blade are probably not original. Note the squared-off notch at the bottom of the blade. Two second quality lures were also made; the "Mentor" and the "Eureka." The Mentor was nickel plated and had an inexpensive swivel. The Eureka was made of polished tin and was available with either a twisted wire leader or an inexpensive swivel. By 1895 – 1896, these lures were no longer listed. $100.00 – 150.00.

C. This lure is also a "Windsor," although it does not have the squared-off notch at the bottom of the blade. The Windsor and Peerless were available either way. Two second quality lures, without the square notch, were also made. They were the "Argus" and the "Columbia." The Argus was nickel plated and had an inexpensive swivel, while the Columbia was made of polished tin and came with either an inexpensive swivel or a twisted wire leader. Both of these lures were listed through 1900, as were the Windsor and the Peerless. $50.00 – 75.00.

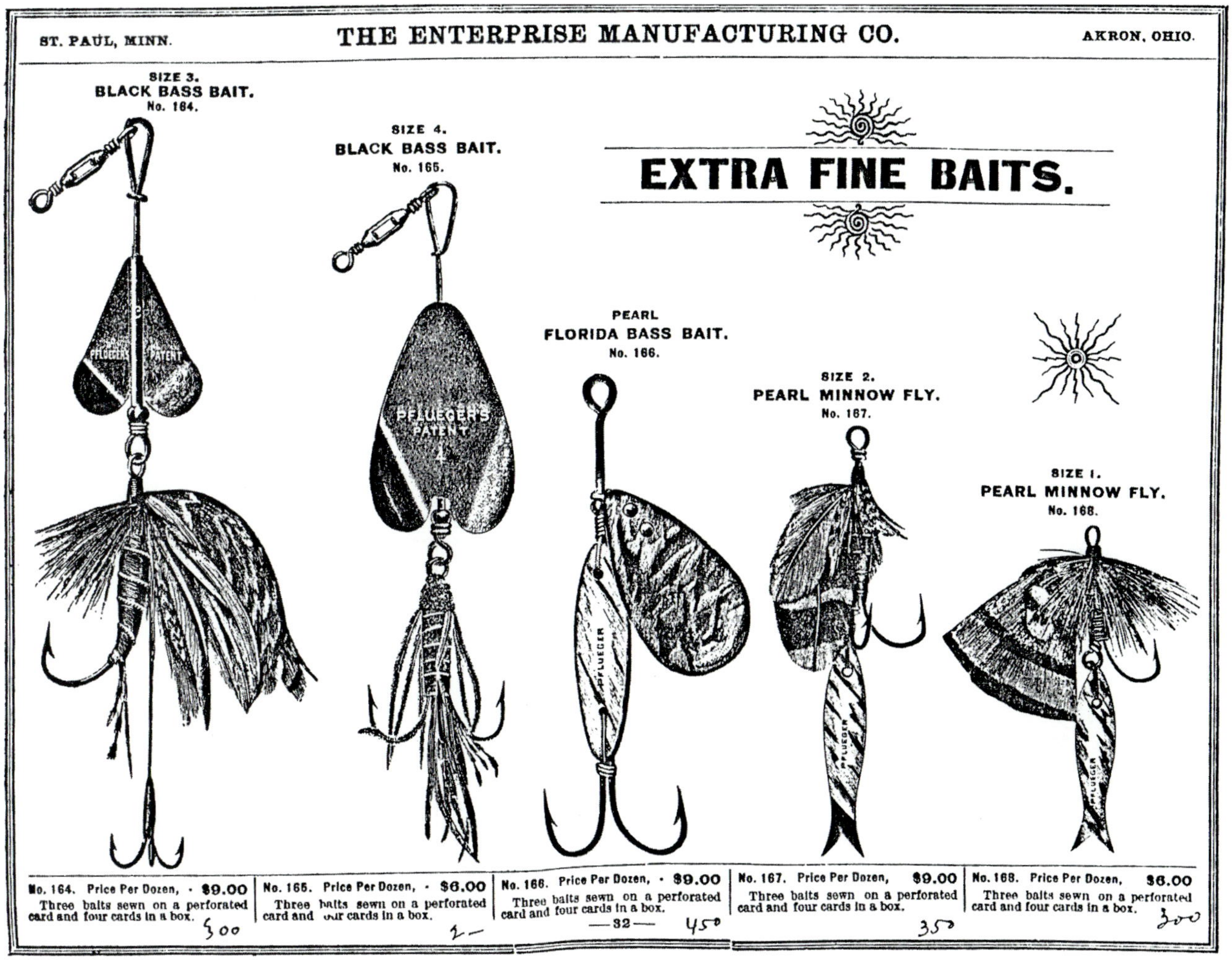

ST. PAUL, MINN. THE ENTERPRISE MANUFACTURING CO. AKRON, OHIO.

EXTRA FINE BAITS.

SIZE 3.
BLACK BASS BAIT.
No. 164.

SIZE 4.
BLACK BASS BAIT.
No. 165.

PEARL
FLORIDA BASS BAIT.
No. 166.

SIZE 2.
PEARL MINNOW FLY.
No. 167.

SIZE 1.
PEARL MINNOW FLY.
No. 168.

No. 164. Price Per Dozen, - $9.00
Three baits sewn on a perforated card and four cards in a box.

No. 165. Price Per Dozen, - $6.00
Three baits sewn on a perforated card and four cards in a box.

No. 166. Price Per Dozen, - $9.00
Three baits sewn on a perforated card and four cards in a box.

No. 167. Price Per Dozen, $9.00
Three baits sewn on a perforated card and four cards in a box.

No. 168. Price Per Dozen, $6.00
Three baits sewn on a perforated card and four cards in a box.

—32—

A.

A. Page (reduced in size) from the 1892 catalog. The two baits on the left are fancy versions of the Irvin Black Bass Bait. The Irvin baits were made in six sizes and available in both luminous and non-luminous. A photo of the Irvin bait is shown on the next page. In 1895 – 1896, a second grade of baits was added and in 1900, a model with red paint on the reverse side. The Extra Fine Irvins were available through 1900. The center lure is the Florida Bass Bait. This bait was made in one size. It is listed in the 1898 catalog but not in the 1900 edition. The two baits on the right are the Pearl Minnow Flys. These two lures are listed until 1898 but are not found in the 1900 catalog.

B. The size 2 Pearl Minnow Fly. $350.00 – 500.00.

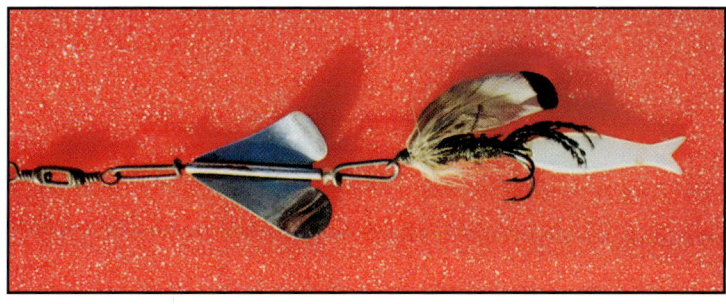

B.

ENTERPRISE MFG. CO.

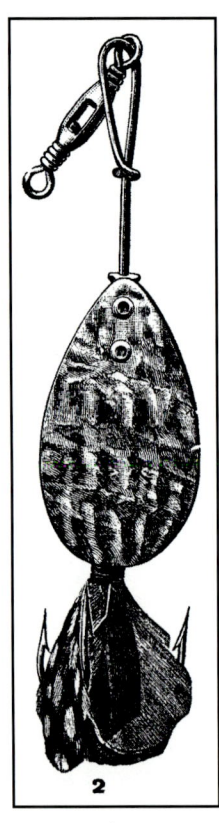

A.

B.

A. The Fine Mottled Pearl Spoon. This cut is from the 1892 – 1893 catalog and shows the exact size of the No. 2 spoon. It was made in five sizes and available in luminous and non-luminous.

B. This photo illustrates the nickel plated cap that was added in 1894. The patented reversible hinge (clevis) was also added in 1894. This lure was in the line through 1900. $30.00 – 40.00.

C. The Irvin Baits. $15.00 – 25.00.

D. The Florida Bass Bait. $350.00 – 500.00.

C.

D.

ENTERPRISE MFG. CO.

Pflueger's Fish Spearing Decoy Minnows. These minnows were made of rubber and were not equipped with hooks. Their purpose was to lure Pike and Muskallonge within range of the spear. They were originally made in four sizes: 2, 2½, 3, and 7 inches. These sizes correspond exactly with the sizes of the Admiral bait and the Muskallonge Trolling Minnow. They undoubtedly shared common molds. The Decoy Minnows were introduced between 1887 and 1892, and were made in both luminous and non-luminous. By 1895 – 1896, they were available in luminous decorated, luminous silver, non-luminous plain, and non-luminous decorated. 1895 – 1896 also saw the addition of a 5" size. In 1898, they were advertised as having fins. They were listed through 1900. $500.00 – 750.00.

AMERICAN PICKEREL, OR PIKE.

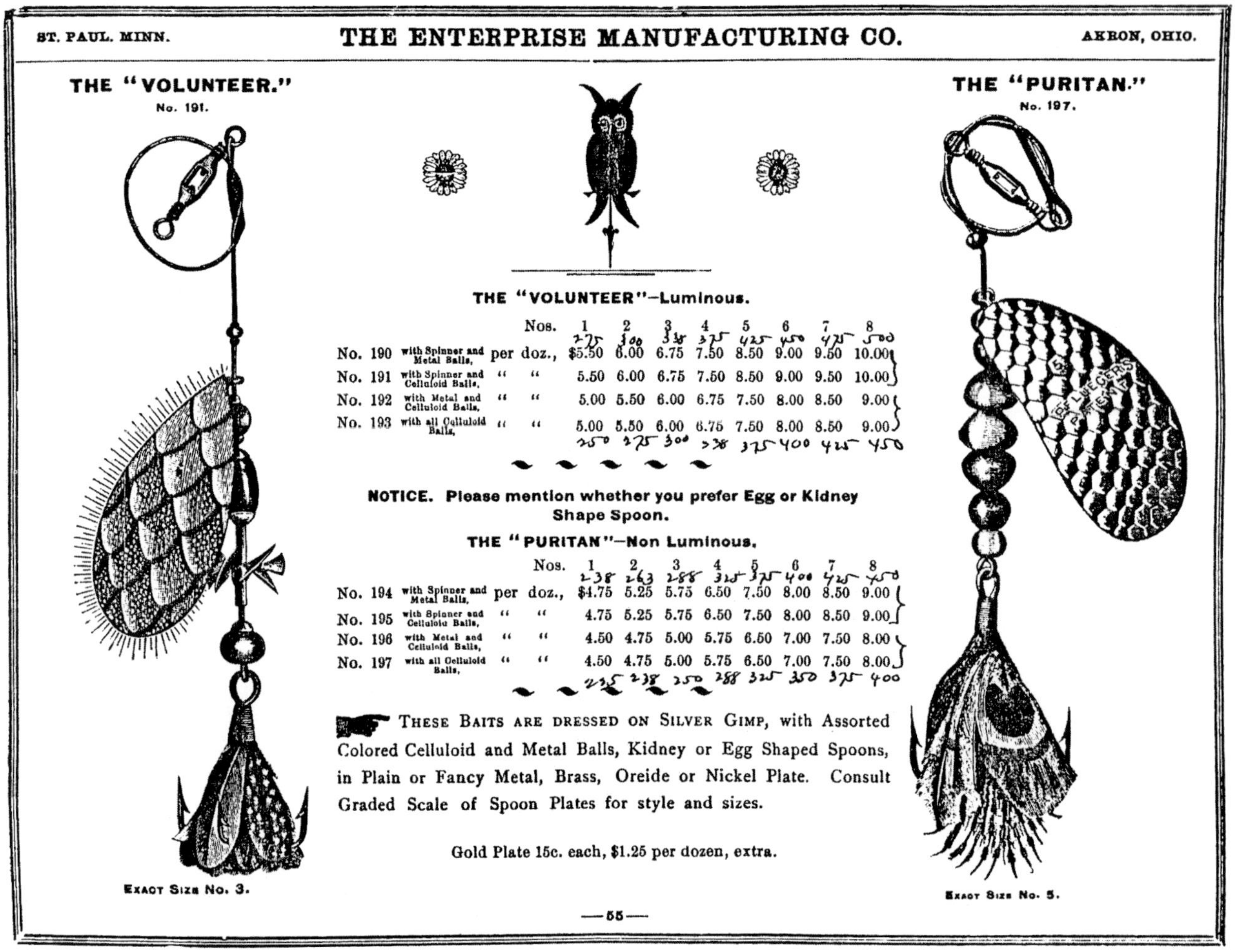

ST. PAUL, MINN. **THE ENTERPRISE MANUFACTURING CO.** AKRON, OHIO.

THE "VOLUNTEER." No. 191.

THE "PURITAN." No. 197.

THE "VOLUNTEER"—Luminous.

		Nos.	1	2	3	4	5	6	7	8
No. 190	with Spinner and Metal Balls,	per doz.,	$5.50	6.00	6.75	7.50	8.50	9.00	9.50	10.00
No. 191	with Spinner and Celluloid Balls,	" "	5.50	6.00	6.75	7.50	8.50	9.00	9.50	10.00
No. 192	with Metal and Celluloid Balls,	" "	5.00	5.50	6.00	6.75	7.50	8.00	8.50	9.00
No. 193	with all Celluloid Balls,	" "	5.00	5.50	6.00	6.75	7.50	8.00	8.50	9.00

NOTICE. Please mention whether you prefer Egg or Kidney Shape Spoon.

THE "PURITAN"—Non Luminous.

		Nos.	1	2	3	4	5	6	7	8
No. 194	with Spinner and Metal Balls,	per doz.,	$4.75	5.25	5.75	6.50	7.50	8.00	8.50	9.00
No. 195	with Spinner and Celluloid Balls,	" "	4.75	5.25	5.75	6.50	7.50	8.00	8.50	9.00
No. 196	with Metal and Celluloid Balls,	" "	4.50	4.75	5.00	5.75	6.50	7.00	7.50	8.00
No. 197	with all Celluloid Balls,	" "	4.50	4.75	5.00	5.75	6.50	7.00	7.50	8.00

These Baits are dressed on Silver Gimp, with Assorted Colored Celluloid and Metal Balls, Kidney or Egg Shaped Spoons, in Plain or Fancy Metal, Brass, Oreide or Nickel Plate. Consult Graded Scale of Spoon Plates for style and sizes.

Gold Plate 15c. each, $1.25 per dozen, extra.

Exact Size No. 3.

Exact Size No. 5.

—55—

A.

A. 1892 catalog page (reduced) showing the "Beaded Baits." Introduced between 1887 and 1892. The luminous model was originally called the "volunteer" and the non-luminous was the "Puritan." Either was available with a kidney or egg-shaped blade. By 1885 – 1886, it was listed as the "Egg Beaded Bait" and the "Kidney Beaded Bait." It was cataloged this way through 1900. After 1897, it was available only with celluloid balls. It is shown with the patented clevis in the 1894 catalog and thereafter. The early models can be identified by the red glass bead above the blade.

B. There evidently was a predecessor to the Beaded Bait. This ad is from an 1886 *American Field* magazine. Pflueger undoubtedly acquired this patent from the Nye Creaser Co.

THE HAMILTON.

PATENT APPLIED FOR

Best Bass and Pickerel Spoon ever made.

Made in two styles. Five sizes in each style. (Cut is size of No. 2.) Style A, dark feathers, black and yellow celluloid beads, gold spoons. No. 1, $1; No. 2, 85 cts.; No. 3, 75 cts.; No. 4, 75 cts.; No. 5, 75 cts. All five sizes, $4. Style B, light feathers, red and white celluloid eads, silver spoons. No. 1, 75 cts.; No. 2, 60 cts.; No. 3, 50 cts.; No. 4, 50 cts.; No. 5, 50 cts. All five sizes, $2.75. Hooks re best bright steel. Gimp is tied directly to hook. Sent by mail on receipt of price, style and sizes wanted. Send for rcular. Mention this paper. (See ad. of Nye Creaser next week.)

24-23-tf alt **THE NYE CREASER CO., Monmouth, Ill.**

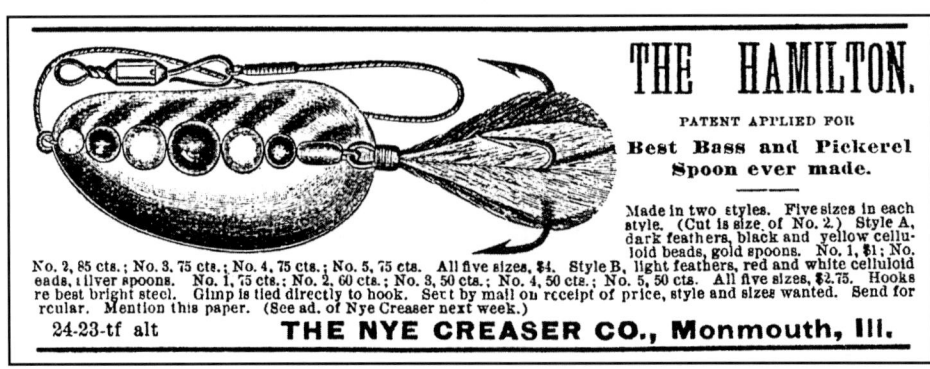

B.

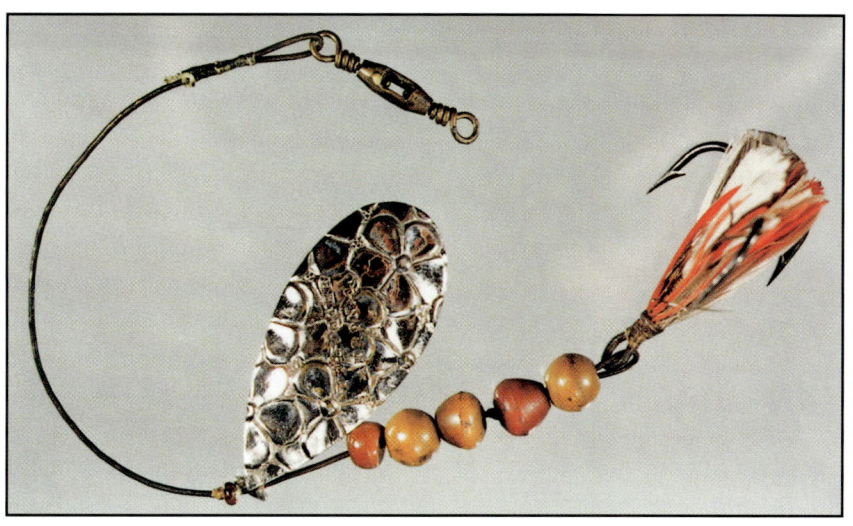

A.

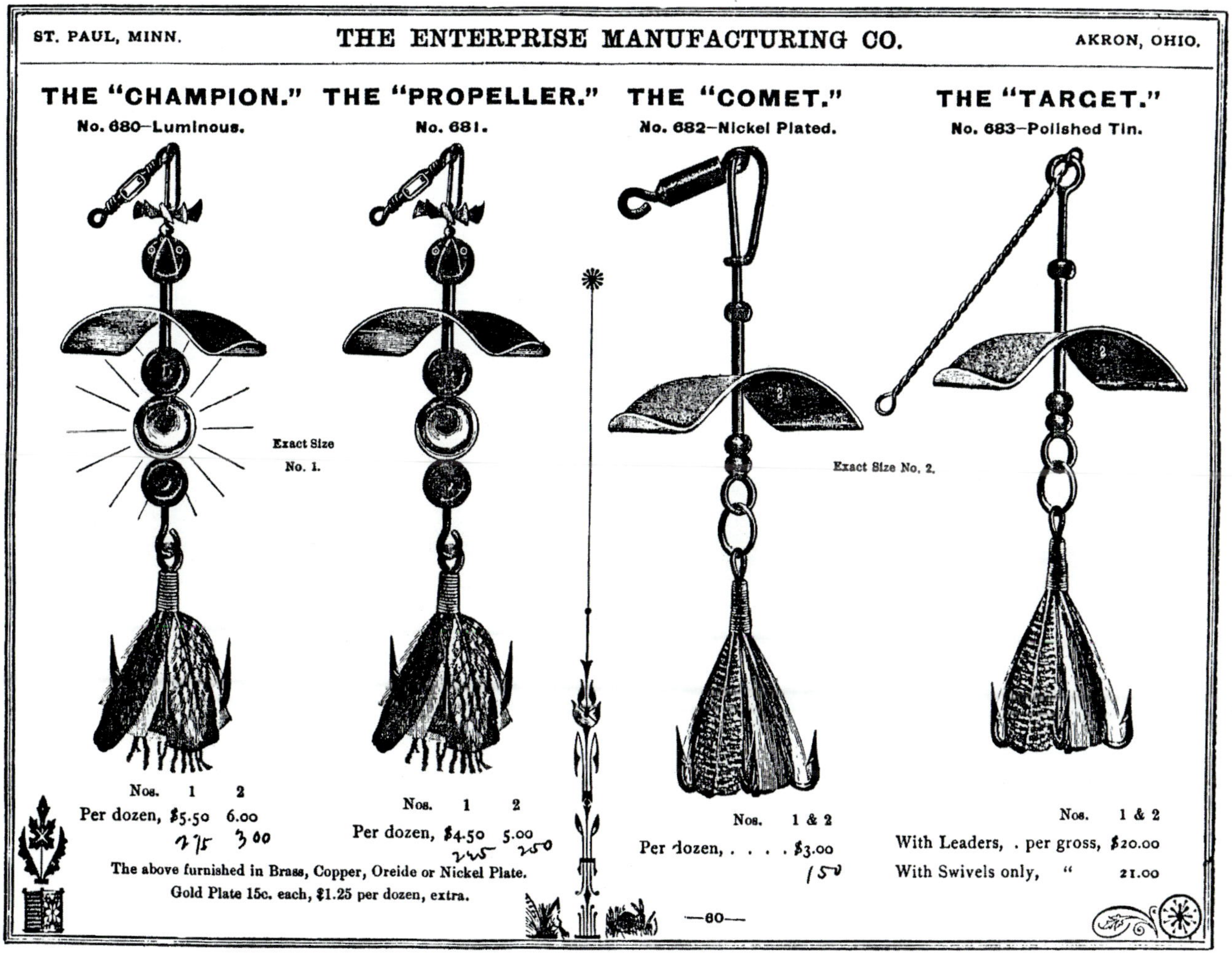

ST. PAUL, MINN. THE ENTERPRISE MANUFACTURING CO. AKRON, OHIO.

THE "CHAMPION." No. 680—Luminous.

THE "PROPELLER." No. 681.

THE "COMET." No. 682—Nickel Plated.

THE "TARGET." No. 683—Polished Tin.

Exact Size No. 1.

Exact Size No. 2.

Nos. 1 2
Per dozen, $5.50 6.00
2 75 3 00

Nos. 1 2
Per dozen, $4.50 5.00
2 25 2 50

The above furnished in Brass, Copper, Oreide or Nickel Plate.
Gold Plate 15c. each, $1.25 per dozen, extra.

Nos. 1 & 2
Per dozen, ... $3.00
1 50

Nos. 1 & 2
With Leaders, . per gross, $20.00
With Swivels only, " 21.00

—60—

B.

A. An early example of the "Beaded Bait." This one has the very attractive Clover Leaf blade design. Note the small red glass bead above the blade. $250.00 – 350.00.

B. These lures were introduced between 1886 – 1887 and 1892. The illustration is a reduced page from the 1892 catalog. They were gone after the 1895 – 1896 season.

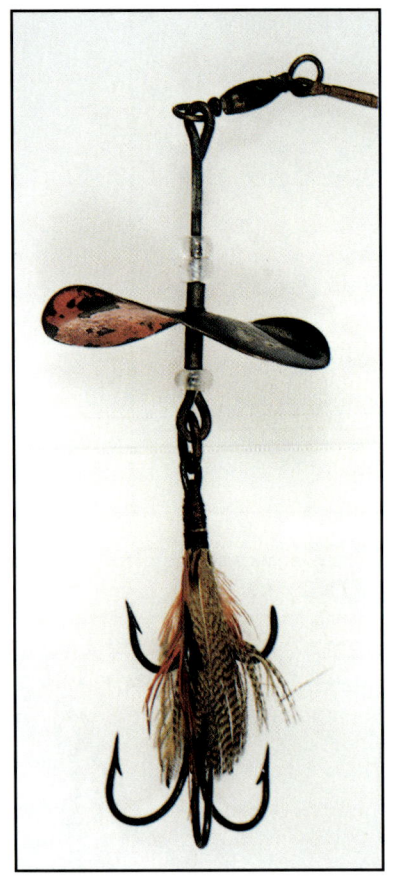

A.

B.

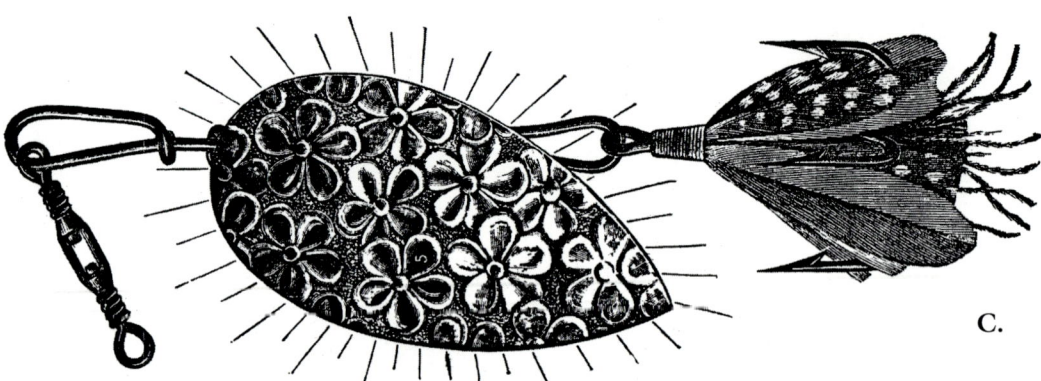

C.

A. The "Target." The hooks have probably been changed. $250.00 – 350.00.

B. The "Propeller." This lure is missing the Clover Leaf spinner on the top. The Clover Leaf spinner was very fragile and is seldom found. $350.00 – 500.00.

C. The "Minne-Ha-Ha Spoon." This spoon was introduced between 1886 – 1887 and 1892. The above shows a cut from the 1892 catalog. Note that the eye of the blade is at the large end. The non-luminous version was called the "Merrimac." A cheaper, nickel plated model, with an inexpensive swivel, was called the "Cayuga" spoon. A polished tin version, with a leader instead of a swivel, was called the "Kenosha." All models were available in 12 sizes. They were unavailable after the 1895 – 1896 season but show up again in the 1900 catalog as the "Montreal" baits. By then the "Kenosha" had been dropped from the line. $250.00 – 350.00.

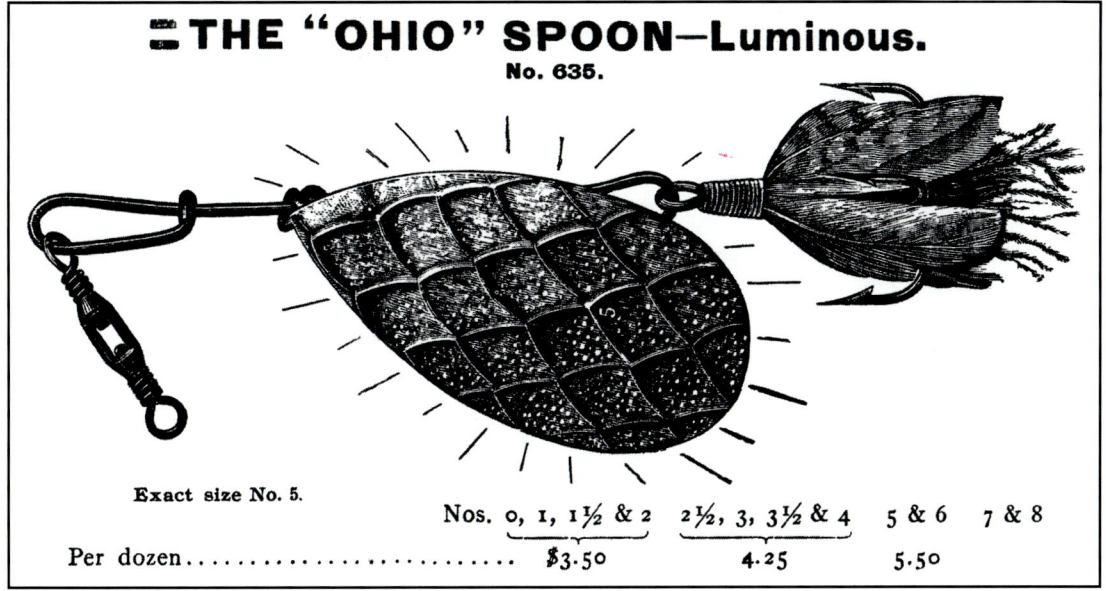

A.

A The luminous "Ohio" spoon. This was added to the line sometime between 1887 and 1892. The cut above is from the 1892 catalog. A non-luminous version was called the "Paragon" spoon. Two lesser quality versions were made: the "Conqueror," which had a less expensive swivel, and the "Dominion," which was equipped with a wire leader. The Conqueror was nickel plated, and the Dominion was polished tin. By 1895 – 1896, there were called "Pflueger's Fine Egg Shape Baits." The Conqueror had been renamed the "Oval, second quality." They were all missing from the 1897 and 1898 catalogs, but reappear in 1900. The 1895 – 1896 catalog states that the Ohio and the Paragon were available in the following patterns: Hammered, Clover Leaf, Fish Scale, and plain metal. From 1894 on, they are shown with the patent clevis. All of the above lures were referred to as "fast motion baits."

B. Two large muskey sized "Ohio" spoons with a "Royal Ball" spoon between. More about the Royal Ball spoon later. $350.00 – 500.00.

B.

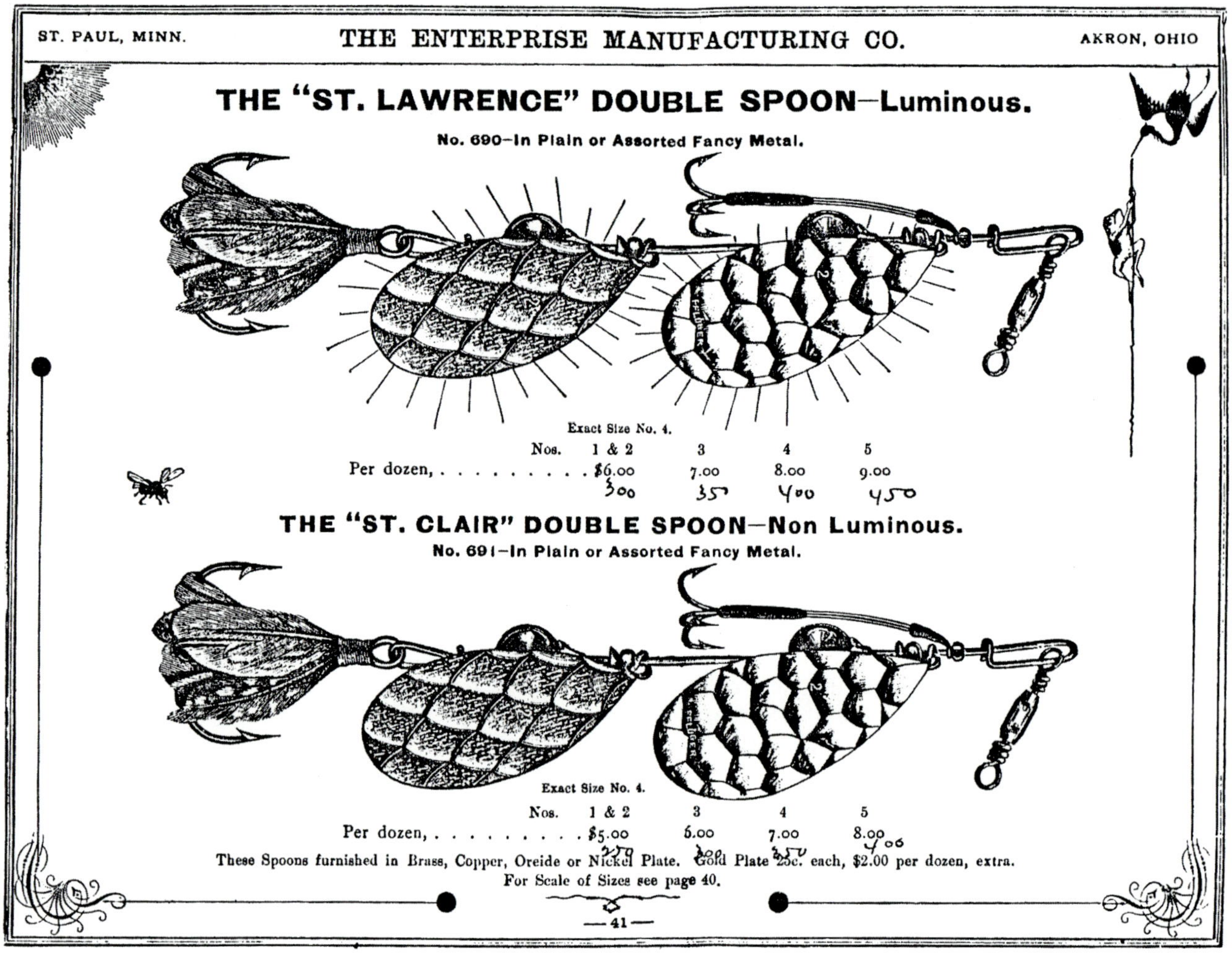

ENTERPRISE MFG. CO.

THE ENTERPRISE MANUFACTURING CO.
ST. PAUL, MINN. — AKRON, OHIO

THE "ST. LAWRENCE" DOUBLE SPOON — Luminous.
No. 690 — In Plain or Assorted Fancy Metal.

Exact Size No. 4.

Nos.	1 & 2	3	4	5
Per dozen,	$6.00	7.00	8.00	9.00

THE "ST. CLAIR" DOUBLE SPOON — Non Luminous.
No. 691 — In Plain or Assorted Fancy Metal.

Exact Size No. 4.

Nos.	1 & 2	3	4	5
Per dozen,	$5.00	6.00	7.00	8.00

These Spoons furnished in Brass, Copper, Oreide or Nickel Plate. Gold Plate 25c. each, $2.00 per dozen, extra.
For Scale of Sizes see page 40.

— 41 —

A.

A. A page (reduced) from the 1892 catalog. These lures were added to the line sometime between 1887 and 1892. They continued in the line through 1900 and were made in five sizes. In 1900, six sizes were available. The patented clevis was added in 1894.

B. The "St. Lawrence" double spoon. $175.00 – 200.00 (upper); $100.00 – 150.00 (lower).

B.

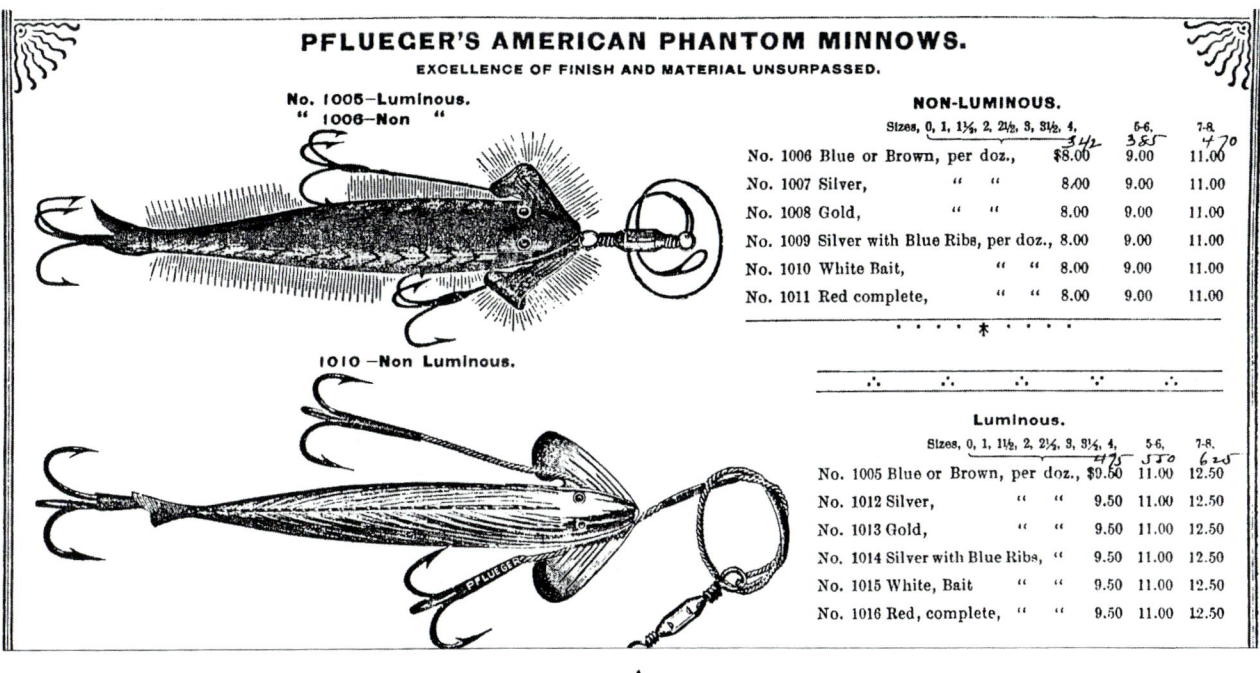

A.

A. Pflueger's American Phantom Minnows. The cut is from the 1892 catalog. The American Phantoms were listed continuously through 1900. They were available in 12 sizes and 12 color combinations. In 1895 – 1896, a series of porpoise hide and sole skin phantoms were introduced. These were also available in 12 sizes and 12 color combinations, including luminous and non-luminous. They were designated as the 1300 series, and numbered 1300 to 1311. The 1300 series does not appear in the 1897 or 1898 catalog, but they reappear as the "Indestructible Phantom Minnows" in the 1900 catalog. These were made of extra thick silk and were warranted not to crack or peel. That year also saw the introduction of a second grade Phantom made in six non-luminous colors. These were listed as the 1400 series and numbered 1410 to 1415.

B. Pflueger's American Phantom Minnows. $25.00 – 35.00.

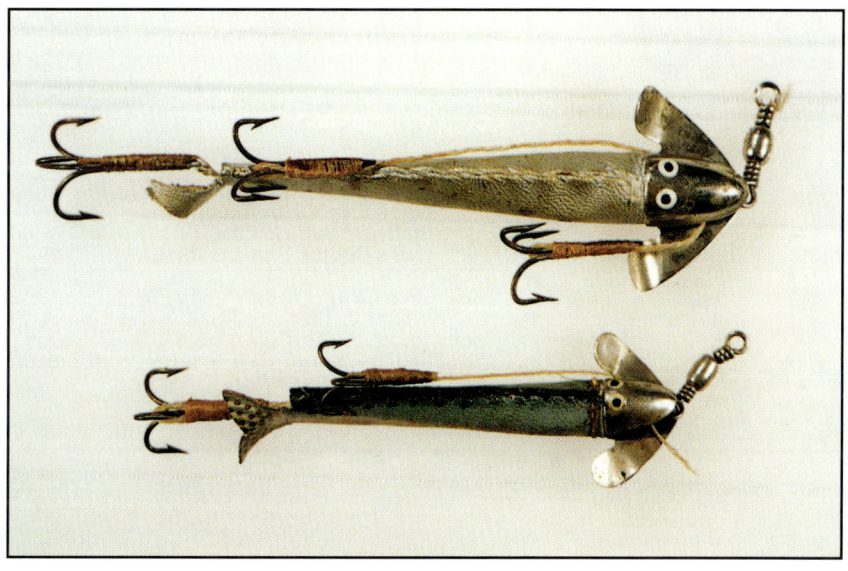

B.

ENTERPRISE MFG. CO.

Pflueger's Phantom Spinners
A Killing Combination for All Game Fish.

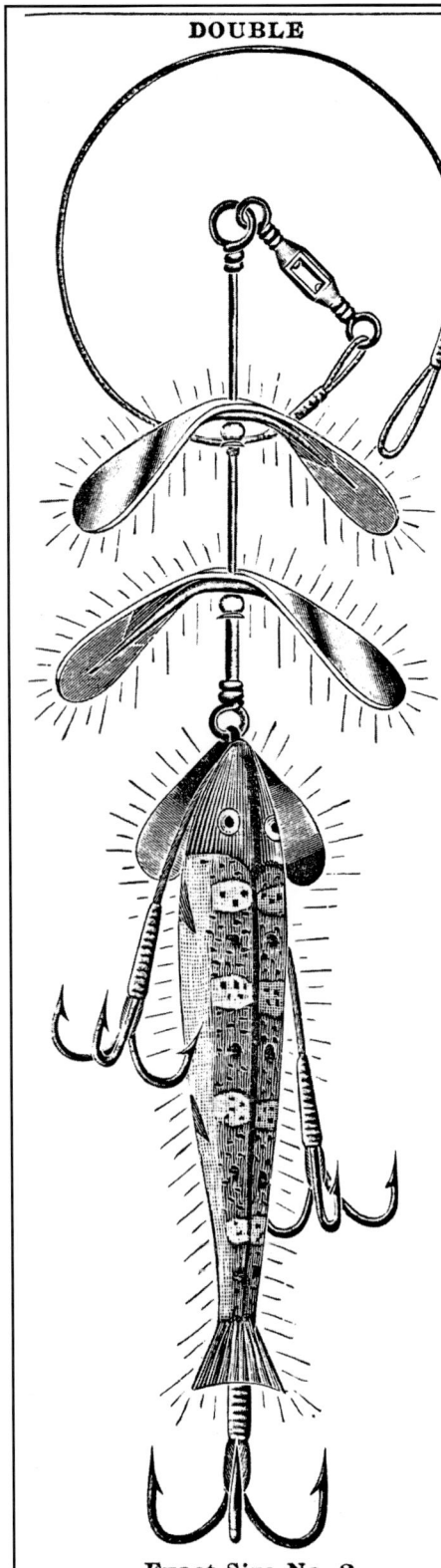

Exact Size No. 2

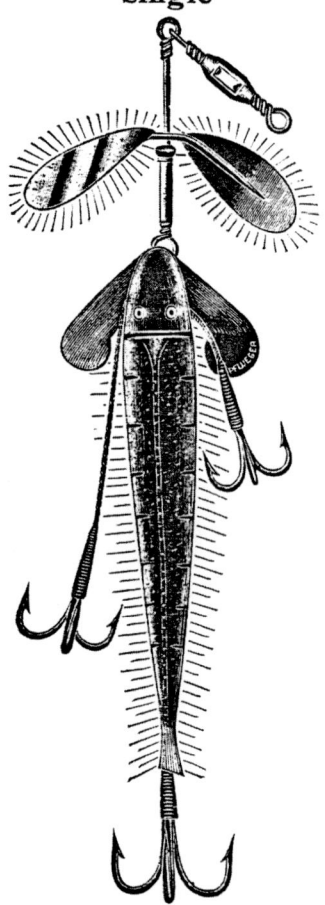

Single

Exact Size No. 1

Minnows made of best-quality silk, painted true to life. This Spinner has all of the merits of the Phantom Minnow and our celebrated Akron Spinner, combined. The double Phantom Spinner is especially killing; the blades revolving opposite to each other over the Phantom, make an attraction which game fish cannot resist.

	Size......	1	2
No. 1019—	Single Luminous..........Per dozen	$8 30	$10 55
" 1020—	Single Non-Luminous.... " "	6 85	8 40
" 1021—	Double Luminous .... " "	9 65	11 80
" 1022—	Double Non-Luminous... " "	7 90	9 45

For Gimp Leaders add $1.00 net per gross extra.
Spinner Blades furnished either Nickel, Brass or Gilt at same price. Unless specified will send Nickel.
Packed—Sewed on a Bronze Printed Card; one Bait in a box, six boxes in a carton.

The "Pflueger Phantom Spinner." This bait first appears in the 1897 catalog as a single only. The 1900 issue shows the addition of a double spinner.

ENTERPRISE MFG. CO.

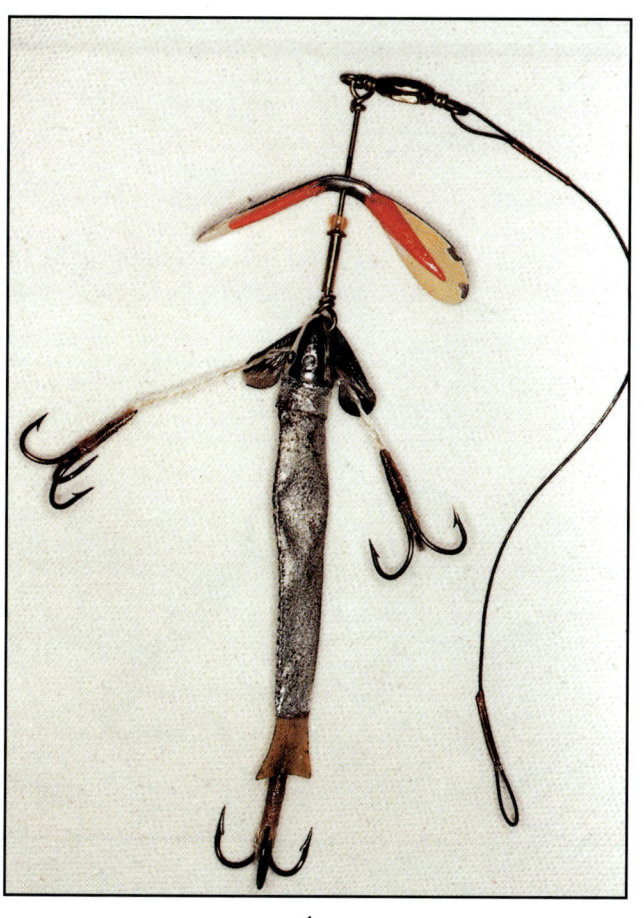

A.

B.

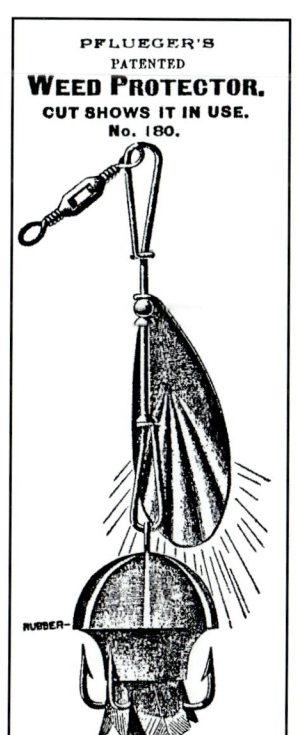

C.

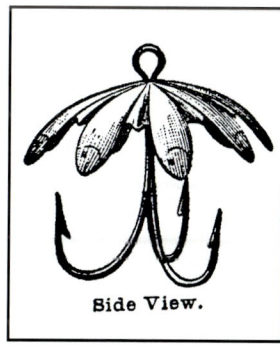

D.

A. The single "Pflueger Phantom Spinner." $100.00 – 150.00.

B. Two interesting lures made by Pflueger. Probably experimental. The one on the left has what appears to be the head of a Flying Helgramite. They both closely resemble a later Pflueger Co. lure called the "Red Devil." No value established.

C. Rubber weed protector. This device was manufactured under Patent No. 432,436. Ernest Pflueger was granted this patent on July 15, 1890. The cut shown is from the 1892 catalog.

D. In 1894, a new type of protector was made available, replacing the No. 180. This protector was made in both a minnow and a feather pattern. It was continued in the line through 1900.

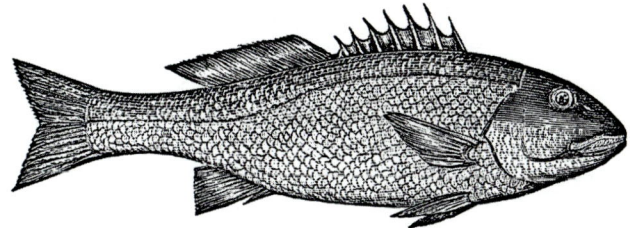

THE RED SNAPPER.—*Lutjanus aya.*

161

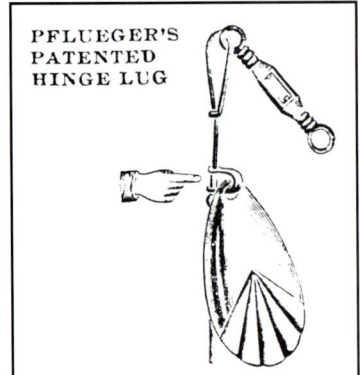

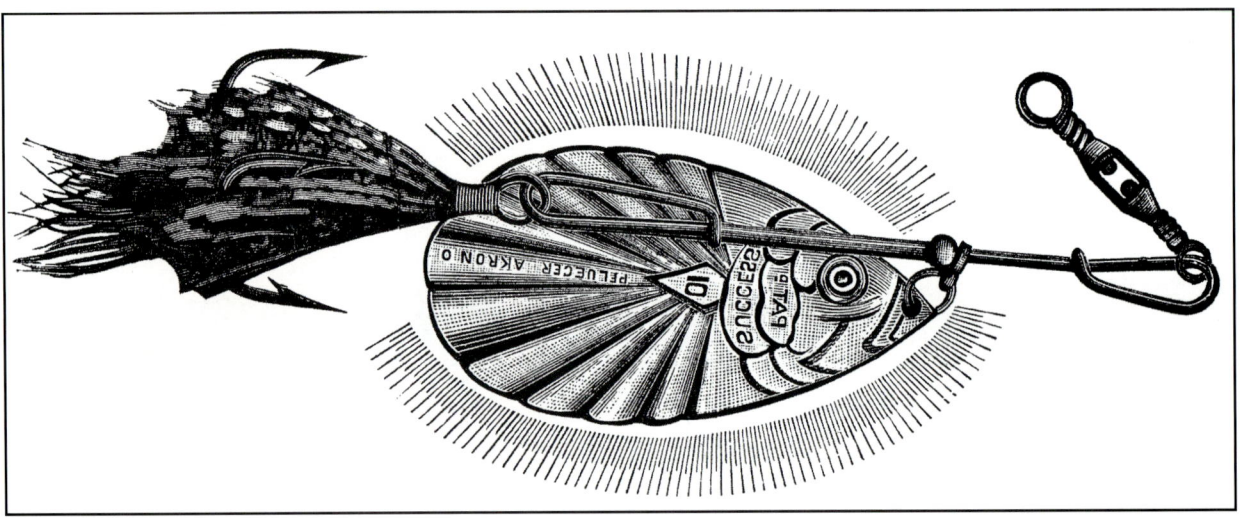

A. A cut from the 1892-93 catalog illustrating the luminous "Success" spoon. A non-luminous version was called the "Clipper." Another model, designated the No. 135, was nickel plate on the convex side and copper on the concave side. Note the hinge lug on this bait. It consists of a split ring attached to the blade, and that, in turn, is attached to a figure-eight-shaped connector slid onto the shaft. This unique attachment is found only in the 1892 – 1893 catalog. I have never seen this attachment in use on a lure.

B. Subsequent catalogs illustrate the hinge as shown in the corner inset above. The 1900 catalog points out the addition of a small tube between the lips of the lug (clevis) to prevent squashing. The No. 135 does not appear in the line after 1896. By 1900, the "Clipper" was described as being nickel plated with a red painted reverse side. 1900 also saw the addition of No. 143; a lure similar to the Clipper but of second quality. All of the above lures were also furnished (after 1894) in copper, brass, and oriede. Gold plate was 15 cents extra. They were made in twelve sizes.

C. Example of the "Success" spoon using a later type clevis. $50.00 – 75.00.

A. The luminous "Pirate" spoon. This lure was introduced between 1887 and 1892. A non-luminous version was called the "Royal Ball" spoon. These spoons were made in 12 sizes. The patented hinge lug was introduced in 1894. The 1895 – 1896 catalog lists the "Egg Ball Bait," a second quality lure. By 1900, the "Kidney Ball Bait" had been added to the line. This lure has a kidney-shaped blade and was available in luminous and nickel plate with red paint on the concave side. This bait was also made in a second quality version. All were also available (after 1894) in brass, copper, and oriede, with gold 15 cents extra. The lure in the photograph has the "shell" design. $350.00 – 500.00.

B. Cut from the 1892 – 1893 catalog. This bait is in the hammered finish.

A.

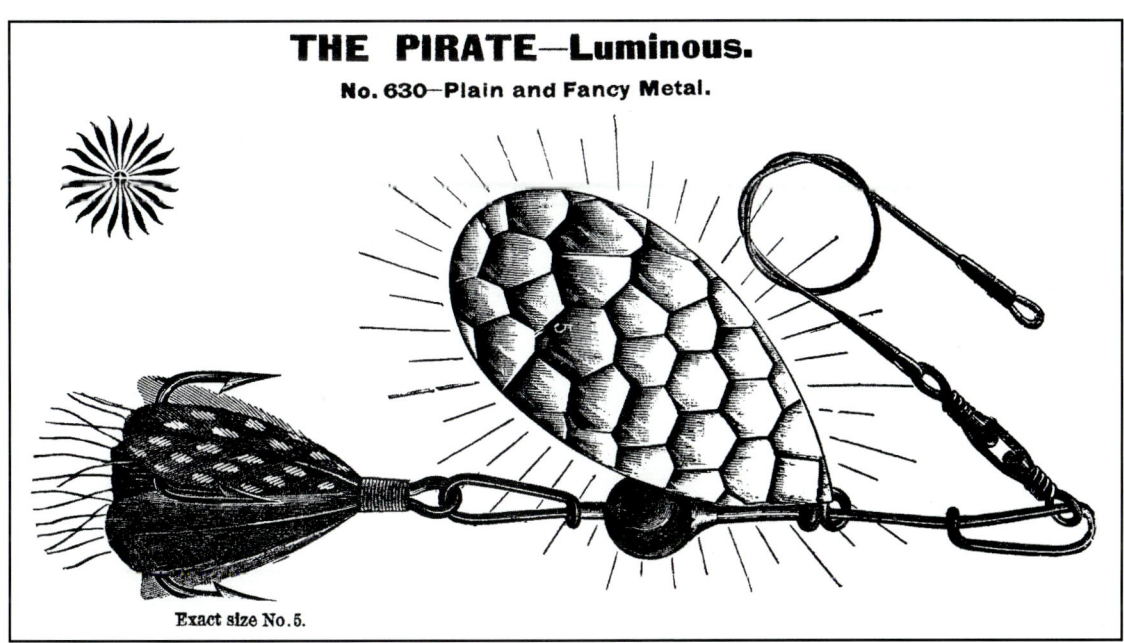

B.

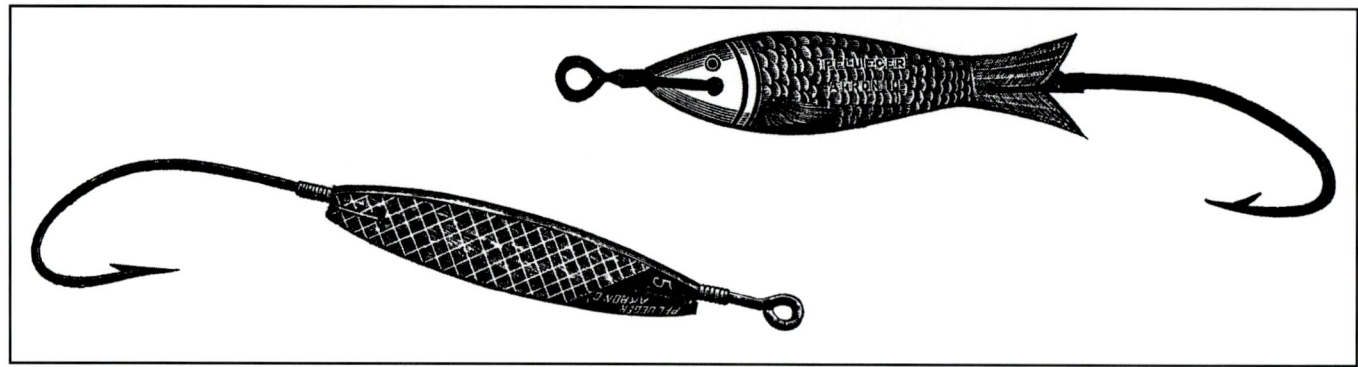

A.

A. Left: The "Figured Pearl Squid." This lure was introduced between 1887 and 1892. It was made in five sizes and was available in white or stained. It was not listed after 1896. No value established. Right: The "Pearl Minnow Squid." This lure was introduced between 1887 and 1892. It was made in five sizes and was available in white or stained. It was not listed after 1896. No value established.

B. "Allen's Patented Abalone Bait." This lure had a pearl blade. It was introduced between 1890 and 1892. The 1892 catalog states that the Enterprise Manufacturing Co. was the exclusive agent for this bait. It was gone from the line by 1893. It probably duplicated the "Fine Mottled Pearl Spoon," a lure that survived until after 1900. The Allen's Bait was made in 12 sizes and finished in luminous, red paint on one side, and pearl on both sides. Note the figure eight hinge used in 1892. This patent had been assigned to Edward T. Allen by H. E. Skinner of San Francisco, Ca. Enterprise evidently obtained the rights to produce the bait from Allen. $150.00 – 250.00.

C. The "Plain Pearl Squids." These lures were listed by 1892. They were made in five sizes and were available in white and stained. They were listed through 1900. $20.00 – 30.00.

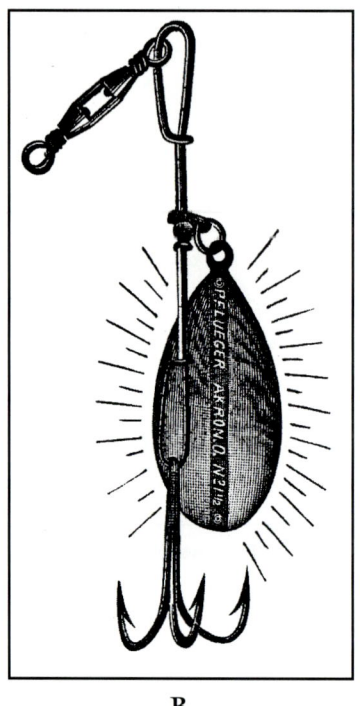

B.

C.

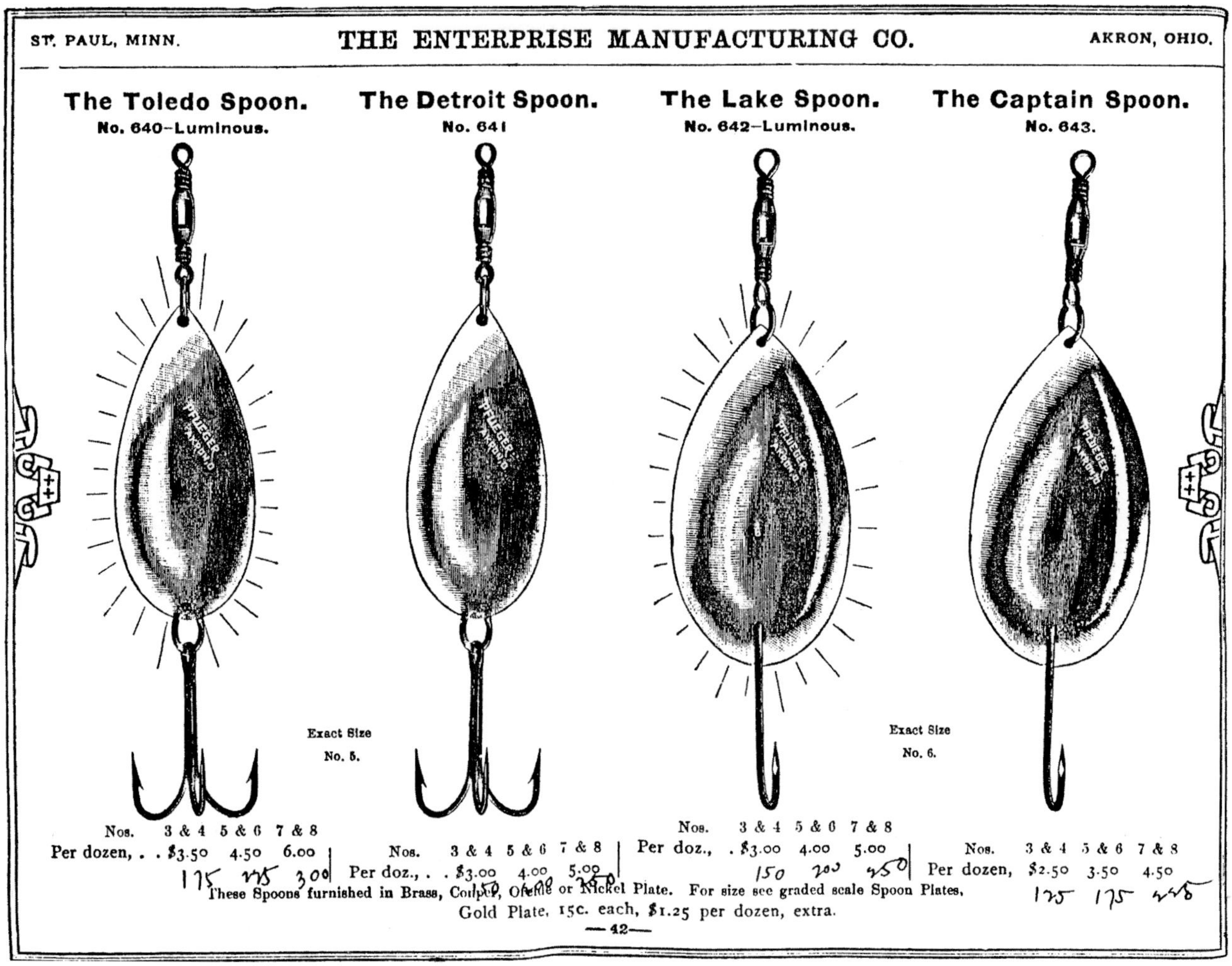

ENTERPRISE MFG. CO.

THE ENTERPRISE MANUFACTURING CO.
ST. PAUL, MINN. AKRON, OHIO.

The Toledo Spoon.
No. 640—Luminous.

The Detroit Spoon.
No. 641

The Lake Spoon.
No. 642—Luminous.

The Captain Spoon.
No. 643.

Exact Size No. 5.

Exact Size No. 6.

Nos.   3 & 4   5 & 6   7 & 8
Per dozen, . . $3.50   4.50   6.00

Nos.   3 & 4   5 & 6   7 & 8
Per doz., . . $3.00   4.00   5.00

Nos.   3 & 4   5 & 6   7 & 8
Per doz., . $3.00   4.00   5.00

Nos.   3 & 4   5 & 6   7 & 8
Per dozen, $2.50   3.50   4.50

These Spoons furnished in Brass, Copper, Or Nickel Plate. For size see graded scale Spoon Plates, Gold Plate, 15c. each, $1.25 per dozen, extra.

—42—

A.

A. Page (reduced) from the 1892 catalog. These lures were introduced sometime between 1887 and 1892. They are all listed until 1897. In 1897, the "Toledo" and "Detroit" spoons were replaced with the "Imperial Spoon." The Imperial is shaped exactly like the Toledo and Detroit and was available in luminous and non-luminous. The Imperial was manufactured through 1900. The "Captain" and the "Lake" spoons were also made through 1900. The Toledo, Detroit, Lake, and Captain were made in six sizes. The Imperial was made in eight sizes. $20.00 – 30.00 each.

B. The "Cyuga Lake" spoon. This spoon was introduced between 1887 and 1892. It was made in four sizes and came in eight different finishes, including luminous. It is similar to the Lake and Captain spoon, but of a more slender design. It was made through 1900. $20.00 – 30.00.

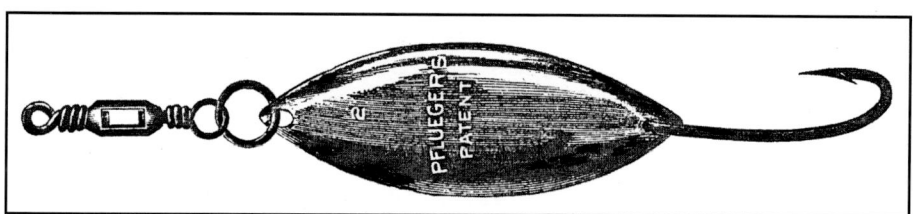

B.

165

ENTERPRISE MFG. CO.

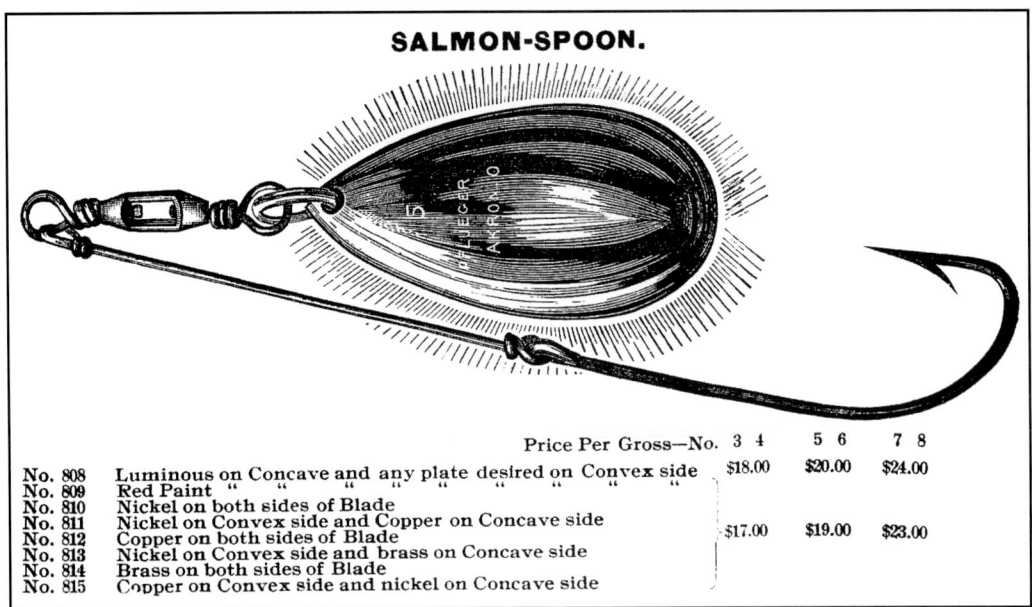

A.

A. The "Salmon-Spoon." This lure was introduced between 1887 and 1892. It was made in six sizes and a variety of finishes including luminous. It was listed through 1900. $25.00 – 50.00.

B. Pflueger's "Skittering-Spoon." This bait was introduced between 1887 and 1892. It originally came in six sizes, but after 1894, it was available in 10. It came in numerous finishes including luminous. The word "skittering" refers to a method of fishing whereby the lure is jerked or drawn along the top of the water. $15.00 – 25.00.

C. Cut is from an 1875 book by Genio C. Scott titled, *Fishing in American Waters*. Genio says, "The angler should use a rod of from 13 to 15 feet long, flexible, but strong. Stand near the bow of your punt, and skitter the lure along the surface of the water, near the margins of the lily-pads." The "Skittering-Spoon" was in the line through 1900.

B.

C.

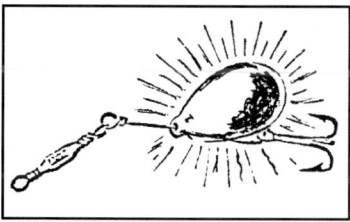

A.

Photo courtesy of the Tom Penniston collection.

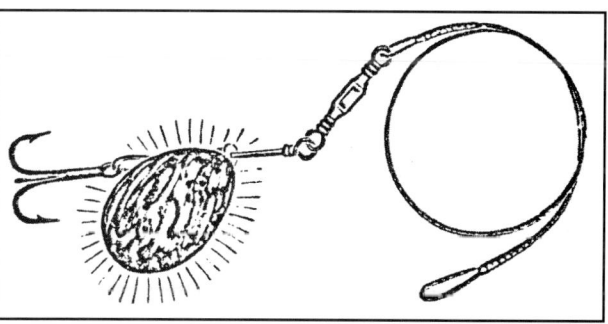

B.

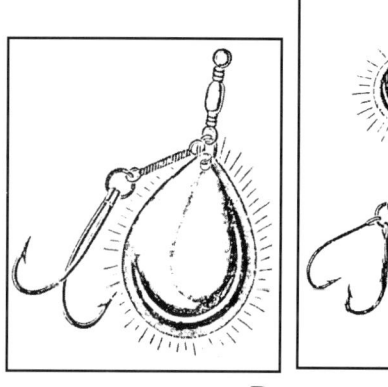

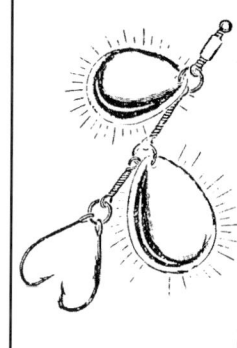

D.

A. A group of 19th century anglers with their long three-piece skittering rods. A fine looking group. Photo courtesy of the Tom Penniston collection.

B. The "Pearl Emeric Spinner." This lure came in six sizes and was available with luminous paint on the concave side and pearl on the convex or pearl both sides. It was made of the highest quality pearl shell (abalone). The line tie was riveted to the shell blade. $15.00 – 25.00.

C. The "Original Emeric Spinner." The Emeric was made in both 1st and 2nd quality. The 1st quality came in luminous with a gut leader. The 2nd quality was not available with luminous paint and it had no gut leader. Both qualities were made with a combination of silver, nickel and copper finishes. $10.00 – 20.00.

D. The "Western Bait." This bait was made in seven sizes and came in luminous and non-luminous paint. It came in a combination of silver, brass, copper, and nickel finishes. They also made a double Western Bait in the same finishes. $10.00 – 20.00 each.

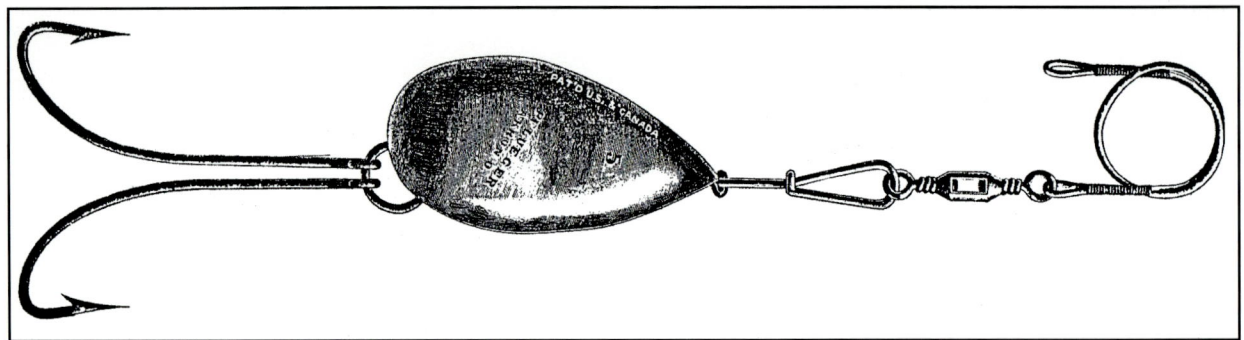

A.

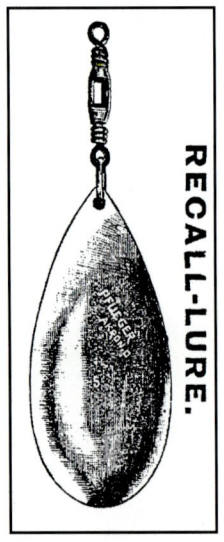

B.

C.

A. The "Commodore" spoon. This lure was introduced between 1887 and 1892. It was originally available in nine sizes and came in eight different finishes, including luminous. It was still listed in 1900, but by then was made in only six sizes. $20.00 – 40.00.

B. The "Recall-Lure." This lure made its debut between 1887 and 1892. It was made in six sizes and was available in eight different finishes, including luminous. In the 1895 – 1896 catalog, its name was changed to the "Puget Sound Bait," a name it retained through 1900. $20.00 – 30.00.

C. Pflueger's "Fine Fluted Spoon." This lure entered the line between 1887 and 1892. It is an exact duplicate of G. M. Skinner's Fluted Spoon. Skinner's bait was patented in 1874, so it is probable that his patent had expired before Pflueger's was marketed. Many of the trade houses during this period also carried a line of Skinner look-alikes. The "Fine Fluted Spoon" was originally made in 12 sizes and available in four finishes. The 1892 – 1893 catalog shows the blade with a soldered eye, but by 1894, it was made with the patented hinge lug (clevis). 1895 – 1896 saw the introduction of second, third, and fourth quality lures. The first quality lures were luminous and non-luminous nickel plated but of a lesser quality. Fourth quality lures were made of polished tin. These spoons were made through 1900 and many years thereafter. $10.00 – 15.00.

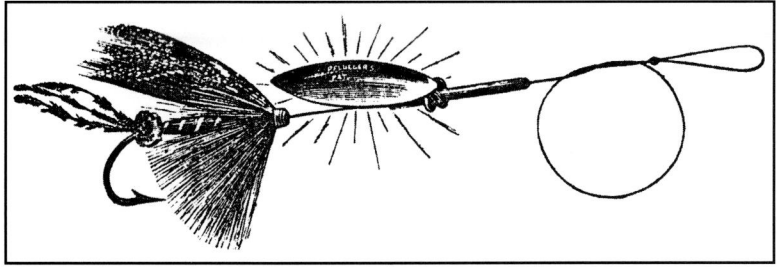

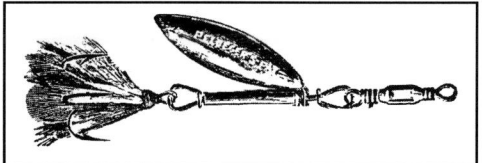

A.

B.

A. The Bass and Trout spinners. These baits were introduced between 1887 and 1892. They were originally made with kidney and egg-shaped blades and were available in luminous and non-luminous. By 1900, they were available in second quality and a number of blade shapes. $30.00 – 40.00.

B. The "Roanoke Spinners." These lures were introduced between 1887 and 1892 and were available in three sizes. They were made with luminous and non-luminous finishes. The 1900 catalog states, "The Roanoke Spinner is one of our oldest and best tried baits." $10.00 – 15.00.

C. A catalog page (reduced in size) from the 1892 catalog. These lures were still available in 1900. $30.00 – 40.00 (Pet); $30.00 – 40.00 (Daisy); $30.00 – 40.00 (Catskill); $10.00 – 20.00 (Sydney); $10.00 – 20.00 (Adirondack).

ST. PAUL, MINN. THE ENTERPRISE MANUFACTURING CO. AKRON, OHIO

Pflueger's Pet Spinner.
Exact Size.

Per Dozen.
No. 208, Luminous..........$4.50
No. 209, Non-Luminous..... 3.50

Pflueger's Daisy Spinner.
Exect Size.

Per Dozen.
No. 200, Luminous $4.25
No. 201, Non-Luminous... 3.25

Pflueger's Catskill Spinner.
Exact Size.

Per Dozen.
No. 206, Luminous..........$4.50
No. 207, Non-Luminous...... 3.50

Pflueger's Sydney Spinner.
Exact Size.

Per Dozen.
No. 202, Luminous..............$3.50
No. 203, Non-Luminous.......... 2.50

Pflueger's Adirondack Spinner.
Exact Size.

Per Dozen.
No. 204, Luminous.........$4.00
No. 205, Non-Luminous.... 3.00

NOTICE. All of the above Spinners are sewn one on a neatly printed card and one dozen Spinners of a pattern in a box.

— 14 —

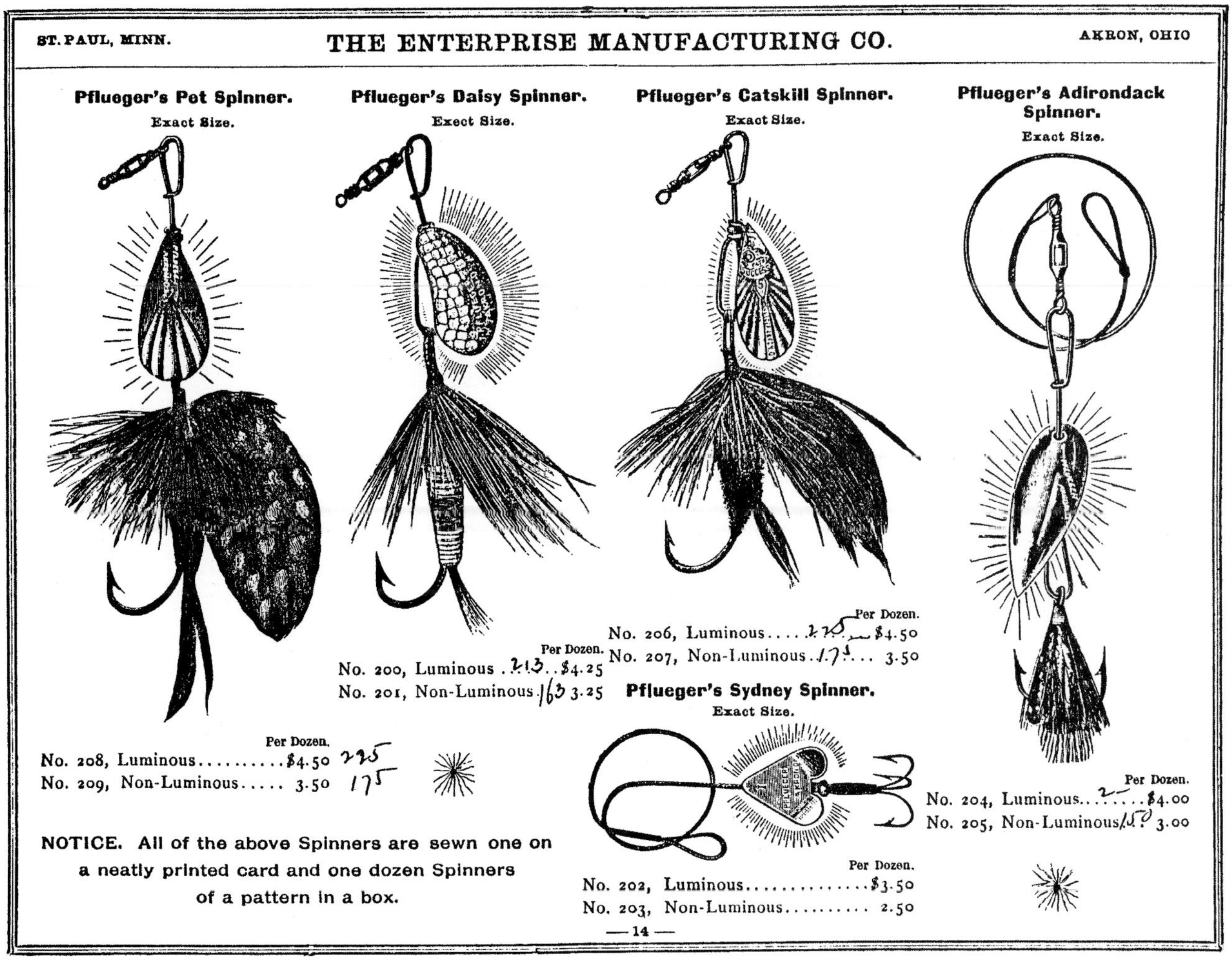

C.

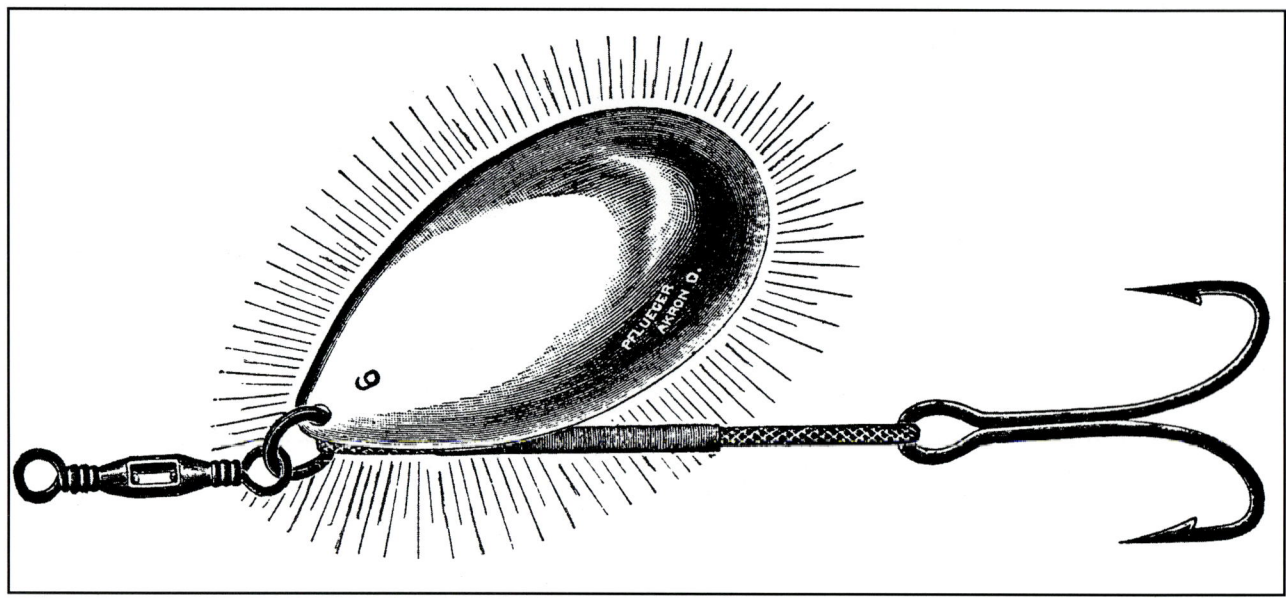

A.

A. Pflueger's "Salmon Troller." This lure is first listed in the 1894 catalog. It was originally made in six sizes and was available in luminous and non-luminous. It has an extra-strong, braided line shaft. In 1895 –1896, it was available in eight different finishes, including luminous. It was in the line through 1900. $25.00 – 40.00.

B. The "Joseph" spoon. This lure was introduced between 1887 and 1892. It was originally made in six sizes and finished in luminous and non-luminous. It has a coil spring on the concave side that keeps the blade away from the shaft. This configuration is similar to a bait patented on July 10, 1883, by Louis Kessler of Ludington, Michigan. Kessler's patent differed from the Joseph spoon mainly in that it used two coil springs instead of one. By 1895 – 1896, it was called the "Perfect Revolving Heart Bait," and was available in a second quality, nickel plated version. It was listed through 1900. $150.00 – 200.00.

B.

ENTERPRISE MFG. CO.

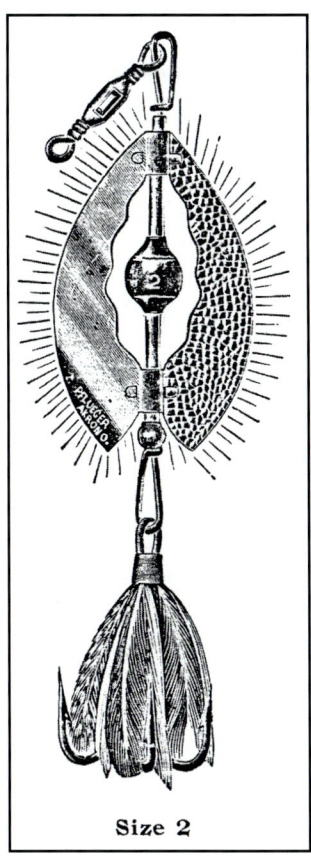

Size 2

A.

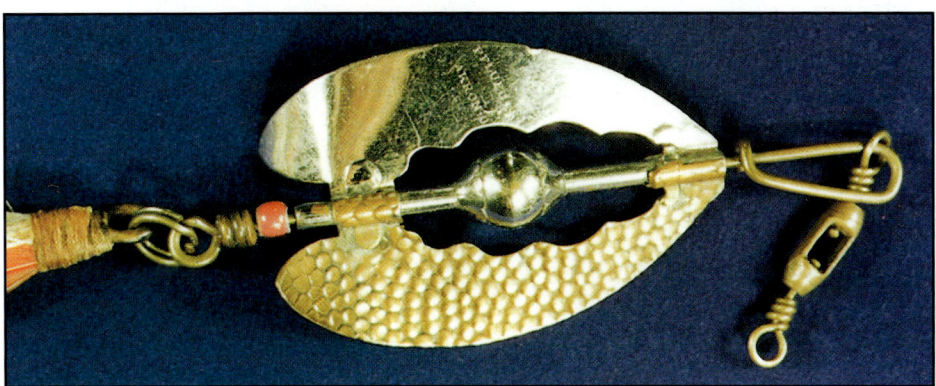

A. Pflueger's "American" spinner. This lure is first listed in the 1894 catalog. John B. McHarg patented the American spinner on Aug. 10, 1886. The Enterprise Co. was probably manufacturing it under a license from McHarg. Pflueger's American Spinner is distinguished from McHarg's by the small tabs that hold the two halves of the blade together. McHarg's were held by a soldered overlap. The American was made in six sizes and was finished in luminous and non-luminous. By 1900, it was available in a second quality. The second quality lure is distinguished by a plain ball in the center and the use of metal washers instead of glass. The American spinner is a beautiful lure. If it were a rare lure, it would be expensive and highly sought after. Top spinner: $50.00 – 75.00; bottom spinner, $25.00 – 35.00.

B. The "Casting Minnow." This bait was introduced between 1887 and 1892. It was available individually as the No. 715 luminous and No. 765 non-luminous, or in the No. 2 Soft Rubber Insect Assortment. By 1895 – 1896, a larger No. 3 had been added. Both lures were listed through 1900. $10.00 – 20.00 each.

C. "Froggie." This lure was introduced between 1887 and 1892. It is listed individually as the No. 713 and was also sold as part of the Soft Rubber Insect Assortment. It was available in luminous and non-luminous. Froggie was listed through 1900. $15.00 – 25.00.

C.

B.

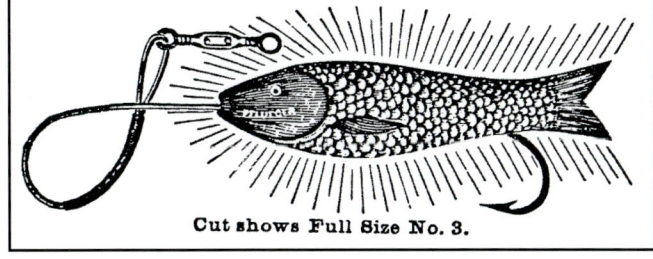

ENTERPRISE MFG. CO.

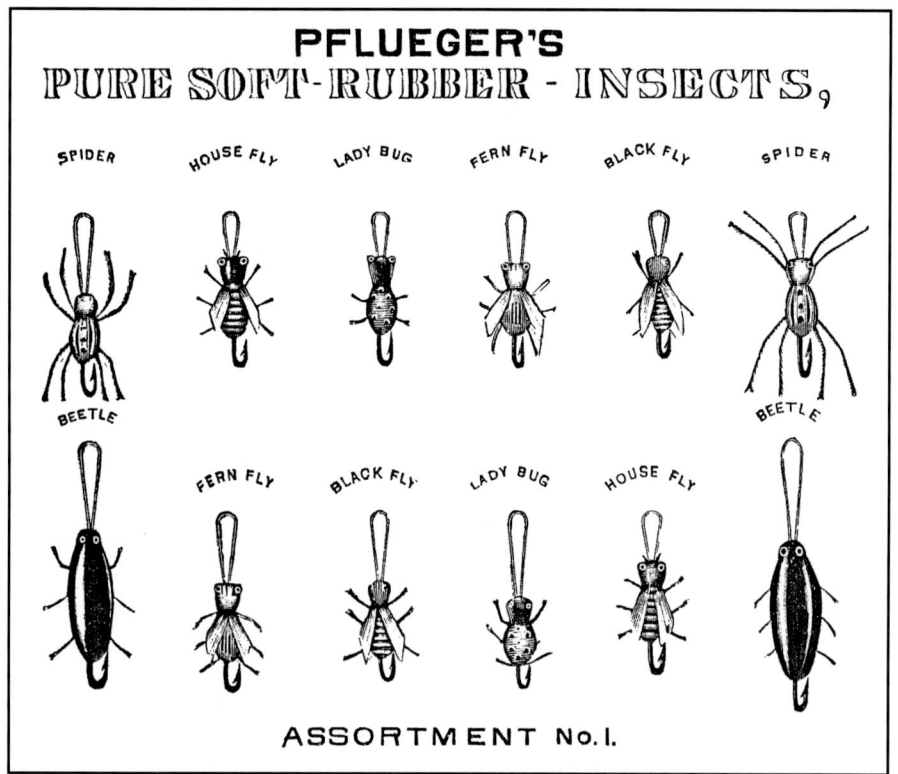

A.

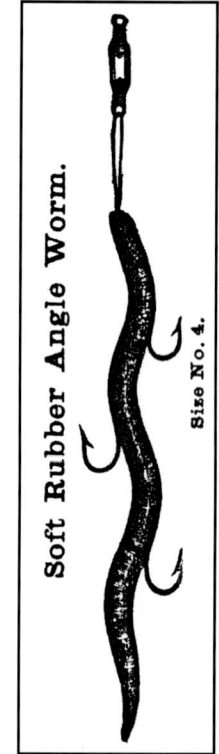

B.

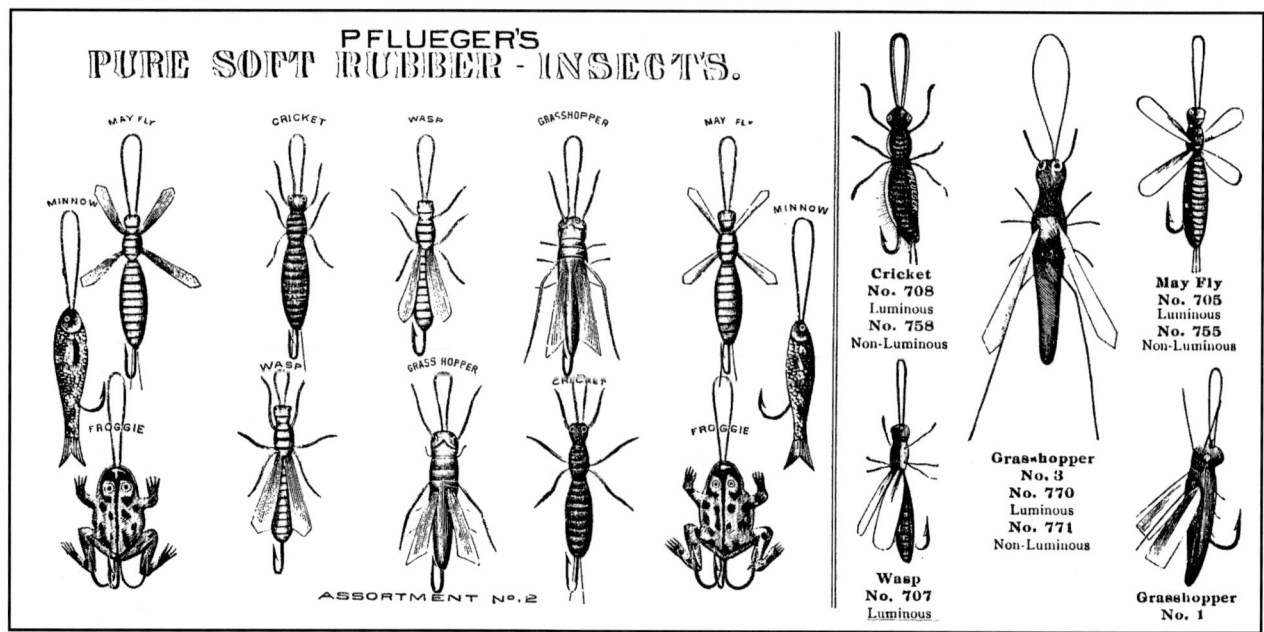

C.

The Soft Rubber Insects were introduced between 1887 and 1892. The Soft Rubber Angleworm is first listed in the 1894 catalog. The insects are listed continuously through 1900. They were available in assortments and individually. The Worm was made in six sizes and was available in luminous and non-luminous. It was listed through 1900. **A.** $5.00 – 10.00 each; **B.** $20.00 – 40.00; **C.** $10.00 – 15.00 each.

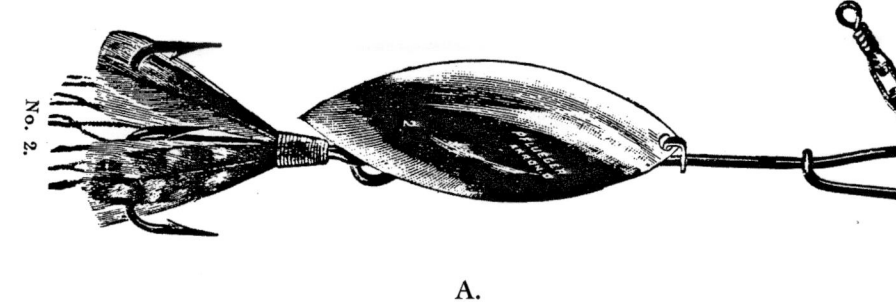

A.

A. The "Muskallonge Spoon." This lure was shown in the 1898 catalog and listed as "recently improved." It was also shown in earlier catalogs as far back as 1894, but always as a part of a boxed set of miscellaneous lures. The first year it was shown as an individual item was 1898. It was made in four sizes and was finished in luminous and non-luminous. It was still available in 1900. $10.00 – 20.00.

B. The "Holt Spoon" made its debut in the 1894 catalog. It was made in three sizes, Nos. 6, 7, and 8, and was furnished with luminous or red paint on the concave side. It was still listed in the 1900 catalog. $20.00 – 40.00.

C. Tacoma Trout Bait. This lure appeared in the 1894 catalog. It was originally made in four sizes, Nos. 1, 1½, 2 and 50. No. 1½ had a single spinner, while Nos. 50, 1, and 2 had double spinners. Size 50 was the smallest and size 2 the largest. In 1895, a No. 70 was added. This lure had double kidney-shaped blades. The addition of a No. 1¾ was also in 1895. This was a medium size between No. 1 and No. 2. By 1900, there was a No. 60 (a small tandem kidney spinner), and a No. 3 (one size larger than the No. 2). These lures were available in luminous and other standard finishes. $10.00 – 20.00.

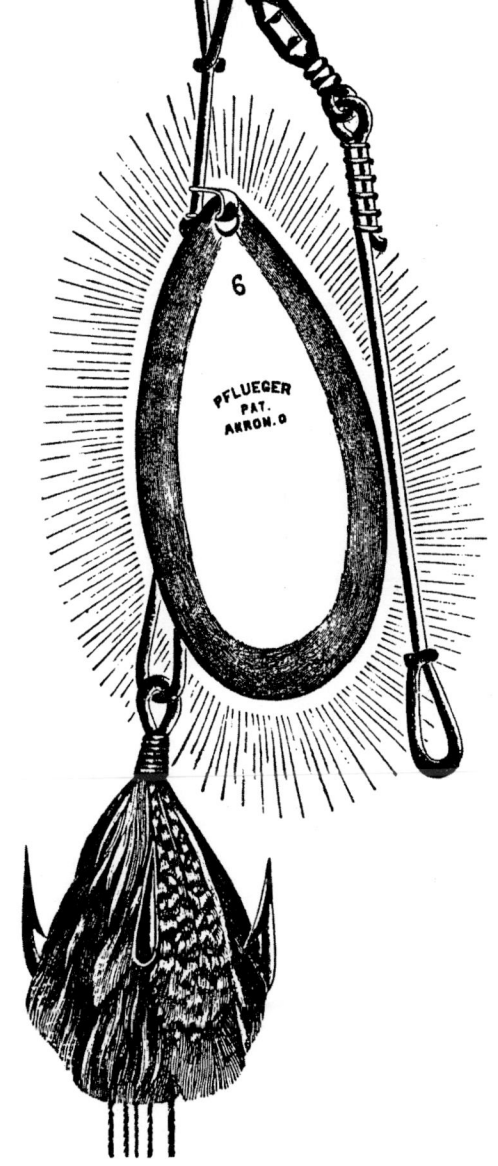

B.

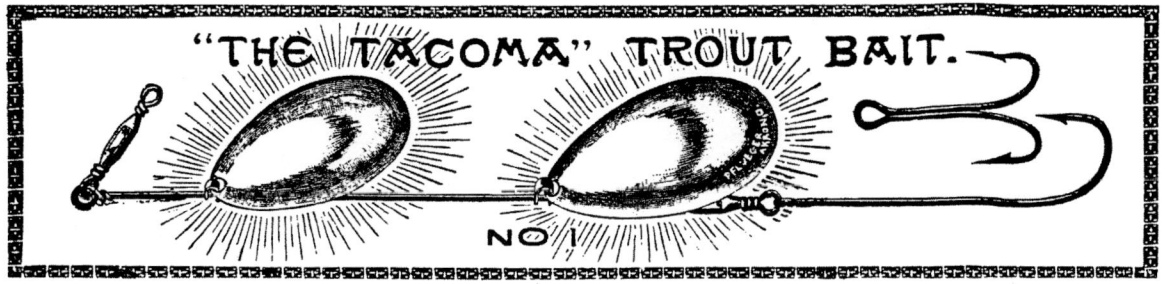

C.

A.

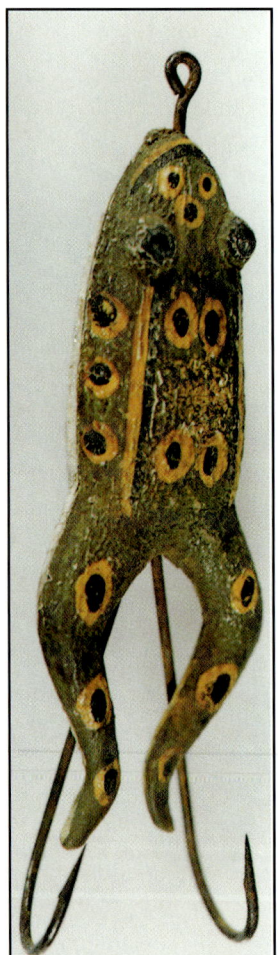

A. "The Floating Meadow Frog." This lure appears in the 1900 catalog. The catalog states that the frog is "improved" which indicates that it probably was available in 1899. It was made in luminous and non-luminous, both supplied with a swivel. The luminous frog was listed as the 774 and the non-luminous as the 775. A swivel on either the floating frog or the sinking version would indicate an early example. $75.00 – 125.00.

B. "Frog No. 3 with Swivel." This is the sinking version. It was also available in luminous and non-luminous. Later versions of this frog are found with the legs secured with thread as on the floating model. The luminous frog was listed as the 766 and the non-luminous as the 767. The cut is from the 1900 catalog. By 1916 this frog was called the "Conrad Frog." This lure was more than likely available in 1899. $50.00 – 75.00.

C. Cut of "The Floating Meadow Frog" from the 1900 catalog.

D. Later version of the 766 frog. $50.00 – 75.00.

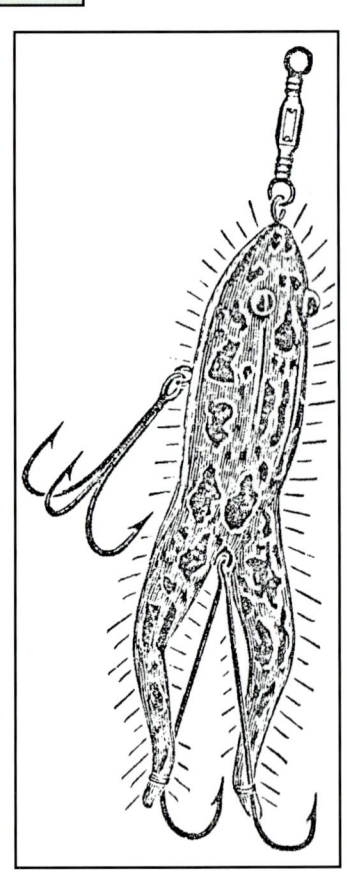

C.

D.

B.

The "Eclipse Spinner." This is a four-bladed lure made to be used with bait such as minnows or worms. It is a combination of hammered and plain metal in three assorted platings, brass, nickel and copper, and came in luminous and non-luminous. It is found in the 1900 catalog. $20.00 – 40.00.

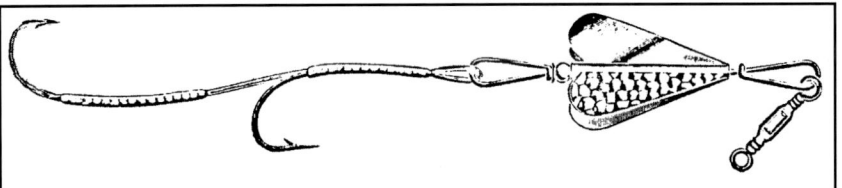

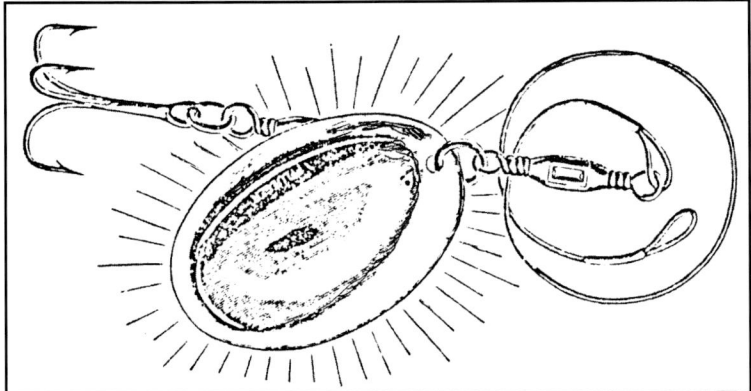

The "Wilson Bait." It is very similar to the Skittering Bait but has a turned-up lip on the fore end that gives it a wobbling motion. It came in 10 sizes and in luminous and non-luminous. Also various combinations of nickel, copper, and brass blades. It was found in the 1900 catalog. $10.00 – 20.00.

The "Bucktail Minnow Spoon." The spoon came in four sizes and could be obtained in either silver, nickel, brass or copper blades and either luminous or non-luminous. $25.00 – 50.00. There was also a "Bucktail Casting Spoon." This was a fluted spoon with a trailing single bucktail dressed treble. It came in three sizes with the blades finished the same as the Bucktail Minnow Spoon. These lures were found in the 1900 catalog.

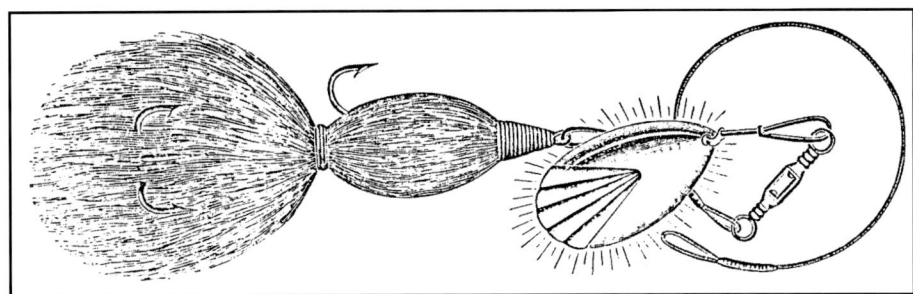

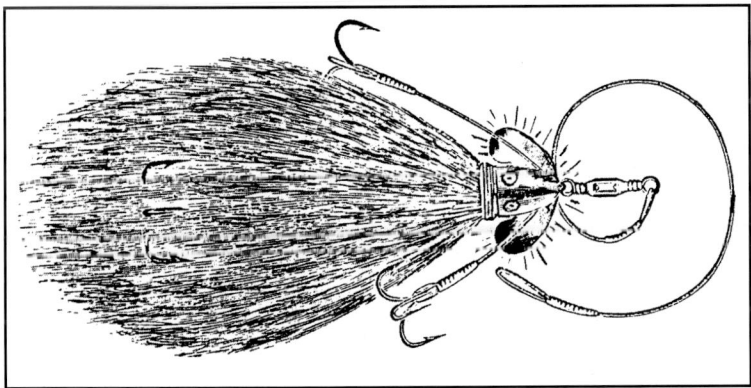

The "Bucktail Phantom Minnow." It came in three sizes and with either a luminous painted head or a nickel plated head. This lure was found in the 1900 catalog. $50.00 – 100.00.

The "Summit Spinner." The ad says "wings are deeply cupped or bowled." It came in two sizes and in luminous and non-luminous paint. Blades were available in combinations of silver, brass, copper, and nickel. This lure was found in the 1900 catalog. $20.00 – 40.00.

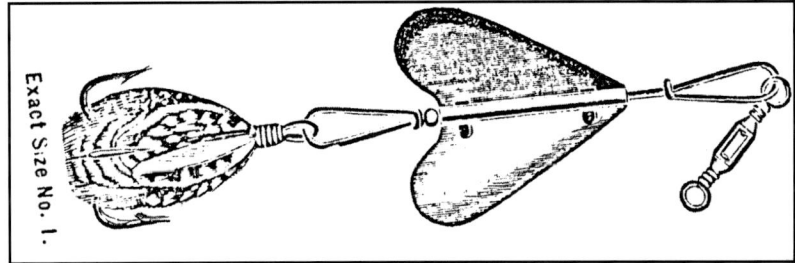

A.

A. Mumford's Safety Hook and Bait Box. This little tin box is done up in typical Victorian style, complete with butterflies and flowers. Note the notches on lower part of the open box. This is to allow access to the box without shearing off the line on the sharp tin lid. They also made a double box with two lids. No value established.

B. "Pflueger's Combination Reel and Line Dryer." The ad says, "Made of well seasoned hard wood and firmly put together. Furnished with a lever brake to be operated with the thumb." It was made in three sizes and four colors: red, green, black, and blue. $100.00 – 200.00.

B.

A. The "Beaded Trolling Spinner." I don't know why they call it the Beaded Trolling Spinner; the only bead on it is the bearing under the blade and that is found on most all spinning baits. It was made in two sizes and furnished with a gut trailer and two hooks. It was available in luminous and red paint $20.00 – 30.00.

B. Believe it or not, a Lake Trout flasher rig from 1900. It was called the "Conger Salmon Trout Spoon." It was made in two sizes and available in luminous and non-luminous. There was also a single-bladed version called the "Salmon Trout Spoon." They both came in a combination of nickel, brass, and copper finishes. No value established.

C. The "Lake Tahoe Spoon." This was a flasher intended to be used with bait. It came without a line tie or hooks. It was available in luminous or red paint and came in two sizes. It was made in brass, nickel, and copper finishes. It was found in the 1900 catalog. $10.00 – 20.00.

D. The "Halcyon Spinner." The catalog description states that this lure has been on the market in Europe for a number of years. It was made in luminous and non-luminous. The body was available in polished gold or silver. The propeller was also made in polished gold or silver. It was found in the 1900 catalog. No value established.

E. The "Cyclone Spinner." This lure closely resembles another lure called the P & S spinner. It came in nine sizes and single or double configuration. It was available with luminous or red paint under the blade. It was also made without paint and could be had in silver, nickel, brass, or copper finish. It was made strung on piano wire or on a solid shaft. It is found in the 1900 catalog. $25.00 – 40.00.

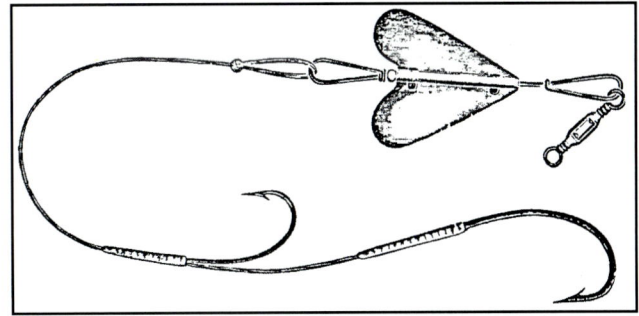

A.

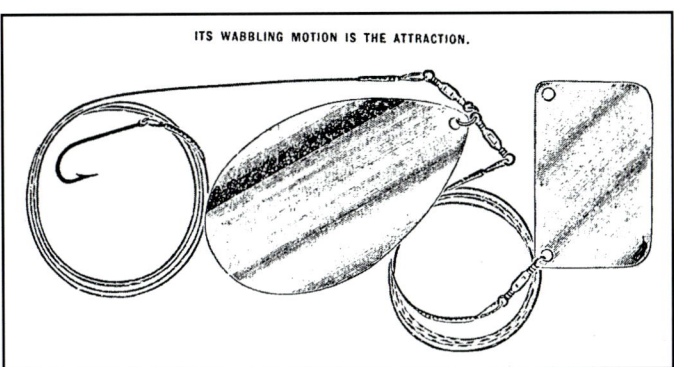

B.

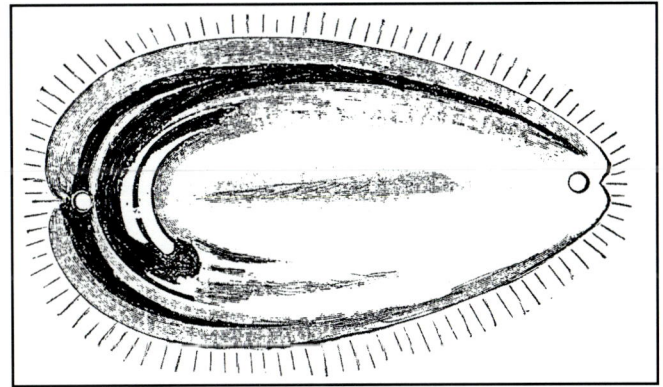

C.

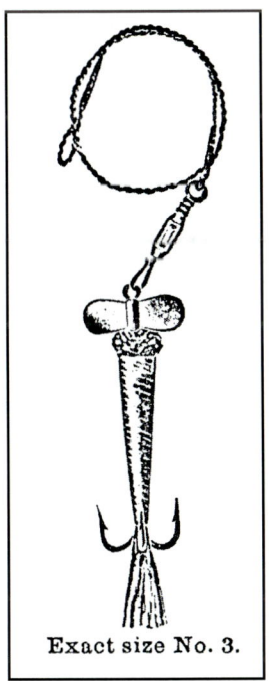

D.

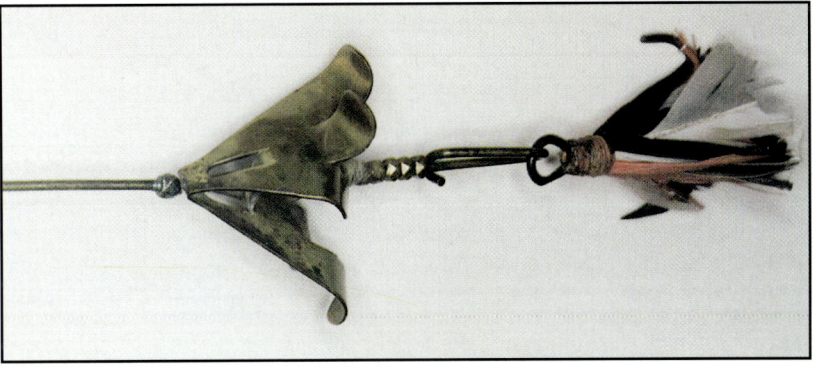

E.

Enterprise Mfg. Co.

Pflueger's Fishing Castle

The latest and most practical invention of the age for enticing all kinds of large, wary game fish. The Castle is made of stained wire netting in two sections, which work on a hinge, and lock with a clasp. The Castle should be charged with live minnows to form an attraction. The lines on the arms of the Castle should be baited with either live minnows, frogs or other natural or artificial bait. The live minnows, swimming in the castle, in their fruitless efforts to escape, attract the fish, who, coming up, will take the baits on the lines.

Supplied with an anchor to hold Castle in a desired place in a tide or running water, also a cork float.

Pflueger patented this contraption on Nov. 7, 1899. It appears in the 1900 catalog. It was sold as a complete kit, consisting of rod, reel, line, and large egg cork float. Prices ranged from $30.00 a dozen to $60.00 a dozen, depending on the quality of the reel and the type of line in the kit. No value established.

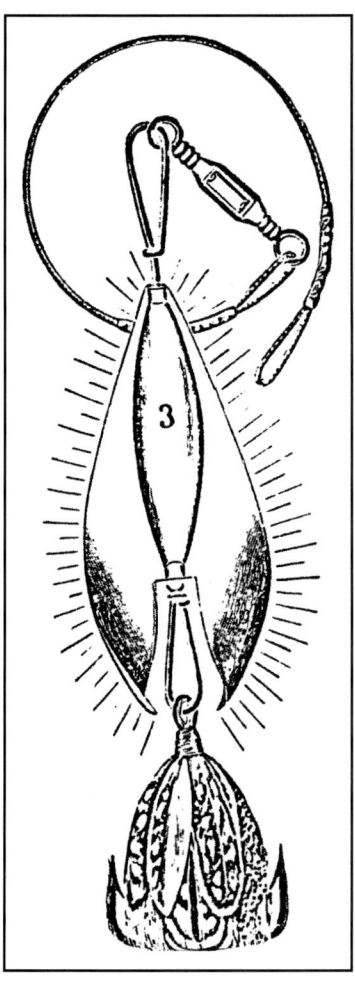

A.

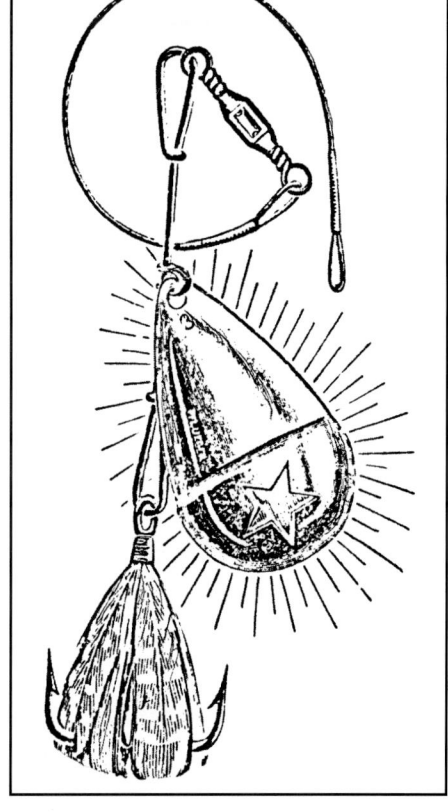

B.

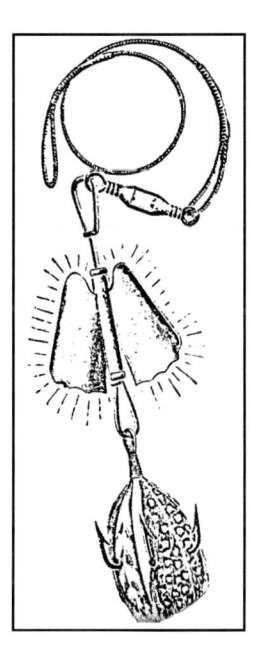

C.

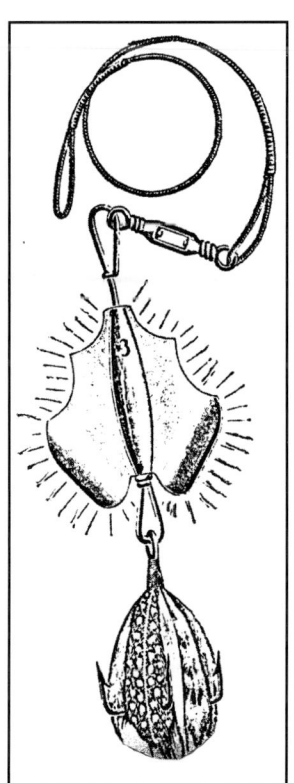

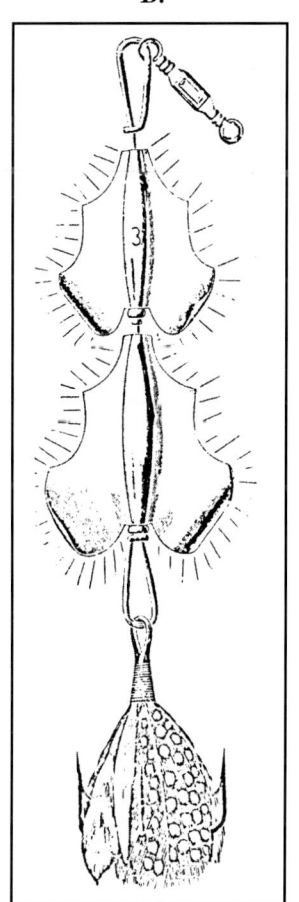

D.

A. The "Whitehall" Spinners. This is an exact copy of the Buel Arrowhead Spinner. It was made in nine sizes and came in first and second quality. It was available with luminous belly and it came in combinations of nickel, silver, and copper finishes. $30.00 – 50.00.

B. The "Star Bait." This is a copy of the Lowe Star Bait. Interestingly the Pflueger Co. bought out the Lowe Co. in 1916 but continued to sell their own Star bait for many years. It was available in nine sizes and could be had with luminous or non-luminous backs. It was made with gold, silver, nickel, and copper finishes. $15.00 – 30.00.

C. The "Buckeye" spinners. This lure is a copy of the old W. D. Chapman Bass Bait. It was made in four sizes and available in luminous and non-luminous. It was finished in either nickel, silver, or copper. $50.00 – 75.00.

D. The "Reversible Propeller." This lure is another copy of a W. D. Chapman lure also called the "Reversible Propeller." It was available with a luminous or non-luminous belly and was finished in either nickel, silver, or copper. $50.00 – 100.00.

Note: **C.** and **D.**. were probably acquired by the Enterprise Co. from the successors to the W. D. Chapman Co. All the lures on this page were found in the 1900 catalog.

This advertisement, from the Dec. 27, 1884 edition of the *American Angler* explains, at least in part, the considerable number of lures manufactured by Pflueger that were patented by other individuals. Pflueger continued to acquire patents and buy up smaller companies throughout their long history. By 1900, Pflueger was without peer; they manufactured more angling related products than any company in the U.S. and continued to do so well into the twentieth century.

Collector's Postscript

Many of the lures described in this chapter were manufactured over a long period of time and differentiating between the old and the new can sometimes be a real problem. Collectors should remember that the common Bulldog Trademark found on many lures wasn't registered until Aug. 3, 1915. Any lure bearing this trademark would have been manufactured after that date. Most old examples are marked simply, Pflueger, Akron, Ohio.

Many of the early lures used glass beads for bearings instead of the more common and newer brass spacers and beads.

Collector's Note

If you have a spinner that you suspect was made by Enterprise but can't seem to find it in this chapter, you should do the following before you give up. Note the shape of the spinner blade and if you find one illustrated that corresponds to it, be sure to read the complete caption. Many of the spinners were made in several different configurations. Some were luminous while others were not. Some had inexpensive swivels while others had no swivel but were attached to a twisted wire. Some were made of nickel plated brass and others were made of inexpensive polished tin. Each one of these had a different name. Read the captions carefully.

John B. McHarg

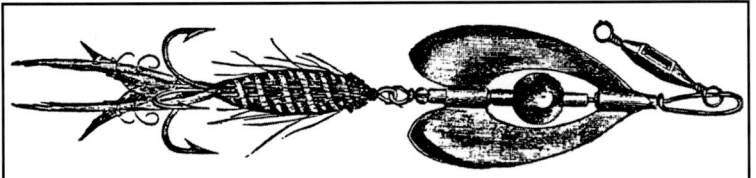

John Brainerd McHarg was born on October 20, 1823, in a small frame house on the south side of West Dominick Street in Rome, New York. He was a descendant of John McHarg who came to the United States from Scotland about the middle of the eighteenth century and settled near Albany, N.Y. His father was James McHarg, a skilled mechanic who worked at the United States Arsenal in Rome. James established the sporting goods business that later would be carried on by his son.

John evidently learned the tackle manufacturing business well, and in 1850 at the age of 27, he entered into business with Jesse J. Armstrong and J. Hildreth. Later on he was also associated in business with his brother D. P. McHarg and Charles Northrup. These companies provided jobs for 10 to 30 girls. He was also for years the senior member of the firm of Hook, Pepper, and Co. This company was founded in 1860 and besides McHarg consisted of John Pepper Sr. and James Hook. This company manufactured fishing rods for the wholesale trade.

John's father is credited with inventing the first jointed fishing pole manufactured in this country, and John patented the first sliding ring reel seat. John also applied for and received three different patents for the improvement of fishing lures. The first was patented on May 4, 1886, and was basically for the application of a metal shield on the surface of a trolling spoon. The second patent was granted August 10, 1886, and was for the "American Spinner." This lure is very similar to the Buel patent "Arrowhead," but instead of a hollow chamber between the blades, it has a reflective ball. The third patent is for the use of the reflective ball in combination with long tube type washers on a common spinner.

John McHarg was a respected member of the Rome community and an avid sportsman. He was an expert angler and fly caster. In 1871 he took third place in the annual New York State Sportsman Club casting competition. Contestants were judged for distance, accuracy, and delicacy. McHarg's cast was 65 ft. using a 12' 6" rod.

John Brainerd McHarg died on December 28, 1900, at the age of 77. The following is from his obituary.

"He was a lover of nature and was never so happy as when among the flowers and brambles he loved so well. His heart was tender toward all mankind and every living creature. For years he was sole representative here of the Society for the Prevention of Cruelty to Animals, and most actively and thoroughly strove for the protection of dumb beasts. Mr. McHarg was a friend to those in need, but his benefactions, though many, were not ostentatious.

In politics he was independent. He favored prohibition and cast his vote along that line when there seemed hope of doing good. In local politics the best man was his choice. In national politics he was a Republican. Mr. McHarg was talented as a writer and was a life-long contributor to the leading sporting papers of the country. He had within recent years written a number of interesting communications for the *Sentinel*, and his reminiscences of the old times in Rome and of the sports and sportsmen of other days were eagerly read and favorably received.

Mr. McHarg was baptized by the Rev. Dr. Gillett but never became a member of any visible church. He was a firm believer in Christianity and died in peace, looking for a better land.

Besides his wife, who was Susan Noble, he leaves four children, Alice McHarg Ferril of Denver, Colorado, and Cora, John, and Susan of this city. One brother, D.P. McHarg of Kansas City, and two sisters, Mrs. J.H. Palmer of Denver and Mrs. J.P. Wolcott of Rome, also survive."

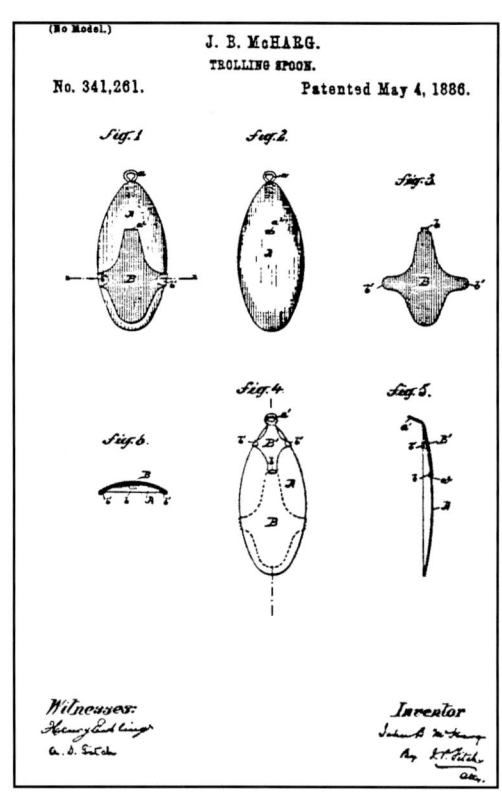

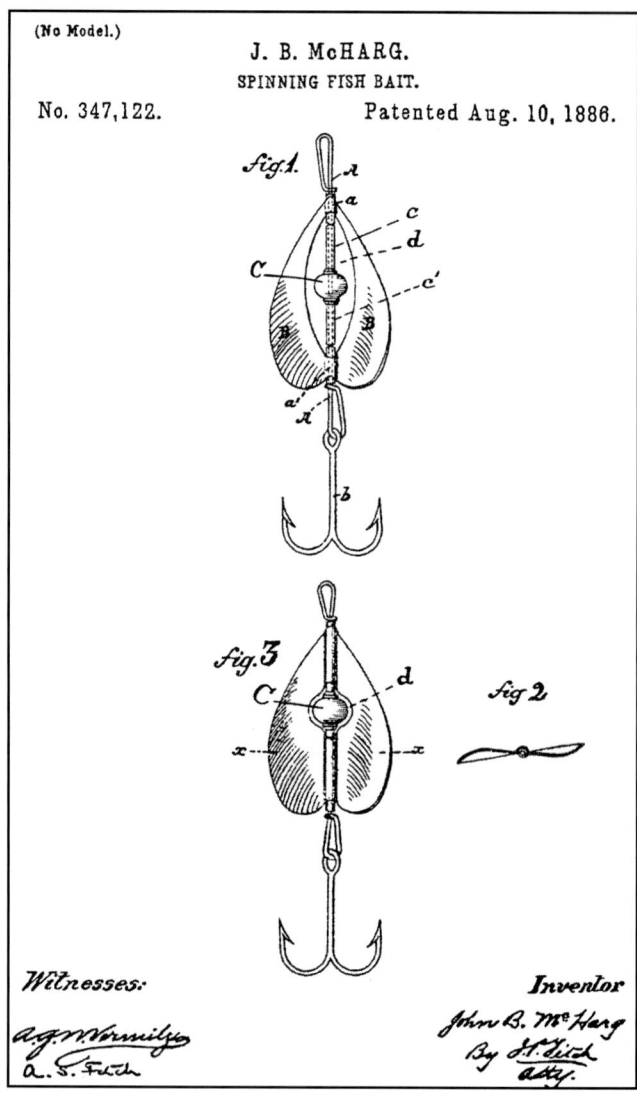

A. May 4, 1886 patent. This patent was for the application of a decorative shield onto the surface of a trolling spoon.

B. August 10, 1886 patent, the "American Spinner." This lure is similar to the Buel Patent "Arrowhead" bait, but instead of a hollow chamber between the blades it has a reflective ball.

C. December 21, 1886 patent. This patent is for the use of a reflective ball in combination with long tube type washers on a common spinner.

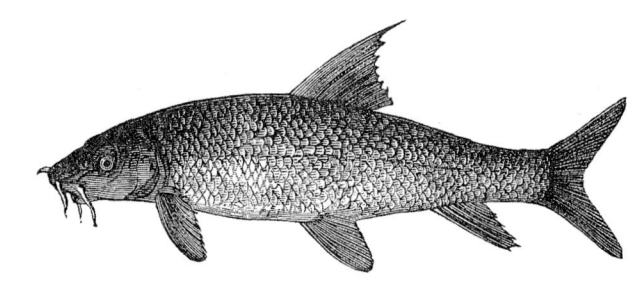

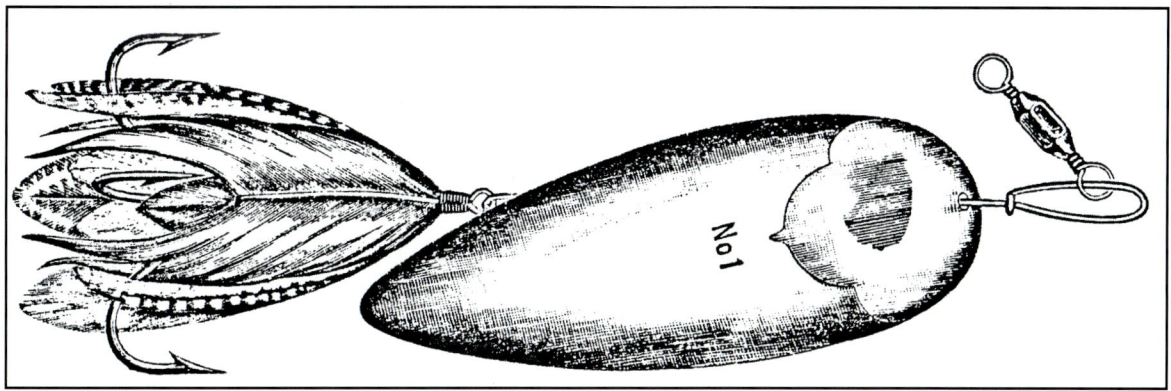

A.

A. Cut from an 1892 Abbey & Imbrie catalog of the "Electric" bait. Although unmarked, this is, in all probability, a McHarg lure. It has the applied shield and wire-wound hooks found on many McHarg baits. It was made in six different sizes and came in either plain or hammered finish. The "Electric" Pike bait was available in burnished tin, Japanned hooks or burnished tin with fly and bright hooks. The 'Electric" Pickerel bait was available in nickel plated brass with bright hooks and swivel.

B. The "Electric" Pike bait in burnished tin with Japanned hooks. The blade is 2⅝" long. $50.00 – 75.00.

C. Abbey & Imbrie's "Fluted Bait." This lure is listed in the 1896 Abbey & Imbrie catalog in eight sizes and was available in polished tin and nickel plated brass. It has the McHarg applied shield and is marked "Pat. May 4, 1886." $35.00 – 50.00.

B.

C.

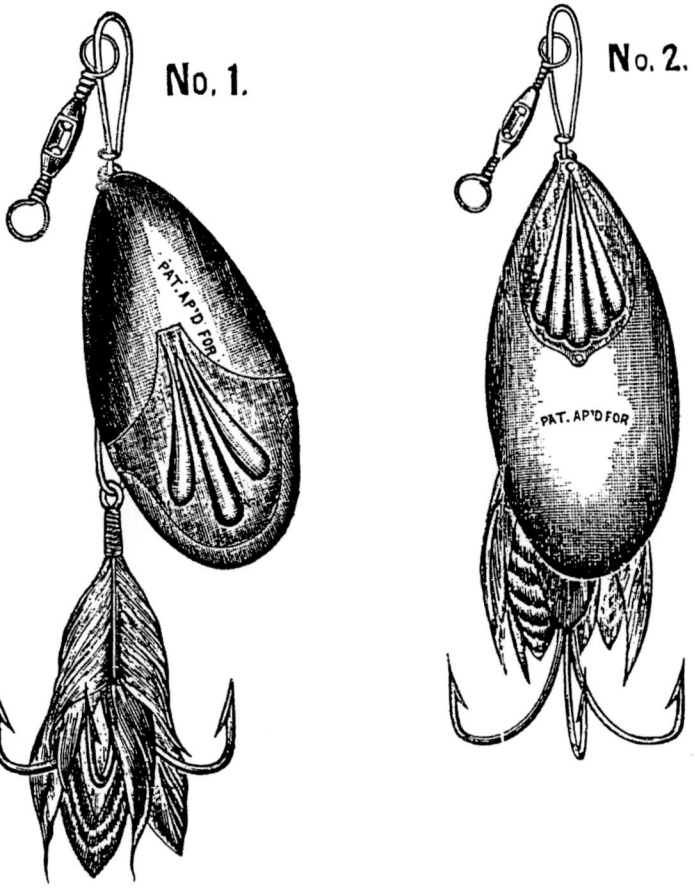

Page from J. B. McHarg and Co. catalog, circa 1886.

A.

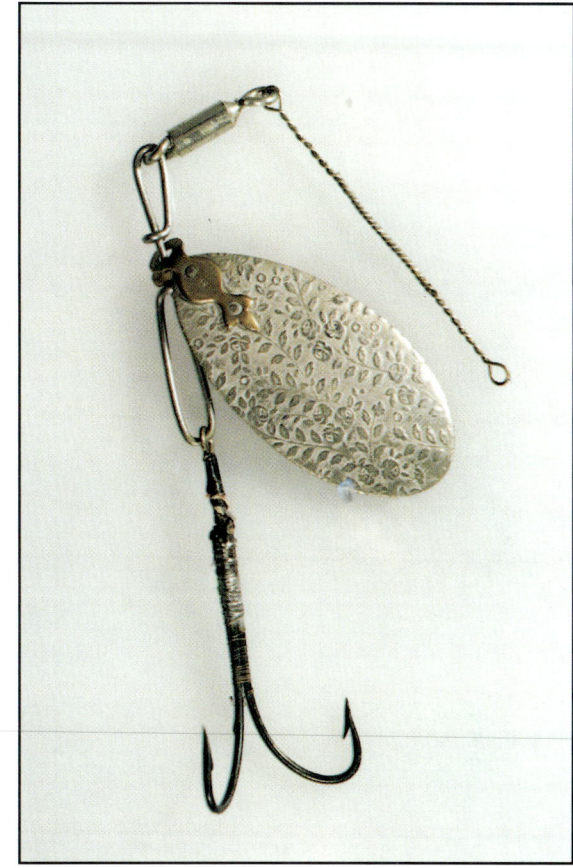

B.

A. The "Fluted Shield Pickerel Bait." It is marked Pat. May 4, 86. The blade is 2" long and has a nickel plated shield attached to the top. It is also marked Abbey & Imbrie No. 3. The other lure is marked Abbey & Imbrie No. 4 and is smaller in size. $50.00 – 75.00.

B. This lure is unmarked but appears to be a McHarg. It has the attached shield and solid swivel found on a lot of McHarg lures. It also has wire-wound hooks, another common McHarg feature. Note the beautiful rose stem pattern on the blade. $250.00 – 300.00.

C. Close-up of the rose stem blade.

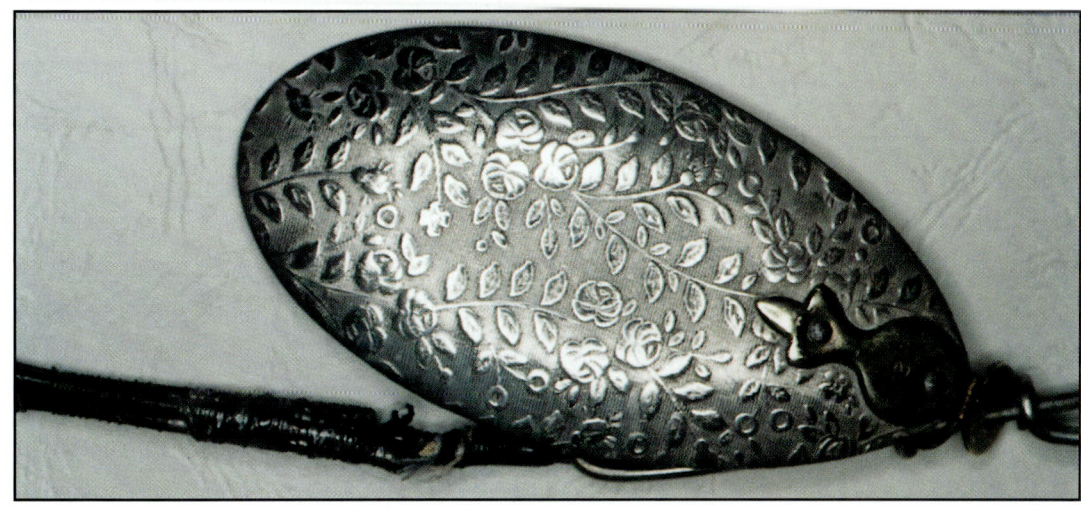

C.

J.B. McHarg

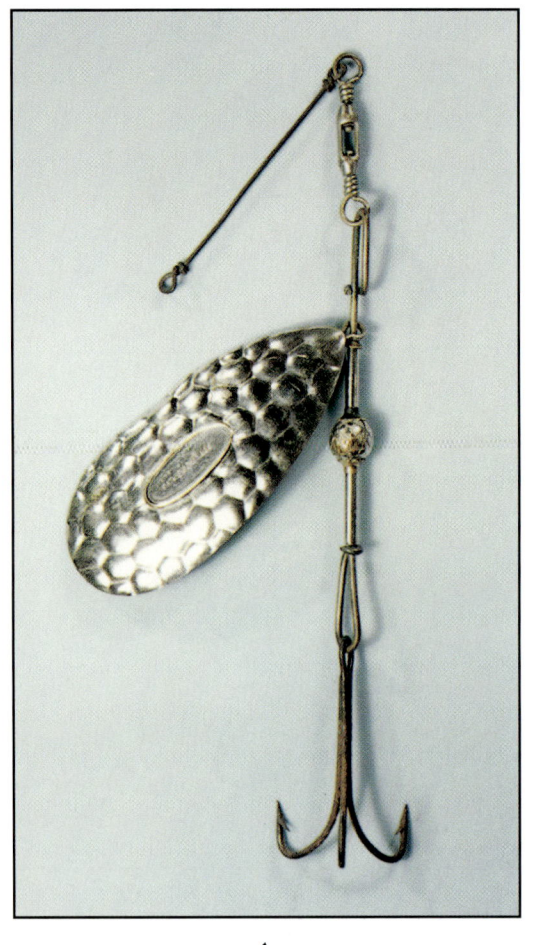

A.

B.

A. Musky sized lure with reflective ball and attached shield. The shield is stamped "Pat. Dec. 21 1886." The blade is 3½" long and has a hammered finish. $75.00 – 100.00.

B. This lure has a heavy cast blade and attached shield marked "Pat. May 4, 1886, and Dec. 21, 1886." The blade is 2" long. Note the fancy segmented ball. $250.00 – 300.00.

C. Another McHarg with the heavy cast blade. This one has an added fly or "Bug." $250.00 – 300.00.

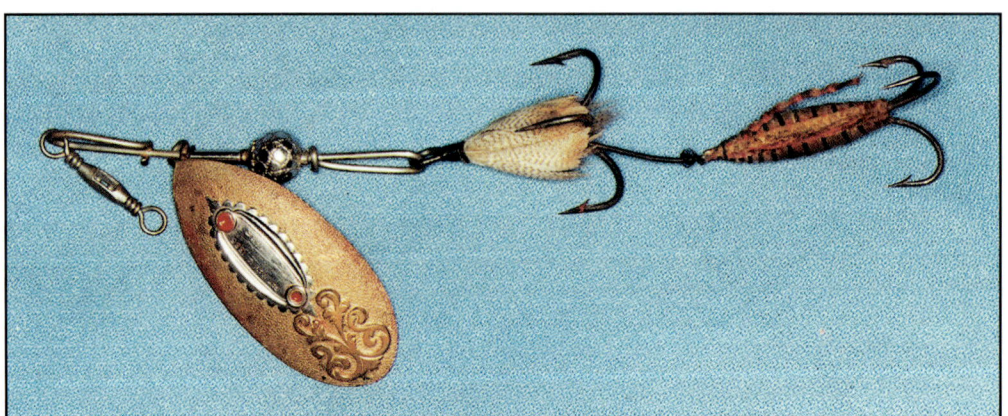

C.

A.

A. This lure, still on the original card, has three interchangeable tails. The one on the lower left of the card originally had a light-colored hackle as a dressing. The tails could be interchanged by opening and closing a formed eye at the rear of the lure. Although the lure is not marked McHarg, the card has attached to it a label bearing the same hunting dog logo as the early "American" spinner on the next page. $75.00 – 100.00.

B. Small triangular-shaped lure marked J. B. McHarg, Rome, N. Y. It is similar to Enterprise's Bass Bait. $20.00 – 30.00.

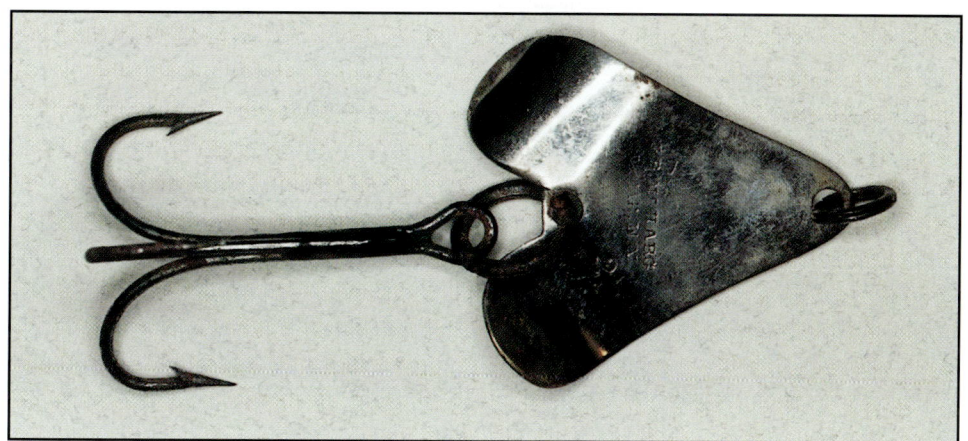

B.

A.

B.

C.

A. McHarg's "American Spinner." This lure is still sewn into its original box. The fly (bug) is attached to a split ring at the rear of the spinner by a small loop of gut. Due to their delicate nature, it is doubtful many flies survived the years. The box is 5½" long. $500.00 – 750.00.

B. The inside cover of the "American Spinner" box. Note: It says Patent applied for. The patent was granted on August 10, 1886.

C. The "American Spinner" with both blades in a hammered finish. These spinners were made in copper, brass, German silver, and nickel plated brass. They can be found in any number of combinations of these materials. $75.00 – 100.00.

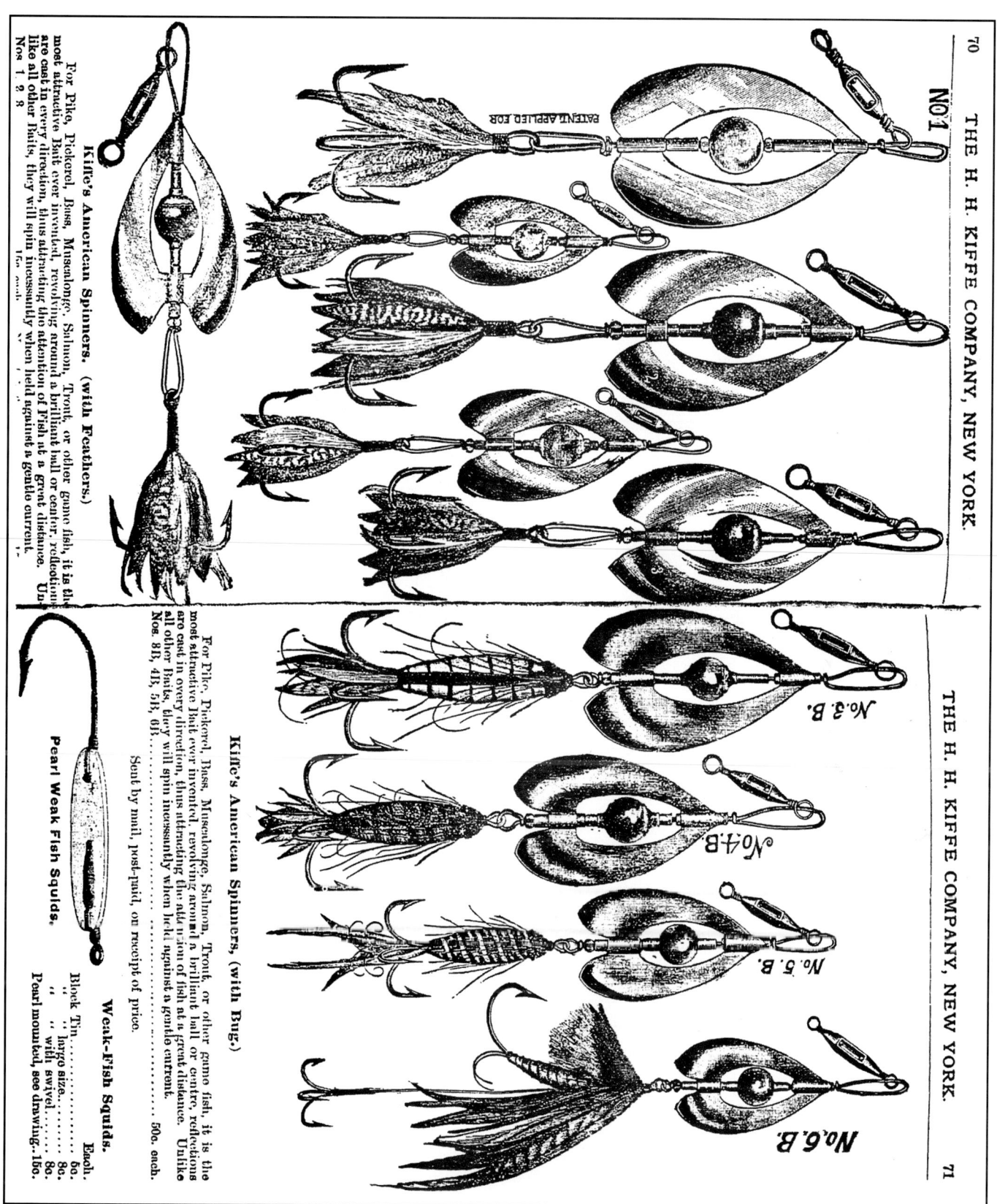

Page from the 1895 H. H. Kiffe Co., New York, showing the variety of "American Spinners" available. The J. B. McHarg Co. made these and other lures for a number of trade houses.

J.B. McHarg

A.

B.

C.

The "American Spinners" shown on this page are representative of the beautiful flies and "Bugs" found on these lures. Note that all of the lures except the one in the upper right hand corner are of similar construction. This lure is constructed with the wings (or blades) attached to the shaft by an overlapped soldered wrap, a method of construction usually credited to the J.B. McHarg Co. whereas, the other lures are attached by rivets. The riveted blades are often found on American Spinners manufactured by the Hendryx Co. The Hendryx Co. was a major manufacturer of fishing equipment during the later part of the eighteenth century and the first part of the twentieth century. It is generally thought that Hendryx didn't start manufacturing lures until the beginning of the twentieth century. However, the 1896 Abbey & Imbrie catalog illustrates American Spinners with riveted construction. The Enterprise Mfg. Co. also made American Spinners. The blades on their lures were attached by the use of metal tabs. See page 196. **A.** $75.00 – 125.00; **B.** $100.00 – 150.00; **C.** $75.00 – 125.00; **D.** $75.00 – 125.00.

D.

John B. McHarg's Best Bass Fly. This photo shows two McHarg bass flies on their original cards. Note the fox with the fish in its mouth trademark. $10.00 – 20.00.

This lure went by several names, including Spinning Coachman, Adirondack Spinner, and Spoon Fly. It was manufactured by McHarg, Enterprise Mfg., Hendryx, Chapman, and probably others. These lures were made in several different sizes. $75.00 – 100.00.

Another beautiful Spinning Coachman. The flies on these lures were heavier bodied than the standard bass fly of the era. They also had a brass eye rather than the gut loop found on regular bass flies. If the fly is tied on a regular eyed hook, it is probably of later vintage. $75.00 – 125.00.

A. Diamond pattern kidney spoon marked J.B. McHarg & Co. Rome, N.Y. No. 3. This lure has the typical McHarg solid swivel and wire wound hooks. $250.00 – 300.00.

B. Dimple pattern kidney spoon marked McHarg & Co. Rome, N.Y. The blade on this lure is 2" long. $100.00 – 150.00.

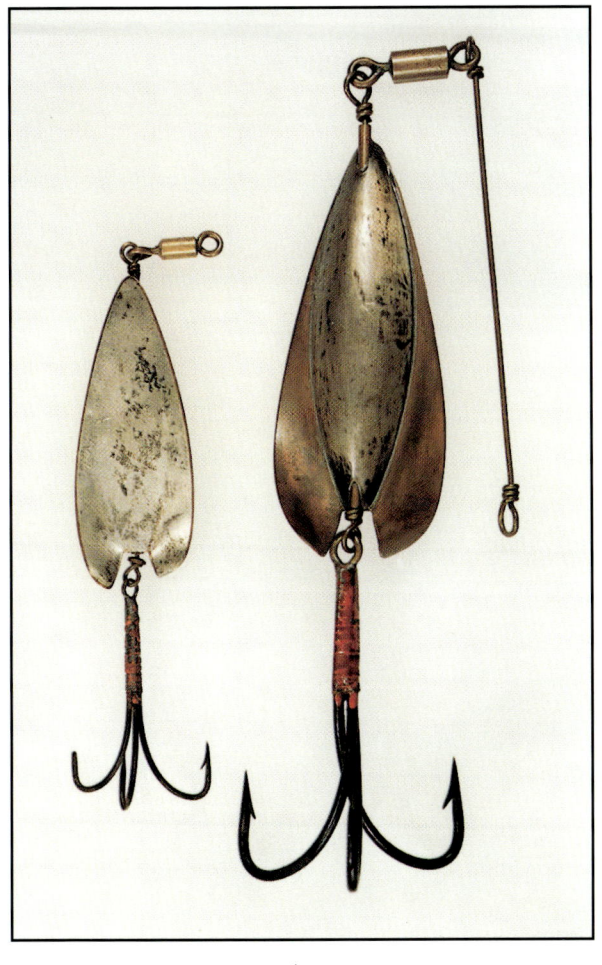

A.

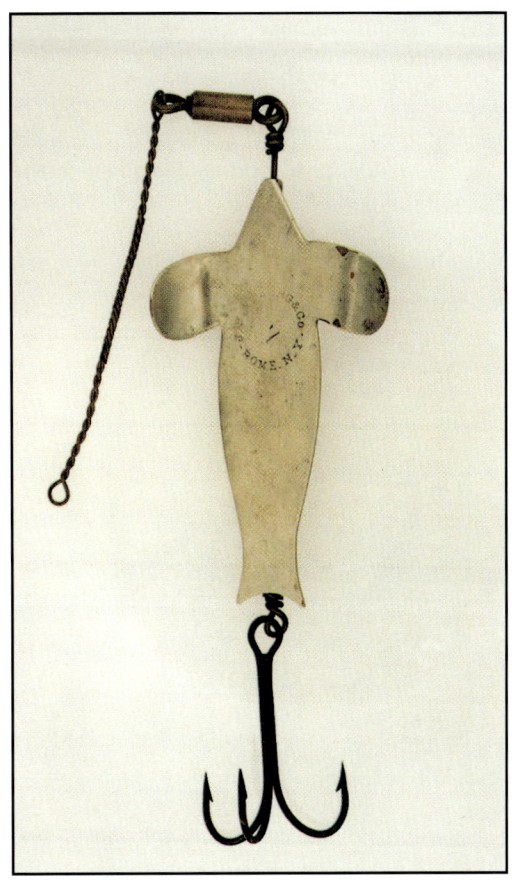

B.

A. These lures are nearly identical to the Buel "Arrowhead" lures. They are copper with a silver wash on one side. The one on the right is musky size. The blades on this bait are 3⅝" long. Both lures have the typical McHarg solid swivel and wire-wound hooks. $50.00 – 75.00.

B. This lure appears to be a copy of the Wm. H. James Spinner (the James Spinner is found in the Miscellaneous section, p. 229). It is marked J. B. McHarg & Co. $50.00 – 75.00.

C. Lure with small oval shaped protrusions. It is similar to lure on opposite page. The blade on this lure is 2" long. It is marked McHarg & Co. $100.00 – 150.00.

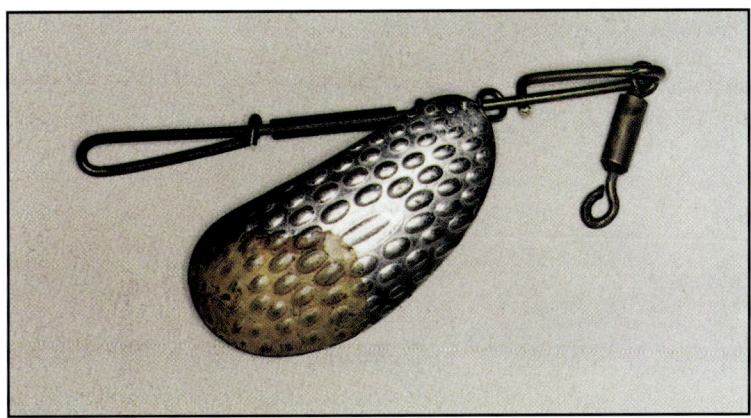

C.

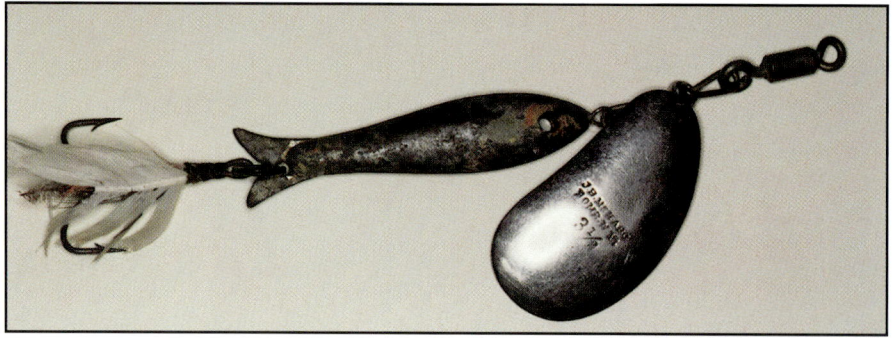

A.

B.

A. "Spoon Minnows." These are small brass minnows preceded by a spinner blade. The lure has a kidney-shaped spoon and is marked J.B.McHarg, Rome N.Y. No. 3½. This bait has holes for eyes. $300.00 – 400.00.

B. "Spoon Minnows." The lure is marked J.B.McHarg, Rome N.Y. No. 5. and has what appear to be small dark glass eyes. $300.00 – 400.00.

C. This lure is thinner than the ones above and has solid yellow eyes. It may have been manufactured by a different company. It is unmarked. $100.00 – 150.00.

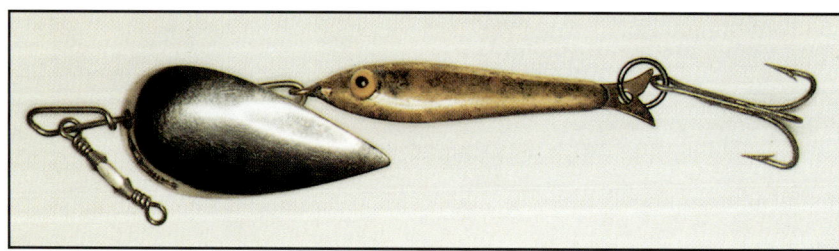

C.

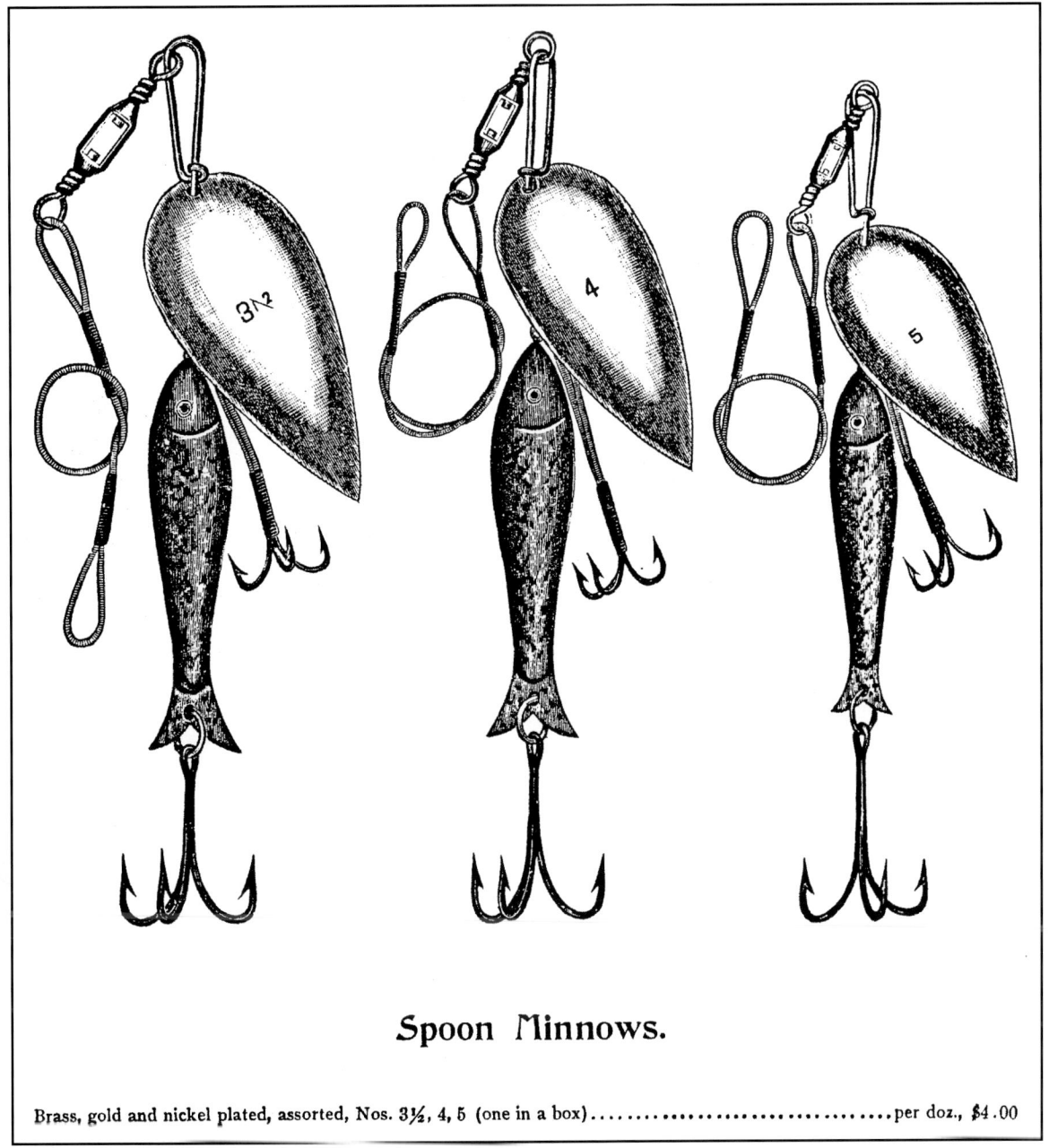

Page from the 1896 Abbey & Imbrie catalog. Abbey & Imbrie used a number of McHarg products.

J.B. McHarg

A.

B.

Collector's Postscript

McHarg lures can be identified in a number of ways. First, of course, look for a patent date and compare it to the patents found in this book. Wire-wrapped treble hooks are another clue, and McHarg often used the solid tubular type swivel. Pflueger's inexpensive lures also used this swivel so if it has a tubular swivel it is not necessarily a McHarg.

McHarg made lures for Abby and Imbrie and several other sporting goods companies. Often his patent dates will appear on lures sold by these companies.

A. Common McHarg Kidney Bait. This lure is marked J. B. McHarg, Rome N. Y. $10.00 – 20.00.

B. McHarg Kidney Bait with patented reflective ball. This lure is marked Pat. Dec. 21, 1886. $20.00 – 40.00.

C. McHarg American Spinner. Note that the wings are wrapped and soldered.

D. Hendryx American Spinner. Note that the wings are riveted on.

E. Pflueger American Spinner. Note that the wings are put on with soldered tabs.

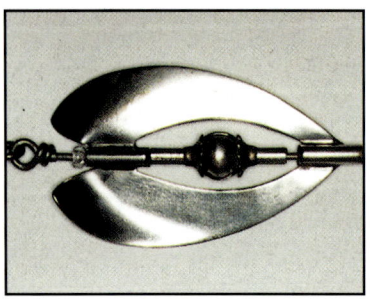

C.

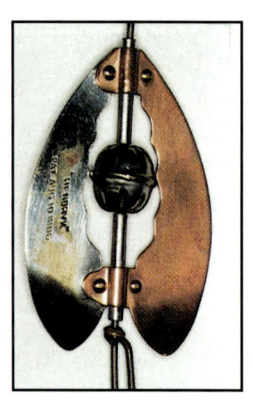

D.

E.

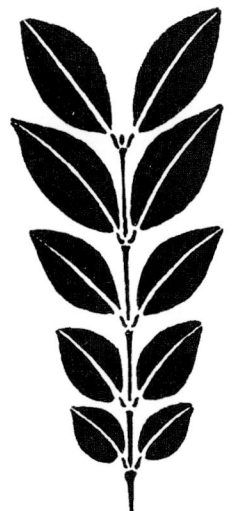

Henry Loftie

Henry Loftie was born February 28, 1839, in Auburn, N.Y. His father was William E. Loftie. He had a younger brother named William.

In 1855 the family moved to Syracuse, N.Y., where William Sr. established a wig and toupee business. Henry and his brother William worked for their father until 1860, at which time Henry went into the hair business on his own. He was very successful, selling his products throughout the country. His brother William continued to work for his father and continued the business after the elder William's death.

Henry was an avid sportsman and in 1887 he founded the Syracuse Split Bamboo Fish Rod Co. In 1888 the name was changed to the Syracuse Fish Rod Co. That same year on Sept. 25, Henry was granted Patent No. 390,028. This patent was for a spoon bait that had a wedge-shaped weed guard on the front and utilized weedless hooks. On Dec. 31, 1889, he was awarded another patent. This was for his "Gang Spoon Bait," a series of spinner blades attached to a single long shaft.

In 1890 the name of the company was once again changed, this time to the Syracuse Bamboo Furniture Co. They continued to manufacture rods and lures but also were making bamboo furniture.

In 1892 the company moved to new and larger facilities in Baldwinsville, N.Y., and on August 30 of that year, Henry was awarded yet another patent. This patent was for a trolling spoon with interchangeable blades.

The company didn't last long in Baldwinsville. Henry sold his interest in the company and in April of 1893, it was closed.

Henry died of pneumonia on May 23, 1917.

Loftie's Gang Spoon Bait. This photo shows two of the five different blades illustrated in the 1889 patent. $75.00 – 100.00.

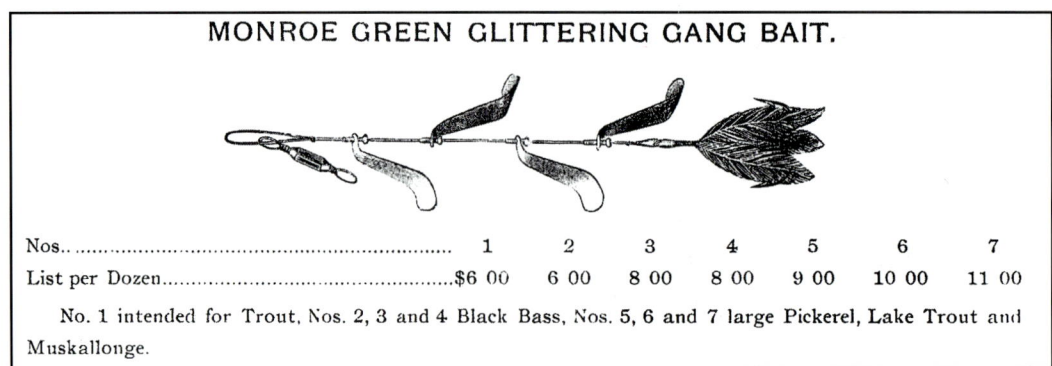

Cut from a turn-of-the-century catalog. Loftie's Gang Spoon Bait appears in several places as the Monroe Green Gang Bait.

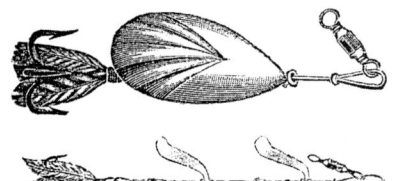

A.

B.

A. Advertisement from the April 7, 1892 issue of *Forest and Stream*.

B. Loftie made a number of lures other than the Gang Spoon Bait. These two are marked LOFTIE SYRACUSE N.Y. $20.00 – 30.00.

C. Patent for the Gang Spoon Bait. The patent refers to the small spinners as "fliers" and the Shaft as the "draw wire." The lure was designed to appear like a minnow when it was drawn through the water. The usual number of spinners or "fliers" found on these lures is four.

C.

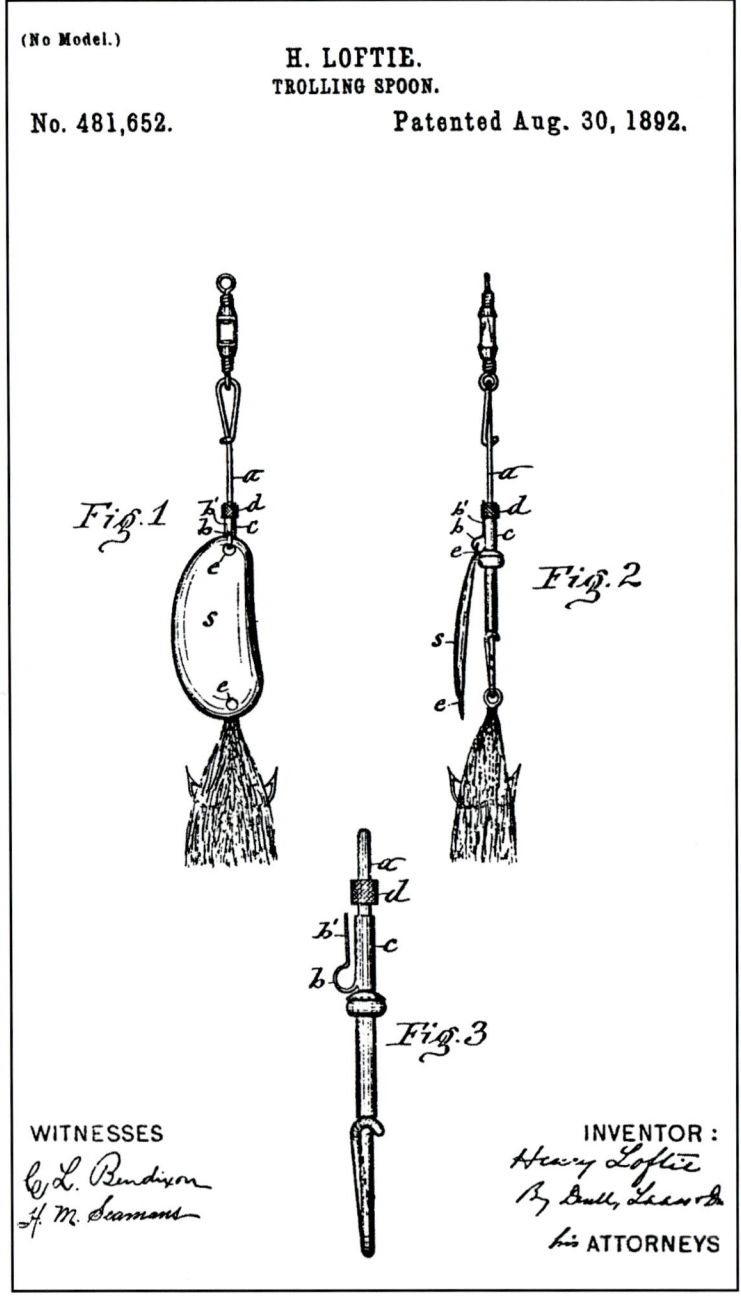

A.

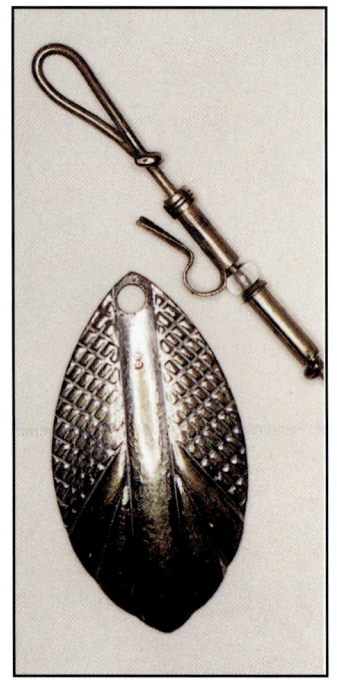

B.

C.

A. Loftie's August 30, 1892 patent. This patent is for a lure with interchangeable spinner blades. Although the concept of an interchangeable blade was not new, the method was. Buel had first patented a lure with interchangeable blades in 1854.

B. An example of Loftie's patent showing the blade removed.

C. An example of Loftie's patent with the blade in place. $100.00 – 125.00.

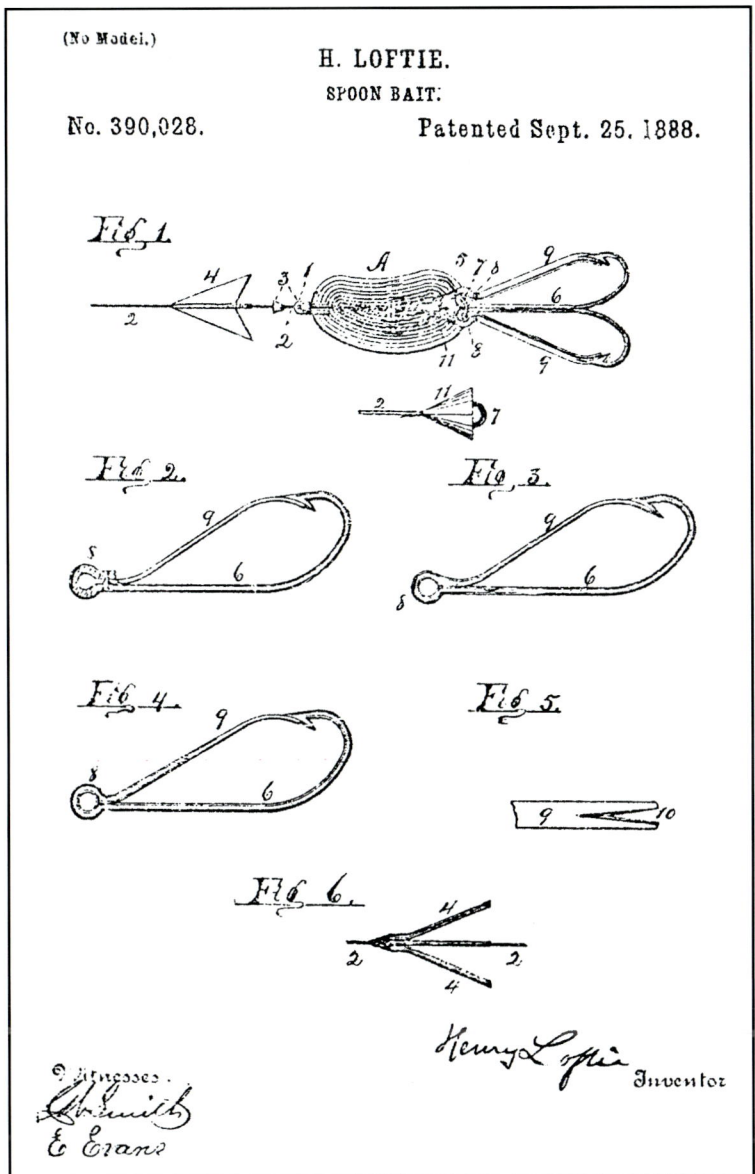

A.

B.

A. Loftie's September 25, 1888 patent. This patent is basically for a bait with wire weed guards and a triangular weed deflector on the front.

B. Lure marked LOFTIE SYRACUSE N.Y. Note the Pflueger patented swivel. $20.00 – 30.00.

John Pepper & Sons

$350.00 – 500.00

John Pepper Sr. was a native of Germany. He came to the United States in 1846 as a child of six years. Soon afterwards his family settled in Rome, N.Y.

By 1860, at the age of 20, he was involved in a rod making business with John B. McHarg and James P. H. Hook. This company was called Hook, Pepper & Co. They made rods for the wholesale trade. As mentioned in a previous chapter, John B. McHarg was the senior partner in this enterprise. The firm was located at 62 James Street and later at 126 James Street in Rome.

In 1890 Mr. Hook retired from the firm, and it became John Pepper & Sons Co. located at 233-235 South James Street. John's sons were Joseph, William, and John Jr. They had probably been employed at the company before the retirement of Mr. Hook.

On May 2, 1893, John Pepper Jr. was granted a patent for what we collectors now know as the Pepper "Batwing" bait.

In 1896 John Pepper Sr. became sole owner of the firm. Son William stayed on as business manager, but sons John Jr. and Joseph went on to establish tackle businesses of their own. The company at this time carried a complete line of fishing tackle. The following is a quote from an 1898 publication titled *The Industrial Advantages of Rome, N.Y.*

"The products of the house comprise a full line of angler's outfits, including split bamboo, lance wood, and all styles of fishing rods, with brass, German silver and nickel plated mountings, trout, bass, salmon, and grayling flies of every variety, and the house carries a large and first-class stock of everything pertaining to a complete fishing outfit, and is in a position to quote prices and compete for trade with the most advanced and progressive houses in the country."

It is not known what happened to John Pepper Jr., inventor of the "Batwing," but Joseph Pepper established the Joseph E. Pepper Bait Co. of Rome, N.Y., and manufactured metal and wood lures well into the twentieth century.

John Pepper Sr. died on June 5, 1919, at the age of seventy-nine.

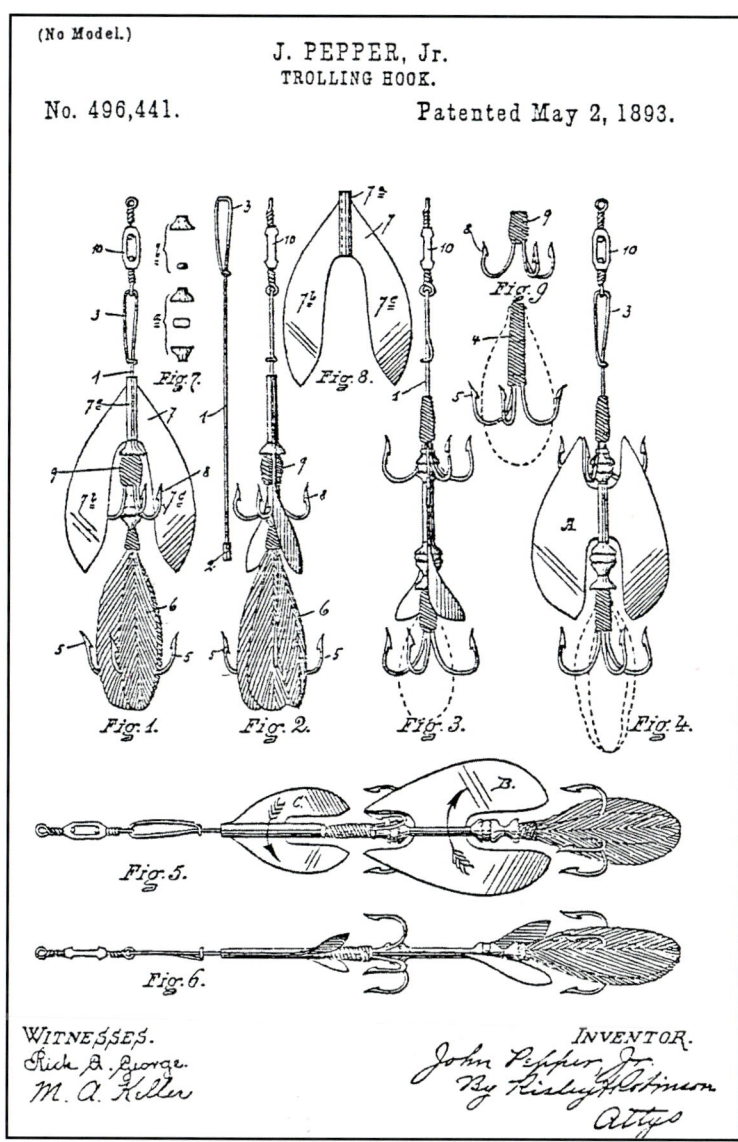

A.

B.

A. John Pepper Jr.'s May 2, 1893 patent drawing for the "Batwing" bait. The text of this patent prattles on seemingly forever about hook position, hook angle, and opposite rotation, but the gist of the thing is that the hooks turn with the spinner for whatever reason. Like many other patents, the finished product appears like the patent drawing but functions like most other lures of its class.

B. John Pepper Jr.'s "Batwing" lure. This has the May 2, 1893 patent date stamped on the wing. It does not have the usual milkglass beads. $200.00 – 350.00.

C. This lure has the "Bug" and milkglass ball of the Pepper baits but instead of the batwing spinner, it has a conventional Adirondack type spinner. $100.00 – 125.00.

C.

JOHN PEPPER & SONS

Pepper "Batwings"

$200.00 – 350.00

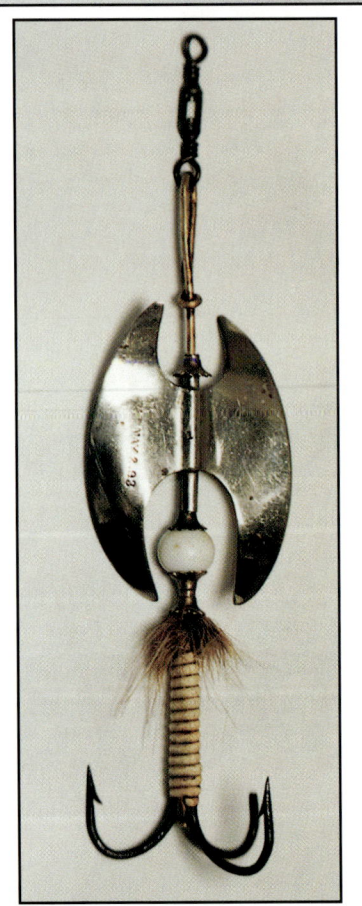

$350.00 – 450.00

Welch & Graves

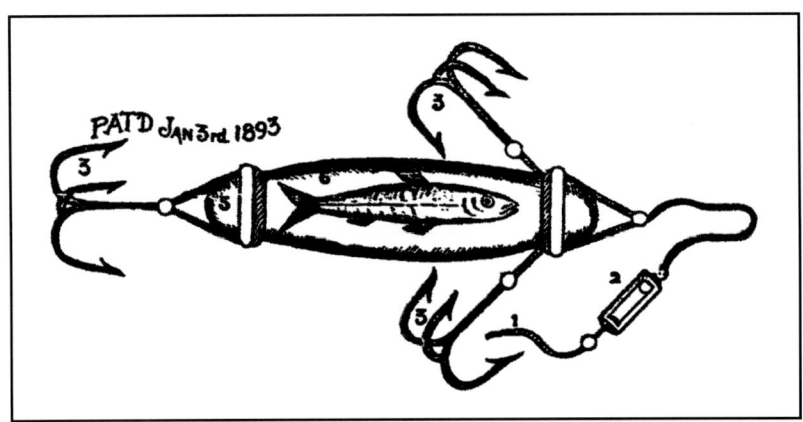

The Welch and Graves "Protected Live Fish Bait" appears to be the first of several glass minnow tubes produced in the United States. This lure was invented and patented by Henry J. Welch of Carthage, New York, and manufactured by Calvin V. Graves of Natural Bridge, New York. They also manufactured two metal lures. One was a spinning lure with Phantom type wings and a clasp to hold a minnow or pork ring bait. The other was fish shaped with an interchangeable center section. This may have been the first U. S. lure to utilize the concept of color change.

The following is from *Haddock's History of Jefferson County 1793 – 1894.*

"Capt. Henry J. Welch, native of Chenango Co. N. Y., born in village of Norwich, N.Y., July 17, 1834. Parents born at Stonington, Conn. Admitted to the bar in Binghamton in 1861. Came to Carthage in 1862, practiced law with Charles Hammond before opening his own office. In Aug. 1864 the 186th N.Y. Volunteer Infantry Regiment was raised and Welch made Captain. After the war he returned to his law practice. He organized the Carthage Fire Department and four times was its president. Was the inventor of 21 patents, among which are the "Pneumatic Horse Shoe" and "The Glass Minnow Tube and Interchangeable Center Fish Bait." Married in 1864 to Zealade, daughter of Orson and Sophia Warren. His home is in the heart of Carthage."

Henry J. Welch died of a heart attack in 1898 while on a fishing trip.

Calvin V. Graves was born around 1844. He enlisted in the 97th infantry at Boonville, N.Y., on February 20, 1862. He served as a drummer boy and later as a musician. After the war he worked awhile as a clothier with his brothers in Boonville, N.Y. He moved to Natural Bridge, N.Y., in the early 1870s. At one time he owned and operated a sawmill and later was involved in promoting a talc mine. During the 1890s he pursued several endeavors including the manufacture of the Henry Welch lures. How Welch and Graves became partners is unknown, but it seems to have worked out for both of them.

Calvin Graves died on April 9, 1907.

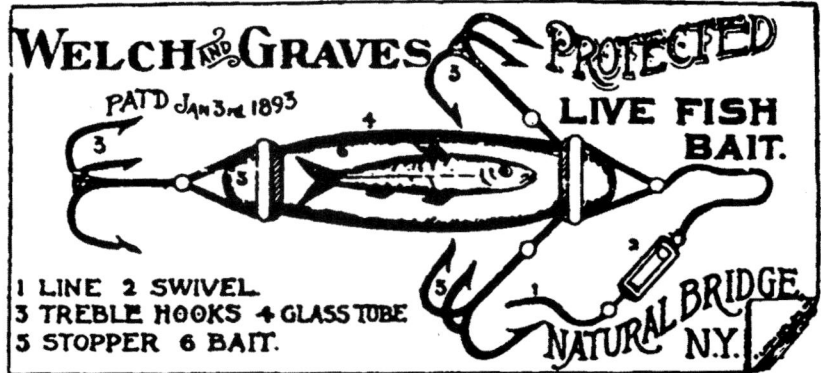

This is a copy of the letter sent to postal patrons all across the nation. The envelope with its 1893 Columbian Exposition stamp is shown on the following page. Note the statement in the third paragraph above. "Don't write to ask questions; life is too short." Maybe arrogance sells lures.

A.

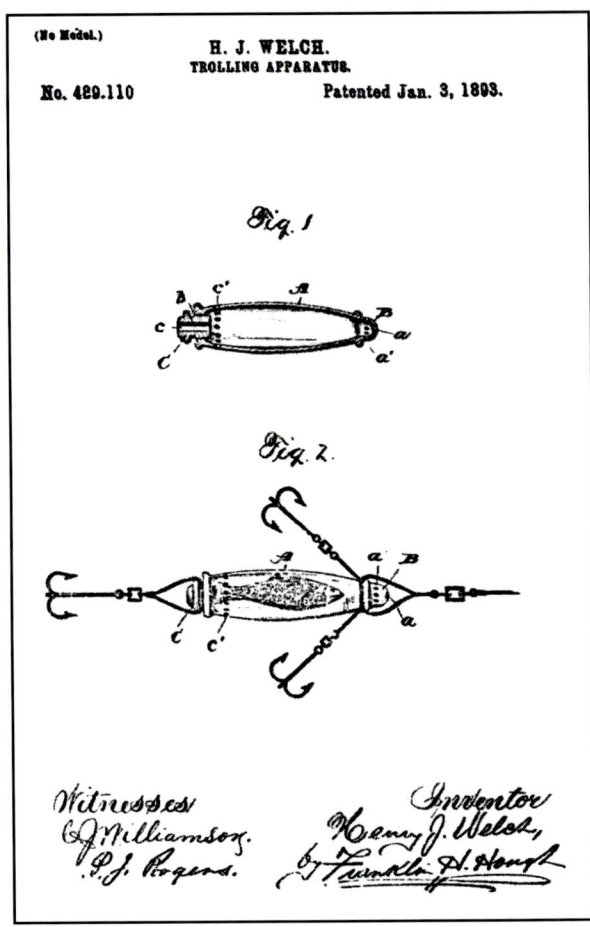

B.

C.

A. The three different sizes of the Welch & Graves minnow tube. They were listed as 3½", 4½", and 5½". $400.00 – 600.00.

B. Patent drawing of Henry Welch's minnow tube. This patent was applied for on Oct. 25, 1892 and granted Jan 3, 1893.

C. Picture of the advertising envelope that was sent to every town in the United States — or at least that was their claim.

A.

B.

A. Box for the Welch and Graves minnow tube. It has the same illustration on the label as the advertising envelope on the facing page. The box is made of wood.

B. Ad of unknown origin, probably 1890s. It is interesting to note that the ad says "weed-proof hooks attached" while the illustration shows regular hooks. Also the spinner on the front is referred to as a wheel.

C. This is the "Improved Protected Live Bait Fish." It is nearly like the one illustrated in the ad, and it does have the weedless hooks mentioned. It does, however, have bent wire shafts holding the hooks rather than the gimp leads shown. $500.00 – 750.00.

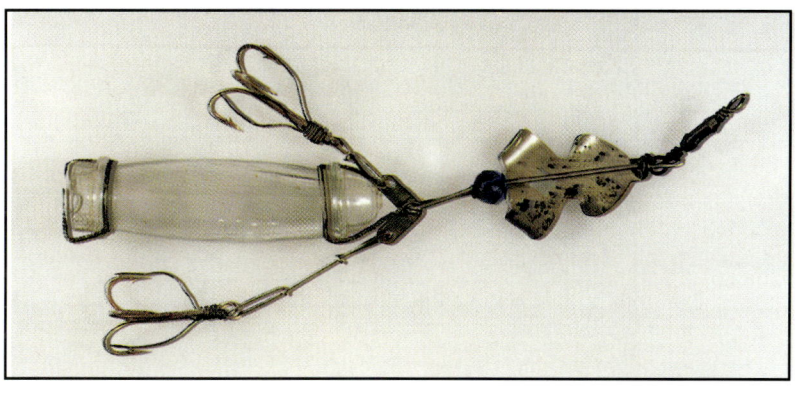

C.

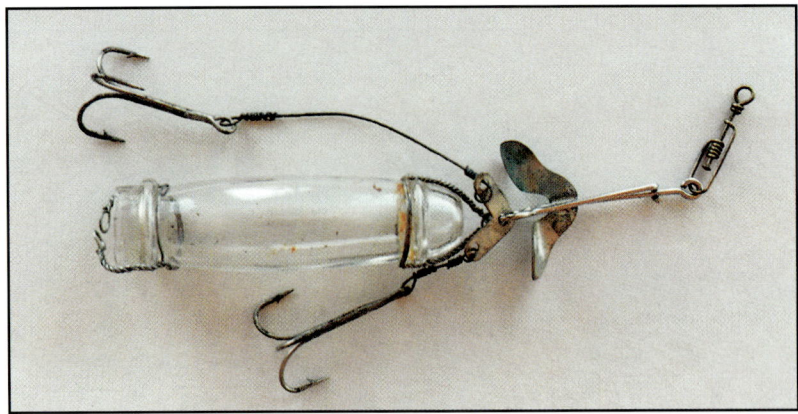

A.

A. Another "Improved" minnow tube. This is very much like the ad illustration on the previous page, except it has a different spinner on the front. This spinner is shown on page 212 in connection with the American Combination Spinner. Also note the strange swivel on the front. $500.00 – 750.00.

B. This lure is also very much like the "Improved" minnow tube but retains its rear hook like the standard tube. All of these lures utilize the small size glass tube. $500.00 – 750.00.

C. Close-up view of this same lure. Note the short twisted wire hook leads.

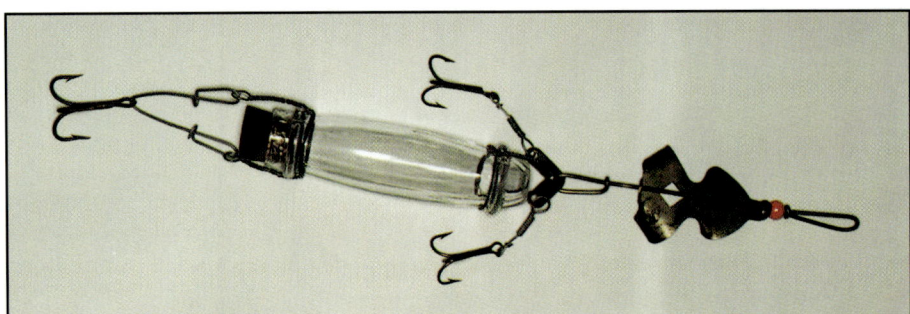

B.

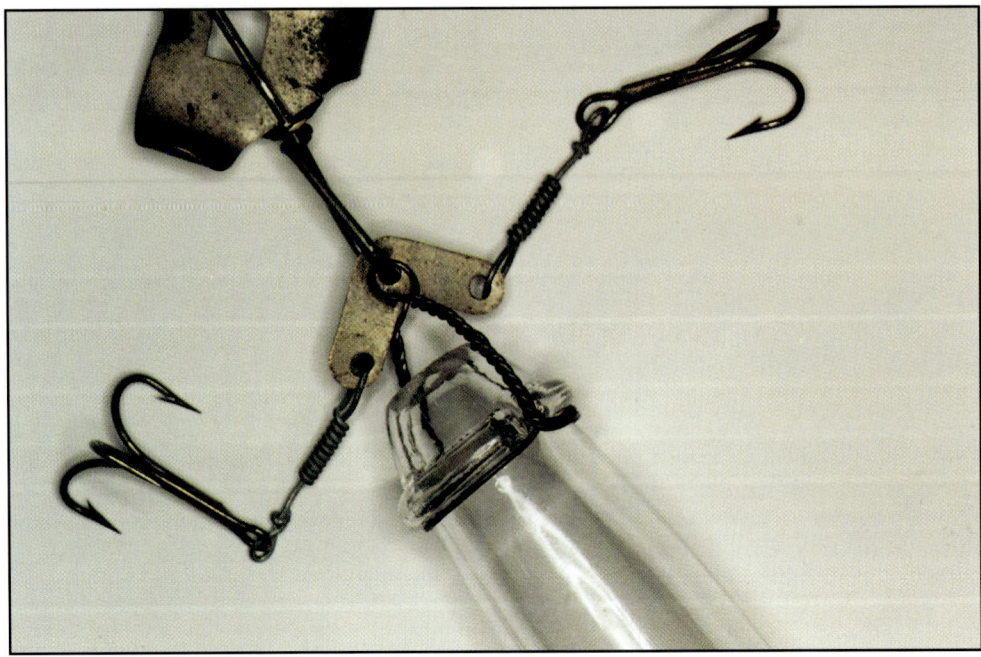

C.

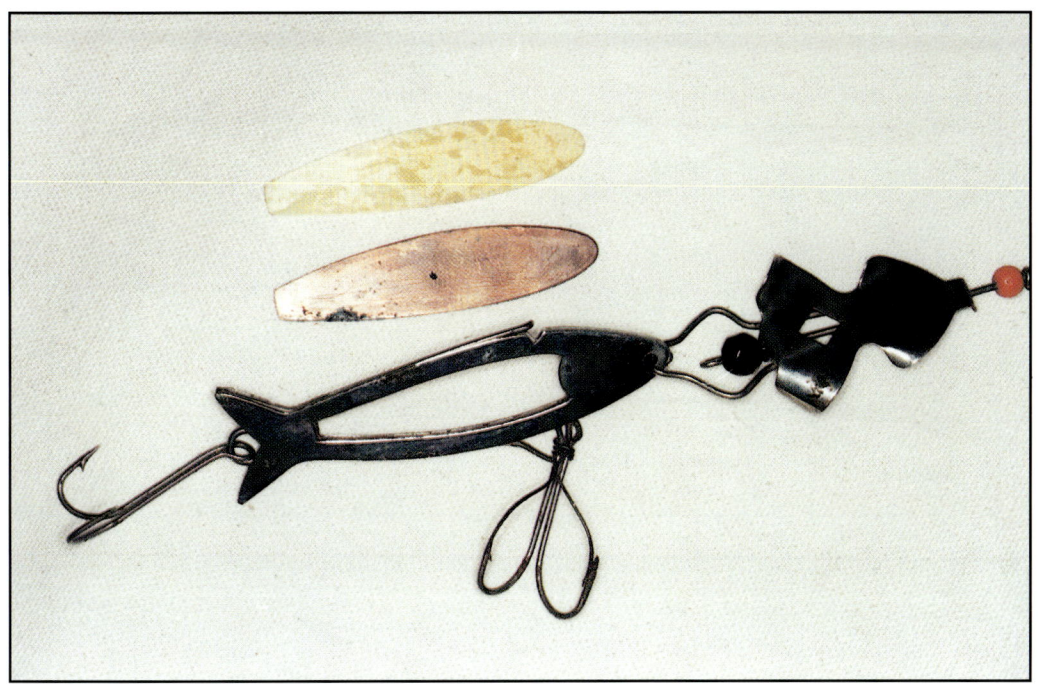

A.

A. For lack of anything better, I'll call this lure the "Changeable Center Fish Bait." In Haddock's *History of Jefferson County* in a short biography of Henry Welch, there is a reference made to his invention of "The Glass Tube and Changeable Center Fish Bait." I used to think this referred only to the Glass Tube and was a description of the tube itself. I now believe that the "Changeable Center Fish Bait" was a separate lure and that the lure is this one. This lure is 3¼" long with the front mounted spinner being 2⅜" long. Each side of the lure is a separate piece of nickel plated brass with a space between. Different colored inserts of celluloid and metal can be put into this space or slot and held in place with a wire retainer. The celluloid inserts have been found in red and yellow. The metal ones in plain brass and nickel plate. This lure has part of the word "patented" stamped into the metal. $1,000.00+.

B. This "Changeable Center Fish Bait" has a different hook configuration than the one above. The celluloid inserts on this bait were marked Patented 1894. $1,000.00+.

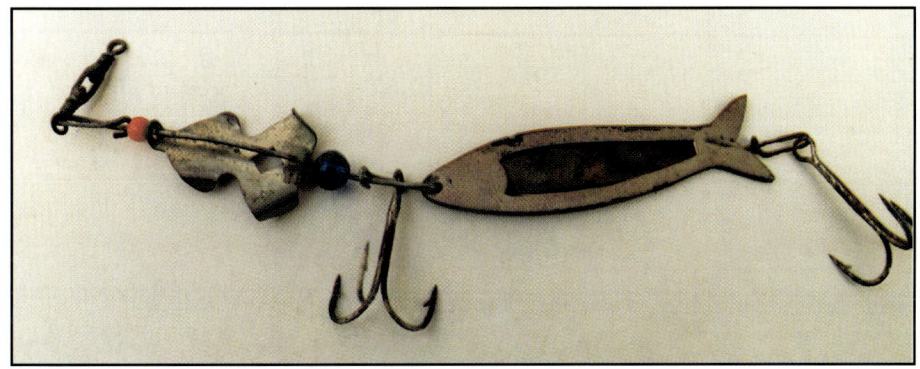

B.

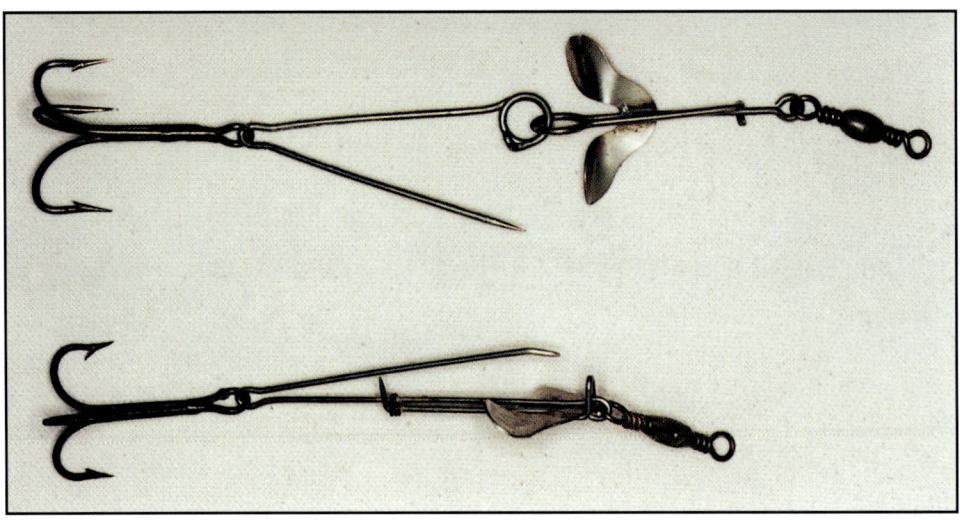

A. This photo shows the two "American Combination Spinners" in the open position. $75.00 – 100.00.

B. Two variations of the "American Combination Spinner." The one on the right utilizes a safety pin type bait holder while the one on the left uses the spinner as a sliding latch. $75.00 – 100.00.

C. Henry J. Welch's patent drawing for a "Fishing Appliance." This was called the "American Combination Spinner" when Welch and Graves manufactured it. It was basically a bait holder with a blade on the front.

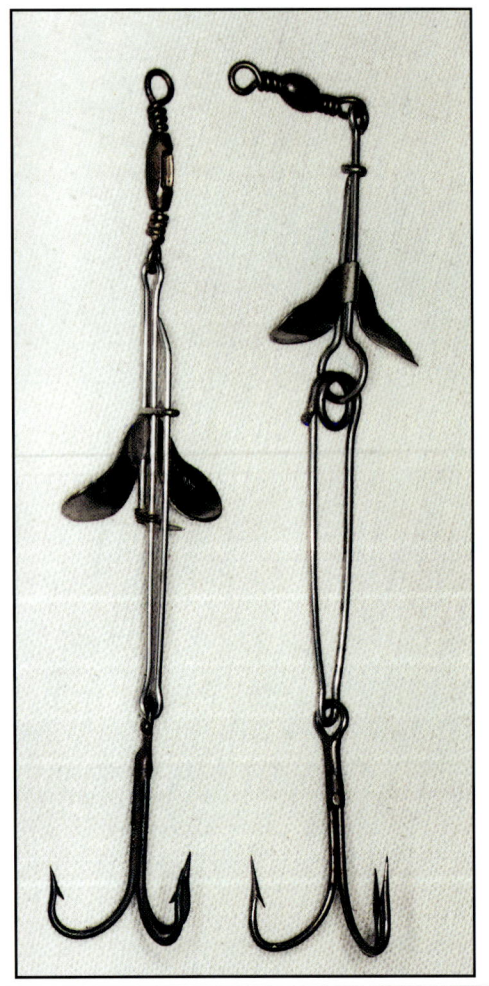

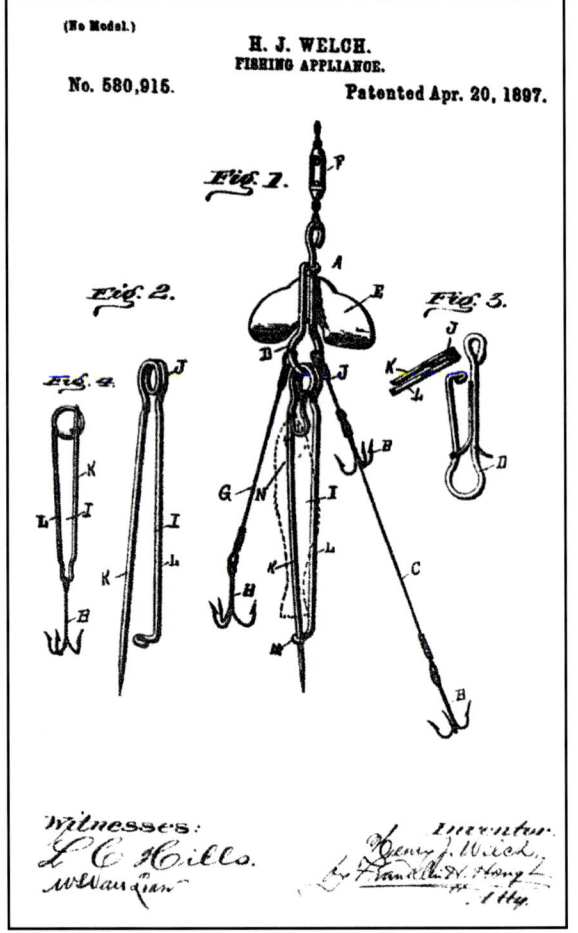

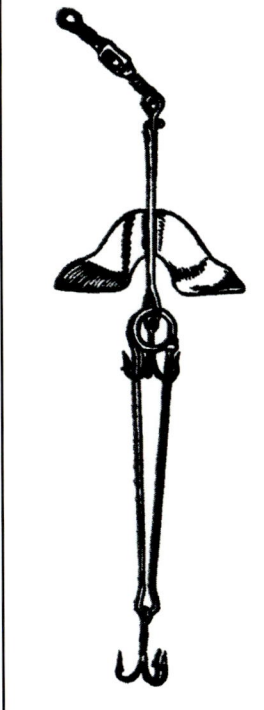 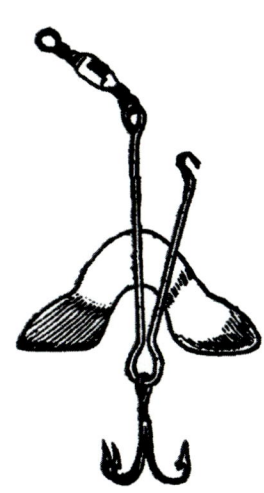  
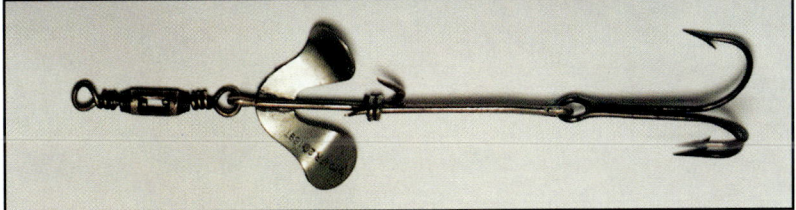
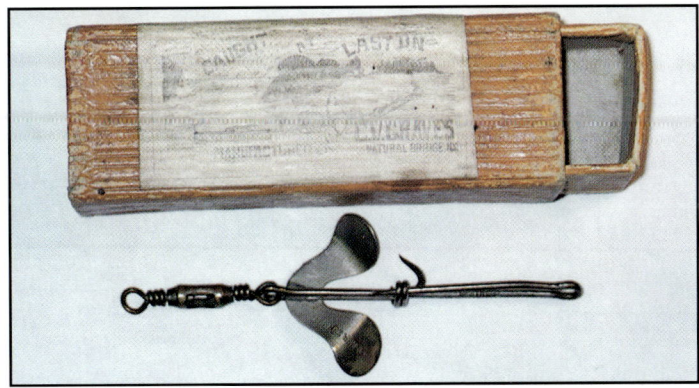

A. Illustration from the instruction sheet sent with the American Combination Spinner.

B. This is a third type of American Combination Spinner. It utilizes a wire ring with attached hook to hold the pin in a closed position. $75.00 – 100.00.

C. Box for the American Combination Spinner. Says, "Caught at last" on the label. $150.00 – 200.00.

James T. Hastings

Chicago, Illinois

"Hasting's Weedless Frog" with its original box. This lure was patented Feb. 5 1895. The patent was for the bent wires that made the lure weedless. This patent is shown on page 216. This frog is 3½" long. In one later ad, this size is called the "Marsh" size. $500.00 – 750.00.

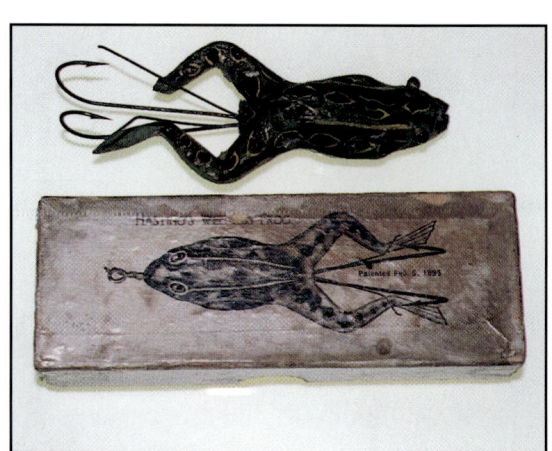

The musky version of the "Hasting's Weedless Frog." This lure was 4½" in length. The early versions, like this one, had bead eyes that protruded from the head of the frog. $250.00 – 300.00.

The underside of the "Hasting's Weedless Frog." The lead triangle at the crotch of the frog provided attachment for the hooks, weedless wires, and the line tie.

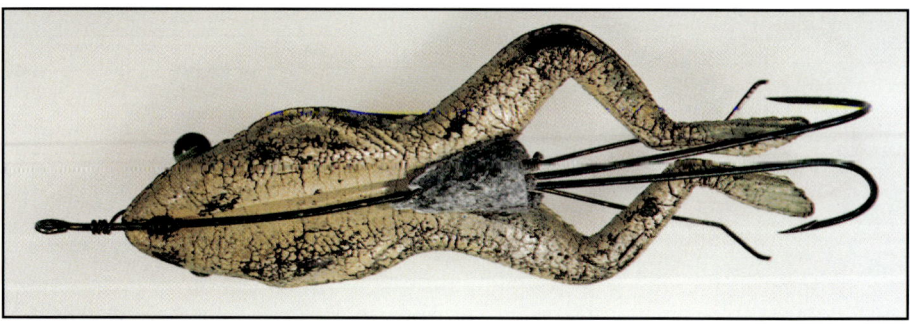

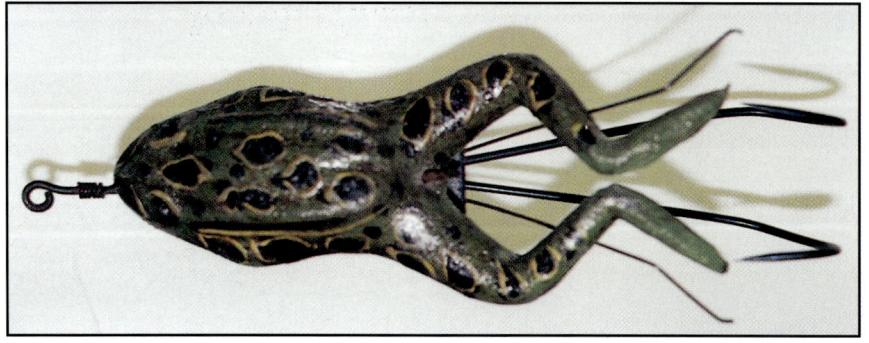

Later version of the "Hasting's Weedless Frog" without the protruding eyes. This is the medium size frog and is listed in advertisements as 3½" long. It was also made in a 2¼" baby size and a 4½" muskey size. After 1909, the medium size was manufactured by the W. J. Jamison Co. of Chicago, Illinois. The Jamison version had a silver belly rather than white as shown above. $30.00 – 60.00.

214

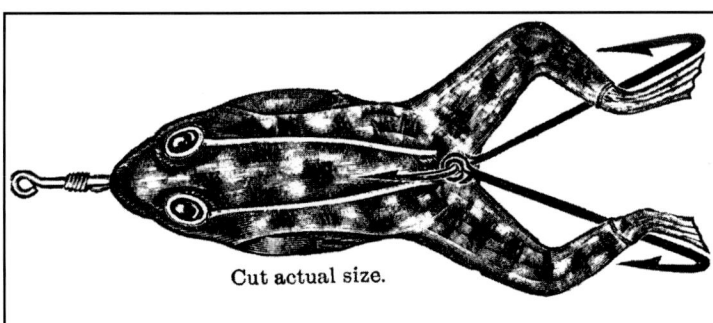

The HASTING NEW RUBBER BAIT-CASTING FROG
WITH CLARK'S IMPROVED HOOK COMBINATION.

This Frog is hollow on the same principle of a hollow rubber ball, hence will float upon the surface. It is very lifelike and indestructible; weighted on the underside and will always drop belly down. The hooks of this improved frog extend down to the toes of the hind legs and are securely fastened to the legs near the feet. *It will catch 'em every time.* The hooks always troll in an upright position, hence really require *no weed guard.* However, the knees act as a weed guard to the trail hooks and the crotch hook is guarded by the back of the frog. *This Frog is a winner.*
Price................$0.70   Sent by mail, postpaid.

A.

Rubber Frogs.
HASTING'S WEEDLESS FROG
PATENTED
48727

These frogs are made of pure rubber making them indestructible, are painted from life by an artist, and are the most natural artificial bait made. They are about the size of a half-grown frog, and always land in the water right side up, the hook being fully exposed to fish biting. It never fails to hook them in the mouth. This bait will not foul in weeds, being "weedless." Hooks can be replaced if broken. It has no superior. But one size on a 6 | 0 Carlisle hook.
Price, for each, with single hook............ $0.75
Price, each, for double, with weedless hook...... .85

B.

A. Cut from "The Wilkinson Co." catalog of Chicago, Illinois. The catalog is circa 1896. Note there are no weed guards on the hooks and there is a third hook at the crotch of the frog. This is similar to the Feb. 19, 1895 patent drawing. Also note the soldered wire wrap directly behind the line tie. This can be seen clearly on the musky sized frog on the opposite page. This wire was used to attach the nose of the frog to the main shaft. On the Jamison Co. version, this wire is not used. Instead a heavy wire loop is used as both a line tie and a nose attachment.

B. Ad from a 1895 Montgomery Ward Co. catalog. This ad shows the frog without the patented weed guards and states that it is available with one 6/0 hook or double weedless hooks. With the single hook it would be like the Feb. 19, 1895 patent.

C. Hasting's Feb. 19, 1895 patent. This patent, granted only a few days after his patent for weedless hooks, is for a lure made of rubber or other flexible material that protects the point of the hook until the material is compressed by the biting fish.

D. Circa 1896 "The Wilkinson Co." ad for a practice frog.

(No Model.)   J. T. HASTINGS.
ARTIFICIAL BAIT.
No. 534,506.   Patented Feb. 19, 1895.

FIG. 1.
FIG. 2.
FIG. 3.

Witnesses: Inventor
J. Halpenny   James T. Hastings
Samuel Griffith   By his attorneys
    Crosby & Hopkins

C.

HASTING'S SOLID RUBBER FROG.   FOR LAWN BAIT-CASTING PRACTICE ONLY

This Frog weighs one-half ounce; this being about the weight of the average casting frog. It is made of the best solid rubber and will stand the same grief of a solid rubber ball. This style of lawn practice in bait casting is very realistic, as this frog goes through the air the same as the natural frog in fishing.
Price, with swivel (swivel not shown in cut),
Each...................................$0.50
Sent by mail, postpaid.

Send 6 Cents for Clark's Angler's and Sportman's Guide.

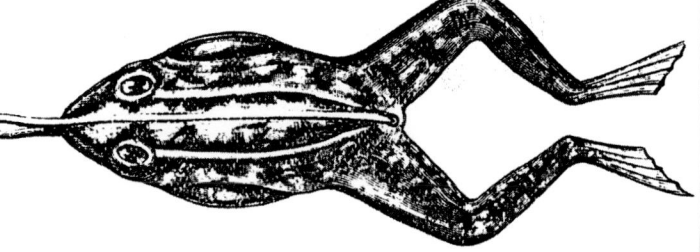

D.

James T. Hastings

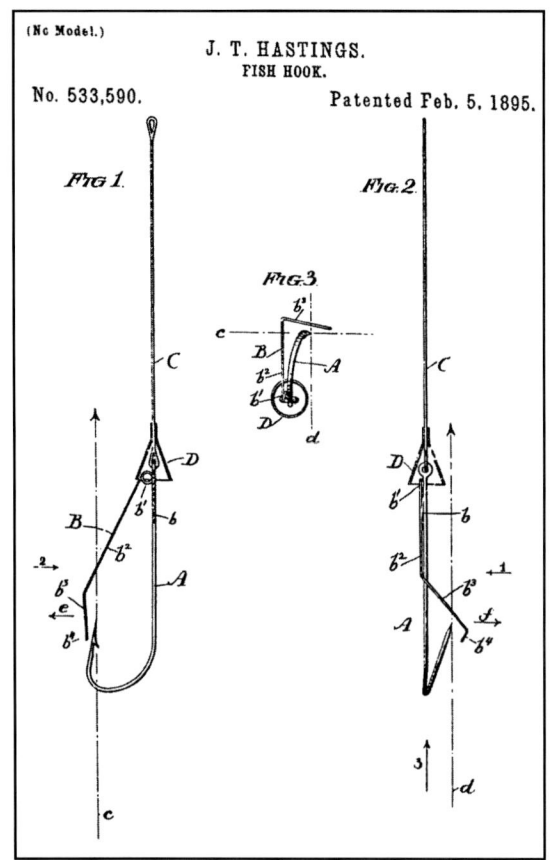
A.

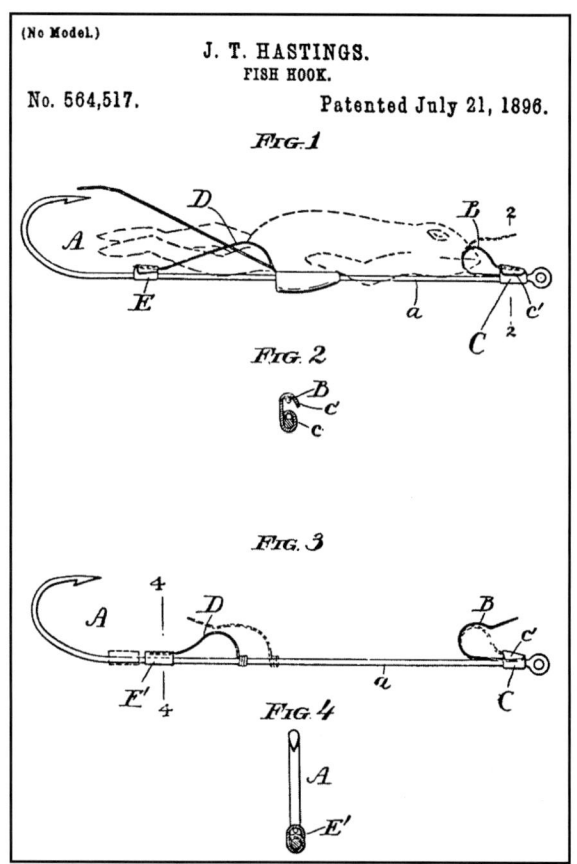
B.

A. Illustration of J. T. Hasting's Feb. 5, 1895 patent. This is basically for a weedless hook using a bent spring steel wire.

B. This patent, granted July 21, 1896, is for a frog or bait harness. Hastings used a similar setup to attach his rubber "Weedless Frog" to its frame. This patent was produced as a frog harness.

C. A 1909 ad for Hasting's Weedless Frog. This must have been shortly before the Jamison Co. began selling them.

D. Reduced copy of the Hasting's Weedless Spoon. Made in four sizes.

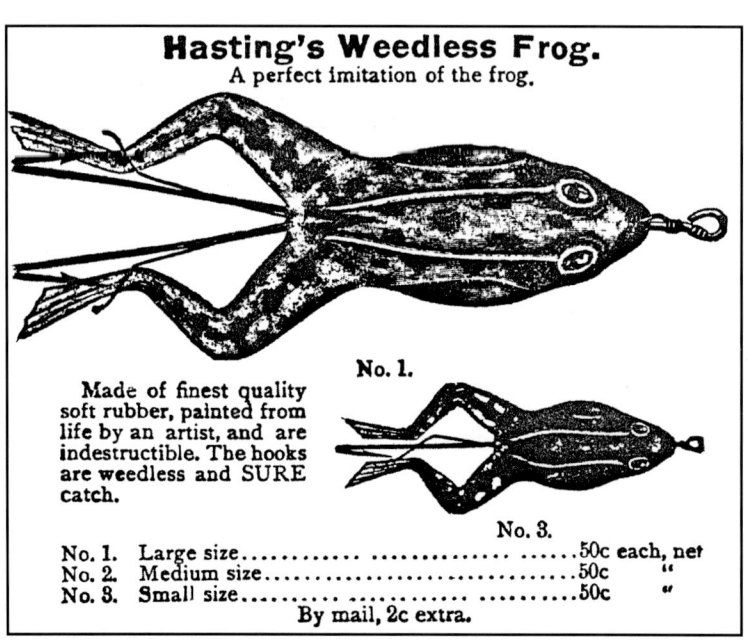
C.

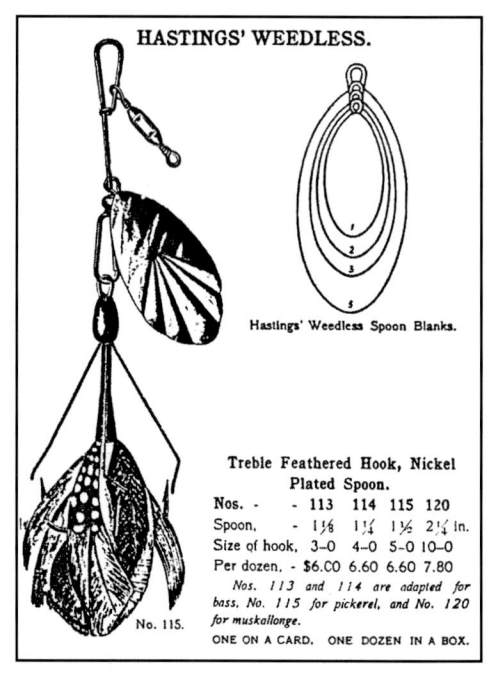
D.

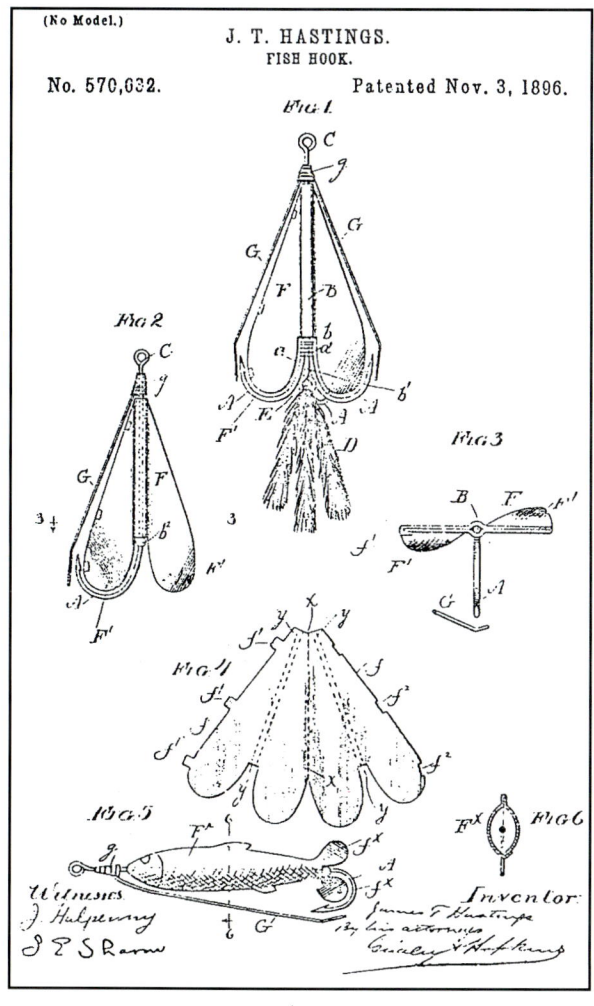

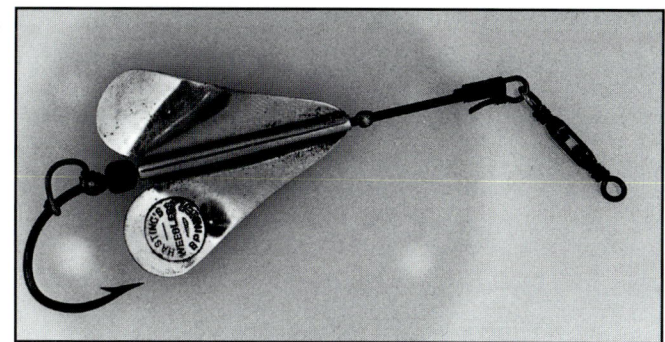

A. Hastings' Nov. 3, 1896 patent illustration. The patent actually calls for the blades on the lure to be removable. On Hastings' production model, they are stationary. Note the weedless metal minnow in the bottom of the illustration.

B. "Hasting's Weedless Spinner." The wire weed guard has been broken off. The lure is marked Hastings Weedless Spinner. The loop on the back is for red flannel. $30.00 – 40.00.

C. 1896 ad from the Wilkinson Co. catalog.

D. Photo and circa 1904 ad for the "Hasting's Casting Minnow." This is a 4½" rubber minnow painted white. It is extremely rare. It probably does not fall within the time frame of this book. The ad is from a Hibbard, Spencer, Bartlett & Co. catalog. $500.00 – 750.00.

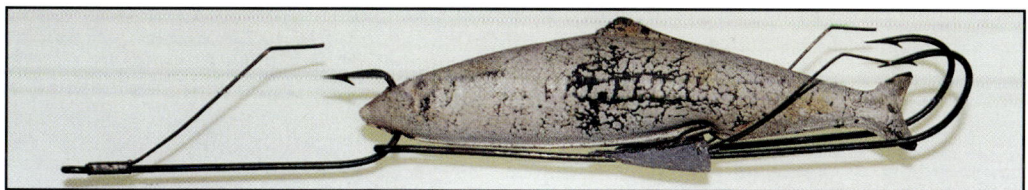

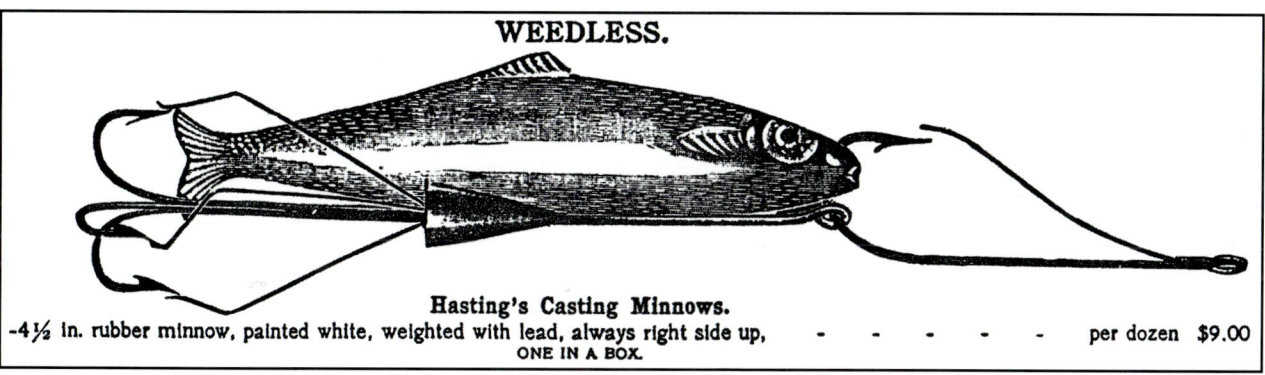

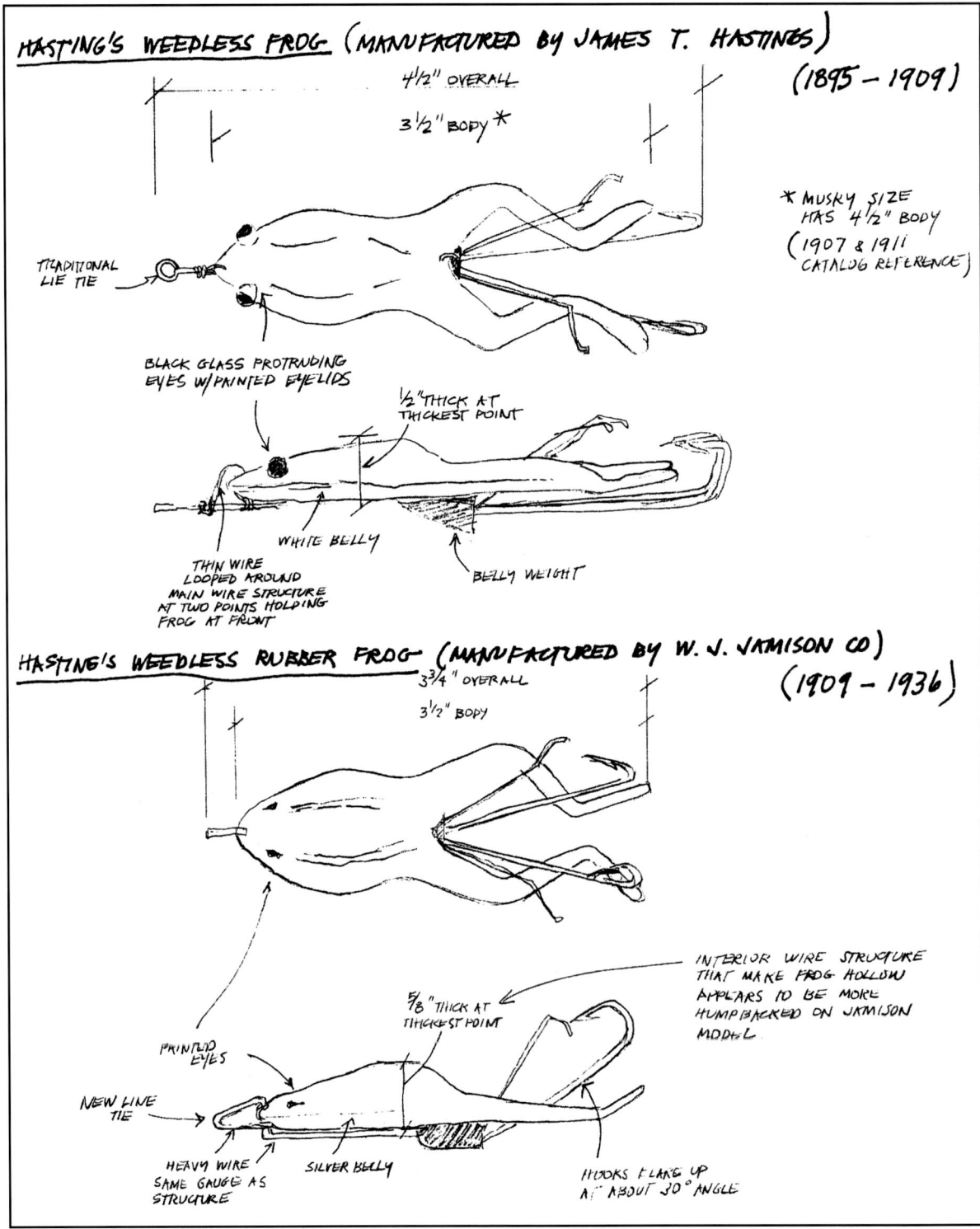

Drawing and text by Steve Lumpkin.

Drawings showing the differences between the Hastings and the Jamison versions of the Hasting's Frog.

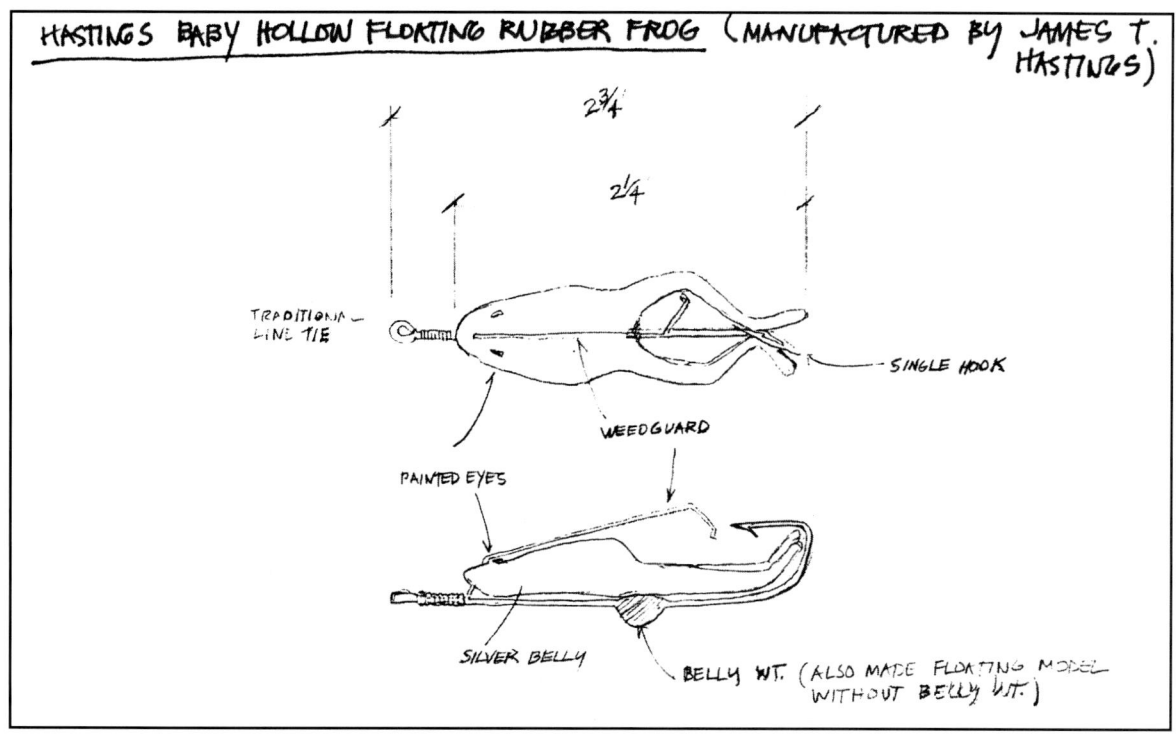

A.

Drawings and text by Steve Lumpkin.

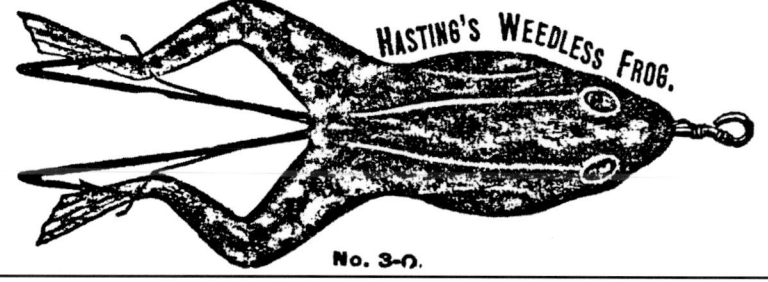

B.

A. Drawing showing the dimensions of the Baby Hasting's Frog. Note that this frog was also available in a floating version.

B. Ad from the 1898 J. F. Schmelzer & Son's Arms Co. Kansas City Mo.

C. Cut from the 1893 *Clark's Sportsman's Guide*.

C.

Charles R. Harris

C.R. Harris was born at White Pigeon, Michigan, in 1848. During his life he lived in Manistee, Niles, and Mackinac City, Michigan and also in Chicago, Illinois, and Williams, Arizona. Besides manufacturing lures, he was in the hotel business and also worked for the Michigan Central Railroad. At least two of the lures he manufactured fall into the time frame of this book. One is the "Harris Cork Floating Frog" and the other is the "Harris Featherbone Minnow." Harris died in 1922.

A.

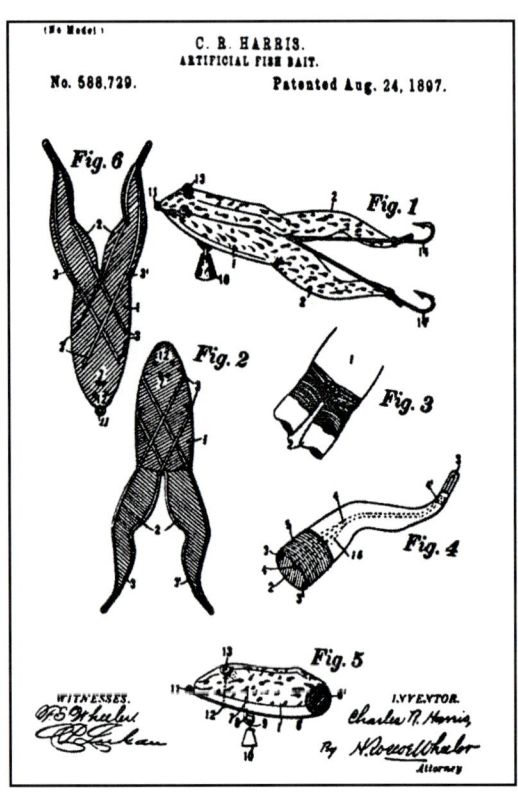

B.

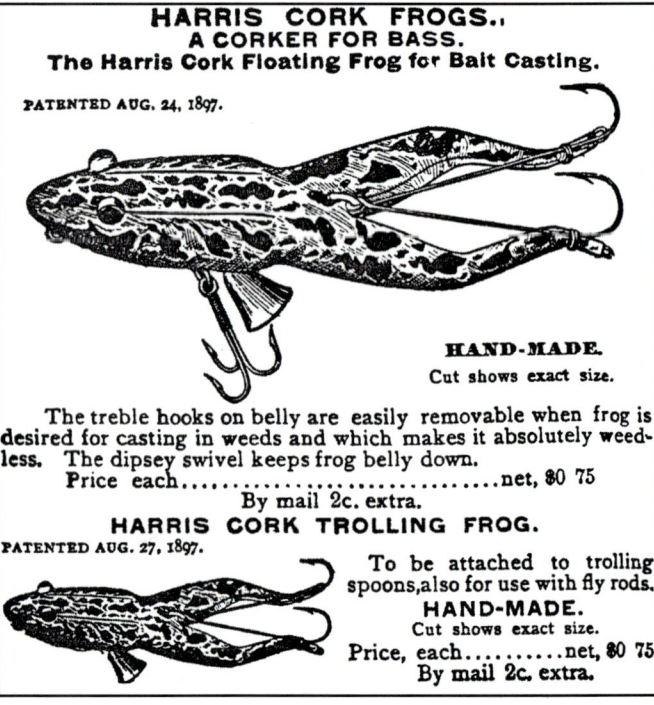

C.

A. The "Harris Cork Floating Frog" and its box. Note it says "Hand Made." This frog is 3" long. It was made in two sizes. $500.00 – 750.00.

B. C. R. Harris' Aug. 24, 1897 patent illustration. This was for his "Harris Cork Floating Frog." The frog was hand made of cork and reinforced with thread wrap.

C. Ad from a Von Lengerke & Antoine catalog, circa 1905.

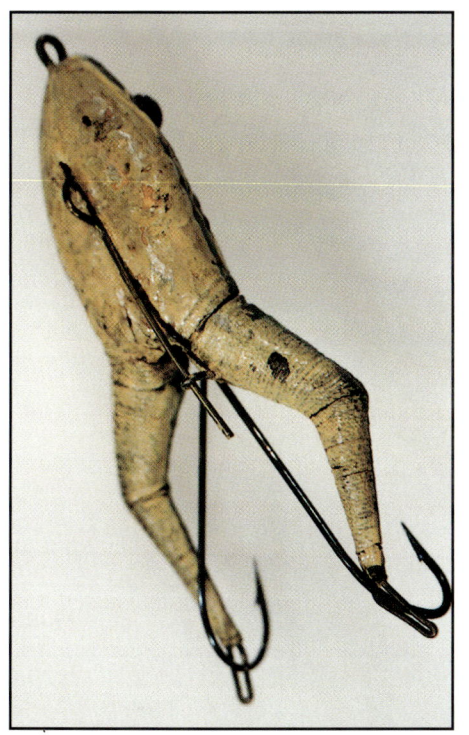

A.

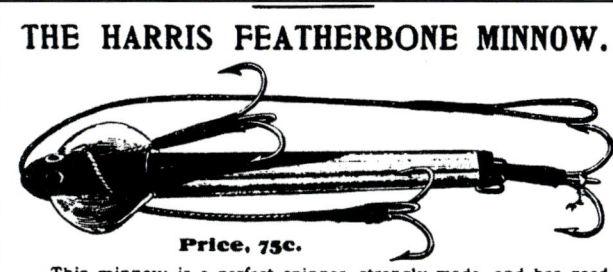

B.

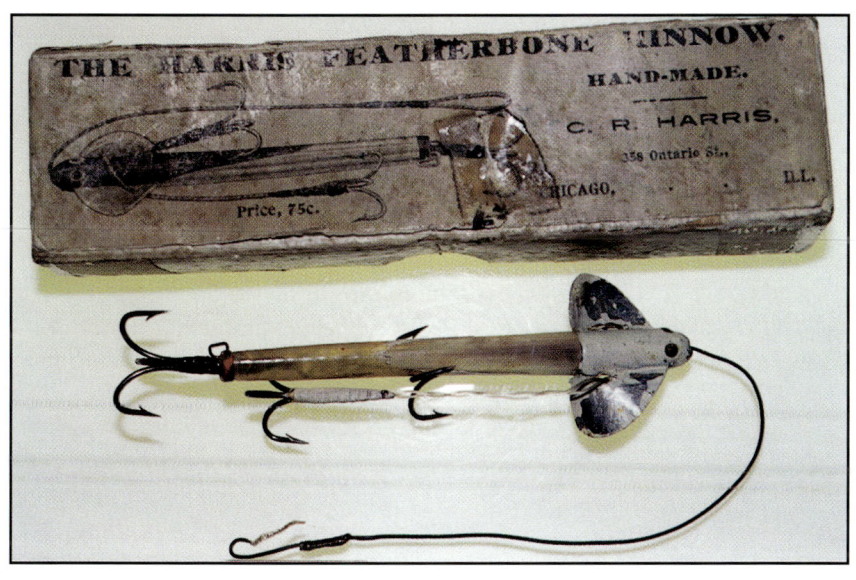

C.

D.

A. Bottom view of the "Harris Cork Floating Frog." Note the brass wire clip that holds the lead weight and hook. $250.00 – 300.00.

B. An 1898 ad for "The Harris Featherbone Minnow." This lure is 3¼" long. Note that it states that it is heavier than a Phantom Minnow. However, it still looks like a Phantom Minnow.

C. "The Harris Featherbone Minnow" in its original box. This lure has a quill body and a heavy metal head. Note the Chicago address. $1,000.00+.

D. The Harris underwater minnow. A rare and beautiful lure. This lure is 3" long. $1,000.00+.

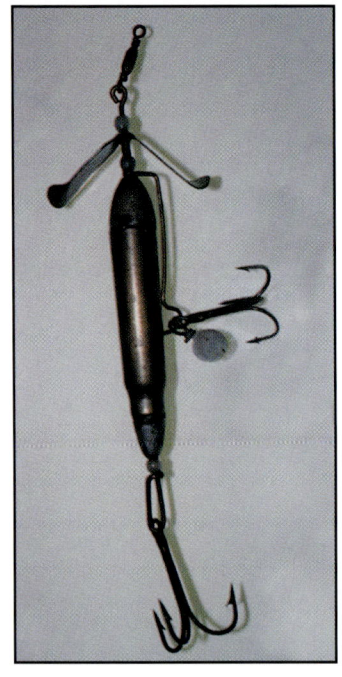

A.

B.

A. Harris "Bullet" bait. This lure is 2½" long. The time frame of this bait is unknown. $350.00 – 500.00.

B. Ad from a circa 1898 Rueben Wood's & Sons Co. catalog.

C. Pair of Harris Featherbone Spinner lures. These lures are approximately 2" long. The time frame of these lures is unknown, but they are similar to the Featherbone Minnow of 1898. $350.00 – 500.00.

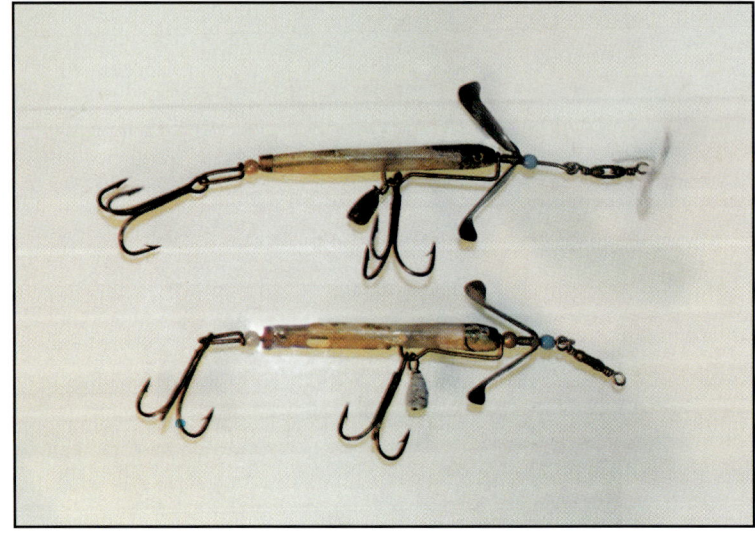

C.

Right: Box for the Harris "Manistee Surface Bait." This bait was manufactured after 1901 (probably after 1905), but I chose to include it anyway because it is the Harris lure most likely to be encountered by collectors and it's neat looking. No value established.

Below: Two and three-hook versions of the "Manistee Surface Bait." The top lure is the most common and has the Harris wire clip hook hanger. $500.00 – 750.00; $600.00 – 800.00; $600.00 – 800.00.

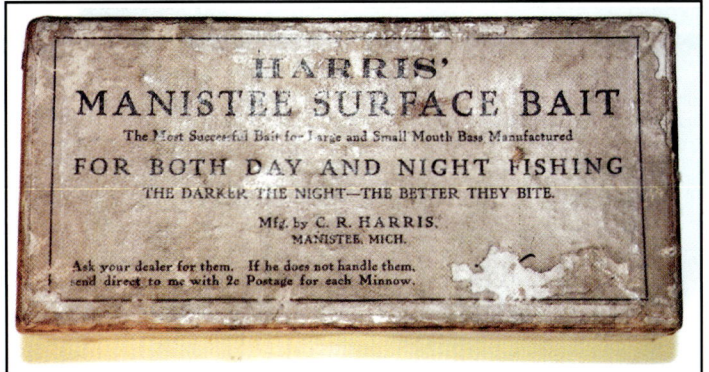

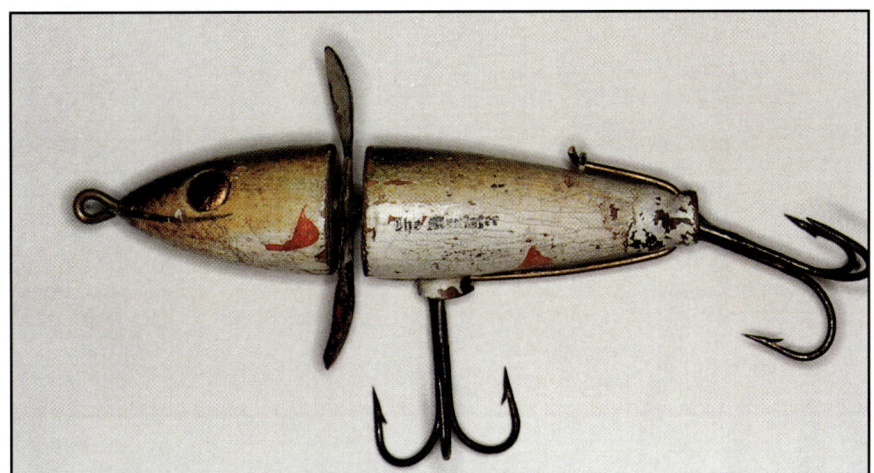

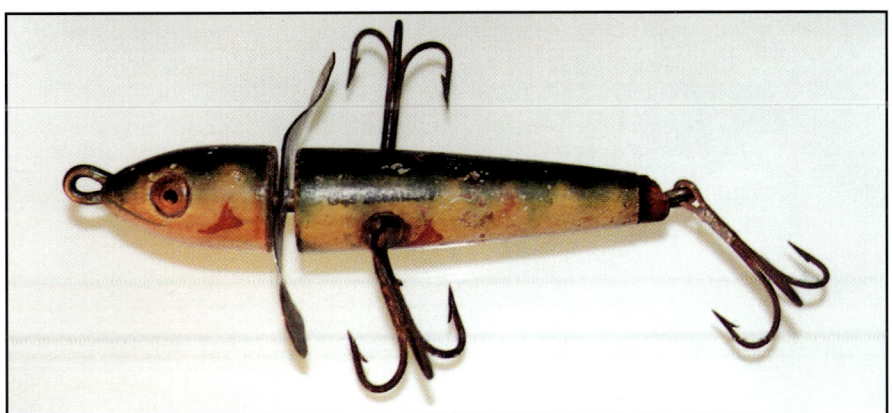

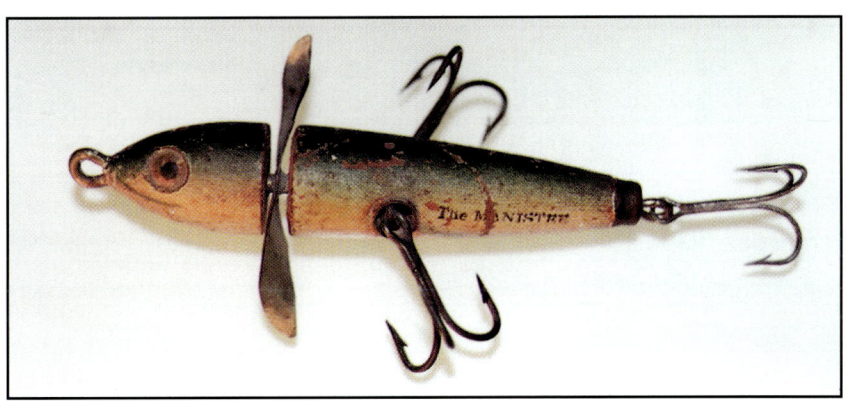

Cover of 1893 *Clark's Anglers and Sportsman's Guide*. It was hand-colored.

Miscellaneous Manufacturers

The following companies and individuals are listed in this category for a couple of reasons. In some cases I didn't feel I had enough information to present an interesting layout and there often was little if any history available. Also a company may have produced only a single lure (albeit sometimes a very interesting lure).

These companies and individuals are not arranged in any particular order.

FREDERIC C.P. ROBINSON

Frederic C. P. Robinson, British subject residing in New York.

Assigned to Thomas J. Conroy of Brooklyn, N.Y.

A. The Robinson Mouse. The Thomas J. Conroy Company of Brooklyn, N. Y. was assigned the patent for this mouse lure. They advertised it in their catalog beginning in 1885. This was before the patent was granted. $200.00 – 250.00.

B. Frederick Robinson's 1885 patent for a hair covered mouse or rat. The patent specifies that the mouse be made of cork or some other suitable material and be weighted so as to float upright in the water.

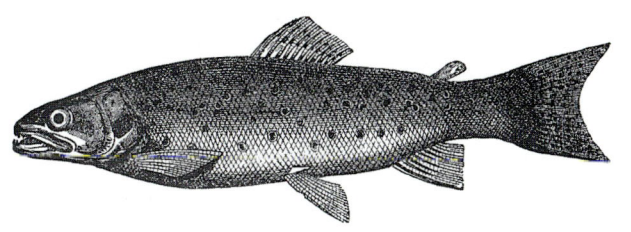

A.

Miscellaneous Manufacturers

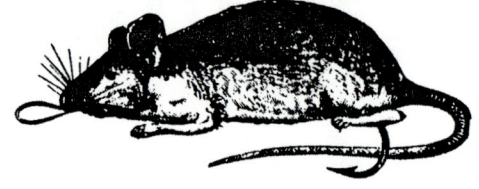

Ad from the Thomas J. Conroy 1889 catalog.

John R. Harlow

Auburn, N.Y.

John is listed in the 1888 Auburn city directory as a manufacturer of trolling spoons living at 24 Lincoln. In the 1900 directory he is listed as superintendent at the Standard Bait Manufacturing Co.

Harlow's trolling lure. $50.00 – 100.00.

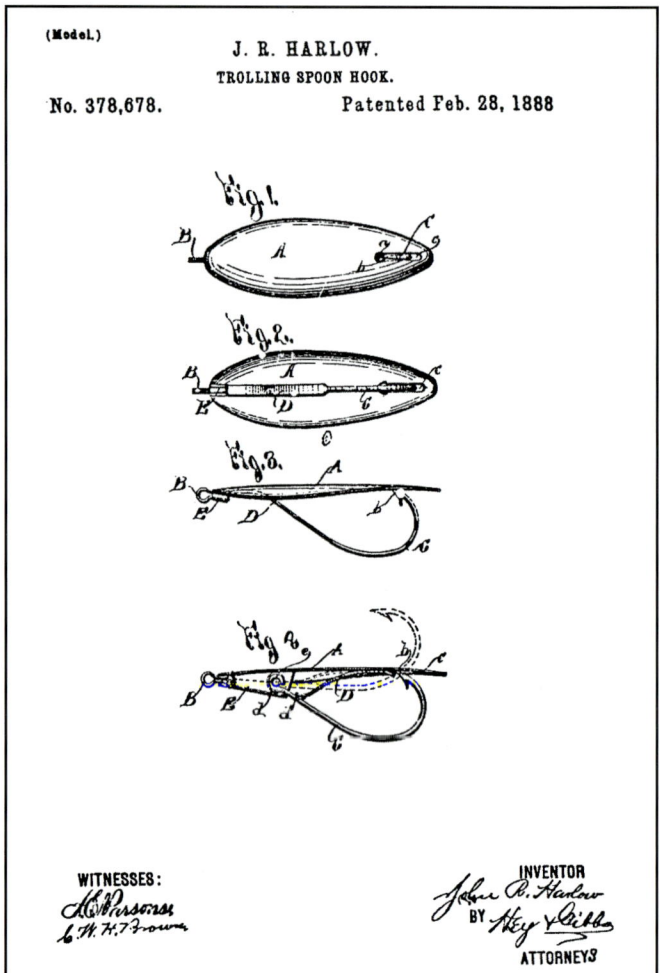

Harlow's 1888 patent for a retractable hook trolling spoon.

Miscellaneous Manufacturers

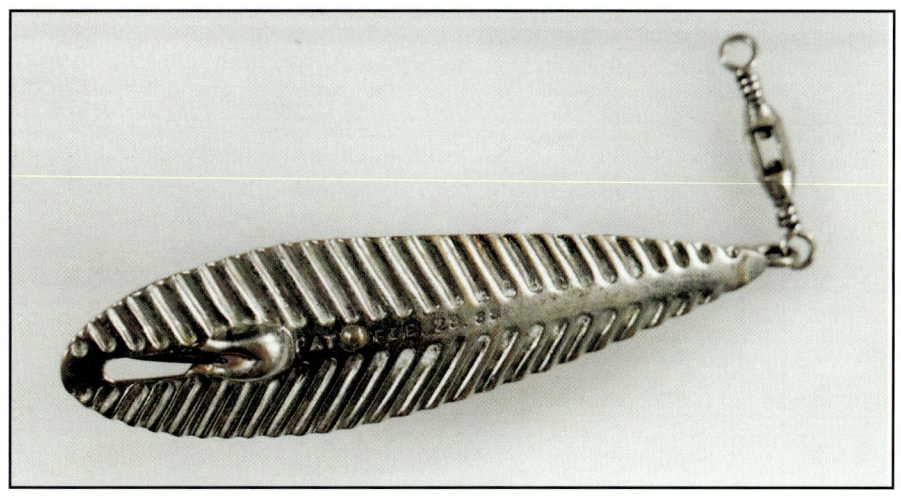

A.

B.

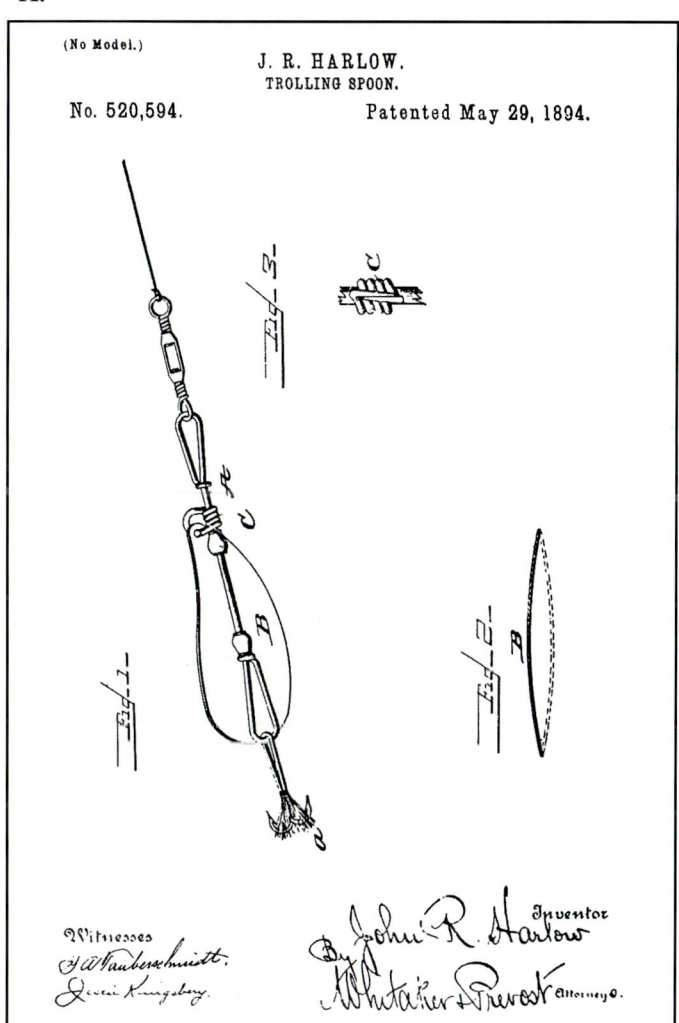

C.

A. Top view of the Trolling Spoon. A Reuben Wood's Sons Co. catalog calls this bait "The Wood's Crown Weedless Spoon." $50.00 – 100.00.

B. Two other spoons manufactured by Harlow. $20.00 – 40.00.

C. This 1894 patent serves two purposes. First relates to the blade being made of a thin pliable metal so that it could be pressed with the fingers and made to reverse itself from convex to concave and vice versa. The second is the clevis that attaches the blade to the shaft. This is made in the manner of a split ring so the blade can be changed at will. I have never seen either of these in use on a lure.

Miscellaneous Manufacturers

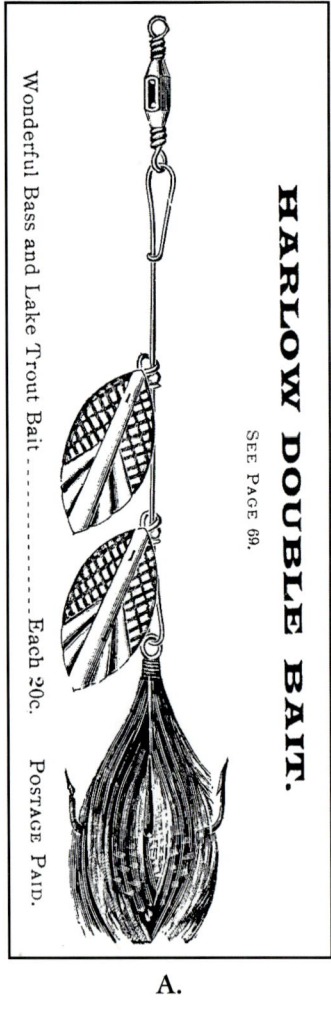

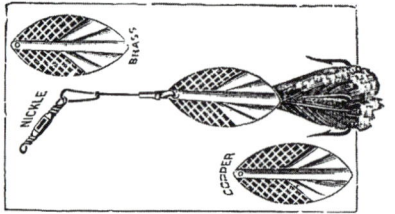

A. Harlow's Double Bait. $20.00 – 40.00.

B. An interesting spinner marked J. R. Harlow. $50.00 – 100.00.

C. Wood's Three Jokers. I don't know who manufactured this, but it was sold by the Rueben Wood's Sons Co. of Syracuse, N. Y. This blade pattern was also used by Henry Loftie of Syracuse, N.Y., and the Enterprise Mfg. Co. I suspect that only one of the companies made this blade.

M.F. Pierce

Marion, N. Y.

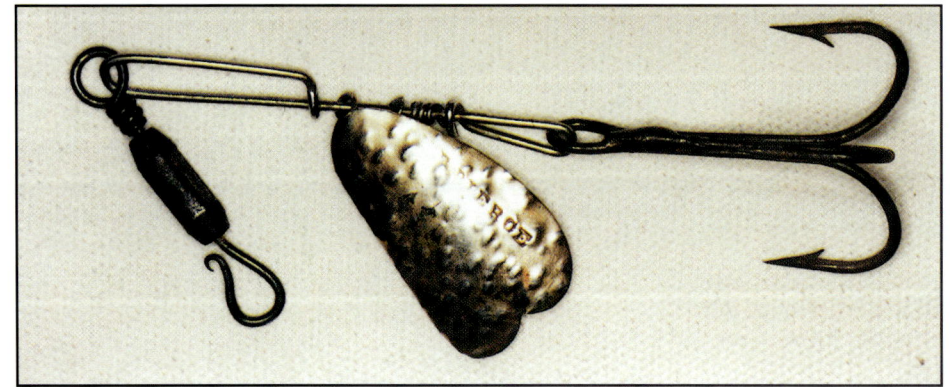

M. F. Pierce spinner. Note the ancient swivel. The blade on this lure is 1⅜" long. $40.00 – 60.00.

Miscellaneous Manufacturers

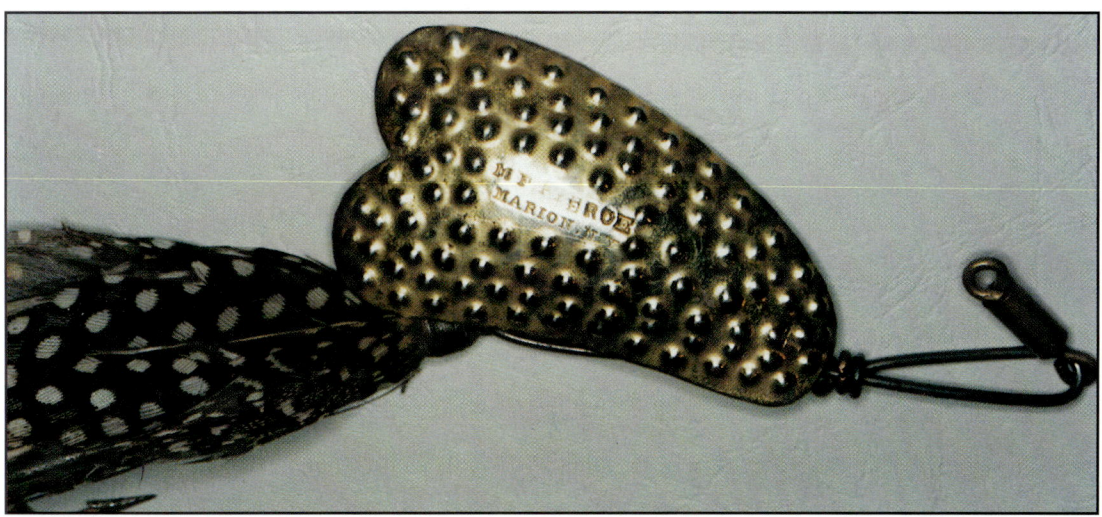

Spinner marked M. F. Pierce, Marion, N. Y. Note the pronounced dimples on the blade and the solid swivel. These are very old lures. $40.00 – 60.00.

WILLIAM H. JAMES

Brooklyn, N. Y.

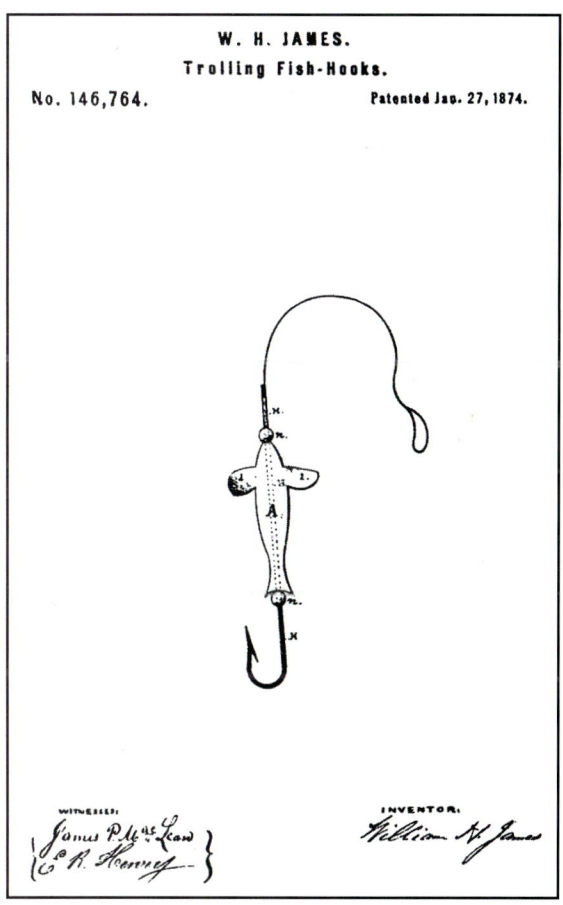

A pair of James patented Trolling Squid lures. Early ads for this lure were usually accompanied by a warning for the buyer to beware of imitations, when this in reality was a rip-off of English lures that had been made for decades. $50.00 – 75.00.

Patent illustration of James Trolling Squid. This patent claims that the wings, or fins, on the lure are novel and useful improvements. This is interesting because any number of English lures were using this principle and had been for years.

Miscellaneous Manufacturers

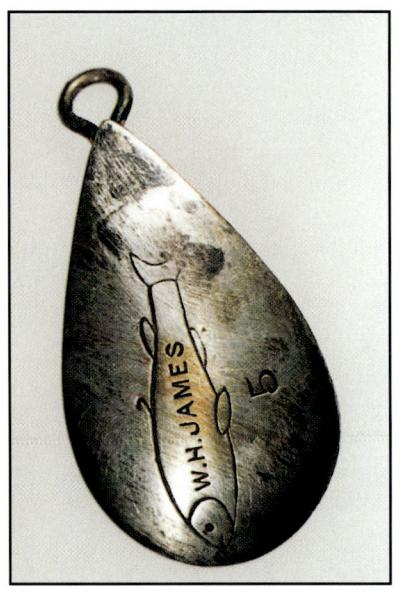

A.

B.

A. Extra large Trolling Squid. The body is over 4" long and it has a huge swivel. This lure came in at least four sizes. The J.T. Buel Co. in later years made a lure that looked exactly like this one. $75.00 – 125.00.

B. W.H. James also made more conventional lures. They usually have the fish logo on the blade. $30.00 – 40.00.

Louis Kessler
Ludington, Mich.

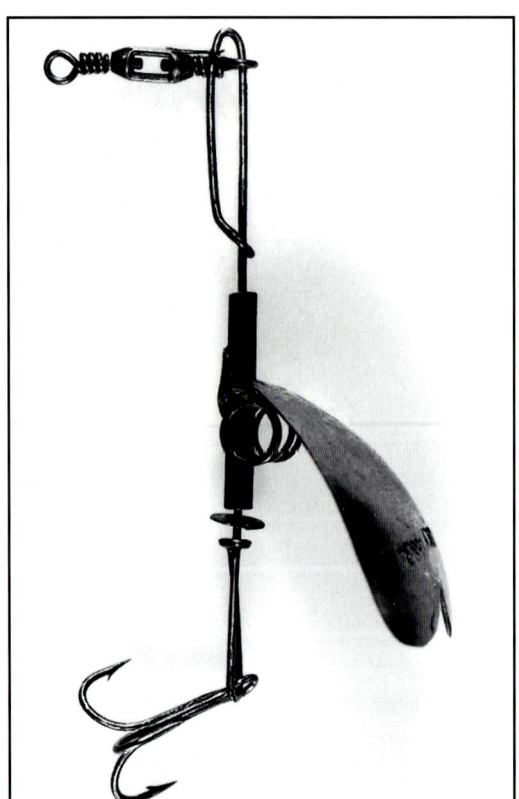

A.

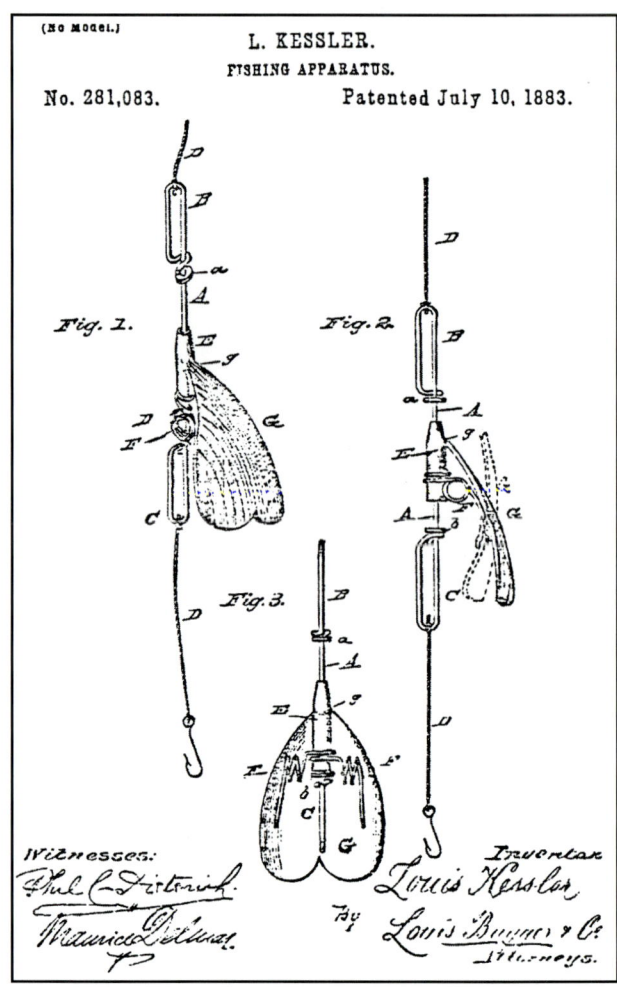

B.

A. Louis Kessler's spinning lure. $200.00 – 250.00.

B. Patent drawing of Louis Kessler's 1883 spinning lure. It features a spring-loaded blade.

230

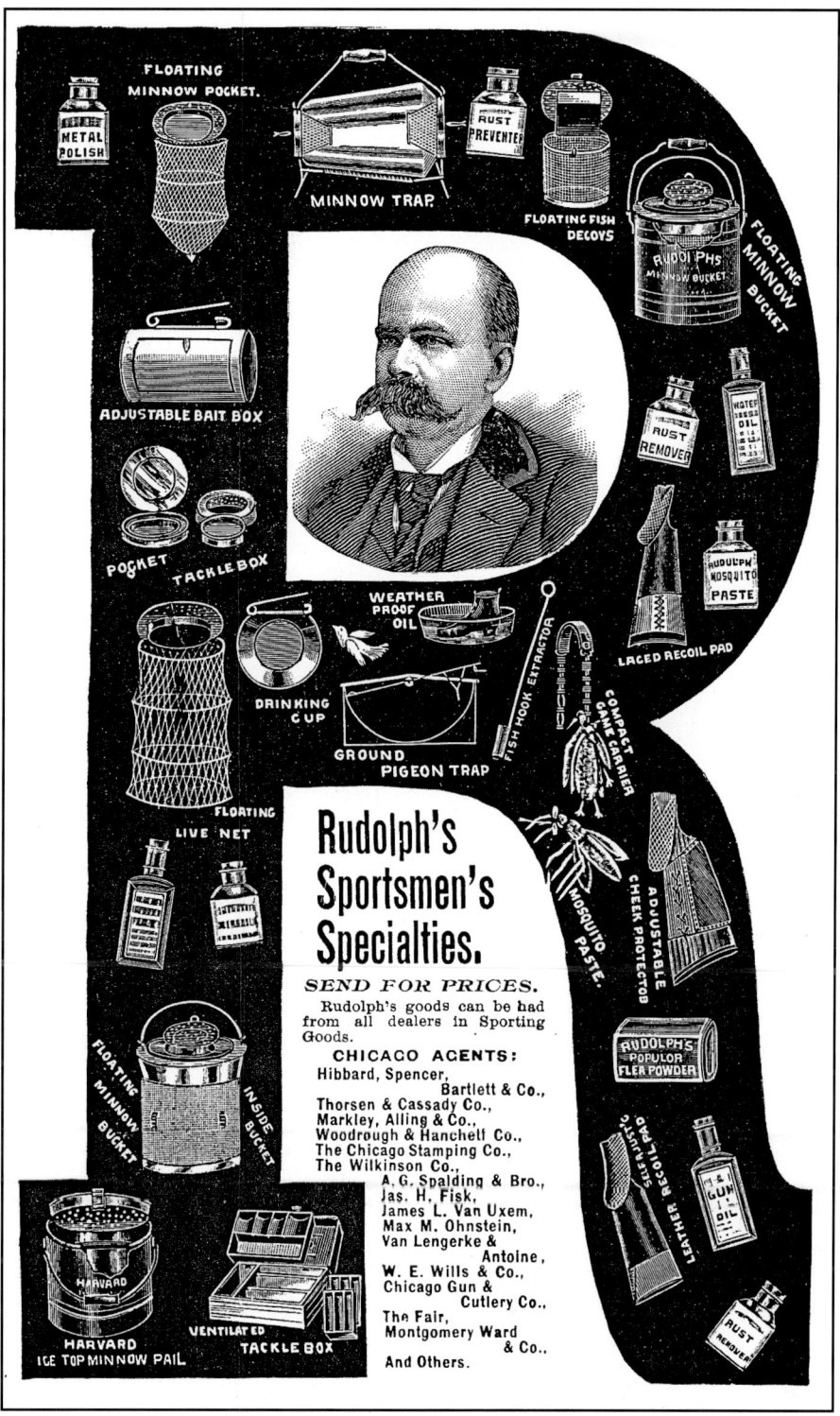

Advertisement taken from *Clark's Anglers and Sportsman's Guide,* World's Fair Edition 1893. Rudolph had a very diversified line of goods. Note the interesting minnow trap at the top of the page.

Miscellaneous Manufacturers

Albert G. Mack

Rochester, N.Y.

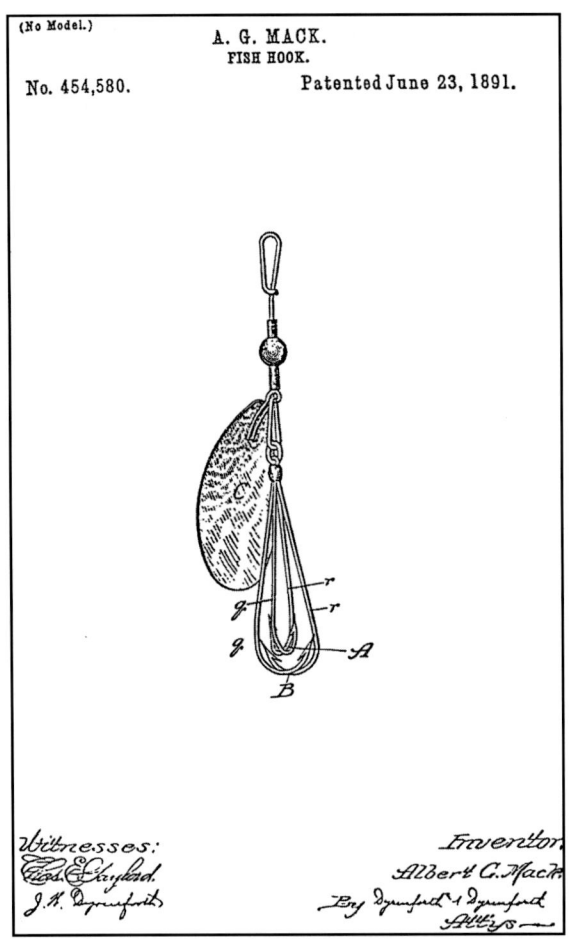

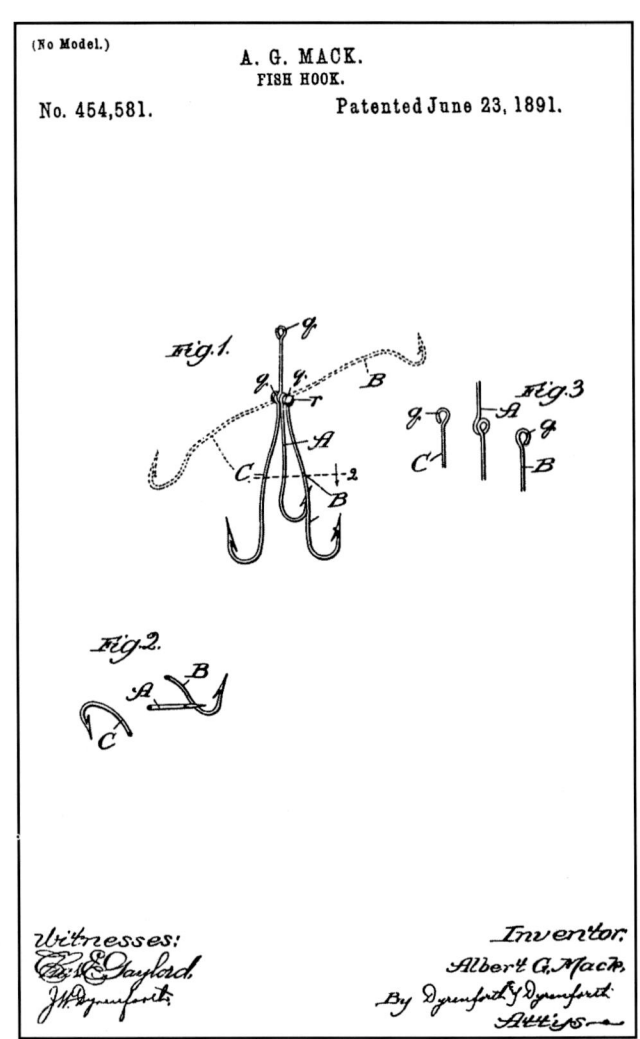

Mack's June 23, 1891 patent for a bait with weedless hooks. Notice that it has four hooks all pointing a different direction and each protecting the other.

This patent was also procured on June 23, 1891. It consists of a baited hook in the center and two longer swinging hooks on the sides. The object was to have hooks ready to intercept a fish coming from any direction.

Mack's "Automatic Weed-Deflecting Bait." $50.00 – 75.00.

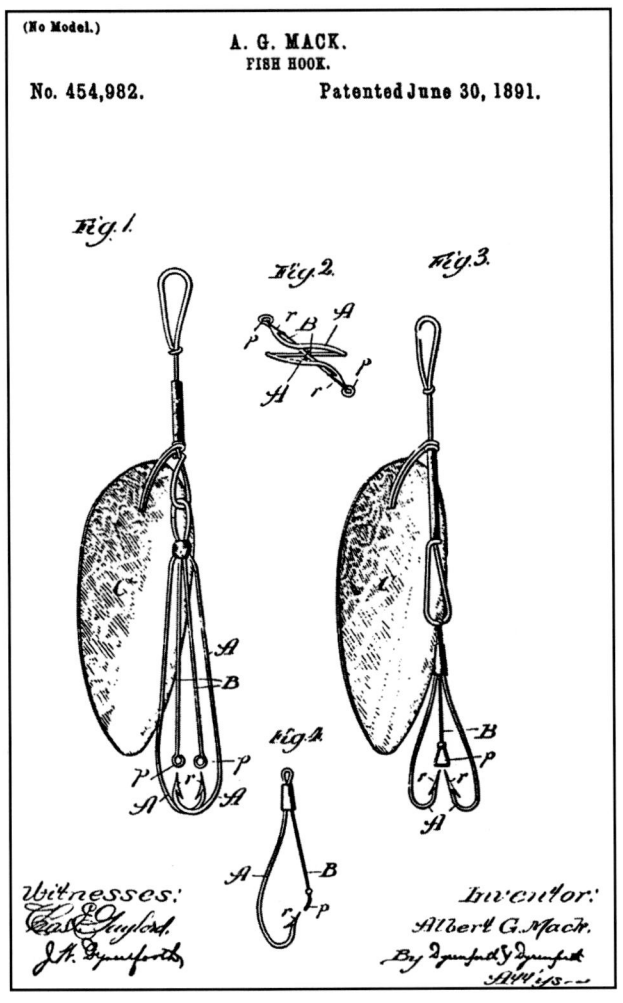

A.

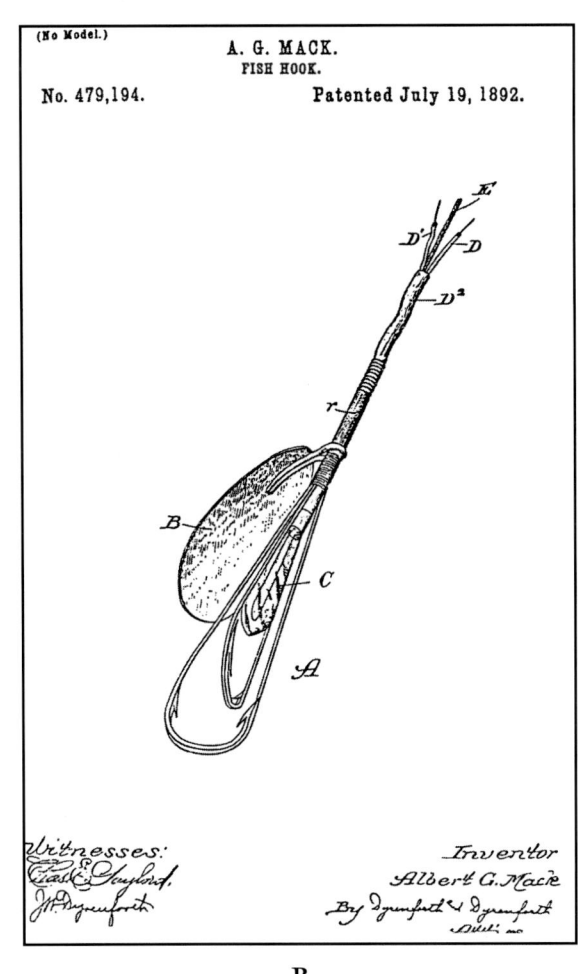

B.

A. June 30, 1891 patent. This is very similar to his June 23 patent except here he is using two hooks instead of four. He has also added a flexible steel weedguard to each hook. This is the lure that he actually produced.

B. Mack's July 19, 1892 patent. This is probably the first patented electric lure. It used wires that ran from the lure to a battery or generator located in the boat or on shore. It is doubtful that it was ever manufactured.

C. 1900 ad for Mack's "Automatic Weed-Deflecting Bait."

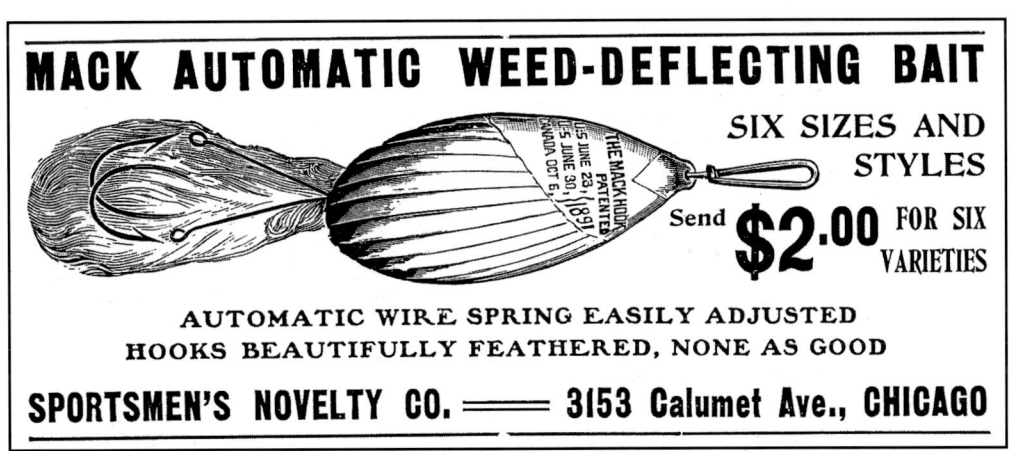

C.

Miscellaneous Manufacturers

W. Delany

Cobourg, Ontario

William Delany was born in 1834 and died in 1912. He was listed as a jeweler. His wife's name was Lavinia.

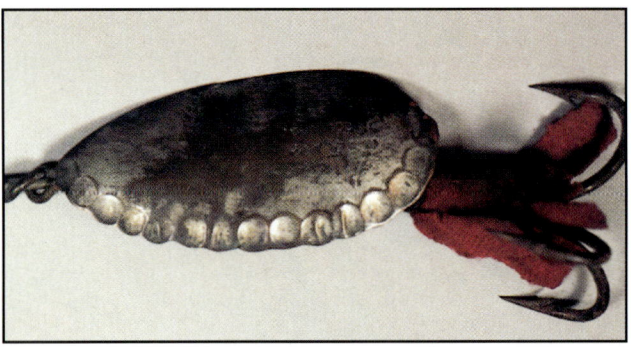

A.

A. Typical crimped edge Delany spinner. $20.00 – 30.00.

B. Group of Delany Spinners. The one on the left shows up in turn-of-the-century Enterprise Mfg. Co. catalogs as the "Coburg Bait." $20.00 – 30.00 each.

B.

Henry Corbin Brush

Brush's Mills, N.Y.

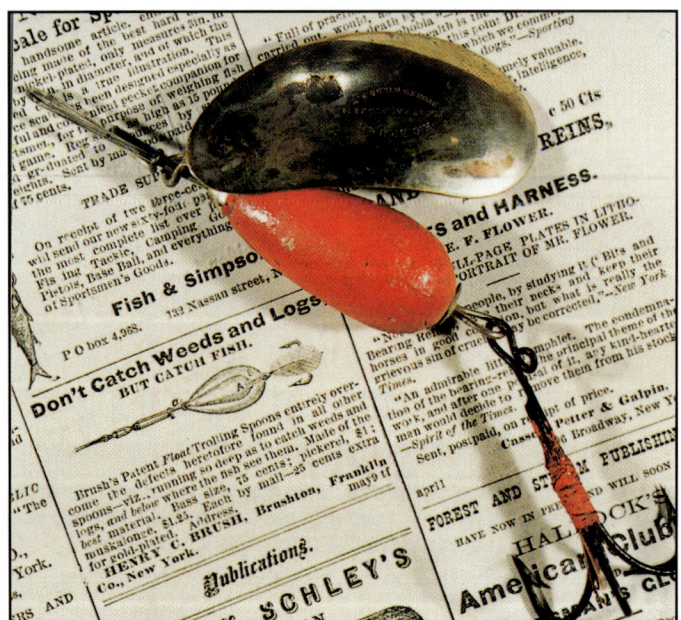

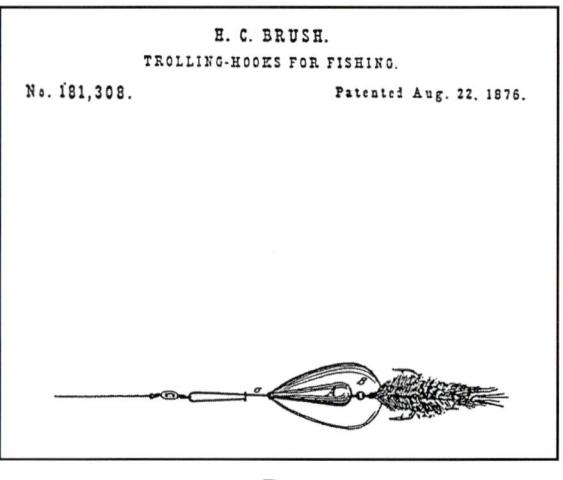

D.

C. Made in three size: Bass 75¢, Pickerel $1, and Muskalonge $1.25. $100.00 – 125.00.

D. Illustration for Brush's Aug. 22, 1876 patent. The basic premise of the patent was the cork body that kept the lure near or at the surface of the water. Some collectors consider this the first wooden lure. I believe the Flying Helgramite is.

C.

Miscellaneous Manufacturers

A fantastic collection of Brush Spinners. All of the colors and sizes are represented.

Archer Wakeman

Cape Vincent, N.Y.

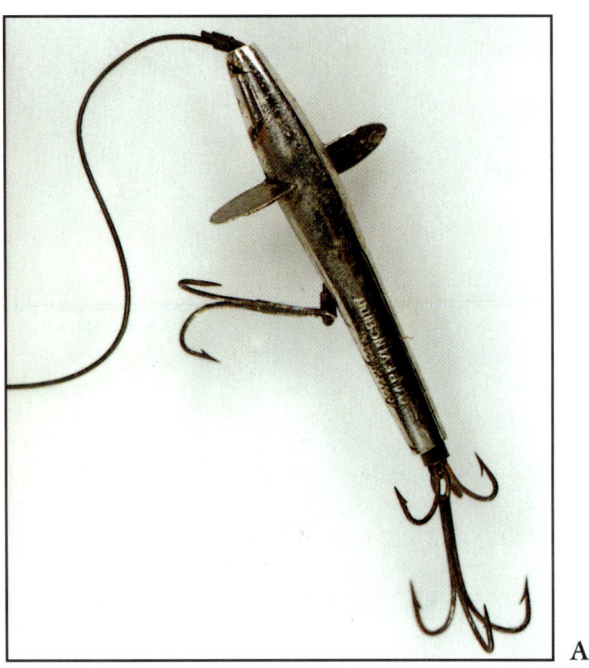

A.

B.

A. Archer Wakeman's first patent, a Devon type lure. $350.00 – 500.00.

B. Drawing of Archer Wakeman's Aug. 5, 1879 patent. It is a Devon type lure almost identical to many English lures.

C. Patent drawing for the "Skeleton Bait." This patent was granted on April 13, 1886. Although basically a minnow harness, it could also be used as a lure without the minnow. This illustration is page 1 of 2. This rendition is nearest to the actual lure Wakeman produced.

D. "Skeleton Bait" showing the size difference between the largest and smallest models. $250.00 – 350.00 small; $750.00 – 1,000.00 large.

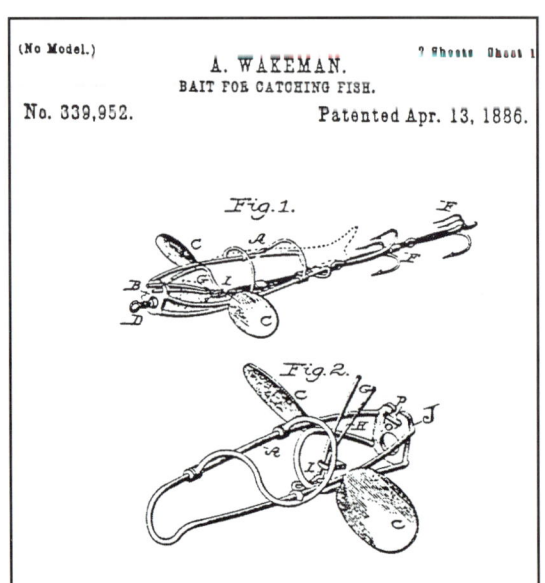

C.

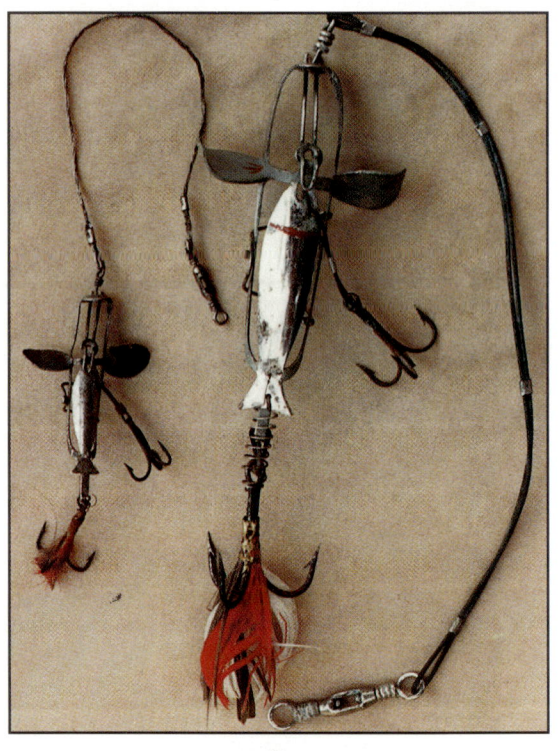

D.

MISCELLANEOUS MANUFACTURERS

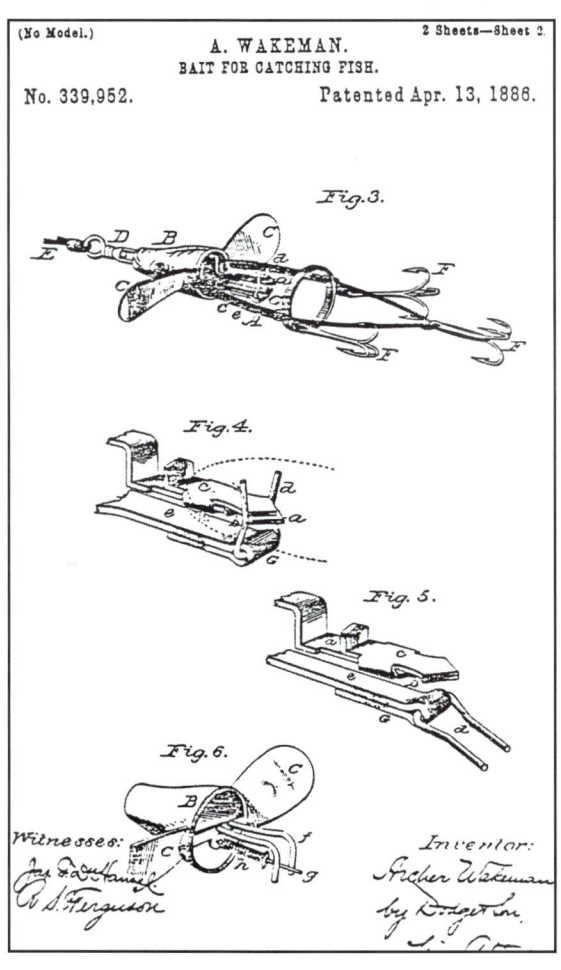

A.

A. Second page of the "Skeleton Bait" patent drawing, shown on the facing page. I have not seen a lure using this design.

B. Skeleton Bait with Box. Note that this lure has a spinner in front of it. The spinners are sometimes marked "Wakeman, Syracuse N.Y."

C. What is probably an older style box.

D. Ad from a circa 1898 Wood's Sons Co. catalog. This ad clearly shows the various parts of the lure. This is useful in determining if a lure is complete.

C.

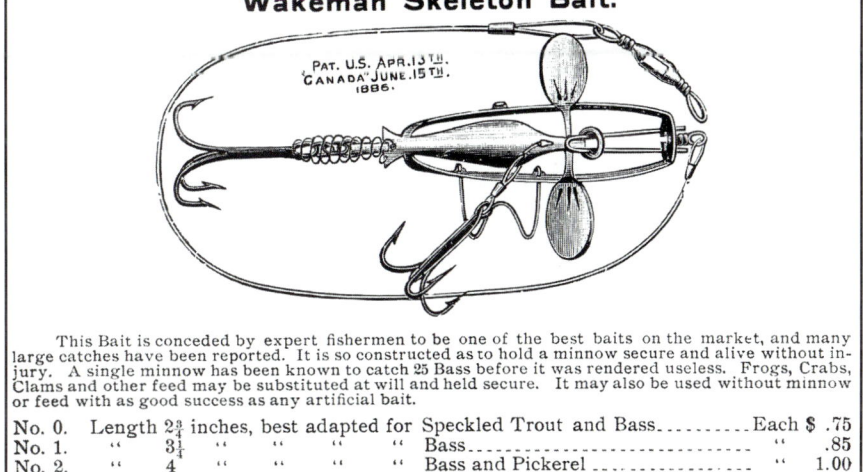

D.

Miscellaneous Manufacturers

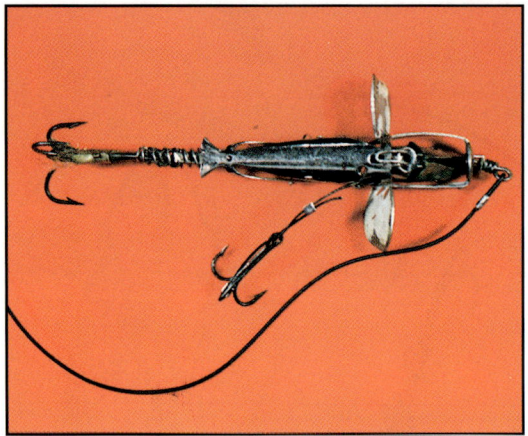

A.

A. Underside view of the Skeleton Bait.

B. Archer Wakeman's patent drawing of a fishing rod that purposely twists the line to make the bait spin. The idea was that you could make a bait spin without it being in motion, as in trolling or casting. Just sit there in a chair on the bank and spin your bait.

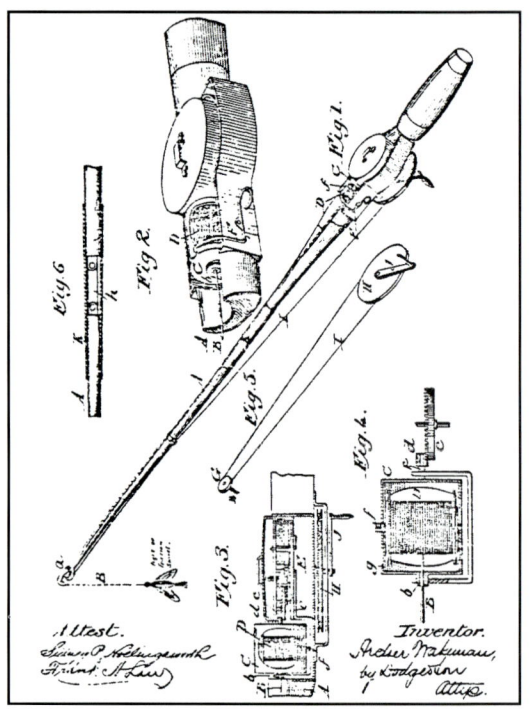

B.

Henry Zuckweiler

Pekin, Illinois

Born 1857, died Aug 6, 1931, he was the son of Louis and Julia Hoerr-Zuckweiler, pioneer residents of Pekin. He was for many years in the saloon business.

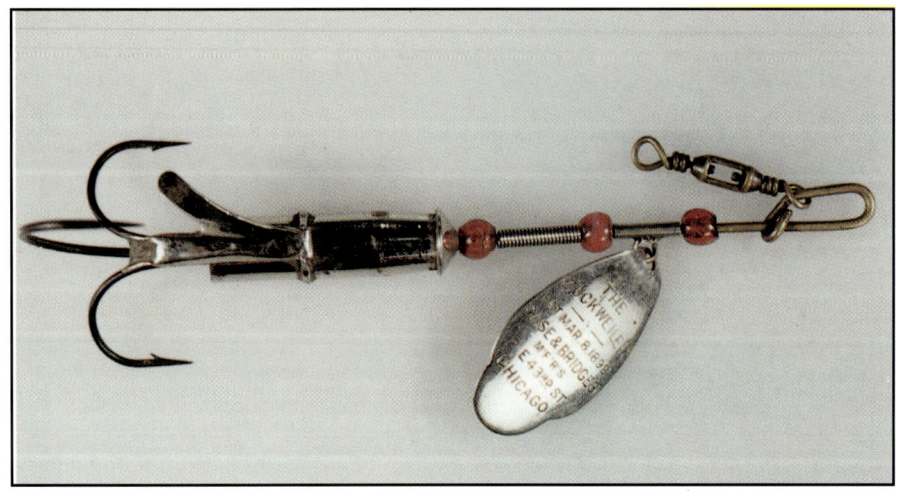

This is a lure with a spring hook arrangement. One hook is stationary and the other two hooks, which are spring loaded, swing up so all three hook points come together and are held in place by a folding weed guard. When a fish strikes and depresses the weed guard, the spring-loaded hooks return to their original open position. Got that? This lure was patented March 8, 1892 and manufactured by Case and Bridges, 2 E 43rd St., Chicago, Ill. $500.00 – 750.00.

Miscellaneous Manufacturers

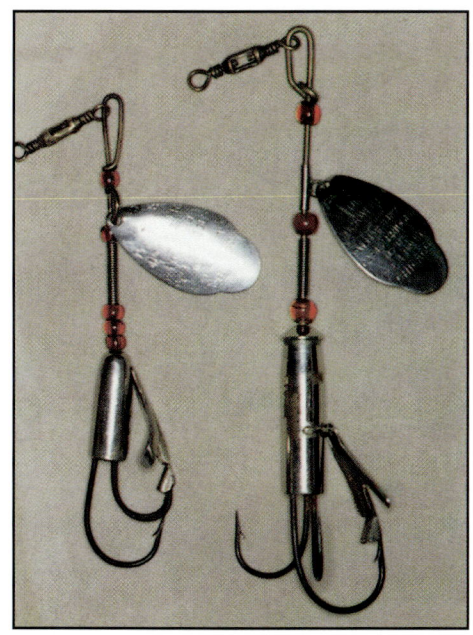

A.

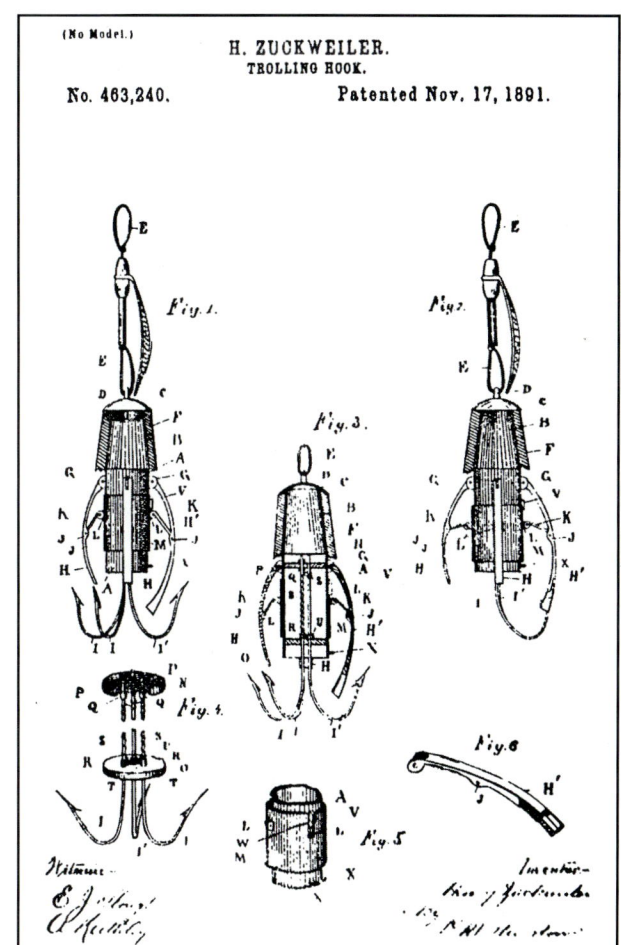

B.

A. Two variations of the Zuckweiler trolling bait. The one on the left is cocked and ready to go. $500.00 – 750.00.

B. Zuckweiler's Nov. 17, 1891 patent illustration.

C. This blade is marked Pat. Apld. for H. Zuckweiler-Pekin, Ill. The patent may have been for a design patent. $30.00 – 40.00.

D. Zuckweiler's Mar. 8, 1892 patent illustration. This patent is most like the actual lure.

C.

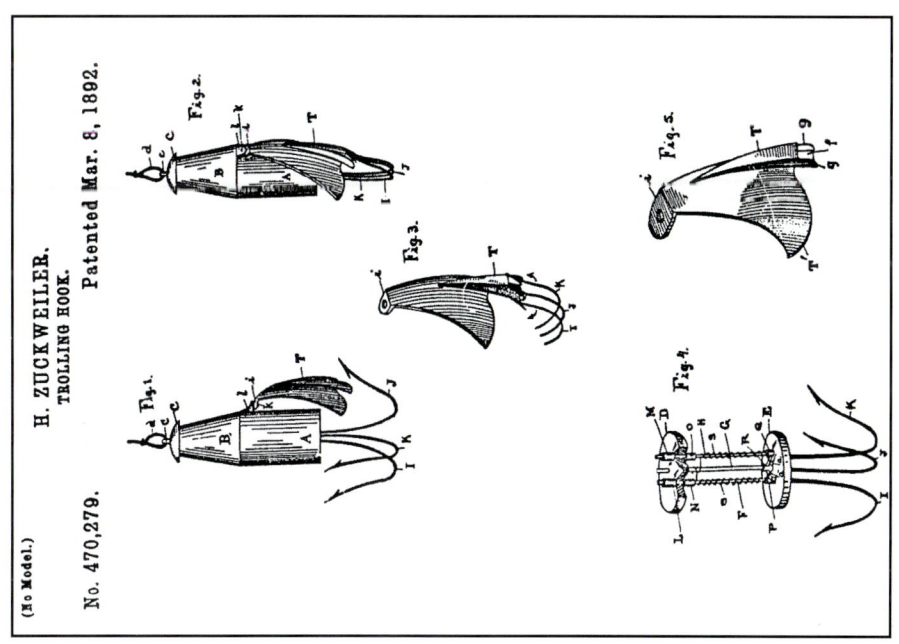

D.

Miscellaneous Manufacturers

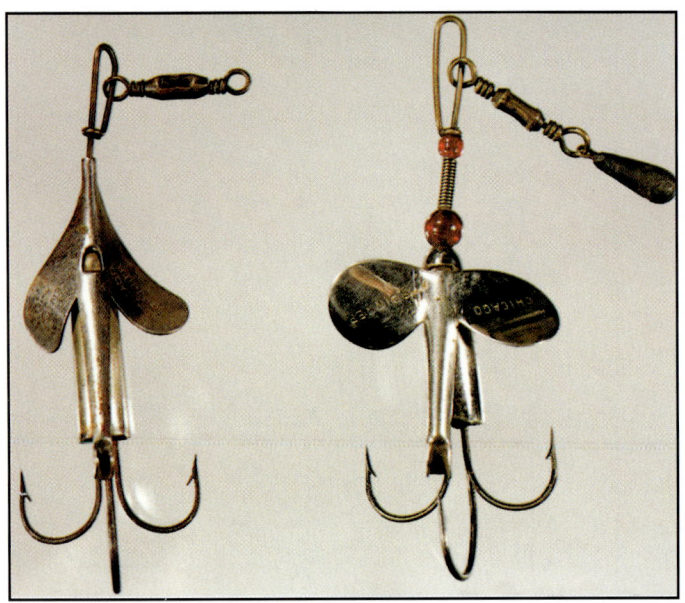

A.

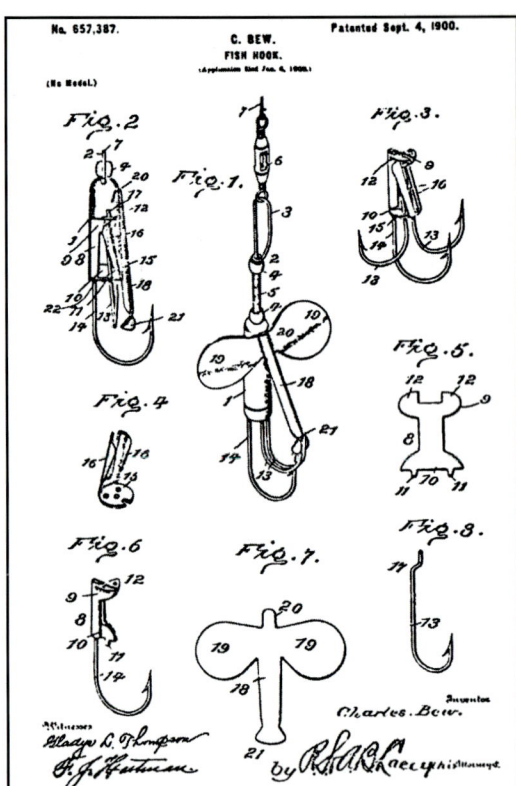

B.

A. Two "Chicago Spinners." The one on the left is marked "patented Sept. 4, 1900," the one on the right just "Chicago Spinner." Both were made on a patent granted to Charles Bew of Chicago, Ill. on Sept. 4, 1900. It is interesting to note that one of the witnesses to this patent was Clinton E. Case. Case and Bridges was the company that manufactured Zuckwieler's Trolling bait. I'm not sure what the connection is here. Perhaps Zuckweiler sold the patent to Case and Bridges and they in turn patented a modified version. $100.00 – 125.00.

B. Charles Bew's Sept. 4, 1900 patent illustration.

BENJAMIN F. BURGESS
Jackson, Mich.

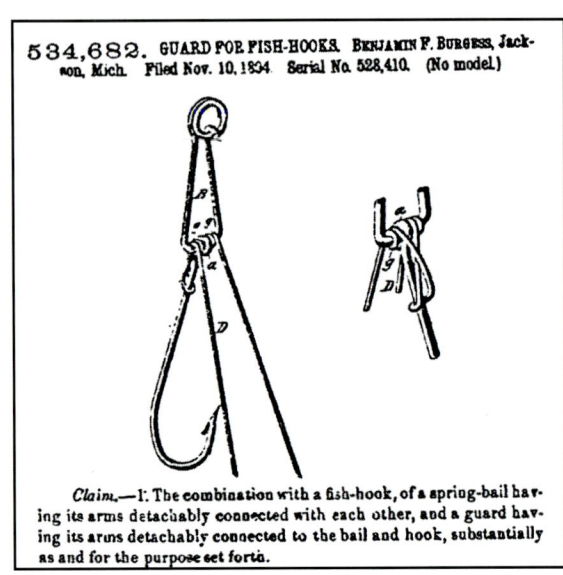

Patent Gazette illustration of Burgess' Sept. 26, 1895 patent for a weedless hook.

Spinner utilizing Burgess' patent. $75.00 – 100.00.

MISCELLANEOUS MANUFACTURERS

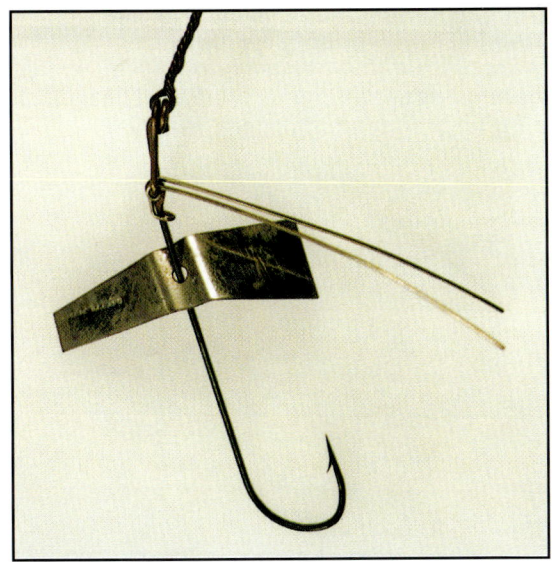

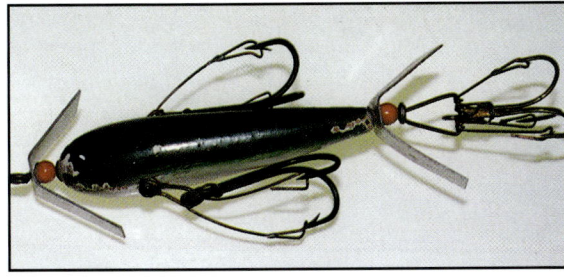

A. Burgess Weedless Hook. This is the Burgess item most familiar to collectors. $20.00 – 30.00.

B. The weedless Burgess Minnow. This lure uses the Burgess weedless patent. Its time frame is not established but it appears to be around the turn of the century. $1,000.00+.

C. Another Burgess Minnow using the Weedless patent hooks. $1,000.00+.

D. Cut from The Wilkinson Co. catalog. Note the different sizes available.

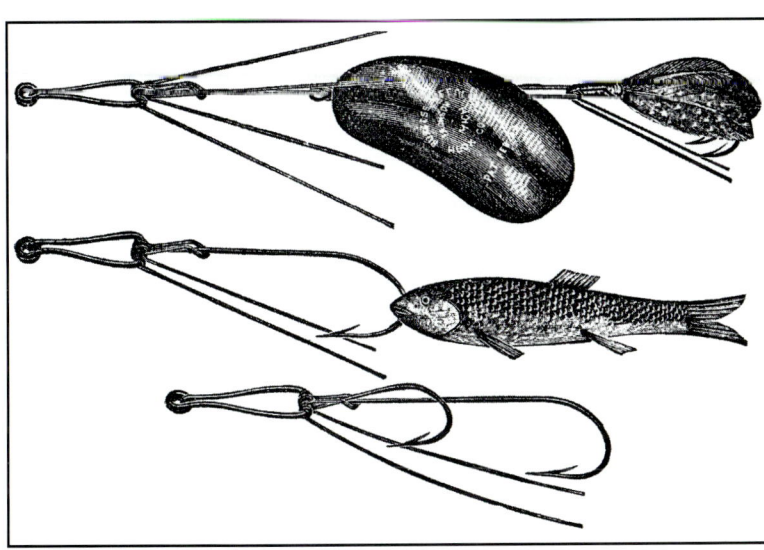

D.

241

MISCELLANEOUS MANUFACTURERS

HENRY E. SKINNER

San Francisco, California
Assigned to Edward T. Allen

A.

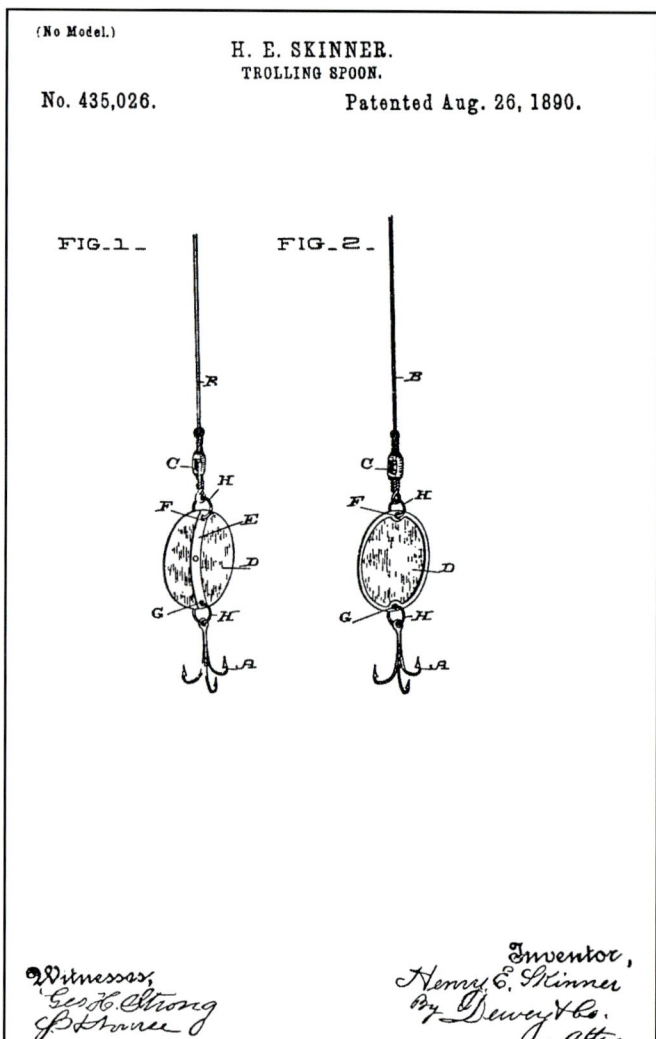

B.

A. Unmarked abalone spoon that has all the characteristics of a Skinner patent lure. $20.00 – 40.00.

B. H. E. Skinner's Aug. 26, 1890 patent illustration. It was for the reinforcement of an abalone shell lure. It was assigned to Edward T. Allen.

C. Abalone spoon bearing Skinner's patent date. This lure is 3¼" long. The Enterprise Mfg. Co. must have acquired the patent rights to this lure. In their 1892 catalog they state that they are the exclusive agent for "Allen's Patented Abalone Bait." $150.00 – 250.00.

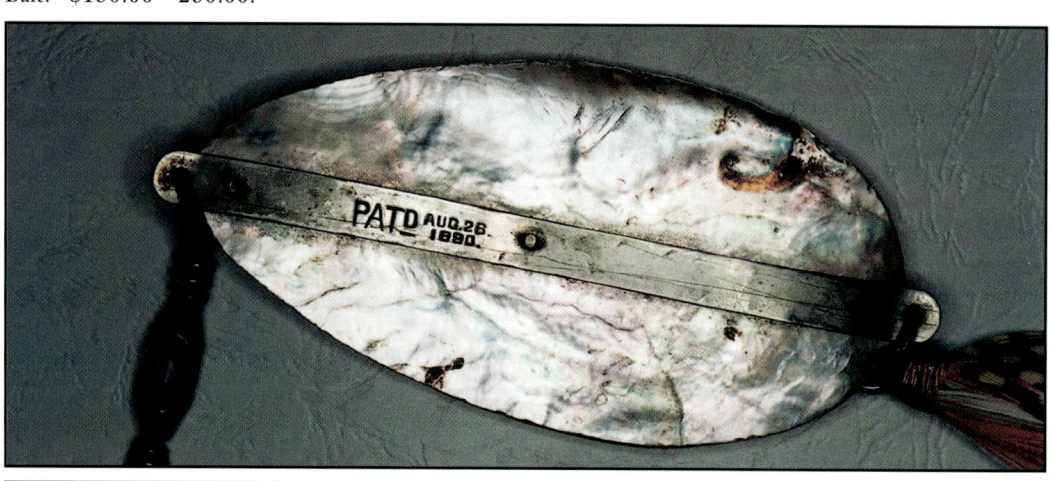

C.

Miscellaneous Manufacturers

Cornelius Lie
Trondhjem, Norway

A.

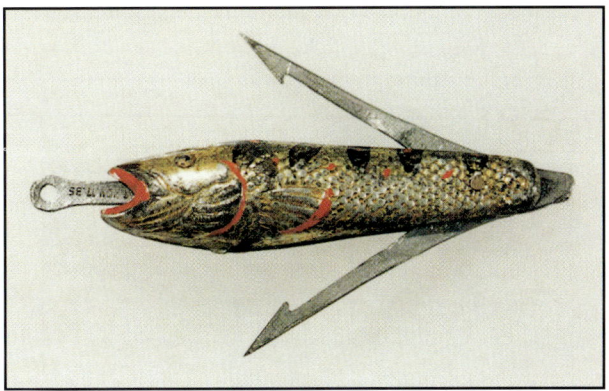

B.

A. Lie Minnow in closed position. $500.00 – 750.00.

B. Lie Minnow in open position. This lure is 2½" long. Note the patent date on the line tie.

C. Cornelius Lie's Nov. 17, 1885 patent illustration.

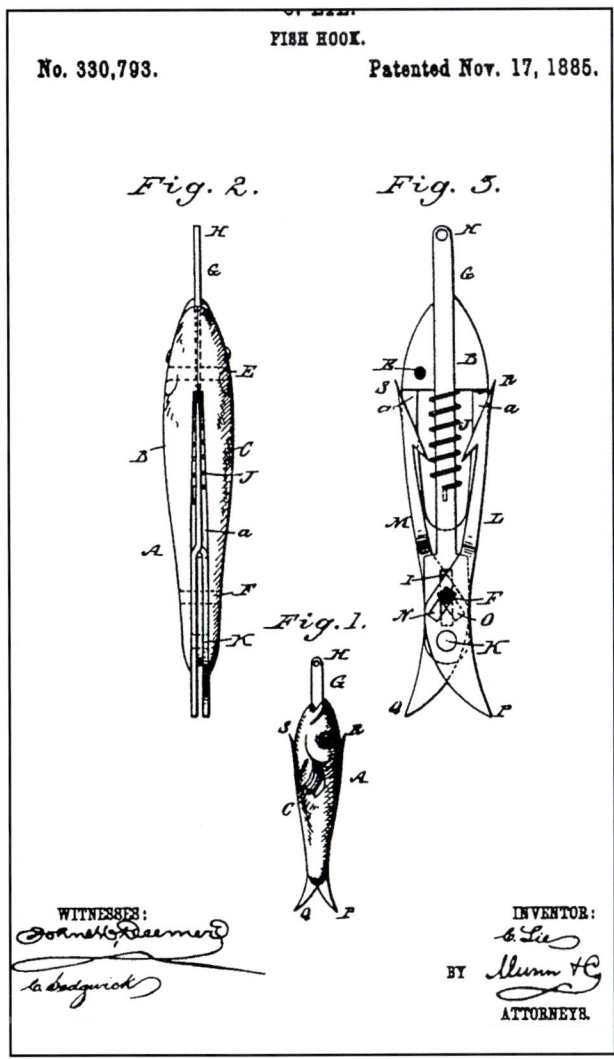

C.

The Westwood Frog
Chicago, Illinois

Ad from a J. F. Schmelzer & Sons Arms Co. catalog. This company was out of Kansas City, Mo. Note that it came in both weedless and plain double hooks. The weedless wires have small coils of wire on the ends like some of the Pflueger frogs. There is speculation that this frog was made by Pflueger for Westwood or Westwood made it for Pflueger. It was also listed in a 1909 Hibbard Spencer, Bartlett & Co. St. Louis, Mo. catalog. It was listed there as being made of solid rubber, 3" in length and non-floating. They were $5.00 a dozen.

Albert Angell
East Orange, N.J.

Albert was listed in the East Orange city directory from 1879 until 1897. He was at various times listed as an inventor and mechanical engineer.

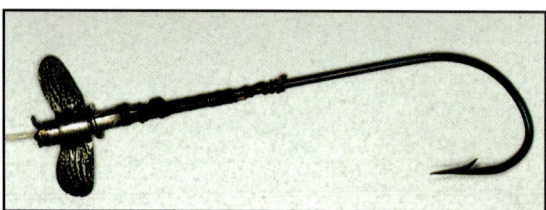

A.

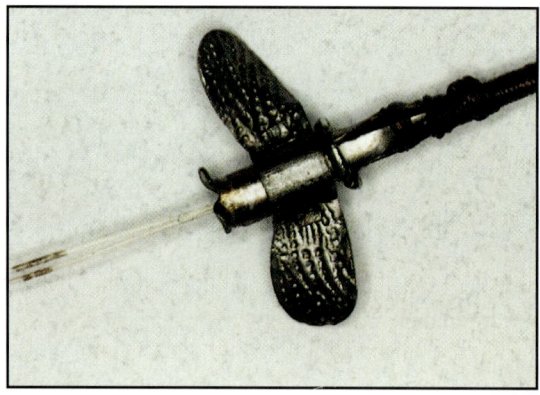

C.

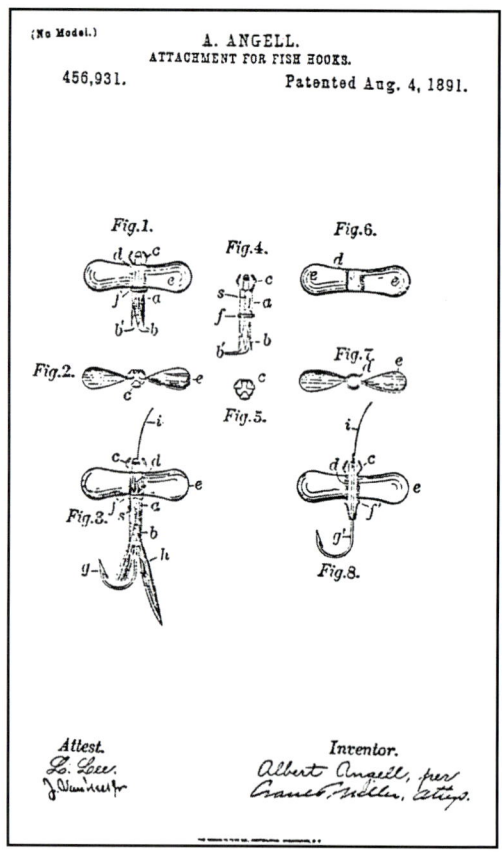

B.

A. Angell's Aug. 4. 1891 patented wings applied to a single hook. $50.00 – 75.00.

B. Angell's Aug, 4. 1891 patent illustration. It was for a small two-bladed propeller.

C. Enlarged view of Angell's Wings. Note the intricate embossing.

D. Advertisement from James F. Marsters 1897 catalog.

E. *Forest & Stream* ad from April 7, 1892

D.

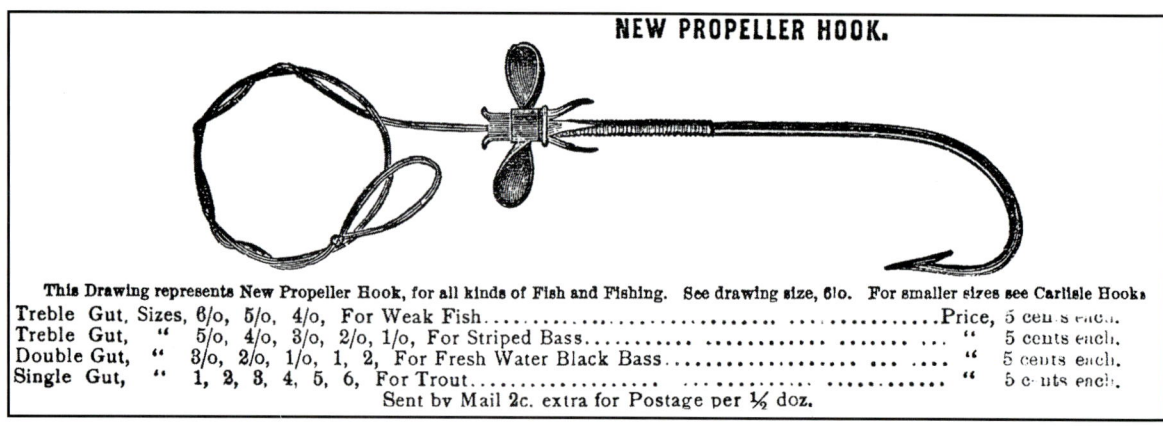

E.

Miscellaneous Manufacturers

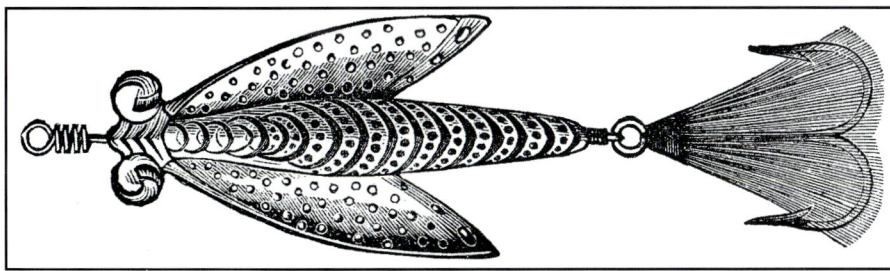

A.

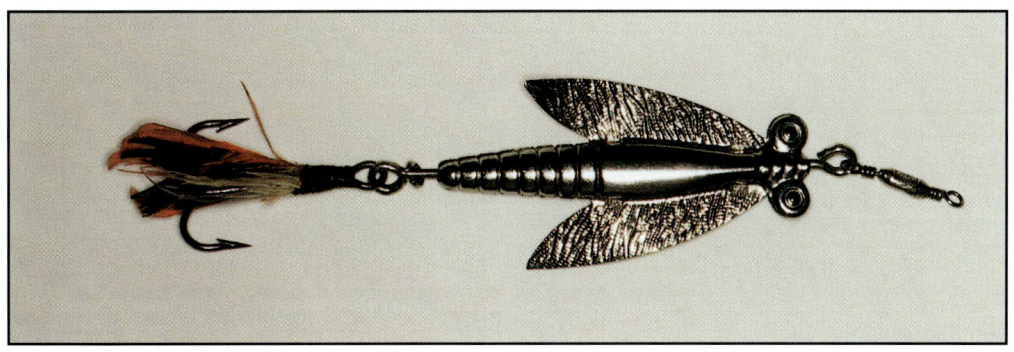

B.

A. Ad from the Wilkinson Co. catalog.

B. The "Excelsior Trolling Fly Spoon." This lure has a 2⅝" body and is 6" over-all. A beautiful and rare bait. $750.00 – 1,000.00.

C. The "Braided Minnow." I have also seen ads for this bait where it was called the "Skittering Minnow." It is made of a wire mesh. It was made in at least five sizes.

D. The "Braided Minnow" by Angell. $150.00 – 250.00.

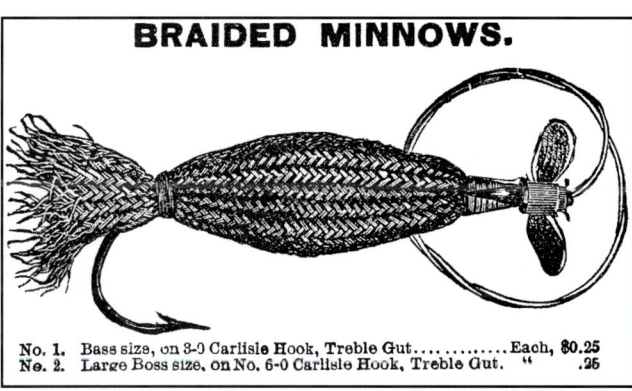

C.

D.

245

MISCELLANEOUS MANUFACTURERS

REVOLVING WINGS.

Cut shows wings adjusted to fly. Adjustable to any fly or snelled hook.

No. 1. Trout size, adapted for Hooks Nos. 6 to 10.
Each..........$0.10

No. 2. Bass size, for Hooks Nos. 2-0 to 4.
Each..........$0.10

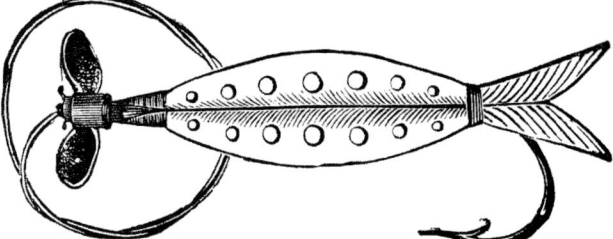

PERFORATED METAL MINNOWS.

No. 1. Embossed Nickel, on No. 6-0 Carlisle Hook, Treble Gut.....................Each, $0.25
No. 2. Plain Nickel, on 6-0 Carlisle Hook, Ringed. Each.................................15

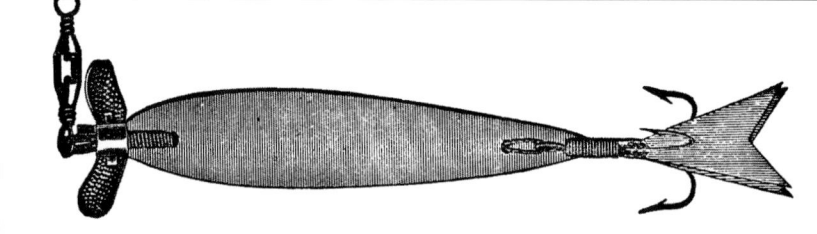

This Drawing Represents Angell's Bass Killer No.20. Price 25c.
Any of the above Minnows sent by mail on receipt of price and 2c. each extra for postage.

These cuts are all from an 1897 James F. Marsters catalog and an 1896 Wilkinson Co. catalog.

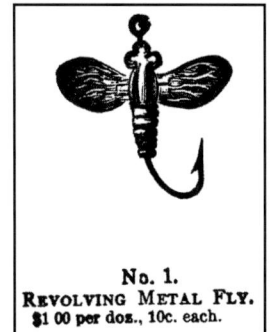

No. 1.
REVOLVING METAL FLY.
$1 00 per doz., 10c. each.

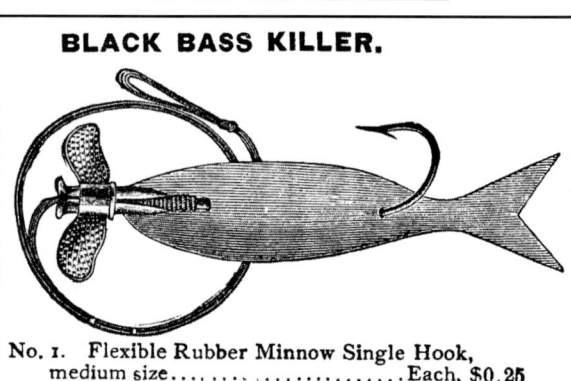

BLACK BASS KILLER.

No. 1. Flexible Rubber Minnow Single Hook, medium size......................Each, $0.25
No. 2. Flexible Rubber Minnow Single Hook, large size......................Each, .25

This Drawing represents Angell's Floating Minnow No. 18. Price 35c. No. 17, 30c. No. 16, 25c.

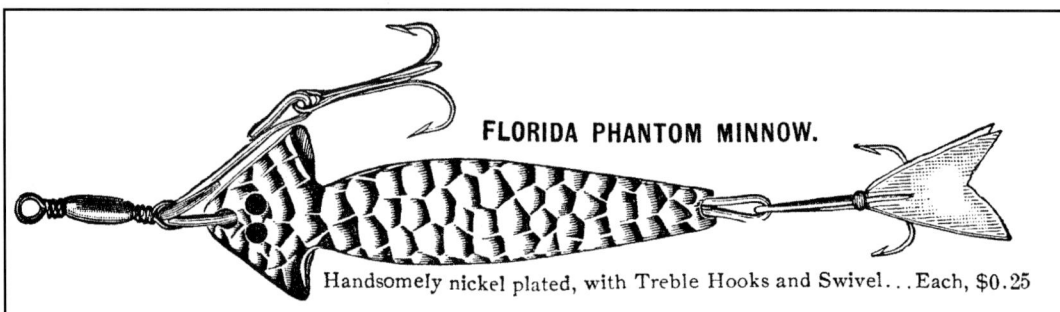

FLORIDA PHANTOM MINNOW.

Handsomely nickel plated, with Treble Hooks and Swivel...Each, $0.25

Henry O. Stanley
Dixfield, Maine

Henry was a fish commissioner for the state of Maine. In an 1873 issue of *Forest and Stream,* it states that in addition to what he was doing for the state he was also raising trout and releasing them into the Rangeley chain of lakes.

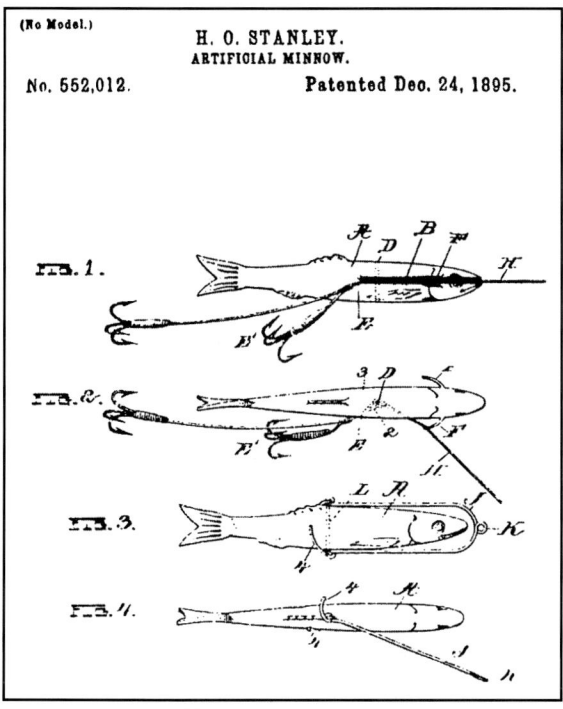

A.

B.

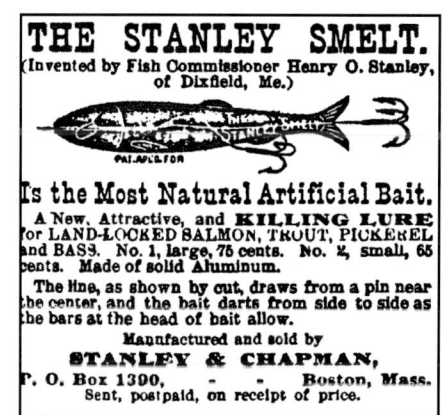

C.

A. Stanley's Dec. 24, 1895 patent. I have not seen this in production.

B. The "Stanley Smelt." This lure is nearly identical to the Nov. 3, 1896 patent. $50.00 – 75.00.

C. Interesting 1908 ad from *Streater's Bible*. This looks very much like the above patent, but is marked patent apld for.

D. An 1899 ad for the Stanley Smelt and the State of Maine Spinner. The State of Maine Spinner appears to be very similar to the English "Archer" minnow rig and several others. Note that the Smelt is made in four sizes, the Maine Spinner in two.

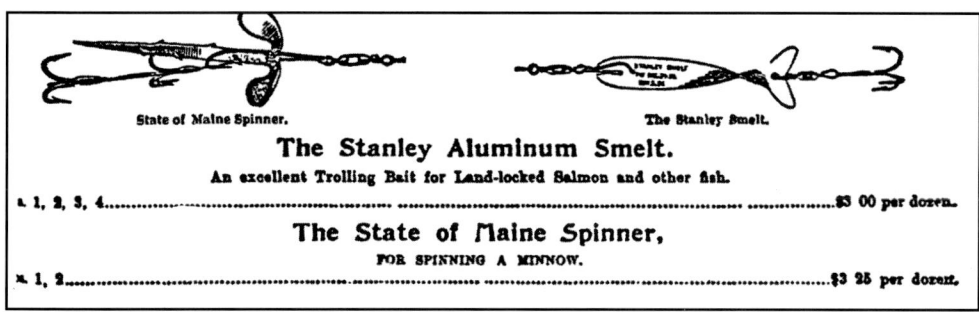

D.

MISCELLANEOUS MANUFACTURERS

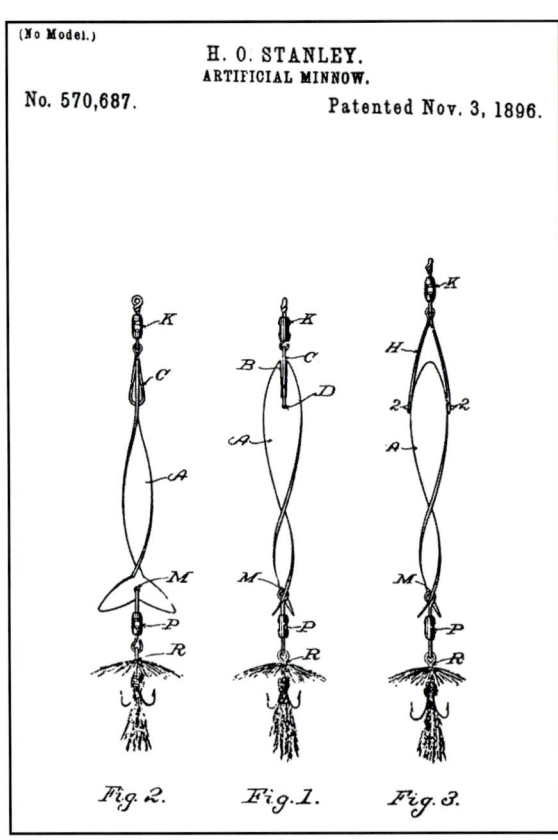

A.

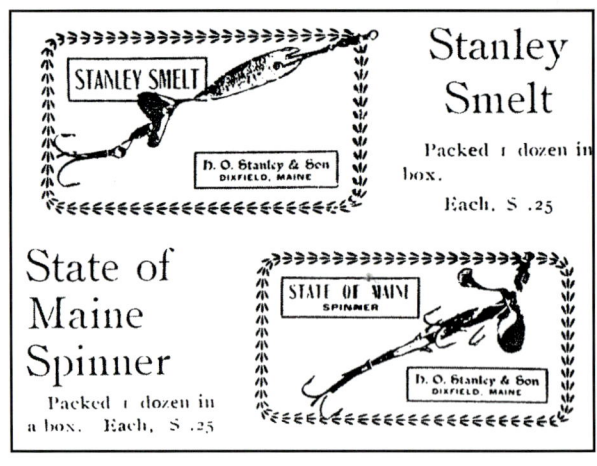

B.

A. Ad from a 1900 Davis Arms Co. Portland, Maine Catalog. Note that it says H.O. Stanley & Son, Dixon, Maine.

B. Stanley's November 3, 1896 patent. This is the lure most familiar to collectors.

E.N. HUGHSON

Clyde, New York

E. N. Hughson was born in the town of North East, Dutchess County, N. Y., October 5, 1821. He was married to Malissa M. Davidson. He was a tin and coppersmith from the age of 13. At the age of 85 he was still active in the trade. His favorite pastimes were hunting and fishing.

E. N. Hughson

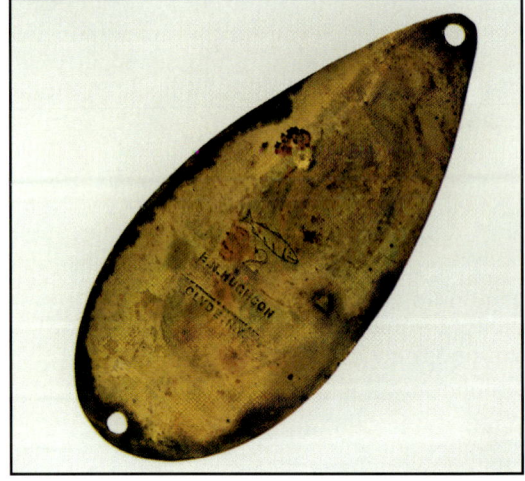

A spoon missing its hook and line tie. There is the image of a fish stamped on the blade. I have also seen Hughson lures without the fish. He seems to have manufactured a rather standard line of spoons and spinners. $20.00 – 30.00.

Miscellaneous Manufacturers

Paul Junod

Celina, Ohio

An 1895 document lists Paul Junod as a jeweler. The 1909 Celina city directory lists him as a jeweler and with the Junod and Co., manufacturers of fishing tackle, office at 110½ S. Main.

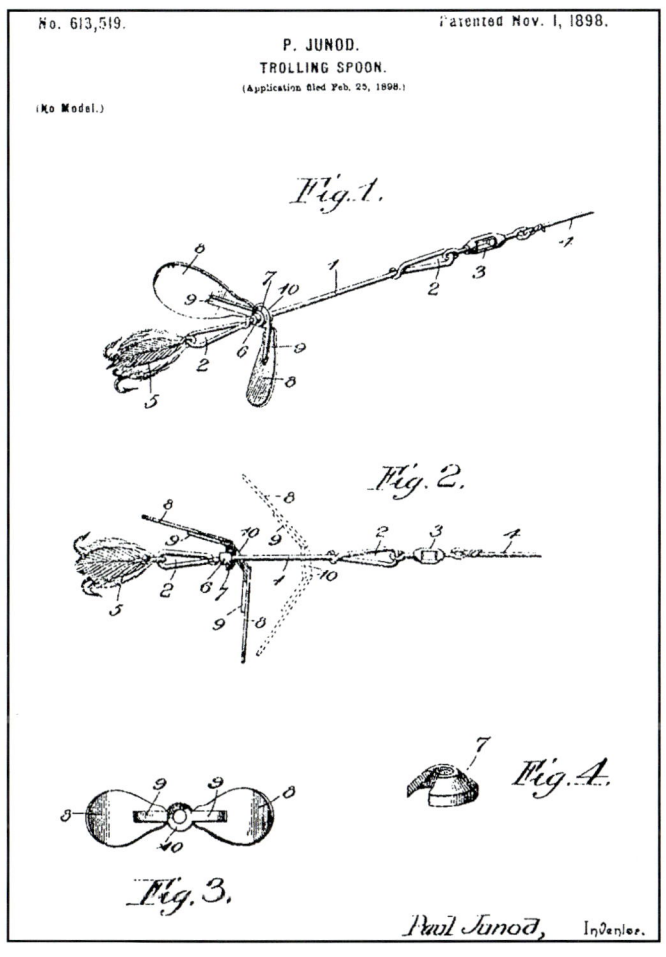

B.

C.

A.

A. A standard Junod Spinner on its original card. This was also made with a single blade. $25.00 – 50.00.

B. Drawing of Paul Junod's November 1, 1898 patent. This patent is basically for a double spinner with propellers that are free to rock sideways and move longitudinally on the shaft in conjunction with concave-convex washers used as bearings. Why he wanted the propellers to do this he doesn't say. He also was granted a patent on December 29, 1903, for the same thing. This patent date is found on the blades of Worden wooden minnows.

C. Unusual single-sided blade on its original card. $25.00 – 50.00.

Mayne C. P. Parker

Indianapolis, Indiana

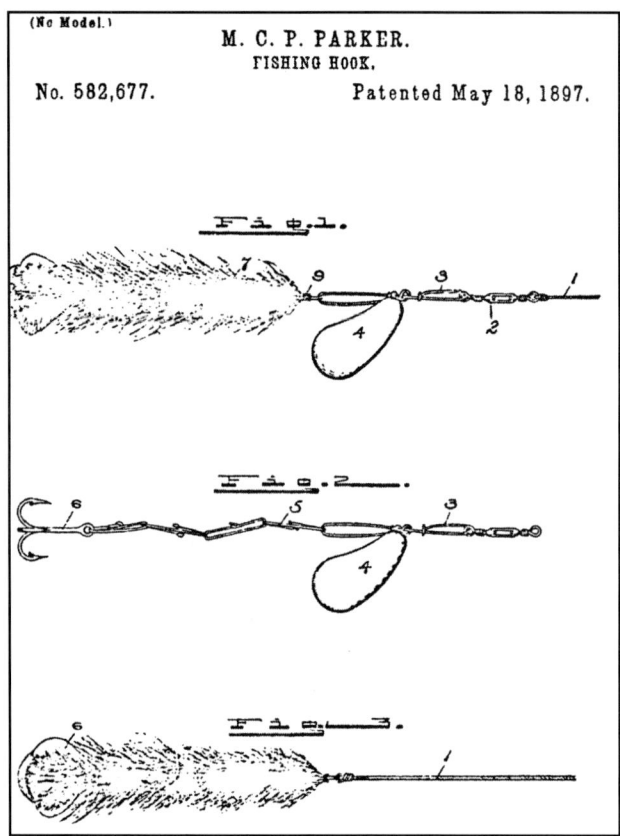

Mayne C. P. Parker's patent drawing for a Trolling worm. He claims in the patent text that it could be manufactured of either hair or feathers.

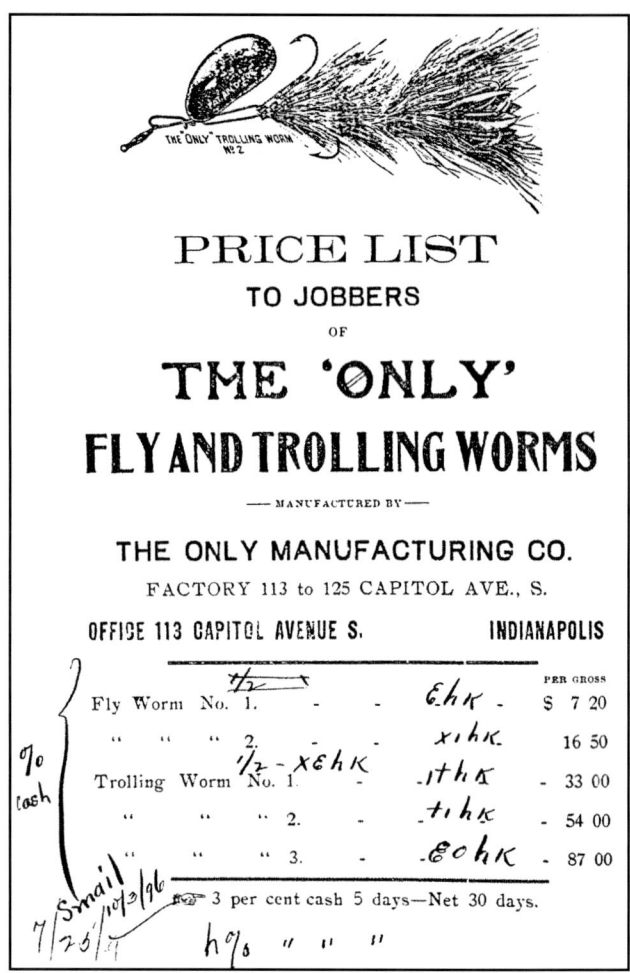

Ad for Parker's trolling worm. Note the date at the bottom. This is before the patent was approved. He applied for the patent on March 30, 1896. There is no mention of a patent in the ad.

A.G. Spalding Co.

Chicago, Illinois

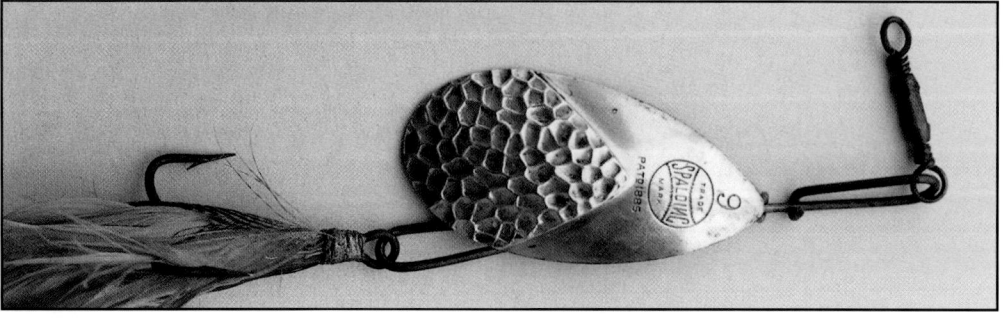

This lure was made in 10 sizes and was available in gold or silver plate. It used a design patent granted to W. T. J. Lowe on Aug. 11, 1885. For more information, go back to page 109.

Andrew B. Hendryx

Hartford, Connecticut

Andrew B. Hendryx was born April 7, 1834, on a farm near Southford, Connecticut. He was a machinist by trade, working for several companies before starting his own business in Ansonia, Connecticut, in 1875. He began by making paper boxes and bird cages. The business was such a success that he soon expanded and moved to New Haven, Connecticut. Over the years his product line increased to include fishing reels. He made thousands of fishing reels during the late 1800s, but lures do not appear in any advertisements until 1900.

These lures were mostly copies of other company's products. One exception was the "Hendryx Propeller." This lure was a three-bladed cone-shaped spinner. It is found in the 1900 catalog of the T. B. Davis Arms Co. from Portland, Maine. Hendryx went on to manufacture several unique lures in the beginning years of the twentieth century.

Andrew B. Hendryx died in 1907.

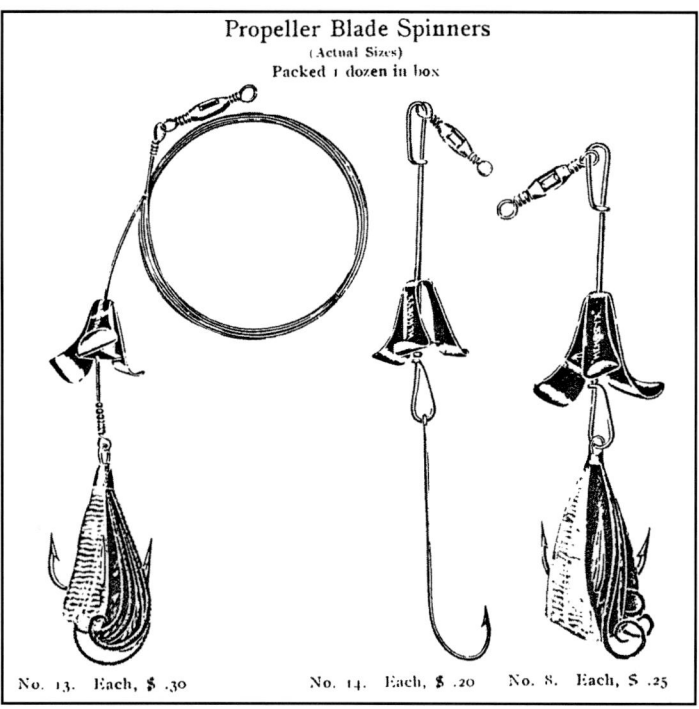

Reduced in size ad from the 1900 T. B. Davis Arms Co. Portland, Maine catalog.

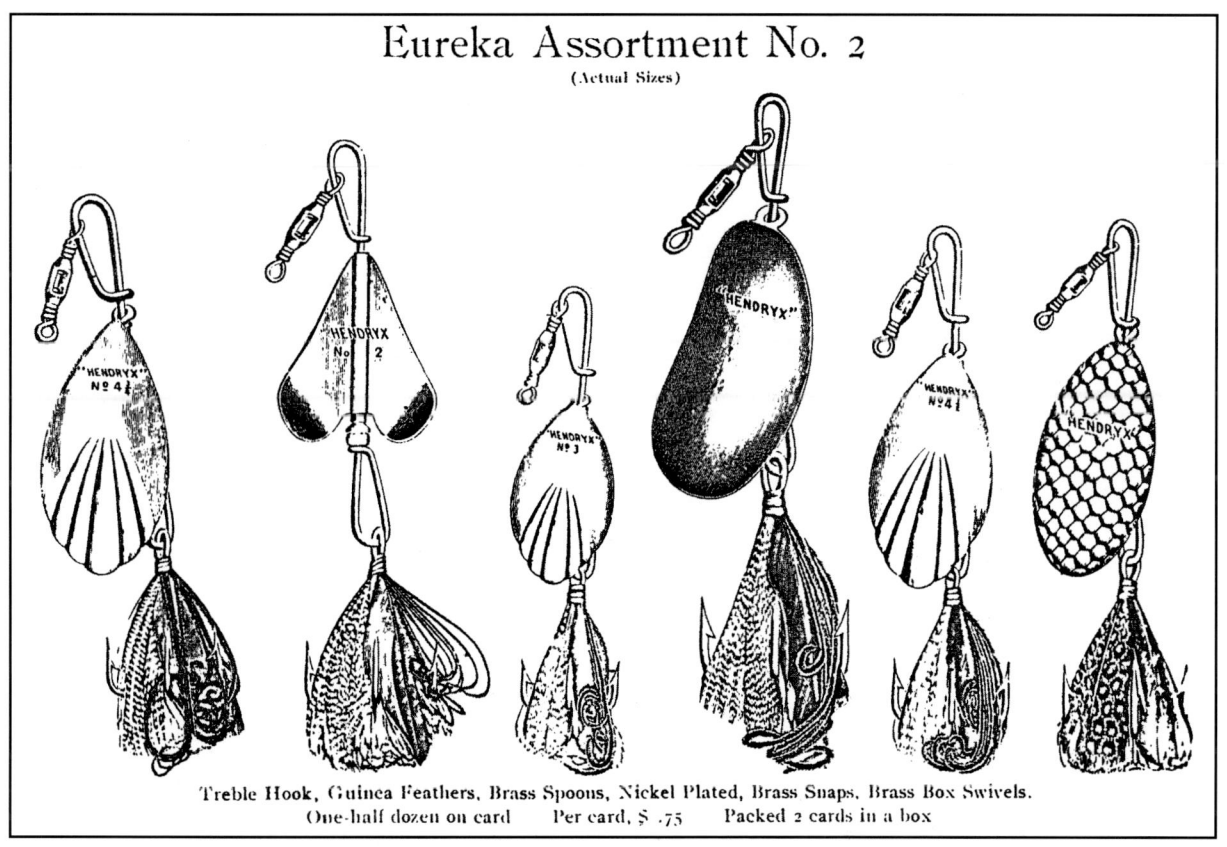

Assortment of Hendryx lures found in the T. B. Davis Arms Company 1900 catalog.

Miscellaneous Manufacturers

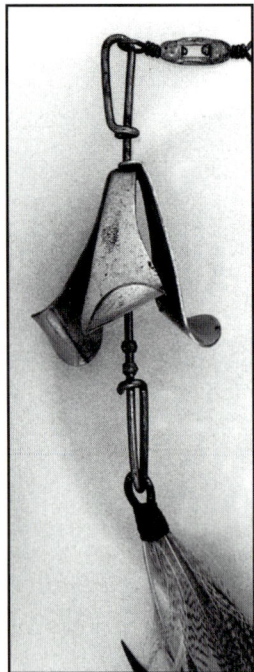

A.

B.

C.

D.

E.

A. The "Propeller Blade Spinner." This appears to be an original Hendryx design. Besides the shaft mounted blade it came on a wire and in a double configuration. It was available in four sizes. $30.00 – 50.00.

B. An assortment of Hendryx lures manufactured around the turn of the century. $10.00 – 20.00 each.

C. An assortment of lures manufactured by Hendryx around the turn of the century. $10.00 – 20.00 each.

D. This lure has been seen with Hendryx markings. $15.00 – 25.00.

E. The Hendryx version of John McHarg's American spinner. Note the rivets holding the blades to the shaft. This was a Hendryx feature, as was the extra large ball in the center. $30.00 – 50.00.

MISCELLANEOUS MANUFACTURERS

M.B. ALLEN

Battle Creek, Michigan

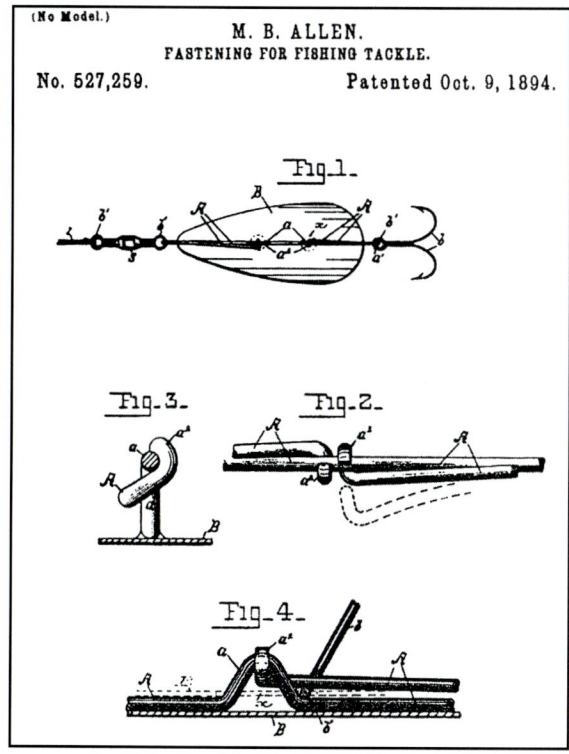

A.

B.

A. M. B. Allen's Oct. 9, 1894 patent drawing. It was for a method of attaching the hook and swivel to a lure using a stiff wire loop that bends back and hooks on itself.

B. A conventional spoon-shaped lure using Allen's patented attachment system. $30.00 – 50.00.

C. Ad from an 1898 Rueben Wood's and Sons Co. catalog and Allen's "New Minnow Casting Spoon." $50.00 – 75.00.

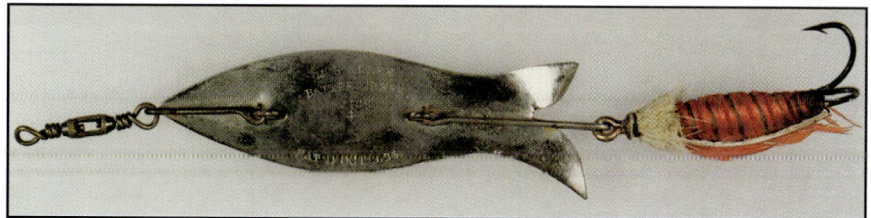

C.

New Minnow Casting Spoon No. 4.

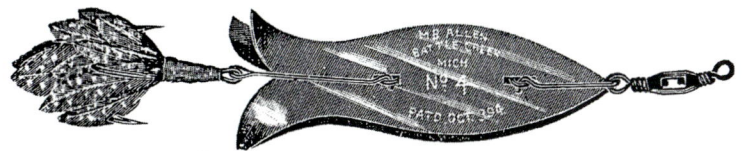

By using one of these spoons the line remains tied in the swivel all day. The objects of this invention are to provide means for the instant and secure movable attachment of the fish hook to the line, also to securely lock the swivel or bait in such a manner that the struggling fish on the hook cannot disengage the latter from the line or swivel; also, to automatically lock the hook to a trolling spoon or other artificial bait, and also to so lock the hook, spoon or bait to the line or swivel, that either may be instantly exchanged for another size or kind; at the same time that the danger of the loss of the fish, or any portion of the fishing tackle caused by the struggles of the fish to escape from the hook, is avoided.

Nickel or Copper..each, 25c. Per doz. $2.50

Miscellaneous Manufacturers

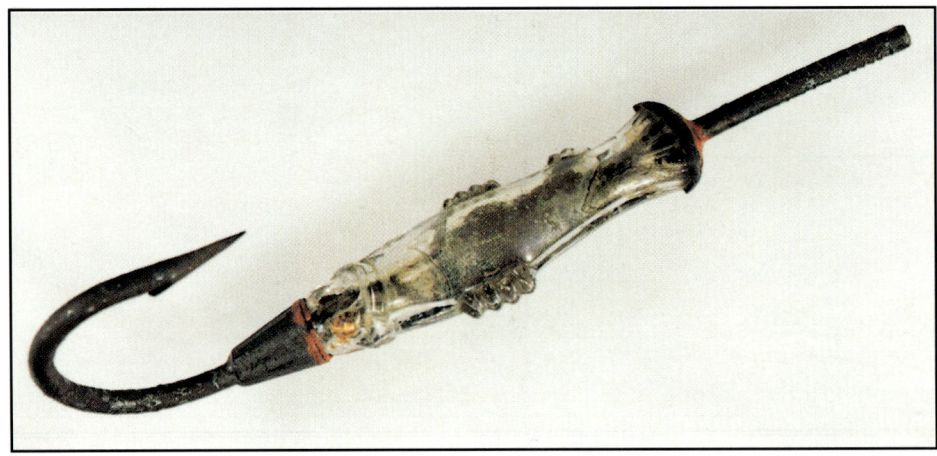

A.

Jorgen Irgens

Bergen, Norway

A. "The Irgens Minnow." This large glass lure, 4½" long, 7½" overall, was coated with silver on the inside. This was to keep it from oxidizing or tarnishing when exposed to air and water, especially salt water. The Enterprise Co. (Pflueger) evidently acquired this patent and used it as the basis for its Crystal Minnow. The Crystal Minnow was much smaller and coated on the inside with Pflueger's luminous paint. $1,000.00+.

B. Jorgen Irgens' Sept. 7, 1880 patent drawing for his glass minnow. He states in the patent that it could be coated on the inside with either silver or gold.

C. Ernest F. Pflueger's Aug. 28, 1883 patent drawing for the luminous Crystal Minnow. Pflueger made only minor changes to the original Irgens' drawing.

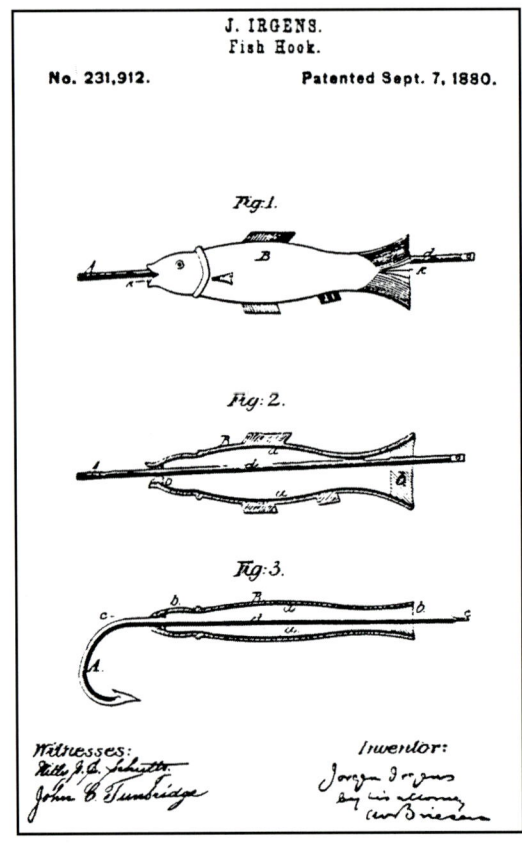

B.

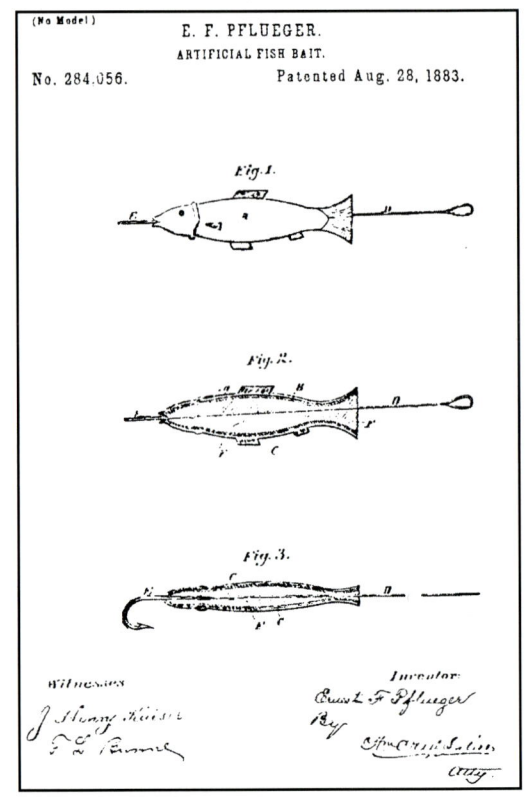

C.

Miscellaneous Manufacturers

Carl J.W. Gaide

Fort Wayne, Indiana

The Fort Wayne city directories list Carl J. W. Gaide from 1888 to 1913. From these we learn that he worked as a watchmaker at three different Fort Wayne jewelers: Trenkley & Scherzinger, P. Scherzinger, and Bruder & Co.

A Fort Wayne marriage index states that he married Sarah A. Hardin on November 9, 1892.

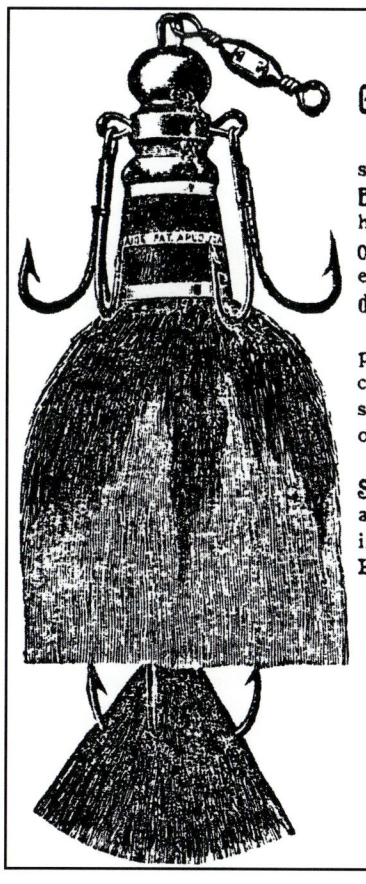

A.

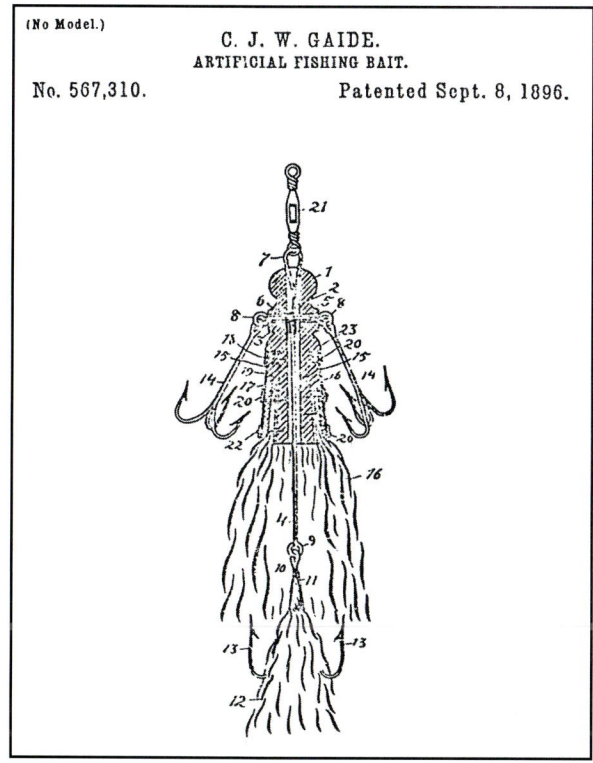

B.

A. Cut from an 1898 J. F. Schmelzer & Sons Arms Co. catalog, Kansas City, Mo. A later catalog published by the Hibbard, Spencer, Bartlett & Co. lists the Gaide bait in two sizes: a small number 3 and a large number 5. The small size was $8.00 a dozen and the large size was $10.00 a dozen.

B. Gaide's 1896 patent drawing.

C. Two examples of the Gaide Bait. The one on the left was used in a trial involving the Shakespeare Co. and the Enterprise Co. It was cut open to show the hook attachment. $1,000.00+.

C.

Miscellaneous Manufacturers

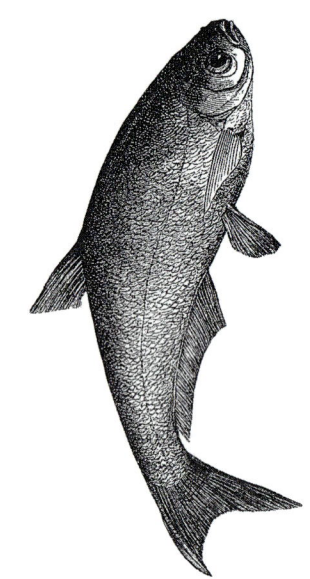

Gaide Bait clearly showing the three bands around the body. This lure 4½" long. $1,000.00+.

Floyd Ferris Lobb
Piseco Lake, N.Y.

Although the Old Lobb spoon reportedly was invented in the 1800s, I believe the box and lure pictured are much later, probably from the 1930s.

The Old Lobb spoon has been reported to have been used since the middle of the nineteenth century. Here's what it says on the box, "Floyd Ferris Lobb was born early in this century, just when and where no one knows. In his youth he was a good musician, writer, and tailor. When about 24 years of age, disappointed in love or for some reason best known to himself, he retired to Piseco Lake, Hamilton Co. New York, in the Adirondack forest, where he lived as a hermit until his death in 1891. Part of this time however was enlivened by a wife. His later years were spent in a cabin quite alone. He was a hunter, trapper, and fisherman, as eccentric as man can be. He designed this bait which bears his name. It has been used for years in Piseco Lake and is there unquestionably more killing than any other blade. In the belief that it will be generally taking (that's what it says!), it is offered to the fishermen in memory of "Old Lobb." $25.00 – 35.00.

Miscellaneous Manufacturers

EDWARD T. DUKES
Quitman, Georgia

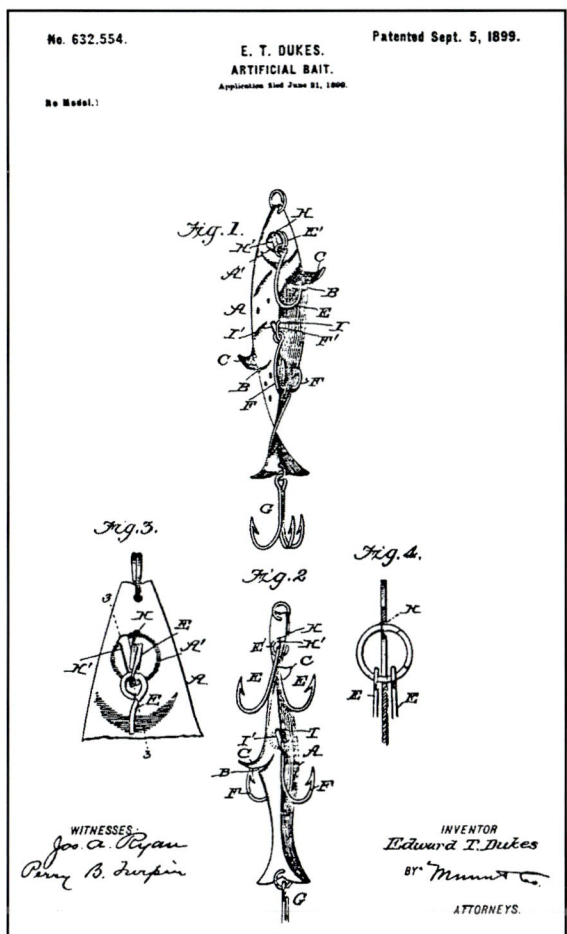

Dukes' September 5, 1899 patent drawing. Fig. 3 in the drawing shows two hooks attached just below the line tie. In the patent text Mr. Dukes states that this hook attachment will, when spinning rapidly, appear as an eye. Like many patent claims, the finished product was somewhat different than the patent. Usually the lure would end up being considerably simpler than the patent claims. In this case he used the line tie to attach the two hooks and painted an eye on the lure. Above right: The "Dixie Minnow." $250.00 – 350.00.

F.S. GRAVES
Albany, New York

Silver-plated spinner made by F. S. Graves of Albany, N. Y. This lure and the two at the top of the next page are typical examples of his work. I believe they fall within the time frame of this book. $25.00 – 50.00.

$30.00 – 50.00

$50.00 – 75.00

W. Harper & W. Smith
Montreal, Canada

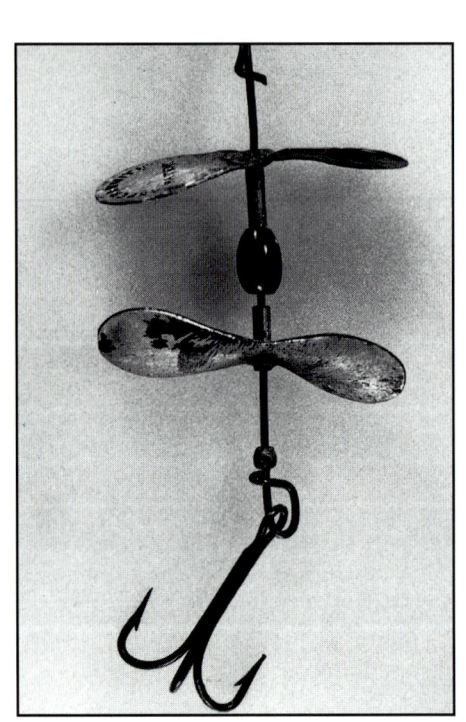

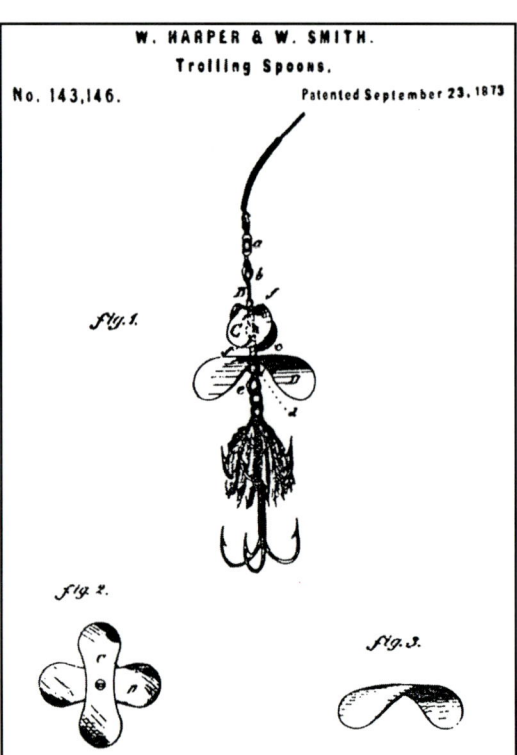

One of the first (if not the first) double-bladed spinners. Patented Sept. 23, 1873. $175.00 – 250.00.

M.W. Votaw and M.E. Thomas

Bowling Green, Kentucky

A.

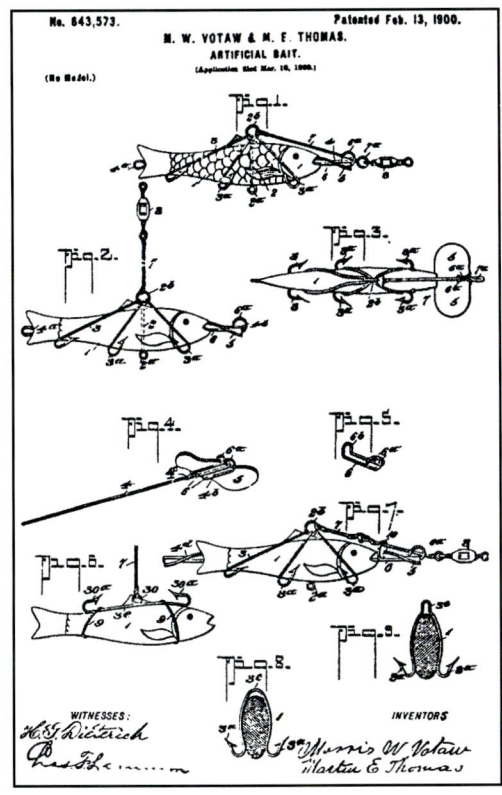

B.

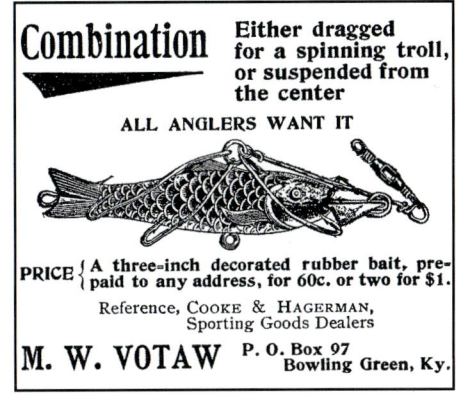

C.

A. The Votaw minnow. The minnow itself was in all probability made by the Enterprise Mfg. Co. of Akron, Ohio. $1,000.00+.

B. M. W. Votaw and M. E. Thomas' Feb. 13, 1900 patent Illustration. This patent was for a lure that could be trolled or fished vertically. It came supplied with a rubber minnow but could also be used as a live bait harness.

C. Ad from the April 1899 *Recreation* magazine. Note there is no mention of live bait. The minnow harness concept may have been problematical. See earlier ad below.

D. An 1898 ad from an unknown source. This lure was evidently advertised and sold a long time before the patent was granted. The poem and ad relate to people being squeamish about hooking live bait.

SURE-CATCH FISH BAIT.

Votaw's Duplex Hooks and Bait Combination (patent pending).

This system of hooks used with either a live or artificial minnow. No hook through live bait to punish or kill it. The most sympathetic lady can use a live minnow in connection with these hooks

Price—A three (3) inch decorated flexible rubber minnow, fully equipped, together with hooks and harness to equip a live minnow, prepaid to any address for 90cts., or two for $1.50.

Dealers, write for circular and wholesale price list.

M. W. VOTAW,
P. O. Box 97, - Bowling Green, Ky.

A MINNOW'S WAIL.

I am nothing but a minnow,
  And you a knowing man;
But now let me teach you something,
  I'm very sure I can.

To be your bait we don't object,
  If in a humane way;
It's always been as you would like,
  Now we would like some say.

The common way of piercing us,
  With hook thrust in the back,
Is too barbarous for these days;
  Of sympathy it's lack.

Be modern, for that it humane,
  And use the Duplex hook;
For then you are just sure to catch
  The finest in the brook.

When harnessed in the modern way
  From danger we are free;
Big fish eating up little ones
  Will be broke up, you'll see.

But they will try it just the same
  As in the days of yore;
But once I'm sure will satisfy,
  They ne'er will try it more.

They've been treacherous now so long
  We want to turn the joke,
And we'll be sure to do it too
  With Duplex for a yoke.

Don't put us on a common hook,
  Or they'll take us away;
Harness us up like this Sure Catch,
  And then they'll have to stay.

      Composed by M. W. Votaw.

D.

E.O. Pealer

P & S Ball Bearing Bait Co.
Sayre, Pennsylvania

In the 1890s E. O. Pealer was a jeweler and fishing tackle dealer in Sayre, Pa. He worked off and on as a train dispatcher and in 1894, along with Thruman V. Sloat, went into the manufacture of his soon to be patented trolling bait.

The lure was at first called the "Pealer and Sloat's Trolling Bait." In 1902 the P & S Ball Bearing Bait Co. was formed. At this time Robert F. Page joined the firm as a partner.

In 1904 the firm went bankrupt and Page became the owner. He evidently (or someone) continued to manufacture the lures as evidenced by the sale of the P & S lures for quite some time afterward.

P & S made lures other than Pealer's patented Ball Bearing Bait but for the most part they were styles common to the industry.

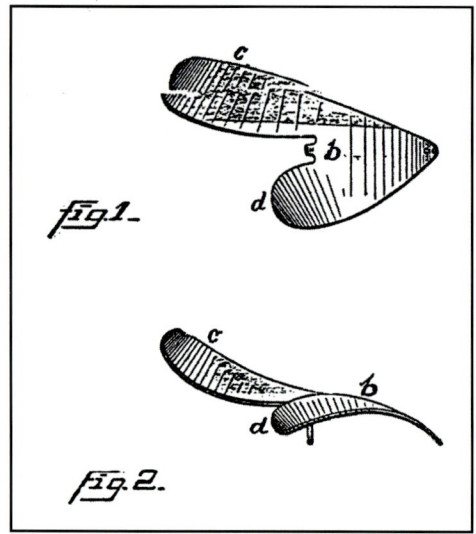

A.

A. E. O. Pealer's Oct. 1, 1895 patent drawing. This is a design patent, number 24,724. In this case it is the design of the blade and not the function that is being patented.

B. E. O. Pealer's Ball Bearing Bait. This lure came in a number of sizes and configurations. Some were on wires and others were on shafts. They made both doubles and singles. $30.00 – 50.00.

C. Large musky size P & S Ball Bearing Spinner. It is shown next to a South Bend Bass Oreno for comparison. The blades on this particular lure were 2⅜" long. It has six faceted beads as bearings. $50.00 – 75.00.

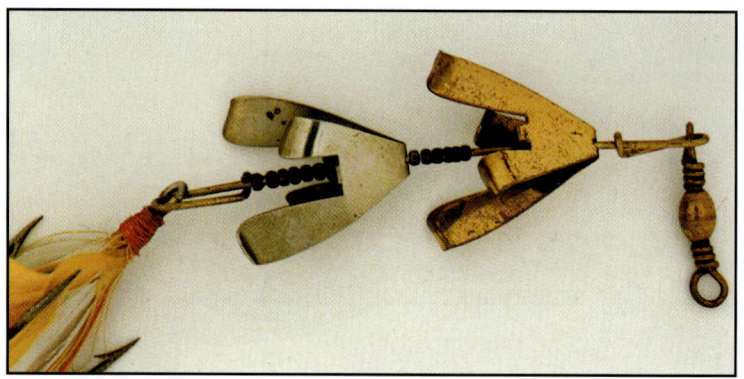

B.

C.

Miscellaneous Manufacturers

Cut from an 1897 James F. Marsters, Brooklyn, N. Y. catalog.

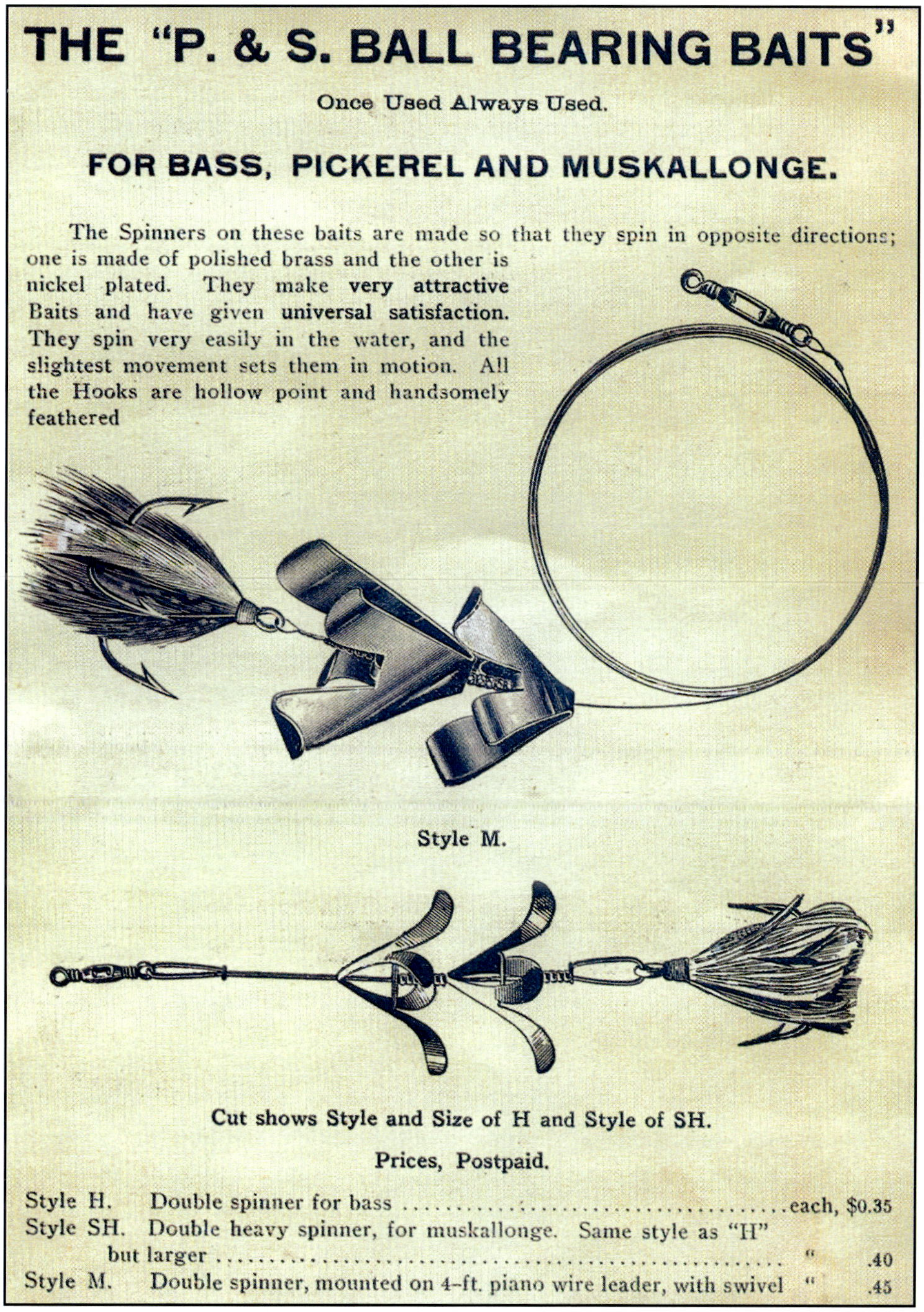

THE "P. & S. BALL BEARING BAITS"
Once Used Always Used.

FOR BASS, PICKEREL AND MUSKALLONGE.

The Spinners on these baits are made so that they spin in opposite directions; one is made of polished brass and the other is nickel plated. They make **very attractive** Baits and have given **universal satisfaction.** They spin very easily in the water, and the slightest movement sets them in motion. All the Hooks are hollow point and handsomely feathered

Style M.

Cut shows Style and Size of H and Style of SH.

Prices, Postpaid.

Style H.	Double spinner for bass ....each,	$0.35
Style SH.	Double heavy spinner, for muskallonge. Same style as "H" but larger .... "	.40
Style M.	Double spinner, mounted on 4-ft. piano wire leader, with swivel "	.45

Ad from a Bullard & Gormley Co. Chicago, Illinois catalog.

The Success Spinner
W.I. Snyder

A.

New York, New York

This lure was made in so many colors, configurations, and materials that it is difficult to determine who is responsible for first putting it on the market. Snyder's name comes up quite often so I'm using him until someone proves to the contrary.

They were made in yellow with gold spots, yellow with white spots, yellow with red head, white with gold spots, white with red head, green with gold spots, brown with gold spots, and brown and green with gold spots.

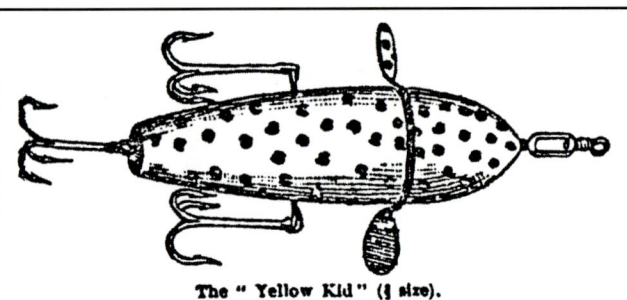

B.

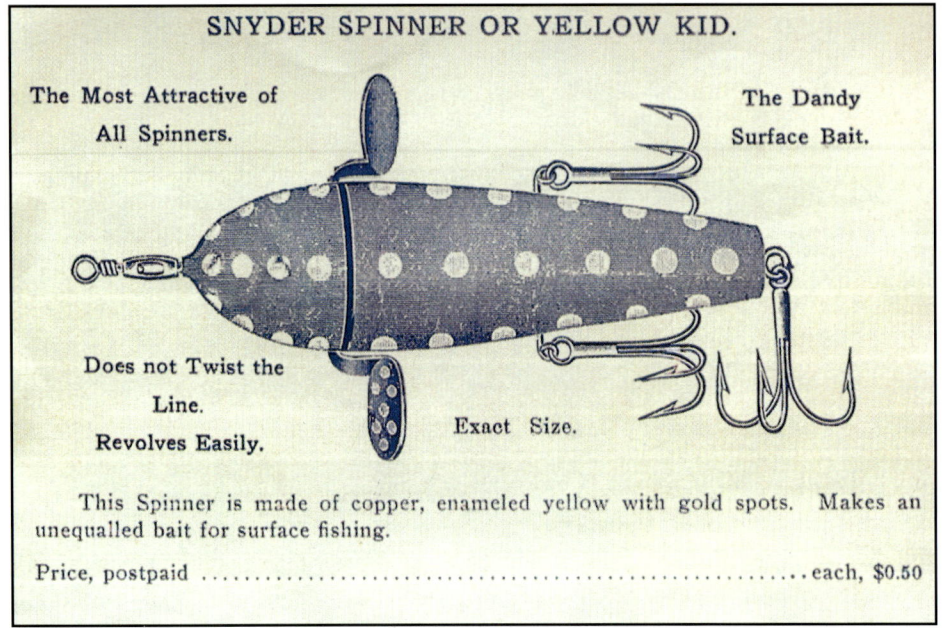

C.

A. Hollow metal lure in its original box. $100.00 – 150.00.

B. An 1899 ad for the "Yellow Kid." This was a common name for this type of lure. They were often yellow with gold spots.

C. A 1906 ad from a Bullard & Gormley Co., Chicago, Illinois catalog.

MISCELLANEOUS MANUFACTURERS

GEORGE H. BACON
Burlington, Vermont

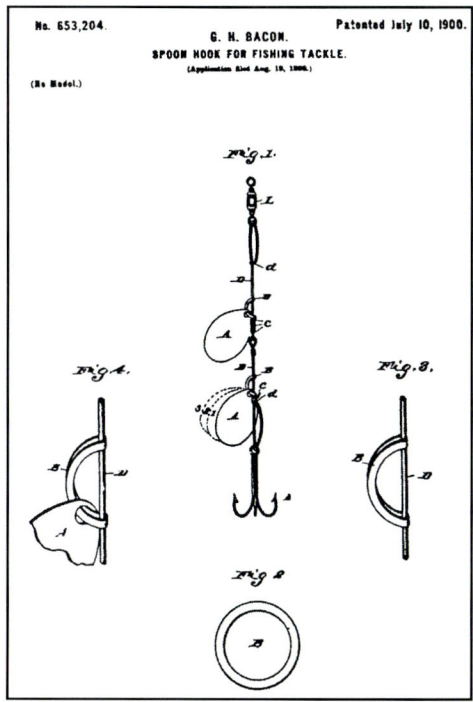

A.

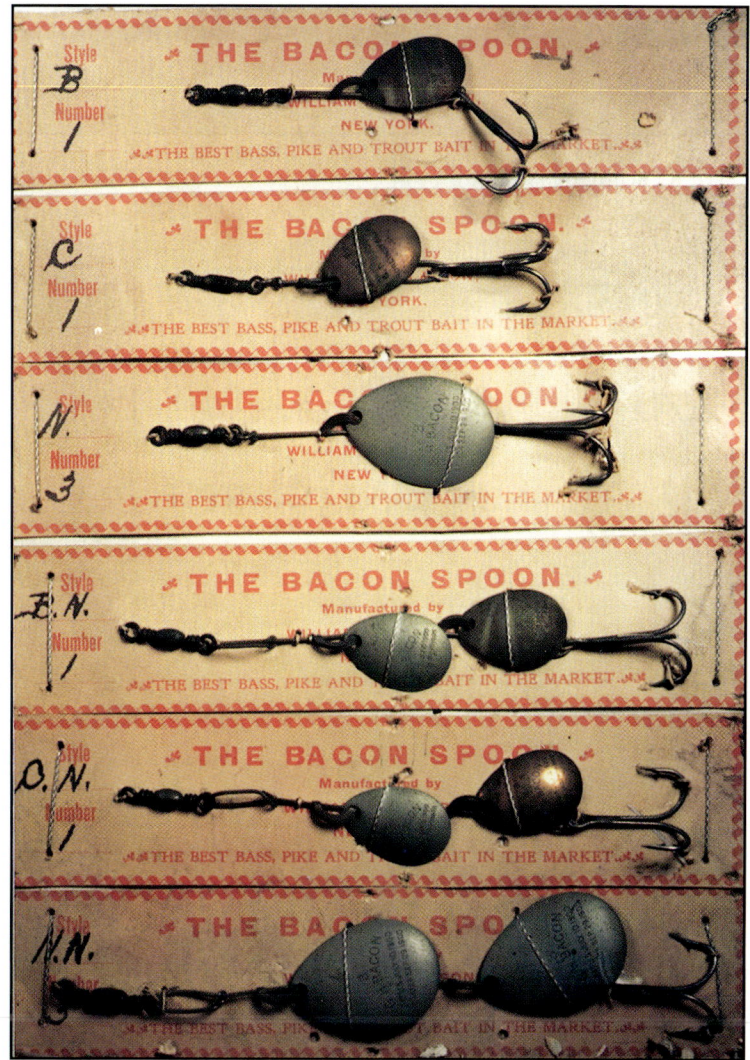

B.

A. George H. Bacon's July 10, 1900 patent drawing. It amounted to little more than an extra large clevis.

B. Bacon spoons still on their original cards. These lures have both the U. S. and the Canadian patents on them. The Canadian patent was granted Sept. 29, 1900. These lures were sold by William Mills & Son Co., N.Y. $20.00 – 30.00 each.

C. 1901 William Mills & Son, N.Y., advertisement from an unknown source.

C.

263

LIVINGSTON S. HINCKLEY

Newark, New Jersey

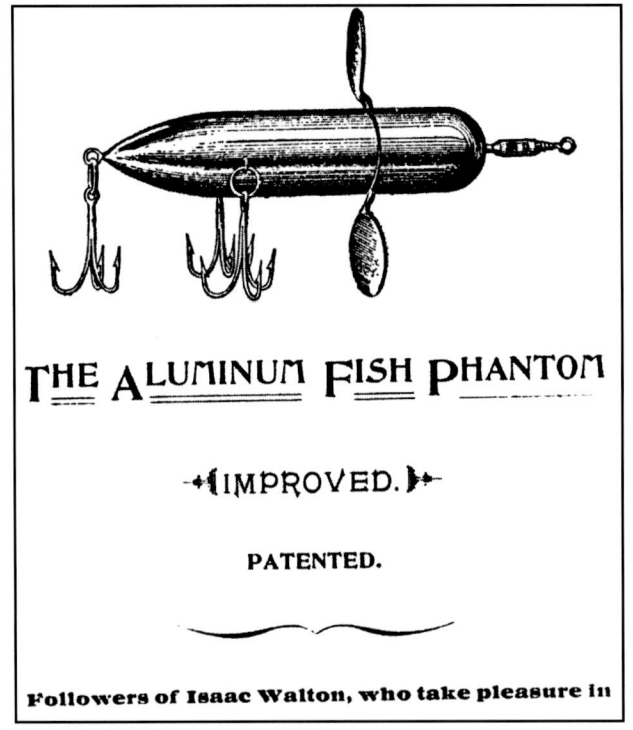

A.

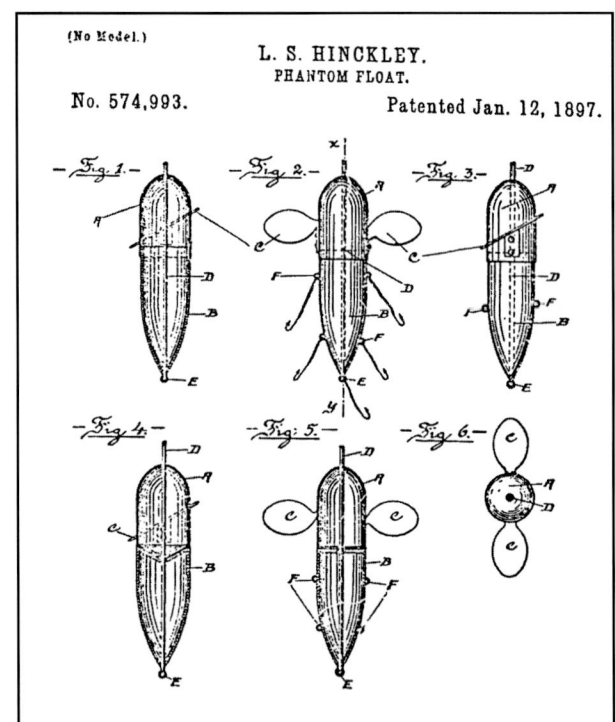

B.

A. Cover of vintage brochure for the Hickley's Aluminum Fish Phantom.

B. Patent drawing for Hinckley's Aluminum Fish Phantom. Made in four sizes, Nos. 1, 2, 3, and 4. Representing 4¼", 3¾", 3", and 2" in length. The latter has only one gang hook at the tail.

C. Hinckley's Aluminum Fish Phantom. This lure is commonly found in plain aluminum and yellow with gold spots. It, like the Snyder lure, was often called the "Yellow Kid" or "Yellow Bird." $50.00 – 75.00.

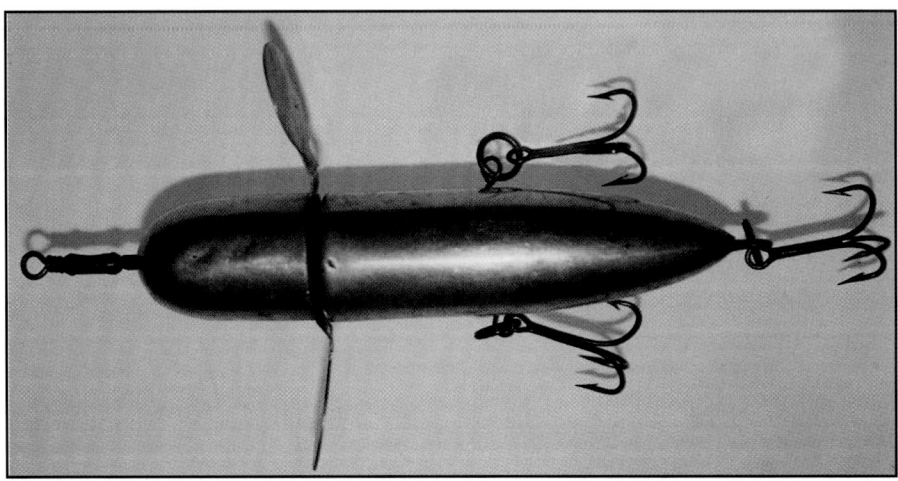

C.

Peter Henkenius
ASSIGNOR OF ONE-HALF TO
James M. Kane

Fort Wayne, Indiana

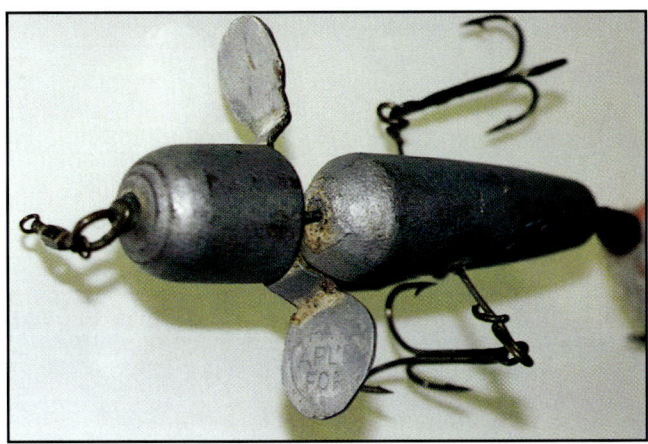

A.

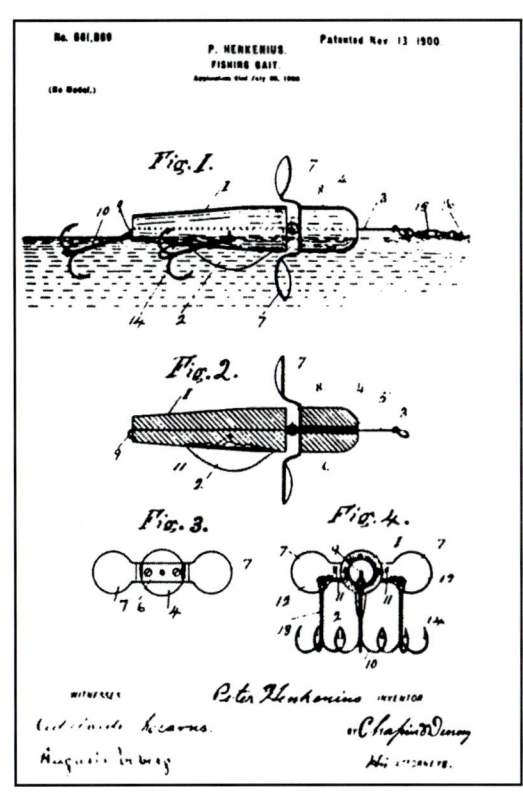

B.

A. The Henkenius Kane fishing lure. This lure is different from the Snyder and Hinckley in that it has a keel attached to the rear section that prevents it from spinning. Thus the hooks are always in the correct position to catch the fish.

B. Patent drawing of the Henkenius Nov. 13, 1900 patent.

C. Henkenius Kane lure. This lure is marked patent pending on the blade. It is 4" long. $750.00 – 1,000.00.

D. Henkenius Kane lure. This lure is marked with the patent date on the keel. It is 3¾" long. $750.00 – 1,000.00.

C.

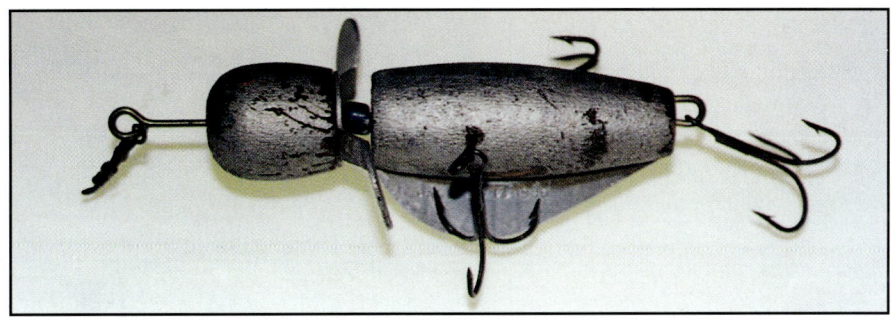

D.

Miscellaneous Manufacturers

W.H. Rockwood
New York, New York
sold by
Abbey & Imbrie
19 Vesey St., New York

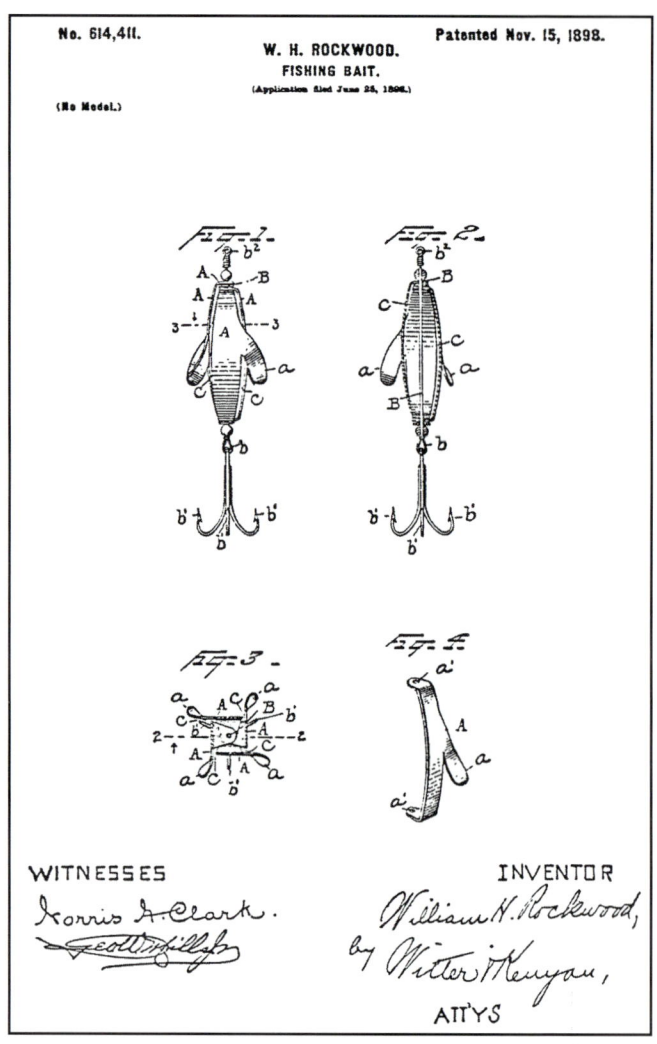

A. Two sizes of the Abbey & Imbrie "Ghost." $150.00 – 200.00.

B. W. H. Rockwood's Nov. 15, 1898 patent drawing.

C. Rockwood's Abbey & Imbrie "Ghost" in its original box. The box states, "Its rotary motion may be regulated by curving or straightening the fins." On the side of the box it says "No. 1" with weedless fly gang and extra treble hook. $350.00 – 400.00.

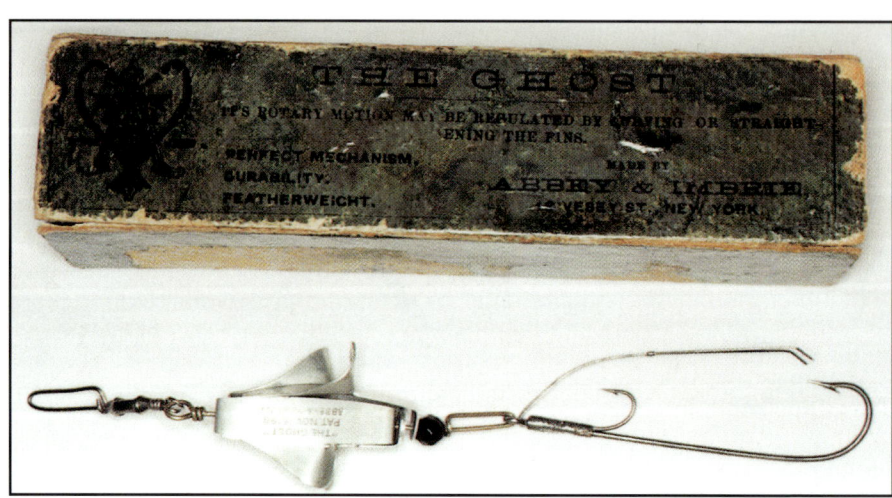

F. A. Pardee and Samuel H. Friend

Kent, Ohio

In 1898 F. A. Pardee and his brother-in-law Samuel H. Friend opened a small machine shop in Kent, Ohio. In this small shop they developed, along with other projects, two of the all-time great fishing lures; The "Pardee Minnow" and the "Kent Champion Floater."

In 1903 Pardee left to study osteopathy in Kerksville, Mo. During the two years he was gone, Samuel Friend took over the operation of the F.A. Pardee and Co. When Pardee returned to Kent in 1905, he turned over the company to Samuel Friend. Friend then renamed the company the Samuel H. Friend Co. (successor to F. A. Pardee & Company). The Samuel H. Friend Co. lasted until about 1908.

The Enterprise Mfg. Co. (Pflueger) later manufactured the Kent Champion Floater, and the Trory Minnow manufactured by Enterprise appears to be a direct copy of the Pardee Minnow (see page 144).

A.

B.

A. Two examples of the Pardee Minnow. They both use an early string through attachment for the hooks.

B. Ad from a July 1900 *Recreation* magazine.

C. Very early Pardee Minnow. Its propellers are different from later models. These may be the propellers shown in the 1900 ad on this page. $1,500.00+.

D. Close-up view of the lure shown at the top of the page. This lure and the other one were acquired at an upstate N.Y. auction that featured many Civil War era items. $2,500.00+.

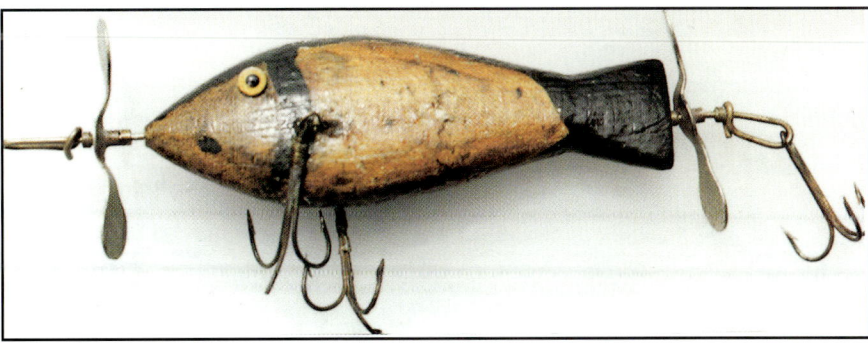

C.

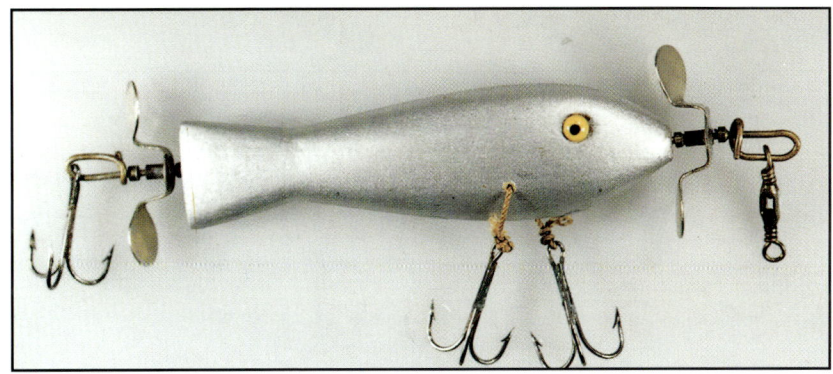

D.

Miscellaneous Manufacturers

The Kent Champion Floater. Although there is no positive proof, this lure was probably made before 1901.

Charles C. Shaffer
Franklin C. Woods

Alliance, Ohio

When Mr. Shaffer invented and produced the "Expert" minnow he was an employee of the U.S. government working for the railway postal service. For this reason he was reluctant to use his own name on a commercial venture, so he named it after his partner and relative, Franklin C. Woods. In an article published in 1921, Mr. Shaffer is quoted as saying that he started the company around 1885. If this is true, the Expert minnow is probably the oldest of the traditional underwater minnows.

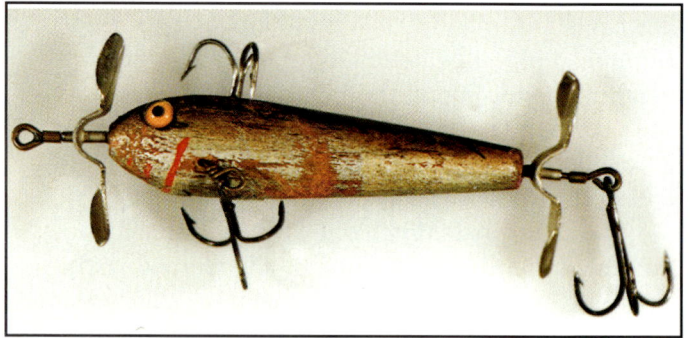

A very early Shaffer Expert, probably before 1900. A May 1908 *Outers* magazine commenting on the "Expert" minnow states their "Expert" wooden minnow has been on the market 12 years and has made an enviable reputation. This would put the Expert's initial production sometime in 1896. $750.00 – 1,000.00.

Early five-hook Shaffer Expert minnow. It is interesting to note that the propellers on this lure look like the propellers in the early 1900 Pardee ad on the previous page, while the propellers on the actual Pardee are different. The Shaffer Experts were also sold by J. C. Holzwarth of Alliance, Ohio, and packaged under the Holzwarth name. $750.00 – 1,000.00.

Later (after 1900) Shaffer-Woods Expert using a through line of silk gut to attach the hooks. This lure also utilizes propellers with holes in them. These props were patented in 1903 by Shaffer. The patent claims the props offered less resistance and the light could shine through the holes onto the lure body. $300.00 – 400.00.

Odds and Ends

Neat pebble grain finish. It appears to be marked with a horizontal diamond near top center, but I can't make it out.

Spinner marked "John Bentley, Jamestown, N. Y." I have seen this lure advertised in the 1920s but it may be older than that. $15.00 – 25.00.

Unmarked lure similar to the later Biff Bait.

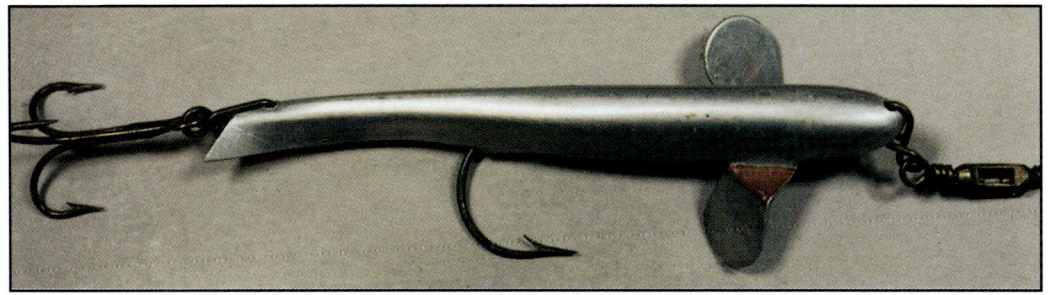

Aluminum lure marked Patent Pend.

Odds and Ends

Neat old lure. Note fancy engraving on body of minnow.

This is a huge Devon type lure. I have misplaced the dimensions of the lure but it was monstrous and with the largest swivel I have ever seen.

Another neat old lure with an interesting offset treble hook.

Odds and Ends

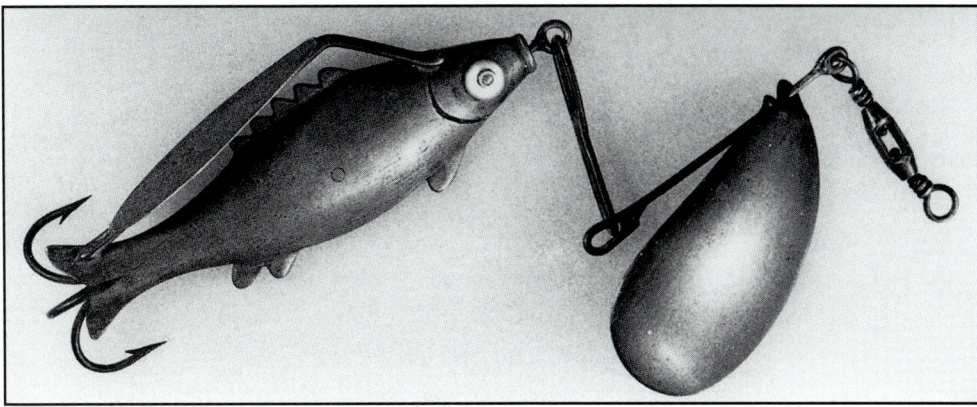

This unmarked lure is made of solid brass. It is so heavy that it has a diving plane in reverse. It was probably used for trolling and the foil on the top kept the lure at a reasonable depth. The eyes are made of abalone.

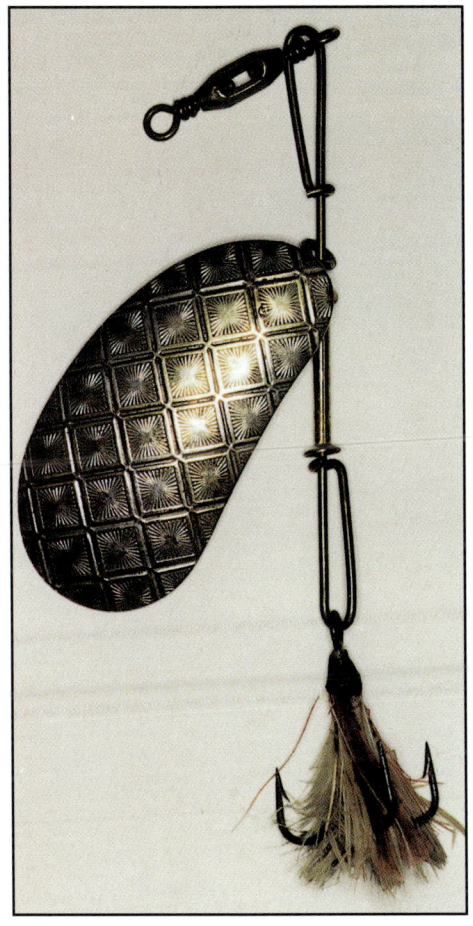

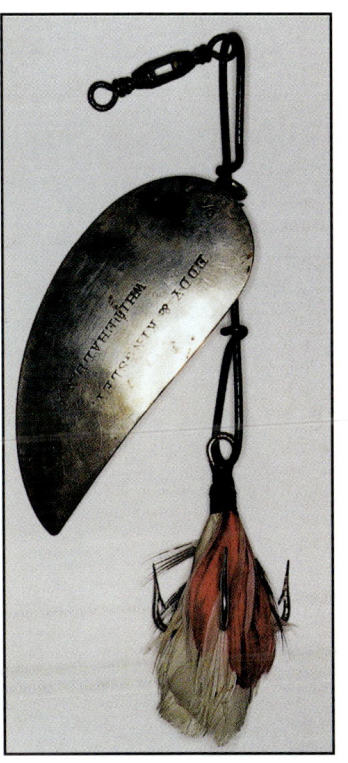

This lure is marked "Backmore." $20.00 – 30.00.

This lure is marked "Eddy and Kingsley, Whitehall, N. Y." $15.00 – 25.00.

This beautiful lure may have been made by Pflueger or McHarg.

Early spinner with interesting design.

MISCELLANEOUS MANUFACTURERS

This cut is taken from a brochure found in a Holzwarth box with a Shaffer "Expert." The brochure also states: "Do not class the 'Expert' with other cheap baits. It is in a class by itself. Not how cheap but how good, our Motto." The "Expert" sold for $1.00 postage prepaid.

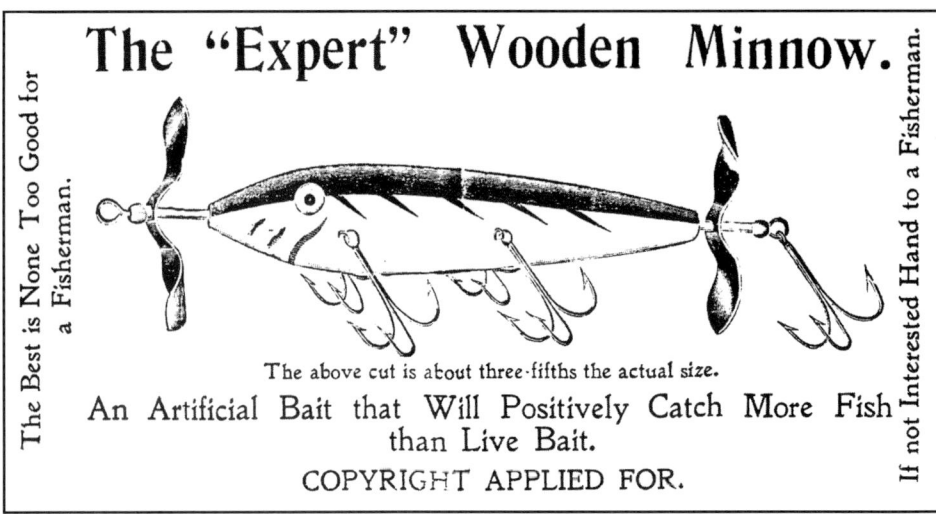

Along with the drawing pictured above, there were several testimonials in the brochure. One of them from C. C. Shaffer himself. The testimonial dated March 4, 1901 is as follows; "DEAR SIR: I have used the 'Expert' Minnow for two years and consider it by far the best catcher I ever used not excepting live bait. I have caught two bass on the same cast with them. Yours Truly, C. C. Shaffer." An unbiased opinion from the owner.

An early cut from an 1800s *Harper's* magazine titled "Pickerel-shooting on the northern lakes."

Odds and Ends

Interesting lure with figures of fish, birds, ships, cattails, snakes, etc. stamped on the surface of the blade.

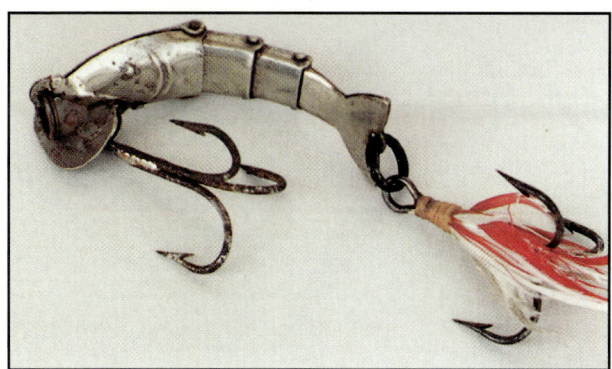

Lure using pinned sections. It would be interesting to see the action of this lure in the water

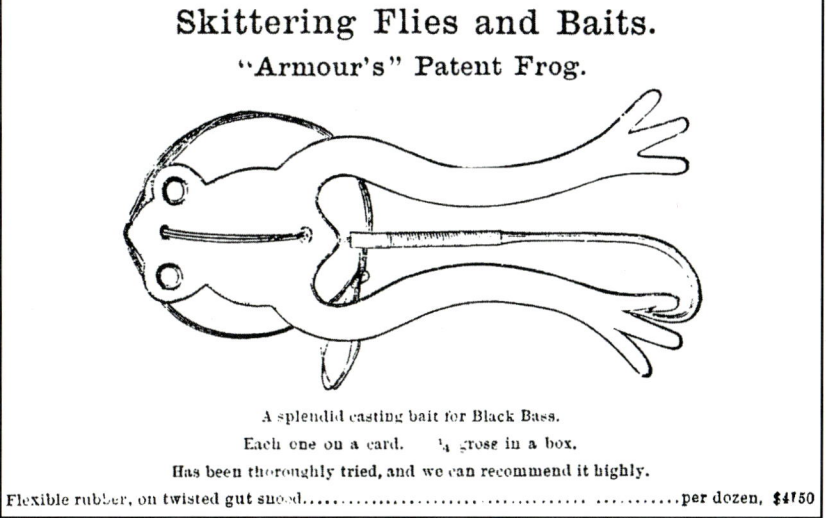

Ad from an 1890s catalog. It was made entirely of rubber.

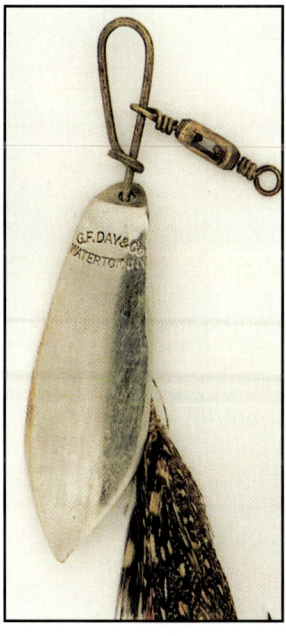

Lure stamped "G. F. Day & Co. Watertown, N.Y." Some of these lures are marked "Day-Pat." These lures are found quite often. I have seen ads for them from the 1920s but some of them are probably older. $15.00 – 25.00.

Art Kimball's trading stock, circa 1982.

Odds and Ends

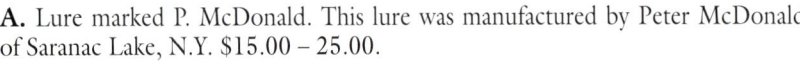

A. Lure marked P. McDonald. This lure was manufactured by Peter McDonald of Saranac Lake, N.Y. $15.00 – 25.00.

B. Top lure is marked "Sportsmans Favorite. Haas Bros. Benton Harbor, Mich." The bottom lure is marked "Sportsmans Favorite. Haas Bros. Wabash, Ind." The Haas Bros. at some point must have relocated or had an operation in both places. $25.00 – 40.00.

C. This blade is marked "J. H. Collins." $20.00 – 30.00.

D. This lure is marked "The Newell Co. Ogdensburg, N.Y." $15.00 – 25.00.

E. This lure is marked "I. W. Lucas Jamestown, N.Y." $15.00 – 25.00.

F. This lure is marked "M. J. Daniels Bemus Pte, N.Y." $15.00 – 25.00.

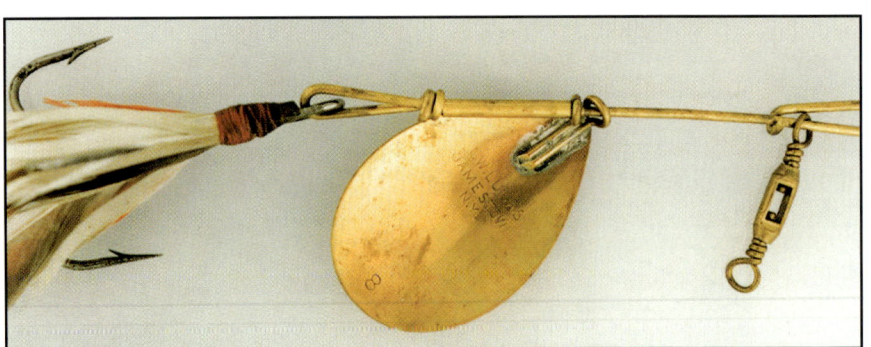

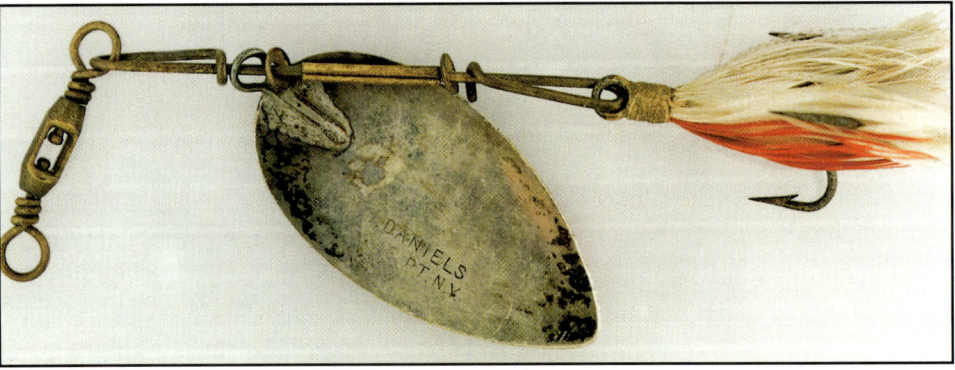

Odds and Ends

A.

B.

C.

A. Part of the John Savu collection of early Pflueger lures.

B. The fabulous "Chautauqua" minnow with its original box. There were a few good lures made after 1901, and this is definitely one of them.

C. A case of the author's former collection of pre-1901 lures, circa 1989. Mostly Chapmans in this case.

Odds and Ends

A set of fluted spinners marked "Mills, New York." This was the William Mills Co. of New York, N.Y. The spinners were probably made by the W. T. J. Lowe Co. of Buffalo, N.Y. $20.00 – 30.00.

Spinner marked "Bouncer, N.Y."

Interesting lure marked "Pat. applied for."

Whence the Plug?

By Sam Stinson

Author's note: This is an article taken from a 1921 issue of the American Angler. *I thought it would be of interest to collectors because of the time frame involved and the subject matter. This article was written nearly 80 years ago and discusses the origin of the fishing plug. Sam Stinson was a popular writer of the period and his work appeared in numerous magazines.*

Isn't it curious how things start? The bass had risen fairly well that day, but they seemed a bit finicky. The evening had turned chilly, as June evenings will, and over our pipes we were holding a post-prandial post-mortem before the blazing log fire; the Magazine Editor, the Artist, the Business Man and I. The Magazine Editor and I had been fishing from the same boat, while the Artist and the Business Man had paired in another.

And there was verbal strife and much abuse, after the manner of men who love each other sufficiently well to feel privileged to call each other names. As bass fishermen we seemed to have but one thing in common. We were all devotees of the plug. But which plug to use, under which conditions? Ah! That was the beautiful, luscious, rosy-cheeked apple of discord.

"Now when we were up in those rushes where we had to pole our way through," said the Magazine Editor, turning his profane attention to me, for his language is apt to be profane even when his voice is most gentle, "if we had discarded our Coaxers for a weedless gang with a frog, or had even tried a strip of pork rind or pickerel belly, we might have —"

"Rot!" I interrupted with the privileged rudeness of a host. "For 12 years I have fished those rushes and until Bill Jamison bobbed up with his Coaxer, I never got anything out of them but promised damnation to my soul. If there is anything in the world more calculated to inspire blasphemy than trying to fish a rush-grown stretch of bass water without a —"

"But the Coaxer was suggested by the old-fashioned pork chunk with a weedless hook," cut in the Artist. "Now, we were fishing all day in open water where we didn't need anything of the kind, and I tried six different plugs before I found that what they wanted was, you can never guess, the old Yellow Kid."

The Business Man grinned. "Fact," he reassured us. "It's a cold fact. Queer how things go. Everything moves in cycles. Hadn't had a rise in two hours. Got out my old mouth-organ. Seemed reminiscent. Don't know what started me, but I struck up "Silver Threads Among the Gold." Heard it the first time I ever went to the theatre, Dan Bryant's Minstrels. Seemed to strike a responsive chord in the bass. Maybe they were old enough to remember it. Put on a Yellow Kid myself, canned the mouth-organ and got that 5-pounder we had broiled for dinner."

"The Yellow Kid was the first plug I ever used," said the Artist. "But the Decker plug."

"The Heddons put out the first plug," exploded the Magazine Editor. "When I was fishing with old Jim Heddon — God rest his soul! — out in Michigan ten years ago, he told me."

"Nix! Nix!" thundered the Business Man. "Cast your eyes toward Lake Hopatcong, New Jersey, if you want the real dope about where the first plug."

"How about Malcolm Shipley, of Philadelphia?" I interposed mildly; but my voice was drowned in a babble of contention that raged through the night. And thus began a quest, the incomplete

FIRST WOODEN MINNOW USED IN THE HEDDON FAMILY
Adapted to trolling and ice spearing for pickerel. Made by the father of the late James Heddon and used by James Heddon on Magacian Lake, twelve miles from Dowagiac, in 1860. Nine inches long

result of which herewith follows; speculative, inconsequential perhaps, but fascinating, I am constrained to think, to any bass fisherman who has become reconciled to the use of the plug through a mass of sophomoric and unpractical criticism, a criticism inspired by an antiquated prejudice against a modern form of sport, a prejudice too strong to allow the critics to find out by practical investigation just what it is they object to. Perhaps they are too virtuous to find out.

"Camouflage! All camouflage. Do you remember, before we got into the war, President Wilson's pronouncement: "We are too proud to fight?"

Well, anyhow, that night's symposium over our pipes before the June log fire started me on a train of thought that has led me far afield. Almost until the gray streaks of dawn warned us that there were bass to be taken on the morrow did we keep going the controversial fires of contention. We got beyond the priority of the plug itself, we abandoned the discussion as to which was the first on the market, we attempted to get back to the very inception of the idea. And we came to naught.

Since then I have delved into libraries. I have haunted museums. I have communicated by correspondence or through personal interviews with many persons, and through devious lines of reasoning I am constrained to the belief that the first breakfast Christopher Columbus had on American soil, or at least after having gone above tidewater, consisted of a big-mouth black bass caught by an aborigine on a plug, crude and prehistoric, but nevertheless a plug. And if any man can say me nay, let him now speak or forever hereafter hold his peace.

The tackle manufacturers themselves, with a few exceptions, I have found to be curiously unresponsive as to the origins of their respective wares. Lake Hopatcong, almost a suburb of New York and believed by many in the East to have given birth to the plug, is barren of substantiation, so far as my communications with the Decker family are concerned. Malcom A. Shipley, a Philadelphia tackle manufacturer, made a surface plug in the late nineties, and it must have been on the market before the Decker Hopatcong plug, although the Decker plug was the first I personally ever saw used.

As nearly as I can recollect, it was in the summer of 1899 that I was fishing at Lake Hopatcong, with old George Decker, as my guide and boatman. He was an older brother of Anse Decker, who later put the lure on the market commercially, and who gained wide publicity by his fishing contest for a stake with W.S. Jamison, the Chicago tackle manufacturer, who at that time was introducing his Coaxer, each contestant using his own plug.

George Decker and I had been fishing all day at Lake Hopatcong with minnows and frogs, strip casting the frogs and trolling the minnows, with very poor success. About five o'clock in the afternoon he squinted at the sun just beginning to be obscured by a black cloud in the West, and drawled: "Bout time fer us to be gittin' some fish. Don't you think so?"

I assured him I did, and he produced from a tackle box the first plug I had ever seen. Rather astonished, but hesitating to show my curiosity, I watched him take a stiff rod, stiffer than a fly-rod but with the reel seat below the hand, and cast this plug just exactly as he had been previously casting a frog, stripping the line in by hand. The short bait-casting rod with the reel above the hand, now in common use, was not at that time known in the East, although it had undoubtedly been introduced in the Middle West.

And much to my mixed amazement and incredulity he got the fish. I remember now the viciousness with which they rose and struck that clumsy-looking contrivance equipped with what looked to me like the paddle-wheel on a miniature steamboat. He gave me an extra one to try, but I naturally made the tyro's dismal failure at getting it out, and soon gave it up, content with watching his performance.

Two or three years later in Philadelphia, I saw the first bass plugs that had ever come to my knowledge commercially, although the Hopatcong plugs had been sold by the Deckers in a small way as guides. I was passing the retail establishment of

THE CEDAR PROPELLOR
The first wooden minnow put on the market by Malcolm Shipley

Malcolm A. Shipley, and saw in his window what he called his cedar propeller. It was of plain, uncolored cedar wood, and differed somewhat in construction from the Decker plug, being equipped with two very light-weight metal propellers, one fore and one aft, connected by a copper wire that extended laterally through the conical body. It bore three treble hooks.

As I was then preparing for a fishing trip to Lake Sunapee, N.H., I entered the shop and purchased half a dozen, and found them so productive of good results that I continued to use them as long as they were manufactured. Although they are no longer on the market, I still have some old ones in my kit that I occasionally doctor up, as their lightness enables me to use them with a fly rod — but I do not advocate this method of fishing unless one uses a rod that for some reason has been discarded for fly fishing.

My research into the origin of the plug led me more and more to the belief that artificial minnows, so called, had been used by individuals and possibly by a few chosen friends of these individuals, long before they were generally known to the angling public. The Middle West, as the home of the short bait-casting rod, seemed to point the way to the origin of its side partner, the plug: for the two go hand in hand. Consequently it was to the Middle West that I turned my attention. In the East it was exotic.

Angling literature gave me no inkling. Frank Forester, the dean of sporting writers in America, would have damned the plug, had he known of it even in its infancy, as he damned the spoon. For, writing of the black bass in *Fish and Fishing,* he says: "It bites ravenously at a small fish or spinning tackle, or at the deadly and murderous spoon, an instrument so certainly destructive that the use of it is properly discouraged by all true anglers as poaching and unsportsman-like." But then he also speaks of the bass's "numerous and exceedingly acute teeth," to defy which "a treble-twisted gut is necessary." In discussing muscallonge, however, he speaks of the effectiveness of "a bait of tin or red cloth made to play quickly through the water," indicating that even then something remotely suggesting the modern plug may have been used for trolling, if not for casting.

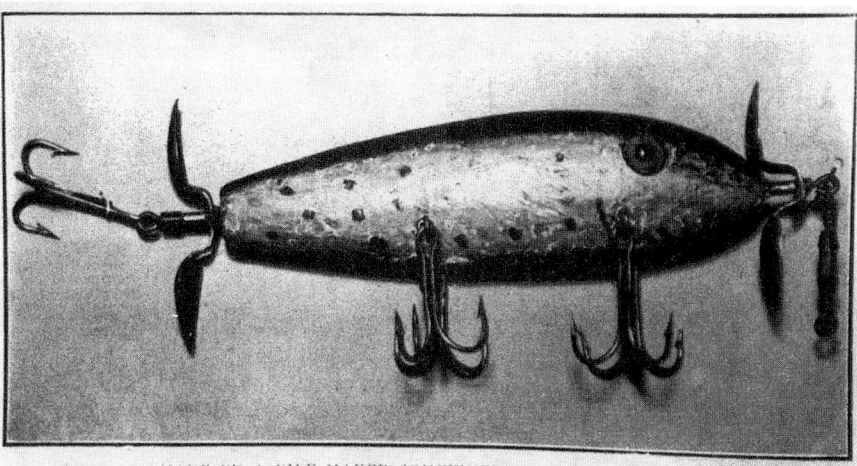

"MADE BY A FILE MAKER SOMEWHERE IN NEW JERSEY"

Indeed there is authentic evidence of this fact as early as 1850, at any rate. The forebears of the family of Heddon, of Dowagiac, Michigan, among the most famed of American fishing tackle manufacturers, can claim this distinction. Although the Heddon lures were not placed upon the market commercially until 1902, the late James Heddon for many years before that date made wooden minnows for the use of himself and his friends. According to his son, Mr. Charles Heddon, as early as 1890 his father was using his wooden baits with the short bait-casting rod.

"In saying that bait-casting was first practiced at that time," adds Mr. Heddon, "I make the exception that there were a few scattering anglers who devised their own equipment, and we seem to have authentic records that bait castings was practiced earlier, but, of course, these were very exceptional cases. My father first made wooden baits exclusively for his own use, originally having no intention of engaging in the art from a commercial standpoint. He was a pioneer sportsman of southwestern Michigan, the first to own a breech-loading shotgun in this county, and was much devoted to field and stream sports. When asked who made the first wooden bait or plug, my father used to always exhibit two types of wooden minnows used by his grandfather in trolling for pickerel on Magician Lake, in this county, as far back as from 1850 to 1855. It is safe to assume that wooden baits in various forms are as old as three quarters of a century."

One of the best-posted men on angling conditions is W.J. Jamison, of Chicago, himself an ardent sportsman and one of the pioneers in the manufacture and marketing of artificial lures for bass.

Whence the Plug?

My request for information developed on his part a keen interest in the subject, and reminiscing in the course of our correspondence, he says:

"The first bass I ever saw taken on an artificial bait was taken in Southeastern Kansas on a phantom minnow cast with a long cane pole. This was about the year 1880, when I was a boy of fifteen. The next day I procured a spoon fitted with a feathered treble and went to the same place and took three nice bass myself, using a long cane pole and wading along the shore. The earliest recollection I have of a wooden bait is of one called the North Channel Minnow, somewhere around 20 years ago. A little later someone somewhere in Indiana put out a plug minnow shaped with holes in it somewhat similar to the Waterwitch, Wagtail Minnow and the Pollywog. This Indiana bait had the hooks attached to strings that ran through the holes connected with the line, allowing you to pull the hooks away from the bait when taking off a fish. About this time Heddon came out with his top-water bait and a little later with his regular minnow. Someone also put out a luminous wooden minnow at that time, but it did not sell and soon disappeared. Another Indiana man took out a patent on a bait like the Decker bait. I believe that was around 20 years ago. The first wobbling wooden plug I ever saw on the market was Heddon's 'Swimming Minnow.' Then the Wilson Wobbler came along, then multitudes of wobblers and wigglers."

Every plug fisherman who has ever lured Mr. Bass from water overgrown with weeds, rushes and lily pads knows the "Coaxer." This was evolved by Mr. Jamison from the pork chunk. He noticed another angler decorating his pork chunk with strips of red yarn, and meeting with much success. This set him thinking. As an improvement on this idea he experimented with a piece of heavy red felt inserted through the pork just under the rind. It made a hit with other anglers who had witnessed the performance, and within a month they were all using the same contrivance. "Finally," says Mr. Jamison, "it occurred to me that I might make an artificial chunk that would carry a hook in the rear. This was early in the winter, but I went ahead and made one out of cork. I weighted a hook, split the cork, and inserted the hook so it stuck out behind. A street carnival was on at the time, and someone brought in a small feather duster, or tickler, I believe they call them, and I noticed the colored feathers and pulled a few of them out and stuck them in the rear end of the bait. I think this was in November. I found a vacant piece of ground not far from where I lived, with about four inches of water in it, and tried the thing out at night by the electric light. It rode beautifully. I kept on all winter working with it, and by spring had about gone daffy over it. And that is how the Coaxer originated."

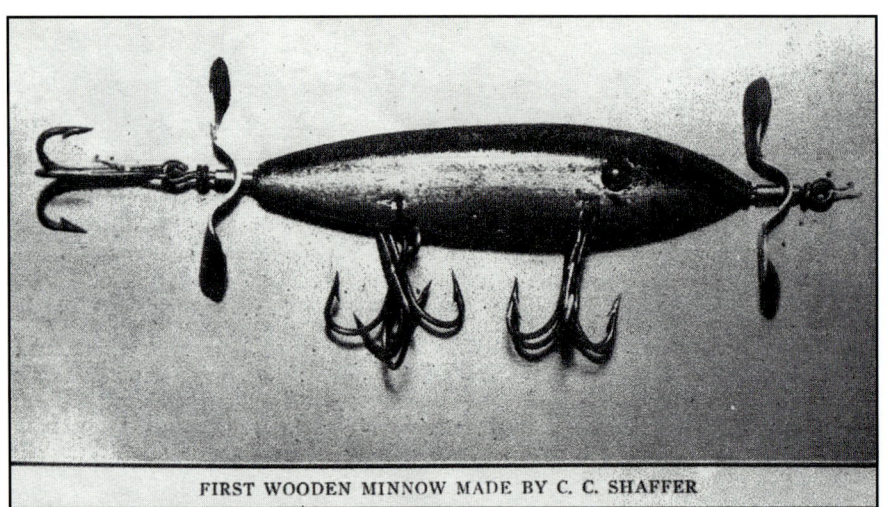

FIRST WOODEN MINNOW MADE BY C. C. SHAFFER

Credit for the origin of the short casting rod belongs to another former Chicagoan, James M. Clark, popularly known to the angling fraternity of that section as "Uncle Jim." Mr. Clark, who is now a resident of Kansas City, was formerly connected with a Chicago sporting goods house, and 30 years ago he introduced to Chicago anglers the six-foot rod. This was a rod of his own design and innovation, and he had a few made to order for his friends and the few customers who were sufficiently far-sighted even then to realize its possibilities. For he was a bass-fishing enthusiast, and was regarded as an oracle, as indeed he was.

My correspondence with Mr. Clark, however, did not result in any claim on his part to the discovery of the plug. With that proverbial modesty of the true angler, with that eagerness to give credit where credit is due, so characteristic of the sportsman, he passes the buck to least, in so far as Mr. Clark has any knowledge (and his experience covers many years of practical trade conditions), he says the first plug to be introduced commercially of which he has any knowledge was known as the Woods Minnow, advertised as the "Expert."

At that time Mr. Shaffer was in the employ of the Government, in the rail-way postal service, so did not consider it advisable to use his own name commercially in connection with the plug. In order to properly introduce it to the trade he named it after a relative, a Mr. Woods. This was about 1885, and although the business was inaugurated in a small way, due probably to a lack of capital, Mr. Clark recollects that the plug was a success from the start.

Mr. Shaffer disclaims any intention of posing as the father of the plug, but he does insist that the "Expert" was the first to be advertised and offered for sale through the medium of advertising. "From the best information I can obtain," writes Mr. Shaffer, "the first wooden minnow was made by a file maker somewhere in New Jersey, and he got the idea from the Indians along the Maine coast."

The file maker, "somewhere in New Jersey" has a rival, however, in a Chicago barber, equally obscure. Robert H. Davis, who knows bass lore from the ground up and who has written much concerning bass fishing with the plug, stands sponsor for the Chicago barber, although unable to give me any definite information about the identity of the tonsorial Piscator.

Antedating Mr. Shaffer's "Expert" were at least two plugs made by the Enterprise Manufacturing Co., of Akron, Ohio. E. A. Pflueger, president of the company, tells me that their first plug was manufactured in 1881. This was an artificial minnow made of hollow glass, mounted with single and treble hooks, and equipped with a spinner at the head. It was filled with a mirror substance, and also had a luminous quality. Artificial minnows of rubber, pearl, and metal followed. The first wooden minnow put out by Mr. Pflueger was the "Comstock." This made its appearance in 1883. It must have been a curious contrivance, as the spinners were mounted on the sides instead of at the head and tail, according to the present method.

But all this doesn't bring us to an understanding of what first inspired the belief that a bass would strike at an object armed with hooks moving on the surface of the water. I myself have thrown a brilliantly-colored empty cigarette box out of my boat and have seen a bass make a rush at it and knock it out of the water. Why? Undoubtedly in uncontrollable anger.

A popular belief is that the plug was originally evolved from the common or garden variety of clothespin. Another is that a woodchopper plying his trade on the shore of a lake noticed the bass rising to the chips as they fell on the surface of the water. James M. Clark, speculating on the origin of the plug, advances the theory that it might be traced back to the English Phantom, or to the Scotch solid rubber Caledonian Minnow. The latter was in use a hundred years ago, and the former, Mr. Clark claims, dates back to the time of Izaak Walton!

Undoubtedly the Indians caught fish by artificial means, probably even before the Christianized paleface bartered firewater and fish hooks for pelts. Evidence of this fact may be seen in the anthropological department of the American Museum of Natural History where, among the Indian relics, one may inspect crude and hookless contrivances for catching fish. These are very remote from the highly colored and enameled lures of the present day, but it is quite possible that through a process of gradual evolution, the finished product as we know it may have come from that source.

The late Alfred M. Mayer, of the faculty of Stevens Institute of Technology, had in his collection of archaeological interest a curious specimen of the handiwork of the American Indian that somewhat remotely suggested the plug. It might be termed an artificial shrimp. Thirty-five years ago Barnet Phillips, at that time secretary of the American Fish Cultural Association, published a paper entitled "The Primitive Fish-Hook," in which he dwelt upon this forerunner of the modern plug, without of course realizing its significance.

Mr. Phillips in describing this lure says, "Occasionally, a savage will construct a lure for fish which rivals the daintiest fly ever made by the most fastidious of anglers. In Professor Mayer's collection there is an exceedingly clever hook, coming from the northwestern coast, which shows very fine lapidary work. A small red quartoze pebble of great hardness has been rounded, polished, and joined to a piece of bone. The piece is small, not more than an inch and three-quarters in length, and might weigh an ounce and a half. In the shank of bone a small hook is hidden. It somewhat imitates a shrimp. The parts are joined together by lashings of tendon, and these are laid in grooves cut into the stone. It must have taken much toil to perfect this clever artificial bait."

This origin of the plug is a speculative filed, fascinating in its possibilities. I admit that I have been able to merely skim the surface, and there are probably many readers of *The American Angler* better equipped than I to solve the moot question.

Front Page Mr. Knowitall.

LURE MANUFACTURERS BEFORE 1901

This list was compiled by the late Dick Nissley of Birmingham, Michigan and given to me for use in this book. Dick always took the time to share new information with me, and although I never met him face to face, I felt he was a friend. We spent quite a bit of time on the phone talking old baits, and after a nice long conversation with Dick, I would always come away with renewed enthusiasm.

Some of the trade houses such as Abbey and Imbrie, Hibbard Spencer, Bartlett & Co., Mecham Arms, James Marsters, and others were not included in separate categories in this book. Although these companies sold lures bearing their trade names, they were generally manufactured by other companies such as the Enterprise Mfg. Co., and G. M. Skinner. Most of these lures were of the garden variety and including them would have been superfluous and tedious. In certain cases, such as the Abbey & Imbrie Ghost, consideration was given to the unique nature of the lure and it was included.

Abbey & Imbrie	New York, N.Y.	1893	Kewell, Chas. H.	San Francisco, Ca.	1900
Alger, Franklin A.	Grand Rapids, Mich.	1900	Lake Baits	Auburn, N.Y.	c1890
Allen, J. D.	So. Otselic, N.Y.	1892	Livingston, J.	Gananoque, Ont.	1895
Allen, Manson B.	Grand Rapids, Mich.	1894	Lobb, Ferris F.	Piseco Lake, N.Y.	1850
Bates, T. H.	New York, N.Y.	1853	Loftie, Henry	Syracuse, N.Y.	1888
Bentley, John	Jamestown, N.Y.	1892	Lowe, W. T. J.	Buffalo, N.Y.	1882
Bingenheimer, A. F.	Milwaukee, Wisc.	1896	Lucas, T. W.	Jamestown, N.Y.	c1890
Brush, H. C.	Brush Mills, N.Y.	1876	McDonald, Peter	Saranac Lake, N.Y.	c1895
Buel, H. W.	Whitehall, N.Y.	1850	McHarg, J. B.	Rome, N.Y.	1886
Buel, J. T.	Whitehall, N.Y.	c1845	Mack's Hook Co.	Rochester, N.Y.	c1890
Burgess, B. F.	Jackson, Mich.	1890	Mann, J. H.	Syracuse, N.Y.	1871
Chapman W. D.	Theresa, N.Y.	1860	Mason, Hiram	New York, N.Y.	c 1890
Chautaqua Lake Baits	Chautaqua Lk., N.Y.	1891	Mill's, William	New York, N.Y.	1897
Cheeseman, L. E.	Saranac Lake, N.Y.	1897	Morse, C. H.	Auburn, Maine	c1900
Clark, C. V.	Hammondsport, N.Y.	1890	New Acme	Syracuse, N.Y.	1885
Clark, Horrocks Co.	Utica, N.Y.	1884	Newell Co.	Ogdensburg, N.Y.	1898
Conroy, J. C. & Co.	New York, N.Y.	c1880	P & S Ball Bearing	Sayre, Pa.	1895
Daniels, J. M.	Bemus Pte., N.Y.	1895	Pflueger (Enterprise)	Akron, Ohio	1880
Day G. F.	Watertown, N.Y.	c1890	Pierce, M.F.	Marion, N.Y.	1887
Delaney, W.	Coburg, Ont.	c1890	Qualman, George	N.Y.	c1890
Gascon, Ade	New York	c1887	Radcliffe, J.	Rochester, N.Y.	1888
Graves, F.S.	Albany, N.Y.	1898	Scheftic, J.H.	Auburn, N.Y.	1890
Haas Bros.	Benton Harbor, Mich.	1895	Schoverlling, Dale & Gutter		
Harlow, J.R.	Auburn, N.Y.	1888		N.Y., N.Y.	1900
Harran E. & Son	Utica, N.Y.	1880	Skinner, G.M.	Clayton, N.Y.	1874
Heddon, J.	Dowagiac, Mich.	1890	Spalding, A.G.	Syracuse, N.Y.	1886
Hendryx, A.B.	New Haven, Conn.	1890	Sterling (attributed to Hendryx)		
Herendeen, G.	Canandaigua, N.Y.			New Haven, Ct.	1890
	Saranac Lake, N.Y.	1898	Thousand Island (Chapman made)		
Hibbard, C.B.	Grand Rapids, Mich.	1884		Clayton, N.Y.	1895
Hildebrandt	Logansport, Ind.	c1890	Waltham	Folsom, N.Y.	1890
Hill, L.S.	Grand Rapids, Mich.	1876	Watson, H.C.	Clyde, N.Y.	c1880
Hughson, E.N.	Clyde, N.Y.	c1890	White Hat Tackle Co. (Treman, King, and Co.)		
James, W.H.	Brooklyn, N.Y.	1874		Ithaca, N.Y.	1890
Ke-Ad Bait Co.	North East, Pa.	c1890	Zuckweiler, Henry	Pekin, Ill.	1891

A Brief History of the Patent Office

At the 1787 Constitutional Convention in Philadelphia on September 5, the clause on patents and copyrights was adopted. The Constitution was signed on September 17 with the provision in Article 1, Section 8, that "Congress shall have the power to promote the progress of science and useful acts, by securing for limited times to authors and inventors the exclusive right to their respective writings and discoveries."

A patent bill was passed on February 16, 1790. The first Patent Commission consisted of three members, Thomas Jefferson being one. The Commissioners examined each patent application to determine its novelty and usefulness. If granted, the patent was in effect for 14 years. No fee was charged but a drawing and model were required. However, in 1793 a bill was passed that put the Patent Office under the direction of the Secretary of State and abolished the examination system. Now all a person had to do was apply for the patent and pay a fee of $30. This, of course, raised money for the government but made the patent system practically useless. A drawing or model was no longer required.

In 1800, when the seat of government moved to Washington D. C., the Patent Office was temporarily set up at the Treasury Dept. In 1802 it was moved to an old wood building know as Blodgett's Hotel. James Madison was Secretary of State at the time and appointed Dr. William Thornton as the first Patent Chief, or Supervisor.

Thornton was a controversial man and was accused, among other things, of a conflict of interest. He was an inventor himself and held several patents. He did, however, redeem himself on August 25, 1814, when he talked the British out of burning down the Patent Office, still housed in Blodgett's Hotel.

The Patent Act of 1836 reestablished the examination system of 1790 and once again it was required that a patent show novelty and usefulness before it would be granted. It was also now required that previous patents be searched for any pre-existing patents of similar nature. An applicant also had to submit a drawing and model. These models could not be more than 12 inches square and the name of the inventor had to be printed or engraved on it.

On the morning of December 15, 1836, Blodgett's Hotel, along with its contents, burned to the ground. Lost were 7,000 patent models, along with all of the records.

The following year Congress appropriated $100,000 for the reconstruction of the Patent Office's Visual History. They had to rely on the patentees and their descendants for the duplication of the drawings and models. Needless to say, not all of the patents were restored. It is possible that a fishing lure patent was granted, lost in the fire, and never restored.

A new building was constructed and occupied in the spring of 1840. It was thought that this building was more than adequate in size. It was for awhile, but after the Civil War there was a tremendous increase in the number of applications. They were running out of room and had nowhere to store the thousands of models. On July 8, 1870 Congress passed a law stipulating that models were no longer required but could be requested by the Commissioner. Many inventors ignored the law and the problem of storage kept getting worse. However, on Sept. 24, 1877, the problem was once again solved by fire.

This fire destroyed the top floor model rooms of the west and north wings. There were an estimated 76,000 models lost, mostly agricultural and mechanical inventions. Once again Congress appropriated money for their restoration. There is no record of the number of models replaced, but by 1880 the Patent Office was overrun with models. They were everywhere, on desks, shelves, under chairs, any place available. The problem was so bad that the patent law was strengthened to make it against the law to send a model, except for flying machines, perpetual motion machines, and special request. The law had come full circle, from requiring a model be sent, to being against the law to send one.

This in effect stopped the flow of models, although, there was still the problem of storing the existing ones. In 1907 Congress decided to sell the collection after giving the Smithsonian Institution six months to choose the ones they deemed the most important. The Smithsonian took only 1,061 models. Three thousand were auctioned off for $62.18 and the rest were stored for nearly 20 years in basements around the capital. They were finally put into an abandoned livery.

In 1925 the Calvin Coolidge administration appropriated $10,000 to dispose of the models. The Smithsonian acquired 2,500 this time, and other museums and inventors took another 2,600. Henry Ford personally picked 25 models of farm machinery which are displayed, along with other patent models, from time to time, at the Ford Museum in Dearborn, Michigan. A representative group of models was laid out in a Washington warehouse for bidders to view and approximately 50,000 were sold for $1,550. This left a mere 125,000 cases of unopened models. As of 1970, many of these cases had remained unopened. O. Rundel Gilbert of Garrison, N.Y., ended up with 75 trailer truckloads of these cases. They are stored in secret barns around Garrison and are being slowly opened and sold at the Patent Model Building in Garrison.

The above information was taken from:
The Art of Invention
by William and Marlys Ray
The Pyne Press, Princeton
Copyright 1974
NOTE: This information is dated, so don't go running around looking in barns near Garrison, N.Y. It is possible, and likely, that the cases have all been opened and disposed of by this time.

Patent Drawings of Unfound Lures

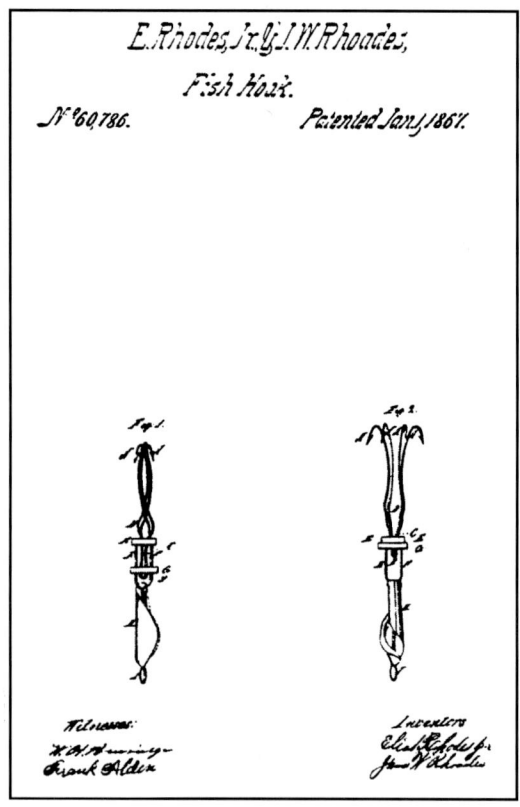

Clyde, Ohio

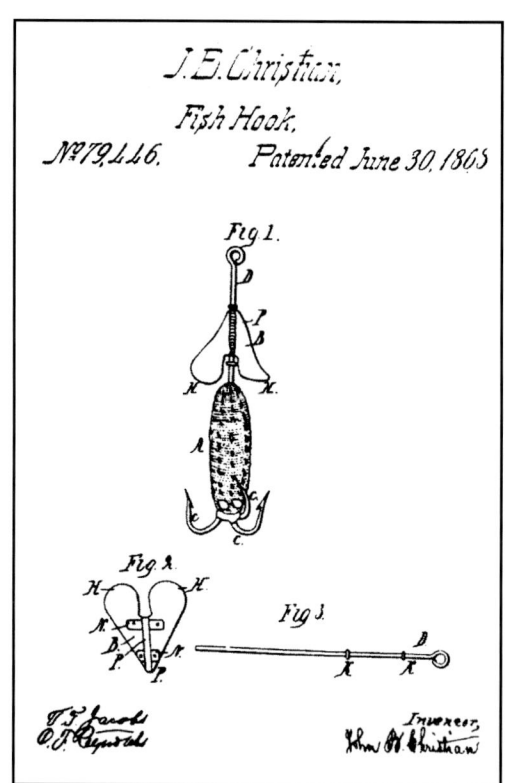

Mount Carroll, Ill.

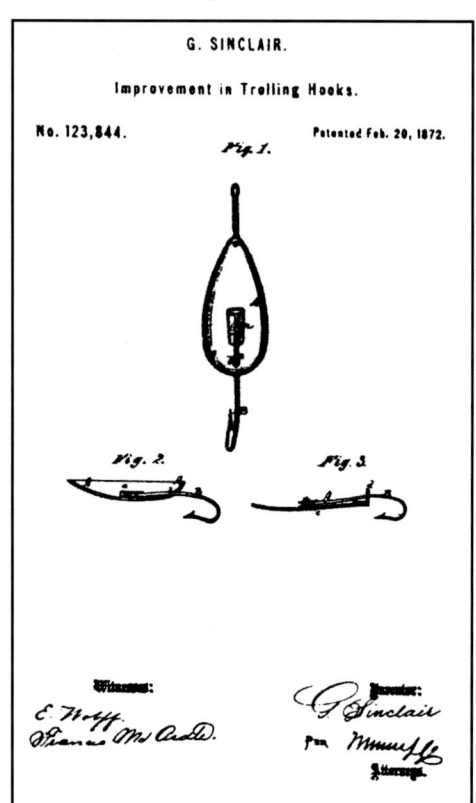

Chicago, Ill.

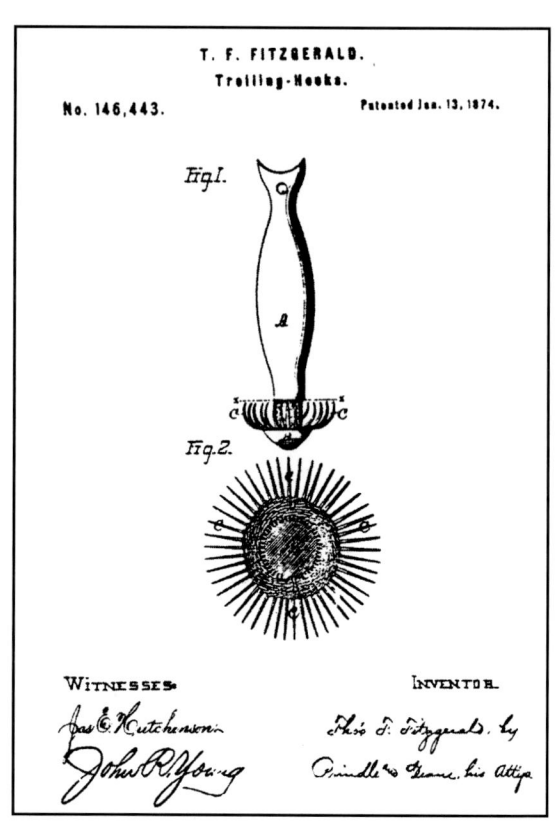

Rockport, Mass.

PATENT DRAWINGS OF UNFOUND LURES

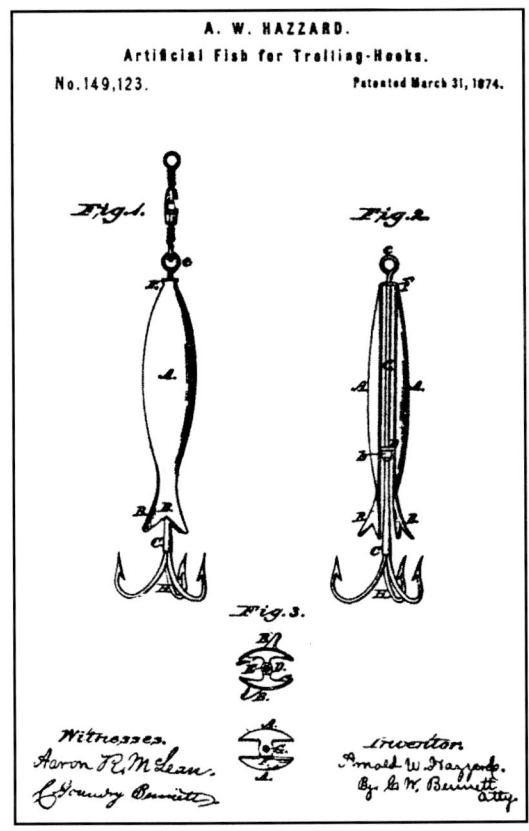

Seneca Falls, N.Y.

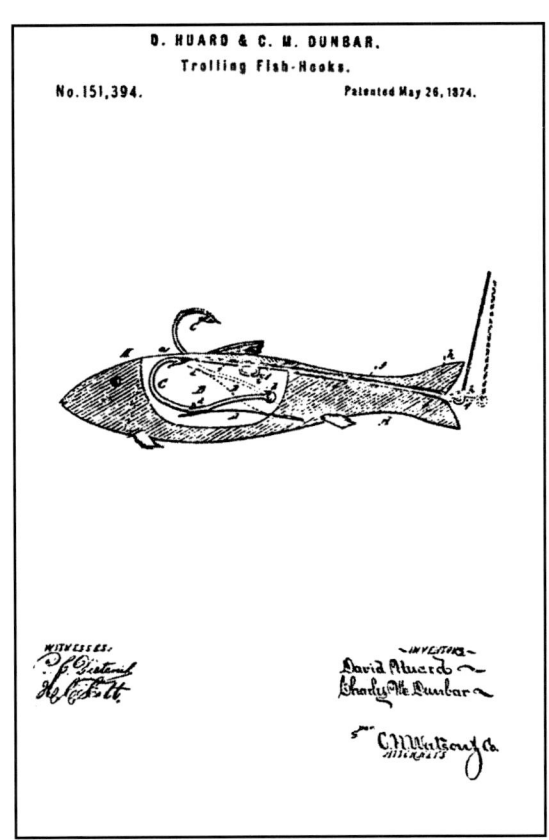

Ashland, Wisc.

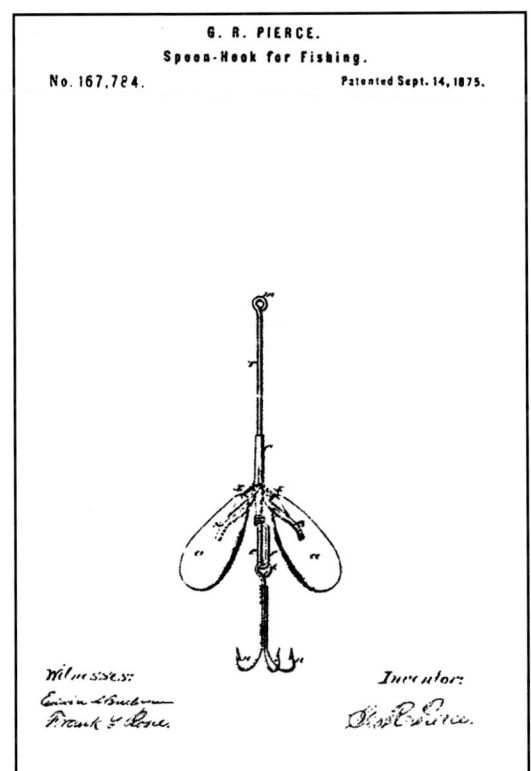

Grand Rapids, Mich.

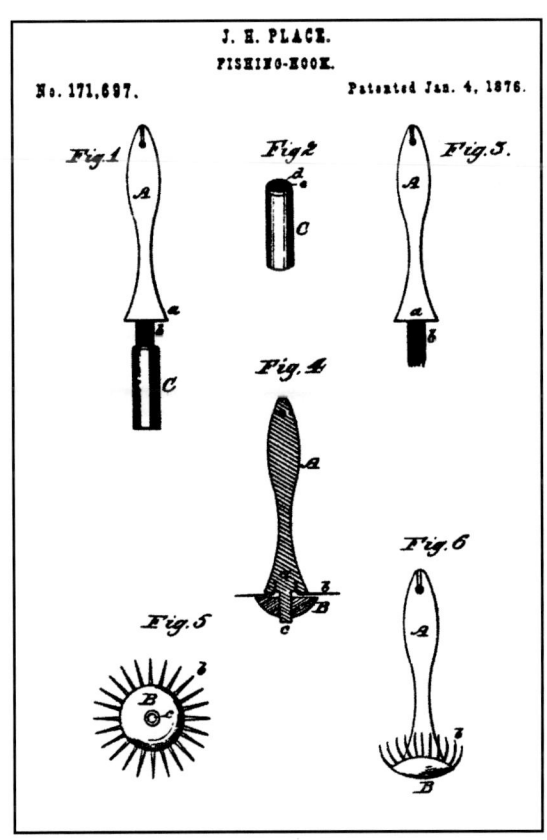

Gloucester, Mass.

Patent Drawings of Unfound Lures

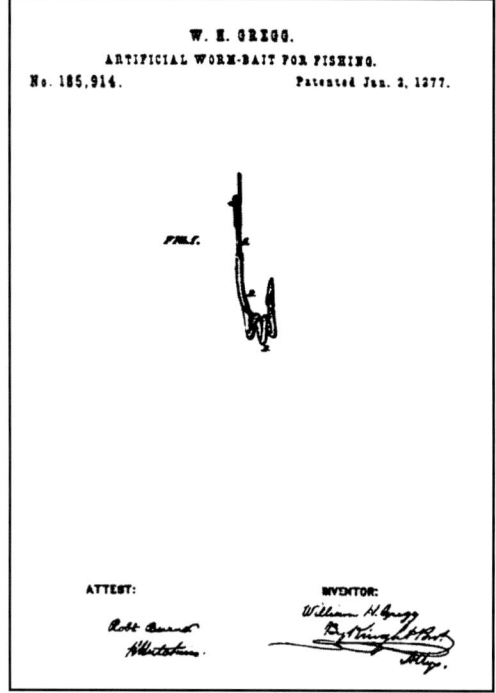

St. Louis, Mo.

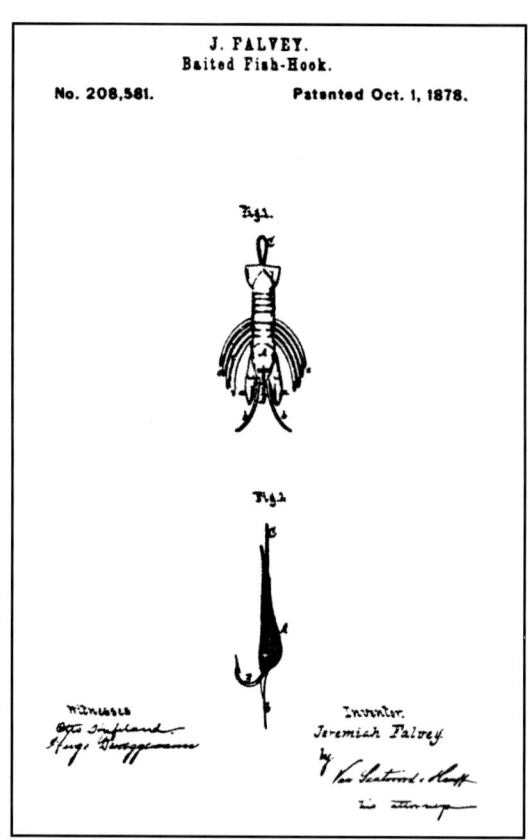

Flatbush, N.Y.

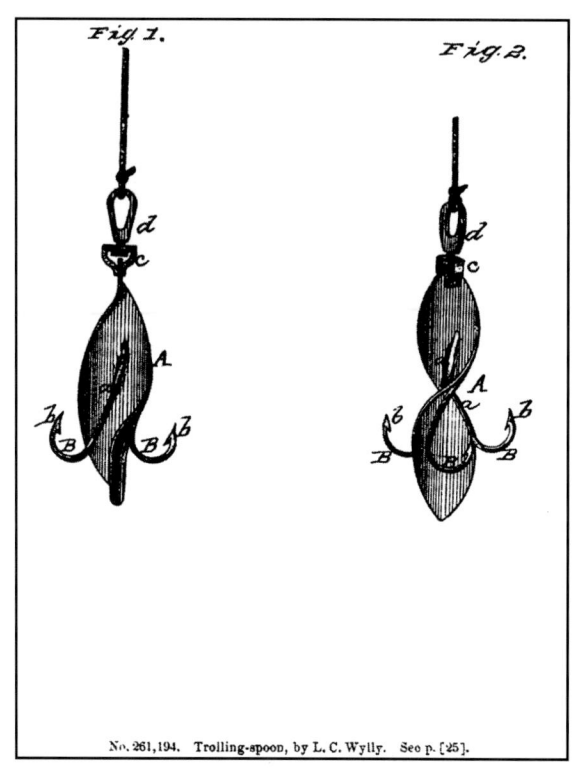

Patterson, Ga. Lewis C. Wylly 261,194

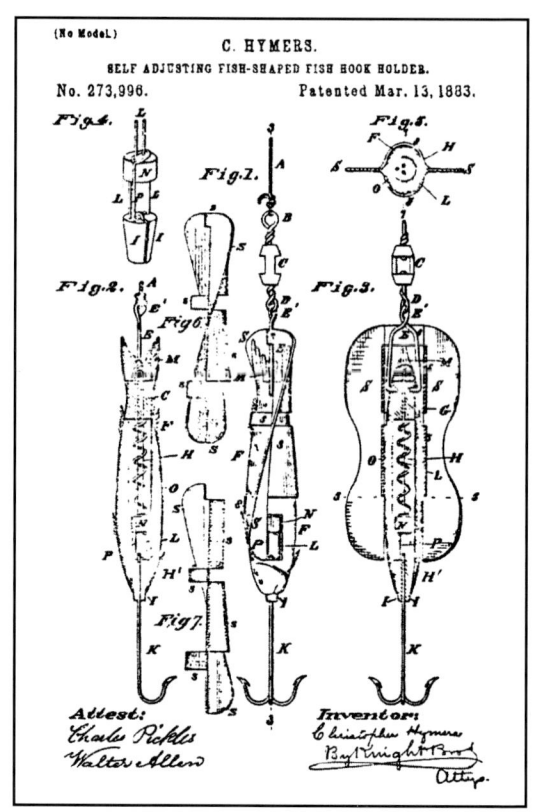

St. Louis, Mo.

Patent Drawings of Unfound Lures

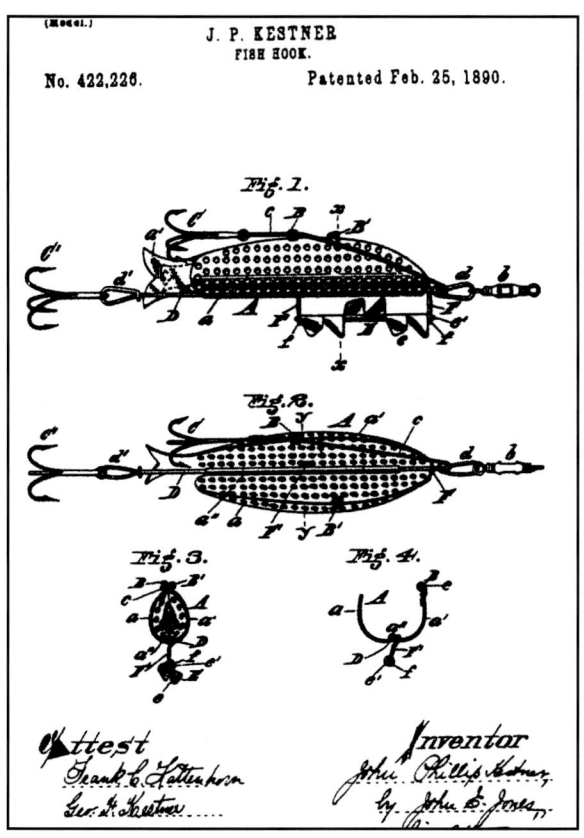

Cincinnati, Ohio

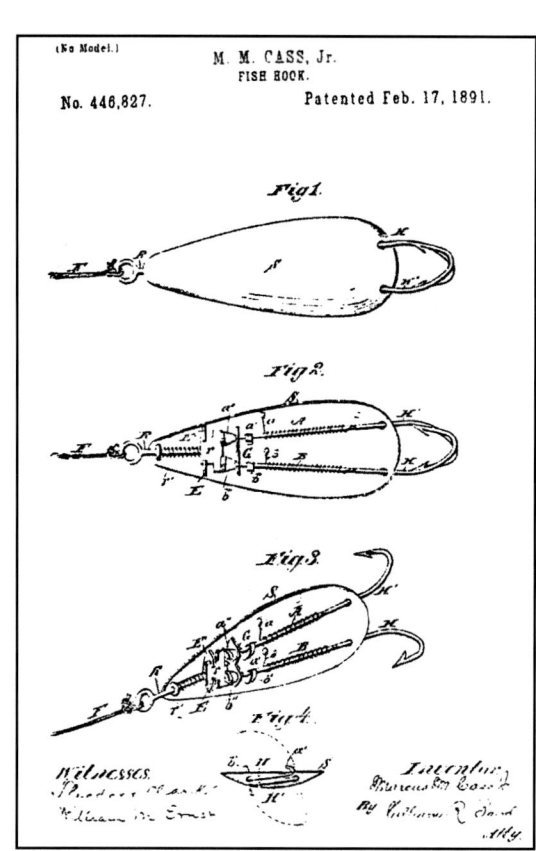

Unknown

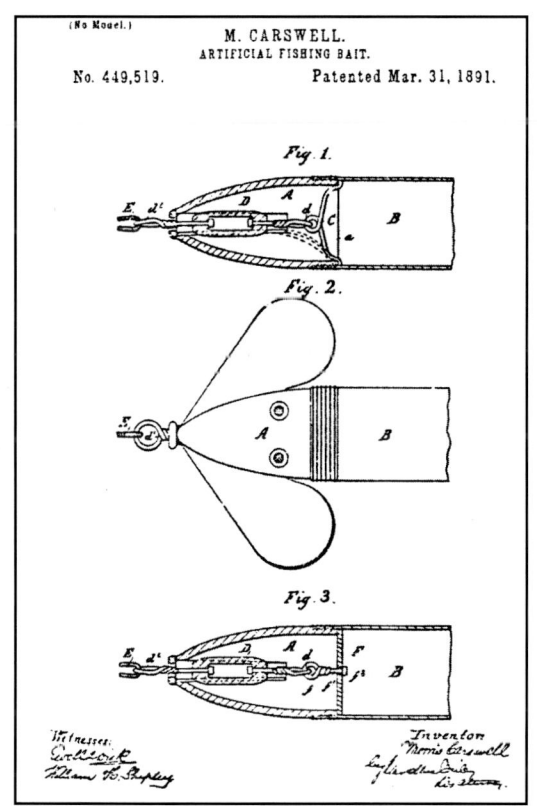

Glasgow, Scotland

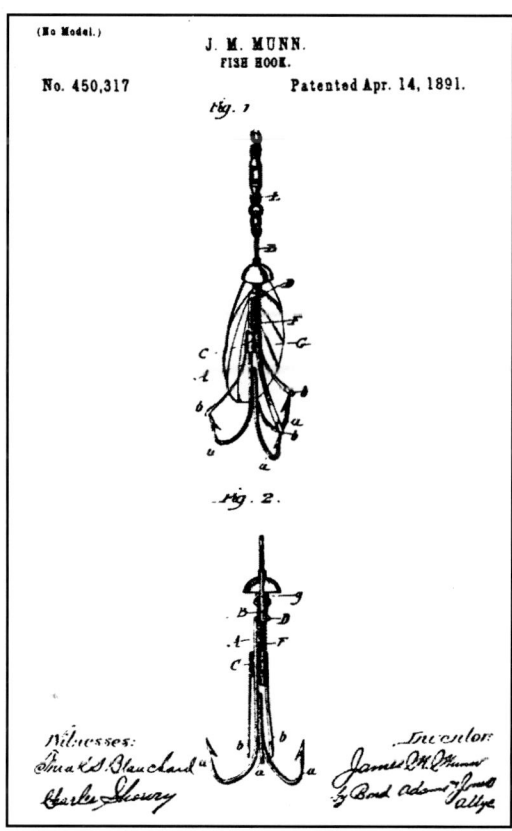

Chicago, Ill.

PATENT DRAWINGS OF UNFOUND LURES

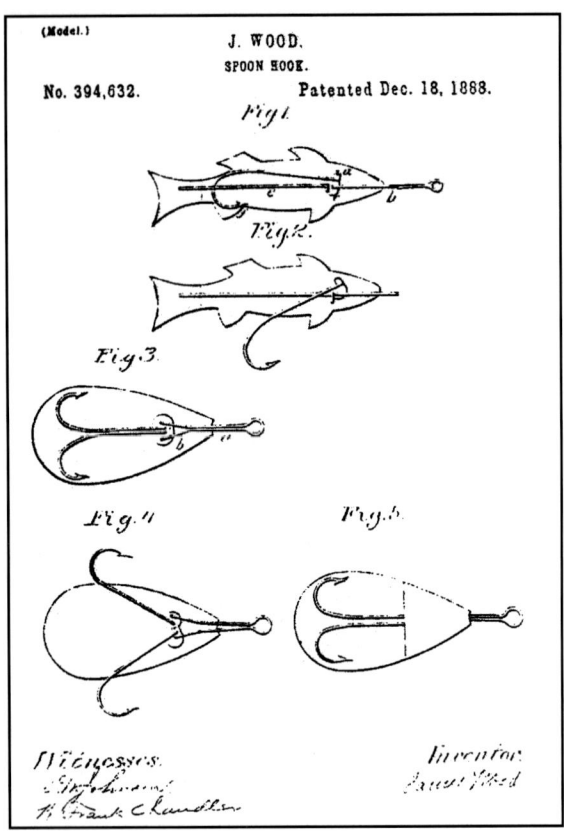

Rochester, N. Y.

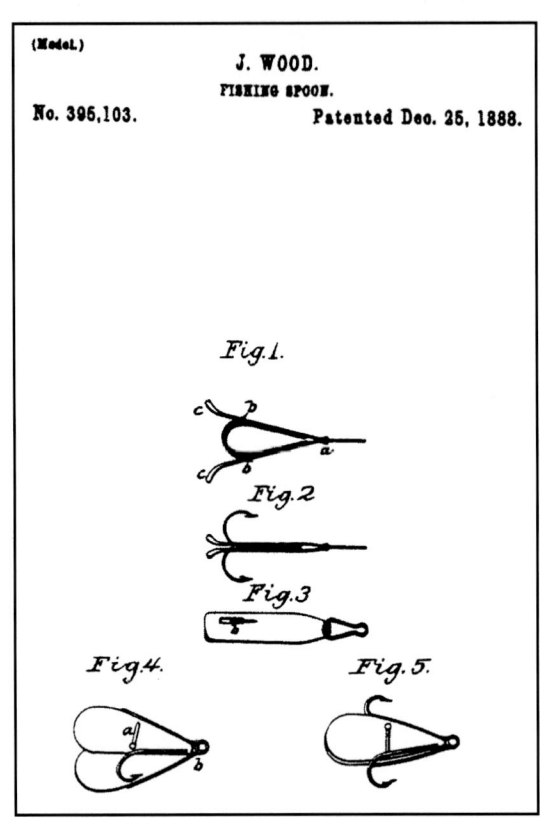

Rochester, N. Y.

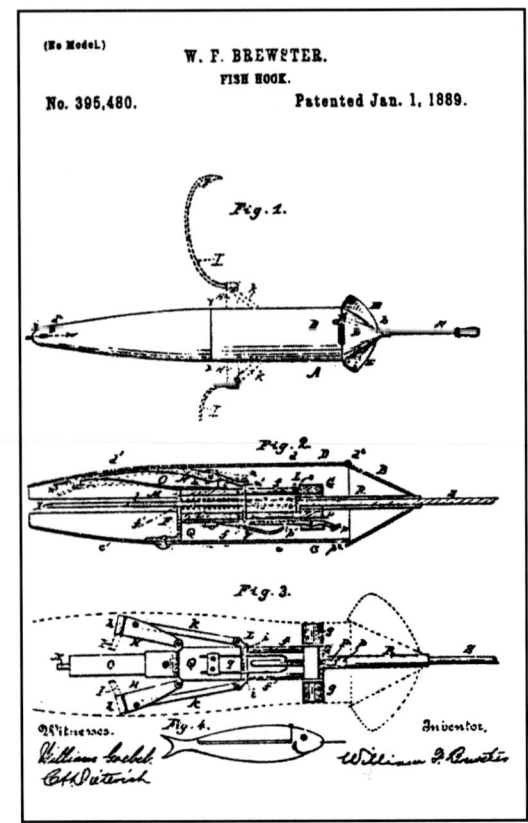

East Orange, N. J.

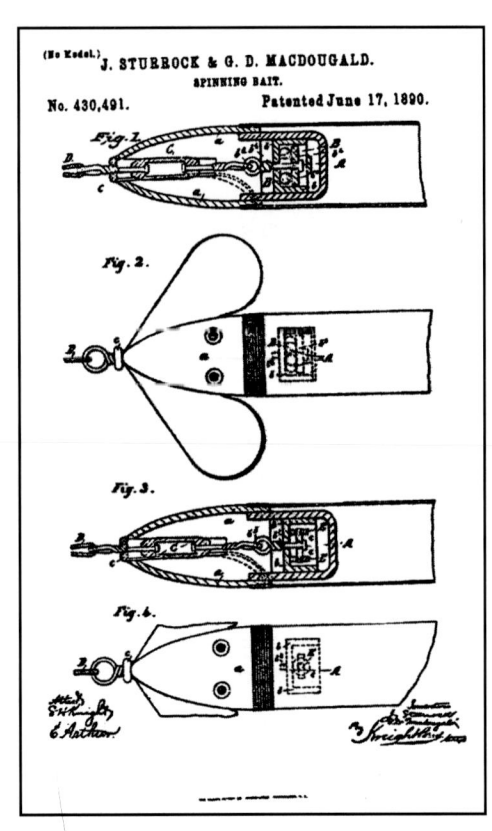

Dundee, Scotland

Patent Drawings of Unfound Lures

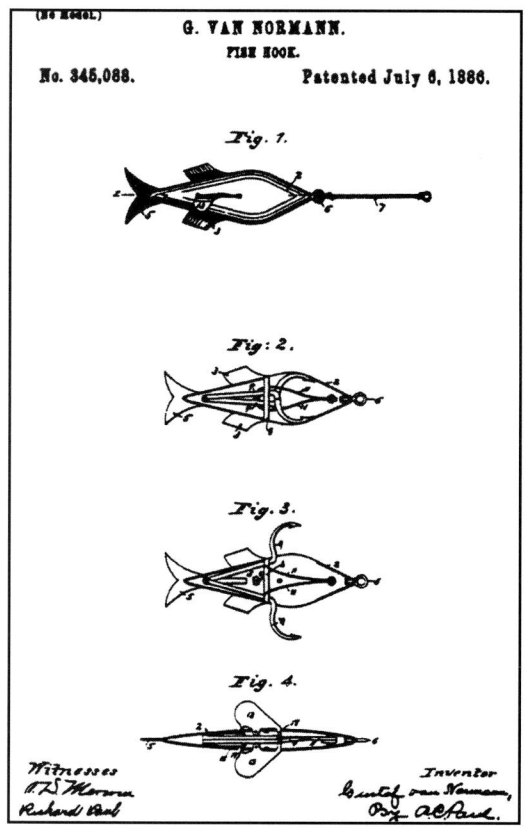

Minneapolis, Minn.

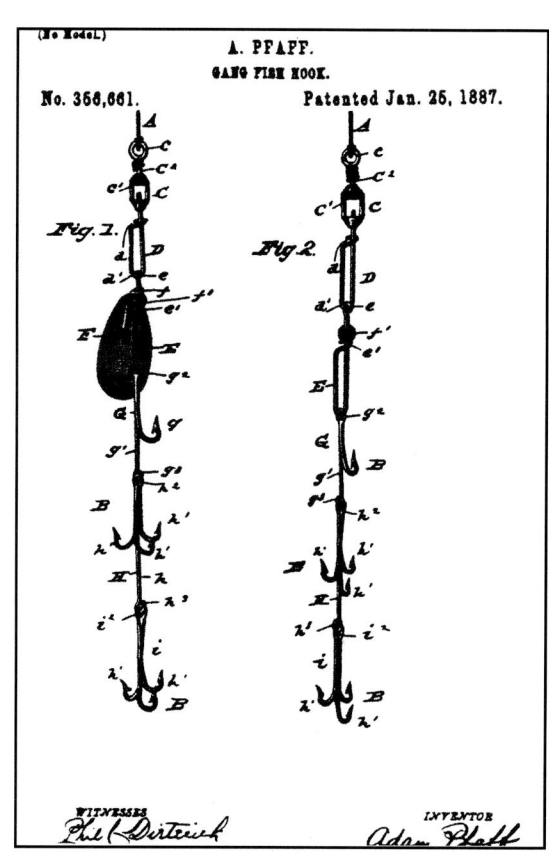

Wayland, N.Y.

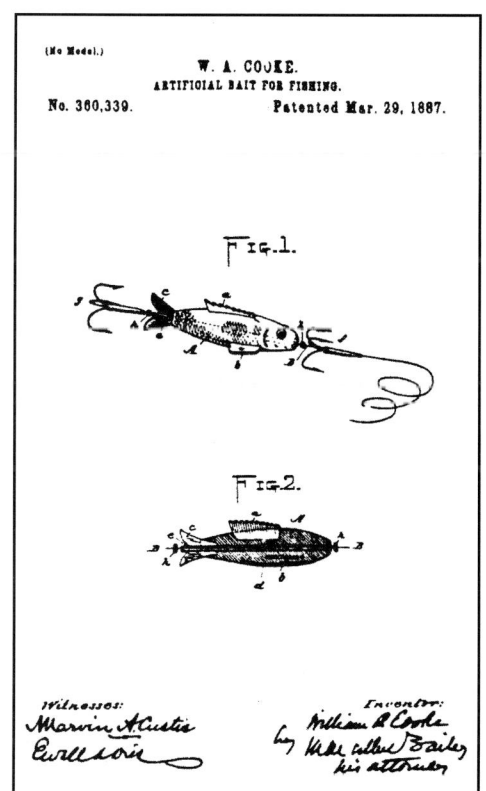

Gaithersburg, Md.

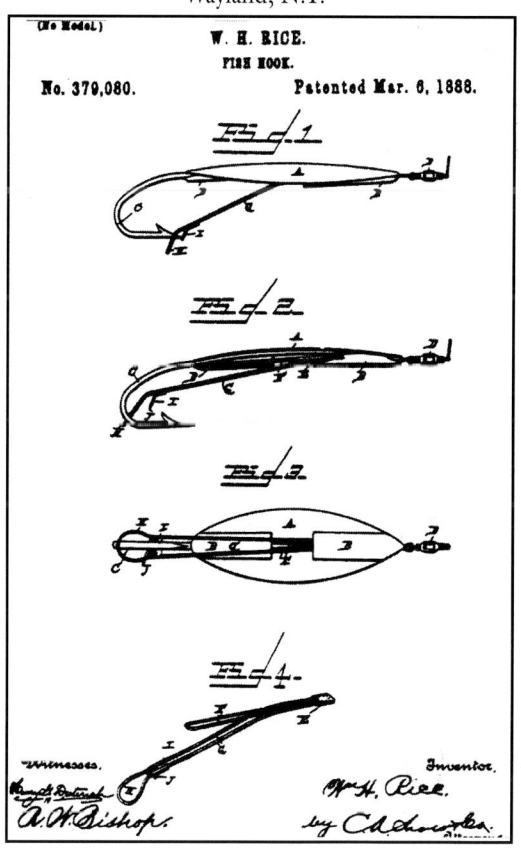

Addison, N.Y.

Patent Drawings of Unfound Lures

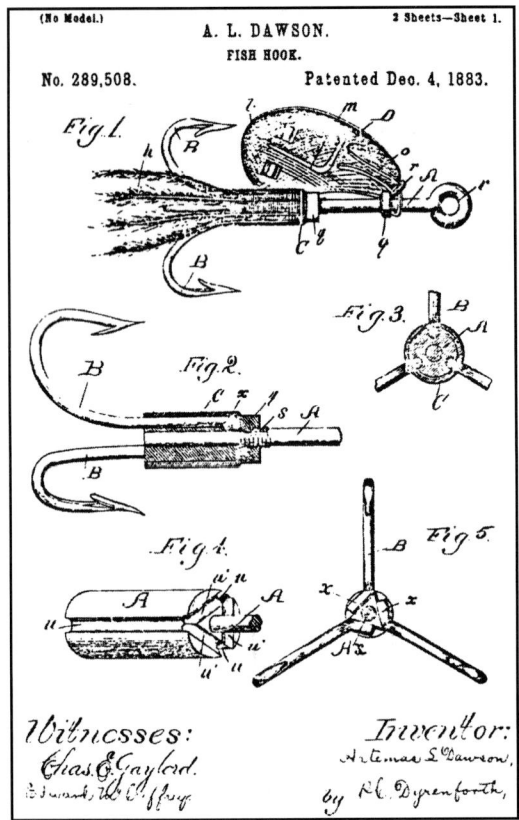

Dakota Territory

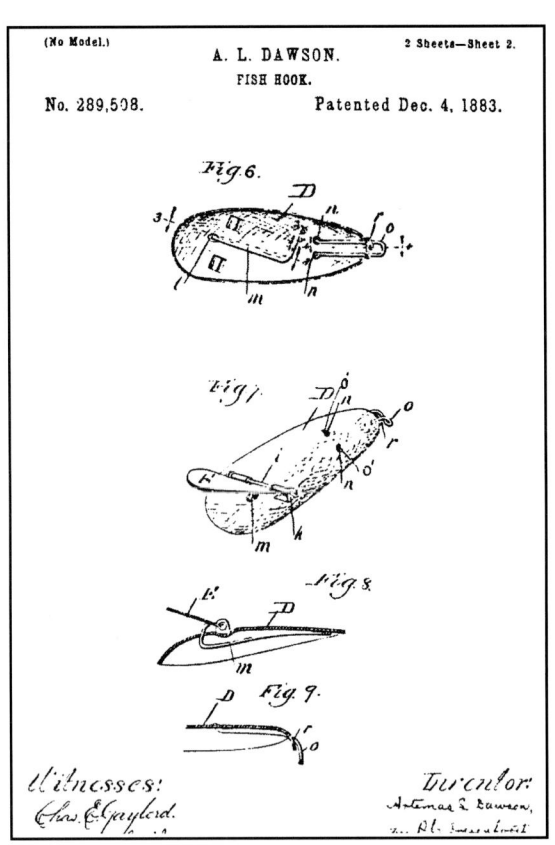

Dakota Territory, second sheet

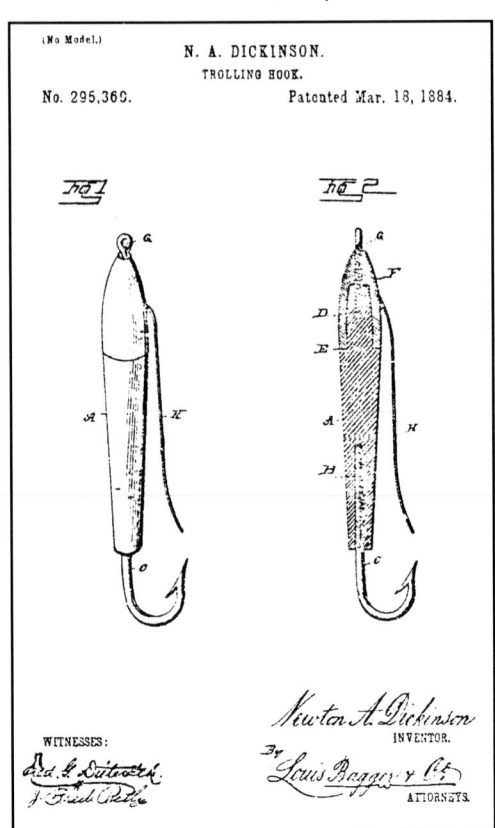

Chester, Conn.

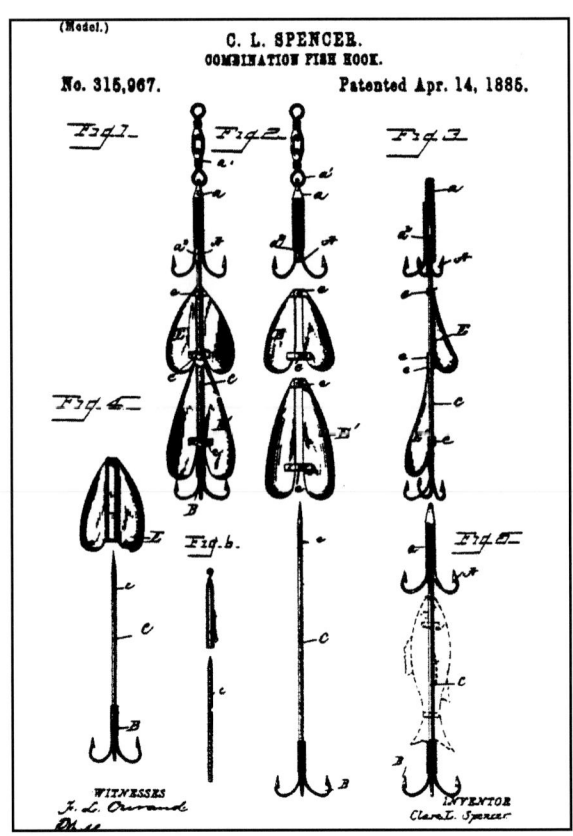

Geneva, N.Y.

PATENT DRAWINGS OF UNFOUND LURES

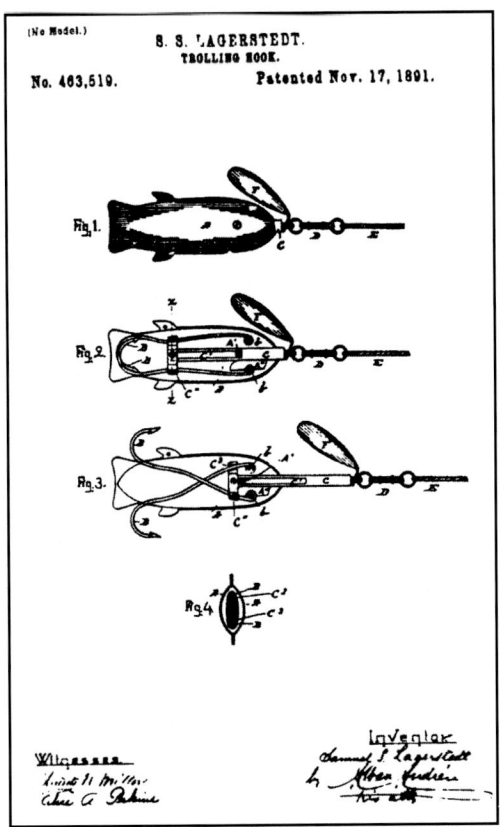

Campello, Mass.

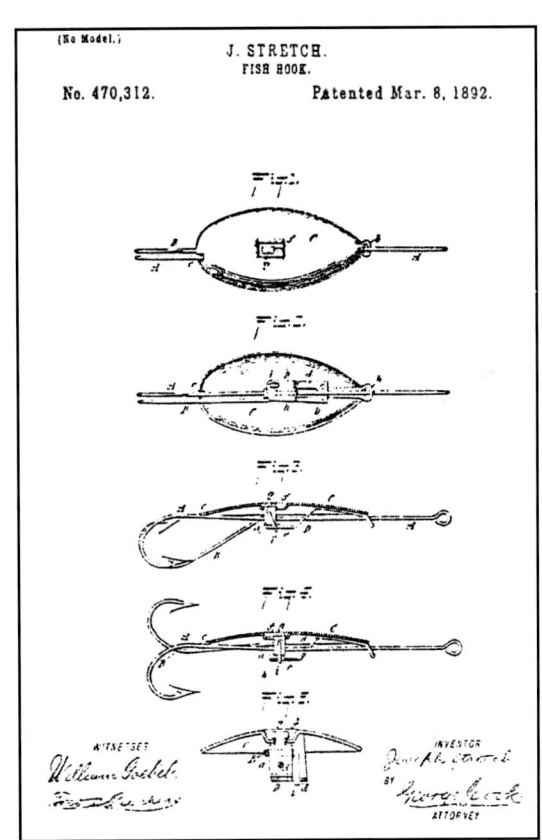

Unknown

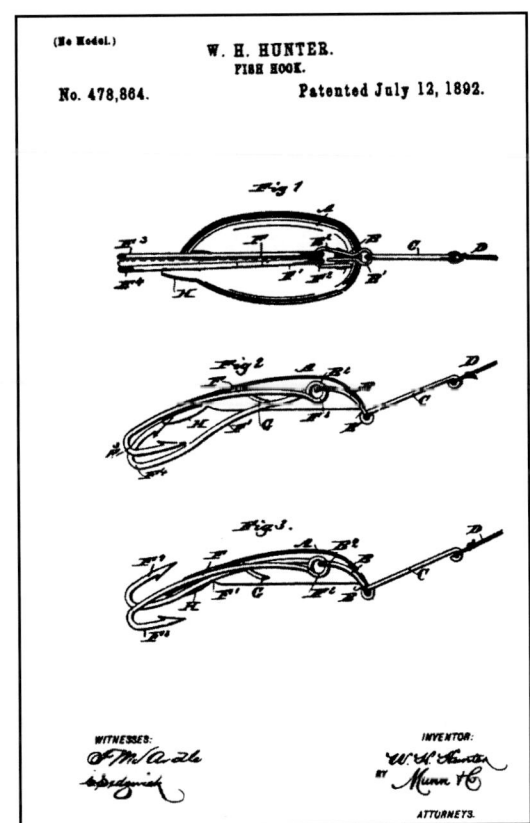

Farmhamville, Iowa

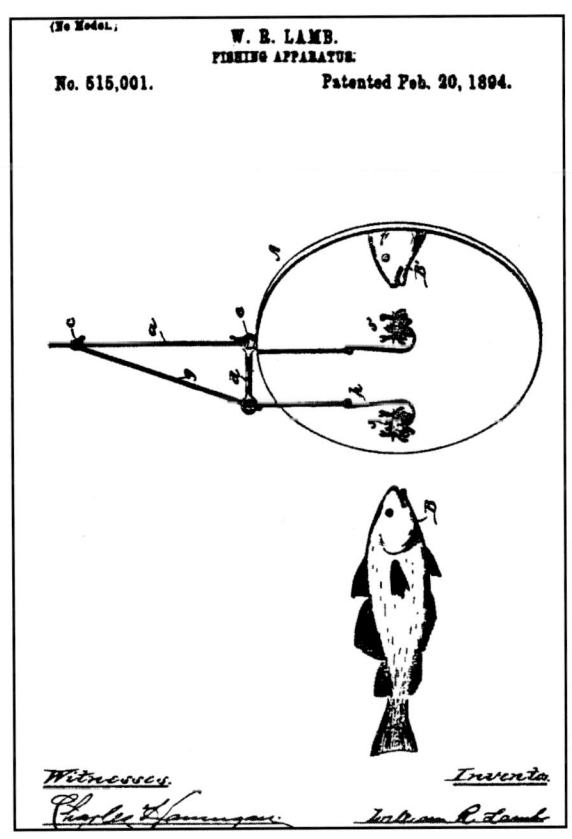

East Greenwich, R. I.

Patent Drawings of Unfound Lures

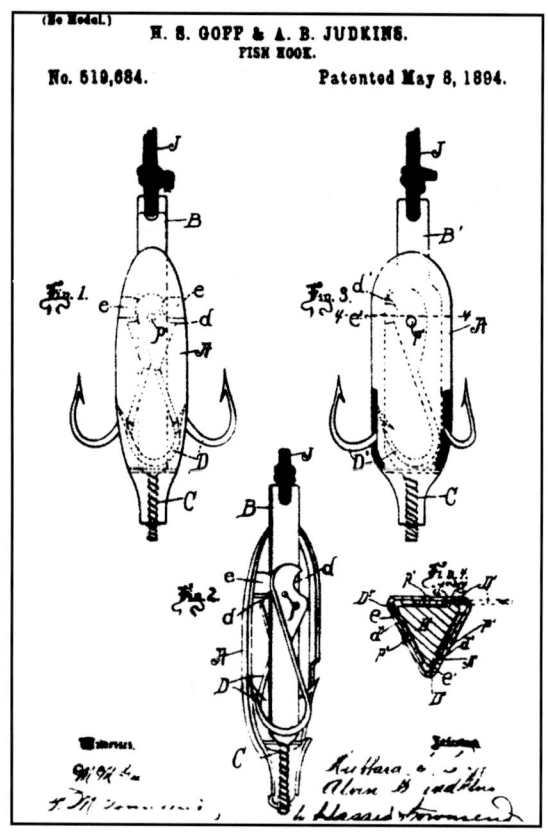

Los Angeles, Calif.

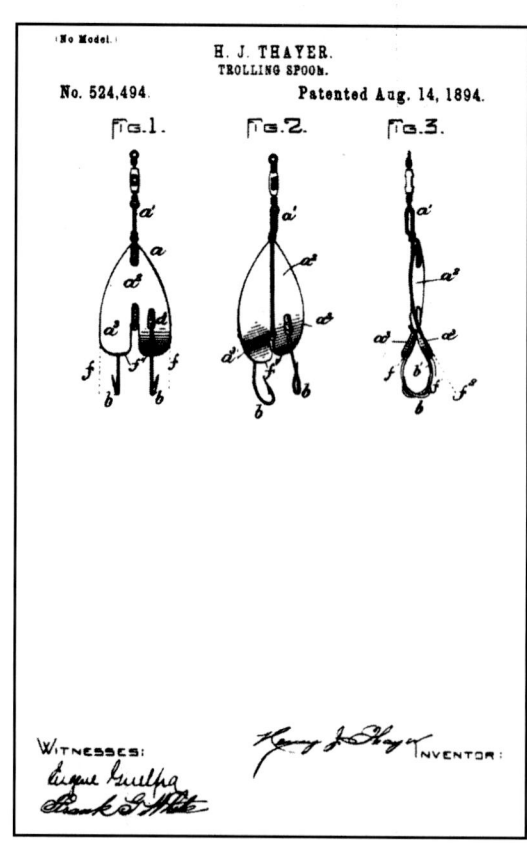

Boston, Mass.

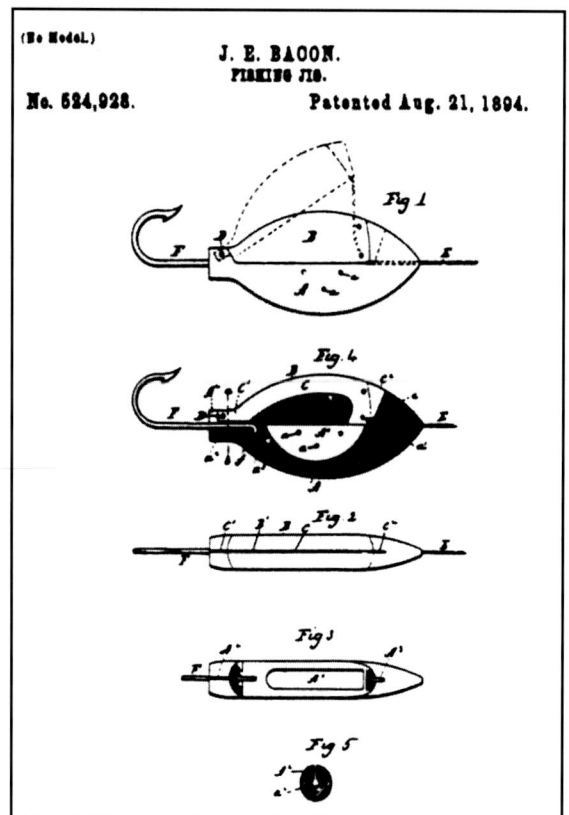

Clinton, Conn.

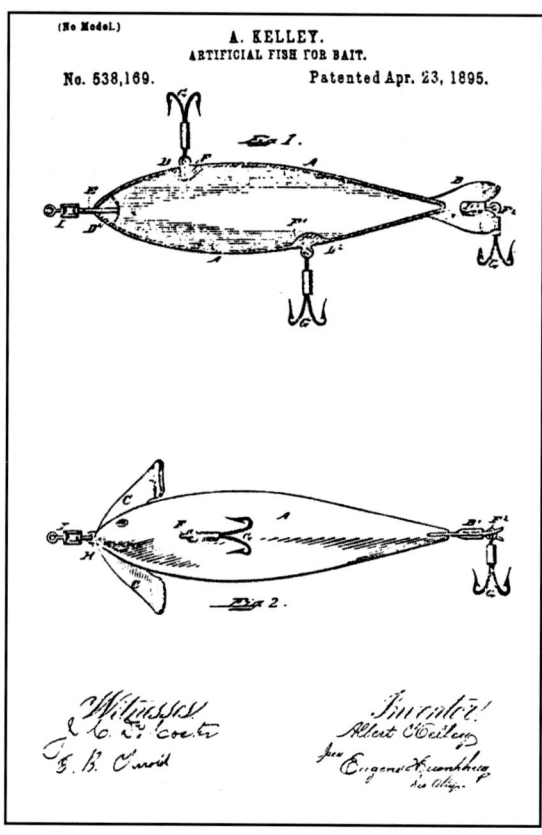

Boston, Mass.

Patent Drawings of Unfound Lures

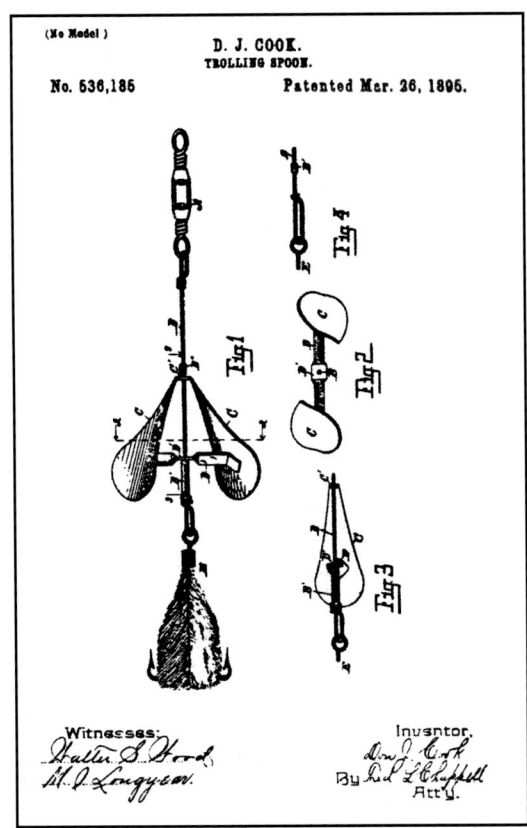

Wakeshma, Mich.

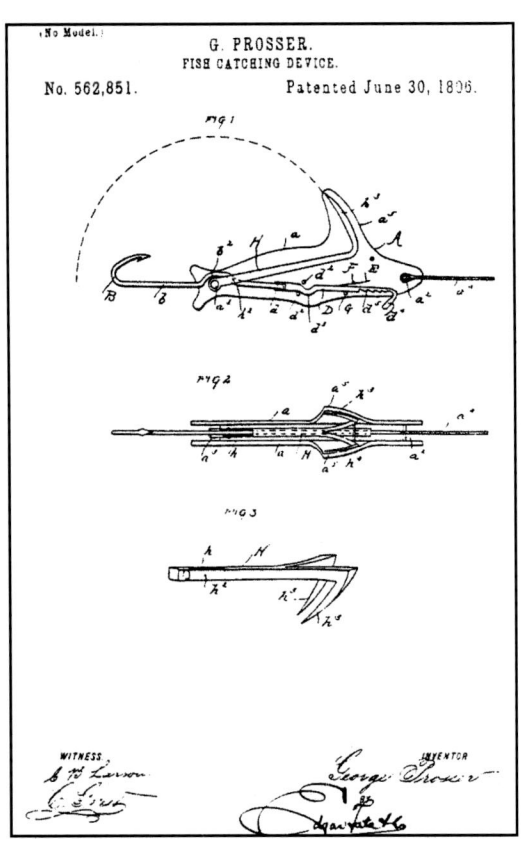

Unknown

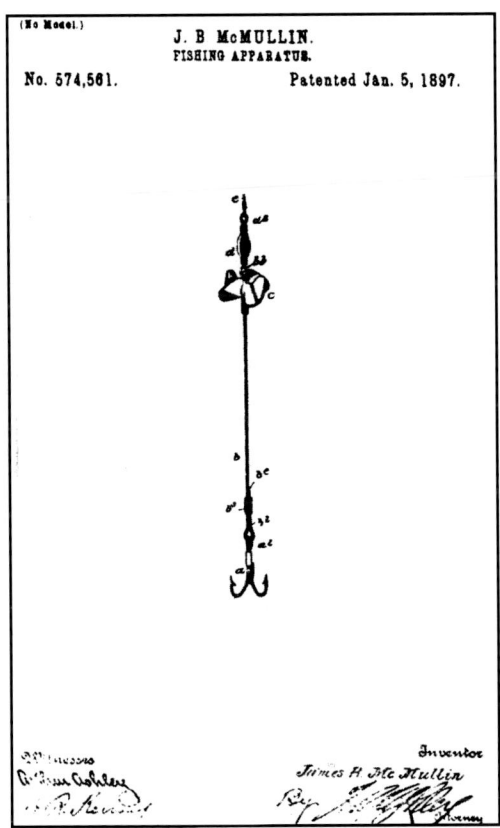

Shakopee, Minn.

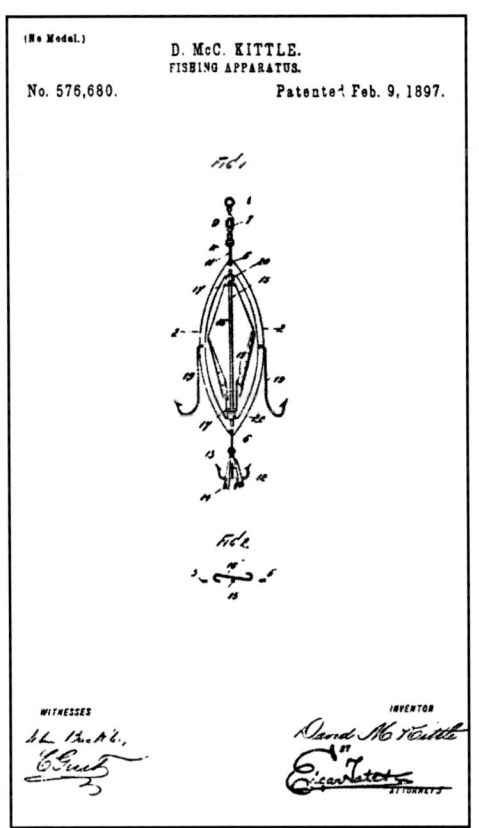

Syracuse, N.Y.

Patent Drawings of Unfound Lures

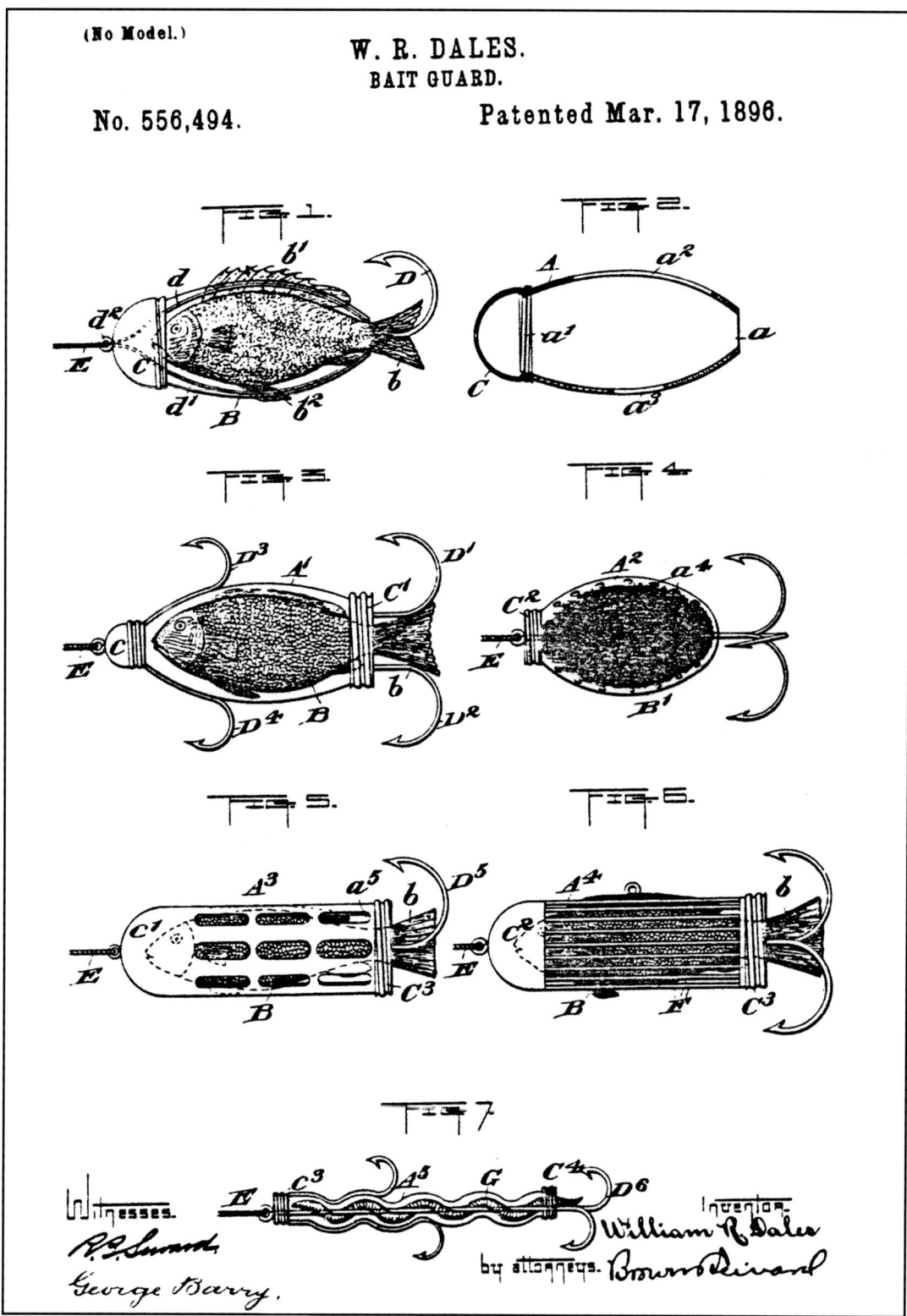

Patent drawing by William R. Dale of New York, N. Y. Basically this is a glass minnow tube, with the difference being part of the bait remains exposed, thus tempting the fish to bite.

Patent Drawings of Unfound Lures

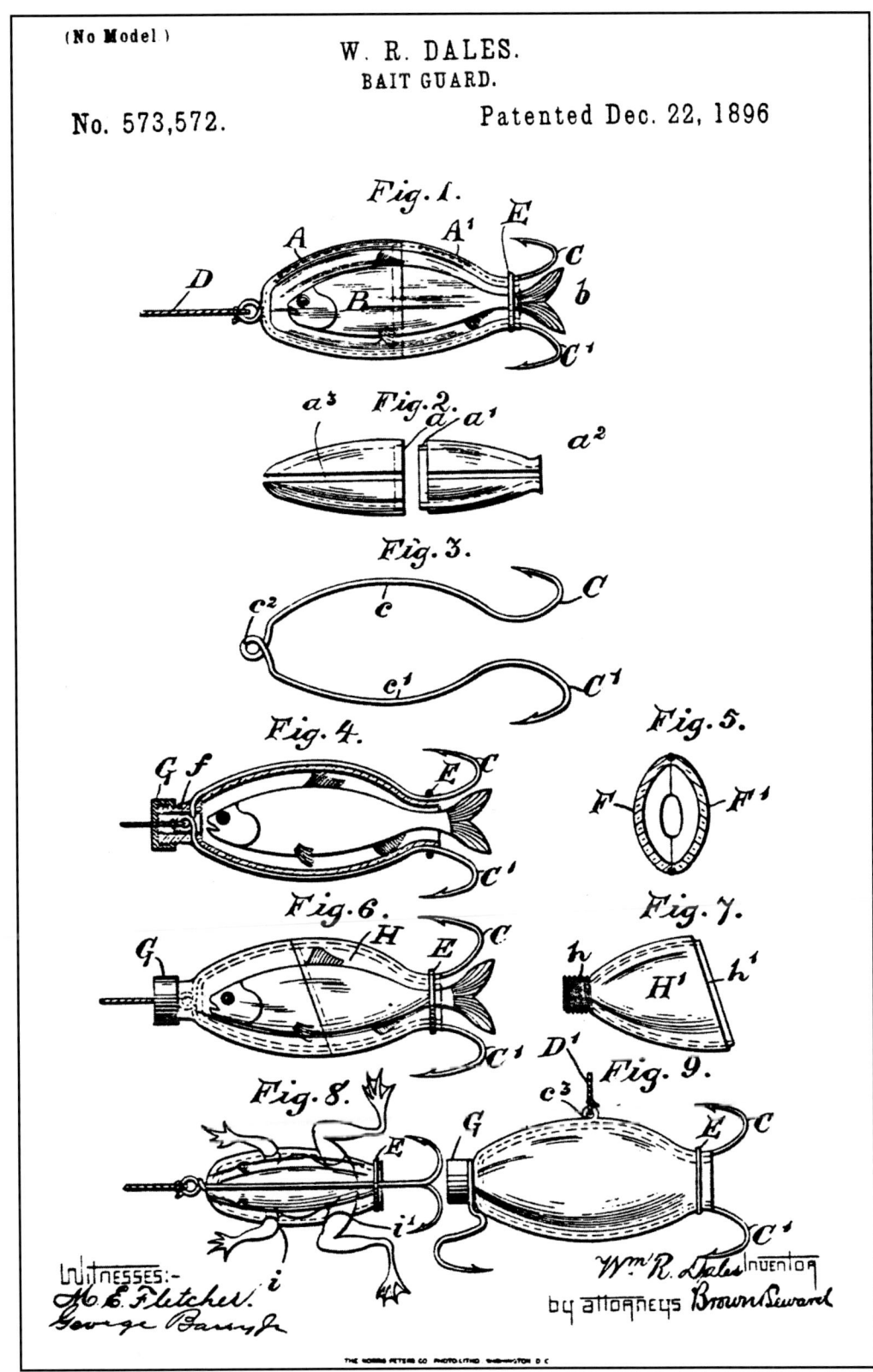

Another patent drawing by William R. Dale. This time his residence is listed as Brooklyn, N. Y. This patent is very much like the one on the opposite page except that in this patent the minnow tube is made in halves to better facilitate placing the minnow in the tube. I can't help but think that these look a lot like the Lurette bait made in Canada.

Patent Drawings of Unfound Lures

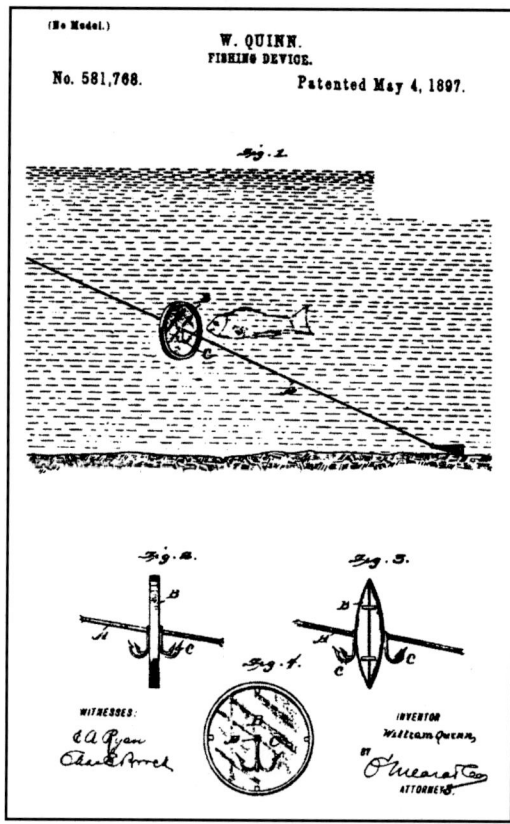

Sturgis, Miss.

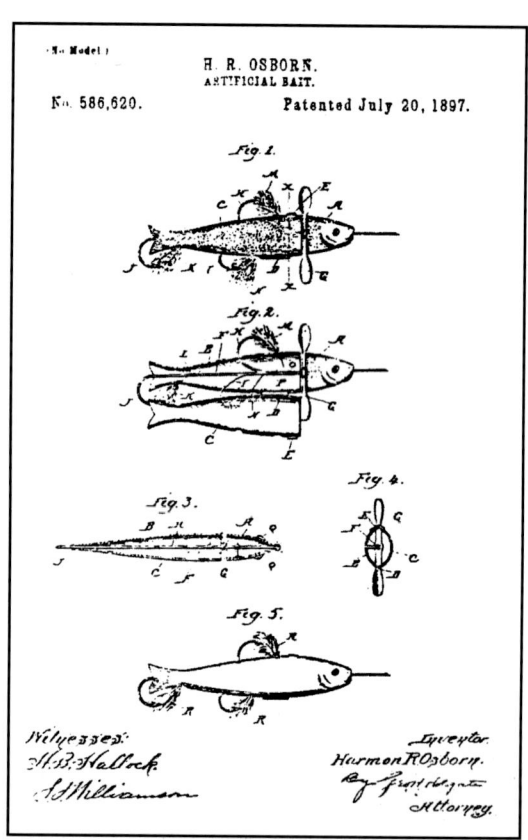

Granville, N. Y.

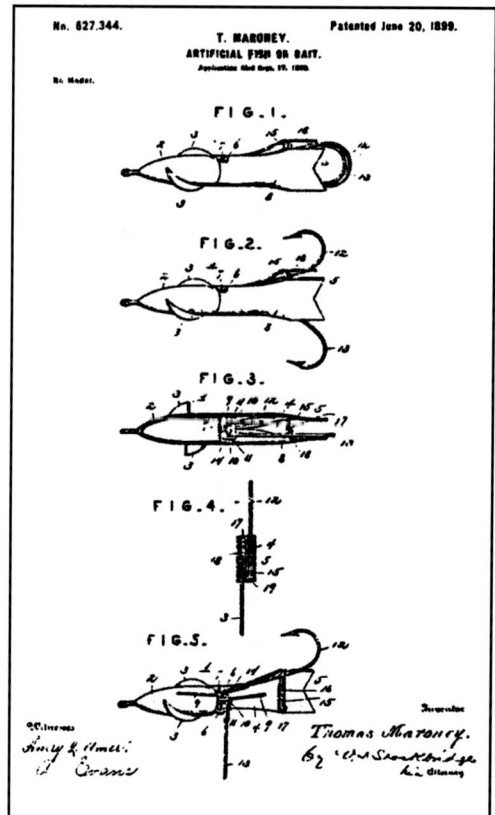

Buffalo, N. Y.

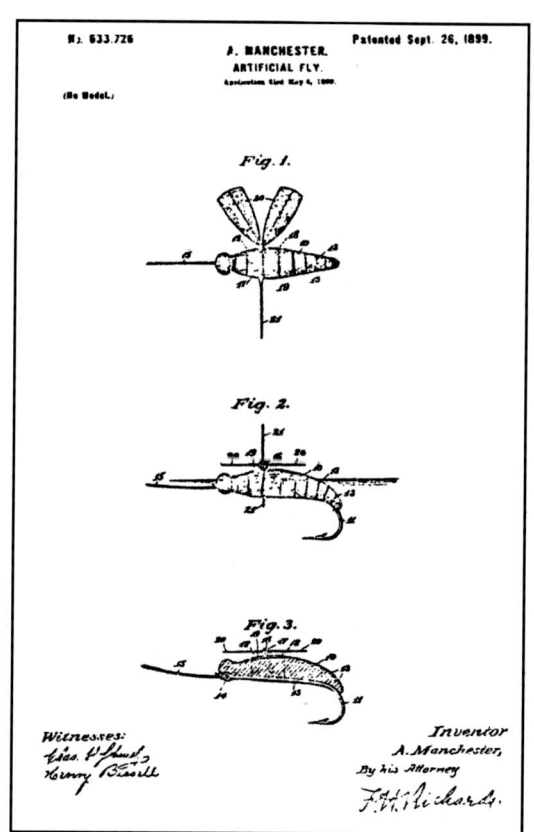

Barkhamsted, Conn.

PATENT DRAWINGS OF UNFOUND LURES

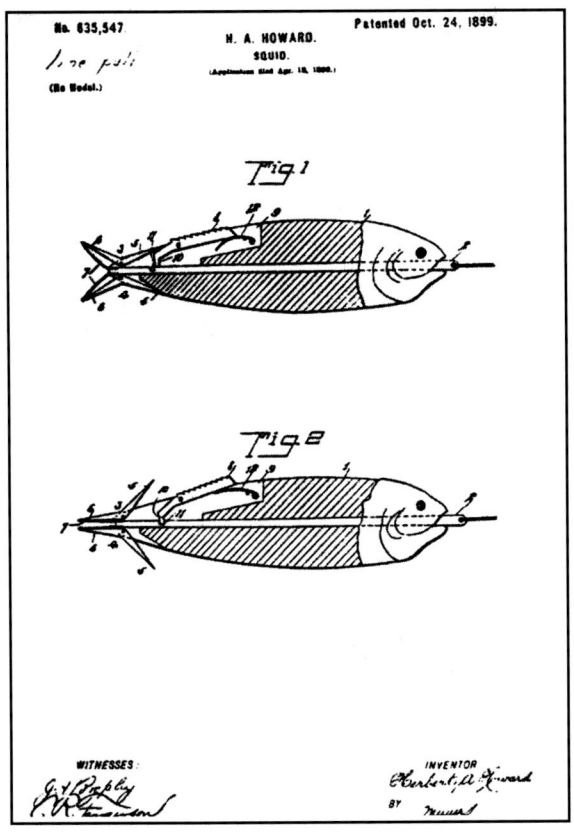

Unknown

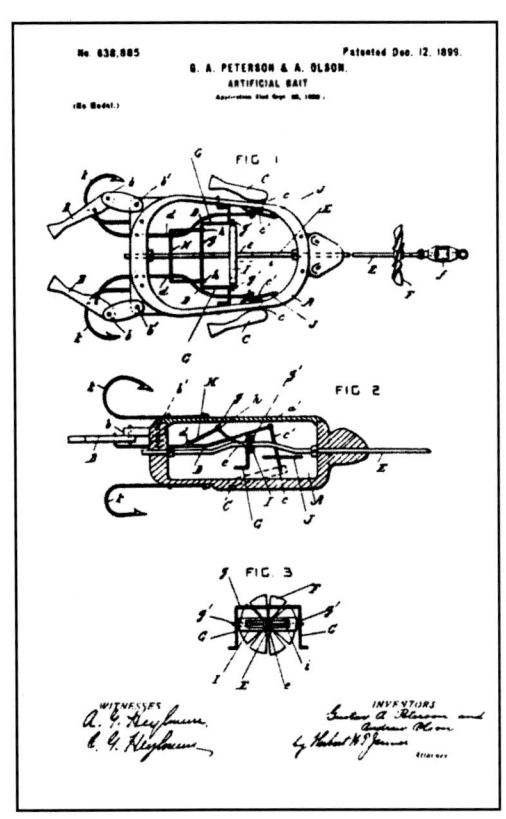

Florence, Mn.

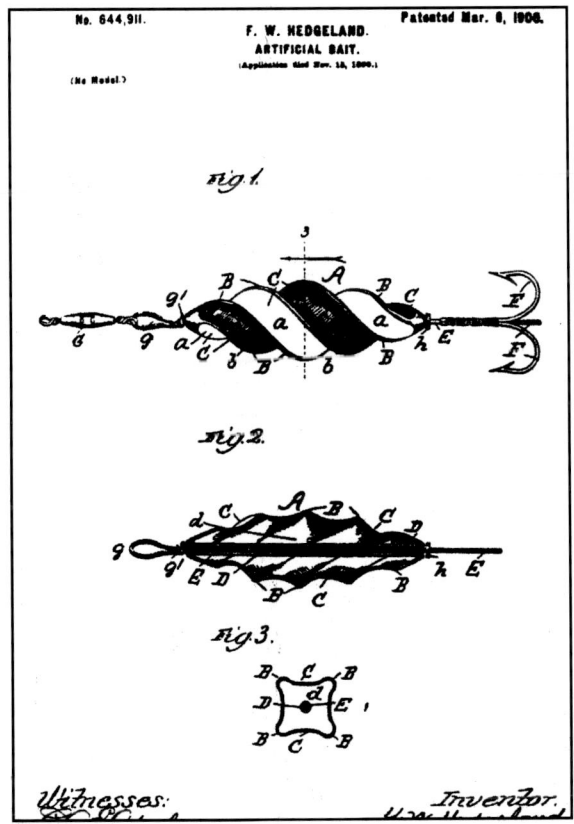

Chicago, Ill.

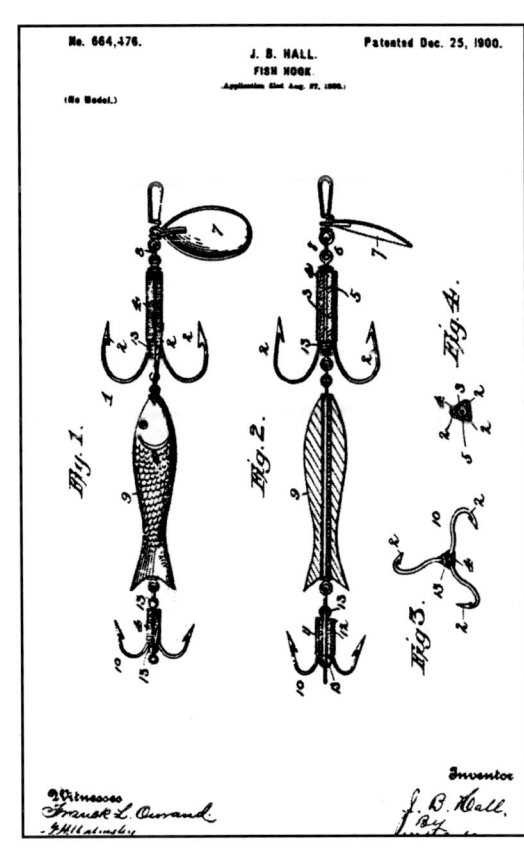

Cleveland, Ohio

Patent Index

Number	Inventor	Description	Date	Page
8,853	J.T. Buel Whitehall, N.Y.	Arrowhead Spinner	Apr. 6, 1852	11
10,771	J.T. Buel Whitehall, N.Y.	Weedless spinner	Apr. 11, 1854	12
11,706	J.T. Buel Whitehall, N.Y.	Changeable spinner blade	Apr. 22, 1856	14
13,068	C. DeSaxe-T. H. Bate New York, N.Y.	Serpentine Minnow	Jun. 12, 1855	21
25,507	Riley Haskell Painsville, Ohio	Haskell Minnow	Sept. 20, 1859	27
54,684	W.D. Chapman Theresa, N.Y.		May 15, 1866	42
60,786	E. Rhodes Jr. & J.W. Rhoades Clyde, Ohio		Jan. 1, 1867	284
79,446	J.E. Christian Mount Carrol, Ill.		Jun. 30, 1869	284
104,930	W.D. Chapman Theresa, N.Y.	Minnow Propeller	Jul. 5, 1870	44
115,434	W.D. Chapman Theresa, N.Y.	Minnow Propeller	May 30, 1871	45
5,291	J.H. Mann Syracuse, N.Y.	Design Patent. Badge shape.	Sept. 26, 1871	84
12,182	J.H. Mann Syracuse, N.Y.	Glass Washers	Nov. 21, 1871	85
123,844	G. Sinclair Chicago, Ill.		Feb. 20, 1872	284
143,146	W. Harper & W. Smith Montreal, Canada		Sept. 23, 1873	258
146,433	T.F. Fitzgerald Rockport, Mass.		Jan. 13, 1874	284
146,764	William H. James Brooklyn, N.Y.	Trolling Squid	Jan. 27, 1874	229
149,123	A.W. Hazzard Seneca, N.Y.		Mar. 31, 1874	285
151,394	D. Huard & C. Dunbar Ashland, Wisc.		May 26, 1874	285
153,854	G.M. Skinner Clayton, N.Y.	Fluted Spoon-Turkey wing	Aug. 4, 1874	89
167,784	G.R. Pierce Grand Rapids, Mich.		Sept. 14, 1875	285
171,697	J.H. Place Gloucester, Mass.		Jan. 4, 1876	285
171,768	J.T. Buel Whitehall, N.Y.	Double spoon	Jan. 4, 1876	18
171,769	J.T. Buel Whitehall, N.Y.	Bait holder	Jan. 4, 1876	16
177,639	Lysander S. Hill Grand Rapids, Mich.	Hill Spoon	May 23, 1876	98
181,308	H.C. Brush Brush's Mills, N.Y.	Brush Spinner	Aug. 26, 1876	234
185,914	W.H. Gregg St. Louis, Mo.		Jan. 2, 1877	286
208,581	J. Falvey Flatbush, N.Y.		Oct. 1, 1878	286
211,906	Lysander S. Hill Grand Rapids, Mich.		Feb. 4, 1879	99
218,345	Archer Wakeman Cape Vincent, N.Y.	Devon type	Aug. 5, 1879	236
231,912	Jorgen Irgens Bergen, Norway	Irgens glass minnow	Sept. 7, 1880	254
254,841	E.F. Pflueger Akron, Ohio	Luminous decorations	Mar. 14, 1882	129
256,843	W.T.J. Lowe Buffalo, N.Y.		Apr. 17, 1882	106
261,194	Lewis C. Wylly Patterson, Ga.		Not Available	286
267,203	Lysander S. Hill Grand Rapids, Mich.		Nov. 7, 1882	100
272,317	E.F. Plueger Akron, Ohio	Luminous paint for lures	Feb. 13, 1883	129
273,996	C. Hymers St. Louis, Mo.		Mar. 13, 1883	286
276,055	W.T.J. Lowe Buffalo, N.Y.		Apr. 17, 1883	107
279,081	W.D. Chapman Theresa, N.Y.	Bird cage spring	Jun. 5, 1883	78
281,083	L. Kessler Ludington, Mich.		Jun. 10, 1883	230
284,056	E.F. Plueger Akron, Ohio	Crystal Minnow	Aug. 28, 1883	254
285,967	W.D. Chapman Theresa, N.Y.	Oil Safe	Oct. 2, 1883	78
289,508	A.L. Dawson Dakota Territory		Dec. 4, 1883	287
295,350	W.D. Chapman Theresa, N.Y.	Allure	Mar. 18, 1884	46
295,360	N.A. Dickinson Chester, Conn.		Mar. 18, 1884	287
295,758	Charles B. Hibbard Grand Rapids, Mich.	Hibbard Spoon	Mar. 25, 1884	102
305,290	W.D. Chapman Theresa, N.Y.	Stamping press	Sept. 16, 1884	79
315,967	C.L. Spencer Geneva, N.Y.		Apr. 14, 1885	
326,886	Frederic Robinson N.Y.	Robinson Mouse	Sept. 22, 1885	225
330,793	Cornelius Lie Trondhjem, Norway	Lie Minnow	Nov. 17, 1885	243
332,879	W.D. Chapman Theresa, N.Y.	Rotating display case	Dec. 22, 1885	37
339,952	Archer Wakeman Cape Vincent, N.Y.	Skeleton Bait	Apr. 13, 1886	36
341,261	John B. McHarg Rome, N.Y.	Applied shield	May 4, 1886	182

Patent #	Inventor	Description	Date	Page
341,954	G.M. Skinner Clayton, N.Y.	Turkey Foot	May 18, 1886	91
345,088	G. Van Norman Minneapolis, Minn.		Jul. 6, 1886	288
347,122	John B. McHarg Rome, N.Y.	American Spinner	Aug. 10, 1886	182
354,721	John B. McHarg Rome, N.Y.	Reflective ball	Dec. 21, 1886	182
356,661	A. Pfapf Wayland, N.Y.		Jan. 25, 1887	288
360,339	W.A. Cooke Gaithersburg, Md.		Mar. 29, 1887	288
378,678	John R. Harlow Auburn, N.Y.	Retractable Hook Spoon	Feb. 28, 1888	226
379,080	W.H. Rice Addeson, N.Y.		Mar. 6, 1888	288
390,028	Henry Loftie Syracuse, N.Y.		Sept. 25, 1888	201
394,632	J. Wood Rochester, N.Y.		Dec. 18, 1888	289
395,103	J. Wood Rochester, N.Y.		Dec. 25, 1888	289
395,480	W.F. Brewster East Orange, N.J.		Jan. 1, 1889	289
418,200	Henry Loftie Syracuse, N.Y.	Gang Spoon	Dec. 31, 1889	199
422,226	J.P. Kestner Cincinnati, Ohio		Feb. 25, 1890	290
430,491	J. Sturrock & G.D. McDougald Dundee, Scotland		Jun. 17, 1890	289
432,436	E.F. Pflueger Akron, Ohio	Rubber weed protector	Jul. 15, 1890	161
435,026	H.E. Skinner San Francisco, Ca.	Abalone spoon	Aug. 26, 1890	242
446,827	M.M. Case Jr. Not available		Feb. 17, 1891	290
449,519	M. Carswell Glasgow, Scotland		Mar. 31, 1891	290
450,317	J.M. Munn Chicago, Ill.		Apr. 14, 1891	290
454,580	Albert G. Mack Rochester, N.Y.	Mack Bait	Jun. 23, 1891	232
454,581	Albert G. Mack Rochester, N.Y.		Jun. 23, 1891	232
454,982	Albert G. Mack Rochester, N.Y.		Jun. 30, 1891	233
456,931	Albert Angell East Orange, N.J.	Angell's wings	Aug. 4, 1891	244
463,240	Henry Zuckweiler Pekin, Ill.	Trolling bait	Nov. 17, 1891	239
463,519	S.S. Lagerstedt Campello, Miss.		Nov. 17, 1891	291
465,215	G.M. Skinner Clayton, N.Y.	Spoon bait	Dec. 15, 1891	95
465,704	G.M. Skinner Clayton, N.Y.	Spoon bait	Dec. 22, 1891	96
470,279	Henry Zuckweiler Pekin, Ill.		Mar. 8, 1892	239
470,312	J. Stretch Not available		Mar. 8, 1892	291
478,864	W.H. Hunter Farmhamville, Iowa		Jul. 12, 1892	291
479,194	Albert G. Mack Rochester, N.Y.	Electric light bait	Jul. 19, 1892	233
479,575	G.M. Skinner Clayton, N.Y.		Jul. 26, 1892	95
481,652	Henry Loftie Syracuse, N.Y.	Interchangeable blade	Aug. 30, 1892	200
489,110	H.J. Welch Natural Bridge, N.Y.	Glass minnow tube	Jan. 3, 1893	208
496,441	John Pepper Jr. Rome, N.Y.	Batwing Spinner	May 2, 1893	203
515,001	W.R. Lamb East Orange, R.I.		Feb. 20, 1894	291
519,684	H. Goff & A. Judkins Los Angeles, Calif.		May 8, 1894	292
520,594	John R. Harlow Auburn, N.Y.		May 29, 1894	227
524,494	H.J. Thayer Boston, Mass.		Aug. 14, 1894	292
524,928	J.E. Bacon Clinton, Conn.		Aug. 21, 1894	292
527,259	M.B. Allen Battle Creek, Mich.	New Minnow Casting Spoon	Oct. 9, 1894	253
533,590	J.T. Hastings Chicago, Ill.	Fish hook	Feb. 5, 1895	216
534,506	J.T. Hastings Chicago, Ill.	Weedless Frog	Feb. 19, 1895	215
534,682	Benjamin F. Burgess Jackson, Mich.	Weedless hook	Sept. 26, 1895	240
538,169	A. Kelley Boston, Mass.		Aug. 14, 1895	292
24,724	E.O. Pealer Sayre, Pa.	Design Patent. P & S Spinner	Oct. 1, 1895	260
552,012	H.O. Stanley Dixfield, Maine	Stanley Smelt	Dec. 24, 1895	247
556,494	W.R. Dales New York, N.Y.	Glass tubes	Mar. 17, 1896	294
562,851	G. Prosser Not available		Jun. 30, 1896	293
564,517	J.T. Hastings Chicago, Ill.	Frog Harness	Jul. 21, 1896	216
567,310	C.J.W. Gaide Fort Wayne, Ind.	Gaide's Bait	Sept. 8, 1896	255
570,632	J.T. Hastings Chicago, Ill.	Weedless Spinner	Nov. 3, 1896	217
570,687	H.O. Stanley Dixfield, Maine	Stanley Smelt	Nov. 3, 1896	248
573,572	W.R. Dales Brooklyn, N.Y.	Glass tubes	Dec. 22, 1896	295

PATENT INDEX/COMPANY INDEX

574,561	J.B. McMullin Shakopee, Minn.		Jan. 5, 1897	293
574,993	Livingston S. Hinckley Newark, N.J.	Aluminum Fish Phantom	Jan. 12, 1897	264
576,680	D. McC. Kittle Syracuse, N.Y.		Feb. 9, 1897	293
580,915	H.J. Welch Natural Bridge, N.Y.	American Combo Spinner	Apr. 20, 1897	212
581,768	W. Quinn Sturgis, Miss.		May 4, 1897	296
582,677	Mayne C.P. Parker Indianapolis, Ind.	Trolling Worm	May 18, 1897	250
586,620	R.R. Osborn Granville, N.Y.		Jul. 20, 1897	296
588,729	Charles R. Harris Michigan	Cork Floating Frog	Aug. 24, 1897	220
613,519	P. Junod Celina, Ohio	Junod Spinner	Nov. 1, 1898	249
614,411	W.H. Rockwood New York, N.Y.	Ghost	Nov. 15, 1898	266
627,344	T. Maroney Buffalo, N.Y.		Jun. 20, 1899	296
632,554	E.T. Dukes Quitman, Ga.	Dixie Minnow	Sept. 5, 1899	257
633,726	A. Manchester Barkhamdsted, Conn.		Sept. 26, 1899	296
635,547	H.A. Howard Not Available		Oct. 24, 1899	297
638,885	G.A. Peterson & A. Olson Florence, Minn.		Dec. 12, 1899	297
643,573	M.W. Votaw & M.E. Thomas Bowling Green, Ky.	Votaw Minnow	Feb. 13, 1900	259
644,911	F.W. Hedgeland Chicago, Ill.		Mar. 6, 1900	297
653,204	George H. Bacon Burlington, Vt.		Jul. 10, 1900	263
657,387	C. Bew Chicago, Ill.	Chicago Spinner	Sept. 4, 1900	240
661,869	Peter Henkenius & James M. Kane Fort Wayne, Ind.	Henkenius Kane Lure	Nov. 13, 1900	265
664,476	J.B. Hall Cleveland, Ohio		Dec. 25, 1900	297
839,917	W.D. Chapman Theresa, N.Y.	Omega Bait	Jan. 1, 1907	63

COMPANY INDEX

Allen, M. B. 253
New Minnow Casting Spoon...................253
Spoon 253

Angell, Albert 244
Angell's Revolving Wings 244, 246
Bass Killer 246
Black Bass Killer 246
Braided Minnow 245
Excelsior Trolling Fly Spoon 245
Floating Minnow 246
Florida Phantom Minnow 246
New Propeller Hook 244
Perforated Metal Minnow 246
Revolving Metal Fly 246

Backmore 270

Bacon, George H. 263
Bacon Double Spoon 263
Bacon Spoon 263

Bate, T. H. 20
Lake Spoon 24
Serpentine Minnow 21, 22
Tin Squid 22

Bentley, John 272

Brush, Corbin 234
Brush Spinner 234, 235

Buel, J. T. 7
Arrowhead - J. Warrin 10
Arrowhead Marked 1852 10
Arrowhead - T. Design 10
Bait Hook 1856 14
Buel H.W. 18
Fly Spoon 15, 16, 17
Patent applied for spoon 9
Pikes Spinner 18
Spring Rods 1854 13
Weedless Spoon 1854 13

Burgess, Benjamin F. 240
Spinner 240
Weedless Burgess Minnow 241
Weedless Hook 241

Chapman W. D. 34
Alfie Lure 38
Allure 46, 47
Allure Type Lure 80
Arrow Shaped Spinner 72
Bait Holder Lure 39
Bass Bait 41, 48, 49
Boss Lure 41, 56
Combination Bait 55
Corrugated Hero Bait 67
Cyclone Bait 63
Daisy Bait 54, 74, 76
Devon Type 64
Double Fish Lure 51

Electric Bait 69
Eureka Baits 81
Excelsior Bait 71
Fish Shaped Spinner Blade 67
Fish Shaped, Two Fins Each Side 59
Fish Shaped w/Curved Lip 50
Fly Rod Lures 80
Four Sided w/Fins Bait 58
Gem Bait 83
German Propeller 66
Hero Bait 67
Hooks to Spoon 79
International Minnow 54
Inverted V Shaped Lure 77
Kilby Bass Double 52
Kilby Bass Single 52, 53
Kilby Minnow 52, 53
Largehead Tapering Body Lure 63
Large Minnow Propeller Type 65
Large Wings Small Body 65
Lure w/1866 Patent 43, 50
Mascot Bait 71
Mermaid Bait 78
Minnow Harness Lure 50
Minnow Propeller 45, 70
Montreal Bait 74, 75
New Bass Bait 75
Omega 62
Perfect Bait 68, 69
Phantom Type 65
Pickerel Bait 75

300

Company Index

Pike Kidney 77
Pike Oval 75, 76
Pike Oval Tandem 75
Reversible Propeller 48
Rotating Display Case 40
Round Spinner Blade 73
Safe Deposit Minnow 57, 58, 59
Sculpin Shaped Blade w/Minnow............64
Sculpin Shaped Blade w/Yarn Wrap 64
Spoon w/offset line tie 79
Spinner w/notch 72, 80
Tandem Spinner 77
Teardrop Shaped Lure 65
Threaded Minnow 59, 60
Water Nymph 61, 72
Whale Shaped Lure 51

Collins, J.H. 274

Daniels, M.J. 274

Day, G. F. 273

Delany, W. 234
Delany Spinner 234

Dukes, Edward T. 257
Dixie Minnow 257

Eddy & Kingsley 270

Enterprise Mfg. Co. (Pflueger) 127
Acme Spoon 150
Adirondack Spinner 169
Admiral Bait 145, 146
Akron Trolling Spoon 130, 133
Allen's Patented Abalone Bait 164, 242
American Phantom Minnow 159
American Spinner 171
Applied Figures, Frog, etc. 142, 143
Argus 150
Bass Spinner 169
Beaded Bait 154, 155
Beaded Trolling Spinner 177
Bolt Spoon 147
Buckeye Bait 136
Buckeye Spinner 179
Bucktail Minnow 175
Bucktail Casting Spoon 175
Bucktail Phantom Minnow 175
Captain Spoon 165
Casting Minnow 171
Catskill Spinner 169
Cayuga 156
Champion 155
Climax Bass Bait 143
Clipper 162
Columbia 150
Combination and Changeable 149
Comet 155
Commodore Spoon 168
Conger Salmon Trout Spoon 177
Conqueror 157
Corrugated Spoon 149
Crescent Bait 149
Crystal Minnow 131, 140
Cyclone Spinner 177
Cyuga Lake Spoon 165
Daisy Spinner 169
Delevan 148
Detroit Spoon 165
Dexter Spoon 131, 135
Dominion 157
Eclipse Spinner 175
Egg Ball Bait 163
Egg Beaded Bait 154
Embossed Kidney Trolling Spoon 136
Empire 136
Enterprise Bait 136
Eureka 150
Excelsior Spoon 136
Figured Pearl Squid 164
Fine Egg Shaped Bait 157
Fine Fluted Spoon 168
Fine Mottled Pearl Spoon 152, 164
Fish Spearing Decoy Minnows 153
Floating Meadow Frog 174
Florida Bass Bait 151, 152
Flying Helgramite 131, 138, 139, 161
Froggie 171
Frog No. 3 With Swivel 174
Governor Bait 146
Halcyon Spinner 177
Hamilton 154
Hard & Soft Rubber Minnows 130, 137
Holt Spoon 173
Imperial Spoon 165
Irvin Black Bass Bait 151, 152
Joseph Spoon 170
Kenosha 156
Keystone Bait 136
Kidney Ball Bait 163
Kidney Beaded Bait 154
Kidney Spoons 130
Kidney Trolling Spoon 130, 136
Lake Spoon 165
Lake Tahoe Spoon 177
May Bug Spoon 141
McMurray Spinner 147
Mentor 150
Merimac 156
Minne-Ha-Ha-Spoon 156
Montreal 156
Mumford's Safety Hook & Bait Box 176
Muskallonge Spoon 173
Muskallonge Trolling Bait 147
New Akron Spoon 148
Nickel Plated Bait 136
Ohio Spoon 157
Original Emeric Spinner 167
Oval 157
Paragon 157
Pearl Emeric Spinner 167
Pearl Minnow Squid 164
Pearl Phantom 141
Pearl Minnow Fly 151
Peerless Spoon 150
Perfect Revolving Heart Bait 170
Pet Spinner 169
Pflueger's Fishing Castle 178
Pfluegers Reel & Line Dryer 176
Phantom Spinner 160, 161
Pike Baits 136
Pirate Spoon 163
Plain Pearl Squid 164
Propeller 155, 156
Puget Sound Bait 168
Puritan 154
Recall Lure 168
Reversible Propeller 179
Rival 150
Roanoke Spinner 169
Royal Ball Spoon 163
Royal Malleable Crystal Body Fly ...140
Salmon Spoon 166
Salmon Trout Spoon 177
Salmon Troller 170
Skittering Spoon 166
Soft Rubber Angle Worm 172
Soft Rubber Insects 172
Soft Rubber Crawfish 130, 134
Soft Rubber Dobson 131, 133
Soft Rubber Frog 130, 132, 133
Soft Rubber Grasshopper 130, 134
Star Bait 179
St. Lawrence Double Spoon 158
St. Clair Double Spoon 158
Success Spoon 162
Summit Spinner 175
Sydney Spinner 169
Tacoma Trout Bait 173
Tandem Spinner 148
Target 155, 156
Toledo Spoon 165
Trory Minnow 144
Trout Spinner 169
Volunteer 154
Weed Protector 161
Western Bait 167
Whitehall Spinner 179
Wilson Bait 175
Windsor Spoon 150

Gaide, Carl J. W. 255
Gaide's Bucktail Bait 255, 256

Graves, F. S. 257
Double Spinner 258
Spinner 257, 258

Haas Bros 274

Harlow, John R. 226
Double Bait 228
Retractable Hook Trolling Spoon 226, 227
Spinner Bait 228
Trolling Spoon 227
Wood's Three Jokers 228

Harper, W. & W. Smith 258
Double Bladed Spinner 258

Company Index

Harris, Charles R. 220
- Cork Floating Frog 220, 221
- Featherbone Minnow 221
- Underwater Minnow 221
- Bullet Bait 222
- Featherbone Spinner Lures 222
- Manistee Surface Bait 223

Haskell, Riley 26
- Haskell Minnow 28-33

Hastings, James T. 214
- Casting Minnow 217
- Weedless Frog 214
- Weedless Spinner 217
- Weedless Spoon 216

Hendryx, Andrew B. 251
- American Spinner 252
- Eureka Assortment 251
- Propeller Blade Spinner 251, 252

Henkenius, Peter & James M. Kane ..265
- Henkenius Kane Lure 265

Hibbard, Charles B. 97
- Heart Shaped Spoon 103
- Hibbard Spoon 102, 103
- Metal Minnow 97, 102

Hill, Lysander S. 97
- Hill Spoon 99, 101
- Peerless Automatic 100

Hinckley, Livingston S. 264
- Aluminum Fish Phantom 264

Hughson, E. N. 248
- Spoon 248

Irgens, Jorgen 254
- Irgen's Minnow 254

James, William H. 229
- Spinner Blade 230
- Trolling Squid 229, 230

Junod, Paul 249
- Junod Spinner 249

Kessler, Louis 230
- Spinning Lure 230

Lie, Cornelius 243
- Lie Minnow 243

Lobb, Floyd Ferris 256
- Old Lobb Bait 256

Loftie, Henry 198
- Gang Spoon Bait 198
- Kidney Bait 199
- Monroe Green Bait 198
- Oval Bait 199, 201
- Patent Bait 200

Lowe, William T. J. 105
- Adjustable Casting Spoon 108
- Buffalo Bait 111, 113
- Buffalo Bait-Double 111, 113
- Buffalo Casting Spoon 119
- Buffalo Casting Spoon w/Aux Hook 120
- Canadian Special 111, 116
- Comstock, Harry 121
- Cupsuptic Bait 115
- Dimple Pattern Spinner 109
- Eclipse Spinner-1st Patent Bait 106
- Fluted Casting Spoon 119
- Fluted Leaf-Muskallonge Bait 118
- Flying Helgramite Wing Lure 125
- Flying Helgramite 125, 126
- Hammered Bait 113
- Hammered Kidney Bait 117
- Heart Shaped Spinner 108
- Kidney Bait 111, 117
- Lake, Salmon, and Muskallonge Bait ..118
- Large Double Blade Spinner 108
- New Fly Star Spoon 114
- New Fly Buffalo Spoon 114
- New Fly Original Fluted Spoon 114
- Original Fluted Bait 111, 112
- Original Fluted Casting Spoon 119
- Plain Leaf-Muskallonge Bait 118
- Second Patent Bait 107
- Spalding Spinner 109, 250
- Star Bait 110-112, 116
- Star Bait-Double 111, 112, 117
- Star Casting Spoon 119
- Star Casting Spoon w/Aux Hook 120
- Fluted Casting Spoon w/Aux Hook 120
- Willow Leaf Spinner 116

Lucas, I. W. 274

Mack, Albert G. 232
- Mack's Weed-Deflecting Bait 232

Mann, John H. 84
- Double Spinner 85
- Heart Shaped Spinner 87
- Kidney Spinner 87
- Kidney Spinner w/Clip 87
- Oval Trolling Spoon 85
- Perfect Revolving Spoon 86
- Shield Spinner 84

McDonald, P. 274

McHarg, John B. 181
- American Spinner 188, 190, 196
- Arrowhead Type 193
- Ball Bait w/Cast Blade 186
- Ball Bait w/Hammered Finish 186
- Bass Fly 191
- Diamond Pattern Kidney 192
- Dimple Pattern Kidney 192
- Electric Bait 183
- Fluted Bait 183
- Fluted Shield Pickerel Bait 185
- Interchangeable Tail Lure 187
- James Squid Type 193

- Kidney Bait 196
- Kidney Ball Bait 196
- Reverse Dimple Kidney 193
- Rose Stem Pattern 185
- Small Triangular 187
- Spinning Coachman 191
- Spoon Minnows 194

Mills, William & Sons 276

Newell Co. 274

Pardee, F. A. & Samuel H. Friend ..267
- Kent Champion 268
- Pardee Minnow 267

Parker, Mayne C. P. 250
- Trolling Worm 250

Pealer, E. O. 260
- P & S Ball Bearing Spinner 260, 261

Pepper, John 202
- Batwing 202-204
- Spinner 203

Pierce, M. F. 228
- Heart Shaped Lure 228, 229

Robinson, Frederic C. P. 225
- Robinson Mouse 225

Rockwood, W. H. 266
- Ghost 266

Shaffer, Charles C. 268
- Expert Minnow 268, 269
- Holzworth Expert Minnow 268, 269
- Woods Expert Minnow 268, 269

Skinner, Gardner M. 88
- Flipback Casting Spoon 96
- Fluted Spoon 90, 93
- Fly Spoon 93
- New Casting Spoon 93, 94
- Plain Spoon 91, 92
- St. Lawrence Muscallonge & Pickerel ..92
- Turkey Foot 91
- Turkey Wing-Kidney 90
- Weedless Casting Spoon 92

Skinner, Henry E. 242
- Abalone Spoon 242

Snyder, W.I. 262
- Success Spinner 262
- Yellow Kid 262

Spalding, A. G. Co. 250
- Spinner 109, 250

Stanley, Henry O. 247
- Stanley Smelt 247
- State of Maine Spinner 247

Votaw, M. W. & M. E. Thomas ....259 Votaw Minnow ....259 **Wakeman, Archer**.......................236 Devon Type ....236 Skeleton Bait ....236-238 **Welch & Graves** 206	American Combination Spinner........212, 213 Changeable Center Fish Bait ....211 Minnow Tube ....208 Improved Minnow Tube ....209, 210 **Westwood Frog**............................243 **Zuckweiler, Henry** 238	Chicago Spinner...240 Spinner Bait ....239 Trolling Bait.......................................238, 239

BIBLIOGRAPHY

Gary L. Miller, *NFLCC Gazette,* Dec. 1987. Unmasking the Manistee.
Harold G. Herr, *NFLCC Magazine,* Dec 1995. The Andrew B. Hendryx Co.
Gerry Barrows, *NFLCC Magazine,* July 1993. Welch & Graves.
Dick Wilson, *NFLCC Magazine,* Jan. 1991. Kent Frogs & Minnows.
Genio C. Scott, *Fishing in American Waters.* 1875
Gerry Barrows, *NFLCC Magazine,* July 1993. Gardiner Mills Skinner.
Bob Groters, *NFLCC Magazine,* June 1995. Early Fishing Lures of Western Michigan
Gerry Barrows, *NFLCC Magazine,* Dec. 1992. The Rome Connection.
Paul Lindner, *The Grand River Valley Review.* First Light Nibbles. 1986
Art and Scott Kimball, *Early Fishing Plugs of the U.S.A.* 1985
Jim Bourdon, *I Love N.Y. Reels and Lures.* 1985
Rich Metcalf, *John H. Mann.* 1986
Rich Metcalf, *Henry Loftie.* 1987
Harvey W. Thompson, *The Spooners.* 1979
Gerry Barrows. *NFLCC Magazine,* Jan. 1994. William T.J. Lowe.

ABOUT THE AUTHOR

Arlan Carter and his wife Loretta live in Fall Creek, Wisconsin, and operate the Northland Fishing Museum and Wildlife Art Gallery in Osseo, Wisconsin. The business, along with an antique fishing tackle display, consists of an art gallery and antique mall.

Arlan has been an active member of the National Fishing Lure Collector Club for the last 20 years. He and his wife host an annual NFLCC club sanctioned meet at Wisconsin Dells, Wisconsin.

Except for four years in the U.S. Navy, Arlan has lived "up north" all his life. During the early 1960s he occasionally attended the University of Wisconsin at Eau Claire and at one time was the owner and operator of several small cable television systems. He loves to fish.

The author with a big one.

NOTE: The author is always interested in hearing from people who have information, catalogs, or photos relating to old lures.

He is also interested in photographing and sometimes purchasing lures. Call toll free 1-800-695-6017 or write Arlan Carter, Box 107, Fall Creek, WI 54742.

Schroeder's ANTIQUES Price Guide

...is the #1 bestselling antiques & collectibles value guide on the market today, and here's why…

• More than 450 advisors, well-known dealers, and top-notch collectors work together with our editors to bring you accurate information regarding pricing and identification.

• More than 45,000 items in almost 500 categories are listed along with hundreds of sharp original photos that illustrate not only the rare and unusual, but the common, popular collectibles as well.

• Each large close-up shot shows important details clearly. Every subject is represented with histories and background information, a feature not found in any of our competitors' publications.

• Our editors keep abreast of newly developing trends, often adding several new categories a year as the need arises.

8½" x 11"
608 pages
$12.95

If it merits the interest of today's collector, you'll find it in *Schroeder's*. And you can feel confident that the information we publish is up-to-date and accurate. Our advisors thoroughly check each category to spot inconsistencies, listings that may not be entirely reflective of market dealings, and lines too vague to be of merit. Only the best of the lot remains for publication.

COLLECTOR BOOKS
A Division of Schroeder Publishing Co., Inc.

Without doubt, you'll find
Schroeder's Antiques Price Guide
the only one to buy for
reliable information and values.

COLLECTOR BOOKS
P.O. Box 3009 • Paducah, KY 42002–3009